Developmental Psychology Today

Contributing Consultants

Justin Aronfreed, Ph.D., University of Pennsylvania

Nancy Bayley, Ph.D., University of California at Berkeley

Ursula Bellugi, Ed.D., Salk Institute for Biological Studies

James E. Birren, Ph.D., University of Southern California

Joan S. Bissell, Ed.D., Harvard University

T. G. R. Bower, Ph.D., University of Edinburgh

J. Anthony Deutsch, D.Phil., University of California at San Diego

Susan M. Ervin-Tripp, Ph.D., University of California at Berkeley

Joseph Glick, Ph.D., City University of New York

Norma Haan, M.S., University of California at Berkeley

Marshall M. Haith, Ph.D., Harvard University

Willard W. Hartup, Ed.D., University of Minnesota

John P. Hill, Ph.D., University of Minnesota

Arthur T. Jersild, Ph.D., emeritus, Teachers College, Columbia University

Jerome Kagan, Ph.D., Harvard University

Kenneth Keniston, D.Phil., Yale University

William Kessen, Ph.D., Yale University

Jane W. Kessler, Ph.D., Case Western Reserve University

Lawrence Kohlberg, Ph.D., Harvard University

Lewis P. Lipsitt, Ph.D., Brown University

Salvatore R. Maddi, Ph.D., University of Chicago

Peter Madison, Ph.D., University of Arizona

Elton B. McNeil, Ph.D., University of Michigan

Harry Munsinger, Ph.D., University of California at San Diego

Henry N. Ricciuti, Ph.D., Cornell University

Carl R. Rogers, Ph.D., Center for Studies of the Person

Pauline S. Sears, Ph.D., Stanford University

Harold W. Stevenson, Ph.D., University of Minnesota

Leland H. Stott, Ph.D., Merrill-Palmer Institute

Sheldon H. White, Ph.D., Harvard University

Developmental Psychology Today

CRM BOOKS Del Mar, California

Preface

The study of human development is a complex business. Consider, for example, the seemingly simple human act of your laughing — or not laughing — at a joke. Your physical state, age, temperament, intelligence, perceptual capacities, family background, social class, emotional makeup, moral values, and education all have something to do with whether or not you find a particular joke funny — and these elements are continually evolving. Think of the jokes that made you roll in the aisles when you were ten. If you can remember any now, you probably won't find them even mildly amusing. Many of the elements that make up your sense of humor — your personality and character — have changed since then. Developmentalists want to know how.

To learn how human character evolves, developmentalists study both the roots of behavior common to all men and the ways in which human beings come to differ from one another. Until quite recently, developmental psychology attempted merely to catalogue physical and behavioral changes at each age and to set up norms. Now, however, exciting new methods and approaches are being used and new findings abound. Even the youngest infants are subjects of experiment, and psychologists are learning much about human capacities and change. Not all psychologists approach the study in the same way, of course. In such a complicated area, now in a period of great vitality, there are wide differences in theories and methods.

This book presents the newest discoveries in the field of human development as well as the theories and findings. It brings together in one coherent and chronological statement what is known about human development today.

Richard L. Roe, Publisher, Social Sciences

Contents

Developmental Psychology Today

Lying in a bassinet is a newborn baby barely a half-hour old. The baby stares vacantly upward; he moves infrequently, and when he does, his movements are jerky and spasmodic. His legs flail, his mouth puckers, and his eyes close. Looking at the infant, one is impressed that he is a whole human being. Everything is there: ten fingers, ten toes, a tongue, all the physical parts of man in miniature.

The change in nine months from two independent cells, the ovum and the sperm, into this complex creature is astounding, but no more astounding than the developments that will occur during subsequent months and years. In a week he will be feeding well, his gaze will be less murky; in three months he will follow events in his world efficiently with his eyes; in six months he will be grasping at toys and sitting; in a year he will be walking; in two years he will be talking; in three years he will be a person, with a name he can say and capable of telling stories about himself; in four years he will be constructing his own miniature world in play; in six years he will be reading about the external world; in ten years he will be a member of a gang of others more or less like himself; in twenty years he will be preparing for a career; in thirty years he will be a father; and then, slowly, his powers will dim, his strength will decrease, his skills will fade, and after six or seven decades he will cease to function as an integrated, vital human being. After seven or eight decades, he will be dead. The details will differ, but in general this is the story of all men. And it is this story, elaborated and presented in great detail, that constitutes the subject matter of developmental psychology.

Unit I
The Meaning of Development

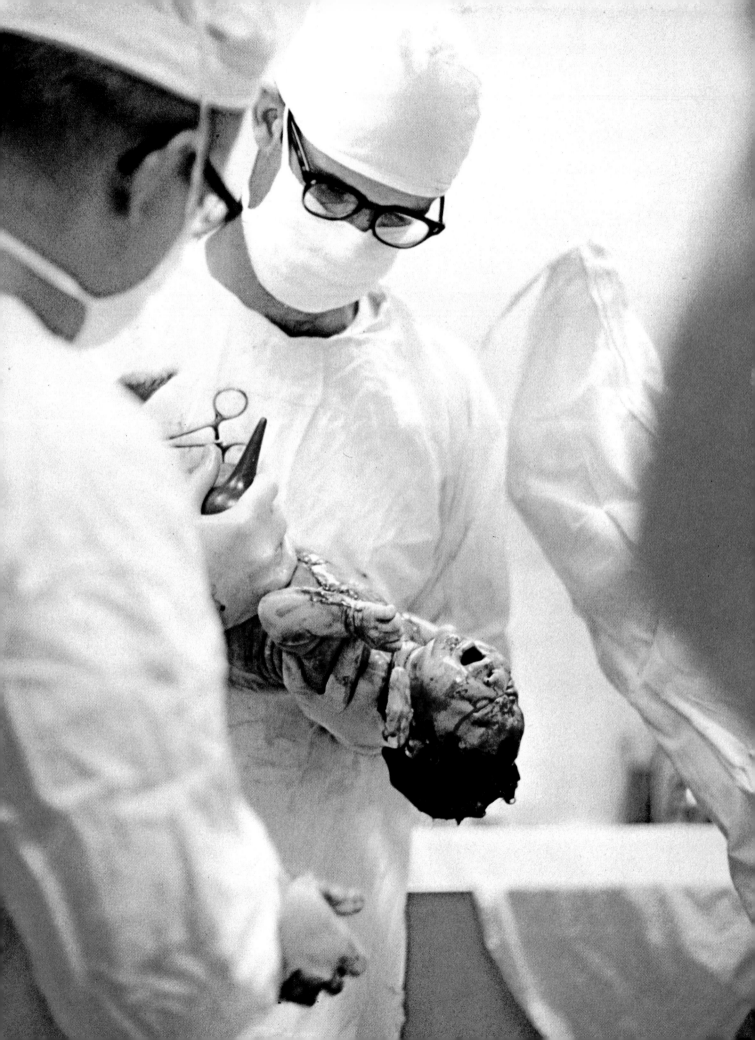

Developmental psychology is concerned with *the description and explanation of changes in an individual's behavior that are a result of maturation and experience.* Let us take each aspect of this definition in turn.

Developmental psychologists are concerned first with the *description* of behavior, for they cannot hope to answer questions about why a human being does what he does until they have a fine-grained, accurate picture of behavior. A behavior is defined as an *observable* act; it can be seen and described in the same way by more than one person. When developmental psychologists talk about behavior, they are concerned with acts, not with the physiological mechanisms underlying the acts. For example, they are more interested in the use of language than in the formation of the sounds of speech and in the use of the hand in grasping than in the neuromuscular activity that permits grasping.

But merely describing behavior is insufficient. Eventually, psychologists hope to be able to *explain why the behavior occurs.* In attempting to provide such explanations, developmental psychologists have constructed *theories*—abstract sets of statements that are logically interrelated. From such abstractions of reality psychologists hope to be able to predict the effects of certain conditions on later behavior, to reconstruct the conditions that led to current behavior, and to devise effective means of controlling future behavior. There is a long way to go yet, but developmental psychology, like any scientific discipline, gains power as its theories become effective in understanding and controlling human behavior.

Developmental psychology introduces the reader to a new way of looking at the human being, of seeing the human being as a changing system dependent upon its biology but constantly subject to the effects of experience. There have been, and at times still are, attempts to separate the effects of biological maturation and of experience on human development. However, these discussions have usually devolved into emotional arguments; the possibility of separating these effects on the development of complex forms of behavior seems to be very remote. Take language, for example. Developmentalists know that the child will not be able to talk until he has attained a certain level of neuromuscular development. No six-month-old speaks in sentences. At the same time, a child living in a relatively unstimulating, unresponsive environment will speak later than children reared in a typical home. In the one case the child is not biologically ready to speak; in the second, the child's world does not offer adequate speech models for learning to speak. But the time and rate at which language will develop in a particular child are the result of an interaction between his level of maturity and his previous experience in uttering, listening to, and being rewarded for the use of language. Arguments (and disillusionment) can be avoided if one does not try to ascribe behavior to maturation *or* experience but instead views both as interdependent and interactive in their effects on development.

1
The Concept of Development

The Meaning of Development

Development implies orderly change. The human being is capable of, and demonstrates, changes in behavior throughout his life. Generally, the rate of change is more rapid during early than later years of life, both because changes in the body are less rapid the older one gets and because with increasing age people tend to establish more stable routines of living. If, however, an infant were placed in a dull, monotonous environment, his rate of behavioral change would probably be reduced; conversely, the rate at which an adult's behavior changes might be accelerated if he had to abandon his everyday routines and adapt to a new and demanding environment. Furthermore, the rate of change of every domain of behavior is not equally great during all phases of the individual's life. For all types of behavior there are periods of rapid development followed by periods of relative stability.

STAGES

It is easy and convenient, therefore, to consider the individual as going through *stages* in his development. The term *stage* is used to describe periods in which the function and relative emphasis of a given type of behavior differ from those at other periods of life. The infant may seem to be focusing all his attention on increasing his mobility, and the teen-ager may devote seemingly inordinate amounts of time to conversing with friends on the telephone. Of course, the teen-ager is also interested in mobility, just as the infant is also interested in other people, but the two types of

behavior have a different emphasis and function at the two periods of the individual's life.

Development occurs in two different ways: continuously, with a kind of accretion of behaviors, like the building up of layers in a pearl; and discontinuously, in a series of rapid glides and jumps. Both processes exist and operate simultaneously in all people; although the observable behavior may appear to be discontinuous, the underlying process by which the behavior is acquired is continuous. The apparent discontinuity in behavioral organization is basic to stage theories of development: there are times during growth when behavioral development appears to advance by means of striking changes in complex patterns of behavior. The behavior that preceded the change is *qualitatively* different from that following the change.

Several developmental theories based on stages are described in this book. Common to all of them—whether by Jean Piaget, Sigmund Freud, or Lawrence Kohlberg—is the definition of stages of development in terms of structure, organization, and process. The following are the criteria of stages set down by Kohlberg.

1. Change from one stage to another involves change in the form, pattern, and organization of an individual's behavior—not just in the frequency and intensity of an individual's responses.
2. Each successive stage involves a new and qualitatively different organization of responses. Not only may the behavior be different and with different emphases in each stage, but the basic rules governing the behavior differ also.
3. Change from stage to stage is inevitable; except in extremely unusual or damaging circumstances, the individual does not respond in terms of earlier modes.
4. The stages in an individual's development appear in a sequence that is fixed and unvarying from individual to individual. Stages are the universals of every human being's development.
5. Stages involve progress toward increasing complexity—each successive stage integrates critical formal aspects of previous stages into a more articulated organization.

Whenever psychologists use the term *stage,* they are making a descriptive, summary statement. It is inappropriate—although sometimes done—to use the term to explain behavior. To say that the infant crawls *because* he is at the crawling stage is redundant. The infant crawls, and a convenient way of summarizing the fact that he is crawling, unwilling to be held, and into all the drawers is to say that he is at the crawling stage. Moreover, he soon will be at a walking stage. The components of walking are being acquired even in the crawling stage, long before he takes his first step: he learns to judge distances, to avoid obstacles, to sit when off balance, and to pull himself up. Thus, although the term *stage* directs one's attention to a particular set of behaviors, one must appreciate that each stage is the product of its antecedents. In the process of mastering the behaviors characteristic of *any* stage, the child is simultaneously preparing for the *next* stage in his development.

PROGRESSIVE CHANGE

Development is progressive. The infant's progress in grasping follows a well-defined series of stages,

Figure 1.1. Learning to write one's language depends on both maturation and experience.

characterized first by reflexive excitation of motor fibers and later by the intricate balance between excitation and inhibition that is necessary for smooth voluntary movement. If we pry open the tight, fisted hand of the newborn and insert a thin rod, the baby will grasp the rod vigorously— so vigorously in fact that he can be lifted partially into the air. The proud father may mistake this as an indication of the baby's tenacity. Actually, the grasp is merely a reflexive response: stimulation of the palm produces a closing of the fingers, and the more intense the stimulation, the tighter the fingers close. The infant does not choose to hold the rod—he holds on because he is reflexively incapable of letting go. Several months later, the reflexive grasp disappears. An attempt to pull the infant will result in immediate release of the rod. The infant cannot yet voluntarily hold the rod, but neither will he involuntarily maintain his grasp of it. Later, of course, the infant can pick up the rod at will, first with the outer portion of his palm and fingers, and by the end of the first year, he will be able to pluck the rod deftly with his thumb and forefinger. A motor response such as grasping offers a clear example of progressive changes in behavior, but other, much more complex forms of behavior, such as thinking, appear to follow similarly well-defined series of stages.

DIFFERENTIATION

Development involves differentiation. Ask a three-year-old to describe a picture. He may say, "Mommy, doggy, baby." The description consists of a delineation of the dominant features of the

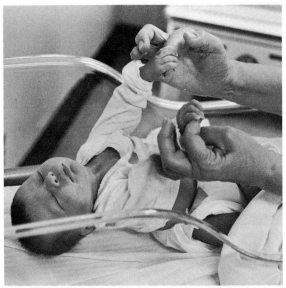

Figure 1.2 (above). The reflexive grasp of an infant a few days old (top) is so strong that he can be lifted partially from his crib; a child several months old (bottom) no longer displays this reflex.

Figure 1.3 (opposite). The child's ability to make progressively finer perceptions of human beings is seen in these drawings, made by children between the ages of five and twelve who were instructed to draw a man as well as they could. (After Goodenough, 1926.)

Figure 1.4 (opposite). The transition from the fetal posture of the newborn to the upright, independent walking of the fifteen-month-old follows a series of progressive stages. The skills used in each stage are prerequisite for the next stage—there are no abrupt changes. Behavior is a cumulative process. (After Shirley, 1933.)

scene. By five, the child will formulate the rudiments of a story. Later, the child may narrate a fully developed, lengthy exposition, including a discussion of the emotional state of the characters, the antecedents of the situation, and its probable outcome. The utterances of the older child are partly a result of his simply having a better vocabulary to call on. But they are also a result of his being able to utilize the vocabulary in discussing a situation, parts of which recall his own experiences, others of which he has heard about, and all of which he is capable of relating to his own complex mental life. With increasing age and experience the individual's complexity and differentiation increase. This example involves language, but the conclusion would be the same if we observed children of different ages playing, drawing, or swimming. With development, there is a transformation of behavior from relatively repetitive and restricted forms to more elaborate and varied ones.

ACCUMULATION

Development is cumulative. Saying that the child is father to the man seems reasonable to us today, but the statement would have met with questioning glances several hundred years ago. Perhaps one of the most significant changes in our attitudes about the human being is our acceptance of the fact that the child is not a man but that his early experiences may have strong effects on the kind of man he will become. Only a few centuries ago, childhood was not regarded as a distinctive phase of development; children were dressed and

treated like diminutive adults. Somewhat later, the distinction between childhood and adulthood was made, but childhood was considered to be the period in which the primary task was the instillation of proper moral values and conduct. Society's present attitude toward childhood is the result of many forces, not the least of which are the writings of Sigmund Freud. In his analysis of mentally disturbed adults, Freud was recurrently led to early experiences in the individual's life that seemed to have profound and lasting effects on later behavior. Freud was a clinical psychiatrist, but support for his observations concerning the influence of childhood experiences on later behavior may be found in more recent formal studies and laboratory experiments.

Thus, when psychologists talk about the development of behavior, they are interested in relatively gross, adaptive changes that are continuous, progressive, and cumulative in their effects. And, importantly, they are interested in describing and understanding the process whereby behavior becomes differentiated into the marvelously complex repertoire demonstrated by the typical adult in his everyday existence.

PHASES OF DEVELOPMENT

There are many ways in which the life cycle can be divided. One of the most obvious is by chronological age. There are disadvantages, however, in using age for this purpose. From birth there are great differences in behavior among individuals of the same age, so efforts to characterize the typical five-month-old, five-year-old, or fifty-year-old are

bound to be misleading. In fact, one of the most common sources of anxiety among parents is baby books that describe behavior at sixteen weeks, forty weeks, and so on. It may be true that the median age at which babies roll over is twenty-four weeks, but many normal, healthy babies first roll over much later—and many do it much earlier. Only when there are marked departures from the normative trends is there reason for serious parental concern. The categorization of development used here, then, is much broader than that implied by age. The divisions of the life cycle described below are called phases rather than stages because progression through stages, as discussed earlier, implies progressive, orderly change and is defined by specific criteria. Phases are broad chronological divisions of the human life cycle. For our purposes it will be sufficient to consider seven phases: prenatal, infancy, childhood, adolescence, youth, maturity, and old age.

Figure 1.5. When Erasmus Quellin painted this "Boy with Dog" (early seventeenth century), little distinction was made between childhood and adulthood.

PRENATAL PHASE

Why should psychologists be concerned with the organism *before* birth? The answer is because they are interested in behavior, and less than ten weeks after conception the new organism begins to demonstrate gross, adaptive forms of behavior. Brush the midfacial area of the young fetus, and it will rotate its head and upper trunk away from the source of stimulation. This seems to be the fetus' first response, but as the fetus develops, it displays much more complex and varied forms of behavior. Mothers find it enthralling, and at times bothersome, to feel the strong stretching movements of the fetus' arms and legs. A fetus may suck its thumb, get the hiccups, or even show primitive breathing movements.

The fetal period is of interest also because of its potential effects on later behavior. Most of these possibilities are still unexplored. Can learning occur during the fetal period? A study by David

Spelt indicates that it can. Spelt showed that fetuses of seven or more months, who are known to respond to a very loud noise, can be conditioned to respond to a vibratory stimulus. The study has never been repeated, so one cannot be sure. Does the mother's emotional state during pregnancy have lasting effects on the new organism? How do drugs, alcohol, or inadequate maternal diet influence later development? It is known that certain viruses, such as that of German measles (rubella), may invade the fetus and cause lasting damage to its central nervous system, producing later effects such as blindness or brain damage. The prenatal phase is the least clearly understood of all the phases, mainly because of the difficulties in conducting satisfactory research, but it is a phase of possibly great importance for the development of behavior.

INFANCY

The prenatal phase is clearly delineated by the fact of birth. There is no such abrupt change in the infant or in his environment to set off the phase of infancy. This phase is perhaps best delimited by considering infancy to begin at birth and to end when the child is able to exist independently of his mother—is capable of feeding himself, of walking, and of talking. Research on infancy has developed rapidly during the past decade, primarily because so many important questions have been raised concerning the early months of the child's life. The questions are of interest not only to parents, psychologists, and

Figure 1.6. These two boys are almost exactly the same age. Although their growth patterns are very different, both are perfectly normal.

pediatricians but also to members of such other disciplines as philosophy, linguistics, and anthropology. Is the infant's mind a *tabula rasa*, a blank slate that is filled only through experience, or are there innate means by which the child perceives the world and organizes his experiences? Does the child's behavior develop through relating stimulus and response, or does the child actively direct his approaches to the world? What effect does the emotional environment of the infant have on his later personality? Do the amounts and types of the infant's experience set boundaries for his later intellectual development? Are there critical periods in infancy during which the child must have certain types of experiences or make certain types of attachments without which he is unable to develop appropriately? There are innumerable questions; some of them can be answered partially, but the answers for others are still merely best guesses.

CHILDHOOD

With the end of infancy and the beginning of childhood, the parents' opportunities to control their child's world begin to decrease. The child begins to need other children as much as he needs his parents. Physically independent, more-or-less self-sufficient, the child resists the efforts of adults to determine what he will wear, what he will eat, with whom he will play, and when he will go to bed. Two of the major accomplishments of childhood are the mastery of language and the learning of social controls. The ability to understand and use language with precision and versatility ex-

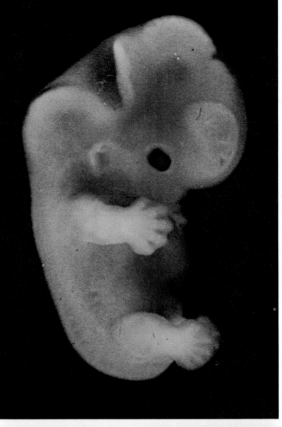

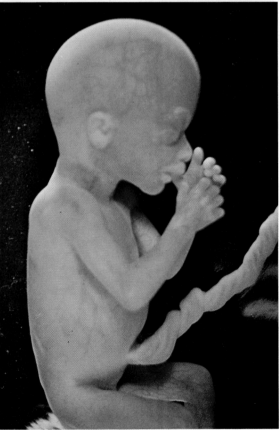

Figure 1.7. Prenatal phase. *(top)* Normal fetus at forty days. Note brain vesicles, eye, ear structure, and formation of fingers and toes. The deep cleft in the brain is the isthmus between the midbrain and hindbrain. *(bottom)* Normal fetus at five months, apparently sucking its thumb. (From Rugh and Shettles, *From Conception to Birth: The Drama of Life's Beginnings,* Harper & Row, 1971.)

tends the child's opportunities for acquiring information and expressing his needs far beyond the capabilities of any other living organism. Learning to exist as one person among many is a difficult task, and it is during childhood that the individual must acquire many basic social skills: he must learn to control his aggression, to take turns, and to behave according to social customs.

The child enters school; he no longer exists in the here-and-now. His behavior becomes increasingly complex, and his thinking, more and more abstract. From the concrete and relatively restricted environment of the infant, the child is propelled into the abstractions of mathematics, the expansiveness of space flights, and the remoteness of dinosaurs. He begins to think propositionally, in terms of "if—then." He carries out series of instructions, formulates rules of conduct for his club, begins to write letters to his friends. During childhood, rate of physical growth is relatively constant, but signs of acceleration begin to appear. The child's appearance begins to change. Long-dormant hormones become active. Childhood gradually ends, and the phase of adolescence begins.

ADOLESCENCE

Adolescence as it is defined by physical changes (an increase in height, changes in bodily proportions, and the appearance of secondary sexual characteristics) is a familiar concept. Adolescence as a distinct social phenomenon has been possible only recently because only a fairly affluent society can maintain individuals in the semidependent

Figure 1.8. Infancy. A robust one-year-old.

Figure 1.9. Childhood. Children actively master their environment.

role of the adolescent. Earlier societies made no distinction between the adolescent and the adult; after the age of seven or eight the individual was considered to be capable of sharing the obligations and opportunities of adulthood.

Whereas childhood is characterized by a dominant interest in members of the same sex, during adolescence there is increasing interest in members of the opposite sex. The adolescent searches for ultimates—truth, love, beauty, and, most important, a sense of self. "What am I?" and "Who am I?" are questions that the adolescent grapples with and, hopefully, eventually answers with comfort. Parent-child relations may become strained during adolescence, with the parents striving to maintain some control and the adolescent seeking self-determination. Because the adolescent is usually financially dependent upon his parents, this struggle may sometimes become bitter for both sides, leading to estrangement or disillusionment.

YOUTH

Social and historical conditions affect both the content and the style of the human life cycle. As was noted above, adolescence as a recognized stage of life is a relatively modern concept. The psychiatric literature before World War I contains little reference to anything besides the biological aspects of puberty. Now, of course, there is a vast amount of literature dealing with the social, psychological, and developmental life of the adolescent. The opportunity for a stage of adolescence was created by the relative affluence and

Figure 1.10. Adolescence. The transition from childhood to adolescence—the period of early adolescence—requires the learning of new roles. During this period comes the shift from friendship only with members of one's own sex to friendships with the opposite sex.

attendant leisure of an industrial society.

There is evidence that in our day we are witnessing the emergence of a new stage of life, which intervenes between adolescence and adulthood. Kenneth Keniston calls this stage *youth*. In this stage are young men and women who are, in the biological sense, adults; most range in age from twenty to thirty. In the sociological sense they are not mature; they have not yet made the commitments—to career and family—that are normally used to differentiate the mature adult from the adolescent. But psychologically, these young people seem to have completed what are usually considered to be the tasks of adolescence: emancipation from family; relative tranquility about sexuality; formation of a relatively integrated self-identity; a synthesis of ego and superego; a capacity for commitment. Most seem to have passed through adolescent rebellion.

These young people—who as yet constitute but a small minority of their age group—are reluctant, unprepared, or unready to enter adulthood. They are ambivalent about the nature of the society to which they must commit themselves and about their internalized social ethics and personal integrity. For many, positive value resides in commitment to change, openness, and fluidity—so that mature commitments are seen as cutting off life's potentialities.

These youths can be found among college and graduate students or dropouts, young radicals, Peace Corps and Vista volunteers, and hippies. Their number is still small, but with the progressive and extraordinary prolongation of education and the rapid, thoroughgoing social change taking place, the stage of youth will become open to progressively larger numbers of young people.

MATURITY

People tend to think of the mature adult as being much more static than the infant, child, or adolescent. Superficially, this appears to be the case,

Figure 1.11. Youth. Members of this emerging stage of life are often ambivalent about both their own values and those of their society.

for there are no universal physical changes that characterize maturity, there are no new approaches to social relations to be acquired, the personality seems stable, and intellectual activities are often at the peak of efficiency. However, there are common problems faced by most adults. How does the adult adapt to being a parent—or not being a parent? How does the adult respond to the death of his parents? Are the plans and preparations that were made for maturity satisfying? Does the adult have a sense of completeness or meaningfulness in his life? What compensates for the fact that he can look forward only to a decrease in his capacities and, ultimately, to death? These are common developmental problems faced during this phase, but they are ones about which, unfortunately, psychologists have only the most primitive understanding.

OLD AGE

Aging is a modern problem, and in a real sense a modern phenomenon. In the Middle Ages, to be forty was to be old. Only during the past few decades have people faced the problems associated with aging. Because of continuous improvement in health care, diet, and the physical environment, a substantial proportion of the American population consists of individuals over the age of sixty-five. Not too long ago, society thought that persons over sixty-five were too old to work and consigned them to lives of idleness and dependence. Is retirement from work a desirable goal? What kinds of physical skills deteriorate with age? What aspects of intellectual activity are most susceptible to the aging process?

Figure 1.12. Adulthood. Most adults take on the responsibility of parenthood, but too little is known about preparation for being a parent or about the changes parenthood works in the adult personality.

Does an enriched environment help to maintain certain types of abilities? Why do some people appear old at sixty, while others continue to lead active, vital lives into their eighties or nineties? The late years of life may be happier and more productive when psychologists are able to answer these and similar questions.

The Methods of Developmental Psychology

Opinions and beliefs about the development of human behavior abound. Philosophers, educators, and religious theorists have been trying to devise theories of behavior for centuries. The conclusions they reached may be profound or petty, insightful or superficial, but regardless of the quality of their thought, these approaches are totally subjective and so, by definition, not scientific. An important step away from subjectivity was taken during the late 1890s and early 1900s, when psychologists adopted the methods that had been used so successfully in the physical and biological sciences: clinical study, observation, and experimentation. The value of these approaches over subjective, introspective methods is that they are more likely to lead to information that is objective, clear, and replicable, and therefore reliably meaningful.

CLINICAL STUDY

Clinical study is an in-depth interview and observation of a child or adult. It may be controlled, that is, the same methods may be applied in a standardized way to each subject, or the psy-

Figure 1.13. Old age. Only within this century have substantial numbers of persons—in technologically advanced societies—begun to live past 65. (See Figure 1.14.)

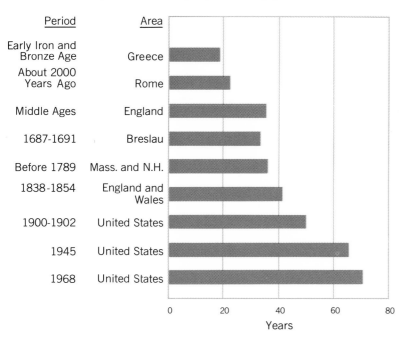

Period	Area	Years
Early Iron and Bronze Age	Greece	
About 2000 Years Ago	Rome	
Middle Ages	England	
1687-1691	Breslau	
Before 1789	Mass. and N.H.	
1838-1854	England and Wales	
1900-1902	United States	
1945	United States	
1968	United States	

Years

Figure 1.14. Average length of man's life at various periods in history. Note the great increase in life expectancy from the start of the twentieth century to 1945.

chologist can vary his approach with each subject. When clinical study is employed with appropriate controls, it qualifies as a method of science and can yield data of great interest. The procedure for the controlled study must be clearly and precisely defined; the investigator is left to his own resources only in such matters as introducing the subject to the clinical situation or maintaining his cooperation, and even these actions may cause bias unless explicitly stated and controlled.

One of the earliest and most productive applications of controlled clinical study is found in the work of Alfred Binet, the French psychologist. Binet was asked by school authorities in Paris to devise a means of picking out slow learners so they could be assigned to special classes. After trying many different approaches, Binet hit upon the idea of asking children a series of questions of progressively greater difficulty. If a child had a chronological age of seven but could answer questions only at the level of the average five-year-old, there was an indication of mental retardation. But such deductions could be made only if each child was asked the questions and presented the materials in exactly the same manner. Without this standardization of procedure there would be no valid basis for comparing the performances of different children. Binet's test and its successors have been used both as clinical tools and as a means of investigating various questions concerning intellectual development.

Another, more recent, application of the clinical method can be found in the studies of the famous Swiss psychologist Jean Piaget. Piaget's theories concerning cognitive development have been based primarily on studies that utilized the clinical method. However, Piaget's clinical method is not standardized in the same way as Binet's. The method used in his earlier studies was a free conversation with a child, in the course of which Piaget asked control questions and also questions aimed at checking the child's hypotheses. Piaget saw disadvantages in both pure observation and in standardized tests, so he chose an intermediate method. The procedures used in his more recent studies are more standardized. A famous Piaget experiment involves two glasses of the same size and shape filled to an equal level with colored water. A child is asked whether the two glasses contain the same amount of water. When the child asserts that the amounts are the same, the water from one glass is poured into a shorter, broader glass, so that the levels of the colored water in the two glasses differ. A six-year-old, when asked whether each glass now contains the same amount of water, will say, "No! This one has more water in it because it is higher." When the water is poured back into its original glass, the child will again say that the two glasses have the same amount of water in them. When he is asked, "How do you know?" he answers, "Because I can *see* that they do!" When he is older, the child recognizes that perception alone is not an adequate basis for making such judgments. Unless Piaget had presented such problems to all children using much the same procedure he would not have known whether the differences in their responses at different ages were the result of

Figure 1.15. Clinical method. Jean Piaget devised the apparatus shown to investigate children's cognitive development. The child is told to adjust the plunger so as to make the red ball knock the green ball into the hole. The same materials are presented to all the children in much the same manner. If the child succeeds, he has demonstrated that he understands the rule that angle of incidence equals angle of reflection.

the differences in method of presentation or of actual changes in the children's cognitive activity.

OBSERVATION

Like clinical study, observational methods are capable of yielding scientifically acceptable data (rather than interesting anecdotes) only if the observations are made in an appropriately controlled manner. The investigator must determine how the behavior will be recorded, whether different observers can record behavior reliably and consistently, and how the behavior will be categorized and analyzed. Also, observations of behavior must be transformed into some manageable type of unit or rating; however objective and detailed they are, the observations are of little value unless they can be measured and quantified.

There are certain aspects of human behavior, particularly those involving behavior in natural settings, for which only observational methods can be used. For example, psychologists may wish to study the effects of racial integration on the social behavior of preschool children. They could use various clinical approaches to assess the children's attitudes toward members of the other race, but what they are really interested in is how confrontations with members of another race influence social behavior. To conduct this study, they must observe the children's behavior before and after the groups have been integrated, or contrast the behavior of children in integrated groups with that of children in racially separated groups. There are numerous ways these observations could be made. One could use a time-sam-

pling method, whereby psychologists observe the children at predetermined intervals and count the number of children engaged in like-race and unlike-race social interaction. One could *count* the incidence of aggressive, dependent, and dominant types of behavior. Before any of this can be done, however, the observers must have clear definitions of the variables with which they are concerned. Will they consider physical contiguity to be an example of social interaction? How will they define aggression? Can two observers, watching the scene at the same time, get comparable results?

One might make descriptive records on tape or in writing of the children's social interaction at different times during the day. To use this method, the psychologist must be sure that he is obtaining a representative sample of each child's behavior, that he is recording the behavior reliably, and that he can devise a means of rating the observational records so that they can be reduced to a quantitative form. If such a study is conducted well, valuable information can be gained about the everyday effects of a potentially important variable on children's behavior—information that can be acquired only through the observational method.

EXPERIMENTATION

An experiment involves the investigation of the effects of particular variables (called *independent variables* because they can be manipulated) on behavior (called the *dependent variable* because changes in behavior presumably depend on the effects of changes in the independent variables).

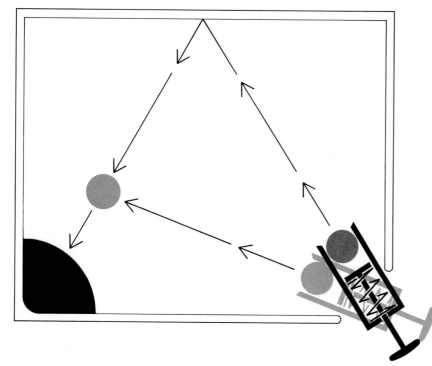

All of the precautions of objectivity, clarity, reliability, and replicability required of controlled clinical and observational study are necessary in using the experimental method. However, it is often much easier to attain these goals through an experiment, primarily because the investigator is better able to control and manipulate the variables under study.

Studying behavior through the experimental method is not as unnatural as some might think, and the method has been employed successfully in thousands of psychological studies. Let us look at a typical example. Two investigators (A. R. Jensen and W. D. Rohwer) were interested in studying developmental changes in children's learning. The subjects for the study were children from kindergarten through grade twelve. They were shown pairs of pictures of common objects. Half of the children at each age level were asked to name each picture, and the other half were asked to construct a sentence relating each pair of pictures. (This was the independent variable: naming the objects or relating them through a sentence.) The subjects then were presented the pairs of pictures and were required to learn the members of each pair well enough so that when one picture was presented they could recall the other picture of the pair. (The number of pictures recalled correctly was the dependent variable.) The results are presented in Figure 1.16, which shows that the children who used the sentence-making method required fewer trials. Also, when children at the same age levels are compared, it can be seen that the children who

made sentences learned the material much faster. This experiment illustrates the powerful effects of requiring the child to relate objects in a meaningful manner through the construction of sentences and thus adds to psychologists' knowledge of learning in children. When materials are meaningfully related, the eight-year-old may learn as well as the seventeen-year-old. It is doubtful that this information could have been obtained so efficiently or so convincingly had other than the experimental method been employed.

THE DATA OF DEVELOPMENTAL PSYCHOLOGY

The average person tends to think of developmental psychology as a source of normative data about development: When should children know their colors? When does the adolescent growth spurt begin? What differences are there in the IQs of rural and urban children? During the early years of the science, developmental psychologists sought to answer such questions. Their interest in normative studies is not surprising, for until some of the major developmental changes in behavior were known, it was impossible to proceed to the next stage, that of attempting to interpret the bases for such developmental changes. Although an interest in normative studies has not disappeared, it has been displaced to a great degree by an interest in the construction of theoretical models. Accompanying this change has been an increasing dependence on the experimental method.

This book relies heavily on discussion of the results of experimental studies, but it also interprets these results in terms of various theoretical

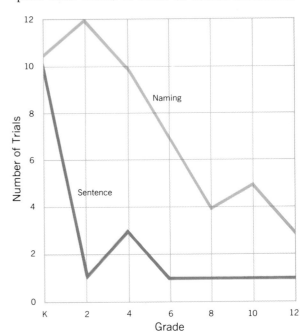

Figure 1.16. The mean number of trials required by children from kindergarten through twelfth grade to learn ten pairs of items. One group learned by naming the items; the other combined the words in a sentence. (After Jensen and Rohwer, 1965.)

positions. The book is not a long narrative of the changes in behavior that occur across the life span, nor is it an exposition of how to rear children or lead the good life. As scientists, psychologists learned long ago that their primary mission is to provide sound and useful information rather than a mere catalogue or an arbitrary list of rules. True, psychologists are always interested in and alert to the applications of psychological data and theories. Even so, they are more likely, for example, to discuss the effects of physical punishment on the child's behavior than to tell the parent that he must always or never spank his child.

THEORIES IN DEVELOPMENTAL PSYCHOLOGY

There is an implicit theory behind every productive investigation. Binet had certain notions about intellectual development before he selected

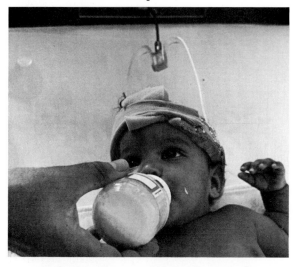

the items for his first intelligence test. Piaget had some idea about children's concepts before he did his first studies with the water glasses. It is not the existence of such ideas but their explicitness and formal organization that distinguish current theories of intellectual development from those of Binet, and Piaget's early work from his later theoretical writings.

There are three basic theoretical approaches to the study of developmental psychology: psychoanalytic, behavioristic, and cognitive. It may seem paradoxical that there is no single, unifying theory, but the explanation is simple: Human behavior has many facets, all of which interact with each other while still maintaining some independence. People perceive, learn, think, and feel. Because each of these components of behavior is so complex in itself, theorists have tended to concentrate on understanding only one. Psychoanalytic theory is for the most part a theory of feeling, a theory of how emotional (affective) states develop and influence behavior. Behavioristic theorists, on the other hand, have been interested in studying learning, the learning both of new information and of social behavior. Cognitive theorists have devoted their attention to thought. Each type of theorist has had something to say about the behavior discussed by the others, but none has attempted to extend his discussion to cover the full range of human behavior.

THE USES OF DEVELOPMENTAL PSYCHOLOGY

This book may well provide you with a new way of looking at the development of human behav-

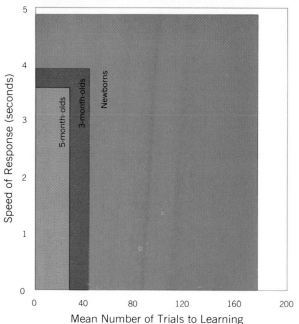

Figure 1.17. Experimental method used to determine how early in life learning (conditioning) can occur. Infants' heads were placed in a light harness, like that shown at top; the harness permitted the automatic recording of incidence and degree of head-turning response. When a bell sounded (CS), the infant's left cheek was stroked, and when he turned his head to the left he was fed milk (UCS). When a buzzer sounded, the milk was presented from the right. The results (bottom) show that the infants learned (CR) to turn their heads to the side indicated by the stimulus, and that although newborns can learn, major developmental changes occur during the first three months of life. (Not shown is the fact that wide individual differences in speed of conditioning exist among newborns; some learned the correct responses in seven days, whereas others required more than a month. (Data from Papoušek, 1967.)

Summary of Methods Used in Developmental Study

Method	Description			Examples in Text
Observational Study Studies Naturalistic Events	Diary Description	Open to diverse phenomena	Describes developmental changes that occur at biographically sampled intervals	Darwin, p. 72 Weir, p. 104
	Specimen Description		Describes intensive and continuing behavior sequences	Schaefer and Bayley, p. 138 Bowlby, pp. 156-157
	Time Sampling	Closed to specific behavioral occurrence	Records selected aspects of behavior in a limited time span	Fantz, p. 73
	Event Sampling		Specific behavioral events (e.g., arguments) are recorded as they occur	Fries, p. 136
	Trait Rating		Specific behaviors, defined beforehand (e.g., aggressiveness), are recorded as they occur	Rheingold, pp. 141-142
Experimental Study Laboratory Setting	An experimenter first hypothesizes a causal relationship. Then, to check his hypothesis, he manipulates one or more (independent) variables in order to study the effect on the specific behavior (dependent variable). All other variables are controlled.			Bower, pp. 109-110 Mundy-Castle, pp. 121-122
Clinical Study Naturalistic or Laboratory Setting	Clinical study refers to a one-to-one interaction between subject and experimenter or researcher — usually a continuous and intensive interchange. It can be open-ended or closed (see Observational Study, above), and this one-to-one type of relationship can be used in a natural or in an experimental setting.			Piaget, pp. 207-208 Bellugi, pp. 216-217

Aims

Any of these methods may have as its goal one of the following:

1. Obtaining NORMATIVE data (what the average behavior is at a given age).

2. Obtaining SYSTEMATIC data (data to support a given theory).

3. Obtaining IDIOGRAPHIC data (what individual differences exist within a given group).

ior. It is easy to view lower organisms with detachment, for their behavior is removed from anything you have experienced. It is more difficult, at first, to look at the behavior of the human being in a similarly objective fashion. But a major message of psychology is that human behavior has its antecedents and its consequences, that there is regularity and a degree of lawfulness in development. With appropriate analysis and objective study you should be able to discover why certain types of behavior occur and how conditions may influence later behavior. After reading this book you should no longer be content, for example, to ascribe a child's aggressive behavior to meanness, but you should demand (and should be able to begin to formulate) a more penetrating analysis of why the child so often attacks other children.

Developmental psychology has grown phenomenally during the past two decades. Is it because methods and theories have reached a relatively sophisticated level? Or is it partly because society has begun to acknowledge the fact that scientific methods can be applied successfully to the understanding of human behavior? Parents face problems in the management and rearing of their children. Teachers are confronted with difficulties in instructing their students. Pediatricians find that a significant proportion of children's illnesses have no physical basis. Social agencies realize the necessity of providing experiences for young children that will improve their prospects for later scholastic and social success. Many questions about psychological development cannot be answered at present, but there is enough sound information and incisive theory for developmental psychology to offer inviting possibilities to anyone interested in understanding—and influencing—the development of human behavior.

Figure 1.18. Characteristics of the three principal methods of psychological investigation.

When one brand-new car smashes into another in a spectacular automobile accident, human beings tend to look for a single cause to explain it—they search for a wheel that was loose, a driver who was drunk, a sign that was inadequate, a street that was slippery. They seldom entertain the likelihood that all four factors could have been involved at once and actually contributed, each in its own way, to the ultimate outcome. Similarly, in explaining human development, people—parents, teachers, and even psychologists—frequently suppose that they need only uncover the one single factor that will fully explain a process or a behavioral outcome. If a child in the second grade is having difficulty learning to read, his teacher may say that he has poor visual acuity, or that his parents tried to teach him reading too early, or that he is lazy, or that he is of low intelligence. We humans, including those of us who pride ourselves on our ability to understand the complexities and nuances of life, are often in search of a single answer when it comes to explaining behavior. In fact, however, few facets of behavior and development can be fully understood by looking at the relationship between a developmental effect and only a single cause.

Any understanding of developmental outcomes must inevitably involve the exploration and documentation of multiple, *interacting* causes. Yet, for convenience, it is necessary to speak of different *classes* of causes in order ultimately to bring them together for joint consideration. Thus, it is convenient to speak of hereditary influences on behavior, even though heredity cannot operate with-

out environmental collaboration. Learning mechanisms are certainly another class involved in the alteration of behavior, even though motivation is intricately implicated with these mechanisms in determining behavior. And there are social influences on child behavior, even though they work differently on persons of different body types, different skin colors, different ages, and even different generations. It is necessary to explore each class of causes individually before beginning to study their complex interactions.

BIOLOGICAL FACTORS

There are two kinds of biological influences on development: one set of factors provides for the maturation of the child; another set of constitutional factors helps provide him with his uniqueness throughout his life span. In the first few years of life biological maturation can be a strikingly regular process, providing for the unfolding of behavior in remarkably patterned and predictable stages. However, maturation does not proceed in a straight line, with a child beginning at a less mature and ineffective stage and proceeding to a more mature and effective stage. Although this is the general direction and nature of the child's development, the movement is more intricate in the child's progression from one stage to another.

In the acquisition of new skills, for example, the child often appears to go through a period between stages: he is trying to abandon his older, lower level of functioning but has not yet become proficient with the higher-level behavior. Thus, disintegration—the falling into disuse of lower-or-

2
Mechanisms of Development

der patterns of behavior—is as important and as visible a part of the developmental process as is the emergence of new, higher-order forms. During the first several months of life, for example, most infants are content to be fed by their mothers. By around one year, however, most children begin demanding that they be allowed to use their own feeding implements. The result is that the child splashes his food everywhere except into his mouth, generally disrupting the business of feeding. Similar apparent setbacks in the process of development are striking during early adolescence. Added maturity often turns a helpful ten-year-old, for example, into a rebellious eleven-year-old. The point is that development is a process of making readjustments and new integrations —and the process can appear to be uneven and risky. In the long run, human growth brings forth new abilities and potentialities, even though it may produce maladjustment in the short run.

PHYSICAL MATURATION

Consider walking as an example of biological maturation. The child's ability to walk matures gradually, through a series of preliminary stages. At birth, the infant has very little control of his posture or movement and remains in basically the position in which he is placed. By twelve weeks an infant lying on his stomach can raise his head up, lifting his chin off the bed. By twenty weeks, the infant sits up with the support of an adult. By six months, he sits on a supportive highchair. By seven months, he sits alone, with no support whatsoever. At eight months, he stands with the help of an adult. By ten months, he crawls, moving himself from place to place with little difficulty. By twelve months, he walks when led. By thirteen months, he walks alone.

Although the ability to walk appears to emerge spontaneously, there are definite organic changes that underlie its emergence. These organic changes are the basic mechanisms of biological maturation. The maturation of various neural pathways is, for example, a prerequisite to walking, as is the growth of certain muscles and bones. The development of these and other neurological and muscular systems basically determines when various functions will emerge in the child. Studies have shown that environmental conditions, experience, and practice affect the rate of biological maturation only under severe conditions.

All parents know the sudden new excitement that comes to the infant when he first begins to creep about freely and then, not too long after, to walk. A whole new environment opens up to the child—cupboards full of pots and pans, drawers, chairs. A simple, gradual process of physical maturation leads to an abrupt widening of the intellectual horizons of the child. He can move about and explore the home he lives in. It is characteristic of most of the great milestones of maturation that they bring the child and later the person to a new environment.

Another developmental change that is a function of biological maturation is the onset of puberty during adolescence. The term *puberty* is de-

rived from the Latin word *pubertas*, meaning age of adulthood. The physiological and bodily changes that occur at this time are due, in part, to an increased output of the gonadotropic hormones of the anterior pituitary gland. This gland, situated in the brain, partially governs and controls the hormonal balance of the body. The gonadotropic hormones stimulate the activity of the gonads, or sex glands, thus increasing the production of sex hormones and the growth of mature sperm and ova in males and females. The sex hormones in combination with other hormones of the body cause the growth of bone and muscle and lead to the typical adolescent growth spurt.

Puberty comes earlier in girls than in boys. On the average, girls start to menstruate at thirteen and boys do not reach maturity until about fifteen. Like other developmental changes that are a function of biological maturation, the onset of puberty is fairly predictable, but there is considerable variation among individuals. The important point is that these biologically determined functions emerge independently of learning—without any particular experiential prerequisites—simply as a result of biological maturation.

In the case of puberty, just as in the case of walking, maturational events throw open a new environment. Society permits the adolescent to have some of the rights of the adult, and it punishes him if he cannot sustain some adult responsibilities. The adolescent, like the toddler, explores that environment. Now it is an environment of legal, political, financial, and religious institutions—the apparatus of the social system in which the adolescent will soon take a part.

On the whole, maturation is a complex orchestration of physical change in the child that brings about psychological change in part because it permits the child to progressively enlarge his physical and psychological environment. As new opportunities are opened, they are seized upon. The child, an organism built to learn, explores each new environment and learns from it.

COGNITIVE GROWTH

Psychologists are interested not only in what the child knows at each age but also in how he knows it. They now believe that the child's grasp of his environment changes qualitatively as well as quantitatively as he grows older. Fundamental changes in the nature of the child's thought occur between early childhood and late adolescence. These changes are a result of the emergence of qualitatively different kinds of mental processes, as described, for example, by Sigmund Freud, Heinz Werner, and Jean Piaget.

One might best describe these different mental processes through a model of the mind as a series of computers. With this analogy, there are three computers that operate at different times in human thinking. Each computer has a unique set of input devices, a unique central processing unit, and a unique set of output devices. Table 2.1 displays the computer levels described, along with the learning processes that occur at each level. It also shows the equivalent cognitive stages according to Piaget's theory of cognitive development.

The infant has available to him a low-level, primitive computer. The thought and output of this computer are intuitive or emotional. The computer performs what Freud called primary process thinking. Its thought is emotionally loaded; various ideas are freely associated with one another, and there are many connections among different ideas. The computer seems to combine and confuse projections from the internal, visceral environment with stimuli from the external environment, so that the inside world is not clearly differentiated from the outside world. In general, the computer deals with information in a crude, impressionistic way and is too primitive to analyze experiences into conceptual categories.

The input to this computer comes from all the senses: visceral sensations, tactile sensations, smells, sounds, or visual sensations. The output is generally an emotional response or a motor reaction.

The emotional learning of this computer stays with the child even when higher-order kinds of thought begin to function. The child defines what and who he is—in both objective and spiritual terms—in these early years through basically emotional experiences. He learns where home is and learns that people interact, talk, laugh, and, in general, behave in certain ways there. These basic patterns define an individual's notion of what is comfortable and what is usual behavior. The environment that the child becomes familiar with in his early years, the accents he hears people use in speaking—things he learns about at an

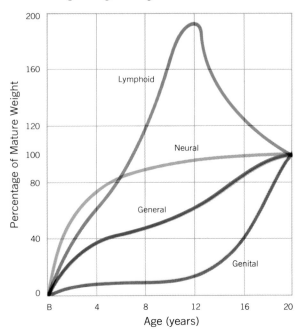

Figure 2.1. The growth rates of the four major categories of organs or tissue types from birth to maturity. Note the steep incline of the curve showing growth in genital organs and tissue during adolescence. (After Scammon, 1930.)

Table 2.1. Summary of Cognitive Development

Computer Analogy	Learning Processes Encompassed	Piagetian Stage and Characteristics
First-order	Classical conditioning Operant conditioning Habituation Chaining Multiple discrimination	*Sensorimotor*—Exists prior to acquisition of symbolic language; infant's intelligence displayed in his actions. *Preoperational*—Thought not usually organized into concepts; no mental representation of a series of actions. (See Chapter 11.)
Second-order	Concept learning Principle learning	*Concrete operations*—Operation of conservation present; child can simultaneously reason about a whole and its parts; ability to serialize. (See Chapter 15.)
Third-order		*Formal operations*—Can consider many possible solutions to a problem; thinking is self-consciously deductive; abstract rules used to solve a whole class of problems. (See Chapter 20.)

emotional level—these will always be natural to him, regardless of what second behavior pattern or language he might learn later on.

As the child progresses through early childhood, a second-order computer becomes dominant. This computer, unlike the first, is well ordered and rational, dealing with information in an objective rather than a subjective way. Unlike the first-order computer, this one can systematically integrate and synthesize information and experiences. It enables the child to process information in the present and to relate this information to past experiences. With the emergence of this computer, the child's behavior begins to take on organizational, planning, and inhibiting functions. Because the child is able to integrate and synthesize experiences, he can plan strategies of problem solving and can inhibit irrelevant behaviors. Between the ages of five and seven the child

begins to solve problems concretely, using a variety of methods, and it is at this point that the differences between the second-order and the lower-order computer become most evident. It is no accident, then, that the child can cope with school at about the same time as the rational computer takes the dominant responsibility for his conduct.

The third-order computer is similar to the second-order, but it can perform greater numbers and kinds of operations on information—it performs functions like those of the second-order computer but in a more complex way. It is able to deal with more information and to make integrations between very different and numerous sets of information. The third-order computer also works at a more abstract level than the second-order one; it is able to make complex deductions about the world, and it is able to integrate and synthesize abstract ideas as well as concrete experiences. Thus, it is responsible for thinking about thoughts. This computer begins to operate during adolescence.

GENETIC ENDOWMENT

A second aspect of the child's biological makeup that influences his development is his genetic endowment. An individual's genetic structure predisposes him toward certain behavioral traits. It is very rarely possible to exactly identify the genes that determine human behavior traits, but it is often possible to infer that a trait has a genetic basis because it runs in families in certain orderly ways. There is evidence of some genetic basis for the physical and physiological makeup of the individual, his *potential* for intelligence, certain talents for music or mathematics, and predispositions to some kinds of psychopathology.

Herbert Birch and his colleagues have found that in the first months of life many infants display a predominant temperament or behavioral pattern, which may persist relatively unchanged through childhood and into adulthood. These temperamental patterns stem from such relatively independent qualities of behavior as activity level, rhythmicity, adaptability, the tendency to approach or withdraw from new stimuli, mood, sensory threshold, distractibility, and attention span. These patterns of temperament may best be viewed as generally referring to the *how* of behavior. They differ from ability, which is concerned with the *what* and *how well* of behaving, and from motivation, which seeks to account for *why* a person does what he is doing. When psychologists refer to temperament, they are concerned with the way in which an individual behaves. Two children may each throw a ball with accuracy and have the same motives in so doing. Yet they may differ with respect to the intensity with which they act, the rate at which they move, the mood they express, the readiness with which they shift to a new activity, and the ease with which they will approach a new situation or playmate.

Temperament thus refers to the behavioral style of the individual. Its importance lies in the fact that certain characteristics that appear in early infancy continue to characterize the child's behavior during the first several years of life. Thus, an infant's profile on such behavioral characteristics as tempo, adaptability, energy expenditure, and mood are generally found to be consistent with his profile during the later years of early childhood.

The relative importance of endowment and of

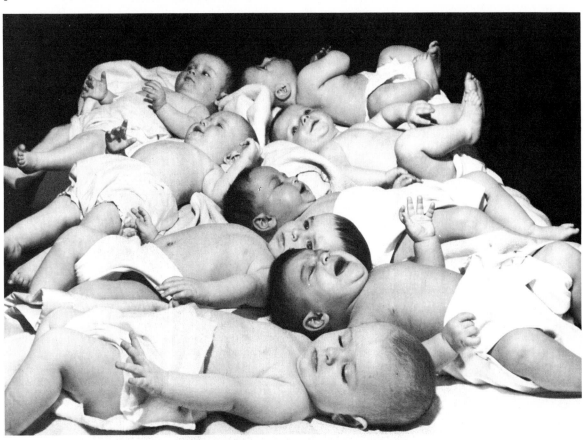

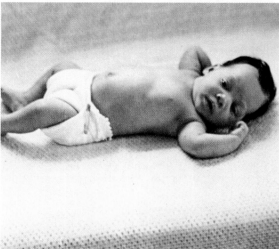

social and environmental factors in forming the child's later temperament has not been clearly delineated. It is clear, however, that degrees of compatibility or incompatibility will come to exist between a child's innate temperament and the attitudes and expectations he meets in his environment; compatibility usually permits healthy development; incompatibility may lead to disturbances in behavior.

Sociocultural Factors

The social and cultural environment provides a general schedule of stages through which individuals pass and a general understanding of the roles appropriate to these various stages. This schedule acts as an external agent regulating the psychological growth of the individual.

As the child gets older, he becomes eligible to participate in new, culturally defined activities, and these activities present him with various expectations and demands. His meeting of these demands serves to change him. The societal stages the child goes through are not independent of one another because entrance into each stage presumes that the last stage has been successfully mastered. Similarly, the stages are not independent of biological maturation because participation in them requires certain degrees of physical, behavioral, and cognitive maturity.

Erik Erikson, in *Childhood and Society*, describes each individual as passing through eight stages, beginning with infancy, progressing through the toddler stage into early childhood, through later childhood into adolescence, and

Figure 2.2. Differences in infants' temperaments can be seen in the first months of life, and this basic temperament may persist relatively unchanged throughout an individual's life.

then into young adulthood, later adulthood, and, finally, maturity (see Table 2.2). Erikson explains

Table 2.2. Erikson's Stages of Man

Chronological Stage	Erikson's Characterization
Oral-sensory	Basic trust vs. mistrust
Muscular-anal	Autonomy vs. shame, doubt
Locomotor-genital	Initiative vs. guilt
Latency	Industry vs. inferiority
Puberty and adolescence	Identity vs. role confusion
Young adulthood	Intimacy vs. isolation
Adulthood	Generativity vs. stagnation
Maturity	Ego integrity vs. despair

Source: Adapted from *Childhood and Society*, 2nd ed., rev., by Erik H. Erikson. By permission of W. W. Norton & Company, Inc. Copyright 1950, © 1963 by W. W. Norton & Company, Inc.

the underlying assumptions of viewing development in terms of these predetermined societal zones. He says that the human personality develops according to steps that are determined by the person's readiness to approach, be aware of, and interact with a widening social horizon. Society welcomes this succession of potentialities for interaction and attempts to encourage the proper rate and the proper sequence of their unfolding. Erikson describes an intricate balance between the individual's maturation and society's expectations of that individual.

As he goes through society's predetermined stages, an individual's understanding of where he is and what society expects of him changes. For example, society's expectations for a married man of twenty-one are very different from its expectations for a twenty-one-year-old bachelor; the young man learns, through a process not unlike osmosis, how he must change for his new role. In normal circumstances, he accepts and is able to fulfill the challenges of society's expectations; he does what society expects of him at various times, and by doing so he is changed by society's developmental schedule.

If an individual does not conform to a general societal norm and is not where society expects him to be at a certain point, he may experience some feeling of inadequacy and tension. For example, the adolescent who drops out of school at sixteen or the young professional who does not get an expected promotion at twenty-nine knows that he is not progressing from one zone to the next—as is expected of him and as his peers are doing—and he is likely to feel unhappy about it. But the societal role structure and how people react to it are complex matters. A person may rigidly define for himself one route through the age norms that he defines as success in life. Actually, there may be many such routes for him and, at any choice point, more alternatives than he recognizes.

INDIVIDUAL VARIATION AND SOCIOCULTURAL NORMS

Societal expectations act as an important guiding force in the psychological development of the child. There are numerous individual variations within this global pattern, however. People who have certain extreme characteristics, for example, tend to have unique patterns of development. General societal norms do allow for individual variation, but there are a good many idiosyncra-

Figure 2.3. An individual's social and cultural environment defines for him his role at the various stages of his development.

sies that cannot be handled by normal social institutions. The public school system, for example, is
only equipped to handle children in the normal
IQ range. Children who fall far below or far
above this range may, if circumstances permit, be
sent to special schools simply because the system
is not equipped to handle extremes. Similarly,
most public institutions are not equipped to handle such unusual traits as kleptomania, and the
school-age child with this problem is likely to be
assigned to a special school. Other unusual characteristics, such as psychosis, epilepsy, and blindness, are likely to be treated in the same way.
Extreme cases that cannot adjust to the system
and that the system cannot accommodate are
removed so that both they and the system can
function better.

Once a child has been steered into a specialized
path, that path itself becomes another developmental force in his life. The mentally retarded
youngster, for example, becomes part of a subculture that acts on him in particular ways.

CULTURAL DIFFERENCES

There are thousands of such variations within the
normal range, some in the form of temporary
choices, some being more permanent choices. Perhaps the best way to illustrate the situation is in
terms of a large number of intersecting railroad
tracks. If an individual makes certain kinds of
decisions, such as the decision to drop out of high
school, he is not likely to reenter some tracks,
such as the track leading to college. Other decisions have only temporary effects on the individual's life, although they, too, act as forces that

serve to influence future development. An example of such a temporary influence is an individual's decision to take a particular high-school or
college course, or to participate in a particular
activity.

Switching back and forth from one track to
another is clearly not a random process. First, the
abilities and unique characteristics of a child as
well as his family background usually prove to be
vital in determining the tracks he will follow.
Second, the effects of biological maturation and
the general societal norms held for individuals in
his culture at his time in history serve to constrain
movement from one track to another. Beyond
that, there is a force that might be called psychocultural inertia: continuing on a given track in
the same direction is extremely likely, but major
changes from one track to another are highly
unlikely.

The railroad track representation can best be
interpreted in terms of concrete life instances. No
two children are born in the same environment—
that is, in precisely the same social milieu. A child
is born into a particular environment, and on the
basis of that environment psychologists can make
certain predictions about where he will be in the
future. They do not expect, for example, that
there will be large moves across social class. Children born in a certain social milieu will find it
very difficult to cross the necessary barriers to
become part of a vastly different social environment. For example, although one of the great
dreams of most American youths is to go to college, it is known that this aspiration is more likely
to be fulfilled if a child's father is a professional

Figure 2.4. A child who is unable to
fulfill the expectations for his social
role—e.g., an unathletic, awkward,
dependent boy—may find himself
miserable and alone for part of his
childhood.

Figure 2.5. Some of the life possibilities
and impossibilities resulting from
high-school tracking.

than if he is an unskilled laborer. In addition to the simple constraints resulting from what is likely and plausible, the principle of psychocultural inertia comes into play; there is a certain psychological and emotional conservatism such that if a child grows up on a farm, there is some doubt that he will be comfortable if transplanted to complex urban settings when he is an adult.

INDIVIDUAL DIFFERENCES

The various social roles acceptable at any one period in a person's life indicate how much individual variation social roles permit and encourage. Tracking in high schools is a good example. In many areas of the country there are at least five different tracks that high-school students are able to follow. The first is the college curriculum, in which students take academic courses as a preparation for enrollment in four-year colleges. The second track is the commercial curriculum, which prepares students to proceed directly into a business or accounting career or into further training (usually at the junior-college level) in commercial skills. The vocational, agricultural, and industrial arts (home economics for girls) tracks prepare adolescents either for direct entrance into a vocation or for further specialized training. The students in each of these tracks are often further divided according to ability.

The high-school culture, of course, consists of more than academically determined roles. It is a complex environment, in which individuals choose a variety of life styles, which they then mold to their own personalities. A study by James

Coleman described in great detail the differences among athletically oriented, academically oriented, and socially oriented high-school males. His study illustrated the fact that there are a wide variety of options available to the adolescent and that once an individual makes a particular choice, the expectations held for individuals who have made that choice become an important force in his subsequent development.

MECHANISMS OF LEARNING

Some of the basic processes of behavioral development can be outlined in terms of the mechanisms involved in learning. These mechanisms are not at all unique to the child; they occur in humans of all ages. As a person grows older, the way he learns does change, but the three computers analogized earlier are all operative in adolescents and adults. Some of the basic mechanisms by which humans learn are described in the following paragraphs.

CLASSICAL CONDITIONING

One of the primary mechanisms involved in the experiential alteration of behavior is classical or Pavlovian conditioning. In this process an initially neutral stimulus is paired with another stimulus that elicits an unconditioned response. Eventually, the neutral stimulus will come to elicit the response. Classical conditioning always involves a purely reflexive response, such as a startle reaction, to a definite stimulus, such as a loud noise. For example, if a puff of air is blown into a person's eye, it is a natural, unconditioned response for the eye to blink. This defensive reflex

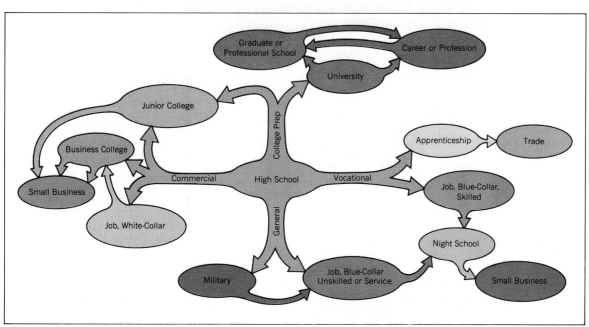

has the effect of protecting the eye from intrusion of foreign matter. If one were to sound a tone just before the presentation of the air puff over a series of trials, the person would eventually become conditioned, so that the tone alone would be sufficient to produce the eye blink.

Classical conditioning occurs during development. For example, a toddler who is commonly fed near a refrigerator in the kitchen usually learns to associate the sight of the refrigerator door closing (an initially neutral stimulus) with the slam of the door, which customarily produces a startle response. The classical conditioning phenomenon may be seen when the infant comes to anticipate the slam by balking or blinking at the sight of the closing door.

Emotions are particularly subject to classical conditioning, as when a child becomes afraid at the sight of an object that once caused him pain or startled him. The classical study of such emotional conditioning was carried out by John B. Watson, the father of American behaviorism. He conditioned a young boy, Albert, to fear furry objects by sounding a very loud noise while Albert was playing with a rabbit. The loud noise startled Albert and made him afraid. This natural and innate reaction to loud noises was transferred to the furry rabbit—as well as to other furry objects such as pelts and even Santa Claus' beard—because the rabbit was engaging Albert's attention when the loud noise sounded. Albert's is a pure case of classical conditioning. There is some controversy over what proportion of learning in in-

fants is classically conditioned. It appears that the amount of learning that takes place through classical conditioning is far less than the amount learned through operant conditioning.

OPERANT CONDITIONING

Operant conditioning involves changes in a child's responses as a result of the reinforcing or rewarding consequences of the response. Organisms tend to engage in behavior that succeeds in producing desirable outcomes. Systematic reinforcement of a response importantly affects the rate at which that response subsequently occurs. Operant conditioning may involve the presentation of a positive event contingent on the desired response. Examples of such positive reinforcers would be the awarding of candy or praise following a response —the reinforcement makes the response more likely. Another kind of reinforcement is called negative because it involves termination of an aversive stimulus following and as a result of a response. Responses that get rid of situations people do not like are likely to be tried again in similar situations in the future.

An amusing example of reinforcement occurred when the students in a psychology class got together and decided to condition their professor. When he moved to the left of the lectern, they disrupted the class—coughed, shuffled papers, dropped books. When he moved to the right, they all paid strict attention. By the middle of the term, the professor stayed strictly to the right of the lectern. Standing to the right was positively reinforced by the students' attention and nega-

Figure 2.6 (opposite top). Diagrammatic outline of the classical conditioning procedure. Here a child learns to fear a stuffed animal. In order for conditioning to occur, the conditioned stimulus must either be presented simultaneously with the unconditioned stimulus or must immediately precede it. Presenting the conditioned stimulus after the unconditioned will not produce conditioning.

Figure 2.7 (opposite, right). Diagrammatic outline of positive reinforcement, used here in an operant conditioning procedure to help a six-year-old girl, Jill, interact positively with her classmates. A therapist came to Jill's class, showed all the children a "Jill box," and told them it would buzz whenever Jill did something particularly good. Each time the box buzzed, Jill and all her classmates got candy. Operant conditioning used in such a purposeful way is called behavior modification.

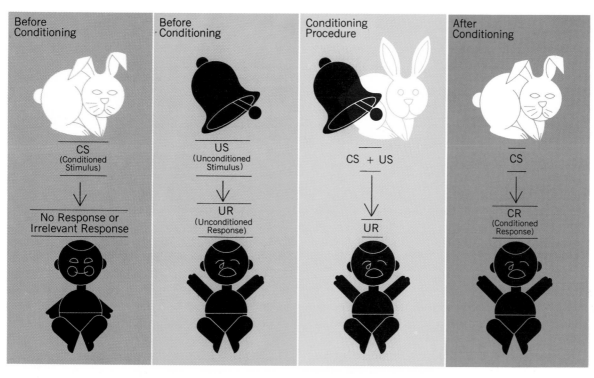

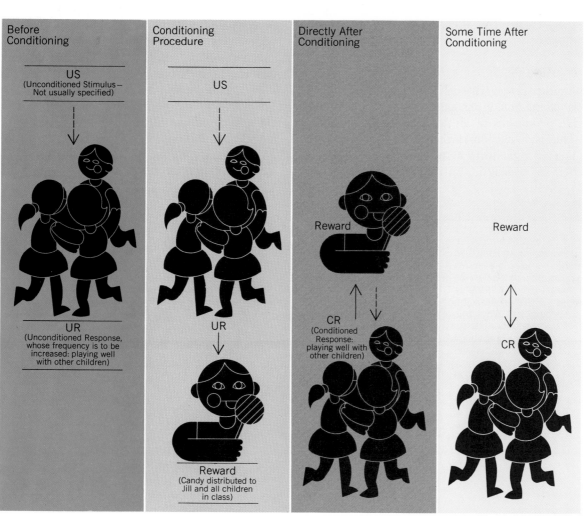

tively reinforced by the ending of the disruptive behavior.

Positive and negative reinforcement increase the tendency of a person to engage in the behavior that produces them. Operant conditioning also specifies a way to inhibit behavior: punish it by arranging that it have undesirable consequences. Suppose that a parent wished to have a child stop sucking his thumb. He might arrange that thumb sucking have undesirable consequences, such as the immediate but temporary shutting off of the child's favorite television program. As each entry of the thumb into the mouth continues to cause the shutting off the television set, the tendency of the child to suck will decrease dramatically.

The operant technique rests on the law of effect, which asserts that responses followed by a satisfying state of affairs will tend to be repeated under similar circumstances in the future, whereas behaviors that produce neutral or disagreeable effects will tend to diminish in frequency. The law of effect has been shown under many different circumstances to exert powerful control over many different kinds of behavior in humans.

HABITUATION

Another process through which behavior changes is *habituation*, a phenomenon that is demonstrable in humans of all ages, including newborns. This phenomenon involves the gradual diminution of response to a stimulus that is presented over and over again. Initially, the stimulus arouses

some sort of behavior, but the behavior becomes less and less arousable as the stimulus is presented over and over again. For example, in experiments children will initially press a button or pull a plunger to produce an interesting picture on a screen, but the response will drop off unless a novel stimulus is substituted for the original one. This phenomenon is often spoken of in terms of the subject's getting used to the stimulus or becoming bored by it. The functional significance of this built-in process is that it enables persons to disregard stimulation in their environment that is of no particular consequence at a given time so they can focus on matters that may be more important for survival or enjoyment. Most babies who are at first disturbed by loud noises in the household, such as telephone bells or a barking dog, will habituate to the noises after relatively short periods.

Learning mechanisms are major contributors to the acquisition of intellectual performance. Learning is basic to the socialization of individuals, and learning processes figure prominently in the personality functioning and adjustment of individuals. For example, if habituation does not occur in the young child, he becomes overresponsive to multiple sources of stimulation, and his learning of such basic skills as reading may be impeded. Similarly, classical conditioning enables the human to take preparatory action in the presence of noxious or threatening stimulation. It is also clear that the judicious application of reward to the young child for socially sanctioned behavior enables parents and society to socialize the

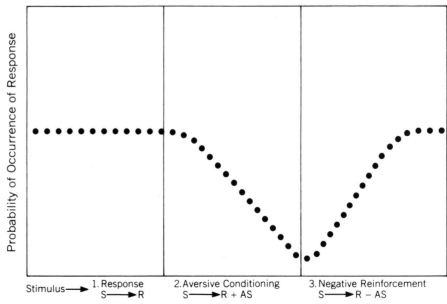

Figure 2.8. Diagrammatic outline of aversive conditioning and negative reinforcement. In aversive conditioning, a punishment—aversive stimulus (AS)—follows the response. When this sequence occurs repeatedly, the probability of the response decreases—sometimes reaching zero. When the aversive stimulus is removed, the probability of the original response occurring increases.

Probability of Occurrence of Response

Stimulus⟶   1. Response   2. Aversive Conditioning   3. Negative Reinforcement
            S⟶R   S⟶R + AS   S⟶R − AS

infant. All learning, however, takes place against a backdrop of biological limitations and the child's personal experiential history.

Complex Manifestations of Learning

The mechanisms set out above are at the base of the more complex manifestations of learning. For example, a type of learning called *chaining* consists of putting together behaviors that were previously learned by means of conditioning, and chaining underlies the more complex types of learning discussed below.

CHAINING

Chains consist of a sequence of nonverbal behaviors or of verbal associations, which can vary in length from the acts involved in buttoning to those involved in reciting the Boy Scout Oath. Each link in the chain must have previously been learned—from external cues—and the links then must be put together to produce the desired outcome. Chains are an important but not very complex form of learning.

Naming is probably the simplest of verbal chains. When a child is shown a ball and told its name, two links in the association are required for the child to learn the word. The first is discriminatory: the child's attention must have been drawn to the special properties of *ball*—roundness, bounciness, it rolls. The second link is the conditioning to associate the sound "ball" with the properties he had previously distinguished.

When several simple chains have been learned, they may be combined sequentially (my ball) or

in one of two other important ways: *multiple discrimination* or *concept learning*.

MULTIPLE DISCRIMINATION

Multiple discrimination is essentially the establishment of numbers of different chains. It takes place, for example, in learning the vocabulary items for a foreign language. Young children learn to discriminate among many classes of things in their environment and learn the distinguishing names for these items: dump truck, fire truck, garbage truck, ice cream truck. This kind of learning plays an important role in more complex learning activities, such as concept learning.

CONCEPT LEARNING

Putting things into a class and responding to the class as a whole is a definition of concept learning. Given a number of objects that may vary widely in appearance, an individual learns to respond to them in terms of some abstract property they all possess. The capabilities that were established by multiple discrimination are a prerequisite to the learning of concepts, that is, an individual must have firmly acquired a set of chains (verbal or not) to represent the characteristics of the members that will compose the class. Concept learning is not necessarily verbal; a pigeon that has learned to respond to a lighted round key (and to ignore unlighted ones) to get food and that then responds to a lighted square key (and ignores unlighted round ones) has put lighted keys into a class and responds differently to lighted keys than to unlighted ones. In most

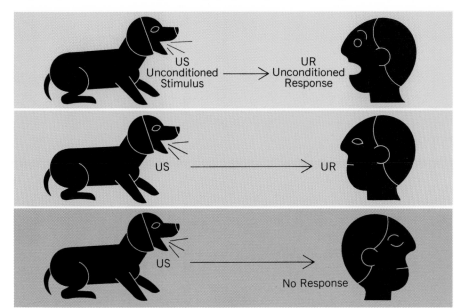

Figure 2.9. Diagrammatic outline of habituation.

cases, however, people do employ language in the learning of concepts. In fact, people largely organize their world by means of concepts: concepts of objects—chairs, animals, vegetables; concepts of place—up, next to, in front of; concepts of events—go, put, stop. All these are concepts that most children learn before age four. The use of concepts frees human thought and expression from the domination of the physical environment.

It may be that the process of conceptualizing is different in children than in adults; in children what takes place is truly concept *learning*, whereas in adults the process might better be called concept *generalizing*. The different kinds of concepts (superordinate, relational, and analytical) and how children use them are discussed at length in Chapter 15.

PRINCIPLE LEARNING

A principle may be defined as a relationship (chain) between two or more concepts. The concepts that are to be linked must already have been learned. For example, "trains go on tracks" relates the four concepts of train, track, on, and go. This principle is a relatively simple one; a child can demonstrate that he has learned this principle not by repeating it but by demonstrating it. If some toy trucks, automobiles, and trains are set before the child, with toy train tracks and other kinds of roadways, and the child runs the train along the track, it is clear that he has learned the principle.

For the most part, it is only young children who learn principles in isolation—"stoves are hot." Older children and adults typically learn related sets of principles that are part of a larger topic. For example, "Salt is composed of the elements Na and Cl" is only one principle in the hierarchy of principles that make up the study of chemistry.

By combining old principles into new ones, people can solve problems that are new to them—although the solution arrived at may not be new at all to other people. Problem solving occurs every day in the life of most people—a housewife decides how to place furniture in a room; a lawyer decides how to plead a case; a plumber repairs faulty piping. From time to time, people come up with solutions that are entirely new—and this may be defined as creativity.

The mechanisms of learning are set out in Table 2.1, which ties them in with the computer analogy discussed earlier in this chapter and with the stages of cognitive development described by Jean Piaget.

AN OVERVIEW OF MECHANISMS

Development is not a simple linear progression upward through better and better stages. On the contrary, the process of psychological growth often brings setbacks, in the form of periods of unhappiness, stress, trouble, and difficulty. In this process, the individual generally moves from a lower-order stage through a period of confusion, emerging with new, higher-order abilities that supersede his previous abilities. The transition from one level of performance to another is not always smooth; it involves troubled moments when a lower-order ability is in the process of disintegration and a higher-order ability has not yet emerged.

We have seen that biological maturation is a primary mechanism of development. It leads to physical, behavioral, and cognitive changes in the individual. Particular behaviors, such as walking and language, emerge as a consequence of the predetermined schedule of biological maturation that is a part of the individual's genetic makeup. It is remarkable to observe these behaviors emerge with no apparent experiential precursors. Actually, basic neurological and physiological changes underlie the emergence of these behaviors. Such organic changes also underlie the cognitive changes that occur during development, including the shifting in organization from one level of information processing to another, higher level.

We have also seen that genetic endowment plays an important part in the child's development. Various temperamental characteristics such as distractibility and irritability, for example, interact with the child's environment in various ways, sometimes successfully, sometimes leading to behavior problems. During growth, particular genetically determined individual characteristics manifest themselves. In general, growth is a process of differentiation in which the particular abilities and idiosyncrasies of each individual become manifest and interact with the environment.

There are two distinct kinds of differentiation that occur during the child's development. The first is a function of the particular individual's genetic endowment—differentiation due to intrinsic, biological factors. The second kind of differentiation is a function of the particular individual's interaction with social and cultural factors—differentiation due to the extrinsic, social environment. As these differentiations occur, the new social roles that an individual assumes become a force influencing his later development.

Learning is the final fundamental force in the child's development. Learning occurs as a result of the consequences of the child's behavior when he encounters new experiences.

These, then, are the mechanisms of development. Each plays its role in the drama of growth, but none appears singly on the stage. There is always multiple causation in development. Each type of mechanism is implicated to some degree in every developmental event, and the human intricacies of development require the harmonious cooperation of each of these mechanisms. The rest of this book is an essay in praise of such cooperation in the service of progress toward maturity.

A newborn baby is both an end and a new beginning. The gestation period of growing inside the mother's body, the first and in many ways the most important phase of life, is suddenly ended by birth. No other developmental period will ever again end so dramatically in so short a time and so absolutely finally. Birth represents both separation and deprivation, independence and the necessity of self-reliance. No longer will the baby be able to rely entirely on the resources of the mother's body; he must rely on his own. Much that will mark or distinguish the child for the rest of his life has already happened. The baby's heredity, fully determined some nine months earlier at conception, has already expressed itself in the initial physical form and psychological temperament of the infant. Any inadequacies in the mother's condition during pregnancy have already worked their often-irreversible damage on the child. And the dangerous and potentially fatal birth trauma has only just recently been survived. But in the vast majority of normal cases, a bright, hungry, active, inquiring, responsive infant enters the world equipped with a healthy and growing body and a rapidly expanding motor, sensory, and mental capacity that admirably fit him for the beginning of life. It must be granted that a great deal has already been determined at birth and that the child's family, society, and culture will determine much more as he grows. But the adult cannot be known with certainty from the child. At birth, the infant faces the challenge of his very own, particularly individual development.

Unit II
The Beginning of the Life Cycle

The seven stages of the life cycle
are symbolized by the illustrated
boxes accompanying each of
the seven unit openings. One box is
removed from the set as each
life stage is considered.

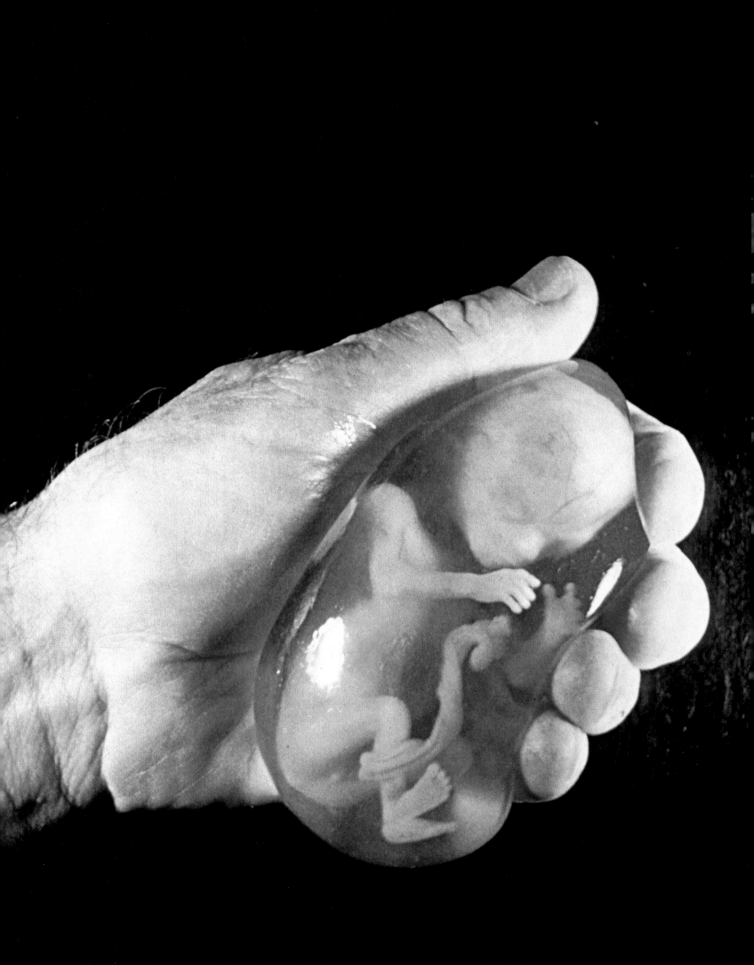

Previous to the nineteenth century, people held a variety of beliefs and superstitions about how a human being is formed at the beginning of life. Medieval artists depicted the child in the womb as a miniature man, complete with all human features and involved in a variety of motor activities. But Leonardo da Vinci, in his notebooks of 1510–1512, made several sketches of the unborn infant, indicating in the margins that the infant in the womb is immobile and essentially a part of the mother, sharing her blood and making use of her other organ systems.

In the seventeenth and early eighteenth centuries, biologists were divided into two camps: the *ovists* held that the prefabricated baby is contained somehow in the mother's ovaries and that the sperm merely serve to incite the expansion of the already-made baby; the *homunculists*, on the other hand, said that the preformed man exists in the head of the sperm, which uses the womb as an incubator in which to grow. These two views, together called the emboîtement (encapsulation) theory, were effectively demolished in 1759 when Kaspar Wolff postulated that both parents contribute equally to the organism and that the life of an individual begins as a bunch of globules. More than fifty years later Karl von Baer substantiated this theory when he discovered the mammalian egg cell under his microscope.

In the second half of the nineteenth century, study and knowledge of embryology became widespread. The discovery of the nature of the cell, the publication of Darwin's *On the Origin of Species*, and George E. Coghill's systematic observation and reporting of embryonic behavior all contributed significantly to current knowledge of prenatal development.

CONCEPTION

The life of each and every one of us began with the uniting of two cells into one at the moment of conception. Of the two cells, called *gametes*, one, the sperm cell or *spermatozoon*, came from our fathers, and the second, the egg or *ovum*, came from our mothers.

An ovum is a tiny speck barely visible to the naked eye but still some 85,000 times greater in volume than the tadpolelike sperm. A woman produces one mature ovum approximately every twenty-eight days, and this ovum is receptive to male sperm for about one day after it has left the ovary and is in the process of traveling down the Fallopian tube to the uterus. During normal heterosexual intercourse, spermatozoa (continually manufactured in the male testes, so that the man is almost always fertile), which are suspended in a fluid called *semen*, are released by the male and enter the vagina. The semen may contain anywhere from 20 million to 500 million spermatozoa per cubic centimeter, all capable of fertilizing the ovum. A small percentage of these sperm manage to propel themselves, by lashing their tails, through the *cervix*, the opening connecting the vagina and uterus, and eventually make their way to the Fallopian tube. Inside the tube the surviving spermatozoa wait for an ovum; if one arrives,

3
Prenatal Development

they surround it, and one sperm cell eventually penetrates the outer membrane of the ovum and makes its way to the cell's nucleus. The sperm and ovum thus unite to form a single cell, the *zygote*, which will soon develop into a new human being.

EARLY STAGES OF PRENATAL DEVELOPMENT

Prenatal development falls into roughly three stages. During the first two weeks after conception, called the *germinal period*, the fertilized egg is primarily engaged in cell division. In the six weeks following the germinal period, the *embryonic period*, the organism begins to take shape and its various organ systems begin to form. Thereafter, from approximately eight weeks after conception to birth, the developing organism is called a *fetus*. The total gestation period usually lasts about 280 days, or nine calendar months, calculating from the beginning of the mother's last menstruation. The fetus' age, then, is referred to as its *menstrual age*.

THE GERMINAL PERIOD

Almost immediately following fertilization, the zygote begins the process of cell division that will eventually result in a human body made up of many billions of cells. It is estimated that the fertilized ovum takes about three days to progress through the Fallopian tube to the uterus, where it floats freely for another four or five days before becoming attached to the uterine wall. While floating around in the uterus, the cluster of cells

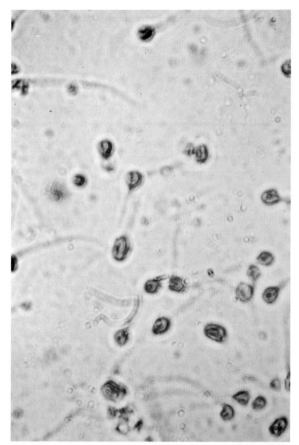

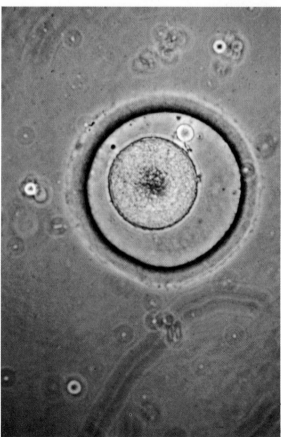

Figure 3.1. Living, active human sperm, highly magnified. The waving tails propel the sperm, and the head contains the nucleus, which carries the twenty-three chromosomes. (From Rugh and Shettles, 1971; courtesy Dr. L. B. Shettles.)

Figure 3.2. Living human ovum. (From Rugh and Shettles, 1971; courtesy Dr. L. B. Shettles.)

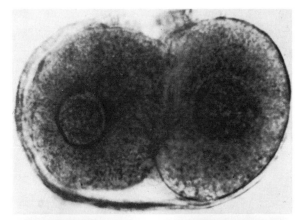

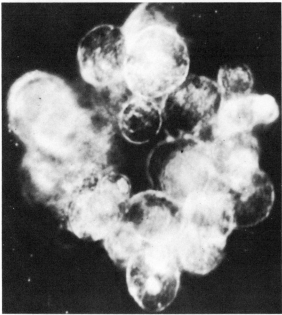

forms what is called a *blastula*, a hollow sphere that soon fills with fluid (see Figure 3.3). As the number of cells in the blastula increases, some move outward and mass at one end. As the structure begins to differentiate itself into different parts, it becomes known as a *blastocyst*. Most of the blastocyst will be devoted to the housing of the growing organism: the cells surrounding the cavity come to form the protective *chorion* (the outer sac) and the *placenta* (the organ that forms in the uterine lining and through which the developing organism receives nourishment and discharges waste). The inner mass of cells comes to form the *amnion* (the inner sac), the nonfunctional yolk sac, and the *body stalk*, which will become the *umbilical cord* and the *embryonic disk*, from which the embryo itself will emerge. The embryonic disk is in turn made up of two cell layers, the *ectoderm* (upper layer) and *endoderm* (lower layer). The line at which the two layers meet will soon become a third layer, the *mesoderm*. From these three primary germ layers, cells are differentiated that will become various body tissues: the ectoderm is the source of cells for the skin, the sense organs, and the nervous system; the mesoderm is the point of origin for the muscular, circulatory, and skeletal systems; and the endoderm gives rise to some of the digestive glands and the alimentary canal.

By the end of the germinal period the organism is enclosed in a double-walled membrane (the chorion and amnion) that extends out of the placenta in the form of a balloonlike sac filled

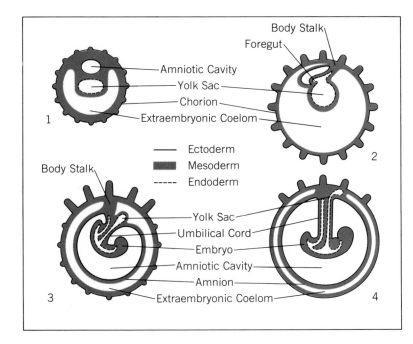

a
b

Figure 3.3. (a) Human egg at the two-cell stage of division. (Courtesy Carnegie Institution of Washington.) (b) When the fertilized ovum has divided four times, the resultant sixteen-cell entity is called the morula. These sixteen cells are similar; differentiation has not yet begun. The blastula is the subsequent stage of development. (Courtesy Dr. L. B. Shettles.)

Figure 3.4. Stages in cell differentiation leading to development of the embryo and the membranes that support it. (From *Embryology*, 6th ed., by J. B. McMurrich. Copyright© 1920 P. Blakiston's Son & Co. Used with permission of McGraw-Hill Book Company.)

with amniotic fluid in which the organism itself floats. So far so good; life is well on its way.

THE EMBRYONIC PERIOD

During the second week of its existence, the blastocyst embeds itself in the spongy wall of the uterus, and thereafter it is referred to as an embryo. Tiny tendrils from the outer layer of the organism's self-created environment take root in the uterine wall; they soon take shape as capillaries, called the *chorionic villi*, that are linked with the developing umbilical veins and arteries. The villi, together with the surrounding maternal tissues, eventually become parts of the placenta.

During the embryonic period the various organ systems start to emerge. The heart, a U-shaped tube, is usually beating by early in the fourth week and is, in proportion to the embryo's body, nine times larger than the adult heart. Blood begins to flow through the microscopic veins and arteries. There is a simple brain, rudimentary kidneys, a liver. a digestive tract, and a primitive umbilical cord. Yet the month-old embryo is only about one-fifth of an inch long, which is still about 10,000 times larger than the original fertilized egg. As shown in Figure 3.5, the embryo is markedly curved and there is a distinct head fold, which contains swellings and markings that will eventually become the jaw, eyes, and ears of the growing individual.

By the end of the embryonic period, the organism reaches a length of about one inch. What look like the gill slits of a fish are really the forerunners of the throat, esophagus, jaws, and

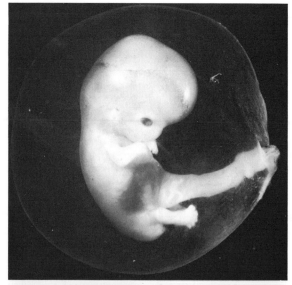

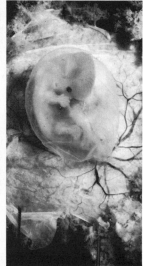

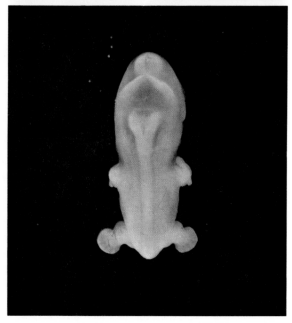

Figure 3.5. The embryonic period. (Color from Rugh and Shettles, 1971.)

external ears. What appears to be a primitive tail eventually becomes the tip of the adult spine; the tail reaches its maximum length at about six weeks and thereafter slowly recedes. The head is clearly distinct from the rounded, skin-covered body and accounts for about half the embryo's total size. The eyes have come forward from the sides of the head and eyelids have begun to form. The face clearly contains ears, nose, lips, tongue, and even the buds of teeth. Limb buds grow, too, and become paddle shaped. The fingers have begun to appear, first merely as ridges but later as separate entities (see Figure 3.6).

Even before the embryo enters what is called the fetal stage, the brain sends out impulses that coordinate the functioning of the other organ systems. The heart beats sturdily, while the stomach produces minute quantities of some digestive juices, the liver manufactures blood cells, and the kidneys extract urea from the blood. The endocrine system has taken shape: the adrenal medulla secretes epinephrine, and the testes in the male embryos begin to produce androgens. Even isolated reflexes can be elicited. However, all these functions are in very primitive form and must develop for several more months before they can be considered fully functional.

The Fetal Period

The actual physical event used to determine the change from the embryonic to the fetal stage is the appearance of the first bone cells about three months after conception. Because the fetal period composes the major portion of prenatal develop-

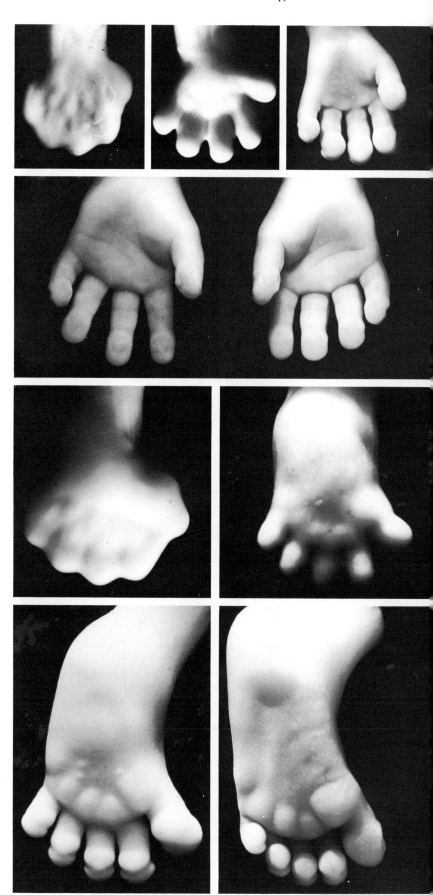

Figure 3.6. Development of hands and feet. In the fifth week hands are a "molding plate" with finger ridges. In the sixth week finger buds have formed. In the seventh and eighth weeks the fingers, thumbs, and fingerprints form; note the prominent touch pads. In the third month the pads regress, and hands are well formed. The feet begin to form in the sixth week, and forty-eight hours later have large toe ridges. The heel appears by the end of the sixth week and grows out in the next five days. In the third month feet are well formed.

ment, it is best to further divide it by discussing fetal development on a month-by-month basis.

THE THIRD MONTH

By the end of the third month, the fetus is about three inches long, and the head continues to be relatively large, with a high, prominent forehead, a prominent nose, external ears level with the lower jaw, and eyelids that are sealed shut (see Figure 3.7). Buds for all twenty temporary teeth are formed, and vocal cords appear. The ribs and vertebrae of the fetus turn to hard cartilage. The fingers are well developed, and fingernails and toenails are forming. The external genitals undergo marked changes, and it is possible to determine the sex of the fetus by inspection.

By the end of the third month the fetus shows a distinctive individuality. Although at this age the fetus weighs only an ounce, it is already quite active. It can kick its legs, turn its feet, close its fingers, bend its wrist, turn its head, squint, frown, open and close its mouth, and perform other such actions.

THE FOURTH MONTH

During the fourth month the growth of the lower parts of the body accelerates so that the head size is now only one-fourth of the total body size. The fetus doubles in length to almost six inches and increases in weight to about four ounces. Most of the bone models have been formed by four months, although *ossification*, the replacement of cartilage by true bone, will not be complete until many years after birth. Reflexes become more

brisk as muscular maturation continues, and movements can often be readily perceived by the mother (the first ones she feels are known as the *quickening*).

THE FIFTH MONTH

By the end of the fifth month the growing fetus is about one foot long and weighs about a pound. Its skin structures begin to attain final form, and the sebaceous glands have appeared and are functioning. Fingernails and toenails have formed, the bony axis has become quite straight, and much spontaneous activity occurs. The fetus sleeps and wakes much as a newborn does, but it also undergoes torporous periods not found in the newborn. It even has a characteristic lie, or favorite position in which to sleep. A five-month-old fetus may survive briefly outside its mother's body, but it usually dies because of its inability to maintain the necessary breathing movements.

THE SIXTH MONTH

In the sixth month the growing organism adds about two more inches and gains almost another pound. The eyelids, which have been fused shut, open to reveal completely formed eyes—the fetus may open and close its eyes and look up, down, and sideways. Abundant taste buds (more than in infants or adults) appear on the tongue and in the mouth. Eyebrows and lashes may have formed. A fine, woolly fuzz, the *lanugo hair*, appears on most of the body; however, most of this lanugo will disappear if the fetus goes full term. At this age the fetus has a grasp reflex and will soon be

Figure 3.7. Growth of the fetus. (From Rugh and Shettles, 1971.)

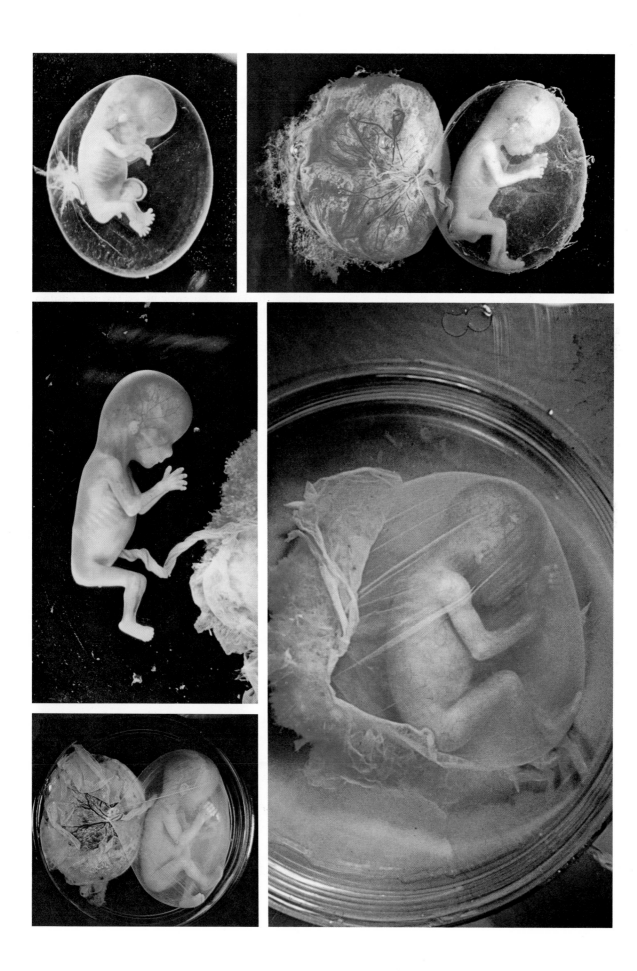

able to support its weight by holding on to a rod with one hand. In the sixth month the fetus also is capable of making slight but irregular breathing movements and may hiccup.

THE SEVENTH MONTH

By this time the organism is capable of independent life. The cerebral hemispheres cover almost the entire brain, and the fetus can perform a variety of specialized responses. The seven-month-old fetus is usually about sixteen inches long and weighs about three pounds. The hair on his head may grow long. Also by this time, one or both of the male testes may have descended into the scrotum. If born during the seventh month, the baby is able to cry, breathe, and swallow. He is highly sensitive to infection, and he needs a highly sheltered environment, such as an incubator, in order to survive.

THE EIGHTH AND NINTH MONTHS

During the final period of prenatal development, the finishing touches are put on the organs and functional capacities of the organism. Fat rapidly forms over its entire body, smoothing out the wrinkled skin and rounding out its contours. The fetus is quite active at this stage, although its actions become limited because of the increasingly snug fit in the womb. Its organs step up their activity and its heart rate becomes quite rapid. In the filling-out process the fetus usually gains about a half a pound a week.

At birth the average full-term infant weighs a little more than seven pounds, though weight may vary from five to twelve pounds, and he is about twenty inches long. The normal term of pregnancy is 280 days, but babies born between 180 and 334 days after conception may be able to survive.

THE BIRTH PROCESS

Toward the end of pregnancy, the fetus turns head down and comes to rest with his head in the lower part of the uterus. He is then in position for a headfirst passage into the world. The onset of labor, the process by which the baby is expelled from the mother's body, is probably triggered hormonally, although the specific trigger is unknown. Once begun, labor consists of relaxation of the circular muscles of the cervix and spontaneous rhythmic contractions of the involuntary longitudinal uterine muscles, aided by contraction of the voluntary abdominal musculature. The muscular contractions gradually squeeze the baby out of the uterus and through the vagina into the world.

Labor is usually divided into three stages. The first and longest stage is the period in which the cervix dilates to permit passage of the baby's head; contractions during this time come at progressively shorter and shorter intervals. This stage lasts an average of fourteen hours for first babies but is usually much briefer for later children.

The second stage of labor includes the baby's passage through the vagina and his actual delivery into the world. This stage may last from under twenty minutes to an hour and a half. After the baby has been extracted, the doctor (or midwife) holds him by the ankles and, if breathing has not begun spontaneously, slaps him on the buttocks to get him started. As soon as the blood vessels of the umbilical cord stop pulsating, the cord is clamped and cut. The baby is then quickly assessed for breathing, muscle tone, heart rate, reflexes, irritability, and color to determine if he will need further medical help. For the infant, a long and difficult birth may be accompanied by *anoxia* (reduced oxygen supply), by toxins in the blood supply, or by direct injury to the brain.

The third and final stage of labor consists of the delivery of the *afterbirth*—the placenta with its attached membranes and the remainder of the umbilical cord. This stage takes less than twenty minutes and is virtually painless. The doctor will usually examine the afterbirth to see if it is complete and normal.

Not all deliveries proceed in this normal fashion. In a breech delivery, the baby's buttocks appear first, then his legs, and finally his head. Such deliveries are dangerous because the infant may suffocate before his head emerges. Deliveries involving extensive use of instruments are also potentially dangerous and may result in permanent brain damage. Some babies must be delivered surgically, by Caesarean section, because there are medical complications that would make a long labor dangerous for the life of the mother or child or because the fetus is in an abnormal position.

Environmental Influences on Prenatal Development

Although the intrauterine environment is usually quite stable and varies only within narrow limits, experimental manipulation of the prenatal envi-

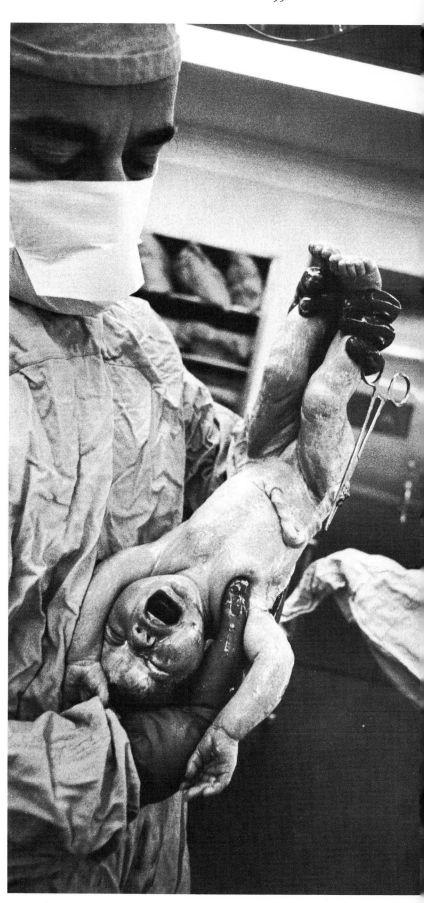

ronment of animal embryos indicates that even minor alterations can produce serious deformities. Some of the agents that have been shown to alter prenatal development in one species or another include poisons, drugs, viruses, x-rays and other radiation, abnormal blood conditions of the mother (anemia), hormone imbalance, vitamin excess or deficiency, lack of oxygen, and iodine deficiency.

These environmental influences have caused such deformities as anencephaly (lack of brain), harelip, phocomelia (deformation of limbs such as that caused by the drug thalidomide), cleft palate, extra or missing members, and sex reversal or ambiguity.

The nature and extent of any environmental influence on the developing organism depend on a variety of factors, including the time of development at which the agent is introduced, the part of the organism affected, the size of the dose, and individual differences among organisms.

Timing is apparently the crucial factor in determining whether or not an abnormality will appear, and if so, what kind it will be. Because various bodily organs develop on a special timetable, if an organ does not develop at the proper time it may never be able to develop fully. Thus, if development is interrupted when the internal ear is being formed (seventh to tenth week), deafness may result. However, the interference does not affect organs that have already appeared or those that have not yet developed. Because the first three months of pregnancy (primarily the germinal and embryonic stages) are critical for differentiation of the body organs, environmental

interference occurring during that time produces most of the defects originating in the prenatal period.

MATERNAL HEALTH

Although the circulatory system of the mother and the developing organism are completely separate, research has shown that certain maternal infections may be transmitted across the placental barrier, enter the fetal bloodstream, and affect the developmental process. Maternal German measles (rubella), for example, may cause congenital abnormalities such as blindness, deafness, brain damage, and heart disease. It is estimated that 30,000 birth defects and 20,000 fetal deaths resulted from the German measles epidemic in the United States in 1963–1965. Other viruses and some bacteria (such as smallpox, chicken pox, mumps, malaria, and syphilis) may infect the fetus so that the disease is present in the newborn.

Severe maternal nutritional deficiencies during pregnancy can affect the developing organism. Deficiencies in vitamins B, C, and D are known to have caused fetal abnormalities and even death. An oversupply of vitamin A also causes developmental defects. Maternal malnutrition or lack of protein can also affect the length and weight of the child at birth.

Several researchers have suggested that the emotional state of the mother may have an influence on the personality development of the child. The mother's emotional state can bring about chemical changes in her body, and some maternal substances may cross the placental barrier to produce changes in the fetus. Research at the level of the rat and mouse has shown that mothers subjected to severe or prolonged stress, sudden exposure to cold, or crowded living conditions can produce offspring whose infantile body size, viability, adrenal size and activity, anxiety level, and learning ability are affected.

RH FACTOR

Blood incompatibilities may also affect the newborn. If the red blood cells of the father are Rh positive and the mother's Rh negative, then Rh antigens (substances that stimulate production of antibodies) may be present in the fetal blood, inherited from the father, while absent in the mother's blood. Antigenic red blood cells pass into the maternal blood from the fetus during pregnancy, resulting in the production of anti-Rh substances in the mother's blood. These anti-Rh substances may then cross the placental barrier in the other direction and destroy the fetal red cells. Because the changes in the mother's blood occur very slowly, a first-born child is rarely affected. However, subsequent children may be severely affected and may require a blood transfusion at birth. Sometimes the fetus may be so severely affected as to require intrauterine transfusion. But under some circumstances pregnancies with an Rh incompatibility are normal and the infant is not affected.

Other environmental factors have possible effects on the growing organism. For instance, smoking on the part of the mother has been shown to lower the birth weight of the baby, and maternal use of alcohol, hallucinogenic drugs, and some medications may also affect the child. Some of the effects may be minor, but others, very damaging, such as those caused by thalidomide.

PRENATAL BEHAVIOR

In the discussion of the physical development of the fetus, some of the behaviors that the organism shows before birth were mentioned. For example, thumb sucking, kicking, hiccuping, and other motor activities have been known to occur in the fetus during its development. But how early in its life is the prenatal organism capable of responding to stimuli, what kinds of responses does it make, and what kind of spontaneous behavior does it exhibit?

In an effort to answer these and similar questions about prenatal behavior, researchers such as Davenport Hooker have studied embryos and fetuses delivered by Caesarean section. Those organisms too premature to be saved are placed in a physiological solution maintained at normal body temperature; the researchers then observe the organism's spontaneous movements and reactions to stimuli and record them on film for later study. Table 3.1 and Figure 3.8 show some of the re-

Table 3.1. Prenatal Behavior

Menstrual Age	Behavior
Less than 8 weeks	No response until about 7.5 weeks, when touching the region around the mouth with a hair may result in a flexion of the neck (bending the head to the side opposite the stimulus).
8 to 10 weeks	Touching the perioral region results in a characteristic response involving a lateral flexion (or bending) of the trunk and neck, usually to the opposite side, an extension of the upper arms, and a rotation of the pelvis, then a return to the original posture.
10 to 14 weeks	Movements become more varied and less stereotyped; when the palms of the hands are stimulated with a hair, the fingers partially close; the toes may show upward and downward flexion if the sole of the foot is stimulated; eyelid muscles contract; all areas of the body but the back and the top of the head become receptive to stimulation by 12 weeks; stimulation of the lips sometimes causes swallowing.
14 to 18 weeks	Movement becomes graceful rather than mechanical; stimulation to facial areas may elicit a facial response alone rather than a response of the entire body; a rudimentary grasping reflex appears— fingers remain closed over a hair drawn across the palm; protrusion of the lips can be seen if the lips are stimulated; stimulation of the chest may evoke thoracic contractions.
19 to 24 weeks	If resuscitated after delivery, the fetus can sometimes carry on sustained respiration briefly; it can make a thin crying noise by 24 weeks; it exhibits a grasp reflex strong enough for the observer to move the upper extremities by pulling on a rod the fetus is grasping; also by 24 weeks, respiration may continue for more than three hours.
25 weeks to birth	Self-sustained respiration may continue for more than 24 hours at 25 weeks; the knee jerk, ankle clonus, and other tendon reflexes can be elicited after the fetus has respired for half an hour; eyes may open and close spontaneously; a very strong grasping reflex has developed; the Moro reflex appears; an audible suctorial response is exhibited at 29 weeks; more spontaneous movements occur.

Source: Davenport Hooker, *The Prenatal Origin of Behavior* (Lawrence: University of Kansas Press, 1952; reprinted 1969 by Hafner Publishing Company, New York).

sponses that Hooker found in fetuses at various ages.

Behavioral development in the prenatal organism corresponds to the development of the nervous system and of the muscles of the body. The earliest responses found in embryos can be elicited by stroking the area about the mouth with a fine hair at about seven and a half weeks of menstrual age. The response thus elicited is a general one involving the upper trunk and neck. As the organism develops, more and more of the body area becomes sensitive to stimulation, and responses eventually become localized to the area stimulated, so that when the mouth area is stimulated, only reflexes in the mouth area are elicited.

Within the last few months before birth, the fetus' behavioral repertoire is essentially the same as at birth and includes grasping, sucking, kicking, and other typical infant reflexes.

GENETIC FACTORS

As stated at the start of this chapter, every person begins his life as a single cell—a zygote—that is formed when the male germ cell (spermatozoon) penetrates the female germ cell (ovum). These germ cells, called gametes, are different from all other cells in the human body because they contain twenty-three separate and distinctively different chromosomes. All other cells in the body con-

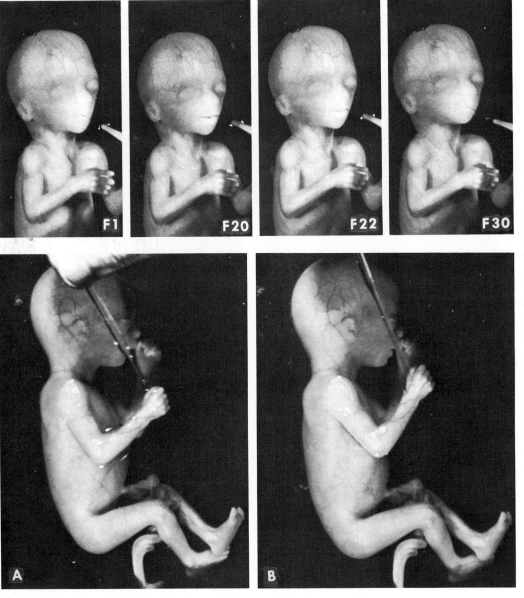

Figure 3.8. (top) Photographs from four frames of a motion picture, which records the reflex following stimulation of the lips and tongue (Fl) of a fetus of 15.5 weeks, menstrual age. The mouth opened (F20, F22), and the tongue formed a groove lengthwise (F20). Further stimulation of the lips was followed by closing them tightly on the stimulator (F30). No other movements accompanied this reflex. The photographs are about 0.7 the size of the fetus. (Figure 19 from T. Humphrey, 1968, *Alabama Journal of Medical Science*, 5, 126-157, through the courtesy of the publishers and the author.) (bottom) By 18.5 weeks, menstrual age, closure of the fingers on a glass rod (A) is accompanied by a grasp sufficiently strong to move the hand (toward the face in this case) as a pull is exerted on the rod. Note that the thumb is outside of the closed fingers and does not take part in grasping. The position of one hand near the mouth is common at this age, in this case the left with the thumb against the upper lip. Photographs are about half the size of the fetus. (Illustration provided by T. Humphrey, Medical Center, University of Alabama at Birmingham.)

tain forty-six chromosomes, in twenty-three pairs.
When the two germ cells combine to form a new
individual, the twenty-three chromosomes from
the mother pair with the twenty-three from the
father, and the new individual's physical and psychological potential are determined.

The makeup of the chromosomes is of utmost
importance to the individual; their implications
for normal and abnormal development will be
discussed in this chapter. Each cell in the thousands of millions that make up the individual's
body will carry a precise copy of the original
twenty-three pairs of chromosomes that came together at his beginning.

GENES

Each chromosome is subdivided into *genes*,
which are the determiners of hereditary traits, and
the genes in turn are largely composed of DNA
(*deoxyribonucleic acid*). In one of the outstanding modern biological breakthroughs, J. D. Watson and F. H. Crick constructed a model of a
DNA molecule, which served to substantiate their
theory about its ability to replicate itself and its
role as chemical code carrier.

The genes are arranged in the same order along
each chromosome in the pair; they appear to be
strung like beads. It is estimated that each zygote
contains 10,000 to 50,000 genes. The great majority of genes are the same for each gamete and so
carry instructions for the same chemical process;
these are the genes that are common to all mankind and confer on us our common humanity. It
is interesting that little is as yet known about how

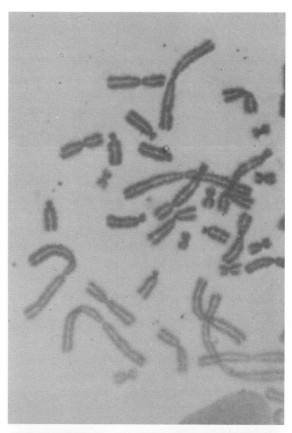

Figure 3.9. Part of the set of forty-six
human chromosomes, magnified 3,000
diameters from a normal human diploid
cell clone in culture. The chromosomes
assume this form during the division
cycle; they are stained with
a dye called giemsa.
Courtesy Leonard Hayflick.
Copyright © the President and
Fellows of Harvard College.

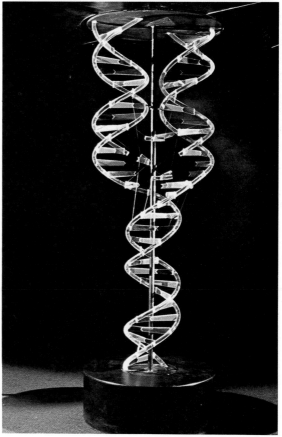

Figure 3.10. Model of a DNA molecule.

the genes common to all men produce their effects. That is, the mechanism of *development* remains a biochemical mystery although the mechanism of *inheritance* is now almost universally accepted. Scientists can explain why a person is born with blue eyes, but they do not yet know why, given two cells with the same set of twenty-three chromosome pairs, one cell becomes part of the brain tissue and the other part of the kidney.

CROSSING OVER

An individual's germ cells lie dormant in the ovaries or testes until puberty, at which time the gametes start forming by a process of division called *meiosis*, shown in Figure 3.11. Before meiosis occurs, the two members of each of the twenty-three pairs of chromosomes in the original germ cell may adhere to each other at various points along their length. The homologous chromosomes may break at these points and exchange corresponding segments. This process is called *crossing over*. Therefore, at the final division in the meiosis process, the gamete's set of twenty-three chromosomes may contain a random assortment of genes from the forty-six original chromosomes. And so, when the gametes combine to form a new individual, half his genes have been drawn at random from his mother and half at random from his father.

DOMINANT AND RECESSIVE GENES

At conception, a gene from the father will be paired with its counterpart from the mother. The genes that pair are called *alleles*. As was stated earlier, most of the gene pairs carry the same instructions. There are genes common to all men, which specify that we will have lungs rather than gills, that our ankle bone is connected with our foot bone, and the like. Some genes carry instructions that are not quite so universal—for example, the genes that determine the eyelid fold that is part of the physiognomy of Oriental populations. Some genes dictate a person's individuality within his population. Still other genes are composed of alleles that carry different instructions within the same cell.

When the two alleles are identical, a person is said to be *homozygous* for that gene. When the alleles carry different instructions, he is said to be *heterozygous*.

One illustration is a well-documented human trait that is known to be defined by a single gene —the ability to taste phenylthiocarbamide (PTC); its two alleles are designated T and t. To homozygotes with the alleles TT, the compound has a bitter taste in solution, whereas to homozygotes with alleles tt, it is tasteless. Because heterozygotes (Tt) also taste the bitterness, it is clear that the activity of the T allele masks that of t.

One more set of definitions is necessary to the discussion that follows. Two individuals with the alleles TT are called *genotypically* alike; TT is their *genotype*. However, two individuals who taste PTC because one has genotype TT and the other Tt are said to be *phenotypically* alike; their behavior is identical although their genotypes are different.

Masking alleles, like T, are called *dominant* in relation to the alleles whose effects they cover; the

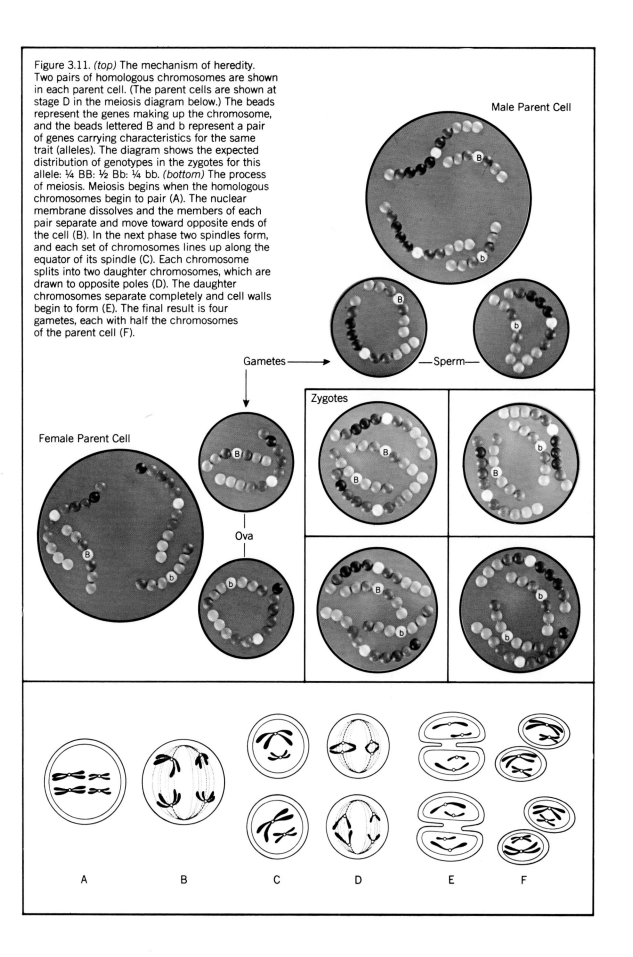

Figure 3.11. *(top)* The mechanism of heredity. Two pairs of homologous chromosomes are shown in each parent cell. (The parent cells are shown at stage D in the meiosis diagram below.) The beads represent the genes making up the chromosome, and the beads lettered B and b represent a pair of genes carrying characteristics for the same trait (alleles). The diagram shows the expected distribution of genotypes in the zygotes for this allele: ¼ BB: ½ Bb: ¼ bb. *(bottom)* The process of meiosis. Meiosis begins when the homologous chromosomes begin to pair (A). The nuclear membrane dissolves and the members of each pair separate and move toward opposite ends of the cell (B). In the next phase two spindles form, and each set of chromosomes lines up along the equator of its spindle (C). Each chromosome splits into two daughter chromosomes, which are drawn to opposite poles (D). The daughter chromosomes separate completely and cell walls begin to form (E). The final result is four gametes, each with half the chromosomes of the parent cell (F).

Male Parent Cell

Gametes →

—Sperm—

Zygotes

Female Parent Cell

Ova

A   B   C   D   E   F

masked alleles are called *recessive*. For some genes, neither of the alleles is dominant, so the heterozygote shows a form of the trait approximately between the homozygous forms.

HEREDITARY TRANSMISSION

The two chromosomes of a pair are called *homologues*. As stated earlier, during meiosis the homologues segregate to different gametes. Using the PTC-taster example again, it is clear that an individual who is heterozygous for this gene (Tt) produces one gamete carrying the T allele and the other carrying the t allele. Because each parent produces both types of gametes in equal numbers and because these gametes will combine randomly in the formation of a zygote, a mating between two such heterozygotes (Tt × Tt) is expected to produce offspring of the three different genotypes TT, Tt, and tt in the ratio 1:2:1.

Half the children, then, will be *genotypically* like their parents (carrying the Tt gene); three-fourths will be *phenotypically* like them (they will taste PTC); but this trait in one-fourth of the offspring will differ from both parents.

The expected ratio of genotypes and phenotypes for traits determined by a single gene can be calculated by constructing a 2 × 2 matrix, as shown in Figure 3.12. The alleles of the gene produced by each parent are entered along separate axes of the matrix, and the cells of the matrix represent the genotypes that will be produced.

Observations of the sort discussed in the preceding paragraphs were the basis of Gregor Mendel's first law of inheritance: the *law of segrega-* tion. Mendel worked with pea plants and postulated that each phenotypic trait of his plants was governed by a separate pair of "elements," which somehow divided and then recombined when a plant produced offspring. It is now known that these elements are the allelic forms of genes, and that meiotic cell division is the basis of their segregation.

Mendel's second law of inheritance, the *law of independent assortment*, describes the simultaneous inheritance of two or more traits that are determined by single genes. For example, an individual who is heterozygous for each of two genes located on different pairs of chromosomes will produce four types of gametes with respect to the two genes. T and t have been designated the alleles of the taster gene, and A and a are the alleles of the gene that produces *albinism* in man (congenital absence of skin pigmentation); AA and Aa individuals have normal pigmentation, and persons carrying the alleles aa are albinos. The four gametes produced by a double heterozygote (TtAa) will be TA, Ta, tA, and ta, and a mating between two double heterozygotes (represented by a 4 × 4 matrix) will produce offspring of nine different genotypes, as shown in Figure 3.13. The expected distribution of phenotypes is a 9:3:3:1 ratio of pigmented tasters, albino tasters, pigmented nontasters, and albino nontasters. Note that $\frac{7}{16}$ of the offspring are expected to be phenotypically different from both parents.

Although geneticists have found that the variation of some traits in humans is governed by single genes (for example, ability to taste PTC,

Parents	Gametes		Expected Progeny Ratio	
			Genotypes	Phenotypes
TT × TT		T T		
	T	TT TT	all TT	all tasters
	T	TT TT		
TT × Tt		T t		
	T	TT Tt	1/2 TT:1/2 Tt	all tasters
	T	TT Tt		
TT × tt		t t		
	T	Tt Tt	all Tt	all tasters
	T	Tt Tt		
Tt × Tt		T t		
	T	TT Tt	1/4 TT:1/2 Tt:1/4 tt	3/4 taster: 1/4 nontaster
	t	Tt tt		
Tt × tt		t t		
	T	Tt Tt	1/2 Tt:1/2 tt	1/2 taster: 1/2 nontaster
	t	tt tt		
tt × tt		t t		
	t	tt tt	all tt	all nontasters
	t	tt tt		

Figure 3.12. Expected progeny ratios for various matings involving the gene controlling taste sensitivity to PTC. (After Murray and Hirsch, 1969.)

albinism, some blood types), this mode of inheritance is the exception rather than the rule. Many structural traits and most behavioral traits have been found to depend on the combined effects of many genes acting together. Traits of this type are called *polygenic* traits, and the complex of genes involved in determining the trait is known as a polygenic system.

Generally, traits determined by a single gene can be classified into sharply defined qualitative categories (for example, taster versus nontaster), whereas polygenic traits show continuous variation on quantitative dimensions. The genes in a polygenic system may be located on the same or on different chromosomes, and each gene in the system is assumed to behave as a discrete unit and to obey the usual rules of transmission—segregation, independent assortment, and crossing over. However, the contribution of each gene to variation of the trait is small and cumulative rather than all-or-none. The action of a polygenic system is analogous to the simultaneous tossing of a large number of coins, where the alleles of each gene (assuming only two per gene) represent heads or tails and the expression of the polygenic trait is determined by the number of heads. The result is continuous variation among members of a population. Examples of polygenic traits are height and intelligence; both the structural trait and the behavioral one display wide ranges in the population. To complete this analogy, environmental conditions could be represented as the independent tossing of a second set of coins, where heads represent facilitative and tails inhibitory environ-

mental effects. The total number of heads, then, in both tosses determines trait expression. Clearly, the range of variation of a polygenic trait will be increased by environmental differences.

HEREDITY AND ENVIRONMENT

When applied to the individual organism, the question of whether a behavioral trait is traceable to heredity or to environment is meaningless because without heredity there is no organism, and without an appropriate environment the organism does not survive to display the trait. With respect to a *population* of individuals, however, it is meaningful to ask how much of the observed variation of a trait is the result of genotypic differences among individuals and how much the result of environmental differences. In the language of genetics, this is equivalent to estimating the *heritability* of a trait—the percentage of trait variance that is attributable to genotypic differences among individuals. Even at the level of populations, absolute answers about heritability cannot be expected because heritability is a measure of the *relationship* between a trait and the population in which it is studied, not a constant property of the trait per se. A trait may have markedly different heritabilities in different populations as a function of the degree of genetic and environmental variability that exists in those populations.

Thus, a trait *must* have zero heritability in a population of genetically identical individuals (because none of the trait variance can be attributed to genotypic differences), but the same trait *might* have substantial heritability in a genetically

TtAa × TtAa		TA	Ta	tA	ta
	TA	TTAA	TTAa	TtAA	TtAa
	Ta	TTAa	TTaa	TtAa	Ttaa
	tA	TtAA	TtAa	ttAA	ttAa
	ta	TtAa	Ttaa	ttAa	ttaa

Expected Distribution of Genotypes
and Phenotypes, Assuming Dominance at Both Loci:

Pigmented Tasters	:	Albino Tasters	:	Pigmented Nontasters	:	Albino Nontasters
9 { 1 TTAA / 2 TTAa / 2 TtAA / 4 TtAa		3 { 1 TTaa / 2 Ttaa		3 { 1 ttAA / 2 ttAa		1 ttaa

Figure 3.13. Expected outcome of a mating of double heterozygotes for two independent genes. (After Murray and Hirsch, 1969.)

heterogeneous population. The heritability of blindness, for example, has increased markedly since 1800 as a result of the elimination of smallpox and other communicable diseases that are potential causes of blindness. Similarly, the equalization of educational opportunities should serve to increase the heritability of IQ scores by reducing environmental differences among individuals. If one keeps in mind, then, that statements asserting a particular trait is 60 percent genetic and 40 percent environmental can be made only for a particular population in a particular environment, one can make a fairly precise quantitative assessment of the importance of heredity and environment in determining some particular trait. Environment in the context of these discussions means any factor that is not subsumed under heredity—psychological environment as well as physical.

LABORATORY STUDIES

Many of the data collected in behavior genetics come from comparison of strains of animals. In general, a *strain* of animals refers to a reproductively isolated population within a given species. Wild rats and laboratory rats are separate strains, as are the various breeds of dogs. If each of two strains has been maintained in reproductive isolation, it is safe to assume that the two strains will differ in the composition of their gene pools. Thus, if under identical environmental circumstances there are behavioral differences between two strains of mice or rats, it can be assumed that the differences are heritable, that is to say, they are genotypic in origin.

Figure 3.14. Various clearly visible hereditary traits are illustrated here.

An inbred strain is a reproductively isolated population (usually maintained under laboratory conditions) in which there has been much mating of closely related individuals, such as siblings and cousins. Because inbreeding increases the number of homozygotes (AA or aa), it tends to reduce genetic variability among members of a population. If intense (for example, brother-sister) inbreeding is continued over a large number of generations, an inbred strain will approach a completely *isogenic* state, that is, one in which all members of the strain are genetically identical. Under these conditions, all behavioral differences between individuals in the population can be assumed to result from environmental differences.

Studies employing the strain-comparison technique have demonstrated the heritability of a large variety of behavioral traits. Strains of mice or rats have been shown to differ in aggressiveness, learning ability, hoarding activity, exploratory behavior, sex drive, alcohol preference, susceptibility to audiogenic seizures, and other traits.

Many studies comparing the responses of two inbred strains to a range of environmental conditions have found that genetic and environmental effects are nonadditive. That is, when two strains of animals are tested in identical environments and on identical tasks, animals from one strain respond differently than the animals from the other strain. R. E. Wimer and his associates, for example, found that one inbred strain of mice learned a task faster when they practiced it at short intervals—every five to forty seconds. A second inbred strain learned the same task much faster when they practiced it only at twenty-four-hour intervals. Other studies have produced evidence that most individuals in one strain of mice are affected by handling or electric shock during infancy and display increased emotionality as adults, while another strain's adult behavior is not affected at all by the same amount of shock or handling.

HUMAN POPULATIONS

Animal studies of heredity-environment interaction are significant for understanding human psychological development because they demonstrate that the universality of behavioral definitions is sharply limited by genetic population differences. Human races are Mendelian populations, which differ in the relative frequencies of various alleles in their gene pools, and different individuals may obey different laws of behavior because they are members of different Mendelian populations. The fact that races are genetically different implies that one should expect to find behavioral differences between them, just as one finds morphological and physiological differences. However, in any discussion of racial differences it is important to remember that populations, not individuals, are being described. The principles of genetic transmission ensure wide diversity *within* races; thus, particular individuals in one race may be phenotypically more similar to members of another race than to members of their own group.

Racial differences are already well documented for at least two psychological traits: color blindness and ability to taste PTC. Approximately 30 percent of American whites are PTC nontasters, whereas 6 to 11 percent of Chinese and only 3 to 9 percent of native Africans are nontasters. The frequency of various forms of mental illness has also been found to differ among races and other Mendelian populations. For example, in contrast to most other populations, manic-depressive psychosis is reported to be more frequent than schizophrenia in the mental hospitals of India and among the Hutterites, an isolated religious sect living in Canada and the northern United States. The latter findings must be interpreted with caution, however, because the observed differences could have a cultural rather than genetic basis.

TWIN STUDIES

Controlled breeding experiments are not possible in human behavior genetics, but useful information may be obtained through the study of phenotypic similarities and differences within families and between twins. If genetic differences contribute to variation of a given trait, it is expected that blood relatives will resemble one another in expression of that trait more than do randomly selected individuals and, furthermore, that the degree of phenotypic similarity between relatives of various categories (siblings, cousins) will depend on the degree of genetic similarity the relatives hold. Phenotypic similarity with respect to *qualitative* traits, such as color blindness, is usually expressed as a *concordance rate*—defined as the proportion of cases in which both individuals show the same expression of a trait. Phenotypic similarity with respect to traits that can be measured *quantitatively*, like IQ, is usually expressed

by a statistical index known as a *correlation coefficient*. (See the Appendix for a more detailed discussion of statistical methods and terminology used in psychology.) The value of this measure for pairs of relatives can range from a minimum of .00, indicating a purely random degree of similarity, to a maximum of 1.00, indicating perfect agreement of trait scores.

Table 3.2 shows the average degree of genetic similarity (expressed in terms of percentage of genes shared in common) for unrelated persons and for various categories of relatives and gives correlations of intelligence-test scores and concordance rates for schizophrenia for these groups. Table 3.3 is a detailed summary of studies made to ascertain correlations in IQ for persons who are related in various ways or, though unrelated, were brought up in the same environment. It is clear that family resemblance with respect to both IQ and schizophrenia depends on the number of genes shared in common. However, a basic difficulty in interpreting family correlation data is that relatives tend to have similar environments as well as similar genotypes, so that the causes of phenotypic resemblance remain ambiguous. It should be noted, however, that Mendel's law of segregation of alleles provides a substantive basis for explaining the fact that *differences* as well as similarities are found among family members. Just as it can explain how a pair of brown-eyed parents can produce a blue-eyed offspring, it may also someday explain why some family members develop schizophrenia and others do not.

Many investigators have turned to studies of

phenotypic correlation in twins in order to avoid the confounding of genetic and environmental similarity that occurs in family studies. About one-third of American Caucasian twins are monozygotic (MZ) and two-thirds are dizygotic (DZ). Monozygotic twins derive from the splitting of a single fertilized ovum and therefore are genetically identical, sharing 100 percent of their alleles in common. Dizygotic twins result from the fertilization of two ova by two sperm and therefore are no more alike genetically than ordinary siblings; that is, they share, on the average, 50 percent of a common set of alleles. Like-sexed DZ twins can be distinguished from MZ twins on the basis of dissimilarities in physical traits such as hair or eye color, blood type, and fingerprint patterns, or, if these tests are inconclusive, by

virtue of the fact that reciprocal skin transplants will take permanently only in MZ twins.

The general rationale of the twin-study method is that phenotypic differences between MZ twins should reflect environmental influence alone, whereas phenotypic differences between DZ twins should reflect the combined effects of hereditary and environmental factors. Thus, the extent to which intrapair similarity is greater in MZ than in DZ twins should provide an estimate of the heritability of a particular trait in the population studies. Table 3.4 summarizes the results of studies reporting MZ and DZ intrapair correlations and concordance rates for a variety of behavioral traits. Note that the measures for both schizophrenia and intelligence show a large discrepancy between MZ and DZ twins; this difference serves to

Table 3.2. Correlation of Intelligence Test Scores and Schizophrenia

Relationship	Genetic Similarity	Correlation of Intelligence Test Scores*	Concordance Rate for Schizophrenia†
Unrelated	0.0%	.00	0.9%
First cousins	12.5	.29	2.6
Half-siblings	25.0	—	7.6
Grandparent-grandchild	25.0	.34	4.3
Uncle (aunt)-nephew (niece)	25.0	.35	3.9
Siblings	50.0	.53	11.5
Parent-offspring	50.0	.49	12.8

* From C. Burt and M. Howard, "The Multifactional Theory of Inheritance and Its Application to Intelligence," *British Journal of Statistical Psychology*, 9 (1956), 95–131.
† From F. J. Kallman, *The Genetics of Schizophrenia* (New York: Augustin, 1938).

Table 3.3. Correlations for Intellectual Ability: Obtained and Theoretical Values

Correlations Between	Number of Studies	Obtained Median	Theoretical Value*
Unrelated persons			
Children reared apart	4	−.01	.00
Foster parent and child	3	+.20	.00
Children reared together	5	+.24	.00
Collaterals			
Second cousins	1	+.16	+ .14
First cousins	3	+.26	+ .18
Uncle (or aunt) and nephew (or niece)	1	+.34	+ .31
Siblings, reared apart	33	+.47	+ .52
Siblings, reared together	36	+.55	+ .52
Dizygotic twins, different sex	9	+.49	+ .50
Dizygotic twins, same sex	11	+.56	+ .54
Monozygotic twins, reared apart	4	+.75	+1.00
Monozygotic twins, reared together	14	+.87	+1.00
Direct Line			
Grandparent and grandchild	3	+.27	+ .31
Parent (as adult) and child	13	+.50	+ .49
Parent (as child) and child	1	+.56	+ .49

* Value one would expect if genetic factors alone were operating.
Source: A. R. Jensen, "How Much Can We Boost IQ and Scholastic Achievement?" *Harvard Educational Review* (Winter 1969).

substantiate the heritability of these traits. The other findings in Table 3.4 suggest that gene differences play a major role in such traits as manic-depressive psychosis, male homosexuality, and extraversion but a somewhat more minor role in the etiology of suicide and psychopathic personality.

Some investigators have questioned the validity of the twin-study method, saying that DZ twins do not experience similar environments in the same way as MZ twins do. They say, for example, that MZ twins are treated more alike by parents and peers and that they tend to model their behavior upon one another. Each of these factors might serve to inflate MZ trait correlations and lead to overestimates of heritability. To counter this argument, other investigators have compared MZ twins reared apart from an early age with MZ and DZ twins reared together. One study of this

type reported a correlation of .77 between the IQ scores of MZ twins reared apart; in a second study the concordance rate for schizophrenia in adult MZ twins separated for an average of 11.8 years was 78 percent. The fact that identical genotypes subjected to different environments (MZ twins reared apart) are more similar with respect to intelligence and occurrence of schizophrenia than different genotypes subjected to similar environments (DZ twins reared together) suggests the importance of hereditary factors. The role of environment is indicated by the fact that MZ twins reared apart are less similar phenotypically than MZ twins reared together.

A further way to separate the roles of heredity and environment is to compare the correlations between adopting parents and adopted children with the correlation between adopted children

Table 3.4. Behavioral Traits of Monozygotic (MZ) and Dizygotic (DZ) Twins

Trait	Investigator	Intrapair Concordance Rate		Intrapair Correlation Coefficient	
		MZ	DZ	MZ	DZ
Schizophrenia	Kallman (1953)	86%	15%	—	—
Manic-depressive psychosis	Kallman (1953)	93	24	—	—
Psychopathic personality	Slater (1953)	25	14	—	—
Alcoholism	Kaij (1957)	65	30	—	—
Male homosexuality	Kallman (1953)	98	12	—	—
Hysteria	Stumpfl (1937)	33	0	—	—
Suicide	Kallman (1953)	6	0	—	—
Intelligence	Newman et al. (1937)	—	—	.88	.63
Motor skill	McNemar (1933)	—	—	.79	.43
Vocational interests	Carter (1932)	—	—	.50	.28
Extraversion-introversion	Gottesman (1963)	—	—	.55	.08
Depression	Gottesman (1963)	—	—	.47	.07
Neuroticism	Eysenck & Prell (1951)	—	—	.85	.22

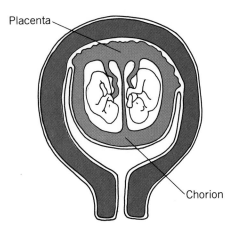

Placenta

Chorion

Figure 3.15. Monozygotic twins, who are genetically identical, also share the same chorion and placenta before birth. (After Arey, 1954.)

and their natural parents. Such comparisons show only a very low correlation between the IQ test scores of adopted mothers and adopted children but almost the usual correlation between the natural mothers and their children who had been brought up by others. Figure 3.17 shows such correlations as found in a study that was conducted by Marie Skodak and Harold Skeels; because IQ scores for the parents were not always obtainable, years of education was used as a rough indication of intelligence.

CHROMOSOMAL ABNORMALITIES

When a cell divides to form a gamete, the process may go wrong. It is possible that during meiosis a pair of chromosome homologues fails to separate, so that one of the gametes has one chromosome in excess and the other cell has one chromosome lacking. The cell with too few chromosomes (22) does not usually survive, but a cell with one excess chromosome may survive to produce an individual with an abnormal number of chromosomes in all his cells. The most common anomaly of this type, where an individual has three rather than two number 21 chromosomes, produces a syndrome of developmental abnormalities called Down's syndrome (or mongolism). The abnormalities include low mental ability (IQ between 20 and 60), thickness and fissuring of the tongue, flattened face, characteristic eyelid folds, and congenital defects (such as heart disease).

The most common cause of Down's syndrome in older mothers is the failure of a pair of chromosomes to separate when an egg is formed; for mothers forty-five years and older, the risk is 1 in 60. Although this disorder is clearly the result of a defect in genetic instructions, *it is not hereditary in origin* because the tendency of meiosis to go awry in this way is not inherited. (It should be noted that when younger mothers—ages twenty to thirty—have children with Down's syndrome, these mothers usually do have one abnormal chromosome, and so it is hereditary. The risk of occurrence for young mothers is 1 in 1,500.)

Aberrations can also occur when a cell divides to form another like itself. During cell division in the early life of the embryo, it is possible that one of the daughter cells receives three number 21 chromosomes and the other, one. The cell that receives only one does not go on to multiply, but the cell with 47 chromosomes does multiply, as do the cells with the normal complement of 46 chromosomes. The individual thus composed of different cell tissues is said to suffer from *mosaicism*; he will show some of the symptoms of Down's syndrome but in a less severe form. Chromosomes other than number 21 can divide abnormally; some of these anomalies are incompatible with development, and although a few individuals do develop prenatally until the time of birth, their abnormalities do not allow them to survive.

SEX DETERMINATION

Perhaps the most varied set of chromosomal aberrations is connected with the determination of an individual's sex. One of the twenty-three chromosomes that the spermatozoon contributes to the

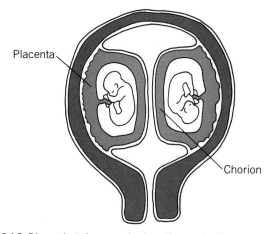

Placenta

Chorion

Figure 3.16. Dizygotic twins may be less like each other, physically and temperamentally, than they are like other of their siblings. The drawing shows that before birth each has its own placenta and chorion; whether there are one or two placentas in the afterbirth permits the doctor to say at time of birth that twins are mono- or dizygotic. (After Arey, 1954.)

zygote is either an X chromosome, which programs the gamete to develop as a female, or a Y chromosome, which determines that the individual will be male. The ovum always contributes an X chromosome, so the normal female zygote has XX, and the male, XY.

One aberration is Turner's syndrome, caused by the individual's having only one X chromosome and no Y chromosome. The afflicted individual looks like an immature female, is abnormally short, and has neither ovaries nor testes. There is also mental retardation, apparently a specific deficit in numerical and spatial ability. Another chromosomal aberration occurs when an individual has two X chromosomes and also a Y (XXY). The developmental symptoms, called Klinefelter's syndrome, include sterility and small testes, although the individuals appear to be males. Mental retardation is also associated with the syndrome. The opposite type of abnormality occurs in males having one X chromosome and two Y chromosomes (XYY). These men tend to be very tall. It has been suggested that they have an abnormally high tendency to crime and aggressive acts, but that remains to be substantiated. Females with three X chromosomes (XXX) appear normal and are fertile, but they also tend overwhelmingly to suffer from mental retardation.

MENTAL RETARDATION

Why chromosomal anomalies should produce mental retardation is not yet known. One possible explanation is that the chromosomal error produces changes in body chemistry. For instance, it

has been shown that in Down's syndrome there is a deficiency of serotonin—a substance thought to mediate transmission of impulses from one nerve cell to another.

There are many such inborn errors of metabolism leading to mental retardation. Among the more common is phenylketonuria. The condition is transmitted by a recessive gene that gives rise to a deficiency in the enzyme phenylalanine hydroxylase. During the first few weeks of life an infant suffering from this disorder will show unusual irritability, have epileptic seizures, and will vomit vigorously. Mental retardation can be diagnosed as early as four to eight months of age from the infant's abnormal hand movements—rhythmic

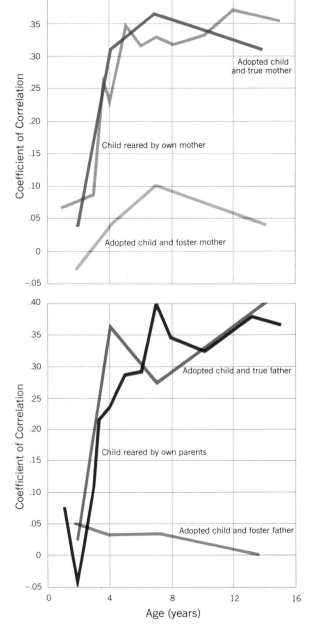

Figure 3.17. Correlations between children's IQ and the educational level of parents or adoptive parents: *(top)* mothers; *(bottom)* fathers. Because IQ scores for the parents were not easily obtainable, education was used as the measure in this study. (After Honzik, 1957.)

pill-rolling movements, irregular ticlike movements, aimless waving of the fingers, and frequent fiddling of the fingers close to the eyes. There may be constant rocking and severe temper tantrums. Electroencephalographic abnormalities are also seen in three-quarters of these children, and their IQs will generally remain at less than 50—if they are not treated. Recent biochemical and medical advances have provided treatment, which, begun early enough, can assure that mentality will be normal in most cases. The treatment consists of a diet low in phenylalanine, as the child lacks the enzyme that would metabolize it in the normal manner.

Another recent documentation of a hereditary

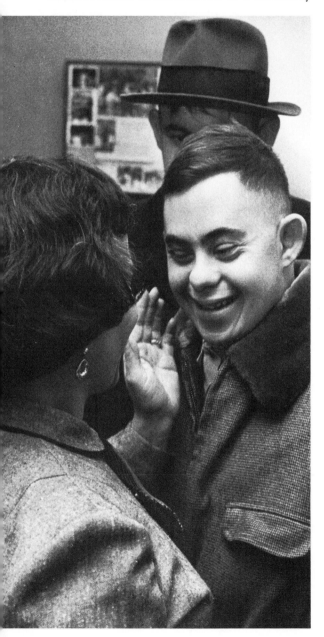

enzyme defect illustrates how biochemists and physicians trace mental and neural abnormalities to genetic aberrations. Daniel Steinberg and his associates studied the families of children who accumulate the compound phytanic acid, which is normally oxidized soon after it enters the body in certain foods. Accumulation of the compound leads to degenerative changes in the nervous system. They saw that 25 percent of a group of siblings were affected with the symptoms of Refsum's disease, although the parents were not affected. They postulated that the affected children were homozygotes carrying both recessive alleles. Testing of the parents proved this to be true. Both parents of affected children proved to oxidize phytanic acid at one-half the normal rate, which indicated that they were heterozygotes with respect to the gene. However, because the amount of phytanic acid they retain is not enough to affect the nervous system, the parents showed no symptoms. Only when they produce zygotes carrying the two recessive alleles does the disease occur.

Although an increasing number of genetic anomalies are being discovered—as a prelude to treating and curing them—the truly amazing fact about genetic determination is that it works so well and so regularly. Beside the intricacies of genetics and amniotic development, the rigors of psychological development will almost, but not quite, appear to be relatively simple. Before facing them, however, it is necessary to take a closer look at the beginning—at the world of the newborn child.

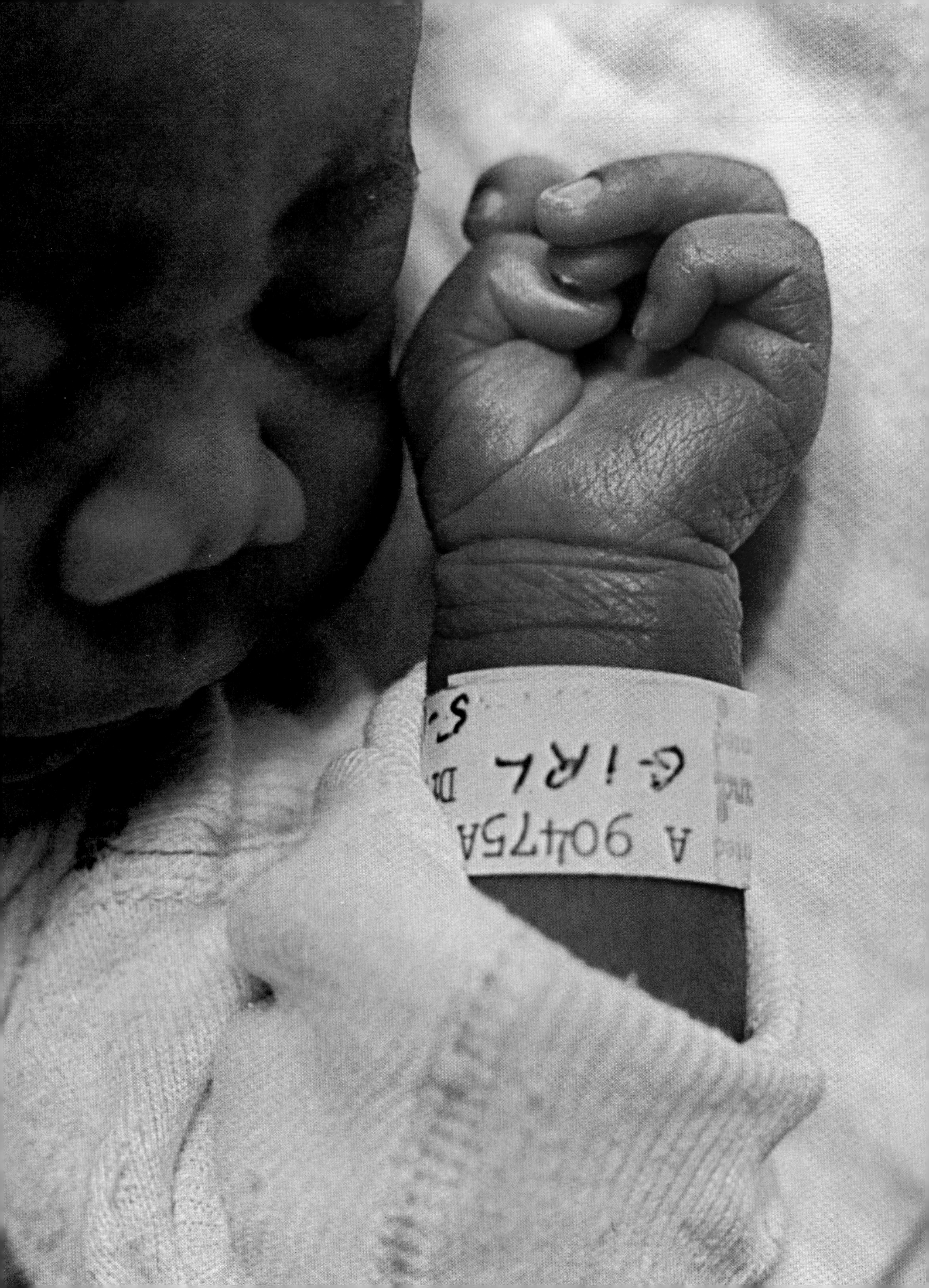
A 90475A
G-iRL

A newborn baby is a curious mixture of competence and incapacity. At the end of his uterine stay, the baby is anatomically very nearly complete; forty of his lifetime total of forty-four cell divisions have taken place; all of his vital organs are formed and functional; to some degree, he sees and hears and smells and tastes; he is certainly able to cry, to move his limbs, to feed, to grimace. To be sure, the newborn is not always seen as lovely. G. Stanley Hall described the infant as arriving with ". . . its monotonous and dismal cry, with its red, shriveled, parboiled skin, . . . squinting, cross-eyed, pot-bellied and bow-legged." But for all his seeming competence, the baby clearly does not possess many of the characteristics that are thought of as particularly human. He does not speak, he does not move away from where he is put down, he has incomplete control of his head and eyes and hands—he does not even show any special response to other human beings —no smile, no snuggling, no joy. William James' oft-quoted lines emphasize the incompleteness of the baby: ". . . assailed by eyes, ears, nose, skin, and entrails at once, [he] feels that all is one great blooming, buzzing confusion."

Perhaps it is precisely this tension between the newborn baby's obvious limitations and his enormous potential—think what the child of twelve to eighteen months of age can do—that has made him the object of intense study over the last hundred years. Attempts to understand human behavior—the differences among people and the commonality of all human beings—lead inevitably to an examination of the child just born.

One of the central tasks of the psychologist of early infancy can, in fact, be seen as presenting the description of the initial state of the human system—the beginning of human development—and most of the present chapter is given over to an account of what the newborn and his world are like. Of course, the newborn child cannot be described without some attention to another important task of the psychologist of infancy—understanding what factors lead to change in behavior over age. Therefore, perhaps a word or two should be said about the major theories of the infant's developmental changes.

THEORIES OF DEVELOPMENTAL CHANGE

Within the study of young infants, two general positions about what causes a baby's behavior to change have been dominant; sometimes they supplement one another and sometimes they are in opposition. The first position, that the baby's behavior is modified largely as the consequence of *physiological maturation*, has been most vigorously defended by Arnold Gesell and his colleagues. They maintain, not that the environment is unimportant, but that the child requires only supportive and quite general outside attention in order to develop normally. Gesell emphasizes the stability and essential conservatism of growth; he points out how well protected the young infant is against minor variations in his physical and parental environment. There is reassurance for new parents in Gesell's description of the baby: "All things considered, the inevitableness and surety of maturation are the most impressive characteristics

4
The World of the Newborn Child

of early development. It is the hereditary ballast which conserves and stabilizes the growth of each individual infant . . ."

The theoretical position most often contrasted with a maturational interpretation of early development emphasizes learning—the importance of *specific experience* in the development of the infant. Proposed in its most radical form many years ago by J. B. Watson and given more recent expression by B. F. Skinner, the attempt to comprehend early development through an analysis of learning supports the hope of many parents of influencing the shape of their children's growth from an early age. If, in fact, children learn from their specific experiences soon after birth (or even before it, as some psychologists have proposed), then parents have an awesome responsibility and opportunity to control the lives of their children.

Not all theorists who believe in the importance of specific experience adhere to the learning position, however. Jean Piaget concentrates on the adaptation of the infant to the subtle demands of his environment, and the psychoanalysts see the young infant as pressed between instinct and reality. Research on patterns of newborn behavior has been influenced by one or another of these several theoretical positions, and it is by no means yet clear which of them will best serve for understanding the baby or what mixture of them all will best represent the complexity of the newborn child.

Methods of Study

Many different specialists have been concerned with the study of the young infant—zoologists,

pediatricians, neurologists, psychiatrists—and many different research procedures have been used. The three systematic techniques that have produced the largest part of our information about the newborn and his world have been *baby biographies*, *normative observations*, and *laboratory experiments*.

BABY BIOGRAPHIES

Although parents have jotted down observations about their babies throughout history, the more formal baby biography came into vogue late in the nineteenth century, at least in part in imitation of Charles Darwin's account of his son's first days of life. The advantages of careful parental description (particularly the authenticity of the baby as a person and the value of knowing homely details of the baby's life) as well as the disadvantages (the bias of affection and the bias of the parent as theorist) are well revealed in a selection from Darwin's observational record:

Anger. It was difficult to decide at how early an age anger was felt; on his eighth day he frowned and wrinkled the skin round his eyes before a crying fit, but this may have been due to pain or distress, and not to anger. When about ten weeks old, he was given some rather cold milk and he kept a slight frown on his forehead all the time that he was sucking, so that he looked like a grown-up person made cross by being compelled to do something he did not like. When nearly four months old, and perhaps much earlier, there could be no doubt, from the manner in which the blood gushed into his whole face and scalp, that he easily got into a violent passion.

Significant contributions to the study of the infant have been made by parents who wrote detailed and analytical notes on what they saw their children do. In particular, much of psychologists' knowledge of the early development of the child's sense of the permanence of objects, of space, and of time depends on the observations that Jean Piaget made of his own three children over the first several years of their lives.

NORMATIVE OBSERVATIONS

The use of normative observation as a way of finding out about infants derives in part from the traditions of natural history and neurological examination and in part from the procedure of intelligence testing of older children and adults. The result is a long inventory of the activities of infants, from the squirming and flailing of general activity to the exact details of the sucking-swallowing sequence. The behavior called *reflexive* has come under peculiarly close attention: the patellar, abdominal, and knee reflexes, the reflexes of the foot, the reflexes of feeding, crying, and grasping, and the reflexes of the whole body, such as the startle response, have been described and analyzed in literally thousands of pages. Later in this chapter, we will take a closer look at several reflexes of the very young infant.

The baby's reflexive behavior has been used to determine whether he is neurologically sound, that is, whether at birth and in the days following birth his nervous system is functioning properly. In general, variations in newborn reflexive behavior permit the diagnosis of only *gross* neurological malfunctioning, and slight variations in the patterns of newborn reflexes do not tell much about the baby's future behavior.

LABORATORY EXPERIMENTS

The most sophisticated and precise methods available for the study of infants are applied in laboratory experiments. The essential features of experimental study—careful description and control of the stimulus materials presented to the baby and a restricted and repeatedly measurable response—can be seen in R. L. Fantz's study of the early infant's perception. The apparatus used is shown in Figure 4.1. The baby lies on his back looking up toward two panels. The experimenter puts contrasting stimuli on the panels—for example, an outline of a human face and a half-white, half-black oval figure—and then observes the movements of the baby's eyes to determine which of the two panels he looks at more often and for a longer time. By varying the kinds of stimuli presented to the baby, the researcher can learn a great deal about what the baby sees and what interests him in his visual world. Experimental procedures have been used extensively in the study of babies, particularly to assess their perceptual abilities and their capacity to learn. Several examples of the results of laboratory study will be reported later in the present chapter and in detail in Chapter 6.

BIRTH: NEW DEMANDS AND A NEW ENVIRONMENT

The birth of the child puts staggering new demands on his capacity to adapt and survive. He goes from an environment where he is almost totally protected from the world to one where he is assaulted by lights, sounds, touches, and ex-

BORN ON Saturday
sixteenth DAY
December 1944
12:15 AM/~~PM~~
Union Memorial Hospital
THE CITY OF Baltimore
NTY OF (none)
STATE OF Maryland.

GIVEN THE NAME OF
Carol Panne McComb.

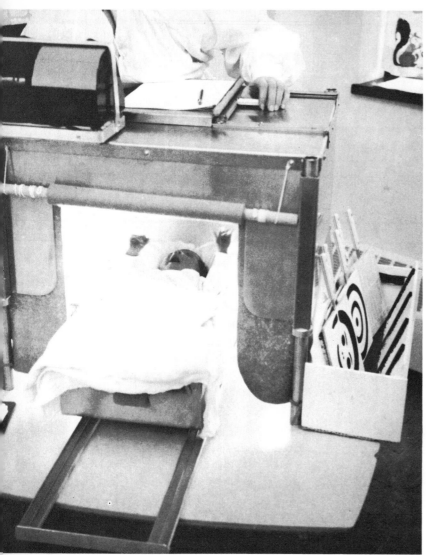

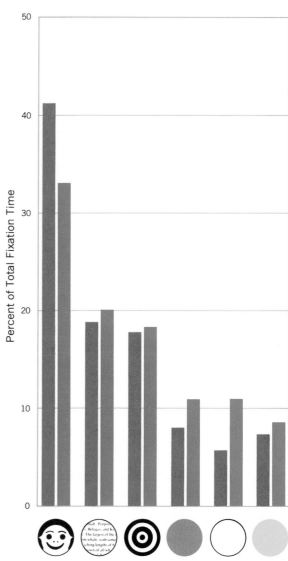

Figure 4.1. *(left)* Infant "looking chamber" used in R.L. Fantz's study of perception in young infants. *(above)* The patterns presented by Fantz to infants two to three months old (green) and infants older than three months (blue). The fixation-time percentages indicate that pattern is more important than color or brightness in infants' responses. (Graph from R. L. Fantz, "The Origin of Form Perception," copyright© 1961 by Scientific American, Inc. All rights reserved.)

tremes of temperature. He leaves a setting where he is supplied automatically with his vital requirements (in a strict sense, the fetal child is a parasite on his host-mother) for one where his own activity must become a part of the process of obtaining food and air. Of course, the physiological and behavioral systems of the newborn infant have evolved over hundreds of thousands of years to prepare him for the dramatic demands of birth. Complex changes, including the opening of new routes of blood flow and the closing of others, occur in his circulatory system to permit the baby suddenly to become an air-breathing organism. Chemical and mechanical changes spur the baby's first breaths, subtle and complex regulations start him on his way to independent feeding, and adaptations of the nervous and endocrine systems make it possible for him to regulate his body's temperature. The most striking evidence for the delicate balance of the infant's readiness to be born can be seen in babies born prematurely. Their deficiencies of adaptation have in the past resulted in damage or death; currently, these infants require artificial support for a few days or even a few weeks in order to survive.

In spite of the newborn infant's ability to adapt to his new environment, he is of course far from able to handle the vital problems he faces all by himself. Unlike newborn spiders, guppies, and guinea pigs, the newborn human infant cannot care for himself. The baby clearly needs the help of others in order to live for more than a few hours, and, in fact, much has been made by developmental zoologists and psychologists of the long period of dependence of the human being. The incompleteness at birth and long childhood of our species contribute to the enormous variation that exists among people and among cultures.

THE INFANT AS A PERSON

Much of the research literature about the newborn infant considers the baby primarily as a member of the human species; it catalogues the uniform and regular features of the baby's behavior—all babies suck, all babies show typical startle patterns, all babies are able to learn something about the surrounding world. What is often omitted in such accounts is a discussion of the differentiating characteristics of a baby, the characteristics that permit one to talk about each baby as unique and individual. Of course, no parent has any doubts about the unique nature of his infant (particularly when the second baby arrives), but the personality of the newborn—the hereditary biasing of his character—has not been as well investigated as some of the uniform marks of humanity in the infant. Nevertheless, it is known that babies differ, and that they differ a lot, on such important aspects of their performance as activity level, willingness to suck, tendency to cry, number and distribution of sleep periods, sensitivity to bright lights and loud noises, and style of adaptation (cuddly as opposed to wiry, for example). It will, of course, matter a great deal whether the kind of baby a person gets fits with the kind of parent he is; there are mothers who can easily manage the quiet, placid infant but who would be put over the edge by an active, squalling baby. The importance of an adaptive fit between newborn child and caretaking mother has barely been opened as a research enterprise. Unfortunately, psychologists are also not confident about how the differentiating characteristics of the newborn infant are related to his later behavior as toddler, adolescent, and adult.

EXPECTATIONS OF PARENTS

The expectations of parents are important to the understanding of the newborn infant for many reasons. Over the last fifty years, Americans have abandoned many of the traditional, grandmotherly sources of information about babies and have become more dependent on the opinions of experts. In this way parents have probably become both better informed and less secure about whether or not they are doing what is best for their babies. Parents have usually subscribed to a modified maturational position in their handling of very young infants: some effects of specific experience can be seen but, by and large, the baby will grow and flourish if he is simply taken good

care of. Very recently, however, there has been an apparent shift toward a commitment by parents to the doctrine that the very young child can be radically influenced by his early experiences in the world. The emphasis on early education, the concern of parents with the child's achievement, and the evidence of the effects of early deprivation have all fed into a new conviction on the part of young parents that what they do with the baby in the first days and months of life is of critical and long-lasting importance. The scientific basis of the child's early susceptibility to variations among the practices of normal parents has not been fully established and much more research needs to be done, but there can be little doubt that the new era of overconcern for very early education has begun to change the relation of baby and parent.

EQUIPMENT OF THE NEWBORN

In awe at Nature's ability to compress all the critical potential of the adult into such a tiny package, one can view the infant from the adult perspective and ask: How is he going to acquire the marvelously complex capabilities of an adult? But there is a second way of looking at the newborn child that has received emphasis only in the last decade or so. Paying less attention to what the infant will become, psychologists ask: With what equipment does the newborn come into the world? What are his own special characteristics?

REGULARITIES AND RHYTHMS

In studying the behavior of any organism, one must begin with observable regularities in that

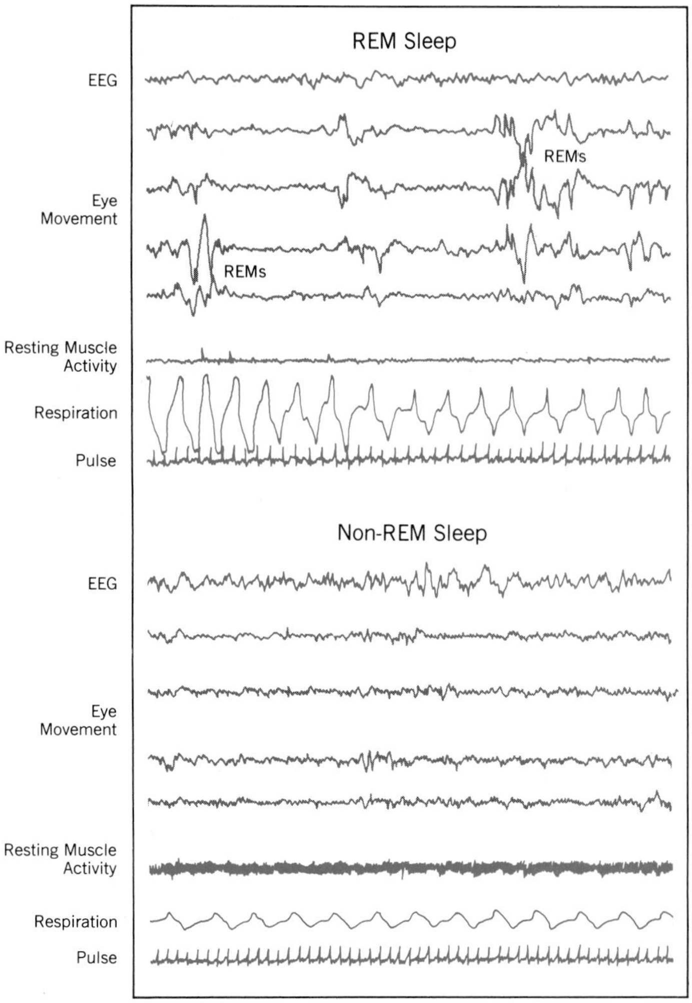

Figure 4.2. Recordings showing the differences between REM (rapid-eye-movement) sleep and non-REM sleep in a newborn. Besides the heightened eye activity during REM sleep, note the absence of muscle activity, the rapid respiratory rate and changing respiratory amplitude. These tracings record a thirty-second interval. (After Roffwarg, Dement, and Fisher, 1967.)

behavior. One of the most interesting aspects of the newborn's behavior, and one that ties him in some sense to all existence—organic and inorganic—is his *cyclicity*. Cyclicity or rhythmicity in the infant can be found at virtually any level one wishes to examine, from brain waves, which occur at rates up to 30 or 40 cycles per second, to sleep cycles with a periodicity of twenty-four hours or so. (Several cycles of shorter duration modulate the lengthy sleep cycle.) There is also the familiar sleep-feed cycle—throughout both the night and the day—of four and one-half hours, encapsulating a cycle of about seventy minutes during which the baby goes from light sleep to intermediate sleep to deep sleep and back again. Again, within this period of seventy minutes there are periods of about twenty minutes of deep sleep bounded on either side by periods of half-sleep, of approximately the same duration. These stages may be differentiated by the amount of eye activity, as shown in Figure 4.2. Within deep sleep there are periods of several seconds within which energy is apparently built up and released through various channels such as startle responses, erections, or spontaneous sucking and movement.

Along with these levels of sleep one can, of course, differentiate several levels of wakefulness. There are at least seven states of consciousness, varying from regular deep sleep to rageful crying. They can be measured by the regularity of the infant's breathing, skin temperature, muscle tone, heart rate, eye activity, bodily and limb activity, brain-wave patterns, responsiveness to stimulation, and vocalizations. A photo showing the way in which the baby is prepared for making these measures is shown in Figure 4.3, which is accompanied by a graph of the actual measurements. Unfortunately, these states do not always change in a regular manner; one of the hallmarks of early life is the caprice of the infant in moving from one state to another. This irregularity has hindered reliable psychological evaluation of the newborn because all measures of infant behavior and awareness are greatly affected by the particular state of the baby's alertness.

The most rhythmic of the newborn's behaviors is familiar to all—sucking. Sucking from birth typically follows a strikingly regular pattern.

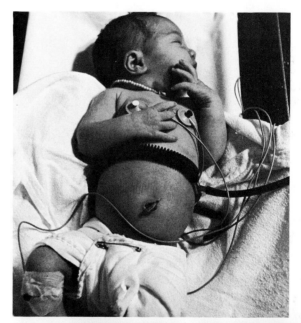

Figure 4.3. Tracings such as those replicated in Figure 4.2 are obtained as shown. The infant is in a stabilimeter crib, which measures his muscular activity. The belt around his abdomen measures respiration, and the electrodes on his chest produce electrocardiographic records. When REM recordings are made, electrodes are placed at the outer corner of the eyes. Such experimental techniques, used to study sensory and learning processes, are not uncomfortable for the infant.

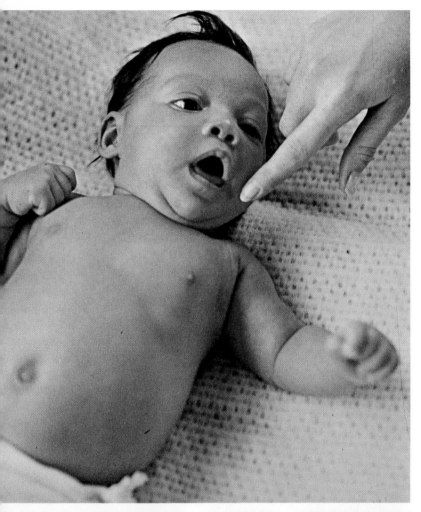

Sucks on a dry nipple occur at about 2.2 cycles per second, a rate that is fairly uniform among most babies. Babies suck in small burst-rest cycles; for example, a baby may suck five to seven times, rest for several seconds, then suck five to seven times, rest for several seconds, and so on. Babies may vary in the number of sucks per burst or in the time interval between bursts, but most babies seem to adopt some burst-rest cycle. And the baby shows strikingly regular physiological rhythms—such as in heartbeat, breathing, and peristalsis.

REFLEXES

Far better known than the rhythms with which the baby comes into the world are the reflexes, which for various reasons have attracted the interest of neurophysiologists and pediatricians. Many of these reflexes are argued to be atavistic—carryovers from an older phylogenetic ancestor—and many of these reflexes are interpreted by students of the newborn as evidence of noncortical functioning. Sucking is often referred to as a reflex in the newborn baby, but many would argue that sucking behavior, as will be shown later, is much too complicated to qualify as a reflex. One reflex closely related to sucking, however, is the *rooting reflex*. If the alert newborn is stimulated by touch around the mouth, he will move his head and mouth toward the source of the stimulus. This reflex presumably seems to guide the baby's mouth to the mother's nipple once he is in range. Another well-known reflex is the *Moro response*. When the baby's head falls backward, he stretches his arms outward and then brings them

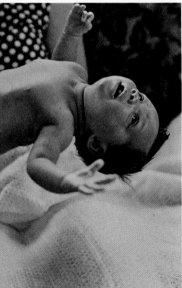
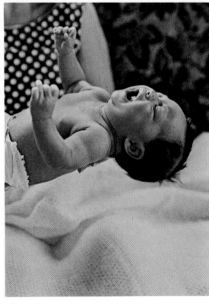

Figure 4.4. The rooting reflex.

Figure 4.5. The Moro response.

together over his chest in a grasp gesture. This reflex is thought to be a carryover from the apes, for whom it would be relatively adaptive for securing either a part of the mother or a tree limb when there is loss of support. Reflexive finger grasping, typically strong enough at birth to support full body weight, presumably served to supplement the Moro response under crisis conditions and to permit attachment to the primate mother's furry chest so that her arms could be free for climbing and nursing.

Several other reflexes exist whose survival role is relatively obvious: babies turn their heads to avoid blankets or pillows that obstruct their breathing; close their eyes to bright lights; twist their bodies or move their limbs away from the source of pain. Pressure on the palms, possibly indicating hand location of the breast, produces suckinglike mouth movements when the baby is hungry.

The role of other reflexes is less obvious in evolution. Babies place one foot in front of the other in a stepping motion when they are held with their feet firmly placed on a platform: they exhibit vertical crawling motions in their cribs when a platform is pressed against the bottom of their feet; and they show whole-body extension when the soles of their feet are scraped (see Figure 4.6). These reflexes are of neurological interest because the adequacy of the lower spinal cord is indicated by adequate foot reflexes. The disappearance of many of these reflexes probably indicates the onset of activity of cortical inhibition centers, which occurs near the end of the second month of life. It is worthwhile to note that some

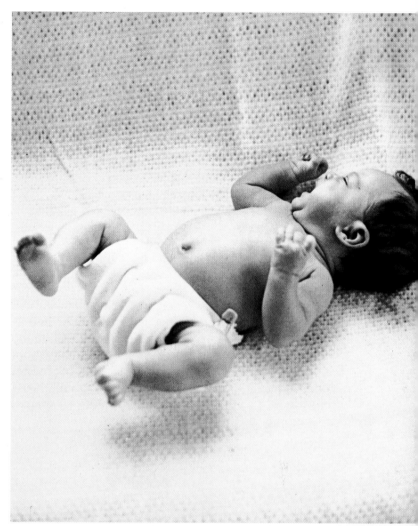

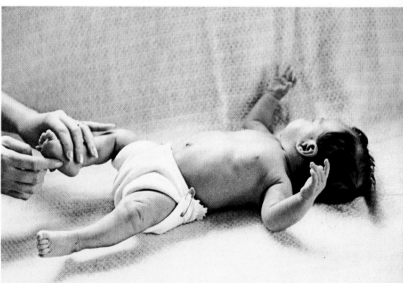

Figure 4.6. Extension of the body as a reflex reaction to scraping the sole of the foot.

reflexes appear to develop later in life; for example, the eye-blink reflex to approaching objects does not appear in the average baby until two months of age.

PATTERNS OF BEHAVIOR

Careful analyses of the behavior of the newborn have recently led investigators to conceive of the newborn not primarily as a bundle of reflexes but rather as an organism that possesses several congenitally organized patterns of behavior. These patterns of behavior seem more complex than simple reflexes and substantially more important for development. Sucking is an excellent example. When a baby sucks, he must coordinate three different, somewhat antagonistic, functions: breathing, sucking, and swallowing. Swallowing apparently depends on the amount of milk in the baby's mouth because swallowing never occurs when a pacifier is exercised. The baby swallows between an inspiration and an expiration in only .5 second. There is also a rhythmic relationship between sucking and breathing; a baby will suck either once to one breath or twice to one breath. The best coordination of sucking occurs when a suck is made during an inspiration and a swallow is made between an inspiration and an expiration. A kind of hierarchical relationship exists among these three mechanisms, with swallowing controlling sucking and sucking controlling breathing.

Even more fascinating than the complicated relationship between swallowing, sucking, and breathing are the mechanics of the sucking act. In order to extract milk from a nipple, the baby must establish a closed-air seal around the nipple with his mouth. He is aided in this task by the lips and by fat pads on the inner and outer portion of the gums. An additional set of pads on the inside of the cheeks keeps them from collapsing when negative pressure is established inside the mouth. The baby does not suck like the adult taking liquid from a straw. The adult establishes negative pressure by chest inspiration, but the infant uses what is called mouth sucking. After the nipple is suctioned into the mouth, the jaw and curved tongue are raised, and then the tongue squeezes the nipple against the hard palate at the top of the mouth, pressing out milk from the nipple by moving it from the front to the back of the mouth. Finally, with the closed-air seal still intact, the baby drops his lower jaw, thereby increasing the size of the oral area, which, in turn, produces negative pressure and draws more milk into the nipple. Remember, all of this takes place in coordination with breathing and swallowing *twice each second.*

So the whole process of sucking is quite complicated. It has, in fact, challenged the ingenuity of investigators for more than sixty years. A huge technology has evolved around the development of procedures for measuring sucking. Early inves-

tigators attached chin straps to the baby that were connected through a system of levers to a heated stylus that wrote; as the chin moved up and down, so would the stylus' tracing. Today one of the more sophisticated procedures employs x-rays in an analysis of the movements of the jaw.

RULES

What is it that ties the simple and organized behaviors of the baby to his various internal states and to the state of the outside world? It seems as though nature has endowed the newborn with general rules for behaving in certain situations. Again, sucking is a good example of this concept. If sucking were merely a reflex response to a nipple in the mouth, the baby would suck at any time, but it is well known that he will not. A baby who is drowsy or sleepy or completely satiated with milk will not suck, although it is generally true that when a baby is hungry, he is also alert and awake.

It is possible that the baby does not recognize hunger per se but that hunger arouses the baby and, in a state of arousal, the baby sucks. Investigators have fed babies to satiation and then, instead of permitting them to fall asleep, have aroused them by placing one foot in cold water.

This act aroused the babies and they sucked just as much as they would have if they were hungry; therefore, it appears that one of the rules with which the baby comes into the world is: if aroused and nipple is in mouth, then suck.

There appear to be other, more complicated rules relating the baby to the outside world. For example, investigators have known that babies will follow a moving object or respond to light at birth, but these behaviors were thought to be reflexive. One might predict from this reflex notion that babies would close their eyes in darkness, regardless of state. Recent investigations have shown, however, that if a baby is alert and awake and lights are shut off—that is, if he is placed in complete darkness—his eyes will open widely and he will begin to search, seemingly for light. If a light is then turned on but the baby has only a white patternless field before him, he will continue to move his eyes around. If a form is placed in his field of vision, the baby will focus on it and move his eyes back and forth over the salient edges. Therefore, it appears that the baby comes into the world with almost a programmed set of rules for responding visually in his environment. These rules might go something like this: if awake and alert, open eyes; if see no light, start searching; if see light but no pattern, keep searching; if see pattern, hold and follow edges.

Another example of an extremely adaptive rule with which the baby seems to come into the world may be called *habituation*, which appears to be a device that the baby uses to sort out the

Figure 4.7. In this perception experiment newborn infants were presented with a large black triangle on a white field. Infrared marker lights placed behind the triangle permitted the movement of an infant's pupil to be traced and photographed. The eye movements of a control group of infants were also recorded (not shown here). Although the results show that the ocular orientation of the experimental infants was more toward the vertices of the triangle, most interesting is the vast range of individual differences even newborns show in their way of looking at things. (After Kessen, 1967.)

overwhelming number of stimuli into significant and insignificant categories. For example, if a baby is presented a tone for the first time, he may open his eyes, stop sucking, and appear to be listening to what is happening in the environment. If no significant event follows the tone but it is presented over and over again, eventually the baby will no longer attend to it. Habituation is one of the first indicators of learning in the new-

born baby—by this process he is able to be somewhat selective in his responses.

CAPABILITIES OF THE NEWBORN

Throughout centuries of civilization (and indeed well into the present century), it was widely believed that the newborn child could not sense the usual physical energies in its environment. It was held that he could not see, hear, smell, or taste

but could only feel cold, pain, and hunger. Presumably, the source for this belief was that the infant merely lay in his crib, obviously incapable of grasping or reaching out or manipulating his physical world. Because theoretical biases had led many to believe that knowledge could only be gained by physical interaction with the environment, the infant was thought to be unable to learn. However, it is now known that, permitted a fairly broad range of experience, the baby's eyes are freely able to move, and it is clear that babies can learn from observing relations between events. Evidence now shows that the newborn is a far better-equipped organism than had been originally believed.

As stated earlier, the newborn responds to light; his pupils contract when a light is presented and dilate when it is dimmed. The baby can also hear; it is not difficult to produce a startle response by presenting a loud bang or sudden noise. It also appears that the baby can smell; he will turn his head away from noxious odors. He can taste, and most certainly he senses tactile stimulation. As stated above, it is known that the responses he makes to inputs are not all reflexes. Investigators have carefully measured the eye movements of newborn babies as they looked at homogeneous white or black visual fields and when they looked at patterned stimuli. The baby's spontaneous behavior was very clearly different in the latter case —the baby appeared to be examining the visual patterns by moving his eyes back and forth over their edges.

Even though it is known that the baby can sense various kinds of physical energies, it is still not known what the baby's perceptual world is like. It is not known, for example, whether he sees all elements of a face—two eyes, a nose, a mouth, two ears, a chin, hair—as separate parts, or whether he naturally combines this bewildering number of stimuli into one simple face.

The recent evidence of sensitivity to visual patterns and the emphasis on early infant learning have been widely publicized. Witness the tendency of this generation's parent to arrange mobiles and other visual toys for infants—even as early as the first day home from the hospital—as opposed to the previous generation's belief that the child should not be distracted from the sleep that he needs in order to develop normally.

In their enthusiasm to acknowledge the newborn's skills, however, psychologists must not overestimate (as before they underestimated) what he can do. It is well to reconsider the things that he cannot do, in order fully to appreciate the job that lies before him. For instance, the child must learn a language, he must learn how to relate to an increasingly hostile social world, he must learn about the existence of objects separate from himself, and he must learn the conceptions of space and time, to say nothing of the culture's rules—religion, manners, and morality. All of these developmental milestones are discussed in future chapters.

ADAPTING TO THE WORLD

Given that the baby has many ways of sensing events in the outside world, and given that he has certain coordinated patterns of behavior for meeting certain environmental situations, what then are the mechanisms for his adaptation to the world? How does he come to know more about the world?

HABITUATION AND LEARNING

One mechanism for adapting to the vast number of stimuli impinging on the baby's receptors has already been discussed: habituation. Habituation is akin to a rudimentary kind of learning. It permits the child to ignore certain aspects of his environment. A more complex kind of learning is that discovered by the famous Russian physiologist Ivan Pavlov. Pavlov showed that behaviors originally attached to one stimulus event may become attached to a second event if the two events occur together. The stimulus acquires the capability to signal that a second event is imminent, and the two events become associated. This process, called conditioning, was first studied in dogs but has also been examined in newborns. Babies can learn to associate a presumably neutral event, such as a sound or a light flash, to a stimulus (a nipple) that normally elicits sucking behavior. When a tone is presented over and over again and each time is followed by the presentation of a nipple to the baby's mouth, the baby will begin to suck when the tone alone is presented. Psychologists say that the baby has *learned* the association between nipple and tone, which was set up artificially in the laboratory.

One elaboration of this procedure may be used to study the ability of infants to discriminate different sounds. The baby lies on his back, his head in a movable headrest, while one of two sounds is presented to him. If he turns his head to the right, he is rewarded with milk. He must learn to turn his head one way after one sound and the other way after the other sound (see Figure 6.3). After the learning takes place, as shown in the figure, one can see that the baby protests when his expectation, established over several daily experimental sessions, is violated. Some investigators have held, based on this basic kind of conditioning principle, that babies can learn, for example, love of mother through the association of her face, her touch, and her voice with reduction of hunger and pain. However, other investigators hold that what can be demonstrated in the artificial environment of the laboratory is not necessarily what occurs in the home.

SELF-GENERATED BEHAVIOR

Piaget has held that babies do not learn to associate any two stimuli. Rather, associations are learned between external events only when those events elicit similar actions. Infants learn by acting on the outside world with the congenitally organized responses that they have at birth. A baby does not respond, for example, to a mobile in the usual sense. Rather, he uses the mobile to exercise his organized eye-movement patterns; it is a convenience for performing his visual calisthenics. This theoretical position, holding that the baby explores his environment with biologically given behavioral patterns, fits the observable facts reasonably well in some cases; for example, as everyone knows, a baby puts almost everything in his mouth. Presumably he is using his organized

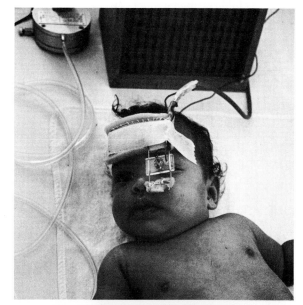

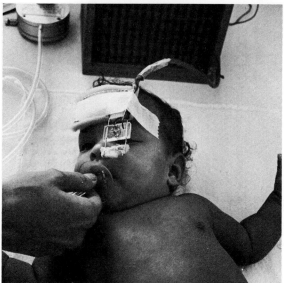

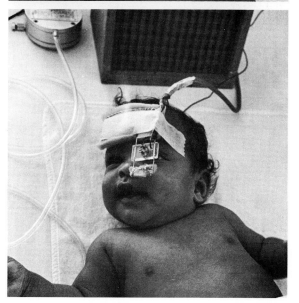

sucking and mouthing response to explore new objects in the outside world. Jean Piaget would say that the infant is imposing his organized oral behavior onto the external objects. This principle could be applied similarly to looking, grasping, and other early responses.

But, of course, new behavior patterns emerge that did not exist at birth. Piaget holds that these patterns develop quite slowly and appear only when a presently available behavior is not suitable for exploring or understanding a new event. In such a case the baby may modify his behavior, producing a kind of compromise response better suited to the characteristics of that object. However, if the event requires too much adaptation of the baby's behavior, the baby will ignore the event rather than accommodate his behavior to it. This way of viewing infant behavior is quite different from the older American view. American psychologists have emphasized the stimulus or the event in the outside world rather than the behavior of the infant. Many investigators have wanted to say that the baby responds either with a reflex response to an external stimulus or with a response that has become conditioned to a reflex. Probably, as in most controversies of this sort, the truth lies somewhere in the middle.

CHILD-REARING PRACTICES

The recent emphasis on early learning and the psychologists' assertion that the mother plays a crucial role in a child's development have led to a certain amount of anxiety among mothers. Mothers are concerned about this burden and often worry about the permanent effects of particular

Figure 4.8. A learning (conditioning) experiment being carried out in L. Lipsitt's laboratory. The attachment to the baby's forehead produces a mild puff of air and records the eye blinks elicited. A tone is then paired with the air puff. After a number of such presentations, the tone alone comes to elicit the eye blink.

experiences. The best evidence available suggests that the single-experience trauma that would permanently affect the child's life is extremely rare. The general tenor of the home life and the general attitude of the parent toward the child are most important in developing his feelings of security and competence. However, love is not the only requirement of the infant. Certainly he needs stimulation of all kinds, but whether or not he has a mobile over his head for one week in the third month of life will have little (if any) effect relative to the *general* attitude of the parents toward education and the provision of a stimulating environment for him throughout his childhood. It is the daily persistent experiences that are important in the child's psychological development.

It is interesting to note how dramatically differ-

ent are child-rearing practices in various cultures and in various generations within a culture. Most people are well aware of the variations, over the past few decades, in opinion on toilet training, breast versus bottle feeding, schedule versus demand feeding, and the oscillation that has taken place between the notion that the child should be strictly raised and continually kept in line and the notion that one should spare the rod and spoil the child. In a decade or so, it will be interesting to look back at practices now adhered to rigorously simply because pediatric theory has taken a certain direction. One must admire the natural durability of the child and his ability to thrive in spite of the vacillations in raising him.

In the face of an examination of cultural differences in child rearing, the oscillations in our own culture seem quite mild. One recent study in

Europe has pointed up some very substantial cultural differences in upbringing and in the philosophy of what is important to the baby in his early days. In one European country the baby is kept in a very cold room; his daily schedule is controlled very rigidly around the clock. He is permitted to feed for ten minutes and then, independently of the amount consumed, he is put in his bed, bound tightly, and all lights are shut off—there is no visual stimulation around him whatsoever. The doors are tightly closed so that his crying will not bother others; he is not picked up when he cries. Contrast this environment to the typical American middle-class environment, where the baby these days is literally flooded with mobiles and patterns, his environmental temperature variation is held within a very small range, and his clothing is kept as loose as possible so that he may thrash about. One could hardly imagine a greater contrast between two styles of upbringing; yet there is little evidence of permanent differences between babies from the two cultures that can be based on the differences in the way the babies are treated.

And so we see that even the newborn infant is a complex organism, possessed of reflex responses, enormous sensory capacity, the ability to learn, and, most critically, a set of intricate behavioral rules and strategies that permit subtle and sophisticated adaptations to novel circumstances. The infant is an organism that is already biased toward a particular and individual personality and that has a reassuring capacity to resist the modest vagaries of environmental facts and parental foibles. If the infant is to survive, it has no other choices.

In the course of just the first two years of life, a normal infant develops the ability to talk with his parents and other people and to understand what they say to him. The infant's emotional repertoire expands from two—arousal or quiet—to many —jealousy, shame, love, hate, fear, joy. The child gains some twenty pounds in weight and a foot or two in height. He changes from a sensory being that can only partially perceive his world to a thinker who not only perceives the world in detail and acts effectively on it but also plots his actions, remembers his past, and dreams of his future. The child's social capabilities expand, with language, far beyond the smile and coo that he brought into the world. His position in society changes also, from one of total dependency to one of complex and expanding social ties and roles both within the family and, increasingly, with outsiders. In these first two years, the infant begins to become the adult, and habits and customs, joys and terrors, laid down now may follow him all the rest of his life. This unit is about how and why these changes take place.

Unit III
The Dawn of Awareness:
The First Two Years

At birth, all normal infants are recognizable as members of the human species, but marked structural differences have existed among them since soon after conception. Infants differ in such physical variables as height (length), weight, muscularity, hairiness, dental development, and a host of other measurable characteristics. As the young child grows, these physical differences persist. Some, such as height and weight, become more pronounced; others, such as hairiness, less pronounced.

Psychologists who are interested in studying growth set up *norms* of development, based on the central tendencies (such as averages) and variabilities of healthy children. However, only a minority of children actually conform to the average. Most are above or below average. Also, it is a rare child who follows the same course in all of the physical variables that are measured in studying growth. One child may follow the norm in weight gain but be exceptionally tall; another may be the reverse. *Individual patterns are the rule.* Moreover, not only does one child differ from another in relation to norms of growth, but an individual child will grow and develop in spurts and plateaus that cannot be predicted from his own history or from the norms. Individuality prevails.

SYSTEMATIC STUDY OF GROWTH

Despite the rule of individuality, a systematic study of growth is necessary in order to obtain knowledge about the cause-effect relationships between physical growth and both inherited factors and relevant environmental situations. Psychologists strive to understand the average, normal, and healthy patterns of growth so that they can identify conditions that operate to lower a child's efficiency or to hinder growth. Once the causes are known, there is the possibility of doing something to control abnormal growth patterns.

Dietary deficiencies are a common cause of abnormal patterns of growth. If, for example, one of two groups of average babies is fed a protein-deficient diet while the other is fed a protein-rich diet, the deficient children will grow to be less tall and less well-muscled, on the average, than will the well-fed children. Comparison of the growths of the two groups shows that the diet produces a difference in growth. Comparison of the growth of the two groups to the norms of growth establishes that it is the deficient children who are growing less well than the average, while the other children are growing according to the average. This sort of experiment has been done in laboratories with a variety of animals, and it points to diet as a central environmental determiner of normal physical growth. Unfortunately, experience in underdeveloped countries and among the various socioeconomic strata in our own country has emphasized the contribution of diet to growth. Once diet has been isolated as a cause of abnormal growth, however, dietary supplements can be instituted to promote normal growth.

The *process of growth* may be thought of as a series of interactions between the growing organism and its environment. In this process the child *grows*, becoming larger. He *develops*, becoming increasingly complex in his body structure and its

5
Physical Development

functions. He *matures*, approaching ever more closely his mature size, organic structure, and body build. These three aspects of growth continuously interact with and facilitate each other.

STAGES OF INFANCY

To provide an overview of physical development during the first two years, Table 5.1 gives some of the milestones of development during those years. Although the accent in this chapter is on physical development, some salient features from the development of vocalization and language are included for perspective and because they will be useful in understanding that aspect of development in Chapters 9 and 12.

Many developmental psychologists divide the first two years of human life—the period of infancy—into seven more-or-less definite stages, each delimited at least approximately by the child's chronological age. The labels given these stages do not imply that the behaviors described exist only at that stage; preparation for the behavior may have begun earlier, and the behavior may continue throughout life. These stages point up either a characteristic that predominates during the period (Crying Period) or a qualitatively new way of behaving (Eye-Hand Stage). The stages outline the important trends in physical development over the first two years.

☐ *Postpartum Stage* The effects of the physical act of birth are noticeable during the first week of life. During this time the infant's physiological reactions stabilize with respect to his environment, and some effects of the prenatal environment—

such as drugs given to the mother during delivery —gradually wane. Genetic determinants, established at conception, persist throughout the lifetime of the individual.

☐ *Crying Period* The amount of time spent crying varies a great deal from child to child and depends on many factors, inherited and environmental. But there is a discernible trend in the average child: By twelve weeks of age the amount of time spent crying is markedly reduced. The crying period thus extends from the first to the twelfth week. During this period there is also an increase in vocalizations other than crying, perhaps because the decrease in the frequency of crying allows more time for other vocalizations. The infant also comes more and more to pay attention to things that go on around him. Crying may increase again during a later period, but its causes are different. During the crying period the child cries mostly because of bodily pain and distress; later he cries from fear or frustration.

☐ *Perceptual Period* During this period, which occurs mainly in the third month of life, the infant begins to show evidence of real visual involvement in the world around him. He comes to respond to repetition and shows signs of boredom (technically, habituation) when the same scene or object is presented to him over and over again. Also, the first appreciations of three-dimensional perceptions appear.

☐ *Eye-Hand Stage* During the period from four to seven months, many things happen to the developing child. Perhaps the most important of these is the development of eye-hand coordina-

Table 5.1. Developmental Milestones in Motor and Language Development

Age	Motor Development	Vocalization and Language
12 weeks	Supports head when in prone position; weight is on elbows; hands mostly open; no grasp reflex.	Markedly less crying than at 8 weeks; when talked to and nodded at, smiles, followed by squealing-gurgling sounds usually called *cooing*, which is vowellike in character and pitch-modulated; sustains cooing for 15–20 seconds.
16 weeks	Plays with a rattle placed in his hands (by shaking it and staring at it); head self-supported; tonic neck reflex subsiding.	Responds to human sounds definitely; turns head; eyes seem to search for speaker; occasionally some chuckling sounds.
20 weeks	Sits with props.	The vowellike sounds begin to be interspersed with more consonant sounds; labial fricatives, spirants, and nasals are common; acoustically, all vocalizations are very different from the sounds of the mature language of the environment.
6 months	Sitting: bends forward and uses hands for support; can bear weight when put into standing position, but cannot yet stand holding on; reaching: unilateral; grasp: no thumb opposition yet; releases cube when given another.	Cooing changes into babbling resembling one-syllable utterances; neither vowels nor consonants have very fixed recurrences; most common utterances sound somewhat like *ma*, *mu*, *da*, or *di*.
8 months	Stands holding on; grasps with thumb opposition; picks up pellet with thumb and fingertips.	Reduplication (or more continuous repetitions) becomes frequent; intonation patterns become distinct; utterances can signal emphasis and emotions.
10 months	Creeps efficiently; takes side steps, holding on; pulls to standing position.	Vocalizations are mixed with sound-play such as gurgling or bubble blowing; appears to wish to imitate sounds, but the imitations are never quite successful; begins to differentiate between words heard by making differential adjustments.
12 months	Walks when held by one hand; walks on feet and hands—knees in air; mouthing of objects almost stopped; seats self on floor.	Identical sound sequences are replicated with higher relative frequency of occurrence, and words ("mamma" or "dadda") are emerging; definite signs of understanding some words and simple commands ("Show me your eyes").
18 months	Grasp, prehension, and release fully developed; gait stiff, propulsive, and precipitated; sits on child's chair with only fair aim; creeps downstairs backward; has difficulty building tower of three cubes.	Has a definite repertoire of words—more than 3, but less than 50; still much babbling but now of several syllables with intricate intonation pattern; no attempt at communicating information and no frustration for not being understood; words may include items such as "Thank you" or "Come here," but there is little ability to join any of the lexical items into spontaneous two-item phrases; understanding is progressing rapidly.
24 months	Runs, but falls in sudden turns; can quickly alternate between sitting and standing; climbs stairs up or down.	Vocabulary of more than 50 items (some children seem to be able to name everything in environment); begins spontaneously to join vocabulary items into two-word phrases; all phrases appear to be own creations; definite increase in communicative behavior and interest in language.

Source: E. H. Lenneberg, *Biological Foundations of Language* (New York: Wiley, 1967), pp. 128–130.

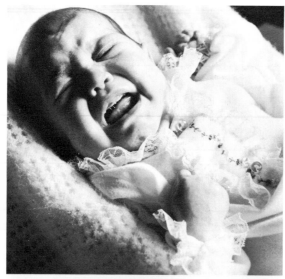

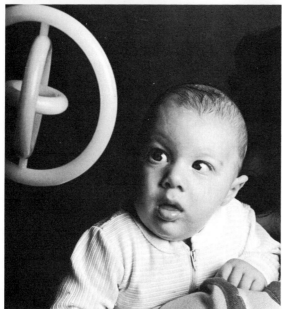

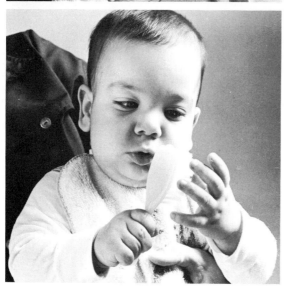

tion, which allows accurate reaching for and grasping of objects. Near the beginning of this stage, reflexive, tight grasping disappears and is replaced with an eye-guided, purposeful reaching for things. In this period, the child seems to become a more human creature by reacting warmly to voices, faces, and happenings.

□ *Transient-Fear Stage* Between about seven and twelve months of age, the trends characteristic of the first four stages continue, and toward the end of the first year a new emotional response appears in the typical child and then gradually fades away: fear of the unknown. This fear may manifest itself as a continuing desire for a security blanket, shyness and sometimes outright fear and flight in the presence of strangers, fear evoked by sudden loss of support, or, quite often, a generalized anxiety. This period is a particularly poor one for moving a child from one home environment to another.

□ *Walking Stage* During the first half of the second year of life, the majority of children—though by no means all—take their first steps. The consequences of this development for the life of the child and his parents are incalculable. Increased danger and increased opportunities only weakly summarize the import of adultlike mobility. Fortunately for parents, the child at this stage is beginning to react well to simple commands, and he may be able to express some of his wants in simple two-word sentences. Positive reactions on the part of parents to these simple requests usually result in a fascination with naming objects. It is interesting that nature provides for the nearly simultaneous development of extreme mobility, adequate comprehension, and at least the rudiments of expressive language at approximately the same time.

□ *Linguistic Stage*   No two-year-old speaks his language very well, but the increase in the use of language during the second half of the second year amply justifies the name of this final stage of infancy. Some children speak and move so well by the end of this stage that they hardly qualify as infants, but the variability in individual developmental patterns is great. The child's range of new physical capabilities expands enormously during this period.

DIRECTIONS OF GROWTH

The direction of growth in humans is in many respects opposite to that of plants. Humans grow in a *cephalocaudal,* or head-to-foot, direction, whereas plants grow from the bottom up. Humans also grow in a *proximodistal,* or center-to-periphery, direction. This pattern of growing seems to follow the fact that the most rapid embryological development occurs in or near those parts of cells destined to be parts of the brain and the nervous system.

Behavioral development seems to proceed in the same directions. The baby can hold his head erect before he can sit, and he sits up before he can walk. He uses his hand as a unit before he can

sustain control over his fingers. Figure 5.3 shows roughly at what ages children gain control over various of their motor behaviors. The ages cited in Table 5.1 are not meant to be standards against which each child must be measured. Although the direction of growth is universal, the rate of growth is individual.

DIFFERENTIATION AND HIERARCHIC INTEGRATION

Nearly all aspects of development proceed by *differentiation* followed by *hierarchic integration.* In physical development, at first the pure number of motor functions that the infant can perform under his own control increases. He gains mastery of movement after movement. Then, interrelations between and among movements begin to emerge—what Heinz Werner called the hierarchic integration of parts into coherent wholes. From simple mastery of the arms as levers, the muscles of the abdomen as lifters of the upper body, and the neck muscles in control of the head, the infant develops hierarchic patterns of purposeful movements in which each separate motor capability is brought into the service of the others in a highly organized way. The infant comes to put together the various simpler movements into the act of sitting up.

CHANGES IN BODY PROPORTIONS

Among the many differences exhibited by newborn infants are great individual differences in the

Figure 5.1. (a) Crying period. (b) Perceptual period. (c) Eye-hand stage. (d) Walking stage.

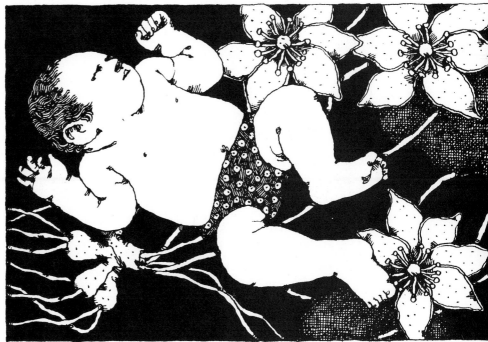

Figure 5.2. The direction of human growth—from head to foot—is opposite that of a plant, which grows from the bottom up.

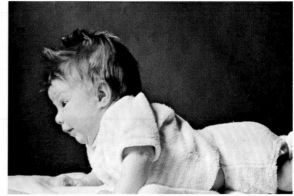
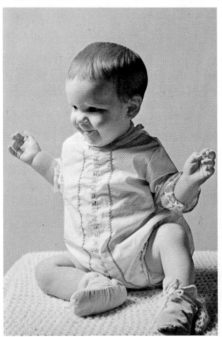

a	b	
c	d	e

Figure 5.3. Differentiation followed by hierarchic integration can be seen in muscular control of motor development. Simple mastery of the arms as levers (a) and of the neck muscles in control of the head (b) permits the infant to develop hierarchic patterns of purposeful movements, such as sitting up (c). These are then combined with developing capabilities, which permit crawling (d), and eventually walking (e).

Figure 5.4. Changes in body proportions with growth. The same boy is shown at various ages. (Adapted from Bayley, 1956.)

relative proportions of various parts of their bodies. These differing proportions lend some infants a long and thin look, some a short and round one, and others, every conceivable aspect in between.

In the first two years of life, the differences between boys and girls in growth rate and body proportion are so slight as to be of no practical significance. Even so early, however, the composition of the male and female bodies differs. Infant girls have proportionally more fat and less muscle as well as less water than boys. Later, girls develop faster than boys, and their growth is generally more steady and stable than that of boys—but these are topics for Chapters 10 and 19.

Body proportions change dramatically from birth through adolescence, as shown in Figure 5.4. From birth to adulthood a person's head doubles in size and the trunk trebles; the upper extremities quadruple in length and the lower extremities increase fivefold. Much of the growth in height during childhood is due to the increase in length of the lower limbs, whereas the increase in the length of the trunk accounts for more of the spurt in height during adolescence. The head contributes increasingly less to total body length, from one-fourth at birth to one-twelfth at maturity.

During the first year of the child's life, he shows extensive growth changes. Body length increases more than one-third, and weight almost triples. A typical infant boy who at birth is twenty inches long and weighs seven and a half pounds, for example, by one year of age will probably be twenty-eight or twenty-nine inches long and weigh about twenty pounds. At two years of age, he will be thirty-two or thirty-three inches long (tall) and weigh approximately twenty-eight pounds. His head during these first two years will grow more slowly than his trunk and limbs, so that his proportions become more adultlike. In addition, his facial skeleton becomes relatively larger, so that his cranium is no longer so out of proportion with his face (see Figure 5.5).

BODY BUILD AND RATE OF GROWTH

There is evidence that rates of maturation and certain types of body build seem to be related. The child who is broadly built, large, and strong is likely to be a fast grower, whereas a slender, long-legged but small, lightly muscled child is likely to be a slow grower (see Figure 5.6 for example). It has also been found that the fast growers usually reach their maximum height at an earlier age than do slow growers, who continue growing for a longer period of time.

CONTROLS OVER GROWTH

Different factors control growth at different stages of life. From conception to about two or three years, growth is determined by the genes, which set the basic pattern, and the environment, which determines the completeness with which genetic factors are able to express themselves. Later, during the childhood years, a hormone from the anterior pituitary gland, in conjunction with thyroxin from the thyroid gland, becomes influential in determining growth. Between the ages of eight

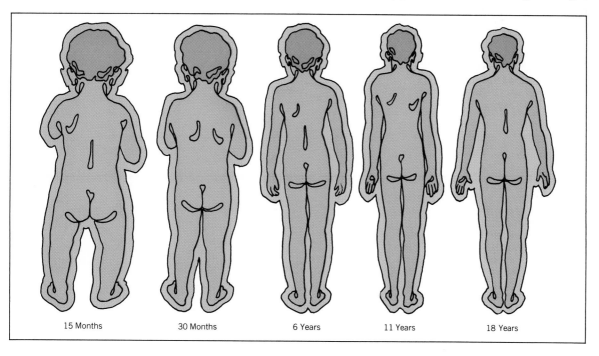

| 15 Months | 30 Months | 6 Years | 11 Years | 18 Years |

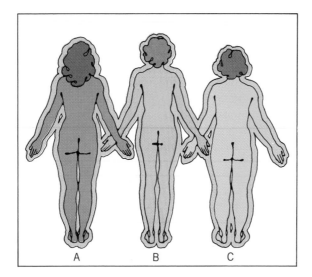

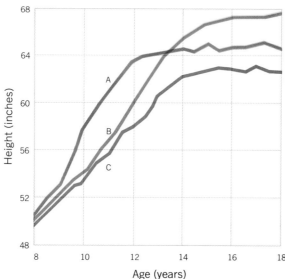

and eleven, additional pituitary hormones begin to function more actively, and as these gonadotropins stimulate the testes and ovaries to produce androgens and estrogens in quantity, the rapid growth and changes of adolescence are initiated (see Chapter 19). These three successively dominating factors that control growth are somewhat independent of each other. They may vary both in their intensity and in their temporal patterns, but at the points of change in their relative influence, certain changes in characteristic growth and build should be expected. This variation again points to the individuality of growth, which severely hinders the exact prediction of the physical appearance and stature of an adult from his size and looks as a child.

METHODS OF STUDYING GROWTH

The various facets of growth are in no way better appreciated than through the various methods of studying growth.

NORMATIVE AGE—CURVES OF GROWTH

The most common way of looking at growth is to compare a child at successive ages with the average of a large group of normal children of the same ages. The resulting individual curves of growth show the child's growth scores relative to the average and the variability of those of the group. Most often a child is compared with other children of *the same chronological age*. However, it is also possible to set up averages or norms on the basis of groups of children that are all the same in another respect—for example, skeletal age.

Figure 5.6. Growth rates for three girls with different body types show that the girls matured differently. Girl A's growth was accelerated; B's was retarded; and C's was irregular. (Adapted from Bayley, 1956.)

Figure 5.5. Changes in facial proportions with growth. The skull outlined at the left is that of a newborn baby; the one on the right is that of an adult. The distance from bottom of the chin to lower lip has been drawn in proportion, so that the differences can be clearly seen. (Adapted from Jackson, 1923.)

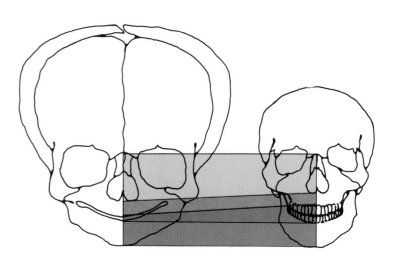

SKELETAL AGE

The sequence of events in human skeletal development is remarkably regular. Early in prenatal life, the skeleton is cartilage, which is only gradually replaced by bone. This process (ossification) begins at *ossification centers* and spreads concentrically. As ossification replaces cartilage with bone, the individual bones in the skeleton increase in width. For a long bone, the primary center of ossification is the *diaphysis,* located in the shaft of the bone. There are usually one or more additional centers at the ends of the bone, called the *epiphyses.*

In order to determine a child's skeletal age, x-ray photographs of the hand and wrist are compared to norms derived from the average individuals in normal groups. The most commonly used norms are those compiled by W. W. Greulich

and S. I. Pyle, whose *Radiographic Atlas of Skeletal Development of the Hand and Wrist* contains x-ray photos of typical children's hands and wrists at each age, up to the age at which ossification is complete. In early childhood, skeletal age depends on the relative size of the ossification centers and the shape and contour of the remaining cartilage on whose basis bone will be formed—the so-called *bone model.* The fusion of bone generated at the epiphyses and diaphyses becomes the significant factor determining skeletal age in later childhood. Figure 5.7 shows x-ray photos from various skeletal ages.

INDIVIDUAL TIME PATTERNS

Longitudinal data on the same individual over long periods of time allow statement of a child's growth relative to himself. A child's own status at

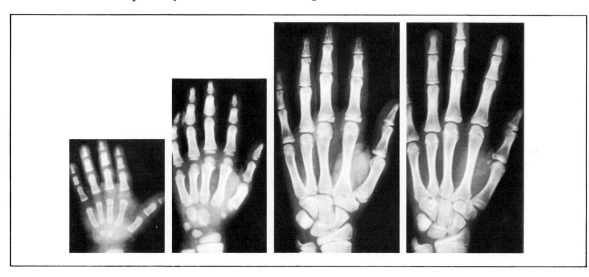

Figure 5.7. Skeletal age. (a) Hand of a boy with standard skeletal age of six months. (b) Boy with skeletal age of five years. (c) Boy with skeletal age of thirteen years. (d) Girl with standard skeletal age of thirteen years. Note the greater maturity of the thirteen-year-old girl's hand, as evidenced by thicker bones and more advanced fusion of the small bones of the hand and wrist. (From Greulich and Pyle, 1959.)

some well-defined period—his height, weight, closure of the epiphyses in the bones of his hand, and so forth—is taken as the standard against which his status at other times is compared. Such time patterns for individuals can be compared to relevant norms in order to detect indications of relative precocity or retardation in the pattern of growth.

"ORGANISMIC" GROWTH

Generally speaking, physical growth, mental growth, and school achievement are all intercorrelated to some extent. W. C. Olson and B. O. Hughes kept longitudinal records of mental capacity, reading ability, height, weight, strength of grip, ossification of hand and wrist, and the appearance of teeth for a number of children. They translated their data for each child into a height age, weight age, and so on, and averaged these "ages" to find what they called an organismic age. Table 5.2 shows the data for a nine-year-old girl whose average, or organismic, age was eleven and a half.

As useful as organismic age may be in summarizing an individual's development, there are some objections to translating one type of unit of measurement into another for the purpose of averaging them into an organismic age. Especially open to question is the comparison of absolute measures, such as pounds of weight and inches of height, with less precise units, such as increments of intellectual ability or changing patterns of skeletal ossification. The latter types of measures have usually been derived from observations on normal samples, reduced to the amount of change

to be expected from one age to another. Such age norms do not take into account the fact that growth is not equal in intensity or extent at all ages, nor that the variabilities of the different types of tests are not equal or alike in their growth trends. Thus, the conversion of separate scores into organismic ages may minimize some evident differences in rates of development and exaggerate others.

DEVELOPMENT OF MOTOR ABILITIES

Sensory and motor functions, basic to all behavior, can be separated only artificially. The sense organs respond selectively to various stimuli, and the resulting responses usually involve some form

Table 5.2. Cross-Sectional Data for Girl Aged Nine Years (108 Months)

Function Measured	Raw Score	Age Equivalent (in months)
Height	60.4 inches	160
Reading	28 items correct	130
Weight	96 pounds	156
Strength of grip	19.7 kilograms	130
Ossification of hand and wrist	x-ray	135
Mental capacity	Tests passed	134
Dental eruption	16 permanent teeth	119
Organismic age		138

Source: W. E. Olson and B. O. Hughes, in R. G. Barker, J. S. Kounin, and H. F. Wright (eds.). *Child Behavior and Development* (New York: McGraw-Hill, 1943), p. 203. Used with permission of McGraw-Hill Book Company.

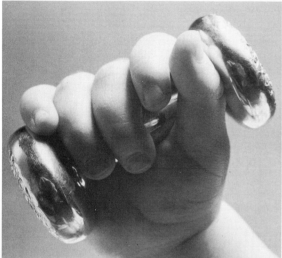

of muscular reaction. Developmentally, the earliest forms of behavior are simple sensorimotor reflexes (see Figure 5.8). During the period of earliest development, when the changes are most rapid, the ability to perform motor functions depends greatly on cortical and muscle development. Gradually, function becomes relatively independent of structure. Once the basic structures are formed and available for use, motor ability depends more on such factors as body build, motivation, and practice.

CORTICAL DEVELOPMENT

J. L. Conel's studies of the postnatal development of the human cerebral cortex demonstrate the basis in the central nervous system of the order of development of motor and sensory functions. It is known that areas of the brain control particular sensory and motor functions; as soon as these areas have developed, the functions appear in behavior.

Between birth and three months of age, the greatest cortical development takes place in the primary motor area of the upper trunk, leg, hand, and head. There is also in this period a rapid advance in myelinization (*myelin*, a neural sheath) of the neural fibers, which serves to channel impulses along fibers and to reduce the random spread of impulses across neurons. At six months there is particularly marked development in motor areas controlling the hand and upper trunk, leg, and head. Between six and fifteen months the motor areas of the brain show less marked growth, but the order in which they attain physiological maturity is: hand, upper trunk,

Figure 5.8. Grasping behavior progresses in the first year of life through a series of stages. At twenty weeks infants can hold things in a primitive way, without firmly grasping them. By twenty-eight weeks they can use their palms to close in on and pick up an object. By thirty-six weeks the forefinger comes into use, and at sixty weeks the child's grasp—with thumb and forefinger opposition—is much like an adult's.

head, and leg. As we have seen, this is the order in which the behavioral development of those parts of the body proceeds.

MOTOR DEVELOPMENT AND COORDINATION

The development of motor coordinations, evidenced first in simple reflexes, appears to depend on the ability of muscles to respond to stimuli; on growth, which gives increased strength to the muscles; and on the development of coordination through practice. Practice strengthens the muscles, stimulates their growth, and promotes learning through the simultaneous stimulation of visual and muscle senses in the eye-hand coordinations involved in reaching, grasping, and manipulating small objects.

In newborn infants these coordinations are seen in such reflex responses as head lifting, various postural adjustments to body position, and reflex grasping. Soon, between one and two months, there are playful bursts of activity in the form of arm and leg thrusts. As the muscles grow stronger, the infant is able to hold his head erect, to push his chest up by his arms, to turn from his back to his side (at four months), and to sit, at first with support; by six months he can sit alone (momentarily). By three months his hands are no longer tightly fisted and he holds a small toy with a grasp that is no longer entirely reflex. The six-month-old will reach for a toy with one hand. (Earlier he tends to "close in on" an object, using both hands simultaneously.) He shows early manual coordination in rotating his wrist, in partially using his thumb in opposition to his fingers, in

grasping, and in trying to pick up pea-size pellets. The eight-month-old sits alone steadily, may be starting to crawl or creep, and picks up small objects with complete thumb opposition. By nine months he can get himself into a sitting position and pull to a standing one by his crib rail. The ten-month-old creeps with agility and can often walk with help, sit down, and bring his hands together for games like pat-a-cake.

The one-year-old can take a few steps alone. In the next six months he will be able to throw a ball, walk backward, and walk up and down stairs with help. The two-year-old walks up and down the stairs without holding on, and by three years he jumps from small heights, runs, walks on tiptoe. The four-year-old can walk a line and can hop a few steps on one foot (see Table 5.3).

Table 5.3. Some Second-Year Items in Bayley's Scales of Psychomotor Development

Item	Age Placement (Months)
Walks alone	11.7
Throws a ball	13.3
Walks sideways	14.1
Walks backward	14.6
Walks upstairs with help	16.1
Walks downstairs with help	16.4
Tries to stand on walking board	17.8
Walks with one foot on walking board	20.6
Walks upstairs alone; marks time	25.1

Source: N. Bayley, *Bayley Scales of Infant Development* (New York: The Psychological Corporation, 1969). Reproduced by permission. Copyright © 1969 by The Psychological Corporation, New York, N. Y. All rights reserved.

MATURATION VERSUS THE ROLE OF EXPERIENCE

Several studies have emphasized the primacy of neuromuscular maturation over experience in determining the infant's acquisition of some skills. For example, Hopi Indian infants are bound to cradleboards during their first year, but they nevertheless walk at about the same time as all other infants who have had more practice in muscular coordination. Another study often cited to support the importance of maturation relative to experience is of twins, one of whom was given six weeks' experience in stair climbing, whereas the other was given only two. Both twins achieved mastery of stair climbing at the same time nevertheless. Figure 5.12 shows that children start to walk at about the same age in five of Europe's largest urban centers, even though the encouragement to walk given children varies greatly from city to city.

But the environment cannot be neglected altogether. Even though practice beyond normal freedom for spontaneous activity may not be essential for motor development, there is no question that some environments promote effective development while others do not. For example, in two of three institutions studied by Wayne Dennis in Iran, infants were handled very little; they were almost always left lying supine in cribs, not propped up. Until the children themselves achieved the sitting position, they remained lying down. They had no toys. Less than half of these children could sit alone when they were between twelve and twenty-one months of age, whereas all normal, noninstitutional American children can

Figure 5.9. Some milestones in motor development. (See Table 5.3.)

sit alone by nine months. The investigator found the same type of retardation in walking alone. As a check against cultural bias, Dennis studied children in another Iranian institution, which offered more handling of the children and possibilities for sitting and crawling. The children at this institution exhibited none of the retardation noted in the first two.

Maturation alone cannot adequately account for the development of behavior; experience and stimulation from the environment make undeniably important contributions to the effects of maturation.

HANDEDNESS

A puzzle in the field of motor development is handedness: only 5 percent of the adult population in the world is left-handed. There is no known genetic or constitutional basis for handedness, and it is certain from the variety of clever and capable southpaws in the world that they are at no real disadvantage in a right-hander's world. The facts suggest a partially experiential basis of handedness. The percentage of lefties decreases from a full 15 percent in the preschool years; rhesus monkeys, who do not encounter human society, split half and half in being left- or right-handed. But it is not at all clear why many fewer than half of the human race start out left-handed nor why right-handedness should be the nearly universal rule throughout the world.

Handedness begins to become evident in the latter part of the first year; almost as soon as the infant can use his two hands independently, he prefers the right. Some lefties persist in their

Figure 5.10. Hopi infant in a cradle-board. Although these infants spend most of their time thus bound, they begin to walk at about the same time as other infants.

Figure 5.11. Infants in a Russian nursery. The effect of institutionalization on infants' motor development—and personality and cognitive development—depends greatly on the type of care the infants receive.

Figure 5.12. The age of first walking in five European cities. (After Hindley et al., 1966.)

preference despite the amazement of parents, the encouragement of right-handed teachers, and the extreme difficulty of dining between two right-handed neighbors. But most people start out right-handed and stay that way. It is said that Babe Ruth was one of the very few truly ambidextrous people. That he chose to pitch baseball left-handed was not based on any natural advantage but rather on the fact that there were so few southpaws available—one of the few competitive advantages available for lefties.

INDIVIDUAL VARIABILITY

There are individual differences in the age at which children master motor and coordination skills. Furthermore, there is great specificity in skills. That is, ability to catch a ball cannot be used to predict ability at high jump, and so on. After early infancy, motor skills are very largely determined by practice. And, as will be discussed in Chapter 6, even very young infants can be retarded or accelerated in responding, depending on the relative deprivation of their environment.

Physical and Social Development

Interrelationships undoubtedly exist between growth, achievement in physical behaviors, and social development. These interrelationships are difficult to document, but they do require some discussion. Erik Erikson has attempted to explain, in his discussion of ego identity, the manner in which physical and emotional development come to be related. He points out that mastery of such a skill as walking helps to make the child a part of his culture; the child becomes one-who-can-walk and acquires a cultural status different from that of one who cannot walk. The resulting cultural recognition—plus the physical mastery itself—contributes to the child's self-esteem.

In conclusion, let us complicate the problem of the interrelationships of physical, social, and intellectual growth even further. Some studies have claimed to detect a link between sheer body size and scores on intelligence tests; these results show that, on the average, larger children tend to score higher than do smaller children. Now, couple this with the finding that larger children may have more than the average self-esteem and it becomes tempting to conclude that larger children have a considerable intellectual, personal, and social advantage. But the cause-effect relationships here are no means obvious. It may be that physical size, rather than chronological age, is simply a better predictor or index of development. It may be that enhanced self-esteem, derived from precocious physical development, gives the child greater latitude and freedom in developing and expressing his intellectual capabilities. It may even be that self-esteem—perhaps learned in the home—is fundamental and that it is self-esteem that allows both physical development and intelligence to express themselves beyond the average. It is in the nature of correlations that researchers do not yet know which account is the true one. Perhaps someday experiments will give the answer; but there are moral, ethical, and practical limitations to experimentation on the development of human children. Presently, it is only possible to indicate the complexity of the various factors involved in the control of human physical development.

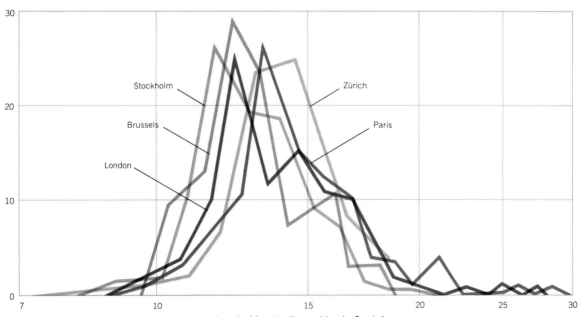

nfancy is one of the most important periods of human life. The infant's experiences and the way he perceives or interprets them are critical for any theory of development; in fact, many psychological theories assert that experience in infancy shapes the entire subsequent course of a human life. The importance of the world of the infant, however, is matched by its inaccessibility. A great deal of psychological methodology depends on being able to speak to and converse with the subject in ordinary language; but infants, almost by definition, don't talk.

METHODS OF STUDYING INFANT BEHAVIOR

The problem of communicating with the infant, of finding out how he perceives things and events in the world around him, has been attacked in a number of ways. The simplest method, and in many ways the most satisfactory, involves direct observation of behavior.

DIRECT OBSERVATION

The information obtained through direct observation can in some cases be entirely unambiguous. For example, if an experimenter moves an object back and forth in front of an infant, and the infant tracks the object with his eyes, the experimenter can be quite sure that the infant not only can track the object but also can see it. However, if he moves an object back and forth and the infant does not track it, what can he conclude? Can he conclude that the infant does not see the object? No, for the infant may see the object and be unable to track it, perhaps because it is moving

too fast. Can he then conclude that the infant can see the object but cannot track it? The answer again is no, because the infant, while able, may be *unwilling* to track that particular object under those particular circumstances. Observation of natural behavior, then, must take into account two processes within the infant: his perception or interpretation of an environmental event and his ability to express or use that interpretation in behavior.

If an experimenter shows an infant an object and he fails to respond appropriately, it is difficult to say whether the failure results from a defect in interpretation or a lack of motor skill. Consider another simple problem. If you show a five-month-old infant a toy, he will reach out and pick it up. If, however, you drop a cloth over the toy before it has been picked up, the infant will sit quiescently and make no attempt to remove the cloth and get at the toy. Why doesn't he try? Is it because out-of-sight means out-of-mind to the infant, so that the object, having vanished, no longer exists for him? Or is it that the child simply lacks the motor skills necessary to remove the cloth and get the toy? The difference between these two interpretations is not trivial. It is very important that psychologists be able to separate lack of conceptual skill from lack of motor skill. Simple observation of natural behavior will not do this; more complicated methods are required.

THE SURPRISE PARADIGM

One of the most widely used methods of studying infants is the surprise paradigm. The rationale

6

Perceptual and Intellectual World

behind this method is simple: If one presents an infant, or indeed any organism, with an event that violates his expectancies or beliefs, then he should be surprised. Surprise can be measured in many ways: by changes in heart rate, respiration, and skin resistance to electricity (galvanic skin potential) or by such behavioral measures of surprise as eye widening, jaw dropping, cooing, squealing, and crying.

This method can be applied to the problem, discussed in the preceding paragraph, of how an infant interprets the covering up of an object. The problem is to find out whether the infant does not remove the cloth to get at the object because he thinks the object no longer exists or because he lacks the skill. If one assumes that he only lacks the necessary motor skills, one can test this assumption with the following event sequence: present him with a toy, cover it with a cloth, remove the toy surreptitiously, and then remove the cloth. Where the toy was, there will now be nothing. (See Figure 6.1.) If the infant continued to believe in the toy's existence while it was out of sight, he should be surprised to see that it is no longer there. If, on the other hand, one assumes that the infant thought the toy ceased to exist when he could no longer see it, he should not be surprised by the lack of the toy but rather by the converse event—when removing the cloth reveals the toy. The results of this experiment indicate that infants are more surprised by the nonreappearance of the object than they are by its reappearance, provided that the time out of sight is less than fifteen seconds or so. It appears,

Figure 6.1. When a screen (in this case a piece of paper) is dropped between a young infant and a toy he is interested in and is left there for longer than fifteen seconds, it appears that the infant ceases to believe in the toy's existence.

Figure 6.2. Some infants' responses can be studied simply by playing peek-a-boo with them. If a person stays hidden behind the crib long enough, does the infant believe the person has vanished and so cease to attend to him? And is he startled if the person then pops up again? Which occurrence surprises him more—the nonreappearance or the reappearance?

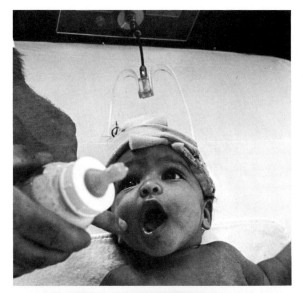

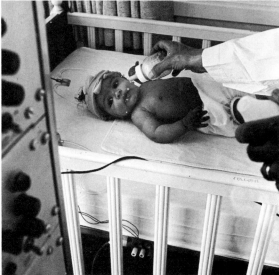

then, that failure to retrieve the object in this simple situation results primarily from a lack of motor ability—not from a conceptual defect.

EXPERIMENTS INVOLVING LEARNING

An infant's learning may also reveal how he interprets events in his environment. Even on the first day of life, an infant can appreciate a contingency between events. In an experiment conducted by Lewis P. Lipsitt, an infant learned that the sound of a bell meant there was a bottle on his right, whereas the sound of a buzzer meant the bottle was on his left. This simple experiment reveals a number of things: The infant can discriminate a bell from a buzzer; he can discriminate right from left; and he can detect the contingency that the experimenter has introduced to his environment. (See Figure 6.3.)

This learning method has also been used by T. G. R. Bower to study the infant's response to vanished objects. Infants were taught to respond in the presence of an object and to cease responding in the absence of the object. The training was so fine that the infants would stop responding as soon as the object was removed. On the critical test trials, the object was not removed; instead, a screen was slowly slid between it and the infant, so that the infant could no longer see the object. The infants continued to respond for some time, indicating that although the object was no longer in sight, it was still in some sense present for them, even though out of sight behind the screen.

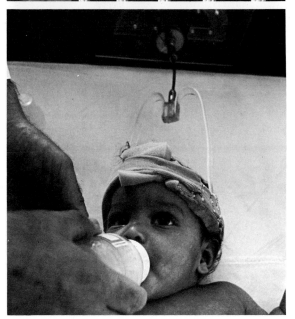

Figure 6.3. One way to enter the infant's world is to present him a learning task. In this experiment, conducted by L. Lipsitt, an infant showed he could distinguish between a bell and a buzzer and could understand the contingency between a sound and the location of the reward.

The methods described here can be used to enter the perceptual world of infants of any age. The basic method of developmental psychology consists of presenting infants of various ages with essentially the same event to discover whether there is any change with age in the way the event is handled. If developmental differences are discovered, the focus of interest becomes the understanding of the processes or mechanisms that generate these changes.

WHAT IS PERCEPTION?

Perception is such a seemingly simple process that it is difficult for many people to understand why it poses problems. In visual perception, for example, the whole process seems very straightforward. Light strikes an object, is reflected from it to the eye of an observer, is focused on his retina, sets off a photochemical process there that produces electrical activity in his optic nerve, which transmits the pattern of activity to the central nervous sytem, resulting in perception of the object. Nothing could be simpler, it would seem. However, there are several properties of perception that cannot be explained by this simple physiological model. For example, we humans see the world as three-dimensional—it extends into depth. There is nothing in the stimulation at the retina that directly resembles the third dimension as we see it. The retinal mosaic is completely flat, yet the world as we perceive it has depth.

To explain certain aspects of hearing poses a similar problem. For instance, we can locate the source of a sound with a high degree of accuracy, but how we are able to do so is a mystery because the ear is essentially a one-dimensional sense organ. Inputs to it are distributed in time, but the temporal dimension has nothing in it to correspond directly to the perceived spatial location of a sound. Olfactory perception, too, requires elaboration beyond the simple physiological model. Although the source of an odor has a definite location, there is nothing in the stimulus at our nostrils that would correspond to the location.

Even what appears to be the simplest of senses, the sense of touch, is not as direct as it first seems. When we feel an object with our hands, we produce a pattern of deformation on our skin surface that is quite unlike the object as we perceive it. We are not aware of the skin deformations when we grasp an object; we are aware of the object. R. H. Gibson showed that under conditions of passive touch—where the object is not grasped but rather is pressed into the hand—adults can even confuse a piece of Swiss cheese with a baseball. To really know how people perceive, then, psychologists must account for the many properties in the perceptual world that are not directly represented in the stimulation at the receptor surface.

STIMULI THAT CORRELATE WITH PERCEPTION

Even though there are no direct representations of the missing perceptual dimensions in stimulation, there are a number of stimulus variables correlated with the perceptual dimensions.

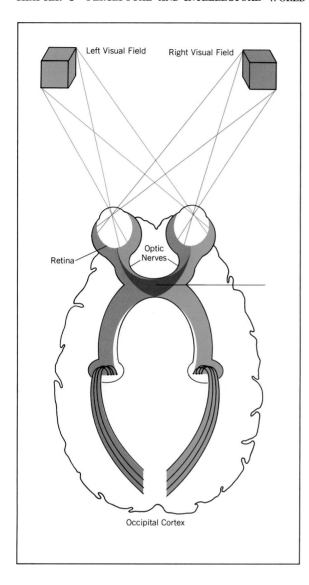

Figure 6.4. The physical process of vision.

HEARING

A sound located to the right of an observer is heard as being on the right, even though there is no right or left in the ear. Psychologists know that a sound coming from the right reaches the right ear a fraction of a second earlier than it reaches the left ear, and the time difference is correlated with its position to the right. The right ear leads the left ear by the largest possible amount if the sound source is to the observer's right on a line extending through his two ears. The size of the time difference declines as the sound source moves into the observer's midline, and it becomes zero at his midline. If an adult dons earphones, and clicks are fed into his ears with appropriate time delay, he will hear not one click followed by another but rather a single click located to right or left, depending on the time difference. The time difference stimulus is thus correlated with the perception of location of a sound source, and adults can utilize the correlation.

The important developmental question is whether infants can also utilize this correlation. Does an infant hear a sound on his right as such? Or does he hear two sounds, one in his right ear, followed by one in his left ear? M. M. Wertheimer attempted to demonstrate some degree of auditory localization ability in an infant a few minutes old by presenting a sound stimulus in various positions around the infant's head. He found that the infant would orient his head and eyes toward the source of the sound, and the accuracy of orientation to right or left was very high. The infant never turned left when the sound was on the right. It seems that a basic correlation, "right ear first means sound to the right; left ear first means sound to the left," is built into the infant's nervous system.

OLFACTION

Just as we have two ears, we have two nostrils, and an odor wafting from the left will reach the left nostril shortly before it reaches the right one. If an adult is presented with two odor-bearing air streams, one leading the other by a few milliseconds, he does not smell two odors but rather a single one that he perceives as positioned to right or left. In olfaction also, then, the perceptual location of the stimulus source is specified by a time difference whose magnitude is correlated with the exact position of the source. Can an infant make use of this correlation? T. Engen, Lewis Lipsitt, and Herbert Kaye presented neonate infants with a wide variety of odors, some of which the infant fixated. He would turn his face toward the source of a pleasant odor and try to avoid less pleasant odors. Both behaviors indicate that infants can localize olfactory sources. Olfactory localization is never very precise, even in adults, so it is unlikely that a small amount of growth in the olfactory system changes the correlation to any great extent.

SIGHT—DISTANCE AND SOLIDITY

The assessment of the infant's ability to locate sounds or odors to his right or left is facilitated by

the ready availability of a directed head-turning response. There is no such simple response available for assessing the missing dimension of vision —distance. Accordingly, experiments on the infant's ability to perceive distance are somewhat more complicated. In adults, distance is picked up by a variety of correlated variables: we have two eyes, each of which sees the world from a slightly different point of view, and so there are slight differences between the images on the two retinas. The magnitude of these differences in the retinal representation of any object is a function of its distance from the observer. These differences can be represented in plane pictures—stereograms—each of which is slightly different from the other (see Figure 6.5). An adult looking at a stereogram is not aware of these differences. Instead, he perceives objects as being at different distances.

Although the use of binocular differences depends on the use of two eyes, adults can perceive depth with only one eye. One correlated stimulus that signals distance to one eye is the change in size of the retinal image of an object as it moves toward one, or as one moves toward it. The closer the object is, the greater is the rate of its size change as it approaches. Adults can use this optical expansion pattern to detect the distance of a moving object when they are stationary, or of a stationary object when they are moving.

Another stimulus that depends on observer movement is the change of an object's position on the retina after a rotary head movement. The

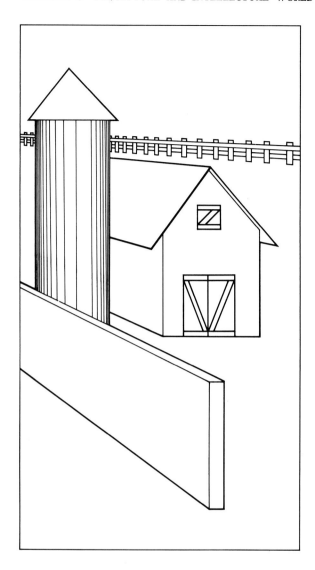

nearer an object is, the farther and faster it moves. And, finally, adults can detect relative distances of objects using only one eye when there is no movement; they use the so-called "painter's cues," such as overlap, texture-density gradients, and perspective diminution.

Can infants utilize these stimulus variables? One way to test distance perception is to employ the avoidance response to approaching objects; Bower has shown that infants a few days old will interpose their hands between their face and an approaching object with the infant's response being determined by the distance of the object. A large object approaching to three feet away and then stopping will not elicit the response, whereas a small object approaching to one foot away will. It is, therefore, not the size of the retinal image that produces the response but the distance of the object. (The response is not produced by air against the face. Air against the face produces a quite different response—head turning rather than head retraction, and no hand movement.) A shadow caster is used to elicit the response, and because in the shadow caster situation there are no binocular differences and no motion parallax stimuli, the response must be based on the optical expansion pattern.

Attempts to demonstrate the infant's ability to utilize the other stimulus variables described are methodologically more complex. The complement of the ability to use stimulus information generated by moving objects is the ability to use information generated by one's own movements.

Figure 6.6. Painter's cues used in this drawing include texture-density gradients, overlap, and perspective diminution-convergence.

Figure 6.5. *(opposite)* If the two slightly different pictures are viewed as shown in the small drawing, each eye sees a single picture. However, the two images may be fused into one and thus give an appearance of depth. Binocular fusion of the disparate images received by the two eyes is said to yield stereoscopic depth.

E. J. Gibson and R. D. Walk studied the latter ability in their visual cliff experiments. Their experiments showed that an infant who is old enough to crawl will not crawl over the deep side of a visual cliff (see Figure 6.8). Even one-eyed infants will avoid the deep side of the cliff, indicating that binocular differences are not necessary for the behavior. However, the infants in these experiments were between eight months and a year old, so it is difficult to say whether the behavior is learned or not. It is also impossible to conclude from this experiment anything about the infant's ability to utilize stimulus information other than that generated by his own movements.

T. G. R. Bower attempted to study the utilization of the other stimulus variables in infants six to eight weeks old by the following means. Infants were trained to make an operant response in the presence of a twelve-inch cube three feet away from them. They were trained not to respond in the absence of the cube. After the discrimination between presence and absence of the cube was perfect, the infants were presented with a thirty-six-inch cube nine feet away. The large cube at the far distance produced the same-size retinal image as the small cube at the near distance, so the only basis for the discrimination was the distance of the two objects. Results indicated that six- to eight-week-old infants could make the discrimination. Furthermore, they could make it even if they were allowed to use only one eye. However, they could not make the discrimination when presented with pictures rather than real objects. These results were interpreted as showing

that infants between six and eight weeks can make spatial discriminations on the basis of motion changes but cannot utilize the "painter's cues" that are present in a picture.

Even though an adult cannot see the back of an object, he perceives it as being solid. The perception of solidity is mediated by many variables, including binocular disparity, relative motion change, and the shading that can be captured in a static display. The grasp response of the infant is a convenient measure of the perception of solidity. An infant who can grasp—even an infant a few days old—will curl his fingers behind a solid object, provided it is defined by binocular differences or motion differences. However, pictorially defined differences elicit no attempts at grasping.

SIGHT—BINOCULAR VISION AND INTERMODAL TRANSFER

Binocular vision and the difference between our two eyes' view of a scene provide one of the most cogent cues to distance and solidity. An adult presented with a binocularly disparate display does not perceive two different views of an object. Instead, he sees a single object at a definite fixed distance. Does an infant have the same ability? In one experiment, infants were presented with a binocularly disparate pair of views of an object, one going to one eye, one going to the other. The display was then changed so that both views went to the same eye. If the infants had seen the binocular presentation as two views, rather than as a unified view of a single object, the transition

Figure 6.7. Stimuli used to test infants' distance and size-constancy perception. The infants were first conditioned to turn their heads to the side when a twelve-inch cube was shown to them at a distance of three feet. (The conditioning was accomplished by having an adult pop up and play peek-a-boo as the reward for head turning.) The test stimuli were a twelve-inch cube at nine feet (A), a thirty-six-inch cube at three feet (B), and a thirty-six-inch cube at nine feet (C). The infants responded to test stimulus A but not to C, which projects the same-size retinal image. Thus, it appears that the infants took into account the distance of the object and its size at the given distance. (From T. G. R. Bower, "The Visual World of Infants," copyright© 1966 by Scientific American, Inc. All rights reserved.)

| | Conditioned Stimulus | Test Stimuli | | |
		A	B	C
True Size				
Distance from Infant (meters)	1	3	1	3
Retinal Size				

to the double view (which can only be seen as two views) should have surprised them. In fact, it did, indicating binocular fusion. Infants thus possess the capacity to integrate their two eyes' views of a scene.

The presence of this capacity allows one to investigate another important perceptual ability, *intermodal transfer*, that is, perception of one sense mode by means of another. When an adult sees an object, he knows that it is hard. The hardness, which is a tactile property, can be picked up by the eye. Infants have the same ability. Bower showed that if infants are presented with a binocularly defined object that exists only optically, they will reach for it, even at a few days of age. Moreover, when their hand gets to the place where the object is seen to be and their hand encounters nothingness, the infants manifest extreme startle and surprise, indicating that they expected their hand to contact some tangible object. The absence of the object surprises them.

Intermodal perception has also been studied in the case of visual-auditory communication. Many sounds come from a visually defined locus in space; the human voice proceeds from a human mouth. E. Aronson investigated the infant's response to a breakup of this correlation. Infants sat facing their mothers, who talked to their infants in any way they fancied. One mother recited the Gettysburg Address to her three-week-old infant. After some time, the mother's voice was displaced so that it appeared to come from a point three feet to the right or left of her mouth. Three-

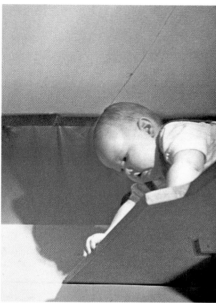

Figure 6.8. Infants will not crawl over the deep end of a visual cliff, even when their mothers motion them to come.

week-old infants are extremely disturbed by the dislocation, indicating that they had detected this association between mouth location and sound location. (See Figure 6.9.)

PERCEPTUAL DEVELOPMENT

In all the capacities so far mentioned, infants seem to be remarkably capable. They have a basic form of space perception, perception of solidity, and some degree of intermodal coordination. This ability does not mean that their capacities do not improve with age; they do. S. Klimpfinger found that the accuracy of space perception increased by about 10 percent between eighteen months and five years, at which point the accuracy of the discrimination was better than in adults. Similarly, K. A. Meneghini and H. W. Liebowitz

found that spatial discrimination, especially at large distances, improved with age. A simple explanation for these developments may be the increase in the size and hence the resolving power of the eye. The stimulus information available for distance discrimination is minimal at large distances. The 30 percent change in size of the eyeball between birth and five years would be more than enough to account for the developmental changes described by these researchers. However, there are other aspects of perception that develop far more than simple growth can account for.

PATTERN PERCEPTION

One of these aspects is pattern perception. A pattern, such as a letter or a human face, can be

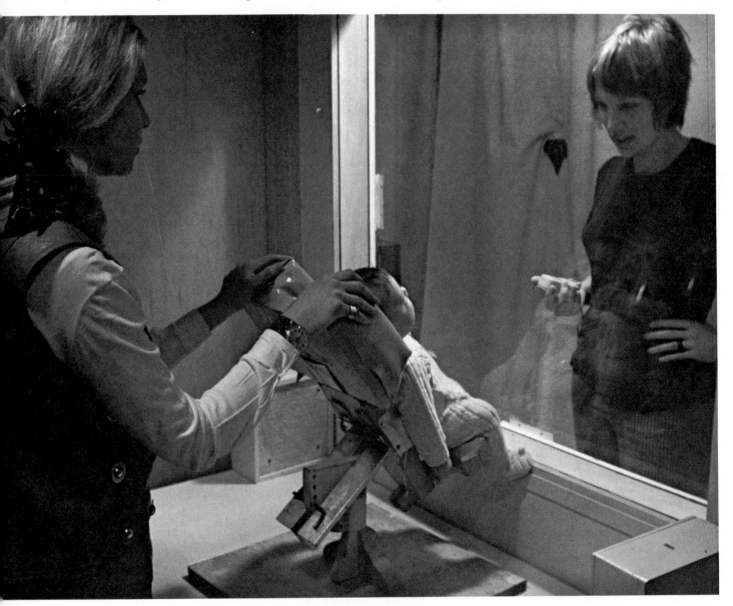

discriminated and identified by adults with great accuracy. Adults almost never confuse faces, even of identical twins; this is not true of infants. The infant response to the face has been very well studied. A young infant sees much less in a human face than an adult does. Thus, infants of under one month show no preference for any of those faces shown in Figure 6.10. These infants will smile at any nodding object that is approximately the size of a human head; the presence or absence of eyes, nose, and mouth are quite unimportant. The only important thing seems to be the motion. By the age of six weeks, eyes have to some extent become important, but any two blobs will also produce a smile; the rest of the features of the face are unnecessary. By ten weeks eyebrows are necessary for best elicitation of the smile, although at this stage the eyes and brows may be very schematic without affecting the infant's response.

By three months, the eyes have to be very realistic to elicit the response. Up to this age, the eyes, the head outline, and the motion seem to operate independently. That is, the eyes need not be presented within a face, the head outline need not have eyes, and the motion need not be that of a head. Past the age of twenty weeks, however, these features alone will not release a smile; the combination is necessary.

Until the age of twenty weeks, the mouth is unnecessary for the smiling response, but at this point, it begins to become important enough so that faces without mouths elicit withdrawal

rather than smiling. Also at about twenty weeks, the approach of a face elicits more smiling than withdrawal. By the age of twenty-four weeks, a broadly smiling face elicits more smiling than a pursed mouth, while angry and wrinkled brows begin to elicit withdrawal rather than approach. By twenty-eight weeks, female faces elicit more attention and vocalization than do male faces, suggesting an ability to discriminate between male and female. Around thirty weeks, infants begin to differentiate familiar from unfamiliar people. Skill at recognizing different faces continues to develop for many years, in fact, up to the age of fourteen; however, by the age of eight months the infant can at least learn all of the information necessary to discriminate a face from a model and to discriminate familiar from unfamiliar faces.

DEVELOPMENTAL MECHANISMS

The simplest developmental mechanism is the process of structural growth. Infants grow very rapidly, and pure growth can produce changes in what are apparently psychological abilities. The eye of a newborn infant is very short by comparison with that of an older child, so the infant must have much less depth of visual field than the adult or older child. Also, the infant eye does not accommodate—it has a fixed focus. Nonaccommodation must mean that, except around the plane of sharp focus, which is about eight inches, the visual world of the newborn is considerably blurred. The normal processes of growth will

Figure 6.9. Experimental setup in E. Aronson's investigation of the effects on infants of voice displacement. The mother's voice is heard coming from the speakers at the side, although the child can see her speaking in front of him.

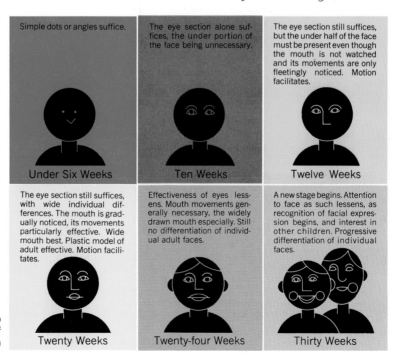

Figure 6.10. Stimuli required to elicit smiling response in infants of various ages. (After Ahrens, 1954.)

Simple dots or angles suffice.

Under Six Weeks

The eye section alone suffices, the under portion of the face being unnecessary.

Ten Weeks

The eye section still suffices, but the under half of the face must be present even though the mouth is not watched and its movements are only fleetingly noticed. Motion facilitates.

Twelve Weeks

The eye section still suffices, with wide individual differences. The mouth is gradually noticed, its movements particularly effective. Wide mouth best. Plastic model of adult effective. Motion facilitates.

Twenty Weeks

Effectiveness of eyes lessens. Mouth movements generally necessary, the widely drawn mouth especially. Still no differentiation of individual adult faces.

Twenty-four Weeks

A new stage begins. Attention to face as such lessens, as recognition of facial expression begins, and interest in other children. Progressive differentiation of individual faces.

Thirty Weeks

both increase the size of the eye (and hence its depth of field) and result in increasing accommodation (and hence in increased clarity of the visual world).

There are processes, however, that depend upon specific input from the environment; if the input is lacking, the developmental change will not take place. Separation of universal growth processes from environmentally induced effects is a very important problem—and a very difficult one. There is a tendency to believe that events normally preceding a developmental advance are somehow a cause of that advance. This assumption is not always necessarily correct. Infants about four months old normally spend a great deal of time watching their hands, and for many years it was thought that watching the hands was necessary for the development of accurate reaching, which follows shortly afterward (see Figure 6.11). More recent research has shown that watching the hands is an artifact of the way babies are cared for in our culture. Until very recently American infants spent most of their time lying on their backs, and they watched the only moving objects available—their own hands. Now that they spend much of their waking time in an upright baby seat, they do not watch their hands but more interesting, worldly objects. Nevertheless, they develop accurate reaching.

It has also been suggested that watching his hand move to and from his face educates an infant's sense of sight because his eyes converge and diverge. It was suggested that this experience is necessary for the development of accurately coordinated binocular vision and that without it, eye movements might not become coordinated. Unfortunately for this notion, blind infants also go through a period in which their unseeing eyes converge and diverge on their unseen hand. The eyes and the hand simply behave together; one does not cause the other. It is clear that psychologists must beware of interpreting a temporal sequence as a causal sequence and of assuming that all the environmental input that precedes or accompanies a developmental advance is necessary for that advance.

LEARNING IN INFANTS

The term *environmentally induced developmental change* corresponds roughly to what most psychologists call learning. There has long been a predisposition to believe that all human knowledge is learned and that a great deal of it is generated by simple conditioning processes. The laws of conditioning have been well studied in animals, and in recent years, there have been numerous attempts to apply these laws to learning in infancy. These attempts, by and large, have not been convincing for various reasons. The human infant appears to be a much more complex learning machine than even the adult of any other species.

OPERANT CONDITIONING

A very basic form of learning is operant conditioning. In the operant conditioning paradigm,

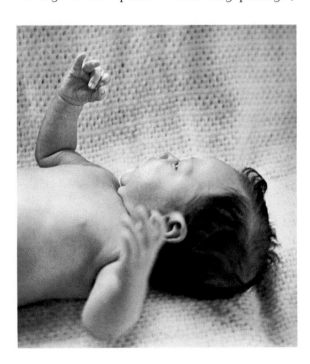

Figure 6.11. Infants about four months old will spend much time simply looking at their hands. For some time, psychologists theorized that this hand regard was prerequisite to the development of reaching capabilities. In fact, however, the invention of the infant seat, which permits infants to spend much time sitting up, proved that hand regard was a function of prevailing child-care procedures.

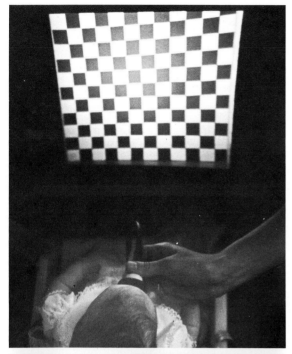

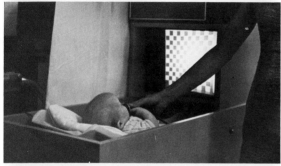

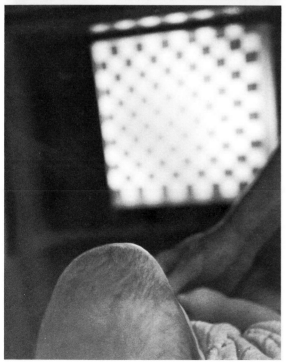

some action of the organism, such as a head turn, is followed by some environmental change. If the environmental change is a *reinforcer*, then the rate at which the organism will engage in the response will increase. For many years it was thought that young infants were incapable of even this relatively simple kind of learning. Attempts to condition ten- or twelve-month-old infants routinely failed. More recent research has shown that the tasks were not too complex for the infants but rather too simple. Even neonates can learn an operant conditioning sequence, as in the bell and buzzer experiments mentioned earlier and depicted in Figure 6.3. However, a sequence that the young infant learns easily may never be learned by the older infant. In part, the problem stems from the nature of effective reinforcement in infancy.

Historically, learning theory has assumed that in order to be effective, a reinforcer must satisfy some simple need, such as hunger or thirst. However, it has rarely been possible to use these reinforcers with human infants. Instead, the reinforcers have been interesting visual displays that are said to satisfy some curiosity drive or need for stimulation. In a recent series of conditioning studies carried out by Bower, the reinforcing event was presentation of a human being for a brief time. This visual event seems on the surface to be a fairly interesting one. However, continuous presentation of this event rapidly led to a loss of interest and a decline in responding—the reinforcer ceased to be effective. The decline could be

Figure 6.12. This experiment, being carried out in L. Lipsitt's laboratory, illustrates both operant conditioning and habituation. The infant, just four months old, is shown a pattern on a televisionlike screen, which he can keep in sharp focus by sucking on the pacifier attached to the screen. Infants will work (suck) with great energy and interest for a while to obtain the reward of the picture. However, they eventually get somewhat bored, do not suck so hard, and the picture pales. When a different picture is made available, the energy put into sucking increases again.

arrested by presenting the event only on every fifth response, but even this routine soon palled. Interest could be maintained for a longer time, however, if the number of responses required to produce the event was left uncertain from reinforcement to reinforcement. These facts are hard to understand given only the terms of classical learning theory.

SELF-GENERATED LEARNING

H. Papoušek has recently clarified the nature of reinforcement in infancy. He found that infants of six months will master quite complex learning tasks, such as making a head turn twice to the right, three times to the left, and once to the right again, *purely for the joy of solving the problem.* His reinforcement was presentation of a white light for a few seconds. The infants in his experiments barely looked at the light, merely checking that it was on to prove that they had solved the problem. Provided the task was changed often enough, the infants continued to learn with this reinforcement over a prolonged period. That the reinforcement was problem solving and not the presence of the light is shown by their refusal to continue responding to the same problem once they had solved it. Failure to learn may thus occur simply because the motivational structure of the task bores the infant, because what most adults assume to be reinforcers in fact reinforce only poorly.

There are other, more complex reasons why older infants may fail to solve a task that younger infants can apparently handle easily. Consider the following simple situation: An infant strikes a key, and a light three feet in front of him goes on. A four-month-old has no trouble mastering this task, whereas an eight-month-old may well have trouble. If, however, the task involves hitting the light itself, which then goes on, the eight-month-old will do as well as or better than the four-month-old. The reason for the difference seems to be that the older infant knows something about causality; he knows, at least, that in his world a cause and its effect are usually in the same place. His imperfect knowledge about causes that are distant from effects prevents him from seeing the connection necessary for learning the problem. Simple learning models can be applied to the human infant only at great risk or with considerable ingenuity.

The structure of an event is far less important in determining what the infant can learn than is his interpretation of the event. As Jean Piaget has always insisted, the environment does not stamp itself onto the child's mind; rather, information from outside is structured and arranged by the child's mind according to rules, and the total pattern of these rules defines the mind of the

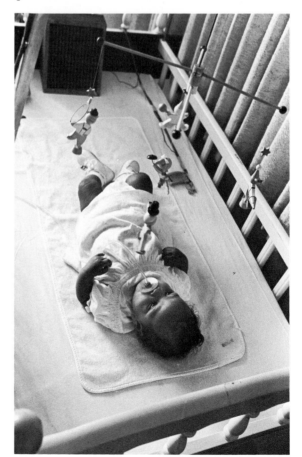

Figure 6.13. In an experiment like the one illustrated here, the researcher makes use of one well-developed capability—the infant's sucking ability—to study learning and preferences. Here, the child's sucking makes the mobile move; the more vigorous the sucking, the more movement in the mobile.

child. Some of the rules antedate experience, whereas others are generated by an interaction of the preexistent rules with environmental events. (See the discussion of *accommodation*, Chapter 11.) The point is that the process is always interactive, involving interpretation. It is never merely a passive reception.

PERCEPTION IN INFANTS

How, then, does the newborn interpret events in the world around him? Psychologists know that the newborn human can perceive the size of an object and its distance from him quite well. He can also track moving objects, provided they do not move too fast. They are interested, however, in more complex variables than these simple perceptual ones. Studies have shown that an infant can perceive an object in much the same way an adult does, that is, he can respond appropriately to its size, shape, distance, color, hardness. However, there are important ways in which his knowledge of objects is incomplete.

MOVING OBJECTS

An infant under four months of age does not discriminate between a moving object and the same object when it is stationary. If an infant is presented an object to track and then the object is stopped, the infant will continue tracking even after the object has stopped. That is, he will continue to follow the object's path of movement even though the object itself has stopped moving. The child's follow-through is not the result of

poor motor control because infants in this situation will also continue to follow quite complicated circular trajectories, which require refined motor control.

It is possible, with suitable optical devices, to present to an infant a stationary object from which another emerges and moves off. This impossible event does not disturb infants of less than about four months, who do not coordinate the concepts of a stationary object and the same object in movement. They do not see a stationary object as the end state of a movement or as something that can potentially move, nor do they perceive a moving object as something that can stop. The two are simply not connected. The connection occurs around the age of sixteen weeks, as was shown in a recent experiment conducted by A. C. Mundy-Castle.

In this experiment an object appearing on the infant's right rises vertically out of sight; then another, *identical*, object drops down on the infant's left and subsequently falls vertically out of sight, while the one on the right rises into view again. The infant subject views a number of such cycles. Although infants below sixteen weeks can quickly learn to look from side to side in order to see the objects, sixteen-week-olds *assume a circular trajectory of a single object*; their eyes do not move simply from side to side but rather describe a circular path that corresponds to the interpolated trajectory of the object. (See Figure 6.14.) Thus, object locations are connected by trajectories for four-month-olds, and an object can move

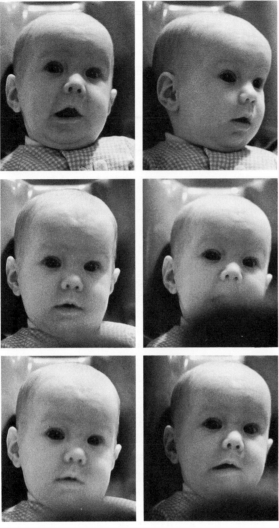

from place to place, even on an invisible trajectory. Furthermore, if the object that vanished on the right does not reappear on the left, the sixteen- to eighteen-week-old—unlike the twelve- to fourteen-week-old—will look back to the right. From such behavior we can infer a belief that an object can change direction.

OBJECT IDENTITY

Although the twenty-week-old child can handle movement events in a mature way, his concept of object has not yet reached that of an adult or older child. Consider the problem of the identity of objects: An object is identical only with itself. Some objects in the infant's world are indeed unique, such as his mother. Does an infant know that he has only one mother? Now, there is a great deal of evidence that an infant can recognize his mother and will respond differently to her than to any other female adult by the age of sixteen weeks, but does this mean he knows he has only one mother? Surprisingly, the answer seems to be no. With suitable optical devices, it is possible to present an infant with three images so that he sees three mothers. If the infant believes he has but one mother, this event should be extremely surprising, and, according to the principles of surprise described earlier, some evidence of startle should be detectable. There is no such evidence in the sixteen- to twenty-week-old infant; he responds to the presence of three mothers with, if anything, more delight than he responds to the presence of a single one. However, the

Figure 6.14. Infant just over sixteen weeks old photographed in A. Mundy-Castle's laboratory while tracking the ball shown in the diagram of the apparatus. The infant starts tracking in lower left photo; follows the ball up until it is out of sight; then *(upper right)* looks to the right in anticipation of the ball's reappearance, assuming a circular trajectory. When it does reappear, the infant tracks it on its downward course.

twenty-two- to twenty-four-week-old becomes extremely upset at the sight of three mothers.

The discovery of the uniqueness of his own mother gradually transfers to other humans and eventually to some objects. Indeed, by the age of seven months or so, the infant seems to have developed a set of extremely complex rules that allow him to define unique objects. In the first place, if two identical objects are simultaneously visible, then the infant never treats either of them as unique. However, presentation of an object all by itself is not sufficient to assure attribution of uniqueness if the object has been seen in different places—even if the infant never sees it in two places simultaneously. For example, if a seven-month-old is shown a desirable toy, then sees it hidden under a cloth, and the toy is spirited away surreptitiously and placed on the table in plain sight, the infant will not accept it: for him it is a substitute. There must be some plausible way for the object to have moved from one place to the other. He will continue to search under the cloth where the toy was hidden, examining the cloth minutely, examining the table surface, looking on the floor, and generally showing that he believes there are two objects in the situation.

This type of performance clearly reflects cognitive skill rather than perceptual ability. The toy is, of course, identical with itself—perceptually indistinguishable. But for the infant, it is not the same toy because there is no way for him to understand to his own satisfaction how the toy moved from its location under the cloth to its

new location in plain sight. This example again shows how the child's ever-developing cognitive skills can generate difficulties that would not occur with a younger infant.

OBJECT PERMANENCE

The problem of permanence has been alluded to several times in the preceding paragraphs. Permanence refers to a conceptual competence, a belief that objects continue to exist even when they can no longer be seen. It also refers to the child's skill in finding objects, which is often used as an index of conceptual competence. As was discussed earlier, even two-month-old infants manifest some belief in the continued existence of hidden objects. If an object the child is watching is covered by a screen, and the screen is then removed to reveal no object, infants of this age are surprised. From this behavior, psychologists infer that the infants believed the object was still there. The belief is time limited, lasting not much longer than ten or fifteen seconds. The reaction also depends very much on the manner in which an object vanishes. A very simple disappearance involves the occlusion of one object by another. In this situation the stimulus information is adequate, so the infant can know that one object is behind the other. Some of the disappearance situations that confront infants are undoubtedly of this sort, but most are not.

Suppose the infant looks away from an interesting object—his mother—and while he is looking away, she leaves the room. When he looks back to the place where she was, she is no longer there, and there is no stimulus information to specify where she is. This kind of situation is not dependent on—and indeed provides no stimulus information to specify—the current location of the vanished object. How does an infant respond to a situation like this? It is difficult to study a situation of this sort in the laboratory because infants do not routinely look away from their mothers, nor can their mothers be relied on to sneak away surreptitiously. However, one can mimic such disappearances. It is possible, using mirrors and special lighting, to make an object vanish without providing any clues to its current location, which is the essence of this problem. To an adult eye, the object seems to fade away like a puff of smoke. How does an infant respond to this kind of disappearance?

Earlier in this chapter, an operant conditioning method of ascertaining how an infant responds to simple disappearance was described. The infant was trained to respond to the presence of an object and not to respond in the absence of the object. If the object disappeared in a simple way —if it was covered by a screen, for example—the infant continued to respond for some time, indicating that the object was still phenomenally existent for him. However, if the object vanished without an indication of where it went, the rate of responding dropped instantly to zero, indicating that the object no longer existed.

One might expect a significant response from an infant if some important object, such as his mother, were made to vanish in this way. With infants under twenty-four weeks of age, one would be disappointed. A young infant will watch his mother dissolve into nothingness with no evidence of upset. This reaction is hardly surprising because, you will recall, infants of this age think they have a large number of mothers. However, as soon as an infant discovers that he has but one mother—the discovery takes place around twenty-four weeks of age—the dissolution of his mother provokes considerable upset and shortly results in searching. The searching is necessarily vague and wide ranging because there is no perceptual information to guide it. The infant may try to crawl to where his mother was, may search all over the room, may even assault the experimenter. The important point is that the search, however oriented, does take place. This behavioral event is novel and indicates a conceptual advance, a belief that, regardless of what he has just seen, his mother must exist somewhere.

This belief is soon extended to other humans, and indeed to other objects. However, the extension of the belief does not facilitate searching, which can only be expedited by the acquisition of specific knowledge about objects. One of the first things the infant more than six months old learns is that some objects are self-mobile. People, for example, move of their own volition. Other objects are inanimate and must be moved. An inexplicable disappearance of an inanimate object is thus likely to provoke an assault on the experimenter, whereas a similar disappearance of an

Figure 6.15. Results of an experiment in object permanence. Infants were trained to respond to a lighted bullseye pattern, set up and lighted in such a way that it could be made to disappear in four different ways. For experimental groups 1, 2, and 4 the object appeared—to an adult eye—either to dissolve away or suddenly "implode" from view. The results show that the object effectively ceased to exist for these infants. Group 3 saw a screen slowly pulled in front of the object until it was completely covered; for these infants the object continued to exist. (After Bower, 1967.)

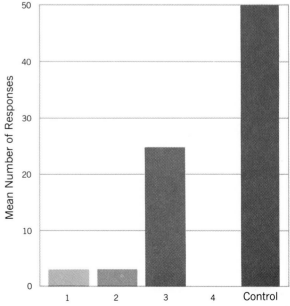

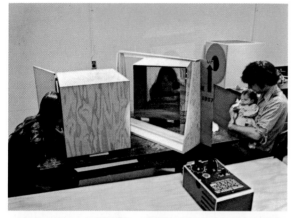

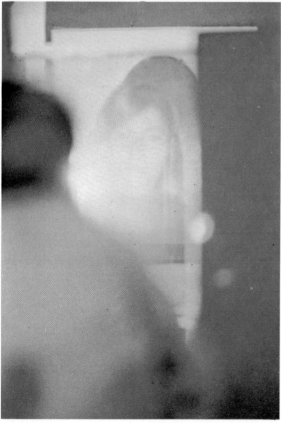

animate object will produce searching. The search is guided by growing knowledge of the characteristics and abilities of the objects in question. In a laboratory situation, unfortunately, it is difficult to study the full range of this part of development because infants quickly become cynical about the causal structure of a psychological laboratory. In order to maintain their sanity, they conclude that mother may go up in smoke, doggy will shrivel to nothing, and sister can pass through a stone wall. Too absurd to suggest searching for long.

CONCEPTUAL STATUS AND PERCEPTION

The development of a concept of an object—which includes a belief in the continued existence of vanished objects and rules for dealing with object identity—is the best-studied part of cognitive development in infancy. The rules guiding the child's behavior based on this concept are initially abstract, specific to each type of stimulus, and uncoordinated. They gradually become coordinated for specific objects, lose their specificity to particular stimuli, and reach a certain level of generality. A similar process of development occurs for causal events. Initially, infants will accept any two temporally contingent events as causally connected. With development, the events must become spatially contiguous as well as temporally contingent. Still later, in the second six months of the first year, the events must be appropriate to one another in some sense that no psychologist has yet been able to fathom.

The infant's interpretation of the world and of

Figure 6.16. Experimental setup showing how a mother's disappearance is effected and how it looks to the infant.

events in the world thus changes dramatically in the course of the first year. The same environmental event may have quite different meanings for infants of different ages whose conceptual structures differ in any of the ways described. A child's differentiation of the object, his development of rules to assign identity, and his acquisition of a sense of object-free permanence are all developmental events that will markedly change the child's interpretation of the simplest environmental event. It is therefore difficult to discuss the effects of environmental stimulation on development in infancy; one cannot even guess at the effects of any stimulus event without knowing the conceptual status of the infant being stimulated. The same event may produce quite different effects on infants whose conceptual levels differ. An infant who has not yet attained an identity rule will not be disturbed to see his mother softly and silently vanish, whereas one who is two weeks older, who *does* have an identity rule, will be considerably upset by this event.

PIAGET'S EQUILIBRATION MODEL

Jean Piaget, from whose work most of the above examples are drawn, emphasizes the way in which the infant's current conceptual level will influence the effects of any environmental input. He has also provided a theoretical model for understanding the interaction between current cognitive level and environmental input. The key concept in his theory is the concept of equilibration. According to his theory, development will not and cannot

take place unless the organism is in a state of disequilibrium. Disequilibrium is induced whenever the organism encounters a situation that produces two or more mutually opposed, partially adapted responses. Both cannot be applied simultaneously; neither is wholly successful. The result is disequilibrium, or conflict between the two cognitive modes. The coordination of these rules, so as to reduce the disequilibrium, is a process Piaget refers to as *equilibration*. Equilibration itself follows very abstract rules.

An example may make this process clearer. The development of a concept of object permanence depends on the prior existence of rules for assigning identity. Thus, an infant must know that he has only one mother before he can work out that she still exists even when he sees her dissolve into nothingness. When an infant first attains an identity rule for his mother, his response to her peculiar disappearance is to accept the nonexistence of the vanished object; any time his mother vanishes to an indeterminate location, he can only interpret this disappearance as the end of her existence. However, she does eventually return. Because he has recently attained an identity rule, he knows that the currently visible mother is the same one as the mother he thought had gone forever, and so a conflict is set up between his interpretation of the disappearance and his interpretation of the reappearance. The conflict induces a state of disequilibrium: the mother cannot both have ceased to exist and have reappeared as the same mother. As a way out of this conflict,

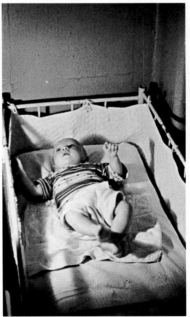
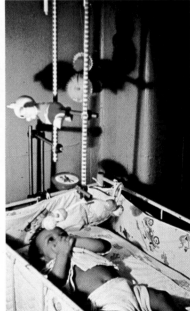

the equilibration process must generate a rule saying that the object in question did exist while out of sight, regardless of whether or not it was clear where she went. The development of conceptual permanence, then, obviously depends on *both* the existence within the infant of an identity rule and the occurrence in the environment of disappearing objects.

ROLE OF STIMULATION

The kind of development described above depends on quite specific stimulation occurring at specific points in development. Nonspecific stimulation also has an important role in development. The mimicking of hand watching by blind infants is illustrative. As was mentioned earlier, blind infants between twelve and sixteen weeks of age move their hands back and forth and to and fro in front of their faces, and their unseeing eyes track the hand from right to left and converge and diverge on it as it moves toward and away from the face. By the age of five months, however, the coordination.has disappeared. The blind infant's eye movements are jerky and uncoordinated and cannot. be brought under control by any external event. Because there is no visual input, the coordinating mechanism degenerates. D. G. Freedman has shown that this degeneration does not happen if the infant receives even a minimal amount of visual input.

A very important aspect of general stimulation is that it nourishes existing coordinations. It is known that deprivation can stagnate develop-

ment, but can the opposite occur? Can enhancement of general stimulation produce accelerated development? There have been only a few studies on this subject, and most of them were concerned with the acceleration of sensorimotor development, particularly reaching. In one experiment B. White and R. Held studied the development of reaching in institutionalized infants. A control group of infants experienced the normal institutional environment, which contains very few things to look at and touch. An experimental group had a massively enriched visual environment, while a second experimental group enjoyed a slightly enriched environment with only one object at a time to look at and reach for.

Although the developmental stages of reaching behavior were the same in all three groups, the slightly enriched group developed faster than the control group, which would seem to indicate positive effects of stimulation. More interesting, however, is that the massively enriched group developed more slowly than the slightly enriched group: a paradox. The resolution probably lies in the fact that the greatly enriched group did little reaching and touching because they had so many things to look at that they had little time left over from looking for touching. Bower has accelerated the development of reaching by about three months simply by giving infants a great deal of practice. Thus, the effects of enrichment in the White and Held study may have been simply the result of practice in reaching.

It is generally true that institutionalized infants

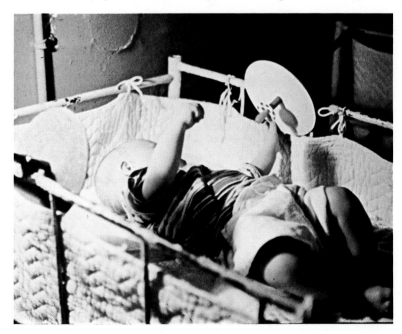

Figure 6.17. Infant's environment in the White and Held experiment: (a) normal institutional, (b) massively enriched visually, (c) slightly enriched —one object at a time to look at and reach for. The slightly enriched group developed reaching behavior faster than the massively enriched one.

in their bland environment attain any given level of cognitive or motor skill at a later age than home-reared infants; this is true of their interactions with people as well as of their interaction with objects. One can usually identify how the institutional environment produces deprivation, and A. Ambrose has shown that the addition of the missing feature will often remove the developmental deficit. However, it is a general rule that an overdose of the necessary stimulation will not produce acceleration.

Characteristic of older infants' play is how they frustrate themselves with difficult tasks. They work on tasks for long periods, often showing signs of frustration, yet persisting for days until the problem is solved. A clear example of this striving for competence in the environment arose in a longitudinal study of the development of the concept of object permanence. In the laboratory experiment, the infants were forever confronted with various hidden objects, as was previously described. Later, in their homes, they were reported to spend hours hiding objects and retrieving them. At a later stage, when the problem in the laboratory was to find an object that had gone out of sight while in motion on a complex trajectory (for example, ricocheted off the wall), the infants in the study would spend hours every day rolling objects under tables, under beds, off walls, and crawling after them until, at the end, they could retrieve a vanished object in this way as readily as if they had x-ray eyes. The encouraging point is that these infants developed evidence of a fully mature object-permanence concept at about nine months earlier than the average. This acceleration was not directly the result of any intervention by experimenters. Rather, the experimenters introduced the infants to the problems and then left them free to program their own development—successfully.

Because psychologists are far from having a complete understanding of the processes controlling the development of cognitive skills in infancy and because the infant makes the best use of available environmental information, it is undoubtedly best to let the infant program his own development. Except for remedying gross environmental deprivation, it is probably best not to interfere with this infinitely complex and successful, self-sustaining, individual process.

Figure 6.18. In their play older infants and young children often pose themselves difficult and frustrating tasks.

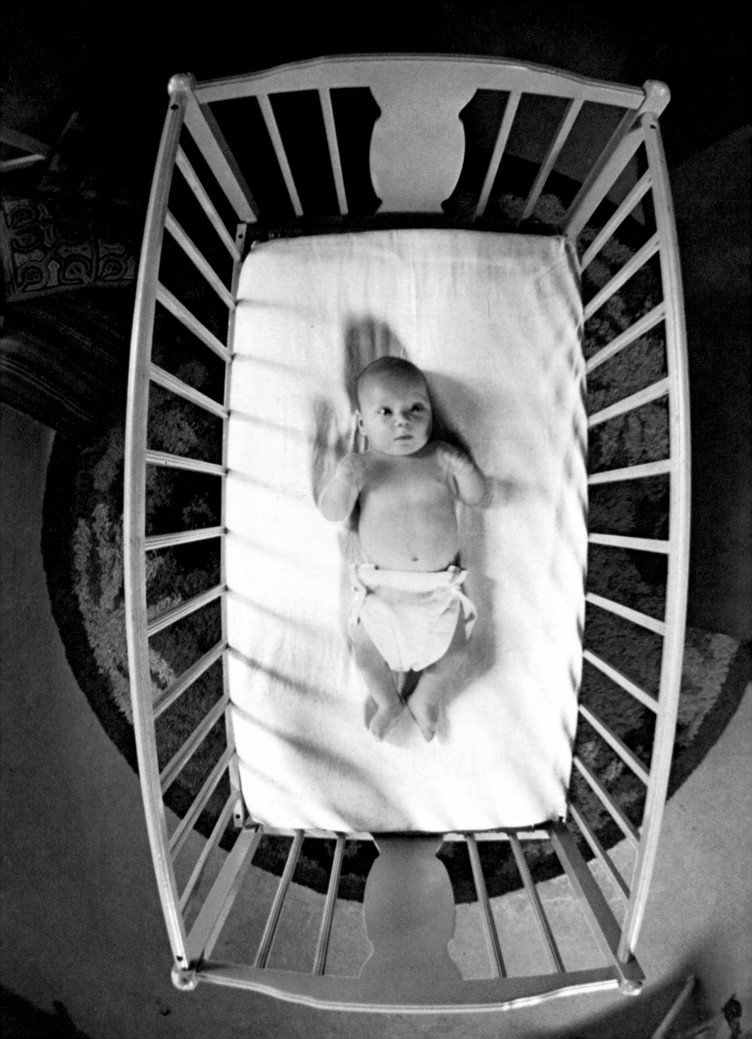

All children, as they grow up, become more and more like adults. By learning from their parents what is correct and valued, from imitating the acceptable behavior of their brothers and sisters, from observing other adults in person and on television, each child absorbs a way of behaving that is similar to the behavior of those around him. Because the people in one child's world are different from the people in another child's, each has a way of behaving that is different from that of others. Sometimes the differences are large, as exist between a child raised in a primitive native culture in New Guinea and one raised in a rich, urban American family. Sometimes the differences are relatively small, as between an American child raised by parents of French heritage and one raised by parents of English heritage in the same small town. But the differences can run deep—involving modes of thinking as well as behaving: approaches to solving problems, the tendency to plan, and basic value systems. The process of psychologically growing into a society is called *socialization*.

The Process of Socialization

Socialization forces a person to become part of his society and to share in its culture. Socialization requires the individual to behave in culturally approved ways and to pay at least lip service to the dominant values, ideals, and motivations of the myriad groups of which he must become a part. The mythical Richard Roe plays many roles all at the same time. He is (1) a male, (2) an American male, (3) an American male whose family is upper-middle-class, (4) . . . whose pro-

fession is architect, (5) . . . who attends an Episcopalian church, (6) . . . who is the husband of Mary, (7) . . . who is the father of Bill and Jean, (8) . . . who is the son of Mark and Ann, (9) . . . who is chairman of the school board, (10) . . . who is boss to eight draftsmen, (11) . . . whose boss supervises him and five other architects, (12) . . . who belongs to Rolling Hills Country Club, (13) . . . who was a lieutenant in the army during the Korean War, and so on. Each of these social roles required that Richard Roe learn his society's expectations for him. The socialization process prescribes acceptable behavior for each role. It also prescribes traits deemed undesirable and discourages their development. The outcome of socialization depends on one's environment—cultural, familial, physical.

Although the products of socialization differ across cultures, many psychologists believe that the same individual and social mechanisms operate in all children in all cultures. The four basic mechanisms are: (1) the desire to obtain affection, regard, acceptance, and recognition from others, and its corollary: (2) the wish to avoid the unpleasant feelings that occur when one is rejected or punished by others; (3) the desire to be like specific people whom the child has grown to respect, admire, or love (called *identification*); and (4) a tendency to imitate the actions of others.

Each of these four mechanisms acts on different aspects of the socialization process, and each of them is relatively strongest at different periods of development.

7
Social Development

Social and Emotional Development

The separation of social and emotional development in the early childhood years (this chapter and the following one) seems to be almost arbitrary. It is difficult to imagine an emotional reaction outside of some social context. Until very recently, however, most psychological studies attempted to observe these aspects of development separately. Either the researchers would attempt to hold one aspect constant while observing the other, or they would ignore one or the other. Consequently, much psychological literature has been categorized either in the area of social *or* in that of emotional development. Before presenting the findings of the literature as thus organized, however, it will be well to discuss the interrelatedness of these two areas and their relation to cognitive development.

Emotion is probably the most difficult psychological entity to define, and differing theoretical approaches explain its occurrence in vastly different ways. For example, if a child experiences the emotion of fear when he sees a dog, Freudian psychoanalysts will explain that, for the child, the dog's fierceness symbolizes his father's anger—that the child, who has had a bad relationship with his father, fears him and transfers that fear to the dog. A social-learning theorist would say, rather, that the child had had a specific experience with an animal from which he learned that dogs are somehow dangerous. Some behaviorists say that all but a few emotional reactions are elicited and learned through classical or operant conditioning in infancy. The exceptions include reactions to painful stimuli or loss of support. Animal stud-

ies have shown that there are species-specific fear stimuli; for example, a duckling instinctively fears a hawk-shaped object.

Fear requires a rather sophisticated level of cognitive development. The feared object must be held in memory, and its appearance (later, its mention alone) must call up the perceptual and emotional experiences connected with the object in the past. The changes in the objects of children's fears shown in Figure 8.3 read like a chart of cognitive development; for example, no children below the age of a year fear the dark, being alone in the dark, or imaginary creatures, whereas a significant percentage of four- to eight-year-olds are afraid of these things. These fears—in contrast to fear of loud noises, for example—require imaginative constructions based on the generalization of past experience interwoven with the manipulation of symbols and images.

Emotion, then, must be considered in its social and cognitive context. The focus of research on the infant as social partner has been concentrated on the mother-child relationship. This is a social relationship in which vast amounts of learning take place—yet what could be more emotionally charged? The importance of these early interactions for the child's later life has been dealt with extensively in psychological literature.

Freud's Theory of Psychosexual Development

Sigmund Freud popularized the theory that infantile experiences are of primary importance for later life. His psychoanalytic theory of the stages of infant development has influenced nearly every

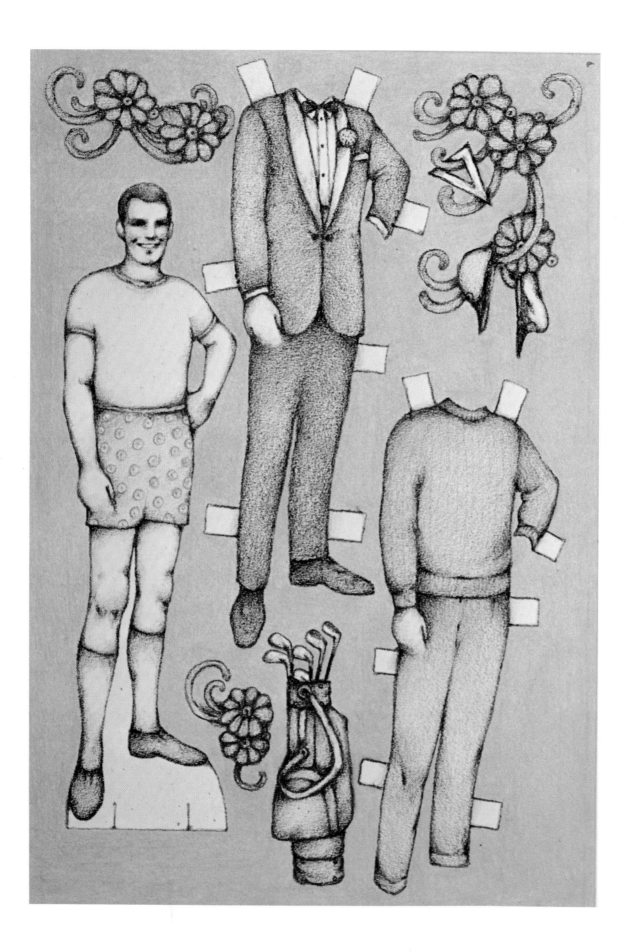

psychological study concerning mother-child relations, whether they dealt with feeding, weaning, or toilet training. Much of the early literature supported Freud's theory, but recent studies suggest that the processes may be even more complex than Freud thought them to be. The following is a brief description of Freud's theory of psychosexual development.

Freud postulated a basic psychological energy, called *libido*, which was inherent in every individual at birth. This energy supplies the sexual drive, whose goal is to obtain pleasure. For Freud, then, all pleasurable impulses are an expression of sexuality. Certain areas of the body are the source of more pleasure than others; these areas Freud called *erogenous zones*: the mouth and lips, the anal region, and the genital organs.

The infant's sexuality is a forerunner of adult sexuality, which appears if development follows the normal progression through the Freudian stages of psychosexual activity. It should be noted that progression through the stages may be interrupted by what Freud termed *fixation* or *regression*. If a child encounters excessive frustration in any of the stages, he may become fixated at that stage. And under certain circumstances, children may regress to an earlier stage of psychosexual activity and expression.

Freud described five stages of psychosexual development. Each is characterized by a different erogenous zone from which the primary pleasure of the stage is derived.

1. *Oral Stage*. Freud maintained that sucking is the main source of pleasure in this stage, which typi-cally continues until some time during the second year of life.

2. *Anal Stage*. The child's pleasure at this stage comes mainly from expelling or retaining feces. Because parents teach the child that feces are nasty and begin to train him to eliminate at certain times in certain places—to socialize him—conflict arises between the wishes, impulses, and powers of the child and those of his parents. This stage lasts until near the end of the third year.

3. *Phallic Stage*. This stage begins when the genital region displaces the anal region as the area of libidinal energy. Both boys and girls show concern for their genitals, which they have discovered to be the source of erotic pleasure. It is during the phallic stage that the Oedipal situation develops: The son develops a sexual attachment to the mother, which creates tension and antagonisms between the father and the son. Ideally, the Oedipal conflict becomes resolved in this stage because the boy's sexual behavior is rebuffed by the mother and because the boy realizes that he is much inferior to the father in strength and authority. To relieve the anxiety that develops from fear of losing the love of both parents, the boy gives up or represses his desires for his mother and identifies with his father. This stage ends at about the age of six.

4. *Latency Period*. In the process of repressing erotic impulses toward his mother, the child's erotic impulses toward all members of the opposite sex are repressed. His personality moves temporarily into a latent stage.

5. *Genital Stage*. At adolescence, sexual interest in the opposite sex reappears, and this stage lasts throughout adulthood.

Successful progress through the psychosexual stages culminates in normal adult heterosexual adaptation.

Figure 7.1. An artist's characterization of Freud's stages of psychosexual development.

MOTHER-CHILD INTERACTION

The relationship between mother and child is a complex one; its intricate details were not considered by Freud in building his broad, general model of development. For example, each child is born with a certain temperament, a certain level of activity and responsiveness; he is an individual. And this temperament may have a great deal to do with his mother's attitude toward him.

THE BABY'S TEMPERAMENT

Although personality is not inherited genetically, each person is born with a particular biological constitution and thus with a particular combination of behavioral *predispositions* and potentialities for development. And each is born into, and will grow up in, a unique and changing environment. The way a child develops socially—the kinds of attitudes toward others he acquires and his eventual competence and adequacy in interpersonal relationships—is the outcome of a continuous interaction between these two factors.

An important early study of the various behavioral predispositions with which babies are born was done by Margaret Fries. By carefully observing the amount and the vigor of bodily activity in neonates, she found that infants varied over a wide range with respect to the actual amount of overall activity, their characteristic muscle tone, and the amount of crying. In terms of these criteria, and under controlled conditions, she classified her infant subjects—all of whom she regarded as normal—into three *congenital activity types:* the active, the moderately active, and the quiet.

What influence may the predisposition to be very active or very quiet have on the child's social development? Parents vary in temperament, too, and are likely therefore to have preferences—conscious or unconscious—for particular types of children. The quality of mother-infant interaction can be significantly affected by the extent to which the baby conforms to, or fails to conform to, these expectations. Thus, the baby's own natural reaction tendencies play an important role in determining the quality of his emotional environment from the very beginning of his life.

A very active baby with high sensitivity to stimulation demands more attention from those who care for him than does the quiet one, and the emotional quality of the interaction he stimulates will vary with the mother's natural mode of approach and emotional attitudes in the care of her baby. She may be inclined to avoid much contact with him, speak to him softly, and minister to him generally with a quieting warmness, which is the kind of treatment the sensitive, highly active baby often needs. Another mother may be much more vigorous in her approach, having more frequent, noisy contacts with him, speaking or singing to him. This care may be better for the quiet infant, who needs social stimulation for his best development. The "good" baby who sleeps a great deal, seldom cries at night, and is so easy to care for is precisely the baby whose predisposition to be overly quiet often invites neglect. His social environment may be, for him, stimulus poor.

Other congenital predispositions, all of which may be profoundly important factors in the

child's social development, have been identified and described. A. Thomas and his co-workers conducted an extensive study in which they relied heavily upon the accuracy of parental observations for their data. They decided that the intimate knowledge mothers gain in the constant care of their infants would be a source of the most meaningful data in this area. They obtained the information by means of a carefully formulated interview procedure. An analysis of their data yielded the following characteristics of infantile reactivity that seem especially important for social development:

1. The *activity level* variable corresponds quite closely to the activity types described by Fries.
2. *Approach-withdrawal behavior* is seen in the child's characteristic initial reaction to any new stimulus pattern, be it food, people, places, toys, or procedures. The behavior of others toward the baby soon becomes conditioned by the infant's approach or withdrawal toward them. The child thus determines the nature of his own social environment, to a degree.
3. The *threshold of responsiveness* is defined as the level of stimulation necessary to evoke a discernible response. Again, the particular level of the baby's characteristic threshold has much to do with both the behavior and the implicit attitudes of those about him.
4. *Quality of mood* refers to the amount of the infant's pleasant, joyful, friendly behavior as contrasted with unpleasant, crying, unfriendly behavior. Mood quality, a predisposition observable almost from birth, interacts in crucial ways with the social aspects of the family environment. The baby who seems to have been "born mad" stimulates different reactions in others than does the happy, bubbling baby.

PARENTAL ATTITUDES

A baby is born into a psychological environment, which may have been created soon after the child was conceived. When she learns she is pregnant, a woman may be eager and joyful at the thought of the new human or she may be in despair. R. R. Sears and his co-workers studied mothers' attitudes toward their pregnancies and found the range of attitudes reflected in Table 7.1.

Table 7.1. How Mother Felt When She Discovered She Was Pregnant

Reaction	Percentage of Sample
Delighted; very happy; had been waiting and hoping for this	50
Pleased, but no evidence of enthusiasm (includes: "This was a planned baby," said matter-of-factly)	18
Pleased generally; some reservations	6
Mixed feelings; advantages and disadvantages weighed about equally	9
Generally displeased, although some bright spots seen	9
Displeased; no reservations	7
Not ascertained	1

Source: Table 11.1 in *Patterns of Childrearing* by Robert R. Sears, Eleanor E. Maccoby, and Harry Levin (New York: Harper & Row, 1957, p. 32).

There are a number of factors that affect these attitudes and their intensities. Generally, the fewer the children in the family, the happier the mother was about her pregnancy: 64 percent of the mothers who were judged to be "delighted"

Figure 7.2. The relationship between a mother and child depends on both personalities.

to find themselves pregnant were looking forward to their first child; of those who already had children, only 34 percent evinced delight. Another important factor was the difference in age between the woman's youngest child and the forthcoming one; two babies may seem to involve more than twice as much work as one.

It is clear that the primary makers of the psychological atmosphere awaiting the child can range from parents who are eager to care for and love him to parents—or a mother alone—for whom the child will be an unbearable, unwanted burden. The long-range impact of negative environments on personality and social development have not been—perhaps cannot be—measured. And the accuracy of prediction—or hindsight evaluation—is complicated by the baby's temperament and the resulting mother-child interaction.

One study, by E. S. Schaefer and Nancy Bayley, analyzed the longitudinal data collected in the ongoing Berkeley Growth Study in order to identify the effects of maternal behavior on the child's emotional and social development. The examiners observed the child-mother interactions and tested the children at intervals over the child's first three years; extensive written observations were made, and from these data behavior rating scales were developed. Analysis of these scales showed two main factors in maternal behavior: love versus hostility and autonomy versus control. The infants' development (they were tested twelve times between the ages of ten and thirty-six months) was rated on the following seven points:

1. Degree of strangeness: shy/unreserved
2. Speed of movements: slow/rapid
3. Amount of positive behavior: negative behavior/ positive behavior
4. Emotional tone: unhappy/happy
5. Activity: inactive/vigorous
6. Responsiveness to persons: slight/marked
7. Irritability (or tendency to be sensitive to and react to stimulation): excitable/calm

Figure 7.3 illustrates the kinds of relationships that were shown to exist between the mothers' behaviors and their children's happiness. In general, there was strong correlation between the love-hostility dimension and the happiness and positive behavior of both sons and daughters.

DIFFERING PARENTAL STYLES

No two sets of parents have precisely the same attitude toward their children, nor do they have similar approaches to rearing them. Researchers have identified the significant variables that affect parental style.

The degree of *emotional involvement* of parents with their child is the first significant variable; it concerns the importance of the infant in the parents' life and the extent to which they are able to involve themselves in his needs and activities. Parental style, insofar as emotional involvement is concerned, can vary from almost complete detachment and indifference to the child to such abiding involvement that everything the baby does is vital to the parents. Higher degrees of emotional involvement are desirable in earliest infancy but can be comparatively stifling for the older child.

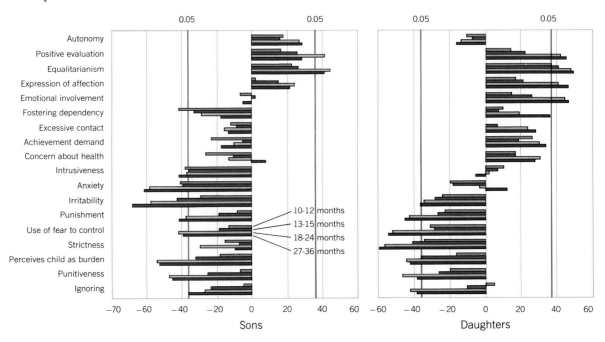

The second major variable in parental style, *individualization*, refers to the parents' ability to discern the child's individual traits—characteristics that require special notice and attention. It also refers to the willingness of parents to treat the child as an entity separate from themselves, as an individual with needs and desires arising independently of parental needs and desires.

The variable of parental *acceptance* of the child refers not only to the parents' like or dislike of the baby but to the acceptance of the infant as he is—as opposed to what they want or expect him to be. This variable is crucial in establishing the differing parental styles inasmuch as the child's behavior and personality will be judged generously or severely, depending on how accepting the parents are of his autonomy.

It may be best to summarize the goals of good parent-child interactions by discussing Erik Erikson's concept of *basic trust*. Erikson sees infancy as the time during which the child learns whether or not the world is a satisfying place to live in. If the child's physical needs—for nourishment, sleep, warmth, and the like—and his psychological needs—for response, contact, affection, and play—are satisfied, he will have a sense of the world as a fine and pleasant place. He will, in other words, develop trust, which Erikson says is basic if the child is ever to become a mature personality (see Chapter 24).

If the child's basic needs are not met (fulfilling his needs does not mean giving the baby everything he wants at the moment he wants it), if he becomes panicky in his helplessness and his world seems always to threaten or frustrate him, he will develop basic mistrust. Basic trust permits the child to react over a wide range of emotional responses, and from this emotional variety, Erikson says, will come openness to experience and the ability to master reality.

How Important Is Mother?

Some evidence for the importance of a mother (much psychological literature uses the term *caretaker*) in social and emotional development has come from studies with animals. The studies with monkeys done by Harry and Margaret Harlow have provided many insights into the tie between mother and infant. These studies deal with *attachment*. The traditional psychological explanation of the growth of the infant's attachment to the mother has been based on the fact that the mother reduces pain and imparts pleasure. The child becomes conditioned to the mother as a stimulus; that is to say, her presence signals the impending pleasure or reduction of distress. The Harlows' studies suggest that the attachment mechanism is much more complicated.

ATTACHMENT IN MONKEYS

In the Harlows' experiments, infant monkeys grew up with two *artificial surrogate mothers* constructed of wire mesh; one of the mothers was covered in soft terrycloth. The monkeys were fed by means of a bottle attached to the mother. Some were fed by the terrycloth mother, some by the wire one. When the monkeys were given the choice of going to either mother, they almost

Figure 7.3. Correlations between maternal behaviors and children's happiness at four age levels. (Adapted from Bayley, 1965.)

always chose the terrycloth one to cling to—even if she had not been the source of nourishment.

Also, when a fear-provoking stimulus, such as a large wooden model of a spider, was placed near the monkey, its initial reaction was to run to the terrycloth mother. After clinging to the terrycloth mother for a while, the young monkey took heart and was likely to venture out and explore the spider. But if only the wire mother were present, the monkey remained fearful.

Clinging is a behavior that young monkeys normally display at birth; it seems to be as natural to them as scanning and vocalizing are to human infants. Clinging seems to be important to the development of the monkey's attachment to the mother.

Because the Harlows' experiments show that infant monkeys do not become attached to the giver of nourishment—the wire mother and bottle —but rather to a clingable mother, the traditional theory of attachment is brought into question.

It is interesting to note that monkeys reared with terrycloth mothers will—after a year's separation from her—run to embrace her and will cling to her passionately. But the monkeys raised with wire mothers did not love them at all after any appreciable separation.

ATTACHMENT IN HUMANS

John Bowlby, R. A. Spitz, and others have postulated the great importance to personality development of the child's attachment to his mother. Their theories, based on a psychoanalytic point of view, also see the mother's role in attachment as

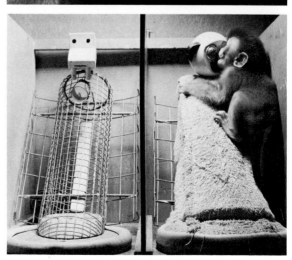

Figure 7.4. Monkeys in the Harlow experiments. When the large toy bear—a fear-provoking stimulus—was placed near the monkey, it ran to the terrycloth-covered surrogate mother for comfort, then later ventured out to explore the bear. If it had only the wire mother to cling to, the monkey remained fearful of the bear.

more complex and vital than simply reducer of distress or imparter of pleasure. The results of many longitudinal studies of children and retrospective studies of adults who were deprived of this attachment have led Bowlby and others to conclude that severe impairments result either when an attachment is not formed or when it is forcibly broken before the age of seven.

The facets of personality found to be most affected in children and adults deprived of attachment are the capacity for establishing affectional ties with others and the ability to control impulse, to put off immediate desires to achieve long-range goals.

Research done by W. Goldfarb has found that even intellectual processes may be affected—especially language and abstraction. When one considers that the mother's role in the earliest years is as molder of the child's experience—she reacts to him as an individual, invents games to amuse him while dressing or feeding him, talks to him— it is not surprising that institutionalized children may be lacking an important part of human experience. Jean Piaget has stressed the importance of experience to cognitive growth; lack of this early experience may well contribute to retardation or impairment of later intellectual functioning.

As with all other aspects of personality, the effects of maternal deprivation vary widely. Psychologists have yet to discover clear evidence of why some infants appear to grow up with good emotional health even though they may have suffered what appear to outsiders to be severely unfortunate experiences with parents or caretakers.

INSTITUTIONALIZATION

No human children are reared in total isolation. The closest human analogy to the conditions under which the monkeys were raised would be an institution (orphanage), where motherless children are raised by caretakers. Even here, study is complicated by a number of factors. One such factor is whether the child had ever been taken care of by his mother before he entered the institution. If so, he was deprived of a mother after having formed an attachment, and his emotional reactions might well be totally different than those of a child who never knew a mother figure. Another complicating factor in studying institutionalized infants is the difficulty of generalizing results from one institution to another. In some, caretakers do little more than prop bottles so the children get nourished and keep them relatively clean but have no time or inclination for play and affection. Other institutions, well enough staffed, may make strong efforts to see that the children are stimulated and cuddled.

Harriet Rheingold conducted a rigorous experimental study of the effects of increased mothering on institutionalized children. The institution from which the children were drawn was better than most: volunteers and hospital personnel were encouraged to talk to the babies and to hold them. This situation made the demonstration of the effects of increased mothering more difficult.

The subjects were sixteen infants between five and seven months of age. Dr. Rheingold herself played mother to eight of these children for eight consecutive weeks. She alone was with them for eight hours a day, bathing, diapering, and playing with them. The other eight infants received their typical institutional care. All the infants were tested once a week during the eight weeks and for four weeks after the experiment. The tests measured social responsiveness to three kinds of people: the experimenter, an examiner who administered the tests, and, at the end of the eight-week period, a stranger. Figure 7.5 illustrates that the experimental babies showed much more social responsiveness to her and to the examiner than did the control babies. (Although not indicated in the figure, they also responded more to the stranger than did the control group.)

When these sixteen children were followed up in foster homes at nineteen months of age, however, no lasting impact from the special experience could be detected. One can only infer why this was so. One possible explanation is that the period of single mothering was too brief to have had a lasting effect. Or perhaps the children in this particular institution were never as severely deprived of attention and affection as are many institutionalized children. One piece of evidence for the latter conclusion lies in the fact that the IQs of the children in this institution showed no decline during their stay—unlike those of many institutionalized children who have been studied.

One poignant and impressive study, made by Harold M. Skeels and Murlon H. Dye, points up the interrelatedness of emotional and cognitive development. They studied two infants—one aged thirteen months with a Kühlman IQ of 46 and the other aged sixteen months with an IQ of

35—who had been transferred from a state orphanage to an institution for the retarded. The mentally retarded women already in the institution doted on the babies, and when the children were tested six months later, not only had their overall behavior changed from apathy to liveliness, but one showed an IQ gain of 31 points and the other, 52 points.

Based on the findings with these two infants, a group of thirteen children—ranging in age from seven months to thirty months and with IQs from 36 to 89, with a mean of 64—were transferred from the orphanage to live with the retarded women. After having been there for periods ranging from six months for the seven-month-old to fifty-two months for the thirty-month-old, every one of these infants showed a gain in IQ. The minimum gain was 7 points, the maximum 58, and all but four gained more than 20 points.

A control group left in the orphanage was composed of twelve infants, ranging in age from twelve to twenty-two months and in IQ from 50 to 103, with a mean of 87. When these infants were retested after periods varying from twenty to forty-three months, all but one of them showed decreases in IQ, ranging from 8 to 45 points—and five of the decreases exceeded 35 points. These findings support the importance of emotional interaction for cognitive development.

Institutionalization, per se, need not be destructive of a child's emotional growth. A natural laboratory setting for the study of the effects of multiple mothering in a semi-institutional setting

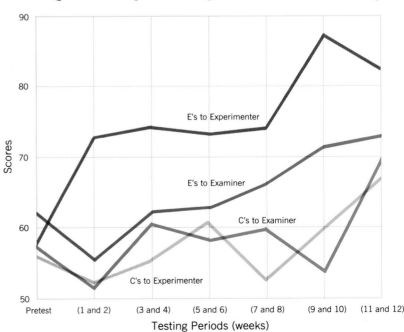

Figure 7.5. The average social responsiveness of the institutionalized infants who had received increased mothering (Es: experimental subjects) and that of a control group of infants in that institution (Cs). Over the twelve periods shown, they were tested in their response to Dr. Rheingold and to the person who administered the tests. (After Rheingold, 1956.)

are the Israeli kibbutzim, collective settlements where mothers work and children are cared for in large groups by a caretaker. In some settlements the children spend only the weekends with their parents. These children have been studied extensively and show no evidence of emotional or cognitive deficiency. The environment of a kibbutz is both warm and stimulating; the experience of these children is nothing like the deprivation suffered by infants in an institution that has only enough staff to keep the babies physically alive.

Child Care

Child-care practices have been the source of much study and much concern to American parents. The influences on their child-care practices have ranged from the behaviorism of John B. Watson to the recently popular common sense of Dr. Spock. Watson saw all behavior as externally determined by conditioned stimuli, unconditioned stimuli, and the learning of habits. In the spirit of science, Watson excluded from consideration all unmeasurable subjective feelings—motives, ideas, will. The carryover to child care was the parents' obligation to condition good habits. The following quote from the 1938 edition of *Child Care*, a United States government publication (the first edition of which was published in 1914 and still being distributed), determined the course of many a life:

. . . Immediately after birth he will begin to form habits, which if they are the right kind will be useful to him all his life. Regularity from birth on is of first importance.

Through training in regularity of feeding, sleeping, and elimination . . . the tiny baby will receive his first lessons in character building. He should learn that hunger will be satisfied only so often, that when he is put into his bed he must go to sleep, that crying will not result in his being picked up or played with whenever he likes. He will begin to learn that he is part of a world bigger than that of his own desires.

When Freud's influence began to be felt in America, he seemed to be championing the free expression of impulse. Parents thought that neurosis arose from society's restraints on free expression, and child care then turned to an emphasis on a refusal to inhibit or frustrate children.

To appreciate the change, consider feeding practices. It was common at the turn of the century to feed babies only when they were hungry. This approach gave way to the apparently more enlightened method of scientifically determined schedules for feeding: from the time that the baby arrived home from the hospital, feeding times of every four hours were maintained—even if the child had to be awakened to eat or if he cried with hunger until the scheduled feeding time. A natural parental resistance to such rigidity was reinforced not only by Freud's emphasis on free expression but also by anthropological evidence about the unnaturalness of scheduled feedings. There followed a general movement back toward feeding the child only when he was actually hungry. Finally, the babies themselves got into psychology by showing that they could individually schedule themselves on their own.

Because Freud attached great significance to the effects of toilet training, both researchers and

Figure 7.6. Children in an Israeli kibbutz.

theorists have dutifully clustered, notebooks in hand, around some fifty years' worth of potties. Little evidence has been produced to support Freud's equation of toilet training with later personality development. All cultures regulate toilet behavior in some way. What seems to be really important, however, is not the child's response to the training itself but the attitude of his parents toward his progress and his response to their attitude. Aggressiveness, fearfulness, guilt, compulsiveness, and the like can be stamped into the child by parental attitudes about almost any given youthful behavior. It just happens that in modern, urban, industrialized societies—where privacy, cleanliness, and sanitation are of paramount importance—parental concern with toilet training is paramount. Therefore, the child's sensitivity to demands made upon him in this area and their impact on his social development are correspondingly great.

What is important is that parents trust themselves to understand their baby and respond to his changing emotional cues.

The Growth of Sociability

As the baby's fund of experience grows, he begins to perceive objects and persons as such. By the time he is four or five months old, he responds differentially to persons in his environment.

INTERACTION WITH ADULTS

At this age he associates the one who cares for him with the satisfaction of his needs and relief from his discomfort. He begins to exhibit an emotional attachment for the caretaker: he *affiliates*.

He experiences love *from* his mother, and in turn he experiences love *for* his mother. One of life's greatest values, the capacity to love, thus seems to depend very largely upon the quality of this early mother-infant relationship. To be deprived of such an experience is to be deprived of a natural condition for developing a *full* capacity to love another person.

In its broader aspects, the affiliative tendency pervades social relationships generally. Children thus become disposed in varying degrees to regard and to approach all human beings with warmness,

with positive expectations, and with what Erikson calls basic trust. The second half of the first year of life seems to be most critical for this development.

The second year of the infant's life is also an extremely important period in social development. By this time the baby is moving about under his own power. He is still, in a sense, completely dependent, but he is beginning to develop a measure of what David Ausubel has called *executive independence*: the ability to satisfy some of his behavioral needs for himself. He is able to move among an increasing number of intriguing objects —including the people—that constitute his growing world. His cognitive development makes rapid progress as he touches, grasps, tastes, pulls, manipulates, destroys—learning from direct experience about the properties and characteristics of the things about him.

INTERACTION WITH PEERS

The social development of children is initially conditioned solely by relationships with adults. From the first crying to be picked up to the eight- or nine-month-old who stretches out his arms toward a grownup to be picked up, the child is learning social reactions. Although there is naturally little peer interaction during the first year, some research has been done to trace the gradual development of enhanced social awareness and of expanded social skills.

Children from six to eight months of age generally relate to their play surroundings rather than to play objects and playmates. Other children are usually ignored. When contact is made, and

Figure 7.7. Growth of sociability in the first two years. *(opposite)* The child under six months usually has little contact with peers. Children from six to eight months do not really relate to each other when they are playing in the same area. *(left)* From nine to thirteen months children compete for toys, and it is at two that children begin to play successfully together—although fighting over toys can still occur.

when it is friendly, it comprises little more than observing, smiling at, or perhaps grabbing at the playmate. When conflict occurs, it is manifested as generalized anger during attempts to obtain some play object that the other child controls.

From nine to thirteen months of age, children respond more to play objects than to playmates. Because of this concern with play material, children tend to fight a great deal during this period as they compete for toys. Unlike the earlier period's conflicts, the fighting is more personal, although the objects, not the playmates, are still the focus, so true hostility is yet to appear.

Infants begin to shift their attitudes toward playmates between fourteen and eighteen months of age. And because the child's play-object needs are largely satisfied, there is a decline in conflict with others.

For the nineteen- to twenty-five-month-old, play objects and playmates are more successfully integrated, and social interaction begins to predominate. Children will modify their behavior in adjustment to their playmate's activity.

Toward Toddlerhood

During the toddler phase—a period of impulsivity —some of the child's experiences cause him to revise his attitudes toward and his relationships with others. His loving attachment to his mother is still strong, but now he begins to see and feel her as restrictive, frustrating, and punitive. In his former complete dependency, those about him were completely subservient to his demands. As he interacts freely with his environment, the so-cialization of his impulses must begin. Property must be preserved; the rights and the welfare of others about him must be protected: his impulsivity must be curtailed. He is, in short, in a most critical period of his social development—a time when the character of his approach to and his dealings with people generally are largely determined. As he learns to cooperate with the authority figures about him and to control his impulsivity, a basic disposition emerges: either to prevail over others or to assume a compliant, submissive role.

The particular form this behavior may take is determined, as has been emphasized throughout this discussion, by the particular pattern of the child's temperamental nature in *interaction* with the significant others about him—more specifically, with the manner in which his impulsivity and his need to explore, manipulate, and learn about his world are handled. A child with a high activity level and high sensitivity to stimulation could develop a disposition to be ascendant in a positive way, to cope vigorously with obstacles, to be a creative leader among his peers. Under different circumstances, perhaps with highly restrictive parents who punish him for his ceaseless activity, the child's frustration could result in hostile feelings and compulsive needs to dominate, to force, to inveigle others to his will. Such basic and pervasive tendencies as to be shy and timid or outgoing and friendly, to be personally responsible or irresponsible—these are among the social dispositions that often have their origin in the child's social experiences during this crucial second year of life, when he is striving for autonomy.

What do infants and young children feel? They cry, they talk,.they giggle and laugh, they break into frenzied excitement and lapse into the sobs of the damned. But are these behaviors really reflections of the sadness, stubbornness, anger, and happiness that we feel as adults? Do infants feel the clammy press of fear, as we do? Do infants have a capacity to love, or does the meaning of love evolve and develop with growth? To what extent are emotional capacities inherited? How are they developed and transformed with age?

Before trying to answer these questions, it is necessary to ask what emotions really are. Even in antiquity, emotion was known to have a physiological component: insulin levels in the blood change; heart rates rise or fall; respiration gets faster or slower. We "feel it in the gut." Indeed, William James speculated that felt emotional experience *follows* visceral arousal—that is, rather than crying because we feel bad, we feel bad because we have been crying. Psychologists now studying the theory of emotion have identified three interrelated classes of events that pertain to emotion: (1) environmental or stimulus events; (2) physiological events; (3) verbal and motor behavior. There is also a fourth element: introspective reports show clearly that there are private feelings, which may or may not be manifested in behavior or speech. However, it is not yet clear how these events interact and influence each other. Is it the case that the body's reactions to the stimulus trigger the emotional behavior we can observe or hear? Or do we simultaneously react both physiologically and by word or deed?

Although the general bodily reactions to emotion are known, specific reactions that occur along with specific emotions have not been delineated. In fact, researchers, such as Stanley Schachter, have shown that emotional behaviors as different as anger and happiness can arise from the same physiological states. Which emotional reaction rises to the surface seems to depend on the environmental and physiological events acting in tandem. For example, a ride on a roller coaster may produce the same physiological state in two persons, one of whom is filled with elation and the other, filled with fear. In fact, on such occasions both emotional behaviors may exist within the same person. These two persons in another situation—say, taking a final examination in a psychology course—may again manifest the same physiological state, yet their emotional reactions could be reversed.

But are emotional reactions in infants exactly like those in adults? If they are different, where do the differences lie? Emotional reactions in adults (the behavior component) appear much more quickly than do the physiological responses that, according to James, are supposed to produce them. In infants under one year, on the other hand, emotional responses—particularly in the case of fear and response to pain—do seem to take longer, long enough to permit the assumption that these responses do follow and are caused by the initial physiological changes. This shift in type of response between infant and adult argues for a significant cognitive base for emotional reactions.

8
Emotional Development

That is, after a person has had much and varied experience with the physiological components of emotions, he can begin to think about his body's reactions, and, as he has more emotional experiences, he can symbolically represent to himself the physiological experience.

In all general discussions of the preceding kind, one must not lose sight of the fact that people differ widely in their emotional behavior. Not only are people's emotional experiences different, but, as discussed in Chapter 7, their basic temperaments have been shown to differ from birth.

Emotional responses are most readily differentiated in terms of whether they are generally pleasant—positive or integrative—or generally unpleasant—negative or disintegrative. Beyond this gross differentiation in terms of pleasure or displeasure, it becomes extremely difficult to identify and classify the many specific emotions observed and experienced by adults, let alone by children, although a variety of schemes for achieving this objective have been developed by different investigators. Specific emotions are sometimes differentiated on the basis of the level of arousal or excitation involved (interest versus delight); sometimes on the basis of the nature of the individual's behavioral response to the eliciting stimulus (rage, expressed by attack, versus fear, expressed in avoidance or flight); sometimes on the basis of the individual's perception of the circumstances of the situation and his relationship to it (jealousy, as a reaction to threatened or actual displacement in a valued relationship, versus humiliation or shame, as a reaction to failure to meet expectations highly valued by one's self and by others whose approval is important).

It is obvious that some of these subtle differentiations and emotional responses require the ability to think analytically about one's self and one's relationship to others in the social environment. Can such emotional responses occur as early as the first two years of life? In fact, what emotional responses are present at birth, if any? At what points in subsequent development can various specific emotions be identified, and what are the stimulus situations that elicit emotional responses during this period of early development? These are some of the principal questions to which research workers have been addressing themselves for many years.

EARLY THEORIES OF INFANT EMOTION

In 1917 John B. Watson and J. J. B. Morgan proposed that the human infant is born with the three unlearned emotions of fear, love, and rage already in his repertoire of responses and that all other human emotions develop from this original trio through conditioning. Watson and Morgan inferred *fear* from the infant's eye blinking, clutching of the hands, and crying upon loss of support or presentation of a loud noise; *love* from the gurgling, cooing, or cessation of crying that occurred when the infant was patted, gently rocked, stroked in the erogenous zones, and so on; and *rage* from the crying, the stiffening of the body, and the arm and leg movements produced by restraining or hampering the infant's movements. Some years later, M. Sherman, who, like

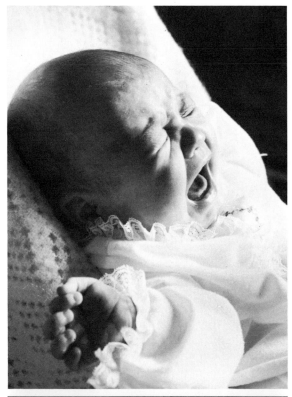

others, was unable to confirm Watson and Morgan's findings, showed that observers tend to make their judgments of emotional reactions in the young infant primarily on the basis of their knowledge of the stimulating circumstances and their own experiences and expectations concerning emotional responses in adults. Without knowledge of the stimuli being applied to the infants, Sherman's observers were unable to agree on what patterns of response could be labeled fear, rage, or love.

It is generally agreed today that in the first few days of life only a state of quiescence or inactivity and a state of increased activation or excitement can be differentiated reliably. Because the latter state is often associated with crying, some psychologists believe that one can speak of negative excitation or primitive unpleasure reactions even at this early point in development. However, K. M. B. Bridges proposed that the excitement of the newborn is neither positive nor negative emotionally and that it is not until the end of the first month that one can reliably speak of negative or distress reaction as differentiated from quiescence. By about the third month of age, the infant begins to show clearly differentiated pleasure responses, seen most readily in the smiling, vocalizations, and heightened bodily activity that constitute the infant's typical social response to the friendly approach of another person. From this point on, as development progresses during the first two years, the infant manifests progressively more differentiated forms of both positive and negative emotional responses.

One framework for describing this progressive emotional differentiation was proposed by Bridges in a study nearly forty years ago. She suggested that out of the distress reactions first observable in a child at one month of age, the more specific negative emotions of anger, disgust, and fear become differentiated by about six months of age, although jealousy is not seen as a distinct negative emotion until close to eighteen months. Similarly, from the delight responses clearly observable by two to three months of age, the more specific positive emotions of elation and affection are differentiated by about one year of age, and by the second year the more serene and sometimes intense emotion of joy is also observable. The validity of these kinds of distinctions and how best to conceptualize, observe, and identify the various emotional responses developing in the first two years of life are both still matters of great concern to investigators in this field.

Fear Responses

Among the most important developmental changes in emotional response in the first two years are those involved in the infant's reactions to and relationships with other people. By approximately five or six months of age, the infant's pleasureful social responses, previously shown to virtually any friendly, talking, smiling person, are manifested more selectively, primarily in response to familiar persons like mother or father. At this point the infant becomes somewhat less positively responsive to strangers, and as the end of the first year approaches, many infants respond to a stranger with considerable distress or fear (sometimes referred to as eight-month anxiety or stranger anxiety).

Separation Anxiety

During this same period of development, the infant's affectional attachments to specific adults, which began to appear at about five or six months of age, become more marked and delineated. Such a specific attachment, or focused relationship, is revealed not only in the infant's positive emotional responses shown selectively toward the mother or other principal caretaker but also by the marked negative reactions and by the strong efforts to regain proximity that often follow even a brief separation from the mother figure. This response is often referred to as *separation anxiety* or separation protest.

Maternal attachment and fear of strangers, which have roughly similar developmental timetables, have been found to be interrelated in a number of other interesting ways—both in humans and in a variety of animal species. For example, if the infant's mother is close by, his fear of strange stimuli is weaker and he is more likely to explore a strange environment. G. Morgan and Henry Ricciuti found that at eight, ten, and especially at twelve months of age babies responded more positively to the approach of a stranger if they were seated on their mother's lap than if they were four feet away from her. At four or six months of age, however, before attachment to the mother had been fully developed, a separation of four feet from her made little or no difference—

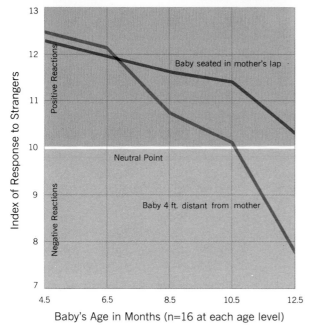

the infants responded positively to the stranger in either case (see Figure 8.2). The influence of the mother's proximity in reducing fear of the strange has been found even when the mother happens to be a cloth-covered surrogate mother to which infant rhesus monkeys had become attached.

FEAR OF STRANGERS

How can the fear of strangers, commonly observed in many infants toward the end of the first year of life, be explained? Arguing from a basically psychoanalytic point of view, R. A. Spitz proposed that the infant's fear of strangers is essentially triggered by the threat of object loss, that is, the presence of the stranger suggests an imminent separation from mother. It is certainly true that some infants may have learned to make this specific association on the basis of their particular experience (the babysitter's arrival, for example). However, many investigators regard the initial appearance of fear of strangers as a special case of the more general fear of the incongruous, uncanny, or unexpected that is observed in the young of many species and in human infants as early as three to four months of age. This negative reaction to the strange or uncanny often is accompanied by a hasty return to mother or to a haven of safety. Fear of the strange and the flight response may well have high adaptive or survival value.

The study of developing perceptual and cognitive capacities may be able some day to explain these changing emotional reactions. For example, a pair of studies by Bower, discussed in Chapter 6, showed that until about twenty weeks of age, a

Figure 8.1. Fear of strangers most commonly appears in children around a year old. Some children never develop this fear to any great extent, and some show it later.

Figure 8.2. Results of the Morgan and Ricciuti study of infants' responses to strangers during the first year. The index to measure response was constructed on the basis of facial expressions, vocalizations, and approach-withdrawal behavior. Note the strong negative reaction of one-year-olds not seated with their mothers. (Adapted from Morgan and Ricciuti, 1969.)

child is not surprised by seeing what appear to him to be several copies of his own mother. However, as soon as he grows to realize (twenty-two to twenty-four weeks) that he has but one mother, the sight of three images of her disturbs him.

OTHER NEGATIVE REACTIONS

Many stimuli obviously produce crying, distress, and primitive avoidance reactions in newborns and very young infants—sudden loud noises, unexpected events, physical pain—and many observers have labeled these responses as fear reactions. It is probably unwise to consider such early responses (before six months of age) as involving *fear* because to fear requires that the infant's cognitive and memory capacities be developed to the point where the stimulus situation can elicit the perceptual and emotional experiences of a particular situation in the past—and that the infant can relate the two situations in a way that permits him to anticipate the outcome of the current one. Some time after six months of age, fears based on the child's emotional experiences undoubtedly do develop. In addition, however, the older infant may begin to learn, from his parents and others, that certain objects or situations—fire, snakes, cliffs—are dangerous and should be feared.

An illustration of the manner in which specific fears change with increasing maturation and development is provided in the early studies of Arthur Jersild and F. B. Holmes, in which parents reported sudden loud noises to be the most common source of fear reactions in the first year, with

fear of animals and fear of the dark being reported relatively infrequently. During the next year or two, however, fear of loud noises tended to decrease while the other fears tended to increase. A summary of these findings is included in Figure 8.3.

Similar developmental trends are reported in a recent study, which indicated that between the ages of approximately five and eighteen months there was an increase in infant's fear responses to strangers, to a grotesque mask, and to a visual cliff, which tests whether an infant will crawl onto a glass surface raised some distance above the floor. Fear of loud noises or of a suddenly appearing jack-in-the-box did not increase over this same period of time.

ANXIETY

Although the terms *fear* and *anxiety* are often used interchangeably, there is a difference between them. Fear is a reaction to a specific stimulus, whereas anxiety is a diffuse, all-pervading sense of fearfulness and emotional distress, which is not elicited primarily by a particular situation or event. For psychoanalytically oriented investigators, anxiety has always been a core concept. Freud and other psychoanalysts have developed a number of hypotheses and views about the nature of anxiety in infancy, based primarily on their clinical experience with adults and more recently with infants as well. According to these views, the earliest precursor of anxiety (or perhaps anxiety in its *primary* form) is represented by those states of excessive excitation observed in young infants

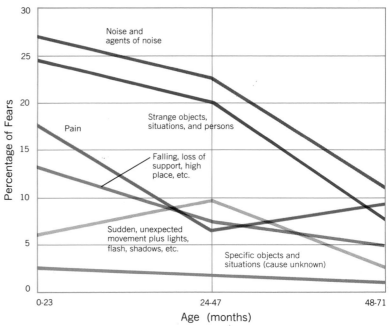

and even in the newborn—especially when there is delay in reducing the initial excitation. Because the infant's mother is the principal agent through which excessive levels of stimulation or physiological need are reduced, the infant soon comes to fear her absence or unavailability as a primary need reducer, so that fear of loss of the loved object (mother) becomes the fundamental form of anxiety later on in the first year of life.

It is extremely difficult, if not impossible, to determine exactly what the infant feels when he is in a condition of excessively heightened stimulation or excitation. As already indicated, some workers are quite ready to label these reactions as anxiety or fear even in the newborn. Other investigators are concerned with determining the way in which an infant's awareness of his own displeasure at excessive stimulation changes with increasing development, becoming gradually more differentiated and linked to specific aspects of his experience with external reality. Spitz, for example, has suggested that the negative reactions of the infant in the first six weeks or so should be regarded as a primitive kind of *unpleasure* rather than as a true emotion of fear or anxiety. By approximately three months of age, when the infant is capable of clearly showing pleasure responses to people, his unpleasure reactions may begin to be associated with specific aspects of his experience; such unpleasure responses may then be seen as representing an early form of fear. It is not until the infant reaches the age of six to nine months, however, that he manifests anxiety proper. According to Spitz, the fundamental anx-

iety in man, which appears by the end of the first year of life, is anxiety concerning possible loss of the loved object. From this point on, anxiety develops and differentiates rapidly, becoming a signal for the approach of any potentially dangerous situation.

ANGER

In addition to anxiety and fear reactions, there are other negative emotional responses that can be reliably observed in infants and are of particular significance during the first two years of life. Anger might be defined generally as an emotional response involving aggressive behavior (or impulse) directed toward some person or object, usually caused by the thwarting or frustration of a desired goal. According to Bridges' observations, early forms of anger can be found in the infant about the sixth month of age. Considering the appearance of anger from a psychoanalytic point of view, A. H. Schmale similarly suggests that early forms of anger are observable shortly before the sixth month of life, just prior to the emergence of specific fear reactions. He considers this early development of anger reactions as reflecting the infant's awareness that gratification is not available from an object or activity that previously provided such gratification when the infant sought it. Frustrated, the infant wants to force an object to provide gratification and so eventually directs aggressive actions toward it. However, it must not be assumed that these early feelings of anger are equivalent to the emotion that is identified in older children and adults as

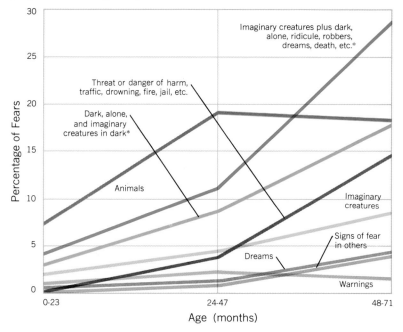

Figure 8.3. Relative frequency of fears at various ages. The graph opposite shows fears whose frequency decreases with age; that at left shows fears whose frequency increases with age. Note how fears change with cognitive growth. The fears were reported either by parents and teachers or by the children themselves. Starred items represent a cumulative tally of two or more items that are also reported separately. (Adapted from Jersild and Holmes, 1935.)

hostility, which involves a desire or attempt to hurt another person. Although these two emotions are closely related and overlapping, it is not at all clear at what point the older infant becomes capable of experiencing hostility as distinct from anger.

It is obvious that the increasing anger reactions shown by infants up to the middle or end of the second year are not simply a reflection of developmental changes. The process of socialization places a variety of demands on the infant and young child as he learns to adjust his patterns of eating, sleeping, toileting, and interacting socially with siblings and parents to the expectations of those responsible for his upbringing. The two-year-old's negativism arises out of his new feelings of autonomy. His growing mobility, his daily-increasing vocabulary, his "need to know" all contribute to his growing sense of "I" as a separate being. And he expresses this sense of himself almost indiscriminately—but not always with the serious intent of digging in his heels. When told that it is bedtime, for example, he may angrily say "no" yet be gathering up his teddy bear and blanket in preparation.

DEPRESSION

There is considerable evidence, particularly from psychoanalytically oriented observations, that under sufficiently adverse environmental conditions—usually involving prolonged separation from the mother—the emotion of depression, or extreme sadness, may be experienced by infants as young as twelve to fifteen months of age. The British child psychiatrist John Bowlby has ob-

served what he regards as depressive reactions in fifteen- to thirty-month-old healthy infants after they had been separated from their mothers and admitted to a hospital or other residential institution. Following an initial phase of active protest and crying (which, as already indicated, are typical manifestations of separation anxiety), the second phase Bowlby describes is one of despair or depression, during which the infant becomes withdrawn and inactive, makes no demands of the environment, may cry intermittently, and seems to show feelings of increasing hopelessness and sadness. Later, the infant gradually moves out of this phase into one of detachment, in which he begins to interact in a pleasant but shallow manner with caretakers and responds in a rather aloof and detached manner when his mother visits.

The depressive reaction of the infant to loss of mother is regarded by G. L. Engel to be so basic that he considers depression-withdrawal and anxiety to be the two primary emotions of unpleasure. Engel also suggests that early forms of depression can be found even in the first few weeks of life, when infants become passive and withdrawn and reduce their activities after prolonged thwarting of their basic physiological needs. Some infants may characteristically respond to thwarting in this fashion rather than by showing the primitive anger responses previously described; others may manifest this withdrawn, inactive, energy-conserving response pattern only after prolonged periods of active crying have failed to provide relief from thwarting or frustration.

JEALOUSY

Jealousy is an emotional reaction commonly observed in young children from about eighteen months of age through three and a half years. When a child thinks that he is being actually or potentially displaced by someone else in his relationship with a special person, usually a parent, his emotional response is to be jealous. Both anger and fear of loss of parental affection are elements in this jealousy. The anger may be directed at the person representing the threat of displacement—perhaps a younger sibling or playmate—or at the parents or at both. Many families have experienced the need to protect the new baby from the jealous toddler, toy hatchet in hand. The outward manifestations of jealousy undergo considerable change with increasing maturity and development, becoming generally less direct and explosive.

SHAME AND GUILT

To conclude this discussion of negative emotions, brief reference should be made to the emotion of shame in infancy. Although this emotion is a particularly difficult one to study objectively in young children, some investigators feel that manifestations of shame can be observed as early as the second year of life. At this point shame or guilt in the infant consists essentially of negative, self-depreciating feelings associated with his recognition of the fact that his actions have failed to meet the expectations or standards of a loved person; his failure is communicated to him by expressions of disapproval or withdrawal of affection. Such a reaction may occur in a two-year-old

who soils his diapers when his parents expect him not to. With increasing age, externally imposed standards or expectations of behavior are assimilated by the child, and he feels shame and guilt at his failure to live up to what are now his own standards.

POSITIVE EMOTIONS

The positive or pleasurable emotions have been far less extensively studied than the negative ones, both in early childhood and throughout the life span. Because negative emotions like anxiety, fear, and anger are often associated with problem behavior, they have attracted a great deal of attention from investigators concerned with the alleviation and prevention of problems of adjustment. However, in recent years psychologists have been showing increasing interest in the role played by the positive emotions in human development.

As indicated earlier, the first clear signs of pleasure or delight in the infant are observable at two to three months of age, primarily in response to the friendly, smiling, talking face of another person. Toward the end of the first year, infants show a great capacity for intense pleasurable reactions in their playful interactions with people and with material objects or toys.

As the infant continues to experience pleasure in his interactions with the particular people with whom he is developing close relationships, one can say that he begins to display feelings of affection, or perhaps early expressions of love. By the end of the second year, the child appears to be capable of experiencing intense feelings of pleasure and happiness associated with particular experiences, events, or people; these intense feelings mark the first appearance of the emotion of joy. The recent writings of S. S. Tomkins place great emphasis on the importance of joy in building and maintaining the crucial social bonds between the infant and his principal caretakers—and between people generally.

During the second year of life, observations suggest that children begin to show the positive feelings that might be identified as pride. Such feelings develop as the child becomes aware that some of his behaviors or activities meet the expectations of his parents, as indicated by rewards of praise, special attention, and affection.

PLEASURE AS THE REDUCTION OF DISPLEASURE

Some of the factors that may play a role in producing such negative emotions as anxiety, fear of strangers, and anger were identified earlier. But how does one account for the initial appearance of various *positive* emotional responses shown by infants in the first two years? Traditional psychoanalytic thinkers have said that early experiences of pleasure derive primarily from gratification of basic physiological needs (hunger, thirst, pain avoidance) and of libidinal (sexual) drives, which, in the first two years, are expressed primarily in oral (feeding, sucking) and anal (urinating, defecating) activities. Objects, persons, or events associated with such need gratification in the infant's experience are said to become sources of pleasure through learning and conditioning. A

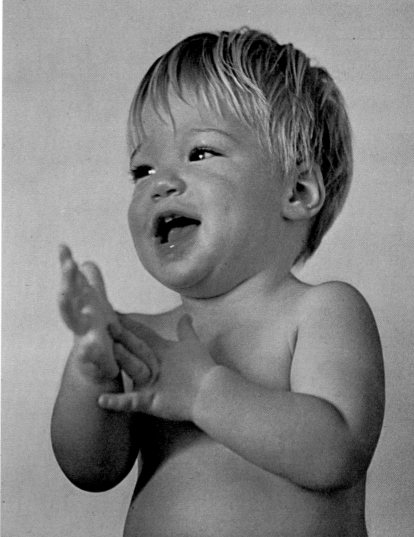

Figure 8.5. Psychoanalytic theory has seen pleasure as constituting the reduction of displeasure (drive reduction), but more recent research results show that many types of experiences or stimuli appear to be intrinsically pleasurable for infants: looking at a smiling face, playing games like pat-a-cake, making new sounds, and mastering new motor skills.

Figure 8.4. Jealousy of a younger sibling can manifest itself as shown here, where—no matter how many other play vehicles are around—the baby's tricycle is the only one worth riding.

similar view is implicit in the approach of psychologists who have emphasized the role of drive reduction as the major motivational determinant of learning. Although the concepts of pleasure and displeasure are not dealt with directly in this approach, it is assumed that high levels of drive (hunger, for example) are *aversive* (or unpleasant), and so people act in ways to reduce high drive. Thus, as in the psychoanalytic view, the reduction of displeasure (which motivates much behavior and learning) is seen as the source of pleasure.

INTRINSIC PLEASURE

In contrast with the foregoing views, there is considerable evidence indicating that a variety of stimuli or experiences appear to be intrinsically pleasurable for infants. (See Chapter 6 for results of studies showing infants' intrinsic satisfaction after solving problems involving perception and, evidently, cognition.) As previously indicated, the human face is a particularly effective elicitor of positive responses in the two- and three-month old infant. Harriet Rheingold has suggested that initially the talking, smiling face of the human, with its changing expressions and movements, represents a complex stimulus that interests and attracts the young infant. Gradually, through a variety of learning experiences, the face or appearance of the parent or principal caretaker becomes an elicitor as well as a reinforcer of a variety of positive emotional and social responses in the infant. Although the learning experiences in-

volved here may well include situations in which the infant associates the parent or caretaker with reduction of his primary needs or drives, the interactions are not limited to these situations.

Some other examples of stimuli that produce smiling or other positive emotional responses in infants include: a soft, high-pitched bell at five or six months of age; a relatively simple visual stimulus, such as a black-and-white cardboard oval that is rotated slowly; and finally, simply bouncing the five-week-old infant's hands together gently as though playing pat-a-cake. Parents know that babies react with pleasure to gentle rocking in a carriage or cradle and to a mother's voice singing a nursery song.

Many contemporary psychologists interested in learning and intellectual development are studying motivation and finding that even infants react with interest, pleasure, and curiosity when they solve some problem that is interesting to them (see Chapter 6).

The Functional Significance of Emotions

Emotions play a very important role in human development even as early as the first two years of life. For example, the child's fear of the strange and unexpected and of being separated from his mother certainly have some adaptive or survival value in that they alert him to potential danger and impel him to act in ways that may help him to avoid such danger. Even the two- or three-month old infant's expression of distress or unpleasure through vigorous crying and increased activity helps ensure that important physiological needs will be attended to.

Similarly, the pleasurable social responses of the infant when his parents care for him and play with him contribute in important ways to the establishment of the social bond or attachment between them; these interactions lay the groundwork for adaptive interpersonal relationships later in life. In contrast, an infant who is often exposed to conditions that generate anxiety, fear, or anger —especially when circumstances make it difficult for the infant to manage these emotions—may suffer personality maladjustment in his childhood and adulthood.

Try to picture how fundamental language is to man. Imagine how you would live in a family and raise your children with no conventional communication. You would be able to teach your child only what he could see you do. There would be some things, of course, he could learn by himself or figure out; not all thinking is verbal: musicians, engineers, and artists make use of aural and visual images and spatial relations. But imagine trying to teach your child what you know of history or what you believe about how society should work without being able to speak to him.

DEVELOPMENT OF SPEECH

Adults use language in different ways for different purposes; the words used to make up poetry, tell jokes, have verbal contests, tell stories, or give short commands may all come from one person's vocabulary, but the ways in which the words are put together and the intonations used in saying them are innumerable. Adults vary in the way they speak with children, and what the children hear in part influences how they learn to speak. The child's caretakers (in most of the world these are older children) may speak to the infant to stimulate, amuse, frighten, punish, command, or instruct him. From this input the child learns whether language is to be feared or enjoyed and what vocabulary style and voice quality to use for different situations.

Infants vary in their use of vocal output from the start, perhaps because of the temperament differences present from birth as well as differences in the use of language around them and the response of others to them. From the time they are born, babies vocalize spontaneously: they cry to signal pain or discomfort or need, they make sounds that seem to indicate pleasure, and, increasingly, they babble for the pleasure of making the sounds. The sounds of joy, called cooing because they seem vocalic to listeners, increase throughout the first months. They occur at times adults think must be happy—after eating, while watching a face smile, when listening to singing, and while looking at or handling objects. After three months, adults can increase the frequency of these sounds by responding to them. From the very start, sounds and gestures are being developed as communicative acts because of how others react. (See Table 5.1 for a summary of vocalization developments in the first two years.) Children in institutions with few adults around may not even cry much because crying is part of the child's social interaction. If no one comes to answer a cry, crying becomes a useless vocalization.

Early in life, deaf infants coo and babble as much as normal children, but after six months of age the richer sound environment of the hearing child shows up in the diversity of his babbling play. When children learn to use words, the playful use of language continues in combinations of nonsense words and in rhyming games, especially under rhythmical stimulation, when, for instance, the child is bouncing in a chair or riding in a car. Babies obviously derive pleasure from sound input too: even children nine months old can be enthralled by nursery rhymes, songs, or stories

9
Origins of Language

although the words are beyond their understanding. Even some adults find themselves lulled by sound and never think to seek the meaning of words in Mother Goose rhymes: What is the *tuffet* that little Miss Muffet sat on? And what exactly are *curds* and *whey?* For several years, in fact, it is the surface of sound, both what they hear and what they say, that attracts children. For them, language is a sensorimotor delight rather than the route to prosaic meaning that it is for many adults. Some excellent examples of sound play were reported in the bedtime monologues of the two-and-a-half-year-old son of Ruth Hirsch Weir, like the following:

> See that
> Walk with feet
> Walk with feet
> Walk with feet
> Two feet
> See
> Twofeet and the horse
> Like all other Indians
> Twofeet had a horse
> Twofeet had a horse
> See cactus
> And the grass
> And the flowers

As children explore objects, they often talk to themselves. This behavior is seen as soon as the child begins to speak, and it reaches a peak in frequency from age four to six, depending on the child; this *parasocial speech* is most frequent when others are within earshot or when the child encounters difficulties, so it seems to be social in origin even though it is often incomprehensible and does not seem to be addressed to anyone in particular. As the child matures, parasocial speech clearly becomes planning language, becomes more understandable, and more often goes underground and becomes inaudible thought. Thus, these early mutterings are for the listener a window to the child's thinking.

Among the earliest forms of speech are routines, or speech tied to situation or gesture: "hi," "bye-bye," "peek-a-boo," "pat-a-cake," "thanks." At first the child seems not to perceive the situational stimulus, such as arrival and departure, that warrants the routine, so the cue is the speech or act of the partner. The child may treat the word as the name of the act: "thanks" is the act of giving, and the child may say it as he gives. An observant parent can work out the rules for the child's usage of these frequent forms.

Many of the earliest utterances of infants seem to order the listener to look at or to hand over an object: "Want dolly"; "See bird"; "Milk." Actually, it may be the listener who interprets these statements as demands for things or acts. Many children simply name objects without wanting to touch them, or they list persons in the household as though checking off their presence; it is not always obvious that the obsessive namer wants much response from the audience. Knowledge of the functions of these early forms of speech remains slight. A little later, predicative statements of facts known to both child and hearer appear, such as "Dolly fall-down." M. M. Lewis dates the beginning of dialogue—where speaker and listener exchange speech—from the middle of the

Figure 9.1. The peek-a-boo game is a routine where gesture and speech are intricately tied; this situation engenders an early form of speech.

second year, but he points out that truly new information comes later. The ability to recognize that a listener should be asked for information the speaker doesn't have, and to offer him only information he lacks, requires a form of social imagination that Lewis says starts to function in the second year. This ability requires cognitive growth, not merely greater verbal skill.

Stages of Speech Development

Human language is a system in which a sequence of sounds, gestures, or graphic signs is related by specifiable rules to its interpretation. When talking about language, one must consider the surface or sensory system, the meanings to be communicated, and the grammar relating sound to meaning. The newborn child must learn to distinguish speech from nonspeech and to recognize which features of speech sounds are important. He must learn enough about the meanings in the nonlinguistic world to have a basis of learning how the two systems are related. He can and sometimes does learn all these things before he begins to speak. In fact, some children who cannot speak at all because of a physical handicap show that they understand completely the function of language and its intricacies. One such child, studied in depth by Eric Lenneberg, was tested in several ways for language comprehension at the age of eight. He was told a short story and questioned about its contents in complex grammatical constructions. There was no doubt that the child had learned to understand what all other children of his area and age understand: English. It is clear

that *having knowledge of a language is not identical with speaking,* and because knowledge of a language may be established in the absence of speaking skills, the former must be fundamental and the latter, accessory.

This part of the chapter, then, will deal with the child's learning to *speak;* the prior, cognitive, functions that underlie *knowledge of a language* are dealt with later in this chapter and extensively in Chapter 12.

Within a few weeks after birth the infant learns to discriminate human voices from other sounds; by the end of the second month he reacts in a way that shows he recognizes friendliness, and he can distinguish male from female voices. In the middle of the first year the child begins to make phonetic discriminations of consonants and correct pitch and stress patterns.

Late in the first year, the child begins to be able to understand commands. By the middle of the second year, it is possible to experiment in his understanding of sentences, and E. Shipley, C. Smith, and L. Gleitman found that a child looks at a ball more often in response to "Throw ball" than to "Throw the ball"; also, he understands "ball" better in the context "Throw the ball" than in the context "Ronta the ball." It is clear, then, that this period of a year and a half of listening has made it possible for the child to identify an object with a sound pattern, to distinguish familiar from unfamiliar words, and to selectively hear certain important parts of the sentence.

It is impossible to overestimate the importance

Figure 9.2. Infants often seem to be peremptorily ordering an adult to hand over something, for example, "Cookie."

to the child's development of listening and comprehending what is heard. It is likely that it is not merely hearing sounds that is important but hearing them under conditions where the meaning is obvious from the situational, physical, or verbal context. In this way, the child can sort out which features of the sound pattern are significant; he would have much more difficulty doing so from a radio or from overhearing adult talk alone.

Observation of the language styles adults use with infants reveals that children are addressed in a special way. "Baby talk" is repetitious and contains many short simple sentences, which would in the earliest stages of development obviously make learning easier. Of course, many features of baby talk in various languages are conventional and expressive and may be quite irrelevant to learning. Because children receive many questions and commands, they can give feedback on whether or not they have understood, and so they generally receive a repetition when they have not. Although contemporary American child-raising mores tend to belittle this baby-talk style, for the first year or so it may facilitate learning.

PRESPEECH SOUNDS

The baby's first vocalizations vary somewhat in form and intensity according to the stimulus: the cry indicating hunger is different from that signaling pain. After three weeks, vocalizations gradually increase in frequency and variety. Some sounds, of course, are physical and digestive mouthings and gurglings. At four or five months of age the primarily vocalic and back sounds begin

to be supplemented by repetitious sequences in which consonant and vowel may alternate, and this sound sequence gives a syllabic impression called *babbling*. The capacity to keep saying the same articulatory sequences over and over again —as in repeating syllables—indicates a great extension of motor control. Examination of strings of babbling shows increased complexity within the string, suggesting a building-up process.

The speech sounds of children from different language communities cannot be distinguished from each other until near the end of the first year, when intonational variations begin to appear. The greater diversity of sounds in the babbling of normal six-month-old children relative to that of deaf children suggests that the hearing of speech sounds stimulates the child. Babbling includes many sounds that an adult cannot make and that the child himself may not be able to say a year later. For this reason, much babbling appears to be motor play, which produces many accidental sounds that have nothing to do with communication.

Near the end of the first year, the child's intonation becomes more and more like that of adult speech; it appears that children can then discriminate pitch and stress. They sometimes produce long, complex sequences of meaningless sounds with the pitch contour of adult sentences. These charming sequences may appear when the child is playing at reading or talking to dolls when no one else is present. By the time such sequences are present, the intonation differences between language communities can be discriminated. The final prespeech stage is the beginning of stable word meanings that adults recognize and can interpret.

FORM OF EARLY WORDS

Early words, unlike babbling, do not sample a wide range of sounds. Indeed, at this stage a child may be unable to imitate sounds he made earlier in playful babbling. The first words tend to be short, of one or two syllables. Typically, the child at first has only one vowel and one or two consonants.

Suppose the child's first word is something like "ba," for "ball." An observer with a tape recorder who is lucky enough to get many examples of a child using this word will find that its pronunciation varies from "bee" to "bow" and that the consonant also varies: sometimes "pa," "va," "da," or "tha." It is because the listener expects to hear and thinks of the word "ball" that he believes the child has a stable pronunciation of it. All languages have this kind of free variation in specch. In adult English an example is the difference between saying "not" with the tongue dropped open or with the tip of the tongue touching the upper palate at the end of the word. In children's early language there is much of this unsystematic random variation.

Some theorists believe that the first units of the child's output may be syllables rather than vowels or consonants. The first consonant distinction children make is often between a stop syllable like da or ba and a nasal like na or ma. At this point, a child will be able to say "ba" and "mama" pur-

posefully. Later D becomes distinct from B, and other consonants like S appear. The order of distinction in hearing is approximately the same as in speaking, except that some sounds whose differences are easy to hear are hard to say; some of these consonant sounds, like R and TH, trip up the articulation of many school-age children. With the vowels, the A may be the first one distinguished from all others. Parents may be surprised to hear that a child who always says "ba" and "mama" will sometimes say "suw" and sometimes "see" for "shoe." At this point the child has only two vowel categories—A and non-A—so non-A words come out in a randomly pronounced

Figure 9.3. At about one year of age, children's speech has the pitch and stress of adult speech, even though the sounds may be meaningless. A child may read a book aloud and sound as if he were telling a whole story—although one understood only by himself.

fashion. Table 9.1 presents the order of emergence of the child's discrimination of various sounds.

Table 9.1. Emergence of Abilities to Hear Sound Differences
(From 10 to 23 months of age)

Order	Ability	Examples
1	Distinction of /a/ from all other vowels	father
2	Discrimination of front from back vowels	she vs. shoe; red vs. road
3	Discrimination of higher vowels from middle vowels	bead vs. bed; book vs. boat
4	Can tell when a consonant* is present	bed vs. ed; dish vs. ish
5	Distinction of nasals and stops	meat vs. beat; no vs. go
6	Distinction of nasal and "liquid" sounds	mess vs. less; new vs. you
7	Distinction between nasals	map vs. nap
8	Nasals and liquids distinguished from sibilants	moo vs. zoo
9	Lip and tongue consonants distinguished	big vs. dig; bun vs. gun; fox vs. socks
10	Stops and spirants distinguished	pull vs. full; do vs. zoo
11	Front and back of the tongue distinguished	done vs. gun; tight vs. kite
12	Voiced and voiceless consonants distinguished	pig vs. big; sue vs. zoo; few vs. view
13	Hissing vs. hushing distinct	seat vs. sheet
14	Distinction of liquids from y	yes vs. less

* Initial consonants are regularly distinguished before final ones, so a child hears the difference between map and nap before he can hear the difference between came and cane.
Adapted from the Russian distinctions. Source: N. Kh. Shvachkin, "The Development of Phonemic Speech Perception in Early Childhood," *Izvestiya Akad. Pedag. Nauk RSFSR,* 13, 1948.

Because the child's repertoire of syllables is very small during the second year, he often repeats syllables. He may say "papa" or "bibi" or "car-car." Also, two different words with different meanings may sound the same because his repertoire offers few possibilities for different word forms. For example, he may say "ba" to imitate the words "flower," "bird," and "ball."

Although the child may use many two-syllable words, the variety of combinations may be limited. The second syllable either may be a repetition of the first or may always contain some particular vowel. For example, a child may use "-ey" in second syllables, so that he says not only "mommy" and "mama" and "daddy" and "dada" but also "baty" or "baba" for "bottle"; one is not surprised by "kagy" for "kangaroo" because in imitating polysyllabic words, the child will either omit the unemphasized syllable or change the word to the pattern he uses, in this case the "-ey" ending.

By the time a child is four he has learned some amazingly complicated aspects of word construction, but he may still have motor difficulties in articulating one or two sounds. These difficulties are not related at all to the basic grand achievement of understanding and producing sentences. Many articulatory delays are spontaneously outgrown. If they persist into later childhood and cause the child to be socially stigmatized, they may play a significant role in his social and psychological development. Figure 9.4 shows the various ages at which children master the articulation of English phonemes.

LANGUAGE AND SPEECH

Language learning takes place during a period of rapid development in the child's perceptual and conceptual achievements, as outlined in Chapter 6. Before a child can retain a stable name for something, he must be able (1) to retain an image of the object named and (2) to discriminate and remember the recurrent features in the sound patterns of the name, which in no two instances are identical as physical stimuli: Daddy's voice saying "kitty" sounds very different from mother's. During the infant's early months, he looks at objects, reaches for them, and later shakes, swings, and feels them. Although touching may not be essential to acquiring images of all stable objects, it is an important component in the acquisition of many images. At the end of the first year, the child refrains more from handling and becomes more interested in watching, pointing—and naming. By the second year, the child will hunt for objects that are absent and fetch them when they are named by others; this behavior requires long-term storage of stable notions of objects and their locations, together with the coded features of their names.

GENERALIZATION

A child's first words usually are very different in their apparent range of meaning from the conventional adult meaning. For example, one child used a single word to refer to a dress, a coat, a white hat, and the carriage she rode in and to ask to go for a walk or report that she had done so. It is easy to see how the use of the word in the

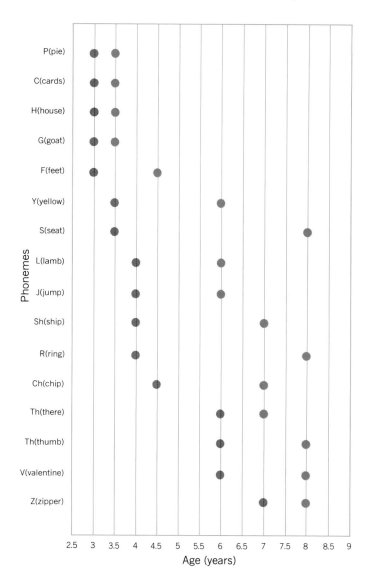

Figure 9.4. The order of articulation of English phonemes. Yellow dots indicate that 75 percent of children can pronounce the given phoneme; blue dots indicate that 95 percent can pronounce it.
(Adapted from Templin, 1957.)

context of dressing her to go out may have led her to include in the meaning all the related things, events, and experiences for which she had no differentiated names anyway. Although many early words are, from the standpoint of adults, nouns, they may be used by the child as if they were not only category names but also referents for actions, requests, and attributes.

Even for nouns the range of reference to objects is far wider than adult categories. One child used a single word to refer to breast, biscuit, a red button on a dress, a bare elbow, the eye in a portrait, and his mother's photograph! Another child, Hildegard Leopold, whose linguist father described her language development in detail, used the word for clock when pointing to a gas meter and to the round hose reel. The perceptual basis for these generalizations is obvious.

Hildegard called any man "papa" when she was fourteen months old. Three months later she called all adults "man" and only her father "papa." At two, she had separate words for father, other men, and women. Hildegard is typical, and parents can tell you of their embarrassment when their child says "Daddy!" to a stranger.

DIFFERENTIATION

The first word for "daddy" may actually mean the category adult or man. The first word for "dog" may actually refer to the category animal. (See

Figure 9.6 for one child's notion and use of the word *dog*.) Because it is often hard for adults to surmise the child's category, instead of teaching him the words "adult" or "animal" to match his category, they try to tailor his categories to his words. They teach children to contrast "daddy" and "mailman," "cat" and "dog." Children are taught to make the conceptual contrasts adults think are important by being given labels for differences adults think they ought to notice, whether these differences are relatively general— "bird" versus "fish"—or particular—"Ford" versus "Chevy." In this way, the child's system of vocabulary and categories gradually becomes differentiated.

The earliest words of children vary markedly between different families and even among children in the same family, according to the interests of a child and those around him. The early vocabulary is likely to include words for the common things the child tries to handle; the people he wants to name; actions he performs like "up" and "off"; names of location; terms for aspects and quantities like "all-done," "no," and "more"; and terms for values and feelings like "want," "mad," and "good."

CONCEPTUALIZATION

As the child grows older, even within the second year, his vocabulary begins to be systematically organized. He learns a series of sex-contrasted

items like man-lady, boy-girl, brother-sister, daddy-mommy. He learns age-contrasted items like mommy-baby, man-boy, lady-girl, hen-chick, sheep-lamb. Thus, the system of meaning underlying his vocabulary begins to take on some of the conventional structure of his society and the rich internal structure characteristic of adult word linkage. Later, superordinate concepts will be learned, like ball plus bat plus doll equals toy; dog plus cat plus cow equals animal. Figure 9.7 illustrates the kinds of concepts the child can grasp at various ages. It is amusing to reflect that the actual range of reference of words like "animal" may have been present long before the child was able to contrast the superordinate and its subordinates (see preceding section).

VOCABULARY

How do children learn vocabulary? Many people believe that imitation is important, but imitation only illustrates that the child has noticed the sound sequence and that the component sounds and their combination are within his pronunciation capacities. Imitation does not show whether the child understands the appropriate context for the use of the word.

One way that children learn meanings is through naming and pointing, where the referent is visible. Most early vocabulary refers to the here and now, the tangible, visible, and sensible. Chil-

Figure 9.6. A fifteen-month-old child's notion of the word *dog*.

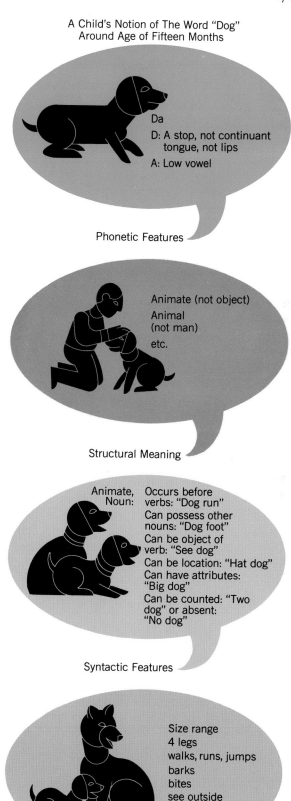

dren who can imitate activities like sweeping and setting the table reveal that they have an organized notion of these as acts, which then can, of course, be named. Many words are learned from verbal contexts alone, just as most adult words are. In general, words that have been heard in the greatest variety of contexts and that have the greatest variety of referents are learned fastest. Frequent hearing of a word alone does not guarantee its retention, which is one reason why travel and reading can lead to rapid vocabulary changes.

Because few situations force us to carefully differentiate between words, many words are synonyms to children simply because they occur in similar contexts. For example, "big" means "strong" and "good" means "happy." Or a child may hear a word in a situation but not really discern its meaning, as when he says "damn" and stamps his foot, as though the word were the name of the gesture, just as "peek-a-boo" is the name of the game. Thus, the learning of new vocabulary does not necessarily lead to the learning of new concepts, even though most adults tend to think it should. Figure 9.8 illustrates how the child's vocabulary increases during the first seven years.

SENTENCES

The most dramatic change in the child's communication of meaning occurs when he puts two items together. As has been pointed out, he may understand the relation between items in sentences he hears before he ever produces sentences; he may even understand this relation when he is

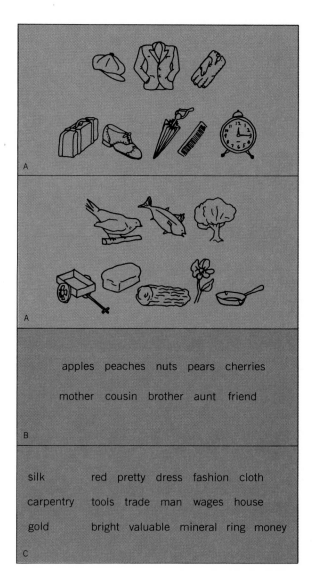

Figure 9.7. These sample test items show the kinds of concepts children can grasp at various ages. (a) First grade: Which of the pictures in the second group goes with the items in the first group? (b) Third grade: Which item doesn't belong? (c) Fourth grade: Which word tells what kind of thing the first word is? Examples are from the Kuhlman-Anderson tests.

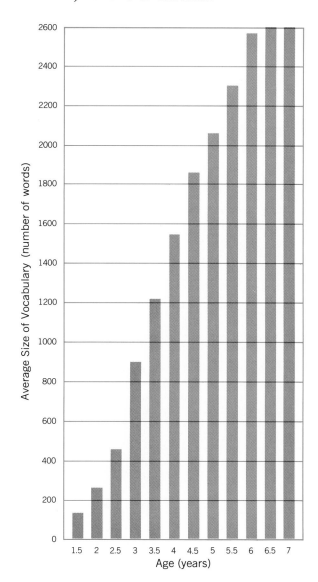

Figure 9.8. Average vocabulary size at various ages. Ten sample groups of children were used in the study. (Adapted from Lenneberg, 1970.)

still producing one-word utterances. Figure 9.10 shows how one child began to use two-word sentences. The earliest sentences researchers have found in samples of children's language (from English, French, Samoan, Luo, and others) tend to convey the following universal relations:

□ **Possession** The child who says "Daddy" when he sees daddy's coat or chair later may say "Daddy coat" or "Daddy chair." If he speaks middle-class English he will frequently say "Daddy's" by the time he is producing sentences three or four words long.

□ **Indicating** Pointing-and-naming behavior becomes elaborated into a longer sequence. As far as it is possible to tell, sequences like the following ones are synonymous at first: "There truck," "Here truck," "This truck," "That truck," "See truck," "It truck."

□ **Location** Along with pointing, the relation of being in, on, or under something else is signaled by a fixed juxtaposition of words: "Baby chair," "Baby car," "Truck up there."

□ **Quantification** Presence, absence, and repetition seem to be aspects of things and actions that are taken into account very early. Utterances like "More write," "Another bang," "No water," and "All-gone puzzle" are among the first sentences. Most of these quantifiers occur alone even earlier.

□ **Conjunction** Although the overt addition of words like "and" and "or" does not appear until later in language development, the earliest sentences contain paired nouns that seem to reflect conjoining or simple associating: "Daddy mommy," "Milk cookie."

☐ *Agent, Action, Object*   Many early sentences select single items or pairs from this set of elements for realization: for example, "Balloon throw," "Mommy back," "Girl write," "Build house," "Get ball," "Daddy fix-on," "Off shoe." Some children put the agent (subject) before the verb, but the object and verb are permutable. It is not until a more advanced stage of sentence production that the child can cope with all three elements or even more in one utterance, and one finds sentences like "Annie more read book."

☐ *Attribution*   Modification of nouns with attributes, like "red truck" and "big ball," appears slightly later than the other basic relations, and sometimes the alternatives available are very limited. Attributes in English normally first appear preceding the noun rather than as predicates.

Certain basic features of these items seem to be present very early. For example, children can make the distinction between animate and inanimate very early. This development is a conceptual one, and in Chapter 6, it is shown how this distinction made a difference in children's search behavior after items were made to disappear. The child knows that animate objects are mobile and so can move out of a field of vision; the child will search extensively for vanished animate objects. Disappearance of inanimate objects, however, causes great puzzlement and frustration. The child may attack the experimenter who caused the object to vanish. Children know that animate nouns can be possessors and agents.

Susan Ervin-Tripp has shown that the development of questions and answers in children who are old enough to engage in dialogue reveals a similar order of development of categories. First there appear questions of "what," "who," "whose," and "where"; next of "what . . . doing"; then "why." Last appear "how" and

Figure 9.9. Psychologists have studied children's first sentences in several language communities, and they have found the same semantic relations taking primacy.

Figure 9.10. Stage 1 grammar of Gia, age nineteen months. Gia has at her disposal: nouns (balloon, ball, etc.); animate nouns (mommy, girl, etc.); verbs (throw, write, etc.); quantifiers (more, nother, a); and Hi. The mean length of her utterances is 1.12 morphemes, and she is able to construct only the four types of sentences shown in parentheses. (Adapted from Bloom, 1970.)

"when." It is clear that animate and inanimate are distinct quite early and that location precedes temporal relations by a significant amount of time.

ROOTS OF LANGUAGE

Wherever psychologists study children's first sentences, they find the same semantic relations taking primacy. These relations either are known to children without learning or have been learned within the first year of life. If they are learned, it is obviously very important to know how the learning takes place because these relations underlie the basic elements of all languages. The origin of language is the subject of much current psychological study.

Several investigators, among them M. D. S. Braine, U. Bellugi, and R. Brown, have found that the elements in these early sentences are not randomly combined. There is a definite order. For example, in expressing the possessive relation, the English-speaking child normally puts the possessor first. In designating or indicating, he puts the indicator word first. Although not all children,

even in an English-speaking milieu, order their words this way all the time in early speech, most of those studied are at least relatively consistent.

Where does this primitive order come from? One obvious source should be the relatively regular order in the brief adult sentences children hear. One never hears children say, "Truck where." Although it is possible to hear adults use this order occasionally ("The truck is *where?*"), the children seem to notice and prefer the predominant order.

ROLE OF IMITATION

One explanation of language learning that used to be commonly accepted is that children learn by imitating. But experiments by S. Ervin-Tripp have shown that children's imitations are no better grammatically than their spontaneous speech at this age. When small children spontaneously repeat sentences, they almost universally make the abbreviations listed below; these patterns are called *telegraphic speech*. The imitations seem to be filtered through their own regular sentence-producing system.

Sentence	*Imitation*
Here is a lemon.	Here a lemon.
Where does that go?	Where go?
What's Dolly's name?	Dolly name?
Is there one, or two?	One, two?
Brought some things here with me.	Things. Brought some things.
The whole Santa's head came off.	Santa head off.
If you open them you will have to take some.	Have take.

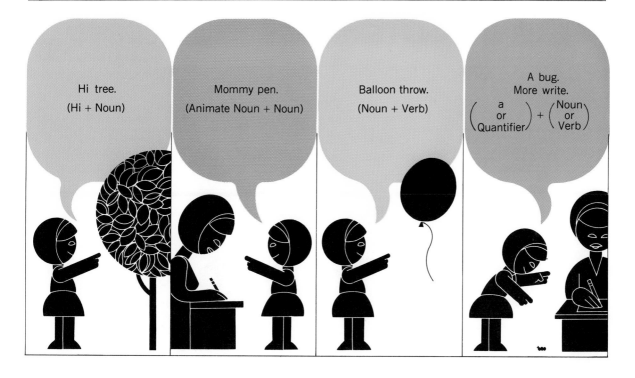

Hi tree.
(Hi + Noun)

Mommy pen.
(Animate Noun + Noun)

Balloon throw.
(Noun + Verb)

A bug.
More write.
$\begin{pmatrix} a \\ \text{or} \\ \text{Quantifier} \end{pmatrix} + \begin{pmatrix} \text{Noun} \\ \text{or} \\ \text{Verb} \end{pmatrix}$

If children do not acquire new knowledge in imitating, do they learn word order by rote memory of sequences? There are several clues that strongly suggest this is improbable. One is that the number of different word sequences children hear is far beyond their rote memory capacity, even if memorization were an efficient way to learn languages. Another significant reason for believing that rote memory is not how children learn language is that they produce novel sequences that they could not have heard adults say: "All-gone puzzle," "Fix on," "The up," "Broken the monkey," "All-gone outside," "See stand up," "All-gone sticky," "Bye-bye dirty." It is very interesting that these utterances have a general pattern, a grammar, of their own. Finnish-speaking children hear both verb-object and object-verb orders because the language is inflected, so it is the inflectional suffixes, not the word order, that identifies parts of speech. Psychologists have observed that some of these children regularize the word order with transitive verbs so that the resulting sentences are unambiguous as to subject and object. Only after they learn inflectional suffixes that identify subject and object does the order become free, as in the adult input.

BIOLOGICAL FOUNDATIONS

The evidence, then, suggests that children's early sentences are *more* governed by order than the language they hear. The children have added something; it seems that order is the simplest grammatical device available to them and one they use spontaneously in converting intentions into speech. If there is some highly regular order in the input, they notice and use it in their own

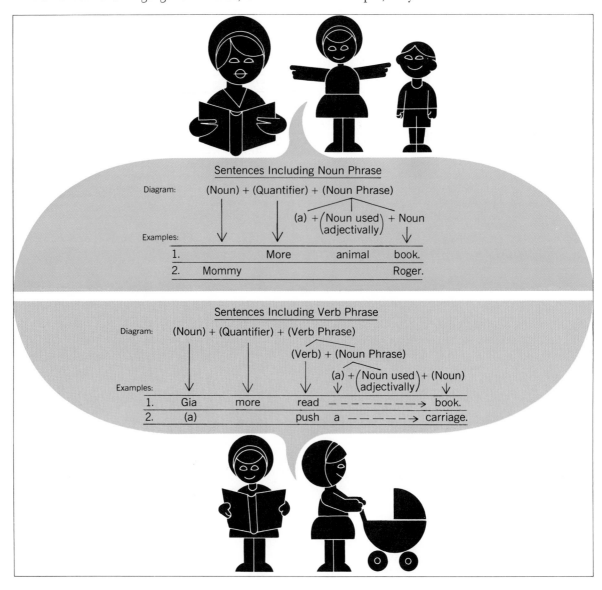

speech; if there is not, they may generate their own order rules and speak consistently within them until their grammar changes and they use some different device for signaling intent. During the earliest stages of developing these order rules, Braine observed the children practicing replacements; for example, once having said, "See hat," the child will try on "See sock," "See horsie," and "See boy" for size.

By the end of the second year, there are several ways in which the structure of sentences becomes more complex. The child becomes able to handle more than a two-part relation, and longer sentences with more complex structures develop. Phrasal units can replace words in the structure: "Here truck" becomes "Here red truck"; "Throw ball" is replaced by "Throw baby ball." Verb phrases may be modified, as in "Annie more read book." Locative phrases become elaborated into prepositional phrases: "Throw ball there" becomes "Throw ball up there" or "Throw ball in chair." An abstract unit in the grammar, the noun phrase, the verb phrase, and the adverbial phrase become necessary to account for the child's behavior, and one could say that these are new concepts. Figure 9.11 illustrates how one child used such phrases.

Although fixed units of time, like "next Sunday" or "for two hours," are hard for children at age two or two and a half to understand, they have already begun to differentiate the present from the nonpresent and to be sensitive to nonassertive modes as reflected in forms like "can," "wanna," and "gonna."

One of the most striking features of the change in language in the third year, to be described in Chapter 12, is that the auxiliary system of the verb, where tense, aspect, and mode are largely signaled, evolves very rapidly. Later yet, children become able to enmesh one sentence within another. These changes in syntax are the most striking yet remaining.

Around the end of the second year, parents are likely to notice that the child is beginning to use the unemphasized grammatical connectors like articles, suffixes, and copulas, which were omitted in telegraphic speech. Until these features become a regular part of the child's grammar, more complex syntactical rules (like the passive), which depend on them, cannot develop. At first the child uses them sporadically. Next he develops a simplified, generalized rule, which yields forms like "feets" and "goed." The child's generation of such overregularized forms—and he is even willing to pluralize nonsense forms like "biks" or "puds"—makes it clear that rote learning plays no part in this part of language learning. The particular phonetic rule that adds a syllable to yield "matches" rather than "matchs" takes longer to develop; when it is first learned, it may upset the earlier system, so the child says "handses" and "footses" for a period. The acquisition of irregular forms like "brought" comes late because the pattern occurs less frequently than the regular -ed one, and children may continue to say "bringed" into the school years. Table 9.2 shows the stages through which a child typically goes in learning plural forms.

Figure 9.11. Stage 2 grammar of Gia, age twenty months. Gia has the same word classes available to her as at nineteen months (see Figure 9.10), but her language shows that she can now construct noun and verb phrases. Although she rarely produces more than two words in a sentence, they are in the proper order, showing that her verb-phrase sentences could, theoretically, be six words long. (Adapted from Bloom, 1970.)

Table 9.2. How the English Plural Develops

Singular	Stage							
	1	2	3	4	5	6	7	8
cup	cups	cups	cups	cups	cups	cups	cups	cups
boy	boys	boys	boys	boys	boys	boys	boys	boys
pud*	pud	puds	puds	puds or pudsiz	puds	puds	puds	puds
bik*	bik	biks	biks	biks, bikiz, biksiz	biks	biks	biks	biks
hand	hand	hands	hands	hands, handiz, handsiz	hands	hands	hands	hands
foot	foot†	foots	foots	foots, footiz, footsiz	foots	foots	foots	feet
man	man	mans	mans	mans, maniz, mansiz	mans	mans	mans	men
house	house	house	houses	houses	houses	houses	houses	houses
box	box	box (singular bok)	box	boxes, bokiz	boxes	boxes	boxes	boxes
orange	orange	orange	orange	orange	oranges	oranges	oranges	oranges

* Nonsense word used to test generalization of the singular-plural contrast to forms never heard before.
† Some children say one foot, two foots. Some say one feet, two feets. A similar sequence of development occurs for both, but only the first is shown here.

The beginnings of language therefore have three roots. One is the biological basis, which gives man the ability to discover and to create the rules and abstract structures that constitute his language and permit him to tie the linear string of speech to the complex structure of meaning by systematic conversion rules. If this biological basis were not present, man would not be alone in having languages of this type; human languages would not be as alike in structure as they are; and children of all levels of intelligence would not find it so easy to learn languages within the first few years of life. Children are not taught their first language. They discover it on their own because their minds are appropriate to the task.

A second major root of language learning is the child's intellectual development as he has commerce with the perceived world around him. Because utterances have meaning, the child proceeds from babbling, when he plays with the surface of sound, to speech, in which some sound differences signal differences in meaning and others do not. His ability to make sense out of what is happening is the basis of his ability to interpret which features of sentences are important and to discover the rules of sentence interpretation. Inevitably, the content of what he can understand linguistically will be affected by his intellectual maturation in very specific ways, such as his ability to perceive temporal relations or hypothetical contingencies.

The third major component of his language learning is his linguistic milieu. Psychologists do not know how much speech or what kind of speech a child must hear to learn a language, but all but the most severely isolated children hear sentences from the time they are born and probably hear them in contexts that frequently indicate their meaning. Can parents change the age at which children pass such basic milestones as understanding specific sound and word contrasts, following directions, understanding first words, sentences, embedded phrases, and relative clauses? So far, all one can say is that such features as vocabulary size, fluency, style, and frequencies of choice of various acceptable forms seem to be trainable—but these features are not the basic ones that are called milestones.

In examining family interaction for the extent to which mothers trained their small children by correcting errors, Brown summarizes his results this way: "It seems, then, to be truth value rather than syntactic well formedness that chiefly gov-

erns explicit verbal reinforcement by parents. Which renders mildly paradoxical the fact that the usual product of such a training schedule is an adult whose speech is highly grammatical but not notably truthful." Although current research has a great deal to say about the descriptive details of language structure as it develops, it still is not known just why, and under what conditions, children's language changes.

Suppose that you had to program a super computing machine so that it could enter the American school system about three years from now. What sorts of things would the machine have to be able to do in order to get along successfully in kindergarten? Certainly it would have to be self-sufficient; no caretaker could follow it to class every day. It would also need abundant social skills, in order to interact effectively and profitably with both the teachers and fellow students. The machine would need a certain amount of emotional stability; an erratic and undisciplined machine would certainly end up at the principal's office or be dismissed. Also, no kindergarten machine could last long without language because the very business of education lives on language as a medium of communication. The machine also would need to be able to think because even kindergarten poses problems to be solved. And if the machine did not acquire one in the natural course of picking up everything else, it would be good to provide it with a personality so that it would be distinctively different from other machines and pupils in the class. The human child needs all the things such a computer would need—independence, social skills, discipline, language, cognitive ability, and personality—and more, too. And the human child develops them to an extraordinarily fine degree in about three years.

Unit IV
The Formative Years: Before Starting School

Although the facts of physical growth are interesting enough in and of themselves, their major psychological impact lies in the fact that sheer changes in physical size radically change even the most fundamental aspects of the child's world. Not only can a bigger child do more with his increased physical and behavioral potentialities, he can also interact in different ways with his physical and human environment. The young infant can neither move nor reach effectively. The toddler is limited to climbing on relatively low objects and to pulling down things that are in reach. True enough, the toddler has the ability to use tools—he can get the dishes off the table by pulling the tablecloth—but with increased physical stature, he can interact directly with the objects on the table. In the human domain, there is no question that the larger and older child is treated differently by parents and others than is the small and physically less capable child. The bigger child also can interact physically with other people in a greater variety of ways. Growth thus underlies the potentialities of development, insofar as it both limits and expands the possibilities for interaction with the environment.

Patterns of growth in infants in the first two to three years of life, while thoroughly individual, are determined largely by genetic factors. But during the childhood years, it is a hormone from the anterior pituitary gland, in conjunction with thyroxin from the thyroid gland, that becomes the major influence on the growth process.

ENVIRONMENTAL INFLUENCES

The glandular determinants of growth can be greatly affected in the later years by a variety of environmental considerations, which can either support or impede normal growth and development. Such factors include diet, general health, and other determinants arising from the socioeconomic background of the child.

THE ROLE OF DIET

Children must have a healthy diet in order to enjoy normal growth and development. Sufficient amounts of high-quality protein provide the material for the building of new cells, necessary for the child's size and weight to increase normally. An adequate intake of carbohydrates provides the child with the enormous amounts of energy that the two- to five-year-old characteristically expends. Finally, the proper amounts of mineral and vitamin components in the child's diet permit proper structural development as well as the utilization of the other nutritional elements.

☐ *Malnutrition* Students of childhood growth have (unfortunately) had numerous opportunities to examine the impact of malnutrition on the young child. Wolff's study of Berlin children dur-

10
Physical Growth

ing World War I demonstrated that the malnutrition they suffered at age five retarded height and weight; however, the restoration of normal diet enabled the children to catch up to their well-fed contemporaries by adolescence. Everyone who has seen news reports on television of the horrors suffered by children—such as those of Vietnam or Biafra—during war can readily appreciate the critical role of nutrition in determining normal, unretarded growth. Many thousands of these young victims of war's relentlessness did not survive the severe malnutrition. Others who managed to live will almost certainly fail to grow normally.

□ *Overfeeding* Ironically, normal patterns of growth may also be upset by dietary excesses. H. Bruch, I. P. Bronstein, and other researchers have found that obesity in children is most often the result of overfeeding; dysfunctions in glandular operation are only rarely responsible. In affluent Western nations like the United States, the opportunities for excessive feeding are great, and it has been demonstrated that an excess of even the healthiest of foods will not produce ever-larger, healthier children but instead can be the root cause of obesity in children, who may in turn become unhappy and socially maladjusted.

CHILDHOOD ILLNESS

A child who escapes serious illness will have a more regular and satisfactory pattern of growth than one who is ill for any length of time because an ill child's energy and resources are channeled into combating his sickness. They are therefore not available to support normal growth. If a child is ill for a short period, as most children are, there should be no difficulty in overcoming the deficit in growth arising out of the illness. But if a child has serious and protracted illnesses, he may be permanently underdeveloped, not from the effects of the sickness alone, but because of the lost periods of reasonably steady growth needed for adequate maturation.

SOCIOECONOMIC STATUS

The setbacks to growth caused by illness are most readily seen in children of the lower socioeco-

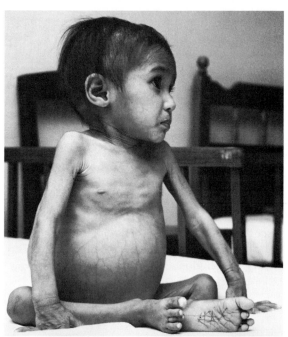

nomic classes. Inadequate medical care and poor diet combine to make the children of poor nations and the poor children of wealthy nations the most likely victims of abnormalities of growth arising out of insufficient diet and long illness.

Inadequate nutrition can have less dramatic but more insidious results than actual malnutrition. Resulting low-energy levels can produce a sluggish child, whose interest is hard to arouse. Undernourished children are more vulnerable to infections of the eyes, skin, and respiratory and gastrointestinal tracts. Because these children are unlikely to have the regular medical care that is an essential prerequisite of middle-class child care, they may consistently suffer from nagging ailments, including badly decayed teeth.

Growth Characteristics

Growth in early childhood, from ages two through five, is not as dramatic as that experienced in infancy. However, it continues to be rapid, and the child's body comes increasingly to resemble what it will ultimately be as an adult.

The average three-year-old boy weighs about thirty-three pounds and is about thirty-eight inches tall. Girls at this age are just a little lighter and shorter. By age five, the average height for boys is betweeen forty-three and forty-four inches, the average weight is close to forty-three pounds, and the average girl's growth has kept pace. The tall, thin, short, or heavy child of two will hold his position relative to his contemporaries at three, four, and five, and his stature during the preschool years is a moderately good indicator of

his adult stature; the correlation has been found to be .70.

In addition to the increase in size, the child undergoes other physical changes in the process of maturation. The head and upper body approach adult proportions, though the rate of their growth is slower than that of the lower body. The limbs grow quite rapidly and the trunk appreciably, so that by age five to six, the child's physical proportions are far closer to those of an adult than to those of the large-headed, round-bodied infant.

By the age of five, the child has attained 75 percent of his ultimate brain weight; by age six, his brain has reached 90 percent of its adult weight. Nerve fibers in the brain and subcranial areas are nearly mature by the end of the preschool period, thus equipping the child for the formal learning experiences of his impending school years.

The child's musculature also undergoes important development during this period. By the time he is ready to enter school, most of the increase in the child's body weight has been in muscle tissue. Development of all the smaller, finer muscles, which will give the individual his ultimate strength and manipulative capabilities, is not complete, however, until adolescence.

The infant skeleton steadily gives way to something more like that of an adult as the limbs and lower parts of the body experience more rapid growth. Infant cartilage is replaced by bone, and the total number, size, and hardness of the skeletal components increase. (See Chapter 5 for a detailed discussion of skeletal age and Figure 5.7

Figure 10.1. Children who are socioeconomically deprived are subject to a variety of health problems because of improper diet and substandard, dirty living conditions.

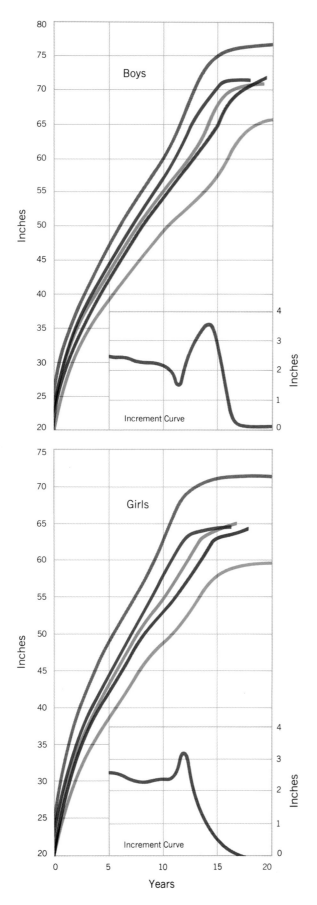

for x-ray photographs of the wrists and hands of children at various skeletal ages.) The entire complement of temporary teeth is acquired by age three, enabling the child to consume adult rather than infant food.

The heart rate of the five-year-old is slower and more stable than that of the infant. Likewise, in early childhood, respiration steadily becomes slower and deeper, and blood pressure also shows progressive increases. It is through all these maturational processes that the preschool child enhances his capacity for more continuous and strenuous effort.

MOTOR DEVELOPMENT

The preschool child, because of his increased mobility, acquisition of language, and developing cognitive abilities, becomes a participant in a much more complex and demanding world than he encountered as an infant. He has steadily acquired the physical equipment that will allow him to engage in many new activities that will test and train his abilities. At play and in nursery school the child has an opportunity to test and refine his new abilities in a broadening range of activities. Running, jumping, manipulating objects, competing with his peers in games and with himself in such tasks as getting dressed are some of the new challenges that his body and mind must confront.

How each child will respond to new physical demands depends on a number of physiological factors. An individual's ability to exert force is limited by the strength of his body's many mus-

Figure 10.2. Curves showing growth in height from birth to maturity for boys *(top)* and girls *(bottom)*. Most children's growth curves will resemble the center one. Accelerated growth is seen in the topmost curve, and retarded growth in the lowest one. The growth curves of those who are tall or short as children *only* because they are fast or slow in maturing, and are not constitutionally tall or short, will resemble those curves just above and below the central one (above, fast-growing; below, slow-growing). (Adapted from Bayley, 1956.)

cles. The degree of speed with which he can move is influenced by the mass of that part of his body being moved. And fast reactions depend on the type of stimuli triggering the reaction, the nerves' transmission of the impulses, the relative complexity of the movement, and the general physical and psychological condition of the child. These factors of strength, speed, and coordination are components not only of childhood play but ultimately of all mature activity as well.

STRENGTH

As size and weight—particularly of muscle tissue —increase, strength is enhanced. From age three on, a child's strength grows until at about age eleven it has doubled. Three- to six-year-old boys and girls exhibit very similar degrees of strength, but after age six the boys begin to outstrip the girls, though not to any great degree until adolescence is reached.

SPEED

Speed is a sensorimotor function that starts to be important in the more demanding play of preschoolers. A major factor in speed is *reaction time:* the interval of time that elapses between the instant a stimulus is presented and the individual's reaction to it. Speed also can be a measure of the absolute time it takes a child to perform a given task. In the preschool years children learn to use their speed in games requiring fast reactions from their minds and bodies, as well as in simple tasks such as running across a playground. In either instance, a child's relative ability to demonstrate speed and speedy reactions will af-

fect his confidence at play and in learning situations, thereby affecting his social development. (The effects of motor abilities on social development will be discussed in a later section.)

COORDINATION

Coordination refers to many aspects of motor performance, including the accuracy of movement, poise, smoothness, rhythm, and ease. Coordination involves far more than mere strength or speed alone and is therefore a better index for determining which child is more able and agile. Coordination is acquired more slowly in the preschool years than are strength and speed because it requires the interplay of more sensory and motor skills that often depend on the maturation of the small muscles—and on practice. Children themselves are very conscious of their own and their playmates' degrees of coordination, and thus a child's relative mastery of tasks requiring coordination can influence his self-sufficiency and self-confidence.

DIFFERENCES BETWEEN BOYS AND GIRLS

To some extent boys and girls differ in body proportions and body form throughout their lives. But the degree of difference in physical makeup and the extent of difference in motor performance are not uniform throughout the entire growth cycle. For instance, the *skelic index,* which measures the ratio of lower limb length to sitting height, can differentiate male from female as early as eight weeks of age. However, this differential is generally no longer observable in children between the ages of five and six, when girls' legs cease to be proportionally longer. In fact, during the preschool period the developmental differences between boys and girls are relatively minor, and discerning them involves fine measurements. In terms of appearance, until puberty the differences between boys and girls are very slight.

For example, greater amounts of subcutaneous fat are found in adolescent and mature girls than in boys. Not only is this sex differential apparent from birth, preschool girls also lose their fatty infant tissue at a far slower rate than do their male contemporaries.

There is an old rule about the growth of children that states that a child has reached half of his adult height by the end of his second year. However, the differences discovered in the growth patterns of boys and girls make this old rule unreliable. In general, it may be said that girls grow up faster than do boys and therefore reach the halfway mark sooner—between the ages of one and a half and two, while boys grow at a rate that allows them to reach their halfway point in height at about two and a half.

It is in skeletal development that girls uniformly outstrip boys at all childhood ages. Girls are somewhat ahead of boys in skeletal development at the beginning of school, and as puberty begins (ten to twelve), the girls start a spurt of rapid development. By age thirteen, the girls are ahead of the boys by two and a half years, on the average.

There are no significant sex-associated variations in motor-test scores during the first twelve years, according to the research of Nancy Bayley. The most significant sex differential among growing children arises from the social implications of physical development. The early-maturing boy has advantages in relation to his male contemporaries, as his status and influence are greater than those of his later-maturing peers. Most evidence for this comes from studies of older children and adolescents, but it is during the preschool years that patterns of social adjustment involving physical ability are first encountered.

Motor Skills

The expansion of the physical activity repertoire of a child is a joy and fascination to his parents and is highly significant in the child's pattern of social development and maturation. There are, of course, large individual differences in the ages at which various children will be able to do different things, as well as differences in the degree of their skill and coordination in each activity. Motor skills are determined for the most part by practice. Furthermore, there is great specificity in skills—each motor skill must be practiced if it is to be performed well. Therefore, ability to catch or throw a ball is in no way related to skill in jumping—mastery of one does not imply the ability to do the other. There is, in fact, only a low correlation between one general area of motor performance and others. For example, demonstrated proficiency in activities requiring manual dexterity has little to do with competence in activities dependent upon strength. Expansion of a child's physical skills is thus largely a matter of

Figure 10.3. Even a motor skill like kicking a ball improves with maturation and practice.

act-by-act and area-by-area training and practice.

Any particular motor skill can be mastered only after the child has carried it through several stages of proficiency. M. V. Gutteridge, after conducting research on more than 2,000 preschool children, produced a scale of motor development for skills. This scale is reproduced in Table 10.1; it can be employed to measure the specific skills of any child.

The Gutteridge scale is particularly useful because it provides four general stages of motor development, within each of which are varying degrees of skill. The first ten degrees of skill mark the progressive acquisition of the ability; the final four degrees (A–D) are exhibited only after the individual has achieved complete competence in

the skill, and thus they involve elaboration and use of the learned ability.

Childhood physical capabilities are not often acquired or practiced in solitude. The preschool child develops and tests his sensorimotor skills among his peers and while doing so experiences critical social development.

SOCIAL IMPLICATIONS OF ABILITY CHANGES

Proficiency or inability in a particular area of motor skill can have considerable influence on a child's ease in social situations and on his general social adjustment. Experimenters have therefore addressed themselves to various childhood skills in order to measure this sensorimotor-social interaction.

Table 10.1. Gutteridge Scale of Motor Skill

Stage	Scale	Degree of Motor Skill
No attempt made	1	Withdraws or retreats when opportunity is given.
	2	Makes no approach nor attempt but does not withdraw.
Skill in process of formation	3	Attempts activity but seeks help or support.
	4	Tries even when not helped or supported but is inept.
	5	Is progressing but is still using unnecessary movements.
	6	Is practicing basic movements.
	7	In process of refining movements.
Basic movements achieved	8	Movements coordinated.
	9	Easy performance with display of satisfaction.
	10	Evidence of accuracy, poise, and grace.
Skillful execution with variations in use	A	Tests skill by adding difficulties or taking chances.
	B	Combines activity with other skill or skills.
	C	Speeds, races, or competes with self or others.
	D	Uses skill in larger projects such as dramatic play.

Source: Adapted from M. V. Gutteridge, "A Study of Motor Achievements of Young Children," *Archives of Psychology* (1939), No. 244. Copyright © 1939 by the American Psychological Association and reproduced by permission.

Figure 10.4. Running is a motor skill that permits the Indians to escape the cowboys and lets you race the wave to the tide line.

Running is perhaps the most typical and easily measured skill among preschool children. Because strength, speed, and coordination all come into play, the opportunities for competition with playmates are almost limitless. In addition, the sight of five-year-olds chasing about at play is a common experience, providing the researchers with numerous test groups. Climbing is also a very good indicator of a physical-social adjustment. Four- and five-year-olds at play will compete with one another by climbing on any available structure, whether it was designed as a climbing toy or not. Children can determine for themselves, by seeing how high and fast they can climb, whether or not they are on a par with their playmates. Jumping, tumbling, and the operation of wheeled vehicles are also subjects of research because they are good tests of proficiency and of the willingness of the child to test himself in a social context.

The child's responses to relative success or failure are good indicators of his social adjustment. Utilizing the Gutteridge scale to measure actual capabilities and comparing the results to both a child's self-evaluation in relation to his peers and to his peers' evaluations of him, researchers can demonstrate the interrelationship of physical advancement and social development.

Throwing is a motor skill related to social adjustment. Inability to throw a ball in childhood can inhibit a child's social development because it is a skill basic to many sports that occupy much of the child's time and dominate much of his social interaction in the school years. Moreover, throwing is basic in humans, related perhaps to early man's need to use the skill for protection and food procurement.

J. A. Hicks studied the throwing of large groups of children from three to six years old, and Wild described the stages through which throwing passes during these years. The results of their work indicate that there is indeed wide variation in throwing skill—from extremely awkward to excellent. However, Hicks and Wild could not determine whether these differences are due to variations in maturation or to practice. In any case, the differences demonstrated that in this fundamental motor skill, any group of children will manifest such varying skill levels that an individual's place and his confidence at play in the group will be influenced by his relative skill.

The child who has achieved proficiency in some motor ability is more likely to be chosen as a leader in athletic and social activities. Those not chosen are consequently less sure of their talent, and they experience some degree of stress and unhappiness. In order to demonstrate how this kind of situation can be influenced, researchers taught five nursery-school children certain skills. The children chosen were all low in their social interactions with their peers. When the children had mastered the special skills taught them, they were paired with others in situations that would allow them to use their new skills. In every case the children exhibited significant changes in their behavior: they asserted themselves, gave directions to the children who did not have their special ability, and in general demonstrated un-

Figure 10.5. The normal activities of childhood represent a celebration of and a delight in the child's developing control over his body's actions.

precedented social ascendancy. The change was not complete; it did not apply to all areas of the children's behavior, only to activities where they could display their specific talents. But children who at the beginning were not considered able to lead or to assert themselves at all had proved that their social potentialities could be tapped.

Erik Erikson has perhaps come up with the best explanation of the relation between physical and social-emotional development. In his examination of ego identity, he indicated that the gaining of physical skills allows a child to become a member of his culture. The possession of culturally accepted skills gives a child an entirely different cultural status from that of his peers who lack them. The skilled child receives the cultural recognition that he is more fully a functioning member of his society, thus adding greatly to his self-esteem.

Physical growth, development, and maturation all combine in contributing to the social integration and personal integrity of the child. For one thing, they make the child appear more adultlike, which enhances society's tendency to treat him as such. The child is striving to imitate and to become adult, and increasing physical resemblance and increasing ability to act like an adult facilitate this goal. The little boy who has the strength and stamina to imitate daddy at play automatically becomes more like daddy both in his own eyes and in those of onlookers. There is enhanced self-esteem for the child from becoming more adult. Cultural integration and acceptance play their role, as do the moment-to-moment approval and encouragement of parents. But probably the greatest boost to self-esteem derives from the child's own internally generated satisfaction over demonstrations of his physical competence. Competence is a real, approved, and glaringly apparent indication that the child is growing up.

Figure 10.6.
Throwing ability, like other motor skills, improves with maturation but becomes stronger and more accurate with practice.

Figure 10.7. The gaining of physical skills both gives a child a sense of competence and allows the child to become a member of his culture.

Cross-cultural and developmental studies both have revealed that there is a great deal of psychological activity occurring in children about five years old. Cross-culturally, there is extraordinary regularity in the time of beginning formal schooling—five-year-olds seem nearly universally to fall prey to this incursion of society. And developmentalists have recently marshaled an impressive list of psychological changes that appear at about the same time. It is still difficult to be sure which is the cause and which, the effect. It might be, for example, that entry into school is responsible for working the changes that the developmentalists uncover. But the changes are of such magnitude—in perception, cognition, and behavior—that it is hard to avoid the conclusion that society is instead responding to the child's developmental readiness for schooling at this time. No matter how this problem finally is resolved, the years from two to five are a period of rapidly expanding growth toward perceptual and cognitive capacities that all come together at the start of school. Specifically, much of what this chapter will discuss in the way of perceptual and cognitive development seems almost by design to prepare the child for learning to read.

Perceptual Development

Recently, innovative methods of studying perception have revealed that even very young infants possess remarkably competent perceptual capabilities. Many of these capacities seem to be built into the human nervous system. During the preschool years, the child's perceptions become more differentiated and more integrated. Because very little research in perceptual development has dealt with hearing, touch, or smell, this account deals only with visual perception.

VISUAL PERCEPTION

A very important perceptual development is the progressively greater ability to differentiate between stimuli. There is an analogous pattern that takes place in infants' progressive differentiation of facial features (see Chapter 6) and in the stages of discrimination that young children go through in learning to read. Children initially discriminate only between open and closed letters, as infants initially discriminate only between faces with eyes and faces without eyes. Children of about four or five ignore the equally important features of letter rotation and reversal—they confuse b and d, p and q. Four-year-olds also ignore such properties as straightness or curvature and thus confuse D and O, although five-year-olds have less trouble with this discrimination. By the time children get to be seven or eight, they use the rotation and reversal features and rarely make errors in letter recognition.

What is the similarity in process between the infant's development of the ability to respond to faces individually and the older child's development of the ability to respond to letters individually? The obvious similarity is the discovery of the features required to identify the object in question. In both cases there is an increase in the number of features detected. Over time, distinctive features—the features that differentiate one face from another or one letter from another—are

11
Development of
Perception and Cognition

Figure 11.1. In early childhood, the individual begins to learn the significance of spatial orientation.

gradually discovered. In part, the discovery process may be the other half of a process of learning *not* to respond to features that are *not* distinctive. Infants respond with a smile to movement at first, but movement is not a distinctive feature of people; it does not serve to differentiate them from one another, and so it soon ceases to attract smiles. Similarly, beginning readers respond to the color of letters and their size, neither of which is distinctive. Responses to these features soon drop out. Response to rotation and reversal is not useful in the world of real objects because an object remains the same even though rotated. It is no wonder, then, that children initially do not attend to rotations and reversals on the printed page; but they must learn to do so if they are to discriminate letters.

In testing young children's perception, one very important point to make is that the child's capacity for making the required distinctions may not be mirrored in his performance. Unless a child is specifically directed to respond to what the tester thinks is relevant or is rewarded for making that response, the child will make only those discriminations he himself regards as relevant. For example, a child may perceive the difference between b and d and yet not judge it relevant. In his experience, a teddy bear, whether its profile faces left or right, is still the same teddy bear.

A recent study has shown that children as young as four or five years can, under the right circumstances, readily distinguish a figure from its reversed form. E. J. Gibson first presented the children in her study with cards on which were printed such standard stimuli as ◁▽ ; below the standard were printed two stimuli, one identical with the standard and the other very different (a picture of a familiar object). The children were asked to pick the stimulus that was exactly like the standard, and they were rewarded by the flashing of a red light when they were correct. This task was, of course, a very easy one, but it served to train the children for the actual test. The test cards contained a standard figure (some geometric form) and below it an identical figure and one that was upside-down or a left-right reversal of the standard. The children made very few errors in matching to the standard on this test. The test results indicate that preschool children can easily discriminate stimuli on the basis of the objects' spatial orientation as long as the task specifically requires a response to this cue—that is, when it is made relevant to them.

As they get older, children do come to regard the spatial orientation of objects as relevant. From their experience with the world—for example, learning to drink from a cup, seeing picture books, and learning the alphabet—they come to know that some things *must* be oriented in certain ways and that changing an object's orientation changes either the thing or its meaning. Also, the learning of labels such as right-left and up-down helps draw their attention to these directions. The role of language in organization of perception and in cognitive development will be discussed in the last section of this chapter.

EDUCATING ATTENTION

One explanation for the development of these discriminations involves the education of attention. In making pattern discriminations the child must learn which features of objects will allow him to discriminate reliably. For example, young infants do not respond to the information within a picture; they attend only to the edges of a picture, responding to it as an object rather than as a representation. J. Hochberg and V. Brooks studied one child who was deprived of pictures in his environment. He had learned the names of people and things but had never seen pictures. At the age of nineteen months, the child was shown line drawings of familiar objects and asked to name them. His performance was significantly above chance. Thus, without prior experience of pictures, this one child was able to identify pictured objects. Does this mean that the ability matures? Or is it learned in the same way as some other perceptual abilities are learned? It seems as if learning to ignore the edges of a picture and to look at its interior, an education of attention, could facilitate the identification of pictorial material simply by ensuring that it is attended to. Once this attentional shift has taken place, a drawing can present many of the distinctive features of an object or a person. Learning to ignore one feature—the edge of a picture—and attend to others—those within the picture—a process that goes on in the normal environment anyway, could thus account for the seeming maturation of the ability to identify pictured objects.

Another perceptual ability necessary to interpreting pictorial information is the judgment of relative depth and distance of pictured objects. W. Hudson studied the responses of Bantus and other native Africans to pictures (see Figure 11.2). All of his subjects could identify the represented objects, but they were unable to identify the objects' location in depth in the picture. Hudson found that Africans with school experience did better in depth judgment than those without it, so he concluded that a specific educational process was necessary to produce this ability. However, the kind of learning involved seems again to be very much education of attention. Pictorial depth cues are not mere convention. They validly represent certain stimulus properties of the real world. However, the depth indicated by these cues in a picture is in competition with the much more powerful information provided by binocular disparity and relative motion, both of which indicate that all of the objects in a picture are in fact at the same distance. Only by ignoring the more potent depth information and attending to the pictorial information can one successfully make depth responses to objects in pictures. Thus the learning involved here again seems to be an education of attention within the perceptual system—learning to ignore some variables in order to attend to others.

The process whereby strategies are developed for selecting which features of things to look at has been studied in lower animals but not in children. In general, it seems that the more varied and diversified the organism's environment, the more features it can attend to. The more varied the objects around an organism, the less likely it is to ignore any feature. An organism surrounded by objects that are all green is unlikely to attend to color because color in its environment is not distinctive enough to warrant attention. If, on the other hand, half of the objects are green and half red, then one would expect the organism to be attentive to color. Similarly, if all the objects in an organism's environment are the same size, then the organism will not attend to size. If there is a wide range of sizes about, then size will be a distinctive feature and will attract attention. In general, the more differences there are between the objects in an organism's environment, the more features the organism will be predisposed to attend to in any novel situation. These principles are well verified in studies of lower organisms, and there is no reason to believe that they are not valid for children as well.

HOW THE PRESCHOOLER PERCEIVES

Young children have difficulty in attending to parts of a stimulus as well as to the whole. In one study that illustrates this difference between younger children (four-year-olds) and older ones (eight-year-olds), the children were first shown complete outlines of objects; detailed parts were then added—one or two at a time—and the children were asked to name the added parts. The four-year-olds were generally much inferior to the eight-year-olds in recognizing the new parts, that is, they could not easily separate the parts from the whole.

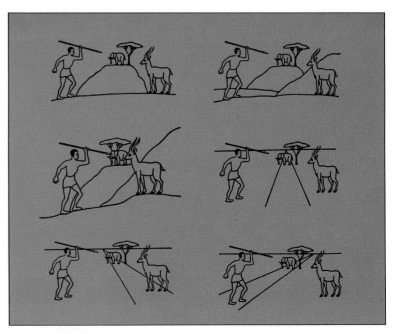

Figure 11.2. Some of the pictures W. Hudson showed to Africans; most were unable to identify the pictured objects' location in depth. (After Hudson, 1960.)

The series of dots in Figure 11.3 is easily recognized by a school-age child as a rabbit, but most four-year-olds would require much more detail to perceive the animal. The preschooler requires more clues—probably because he has had less experience with the world and because his cognitive development is still preoperational (see later in this chapter for Piaget's theory of cognitive development). In some sense, the barely drawn outline of the rabbit implies the concept of rabbit, and children's thought during the early part of these years is just beginning to integrate past and present experiences and to develop representational activity.

It must be emphasized that, as in other aspects of development, there are marked individual differences around these behavioral averages. In some instances a four-year-old will make fewer errors than a six-year-old. These differences are reflected in such things as how well and quickly children learn to read.

Cognitive Development

The adult mind is organized. Healthy adults clearly distinguish between what is within them —their thoughts, feelings, and dreams—and what is outside them—the physical world of objects, the social world of people. The things outside bear relationships to one another. Some are related by being members of the same category of things. The banana, potato, and pork chop are all foods. The hammer, knife, and saw are all tools. Some things are related by means of action. The light switch on the wall is related to the physically dissimilar and spatially remote light on the ceiling. The pressing of a key on the typewriter is usually related to the letter that appears on the blank page.

Adults recognize that some things that appear to be dissimilar are in fact similar. The water that pours from the tap is the same water that is boiled or frozen. Adults accept certain transformations as maintaining the identity of the object that has been transformed. They accept certain different things as equivalent to one another, such as A and a. Some transformations shock people and so are called magic. If I cover something with a handkerchief and it has disappeared when I remove the handkerchief, you are shocked. Your expectations about the behavior of the world are violated.

All of these features of adults' orientation within the world seem so commonplace, so natural, that it is hard to believe we are doing anything other than passively observing the way things are. It is hard to believe that this commonplace organization of things into categories, into stable objects and relationships, into cause-and-effect relationships is, in fact, the product of a long and difficult struggle—a struggle called cognitive development.

The term *cognition* is often used as a synonym for thinking, but cognition is not a special activity, delimited in time, engaged in only at specified periods. Cognition applies to the way in which each of us, smart and stupid alike, comes to know about our world. It is the way that our world becomes organized for us. The story of cognitive

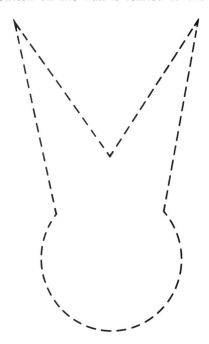

Figure 11.3.

development is the story of how the infant pro-gresses from the "blooming, buzzing confusion" described by William James to the organized, well-ordered world that most adults function in so well.

One of the major features of the organization of the world is the category system, or set of con-cepts, that adults have for packaging their experi-ences into bundles that they can handle. Strictly speaking, the world as people encounter it with their sensory apparatus is composed of discrete, individual experiences. Each object in the world is in some very basic sense unique. An object is always experienced in some particular time and place. Studies of object perception in infants by Jean Piaget and by T. G. R. Bower have shown that the infant occasionally has great difficulty in transcending this particularity. If an object is moved behind a screen, the infant of five months will act as though that object has disappeared. The same sort of argument can be made for any type of experience. For example, on the percep-tual level alone it would be very difficult to see why an orange and a banana would both be classed as fruits. At some point, most children learn this concept. We must recognize, then, that any treatment of cognition has a lot to explain.

The young child seems unable to identify the defining attributes of his concepts clearly and thus falls prey to the breakdown of his concept when some irrelevant attribute is changed. When one cannot distinguish relevant from irrelevant attributes, any change may destroy the stability of one's concepts.

Some of the inconsistency of classification schemes that results from this inability to main-tain a relevant and consistent defining attribute for a concept has been documented by L. S. Vygotsky in his classic studies of conceptual be-havior in young Russian children and by Jerome Bruner and Rose Olver in their studies of concep-tualization styles in American children. Vygotsky presented children with a task that required them to sort a set of thirty-two geometrical objects into four categories. The objects varied from one another in four dimensions. They were of five different colors, six different shapes, two different heights, and two different widths. The correct solution required that the children use both height and width and ignore color and shape to define the four categories. Children were pre-sented with four instances of concepts and were asked to add items that were related to the exem-plar shown. One of the surprising features of younger children's performance was that they would often form concepts that had an inconsist-ent basis. These types of groupings are called *conceptual chaining*. For example, if the object presented to the child was a tall, wide, orange square, one child would add a short, narrow, or-ange circle (thus choosing color as the basis of concept definition); in further extending the con-cept the child would add a tall, wide, green circle (thus shifting his basis from color to shape). Conceptual chains of great length can be built up in this manner, but the conceptual basis for con-struction of the grouping may change each time a new item is selected. The concept is labile in the

sense that now one feature is chosen to define it, and now another. It is clear that concepts formed in this manner are of little help in orienting to the world. Only gradually, with increasing age, do children form concepts that have a consistent basis of definition.

THE MATERIALS OF THOUGHT

There are two aspects to the study of cognitive development: the structural, which describes how the world is organized at a given stage in the development of cognition, and the procedural, which classifies the processes by which this organization comes about. Although the distinction between structure and process is useful for purposes of exposition, in fact they are not separable.

The materials of thought, which are called cognitive units, include images, symbols, concepts, and rules. These mental units are properties of the mind, as temperature is a property of molecules in motion. They are abstract potential forces that provide the child with the ability to make sense of experience, to remember past events, and, eventually, to solve problems. These units are acted upon by cognitive processes, which include encoding, memory, generation of hypotheses, evaluation, and deduction. Because the thought processes of the child before age seven are relatively simple, all the cognitive processes and all the units except images and symbols will be described in Chapter 15.

The *image* is probably the first mental unit to develop. It is a representation of a specific event. The representation is not a photographic copy

Figure 11.4. A test of conceptual behavior employing blocks. (a) The subject is asked to sort the blocks into four categories. Younger children often construct conceptual chains (b); the correct assortment is shown in (c).

but is more like a schematic blueprint that emphasizes the *arrangement of a set of salient elements*. Try to remember your childhood home and note that the image highlights a few critical elements. Perhaps they include an unusual painting in the living room, an old chair in the bedroom, or a ladder leaning against the back of the house. The salient elements supply the image with distinctiveness and differentiate it from images of similar events.

An experiment with four-year-olds may help the reader appreciate the meaning of an image. Each child was given a pile of fifty pictures cut from magazines, many of which illustrated objects he had no name for and found unusual. He looked at each of the fifty pictures for about three

seconds; when he had finished, he was shown pairs of pictures. One member of the pair was from the pile he had examined; the second member he had never seen. The child was asked to point to the picture he had seen earlier. Most of the four-year-olds were able to guess correctly in forty-five of the fifty pairs. One child, presented with a pair consisting of a picture of a slide rule and one of a xylophone, correctly pointed to the slide rule, which he had seen earlier. One must assume that he had some mental representation for the slide rule: *an image of its critical elements*. The match between the slide rule and his image was closer than the match between the xylophone and his image, so the image permitted the child to recognize the correct picture.

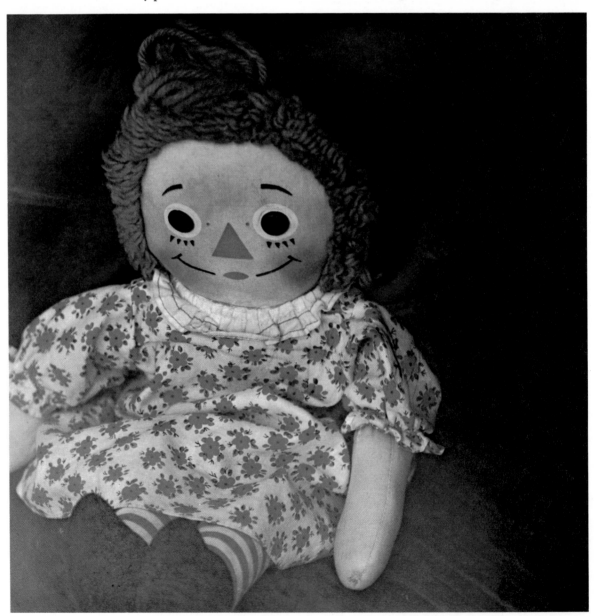

Symbols refer to the next level of abstraction in the representation of experience. Symbols are names for things and qualities; the best examples are the names of letters, numbers, objects, or persons. If the child in the preceding example had said to himself, "That's a ruler" or "That's a slide rule," his correct recognition would have been mediated by his possession of that symbol. The major difference between an image and a symbol is that an image represents a specific sight or sound and preserves the relations in that particular experience. *The symbol stands for something other than the event.* The child who can name the specific arrangement of the three lines that we call the letter A and can point to A when asked possesses the symbol for A. Most children beyond the age of six have both the image and the symbol for letters of the alphabet. Symbols do much of the work of the mind and are used in the construction of the third unit of thought—the concept, to be described in Chapter 15.

The research of Jean Piaget and others has helped to show that while the *content* of the conceptual world that a child may have will be highly variable from child to child and background to background, the organization of this basic information will be characterized by defined developmental levels. The levels do not show individual variation. Thus, this discussion of cognition will be oriented toward the form in which the child has conceptual knowledge and away from the particular content of the child's thought.

Figure 11.5. An image of one's childhood room may have a favorite toy as a salient element.

PIAGET'S THEORY OF COGNITIVE DEVELOPMENT

Piaget's approach provides a necessary corrective to many naïve theories of growth and development that attempt to simplistically answer the question "Why do we develop?"; these theories say that people change by virtue of past experience, which teaches them new things. For Piaget, the possibility of having any experience at all is based on the active tendencies of humans to know—and to work actively to develop their knowledge. Thus, experience is not the answer; it is, rather, the result of fundamental tendencies toward cognitive functioning. A result of some recent experiments by H. Papoušek, described in Chapter 6, indicates that infants as young as six months will solve tasks for the simple pleasure of mastering the solution. It is these tendencies that create what is called the struggle toward knowing —cognitive knowledge.

Piaget's theory derives from two basic sources: a concern with the theory of knowledge (epistemology) and a concern with the biological basis of knowledge. Although some psychologists at-

Figure 11.6 A collage of symbols.

tempt to separate mind and matter, Piaget sees them as integrally related. Piaget sees the higher categories of cognition as deriving from the interplay of the organism with its environment and not as deriving from some special faculty of mind.

Piaget traces the interaction of the human organism and its world over several distinct and definable stages, leading to the end state that characterizes adult Western thought: the sensorimotor stage, which lasts from birth to two years; the preoperational stage, which lasts from two years to seven years; the concrete operational stage, which lasts from seven to eleven years; and finally the stage of formal operations, which comes to characterize adolescent and adult thought. These stages may be seen as a basic description of the different developmental tasks that are solved at each level, and the movement within the stages represents the basic steps taken in solving those tasks. As problems are solved at one level, new problems are created for the next higher level.

The *sensorimotor stage* exists prior to the child's acquisition of symbolic language. During this period, to age eighteen months, the child is essentially involved in perfecting his contact with the objects that surround him. The child comes to adapt his first basic reflex mechanisms to account for features of the objects that these actions present to him. The intelligence of the infant is displayed in his actions. When a one-year-old wants a toy resting on his blanket out of reach, he pulls the blanket toward him to get the object.

This act is not an operation (see the discussion of concrete operations in Chapter 15) but a *scheme of action*. It is a general response used to solve a variety of problems. The act of bouncing in the crib in order to make a toy attached to the crib move is also a scheme of action. The infant has many such schemes. He can suck, hit, bang, shake, or kick, and when a new toy is presented, he will typically exhibit one of these responses. The shaking of a new toy that the child has never seen before provides an example of Piaget's concept of assimilation, one of the two basic principles of his theory.

Assimilation is the incorporation of a new object into an existing scheme. At a given time the child has an existing set of schemes (or operations, if he is older), and new objects and ideas are assimilated to the older, existing ones. The infant's mouthing of a small, blue rectangular object and the adult's recognition of an ultramodern structure as a *chair* both illustrate the concept of assimilation. The process opposed to assimilation is accommodation, Piaget's second basic principle.

Accommodation is the tendency to change one's schemes or operations or make new ones in order to include new objects or experiences. The two-year-old child who has never been exposed to a magnet initially assimilates this toy to his existing scheme and acts toward the magnet as he does toward a familiar toy. He may bang it, bounce it, or try to make it produce a noise. But once he recognizes the unique quality of the magnet—that it attracts metal—he will accommodate his scheme to include it or develop a new scheme of action to deal with magnets.

Mental growth, for Piaget, is the resolution of the tension between assimilation and accommodation. *Intellectual growth* is measured by the growing use of accommodation, the ability to alter old strategies or make new ones to solve unfamiliar problems. Pragmatic flexibility of thought is the key to Piaget's view of intelligence.

The *preoperational stage* bridges the age span from eighteen months to seven years of age; during this period the child encounters reality on an essentially new level, which can be termed the representational level.

One of the basic features of cognition is that adults' encounter with the world is generally in terms of thoughts, rather than in terms of direct action. In some way we deal with the world as we represent it to ourselves (by means of cognitive units). Very often, thinking has been described as a kind of internal dialogue. Although it may not exactly be a process of speaking to ourselves, this description hits upon the basic fact that we deal with thoughts about objects rather than the objects themselves.

During the preoperational stage the elaborate action schemes developed during the sensorimotor period become internalized (nonovert) and hence become available as the vehicle for representational thought. Two basic features of the child's activities during this period reflect this shift from action to representation. The child

begins to imitate the actions of others and even to imitate the actions of objects about him, and he begins to use language. Whereas at the beginning of this period, the only cognitive units he employs are images, later in this stage he can use concepts. One of the basic features of this period is that the imitations become more and more internalized and less overt. Piaget says that these internalized imitations gradually enter into the representational function. Representation involves two aspects; something that is referred to and something that refers to the object, just as the word "book" refers to the object book. Internalized

Figure 11.7. The child in the preoperational stage is able to treat objects as symbolic of other things. For example, he may try to "paint" a tree with water.

imitations take on the function of signifiers, or of things that refer to other things.

The second major activity of the preoperational period concerns the other aspect of the representational act—the formation of *significants*, that which the signifiers refer to. True to his basically constructionist views of cognition, Piaget is not satisfied to state that the object itself is what is referred to by the signifier. For him, the problem of psychological meaning always involves a relationship between things that are represented in thought; the person has no direct relationship to things outside himself, except as they are mediated by his own activities. Piaget sees the significants as deriving from the operation of internalized schemas of the objects and relations that the child encounters. These action schemas, which were originally overt, also become internalized. One can see them at work in the child's play activities: action schemas that had originally been used only in direct activities with objects begin to be used in the absence of the original objects. For example, the two-year-old will treat a stick as if it were a candle and blow it out, or treat a block of wood as if it were a car and move it around, making a noise as it travels. This ability to treat objects as symbolic of other things is an essential characteristic of the preoperational stage. Although the three-year-old uses symbols, his thought is not necessarily organized into concepts and rules. This important process is completed only later, during the stage of concrete operations.

The development of representation during this period provides the child with unique cognitive advantages and at the same time presents him with new kinds of problems. The advantage is that he can integrate events over time, if they are stored in representational form. Action ends when its occasion is over, but representation can be held indefinitely. The integration of past and present that occurs in representational activity also presents great problems for the child. Whereas in the sensorimotor period the child had to solve problems only in the here and now, in the representational period he must do that as well as integrate his present solutions with his past ones. Although this integration will eventually result in a coherent system of conceptual knowledge (derived both from the needs of present action and from past achievements), during the preoperational period problem solving is often accompanied by confusion.

During this period of internalizing formerly overt actions, the child demonstrates a marked egocentrism. The child does not make an adequate distinction between his own perceptions, thoughts, and feelings and those of others. He does not take the point of view of others into consideration, simply because he does not realize that there are different points of view.

In one classic study, Jean Piaget and Edith Meyer-Taylor presented children with a clay model of a mountain range. The children were asked to describe what it looked like from their

own position and then to describe what it would look like to someone taking various other positions around the clay model. The striking feature of children's performances during this period was that they recognized no difference between the positions; everything was described in exactly the same way—as the child himself saw it.

Although this somewhat literal demonstration of egocentrism clearly indicates the type of problem the child has, it does not illuminate the full implications that egocentric behavior has for cognitive functioning in general. To completely understand the relationship, one must recognize the degree to which the adult process of thinking involves the regulative functions of convincing, checking, and proving. In fact, it has been argued that much of an adult's integrated, logical thinking derives from an orientation toward others' points of view and from the attempt to make understandable to others what one knows intuitively. If this is the case, then the child's lack of recognition that others may have a different point of view stands in intimate relationship to his lack of consistency in classification and his difficulties with logical relationships.

LANGUAGE AND COGNITION

The language that adults speak contains in both its semantic and its syntactic organization a vehicle for organizing the world. The way in which words are put together can be seen as the rudiment of a logical system. Some theorists, such as Jerome Bruner, suggest that language learning, the development of adequate terminologies, is one of the tools of cognitive advancement. Others, such as Piaget and some of his major collaborators, suggest that the advancement of language follows rather than precedes the attainment of more elaborate cognitive structures. The issue is still somewhat in doubt. No one has been able to prove conclusively whether language accounts for advanced cognitive behavior or advanced cognitive behavior accounts for language development. However, the arguments for the biological foundations of language are very strong, as discussed in Chapter 9. What is recognized by all developmentalists is that language, thought, and behavior are intricately interrelated. This relationship emerges with both greater clarity and greater complexity—and with increasing cognitive influence—as development proceeds.

Figure 11.8. A characteristic of the preoperational child that has been studied and reported by Piaget is his egocentrism. The child simply does not realize that points of view other than his own exist.

Between the ages of one and a half and four years, normal children all over the world master the basic syntax of the world's thousands of languages. This ability of a small child to learn the complex structure of a language is remarkable. Moreover, each child is exposed to a different sample of the language; that is, he hears a personally unique set of sentences. Yet all children exposed to one language or dialect of that language learn to speak using the same basic syntax. When young children and their parents move to another country with a different language, the children learn to understand and speak the language with an ease and rapidity their parents cannot hope to equal. The saying "So simple a child can do it" is thus literally sound. How did this come to be?

The child's capacity for learning language is not based primarily on his ability to imitate what he hears. Careful parental corrections, expanding the child's versions of his speech. These aspects are all relevant to the child's learning, but there is reason to believe something more crucial is occurring. Though we do not know in the first approximation regard some grammatical regularities and differences from the adult system. Before discussing how children learn language, however, it is necessary to look at some properties of language and to consider what it is that is learned.

Common Properties of Language

All languages are composed of sounds that are combined in various ways to make up the vocabulary of the language. The sounds themselves have no meaning but are bound together (in specified ways) to make up the words. Thus, *b-a-t* and *t-a-b* are different words with different (and unrelated) meanings. Speakers of English can easily recognize invented words that could not be formed from the sound patterns of English—*bnick*—and can differentiate between impossible English words and words that are made up of possible sound sequences—*blick*—but that have no meaning connected to them. (The flexibility of possible combinations allows for the formation of new words, which usually begin in the spoken language and eventually make their way into dictionaries, for example, *smog, fink,* and *motel.*)

All languages have a large but finite vocabulary of words, whose meanings must be learned. One cannot ordinarily guess the meaning of a word from its sound. Some words have more than one meaning: *meet* in *The swimming meet has been postponed* and *We meet on Saturday; light* in *This is a light color* and *This suitcase is light when empty.* Some aspects of word formation are productive; that is, by using affixes, new meanings can be composed: *sad, sadness; begin, beginning; operate, operation.*

However, it is the *syntax* of a language—the underlying rules that determine the form of sentences—that provides for the richest expression of creativity. Except for a few routines, most sentences each person hears and utters are novel. People do not understand sentences by recognizing that they have heard their precise form before. Rather, they understand sentences because

12
Development of Language

they know the rules of combination that make up the syntax of a language. Consider for a moment the sentences in this book. Although they are not difficult to understand, there are probably only a few that are exact repetitions of sentences you have seen or heard before. It is knowledge of the rules of combination—the syntax—that governs how people construct and understand an infinite set of sentences from a finite vocabulary, thus giving language its creative power. Therefore, this chapter will concentrate on how the child learns the underlying grammatical network of regularities in the language to which he is exposed.

KNOWLEDGE OF A LANGUAGE

Children are not usually able to state the rules they know or are using, any more than adults who have not studied linguistics are able to verbalize the fine detail of grammatical rules. Psychologists studying language development use a variety of *indirect* evidence to infer the child's knowledge of rules. Children sometimes make corrections in their own speech, thus displaying knowledge of rules: *I see me in the mirror . . . I see myself in the mirror* or *I seed . . . saw it.* But these instances are relatively rare and only give information on a few scattered aspects of language. To discover children's knowledge of regularities, total patterns of evidence in large samples of children's speech must be examined—the sets of well-formed utterances, the types of omissions, and most important, the sets of utterances children produce that they have probably not heard.

Although the approach to the study of language development in this chapter is relatively new, and although the number of children whose speech has been studied is quite small, the patterns and regularities of development are so striking—across children and across cultures (see Chapter 9)—that a new, more definitive theory of language development must be sought. Language learning as imitation simply does not explain the facts.

OBSERVATION

Roger Brown and Ursula Bellugi studied the speech development of three children, Sarah, Adam, and Eve. At the start of their study Adam and Sarah were twenty-seven months old, and Eve, eighteen months. Adam and Sarah were followed until they were five years old; Eve was studied for nine months (at which time she moved away). These children were selected because they were just beginning to combine words into two-word utterances and because their speech was easy to understand. The researchers visited Adam and Eve at two- or three-week intervals, spending two hours there; they visited Sarah every week for a half hour. During these visits they recorded everything each child said and everything that was said to him.

Between visits, they met in a research seminar with students of the psychology of language to discuss the state of the children's development and to suggest experiments. For example, at one point Adam would sometimes pluralize nouns and sometimes not. It was suggested that he be tested to see whether he could distinguish a correct from an incorrect form. So on the next visit, they asked, "Adam, which is right, 'two shoes' or 'two shoe'?" His answer, produced with enthusiasm, was "Pop go the weasel!" The two-year-old child does not qualify as a model experimental subject. But the recordings over this crucial period in language acquisition nevertheless produced much valuable information. One dialogue between Eve and her mother when Eve was about two is reproduced here.

Eve   Have that?

Mother   No, you may not have it.

Eve   Mom, where my tapioca?

Mother   It's getting cool. You'll have it in just a minute.

Eve   Let me have it.

Mother   Would you like to have your lunch right now?

Eve   Yeah.

Eve   My tapioca cool?

Mother   Yes, it's cool.

Eve   You gonna watch me eat my lunch?

Mother   Yeah, I'm gonna watch you eat your lunch.

Eve   I eating it.

Mother   I know you are.

Eve   Mom, I want more tapioca.

Mother   You do? All right. Would you like to have a cracker?

Eve   Yeah.

Eve   There no more these.

Mother   Are the cookies with the holes all gone?

Eve   It time Sarah take a nap.

Mother   It's time for Sarah to have some milk, yeah. And then she's gonna take a nap and you're gonna take a nap.

Eve   And you.

Mother   And me too, yeah.

Eve   Fraser have moved in that chair.

Mother   Well, I'm not gonna take a nap while Fraser's here. I'll wait until they go.

Notice that both the participants in the dialogue use declarative sentences, requests, negative sentences, questions. There are interesting differences, however, between the speech of the adult and the child. Certain elements are *characteristically* and *systematically* missing from the child's speech; these elements are not optional but are required for full English sentences. The most striking difference is that the auxiliary verbs are missing from the child's speech and present where required in the mother's sentences. In the mother's speech, auxiliary verbs occur with declarative sentences, negatives, questions, and echo statements.

Following are parts of a dialogue between the same child and her mother three months later. Eve's speech has undergone a dramatic change.

Figure 12.1. The child's first verbal interactions usually take place with his mother.

Compare her sentence structures with the sentences in the previous dialogue.

Mother   Come and sit over here.

Eve   You can sit down by me. That will make me happy.

Eve   Ready to turn it.

Mother   We're not quite ready to turn the page.

Eve   Yep, we are.

Mother   Shut the door, we won't hear her then.

Eve   Then Fraser won't hear her too.

Eve   Where he's going?

Eve   Did you make a great big hole here?

Mother   Yes, we made a great big hole in here; we have to get a new one.

Eve   Could I get some other piece of paper?

Mother   You ask Fraser.

Eve   Could I use this one?

Mother   I suppose so.

Eve   Is Fraser goin' take his pencil home when he goes?

Mother   Yes, he is.

Eve   Then we don't see him.

Mother   Nope, probably not. He'll share the paper with you while he's here.

Eve   I will write right here.

Eve   I will put my pencil right here.

Mother   Okay, you do that.

Eve   Now let me draw you a lady.
I can't.
I not how . . . make one.

Mother   You don't know how to make one? You look at Fraser's lady and see if you can make one.

Eve   I can't.
I think I have tear one and I think I can write one.

Figure 12.2. Speech addressed to young children is usually rich with cues. For example, a child who recognizes that a particular piece of clothing means going out in the car—and that going in the car often means going to the dentist or doctor—does not need to be told to "Put on your blue jacket—we're going to the doctor."

The child's sentences selected show a dramatic change. There are auxiliary verbs in negatives, questions, and declaratives. In the short space of three months, then, the child's language system altered quite radically.

TESTING COMPREHENSION OF GRAMMAR

Tests of various sorts are also used to elicit regularities from children. Parents are often misled by a child's response into thinking the child understands most of the language they address to him, but they seldom take into account the restrictions necessary to *test* the child's understanding carefully. A mother may say to her small child, who can speak only two or three words at a time, *Go over to that chair and bring me my knitting.* When the child does so, she may be impressed by his seeming to understand far more than he says. However, the child needs to understand only a word or two of the adult sentence (*knitting* and perhaps *chair*) to be able to comply. In addition, it is very likely that the mother looked in the direction of the chair on which the knitting was prominently displayed; she may have pointed to it and then held out her hand. The linguistic and environmental context of speech addressed to the child is usually rich with cues to aid in understanding.

To test adequately for comprehension of some grammatical rule, it is necessary to eliminate all situational and contextual cues. In the preceding situation, for example, a tester, with hands folded in his lap, might look at the child (not at the object he wants him to bring) and might ask him first, *Bring my knitting to me.* Then, after returning the knitting to its original position, he would ask the child, *Bring me to my knitting.* Perhaps he would try other variations as well: *Me to knitting my bring* and just *Knitting, please.* The point is to establish carefully controlled conditions for testing the child's knowledge of grammatical rules.

SIMPLE ACTIVE AND PASSIVE

Children hear many examples of simple declarative sentences, containing an actor, an action, and the object of that action: *Mommy is eating soup. Sarah is having lunch. Jane feeds her doll. John broke the truck.* In all these sentences the relation between the actor (*John*), action (*broke*), and object of the action (*truck*) is expressed by word order. Also, the first word in all these sentences is

Figure 12.3. One situation in which cues may make speech all but unnecessary is bedtime. The appearance of the pajamas in the mother's hand is the mother's cue to the child, and the child may provide his own cues to the mother by gathering up his crib paraphernalia —blanket, toys, bottle.

a person (*Mommy, Sarah, Jane, John*) and the last word is an inanimate object (*soup, lunch, doll, truck*). Rearranging the nouns in these sentences produces strange results: *The truck broke John. Lunch is having Sarah.* It is possible to construct sentences in which the nouns can be reversed, as in *The boy feeds the girl* and *The girl feeds the boy.* These are *reversible* active sentences. (Although English depends on word order to relate subject to object, there are languages that employ other grammatical means to signal these differences. Russian, for example, uses a system of case endings to indicate subject-object relations, so word order in the adult language is more variable. For each language, children must learn what grammatical means are used to make these distinctions.)

Colin Fraser, Ursula Bellugi, and Roger Brown have developed some tests for the study of children's comprehension of grammar. The child is shown several pictures and must point to the one described by the sentence he hears, or he is asked to act out sentences like *The cat chases the dog* and *The dog chases the cat* by arranging toys that have been set before him (see Figure 12.4). Most children of about three perform well on these tests, and they also observe these relations by correct order in their own speech.

However, not all English sentences have the actor before the verb and the object of the action following the verb. In so-called *passive* sentences, for example, these relations are reordered. Compare: *The truck was broken by John* and *John broke the truck.* The two sentences mean the

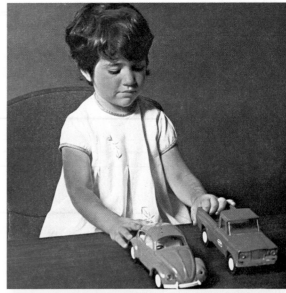

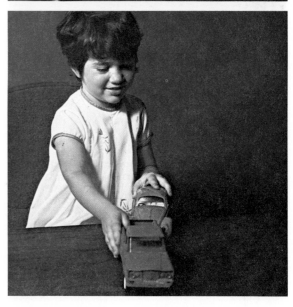

Figure 12.4. Child's performance on active sentences. The experimenter places a car and a truck on the table and then says, "Show me the truck follows the car." The experimenter then puts the vehicles down again and says, "Now show me the car follows the truck."

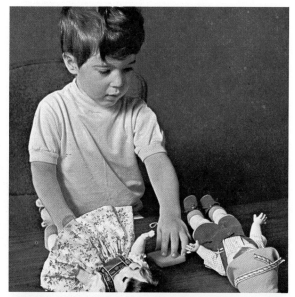

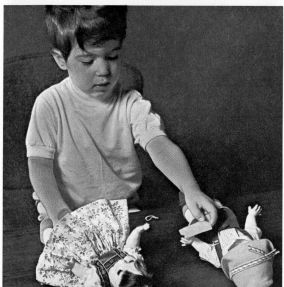

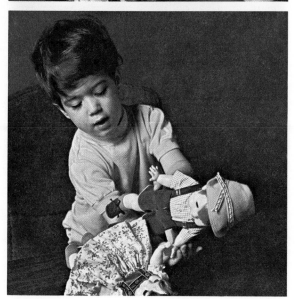

same, but the order of major elements is different. When three-year-olds' understanding of passive constructions is tested as before, by showing them pictures or by asking them to illustrate, for example, *The boy is washed by the girl* and *The girl is washed by the boy,* they seldom point to the correct picture. In fact, they most commonly point to precisely the wrong picture each time. When asked to show *The boy is washed by the girl,* they point to the picture of the boy washing a girl (see Figure 12.5). Because these errors are systematic, it seems likely that young children process these passive sentences as if they were active sentences with some extra, uninterpretable parts.

TENSE AND NUMBER

In most cases, English verbs change form from present to simple past tense: *He teaches at the University; He taught at the University. I walk there; I walked there.* Although a few verbs do not change form from present to past (*hit, hit*), the regular way to form the past for most English verbs is by the addition of *-ed: walk, walked; push, pushed; jump, jumped; ask, asked.* However, many of the verbs used most often form their past tense in an irregular way: *go, went; come, came; drive, drove; break, broke; fall, fell.* Investigators in the field of child language have found that some children learn a number of these irregular past forms as separate vocabulary items early in their speaking life and produce sentences that seem correctly formed: *He came yesterday. It broke. Daddy went out. I fell.* Later, however, when the child discovers the rule for forming

Figure 12.5. Child's incorrect performance on passive sentences. The child is handed a washcloth, a girl doll, and a boy doll. When the experimenter says, "Show me the boy is washed by the girl," the subject puts the cloth in the boy's hand and has the boy wash the girl.

past tenses, the irregular forms that he had correctly produced may disappear for a period and be replaced by overgeneralized forms. The child now may say sentences like: *He comed yesterday. It breaked. Daddy goed out. I falled.*

Clearly, children have not heard forms like these but have constructed them in accordance with regularities observed in the speech they hear. A change from *went* to *goed* is not evidence that the child is regressing; on the contrary, it indicates that the child has, on his own, discovered a regular pattern in language and is using it in his own speech.

During periods of overregularization, the child's speech sometimes seems remarkably impervious to gentle efforts at correction. The following conversation, reported by Courtney Cazden, may serve as an example:

CHILD: My teacher holded the baby rabbits and we patted them.
MOTHER: Did you say your teacher held the baby rabbits?
CHILD: Yes.
MOTHER: What did you say she did?
CHILD: She holded the baby rabbits and we patted them.
MOTHER: Did you say she held them tightly?
CHILD: No, she holded them loosely.

The same pattern of overregularization of certain forms emerges as children discover the regularities governing the description of singular and plural nouns. The English language employs several ways to indicate whether there are one or more objects under consideration. The regular written plural ending is, of course, a final *s* (or *-es* after some sounds, for example, *z*). A modifier may serve to indicate plural: *one spoon* or *many spoons; a book* or *several books; one fish* or *a few fish.* There are also irregular plural forms in English, many of them common words: *foot, feet; mouse, mice; man, men; deer, deer; child, children; tooth, teeth.* These irregular forms, like the irregular verb forms, must probably be learned as separate lexical items.

The linguistic context in English need not indicate whether one object or more than one is being considered. If someone says, *Point to the sheep,* it would be as correct to point to one as to many. The context does not indicate whether a singular or plural noun must follow. Jean Berko has used this fact in constructing a test of the child's knowledge of the rules for forming plurals from singular nouns.

For the test, a child is shown some object for which he has no name. (Large stuffed toys of unfamiliar shape were used in the test shown in Figure 12.6). The tester names these objects with possible but nonexistent English words. He presents the child with one object and says, "Here is a wug." Then he puts down another, similar object next to it and says, "Now there is another wug. There are two_____?" The child obligingly fills in the nonexistent but regular item *wugs.*

From these tests and from observations, psychologists have found that, as with verb forms, the child who had been correctly using some irregular plural forms (*feet, men, mice*) may, for a time, overgeneralize his newly discovered rules

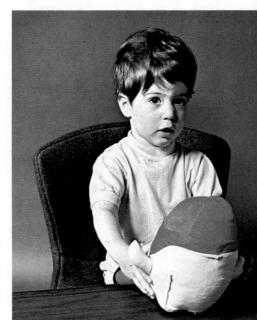

Figure 12.6. The singular-plural test. The experimenter hands the child an object for which he has no name and says "Here is a wug." Then she puts down another and asks the child to finish the sentence: "Now there are two_____."
The child supplies "wugs."

of formation and say *foots, mans, mouses*—or sometimes overcompensate and say *feets, mens, mices*.

The aspects of the child's language-learning process so far discussed are relatively simple ones. It would be misleading to imply that all problems of language learning are so elementary. As one small example, consider some of the aspects the child must learn in order to make sentences correct with respect to number (singular-plural). Because they learn the mechanisms so well as children, few adults ever need to sit down and systematically think about the following requirements for their own language:

1. Only countable nouns take plural inflections. Mass nouns and proper nouns do not (unless one arranges special contexts for them to become countable). Thus, *I have two books* is an acceptable sentence, but *I have two sands* is not; one may say, for example, *I have two grains of sand.*
2. Where applicable, the number of a noun must agree with its modifiers within a noun phrase. It is correct to say *This horse can't win* or *These horses can't win* but not *this horses* or *these horse.*
3. Many pronouns are marked for number and must agree with the number of the noun phrase they stand for. It is correct to say *The boys came here, didn't they?* and *You boys help yourselves* but not *The boys came here, didn't he?* or *John, help yourselves.*
4. There is often agreement in number required across noun phrases in sentences containing a predicate nominative. For example, *This is my book* and *These are my books* but not *This are my books* or *These is my books.*
5. In the present indicative tense, number agree-

ment is required between subject and verb of a sentence. Either *The dog eats the food* or *The dogs eat the food* but not *The dogs eats the food.*

These are a few of the areas in the grammar where number-agreement rules must operate. A child cannot simply learn by rote the semantic bases for the distinction and the correct forms for all singular and plural words—and, in fact, he does not. As with many other aspects of sentence formation, he discovers the intricate grammatical rules that determine well-formed sentences.

Auxiliary Verbs

During the time the second dialogue quoted earlier was recorded, Eve's mother produced a number of sentences with the auxiliary *will*. Nearly all were of the form:
I'll have to buy a new dishpan.
Oh, we'll have to look.
We'll get it later.
I'll fix it later.
You'll ruin it.
That'll be enough.
Yes, and he'll kick you.
You'll go out and play all day.
It'll be a little one.
Notice that in each case the auxiliary *will* was contracted with the subject pronoun: *I'll, you'll, it'll, he'll, we'll.* In the child's speech, instead, the following sentences are found:
I will stand on my knees.
We will buy Becky a new one.
You will gone away.
I will read you book.
They will get dry?
He will have some.
It will work on here, see?

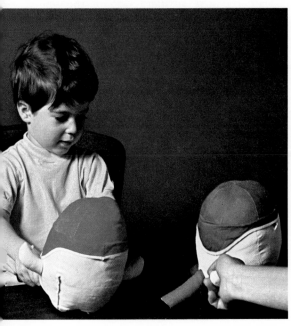

The child produces the noncontracted full form of *will* in her declarative sentences during this period, even though she hears the contracted form in most of the sentences the mother produces. The mother does produce the full form of *will* in questions, of course, as in W*ill it be fun? Will you finish it?* In the three children who were studied carefully (Adam, Eve, and Sarah), the developments were precisely the same, although at different ages and only for a time: the mother said *I'll get it*, whereas the child said *I will get it*.

The children's speech bears a certain relationship to the adult model but is independent from it in characteristic ways. The child's sentences seem at first more precise than the mother's sentences—hardly what one might expect. Language learning, thus, cannot be just a copying process; researchers find these typical deviations from adult speech in children's language at various stages in their development.

THE TAG QUESTION

The results of tests and observations cited in this chapter give evidence that children do not copy precisely what they hear but instead construct sentences according to rules of their own, which they are biologically prepared to do and which they extract from the language around them. One tool that psychologists may find particularly useful in eliciting an older child's knowledge of regularities in English is the tag question:

You'll finish your lunch, won't you?
She's here, isn't she?

John broke it, didn't he?
This can't fall off here, can it?

Tag questions usually request confirmation of the statement they follow. One could substitute single elements (*huh?, okay?, right?*) for the variety of tags and still convey the same meaning in a somewhat less elegant way: *She's here, right? This can't fall off here, huh?* English has a rather complex rule system for generating tag questions, whereas French, for example, has a single invariant form as a tag (*n'est-ce pas?*), which serves the same functions. (This is why one occasionally hears nonnative English speakers adopt a single tag as a question marker: *You can manage this, isn't it?*)

Tag questions are particularly interesting to linguists because the form of the tag is explicitly determined by the syntax of the statement it follows. The grammatical processes involved in forming them are complex and rest on very basic operations of English: the rules for pronominalization, making assertions, negating, and questioning. The grammatical processes are stated below, and the examples that follow each rule are from the speech of Adam when he was about four and a half years old.

1. *Pronominalize* the noun phrase that is the subject of the sentence.

   The man's not bad, is he?
   Me and David are working, aren't we?
   Susie is my sister, isn't she?
   The girls were running, weren't they?
   The puzzle is finished, isn't it?

2. Locate the *first auxiliary verb* of the sen-

tence (or supply the appropriate missing form, usually a form of *do*).

He *was* scared, *was*n't he?
It'*s* tricking you, *is*n't it?
He *can* say Adam, *can*'t he?
He hops like a kangaroo, *doesn't* he?

3. *Negate* the auxiliary verb in the tag if the sentence is affirmative. Use an *affirmative* auxiliary verb in the tag if the sentence is negative.

I *can* hold on like a monkey, *can't* I?
That'*s* funny, *isn't* it?
They *were* jumping, *weren't* they?

He *can't* beat me down, *can* he?
It'*s* not a real watch, *is* it?

Note the special role of the dummy auxiliary *do* in English. It is required for negation and interrogation when there is no apparent auxiliary verb in the affirmative sentence:

It works, *doesn't* it?
She thought that was a tiger, *didn't* she?
Now we have four people, *don't* we?
Adam winned, *didn't* he?

She *doesn't* feel herself moving, *does* she?
It *doesn't* have no eye in here, *does* it?
He *didn't* know what to do, *did* he?

4. *Invert the order* of the auxiliary verb and the pronominalized noun phrase. (Note the order of elements in the sentences and tags presented above.)

Tag questions do not always have the primary function of requests for confirmation from the listener. When the tag is used as a request for confirmation, it must either presuppose shared information on the part of both speaker and listener or assume that the listener has more information than the speaker. Sometimes tag questions are used by parents as prods to influence the child's behavior or to make suggestions: *It goes the other way, doesn't it? Paul would like a turn now, wouldn't he? You are going to wash your hands first, aren't you?* The mother's use of tags with the child is often a gentle way of providing instructions, suggestions, or information.

How does the child learn to produce tag questions correctly? It cannot be a copying process because children do not replicate sentences with tags exactly as they have heard them. On the basis of the great variety of tags children produce that could not have been imitations and the particular types of errors found, it is clear that they construct them according to a set of internalized

Figure 12.7. The tag question is often employed by parents as a gentle prod: "You'll share those with Paul, won't you?"

rules. For example, there are exceptions to the rules for location and copying of the auxiliary verb in the tag. Although the tag for *I'm not helping you* is clearly *am I?* what tag is common for the affirmative: *I'm helping you?* One rarely hears *am I not?* among American speakers. The common English tag is *aren't I?* and that is what the majority of people say. Adam produced the logical missing form when he asked *I'm magic, amn't I?* Certainly he had never heard this form; he constructed it in accordance with his internalized rules.

Adam's mother used tag questions infrequently. Out of the hundreds of utterances addressed to Adam in a two-hour sample, an average of two or three were tag questions. The records kept from the time Adam was twenty-seven months old showed that he produced few tag questions until he was four and a half. In the period just before he began to use them, at about age four, he produced a number of statements followed by *huh?* (the inelegant semantic equivalent of tags). He said things like *I have two turns, huh? We're playing, huh? I have to get black color, huh?* Then, suddenly, in six hours of recorded speech (covering a period of six weeks), the taped records showed sixty-two different statements with tags and no statement followed by *huh?* The number of tags Adam used in these samples was far greater than the number produced by his mother in any set of samples. He did not wait for a response to his questions most of the time but continued his play, talking at the same time. It seemed more like a display of virtu-

osity or an exercise of newly acquired linguistic skill than a sudden desire to have his statements confirmed.

Tag questions appear rather late in the speech of all the children who have been studied. The late appearance cannot be attributed to the length of the sentences; Adam said many sentences that were far longer than his sentences with tag questions before he was four years old. Because tag questions involve the combination of a number of grammatical processes, it seems advisable to look for evidence of the child's learning of the separate aspects before this period.

An example of the kind of study that will be necessary to trace the development of tag questions is suggested by the number of intermediary steps that have been found to precede children's learning of the rules for negation. There are early rudimentary forms (which later are replaced by more complex forms) like *No want stand. Like it, no. No gonna fall. This a radiator, no. No mom sharpen it. No write book.* At a slightly later period, children sometimes say sentences like *You not have one. He no bite you. I not get it dirty.* A few months later one finds that children have mastered the rules for simple negation (*can't, won't, isn't, aren't*) and that they have learned to supply some forms of *do* (*don't, didn't, doesn't*).

Through such a step-by-step procedure, one could trace each of the grammatical processes involved in forming tags and perhaps find that there are rudimentary forms (often different from those the children hear), which are gradually replaced as the child discovers other aspects of the

underlying rule system. It seems likely that such evidence would show that children master all the basic processes before taking the more complicated step of combining them to form tags.

Origins of Language Development

From observation, experiment, and testing conducted by psychologists studying language development, it is evident that children do not learn sentences as memorized sequences. They derive the rules for combining words into sentences by a complex analysis of the language they hear and the way in which it relates to the world. Children's language gives evidence—even from the time they begin to make two-word sentences—of being systematic, regular, and productive. Children analyze and order words, word segments, suffixes, prefixes, agreement rules, and the like and invent new (sometimes overregularized) combinations at all levels of language. Small children, whose cognitive powers are known to be limited in some respects, show a remarkable ability to reconstruct the language they hear. By the time a normal child is five years old, he has learned most of the underlying grammatical rules of his language and is using these rules to understand and construct enormous numbers of different sentences.

In the process of studying children's language learning, psychologists have uncovered evidence for the child's ability to analyze regularities in the language, to segment novel utterances into component parts, and to understand these parts again in new combinations. Children seem to develop

rules of maximal generality, often applying them at first in more instances than required and only gradually learning the proper domain for their application. It seems that children do not need to be specifically taught the rules of grammatical structure any more than they need to be taught the rules of correspondence for recognizing the same object under different conditions of light and position.

Again it must be stressed that the samples of language studied have been from few children and from few languages. However, the samples studied seem to show a remarkably similar course of development among children and across languages. It may be that this similarity reflects universal properties of human language. It may also mean that human cognition progresses in certain universal ways and that children search the language they hear for specific rules in certain orders.

| a | b | c |

Figure 12.8. Even very young children easily demonstrate their understanding of spatial relations. Here the experimenter has asked the child (a) "Show me the zebra is in the truck"; (b) "...on the truck"; (c) "...under the truck."

The years from two to six are the magic years of childhood. Probably at no time in life will the child experience so much that is new, exciting, and pleasurable. And at no time in his life will he be confronted with so many challenges, conflicts, anxieties, and fears. It is a time when the child turns away from the mother and expands his world to include other children, other adults, an expanding environment, and a host of new physical and social skills.

Personality comprises many aspects—consistent behavior, an accordant self-concept, and a set of traits consistent over time. The development of personality during the period of early childhood consists largely of practice of the rudiments of a series of complex lessons that will come to fruition later in life. In combination, innate predispositional factors interact with the environment and the significant persons who populate it to produce an adult human being with a distinct personality.

During early childhood certain areas of personality outweigh most others in importance. These elements include aggression, shame and guilt, dependence and independence, and proper sexual role. These areas are important because experience in each of them fixes a certain portion of the personality and thus lays down a base for future development and the stages yet to come.

AGGRESSION

Most children fight, bicker, and aggress against one another (and adults) at times, and an essential part of human personality is formed in learning the dos and don'ts of managing feelings of hostility and aggression. Many of the lessons learned are the painful ones of conflict with parents and peers and rejection by others. The energetic child experiences more conflict than the passive child, but becomes an active participant in forming his own personality this way. The more passive child acquires a psychic structure that may not be fashioned with his own hand as much as by the hands of others. Thus, aggressiveness may be a positive feature of personality development in cases where independence is one of the valued outcomes of development.

When the growing person enters the period of early childhood, he brings with him an active, influential history of previous experience with hostility, frustration, and aggression, stemming in part from the period of infancy in which he was weaned, toilet trained, and taught preliminary prohibitions. At this point in life, the child has ceased to respond to the mother as the sole representative of the culture; the number of persons with whom he must now interact increases enormously, and an increasing number of these interactions will be laden with conflict. As his exposure to conflict progresses, the child becomes more sophisticated and less primitive in the way he expresses aggression and, if he is successful in his attacks against others, he may develop an aggressive personality that will characterize him throughout his later years.

The young child also begins to understand his own motives as well as other people's, and he learns to deal with these motives in ways that do

13
Development of Personality

not always entail obvious aggressiveness. Until he knows people and their motivations, he may be cowed by strangers and only become aggressive when he is sure he is not likely to be the victim of retaliation. In much the same fashion, the child may acquire the habit of aggressing against those of lesser strength while avoiding conflict with those stronger than himself.

As the normal child grows in experience, aggressive outbursts become internalized and hence mainly symbolic in nature. As he acquires the capacity for indirect action and becomes skilled in psychological persuasion and torture, the amount of his immediate physical aggression decreases accordingly. As the form of the child's aggression changes, so, too, does his ability to nurture anger and keep it alive. The rapid flare-up and instant cool down of his earlier years disappears, and the child learns instead to mount massive sulks, to contain but carry smoldering resentments, and to continue negativism over longer periods of time. The child now swears that he will get revenge if it takes a lifetime. He exaggerates, of course, but his angers do last longer.

There are definite sex differences in aggressive behavior. Boys argue more than girls even though verbal aggressive forms are preferred by girls. Most interchild aggression is between children of the same sex, and much conflict is between children of different ages, with the younger child being the less aggressive of the two. Simply put, the golden years of childhood contain more conflict and exposure to aggression than most of us

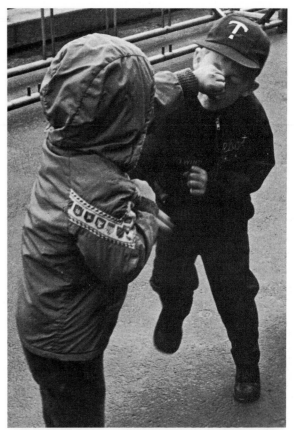

Figure 13.1. Aggression can take the form of either physical or verbal abuse in boys, but girls seem to prefer verbal aggression.

recall. For the developing child, the principal task is to develop a strategic balance between aggressiveness and passive unassertiveness.

Much of human aggressiveness can be traced to frustration; it is impossible to rear children without frustrating many of their needs or heartfelt desires by specifying the times, places, methods, and circumstances in which these needs or desires may be gratified. Children must be taught controlled patterns of social and personal response to frustration in order to make their behavior predictable and, thus, socially dependable and acceptable. Because most young children have a limited repertoire of responses to frustration early in life, part of human personality becomes a reflection of the balance of expressiveness and inhibition the child finally acquires with respect to most of his impulse systems. From simple, direct, aggressive responses the child matures to more sophisticated and indirect means of meeting his problems and achieving his goals.

FRUSTRATION

Frustration is, essentially, a subjective experience or response to the blocked gratification of an individual's needs. The source of frustration may be as simple as a physical obstruction or as complicated as misunderstandings between people. As Elton McNeil has pointed out, the response to frustration will depend upon such determinants as the setting in which it takes place, the intensity of the frustrating experience, its duration, the extent to which the victim sees a way to relieve

his dilemma, and the individual's personal history of success or failure in dealing with states of tension. An additional complication is the apparent or subjective arbitrariness of the frustration; for example, a *person* who interferes with another evokes a more violent response than a sticky door or a high wall, and a *person* who unfairly or needlessly interferes with another provokes more frustration than does an impersonal rule, law, or regulation.

Early theorists at Yale University assumed that aggression was always the result of frustration of one sort or another. Today psychologists know that aggression is only one of many possible responses to frustration and that not all aggression is related to frustration. They know also that the likelihood of an aggressive response is greater when the drive being frustrated is a powerful one, when the frustrating interference is extreme, or when the level of previous frustrations is exceptionally high. In addition, the degree to which hostile feelings will reach overt expression depends on the amount of internalized inhibition of aggressiveness that has been instilled in the individual by parental training and by experience.

LEARNING TO AGGRESS

A number of theoretical explanations of aggressiveness hark back to the parent-child relationship. One theory postulates that an aggressive parent may act as a model for the child: even though the parent may preach nonaggression, the child ignores what the parent says and instead

Figure 13.2. One child's response to frustration.

identifies with the aggressive behavior. Another theory states that parents who are permissive about the aggressive outbursts of their children will increase the frequency with which aggressive solutions will be employed by the growing child in his encounters with the outside world.

Robert Sears, Eleanor Maccoby, and H. Levin interviewed nearly 400 mothers of five-year-old children to explore the relationship between child-rearing practices and aggressive behavior in children. When they measured both the extent to which the mother tolerated aggression and the amount of physical punishment used to deter aggression in the child, they discovered that the mothers with the least aggressive children were those who would not tolerate aggression but did not use aggressive means to stop it. Because the child learns basic lessons about aggression from others as well as from parents when he enters early childhood, this period is one in which lessons learned early are tested in the larger world that surrounds the child.

Aggressive personalities are made, not born, and their origins are formed in what is learned throughout the growing period. The learning of aggressiveness without the necessary social restraints has written many tragic chapters in human history and remains an urgent—but nevertheless solvable—human problem.

Anxiety and Fear

Part of a child's process of maturing involves learning to manage fear and anxiety. Children have a great many fears, and some children grow into adults whose calm exteriors still hide frightened children.

Many childhood fears disappear with time and experience, but as great a number are masked or disguised and persist into adult life as an animate force in personality. This carry-over from childhood is undoubtedly greater than most adults would acknowledge. Such fears may include dread of injury or surgery, of ferocious beasts or harmless pets, of supernatural events or rain, of windstorms or calm seas. More adults are frightened of the dark, for example, than will readily admit it. Frightened adults may simply have learned to live with their fears and to mask their overt expression in order not to be chided for failing to grow up.

Losing fears is not a simple matter. The fears of infancy and very early childhood are immediate and concrete. But as the child grows, he learns to fear many more abstract or nonexistent things. A child who has nothing to fear will often *create* something—a monster, an owl, a bug—to fear. This invention reflects the fact that the child has learned what the world about him *might* contain, that is, he has developed the perceptual and cognitive capacities to know what it is that he should fear, when he should be fearful, and how fear can be used to extract wanted things from adults.

Fear is usually described as a response to immediate and evident danger, whereas anxiety is considered an apprehensive response to *possible* dangers. What a child fears and what makes him anxious differ with age and experience. Thus, re-

leasing a harmless snake in the presence of an
infant or a child up to two years of age evokes
only a curiosity response. Children of ages three
or four are at least cautious about the strange
object, and, after they become four, noticeable
fear responses appear. Interestingly, it is in the
adult population that a severe fear response is
most apparent.

As the child grows up, there is a decline in fears
relating to personal safety because the child becomes more capable of caring for and defending
himself. The child also loses most of his fear of
animals as he acquires a new set of fears and
anxieties about his social status.

Most of the fears of childhood do not correspond to the actual tribulations children undergo
in daily life. Telling someone that what he fears
is statistically improbable does nothing to relieve
his worries. It is apparent that a child will acquire a fear-laden personality in part because he
discovers he is incapable of successfully meeting
life's challenges and in part as a consequence of a
lowered self-confidence based on his own evaluation of his own capacities—as well on the judgments of those who surround him. When a child
is confronted by a massive consensus about his
limitations, he accepts it as a proper evaluation of
himself.

In general, a fearful child is an anxious one. If a
child reacts to threatening situations out of all
proportion to the real danger (as others and even
he judge it), it is likely that his anxious apprehen-
sions will be an integral part of his adult personal-

Figure 13.3. Childhood anxieties and fears.

ity. This anxiety may stem from a series of unresolved inner conflicts, which may invisibly mark
the child throughout life.

Fear and anxiety are vital ingredients in another important component of personality development—the establishment of independence and
dependence.

INDEPENDENCE

In many respects, children in American culture
are independent at an earlier age than their counterparts in European society. In one study comparing American and Swiss children, evidence was
uncovered that the American child matures earlier in certain areas of social development than
does the Swiss child. In this study Leonard
Boehm concluded that American children are less
subjugated by adults, are emancipated earlier
from adult influence, are more dependent on
their peers, enjoy greater freedom of thought and
independence of judgment at an earlier age, and
develop an autonomous conscience earlier in life.
Thus, university administrations should not be
surprised if their nearly mature students act out
characteristics so carefully inculcated in them.

Independence actually begins as early as the
first few weeks of life—the moment the infant
begins to take an active part in interacting with
his environment. When he discovers that the
simplest of his random twistings, turnings, and
movements begins to influence his environment,
he becomes absorbed in the process of active
mastery of the world and acquires his first sense of
independence. With active mastery comes self-as-

sertion, as the child learns to walk, acquires
speech, begins to understand how the world
works and how he can influence it.

In America independence is measured in formal terms and becomes a meaningful part of the
child's life and experience when he reaches five or
six years of age, at which time his readiness for
school is judged by other adults in the society.
Age is not always an adequate measure of readiness for independent experience, but when a child
enters school he must be sufficiently free of ties to
mother and family to learn the academic lessons
that lie ahead of him. The child's needs, goals,
ideas, and skills must all have reached a point of
maturity sufficient to allow him to function as a
free agent in his new, young society.

Aware of the social and personal importance of
achieving this degree of independence, middle-
class parents frequently send their children to
nursery school in preparation for the soon-to-
come formal educational encounter. The importance of such readiness is underscored by the fact
that formal education is directed to the average
child in the classroom. A child who has not yet
reached the level of independence and maturity
needed to master the curriculum will experience
frustration, which will undermine his self-image
and limit his quest for further independence.

With independence comes acquaintance with
society's meaning of success and failure. These
terms are defined in such a relative fashion that
the child soon learns that doing well (as defined
by adults) has more to do with the distance

between his accomplishment and the goals of accomplishment that others have set for him (and that he now accepts as his own) than it has to do with the actual accomplishment itself. He discovers, for example, that his own goals and aspirations change constantly as he grows and becomes more able, and he learns that different people in his environment hold different views of which accomplishments are important in life. Thus, the child's definition of the meaning of success and failure will vary at different times in life—to accord with the views held by those most important to him. The older the child becomes, the more public and apparent will become society's evaluations of his successes and failures and the less wide will become the range of choices available to him. The dramatic beginning of this process takes place in first grade.

DEPENDENCE

Dependent behavior—the desire or need for supporting relationships with other persons—is related quite directly to the experience of anxiety for most developing personalities. When the outcome is uncertain, responses untried, and situations unfamiliar or unexpected, most people feel more comfortable (anxiety free) if they are supported and encouraged by others. The growing child naturally assures himself of freedom from such fear by establishing relationships with others, by stressing his affiliation with supportive people, and by cultivating friends who will supply affection, help, and assistance when it is needed.

In the first years following birth the child is, of course, totally dependent on others for his well-being. With the growth of independence he weans himself from dependency and learns to trust his own resources, capacities, and skills when he is in an anxiety-provoking situation. A child who never experienced anxiety about life would have less need for other people (beyond his first few years). It is only the fact that life confronts him constantly with new challenges and threats that drives him to remain in a protected atmosphere in which others will intervene when the going gets too tough.

Children remain dependent or become independent depending on the degree to which they are taught (and are able) to inhibit dependent urges—urges that warn them of danger or threat and teach them caution in their encounters with the world. Thus, if an anxious mother is herself frightened by life, she will protect the child from encounters that might provoke anxiety or cause him psychological pain; when danger threatens, she will intervene and will provide the protection of a dependent relationship before the child can call on his own resources. She thus signals to him that she considers him incapable.

Whether a child is to become dependent or independent will rest, in great part, on parental reward or punishment for such behaviors. If the child is regularly rewarded and seldom punished for dependent behaviors, he will learn to react in dependent ways. In most families, of course, the growing child will get a mixed and inconsistent set of messages about dependence-independence. He will be urged to be independent in some situations and encouraged to be dependent in others. From these mixed communications he must forge his own version of a balance of dependence-independence and learn to apply each in the appropriate situation. This task is not an easy one, and the truth of childhood is that the developing child fluctuates (often unpredictably) between dependent and independent behavior. The parental problem is no easier. Parents vacillate; they dodge and dart between telling the child, "You are old enough to do it yourself" and "You are too young to be allowed to do that."

In general, boys experience more conflict about dependency than do girls. The social role delineated for females in Western culture is essentially a passive-dependent one, and the movement from early dependence to later "independence" may be a short trip for the female. The expectation that boys will become independent, autonomous human beings makes greater demands on their psychological apparatus.

The typical signs of dependent behavior, according to E. K. Beller, consist of actions such as seeking recognition, attention, help, closeness, or physical contact from others. Independence is apparent when the child is observed overcoming obstacles, taking initiative, trying routine tasks by himself, or carrying activities through to completion. The difference between the two forms of behavior is clearly that of depending on others as opposed to going it alone. And, of course, there

Figure 13.4. Expectations about dependent behavior change with age. A child who clings to his mother on the first day of nursery school is not likely to receive the same reactions from his teacher and peers as one who clings on opening day of first grade.

are expectations set for children according to their age. Relative dependence and independence are judged by behaviors that are age appropriate, and the child out of phase for his age is regularly rejected socially by his peers.

Of the two patterns of behavior, dependency remains more stable over the years for women than for men. Jerome Kagan and H. A. Moss have suggested that these patterns may prevail because Western culture encourages and reinforces dependency in females at the same time as it discourages and punishes it in males. As the child ages, his dependent or independent posture has an important influence on the nature of his relations with his peers. Children dependent on adults interact less often with peers and are less well liked by them. And the base of dependent-independent personality characteristics is established early in the child's life.

THE SEXUAL ROLE

The child must learn to fulfill a number of roles in society and is required to practice the behaviors associated with them. These roles are taught using reward and punishment administered by parents and peers who know the detailed behaviors that the role demands. In part, the child learns these proper behaviors by play-acting or rehearsing the dos and don'ts demanded for an appropriate performance.

One particularly essential set of roles is that of male and female. Before the child even learns that there are two sexes, parents begin a training program (pink for girls; blue for boys) devoted to having their children acquire the proper sex preference and to learning the associated behaviors, attitudes, and feelings that fit each role. These sex roles are, of course, inevitably interwoven with the status society attaches to each role. In general, the male role (with its freedom, authority, and power) is preferred by both sexes while they are growing up. Because sexual behavior is patterned after adult performance, the model provided for the child to study is exceptionally important, as is the quality and stability of the relationship between husband and wife.

According to G. Watson, no matter "whether the growing girl accepts her prescribed role, or rejects it, or vacillates in conflict, she is in trouble." The female role in this, and most other societies, is less exciting and fulfilling than the male role (in a series of public opinion polls it was found that about four times more women wish they were men than men wish to be women).

There is an additional complication in developing the sex role as part of the personality. At one time in this society, as the saying goes, "men were men" and did the kind of work women were unsuited for. Times are changing, however, and as D. G. Brown observed, "One of the more significant psychosocial developments of contemporary American society would appear to be the relatively fluid state of the sex roles of individuals. Within a single generation, significant changes have taken place in the traditional conceptions of what is masculine and what is feminine." Every culture establishes acceptable and unacceptable patterns of behavior and psychological standards for the sexes, and sex-role standards are taught at a very early age.

Traditionally, male dominance is one of the earliest bases of discrimination among human beings. In ancient and primitive societies the prestige of the work determined whether tasks would be assigned to males or females. The historical valuing of male children has long existed and, despite their number, women have been treated as if they were members of a minority group. In fact, there are a great many parallels between the treatment of women and the treatment of Negroes in American society. In much the same way, sex-role social barriers resemble social-class barriers to participation.

Males will grow to discover that the society has defined their vocational role as primary and their role as father and husband as secondary; the reverse is true for women. To fulfill these socially designated roles, boys are reared to achieve while girls are raised to conform. Few of these lessons are begun in infancy, but almost all societies foster achievement and self-reliance in boys and obedience, nurturance, and responsibility in girls when they enter early childhood.

One boy, questioned in a study by Ruth E. Hartley as to what boys have to know and should be able to do, answered: "They should know what girls don't know—how to climb, how to make a fire, how to carry things; they should have more ability than girls; they need to know how to

stay out of trouble; they need to know arithmetic and spelling more than girls do."

Boys think men are very important and able to do whatever they like. Men are the boss, they have the most money, they get the most comfortable chair in the house, and they get angry a lot. Men also are described as being more fun than mothers and are thought to have better ideas.

These observations of male and female behavior and beliefs in early childhood are buttressed by the theoretical system outlined by Sigmund Freud, who was a man. An important feature of Freudian theory is his view of the part psychosexual development plays in the life of the growing child. For Freud, development progresses through a series of stages (oral, anal, phallic) that are characterized by unique psychological, biological, and social events. Each stage makes its imprint on the child's personality and contributes to the success or failure of his encounter with the stages to follow. Personality development in the years roughly from three through six is focused on the phallic stage, in which the rudiments of eventual mature, adult sexuality are practiced. The child must practice the sex role assigned to him by the society if he or she is to be prepared for full sexual participation in the culture.

Freud conceived of these psychosexual stages as fixed sequences in development, but this rather rigid view of the nature of man has been modified by a number of theorists who have since stressed the vital contribution of the role of the ego or self to personality development.

Figure 13.5. Some girls reject the female role and become tomboys.

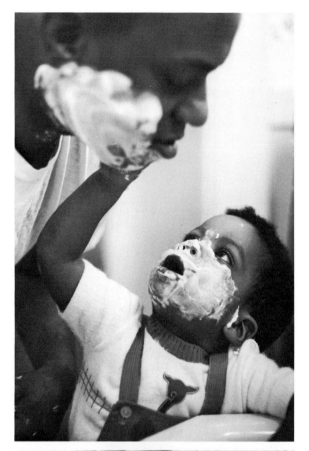

In fact, Freudian theory suggests that the father is the critical model in teaching masculine behavior to the sons while the mother plays a dominant role in teaching femininity to the daughters. Miriam Johnson, however, makes a theoretical case for expanding this conception along a series of dimensions. She insists that it is likely that fathers play a crucial role in the sex-role development of both sons and daughters. She points out that personality development in the child involves making a series of successive identifications and that, following the initial identification of both children with the mother, the girl learns a reciprocal role relationship with the father; that is, in order to learn the dance of life, she uses her father as a model of the partner in the dance.

The development of the sexual part of personality is, again, a vital but incompletely understood part of total development. Like aggression and independence, the outcome of mastering sex roles will forge an important part of adult personality.

Parent-Child Relationships

The nature of parent-child relationships during early childhood is an important determinant of personality development. Family structure may vary from autocratic to democratic and reflect a number of mixes and subdivisions within each category. Thus, equally democratic families may differ in the degree to which each is accepting of children, indulgent of them, overtly affectionate toward them, or protective of them. And, as

Figure 13.6. The acquisition of traditional sex roles starts early.

McNeil indicates, "The relationship between parent and child is not the only factor influencing the pattern of the family. Most American families include other siblings, and at least a few relatives, who are more or less on the periphery of the nuclear family. The number of siblings, their ages and birth order, and the possible influence of the relatives all help determine the pattern of the family, its socialization practices, and consequently, the personalities of the children."

There are a variety of socialization agents that contribute to personality development (school, play, peer groups, and the like), but the family has earliest access to the child and leaves the most indelible mark on his personality. Unfortunately, the family unit has been the single influence most resistant to scientific study. Families differ in terms of parental attitudes toward children, the parental background, the personal characteristics of the parents, the composition of the family (for example, number of parents, number and sex of siblings), the family setting, the behavior of the child, and the overt parental patterns of behavior.

Every child, for example, experiences life differently depending on the age, number, and sex of his or her siblings. And one or more parents may be temporarily or permanently absent from the home at various times in the child's life. The child's ordinal position (order of birth) can influence his experience, and in the same fashion, the spacing between siblings will influence what and when the child learns about life. Think for a moment of all the families with whom you are currently acquainted. It is almost certain that not one of them is an exact duplicate of your own family. Thus, the term *family* refers to a common, yet always unique, experience in growing up.

It is also true that the developing child acquires certain personal characteristics that are in themselves an influence on the behavioral patterns of

the family. At birth or shortly thereafter the child behaves in such a way that he must be responded to and reckoned with by other members of the family. The study of family influence might better be particularized, then, as the study of one-child families, aging families, families with twins, educated families, minority-group families, and the like rather than in terms of an idealized model of the mythical family.

The family must be viewed as a dynamic, shifting, changing, developing entity to which each parent brings a personal set of values, beliefs, prejudices, convictions, hopes, and fears. They are human parents with human limitations, and they are raising children who have needs that may not match those of their parents. It is in this dynamic interaction that personality is fashioned.

There are some vital characteristics of the family setting that must be discussed. Among them are social-class and racial status. It is not possible to speak coherently about personality development without reference to these important cultural subdivisions of our society.

Social Class

Theoretically, a division of social classes into three categories—upper, middle, and lower—can be further subdivided by splitting each class into upper and lower halves. In practice this refinement is untrustworthy because such fine slices differ from community to community, with the percentage of population in each varying substantially. New communities, for example, do not possess the rigid class structures present in older, long-established communities. Still, the social status into which a child is born determines in a substantial way the kind of developmental experiences he will encounter while he is growing up.

The values, child-rearing methods, and life styles of families in the various classes differ, as may their religious affiliations, the number of children the mother will bear, the financial security the family will have, the schools the child will attend, and the associates he will encounter. As M. L. Kahn so ably puts it, "Members of different social classes, by virtue of enjoying (or suffering) different conditions of life, come to see the world differently—to develop different conceptions of social reality, different aspirations and hopes and fears, different conceptions of the desirable . . ." What adults consider desirable, probable, and possible in life will determine the qualities that are instilled in their children. Of all the qualities parents agree a child should have, some will be emphasized to the neglect of others in one social class, and the reverse may be underscored in another social class; for example, lower-class parents may value overt conformity to the prescriptions and proscriptions of society at the same moment that middle-class parents stress the development of self-direction in children. These lessons may be taught casually and with little pressure in one social class but intensely and under close guard in the next social class.

Simply being poor plays an important part in personality development. Being poor impresses it-

self on a child's self-image, may orient him to the present rather than to the future, and may teach him a fatalistic view of life and what can be expected from it. The lower-class child, for example, may have little success in meeting the social demands of his middle-class friends and, if he makes the attempt at all, he will probably be rebuffed and cease to put forth effort to improve his status. It has been said that for many of the modern poor there is no way out or up. Enterprise and hard work seem no longer to suffice in a complicated, technological society.

Now, suppose that in addition to being poor and living in substandard housing, the color of the child's skin is black. He most likely will live surrounded by fellow blacks, who will be similarly deprived and lack exactly what he lacks. He can see, visit, and pass through the white-dominated parts of society, but he cannot share their affluence, possess their privileges, aspire to their goals, or even hope for what they take for granted. The forces that will have an impact on his personality development will be so distinct and so different that they will be totally alien from the forces that impinge on his white middle-class counterparts. A vital part of his self-image will be fashioned by experiences with discrimination and prejudice, and he will be judged not as a person but as a faceless member of a racial group. He will have attributed to him (and will be told he possesses) those characteristics others believe are built into him genetically because of his race. In combination, poverty and minority racial membership will set severe limits on self-development and decrease his chances of becoming what he, as a unique human being, may deem himself to be capable of.

While his black parents will share the value system of the white majority, the teaching practices they will employ will not be the same. The black child may be taught by his mother to be liked, to obey authority, and to conform to social rules even if these lessons will keep him from acquiring a unique personality as a free human being. And when this child ventures into the outside world, he will hear from his black peers a contradictory view about the way it really is and the kind of person he should become. If there is a personality gap, it must be at its widest between parents and children who are poor and black. When formal education begins, these children will find themselves additionally handicapped and unable to use academic excellence as a means of escape from their condition.

As indicated at the beginning of this chapter, the formation of personality in early childhood amounts to practice with the rudiments of a highly complex lesson. It seems fitting to end this account by indicating the savage limitations of poverty and race that will be encountered by millions of members of American society. The forces that act as limitations and inhibitors of healthy personality development in this society may be greater than the forces that work on behalf of it. Perhaps this problem is the most crucial that our society and the individuals within it have to face.

Figure 13.7. Simply being poor plays an important part in personality development— in self-image and orientation to future goals, among other things.

The two- or three-year-old child is delighted by the game of playing house with another person's face. The game begins with a knock on the door—a gentle rapping with the knuckles on the other person's forehead. The child then peeks into the house by lifting the partner's lightly closed eyelid, rings the bell by pulling on the partner's nose, and walks right into the partner's mouth with his fingers. The child extracts peculiar glee from this game, whether the house is played by the partner or by the child himself. The child's interest in such games is apparently related to the tendency of children at this age to react to other people in much the same way that they react to inanimate objects: the child is likely to be interested in looking at and manipulating the eyes, mouth, and even the limbs of another person. A little later, within the second year of life, his relations with others become more truly social, especially with his peers. Cooperative activity is rare at this age, but much of the interaction between two-year-olds seems to be facilitative; that is, children of this age seem to enjoy social contact for its own sake as well as for what it provides in the way of gaining new toys or other desirable ends. Peer interaction at this point also involves considerable rivalry; fighting, particularly over play materials, is very common.

AGE CHANGES IN PEER RELATIONS

The nature of children's interactions with their peers changes dramatically during the third and subsequent years. Mildred Parten, who worked with nursery-school children in the laboratory schools of the University of Minnesota, showed that, as nursery-school children grow older, they engage in fewer solitary activities, they do less passive watching of other children, and they are less inclined toward isolated play. Over this same period, mature patterns of social behavior increase: Friendly, associative contacts between children occur with increasing frequency, and co-operative behavior also rises.

A recent study showed that social rewards are exchanged more frequently among four-year-olds than they are among three-year-olds; the older children more often offer approval to other children, give affection, and yield to the demands of others. They share tangible objects more than do the three-year-olds. In addition, this study found that there is a kind of social reciprocity in groups of preschool children. A very high correlation exists between the frequency with which a child extends rewards *to* others and the frequency with which he receives similar rewards *from* others.

Numerous other aspects of peer interaction change during this period. Dependent overtures made to peers, such as asking for approval and initiating pleas for help, increase greatly, while dependence on adults declines. This increase in peer dependence appears to be a good indicator of normal development because an easygoing, comfortable reliance on peers has been found to characterize preschool children who are particularly well adjusted.

Expressions of sympathy and offers of help are found more commonly in the social behavior of older preschoolers and elementary-school children

14
Social Development with Peers

than in the interactions of very young preschoolers. Ascendance also increases at this time—children become more positive and assertive in their interactions with each other, and they also become more competitive when performance comparisons with other children are involved. Aggressive activity also increases, but in ways that are sexually differentiated. During this period physical aggression increases more for boys than for girls, while verbal aggression appears to increase somewhat more among girls.

Thus, the character of children's interactions with each other changes a great deal during the preschool and elementary-school years. Children become more socially active, and the quality of interaction with age mates undergoes marked change.

EFFECT OF EARLY PEER RELATIONS ON DEVELOPMENT

Psychologists do not fully understand the role played by early contact with age mates in the child's overall development. Students of primate behavior are generally convinced, both from laboratory studies and from studies conducted in the wild, that early contact with peers performs a unique and necessary function in mammalian development. In fact, it is almost impossible to conceive of socialization in species such as the rhesus monkey or the chimpanzee in the absence of peer interaction.

Only a few, unreliable, reports have been published about human children reared under conditions that allowed absolutely no contact with other children. Because almost all these cases have also been marked by other kinds of deprivation (such as lack of normal contact with parents) and most have involved genetic anomalies of one kind or another, one cannot really isolate the psychological consequences of peer deprivation.

ABSENCE OF PARENTS

One study, completed during World War II, strongly suggests that early contact with peers has a compensatory effect on social development when normal contact with parents or parent surrogates is lacking. This finding supports the results of primate studies. Anna Freud's group intensively studied six Jewish children who had lived closely together after their parents were killed in German concentration camps. This intimate contact with peers had lasted from quite early in infancy until the children were about four years of age, when they were brought to England and placed in an orphanage nursery. Observation of the children established two points: Their reactions to the nursery staff were bizarre—they were hostile, uncommunicative, uncooperative, and unaffectionate toward adults—but their behavior toward one another was remarkable for the degree of affection, helpfulness, and closeness they demonstrated. Indeed, it is remarkable that the horrendous early experiences endured by these children had not produced more devastating effects. The fact that the children were not extremely disturbed suggests that the intimate contacts they had had with age mates served a compensatory

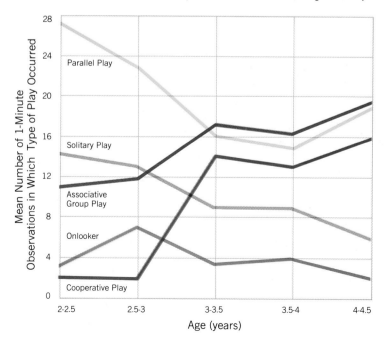

Figure 14.1. Changes in types of play as a function of age. Solitary, onlooker, and parallel play decrease, while associative and cooperative play increase. Sixty one-minute observations were conducted on each child in the study. (After Parten, 1932-1933.)

function for the extreme disruption and hurt that they had suffered.

One cannot extrapolate from the data of a single study to all child-rearing situations. Nevertheless, the suggestion is strong that a child's early contacts with peers contribute in many ways to his socialization. Psychologists know that young children are highly interested in one another and that their behavior toward each other changes in important ways during early childhood. As yet, however, it is not known exactly which features of a young child's behavior derive mainly from peer contact. It is safe to say, though, that these contacts have more than a little to do with producing the behavioral repertoire of the preschool child.

PEER VERSUS ADULT INFLUENCE

Perhaps the issue here is not simply whether young children are influenced in important ways by their peers—this may be taken for granted. Of greater importance is the recognition that influences occur *in conjunction* with adult influences. That is, for most children peer influences are added to adult influences and in this way have their principal effect on a child's behavior. It is true that interaction with peers modifies or moderates the effects of the child's experiences with adults, but most often both these influences operate to reinforce one another.

Although adults are undoubtedly the most significant social influence on the behavior of infants and very young children, development after babyhood should not be regarded as entirely adult dominated. For most children, more-or-less regular contact with peers occurs by the end of the second year. If other children influence the child in any way at this time, then their contribution to socialization must be regarded as significant and vital. For this discussion it is more important to know *how* a young child is influenced by his age mates than to know exactly *what* it is that he is learning from them.

PEER REINFORCEMENT

One important way in which children influence each other is through actions that serve as *reinforcers* (actions or events that affect the probability of a given response occurring subsequently). Social behaviors that carry reinforcing value include approval, affection, attention, and tangible rewards. Such behaviors do not function as reinforcers in every circumstance, and there are many other social acts that have reinforcing potential. Also, it is obvious that the types of events reinforcing one form of activity (aggression, for example) differ from those that reinforce other forms (such as sharing behavior). And because of personality differences, one child may be responsive to behaviors that have little or no effect on another child. Nevertheless, many actions—such as praise and affection—act as reinforcers for nearly everyone in a wide variety of situations.

IN NURSERY SCHOOLS

A recent study by G. R. Patterson, Richard A. Littman, and William Bricker shows how the nursery-school peer group serves to reinforce aggressive activity. These investigators observed two groups of children and recorded reactions to aggression: passivity, crying, assuming a defensive posture, telling the teacher, retrieval of property, or retaliation constituted up to 97 percent of the responses. In other words, a potentially reinforcing peer reaction occurred after nearly every instance of aggressive attack. The data showed that when physical attack was followed by passiveness, crying, or defensiveness, the attacker tended to aggress again relatively soon and toward the original victim. Counteraggression, on the other hand, was associated with subsequent changes in the behavior of the aggressor—he was likely to change his action toward the former victim, pick a different victim, or both. This study clearly points to the peer group as a major force in sustaining or eliminating aggressive activity in young children.

IN THE LABORATORY

The effects of peer reinforcement have been studied in the laboratory as well as in school groups. In the laboratory it is somewhat easier to isolate the factors associated with the potency of a reinforcer than it is in a fast-moving, socially complex place like a nursery school. A recent group of laboratory studies has attempted to isolate some of the factors that affect the impact of praise of one child by another. When one child tells another, "You're doing fine," it facilitates the performance of some children, has little effect on others, and even suppresses the activity of some. Why? The studies discussed in the following paragraphs do not give a neat, thorough answer to

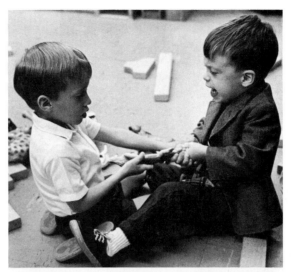

Figure 14.2. Aggression in the schoolroom.

this question, but they have produced some interesting findings.

One factor that influences the effectiveness of peer reinforcement during early childhood is the degree of friendship existing between the subject and the reinforcing agent. In other words, there seems to be a relation between interpersonal attraction and the effectiveness of peer rewards. F. D. Horowitz found, for example, that three-year-old children would pull a lever at a fast rate when they were periodically exposed to the picture of a best friend, at a somewhat lower rate when exposed to photographs of neutral peers, and at the lowest rate of all when a blue light was flashed.

In another study, Willard Hartup found that preschool subjects produce an even faster rate of response in simple tasks when the reinforcing agent is *disliked* than when he is liked. Hartup used a marble-dropping task to assess the capacity of four- and five-year-old children to reinforce their peers. The subject was required to pick up marbles one at a time from a bin and drop them through holes into a container. Verbal approval was periodically administered during this task either by the child's best friend or by a child who was known to be disliked by the subject. Performance in this task, as measured by rate of dropping marbles, was better maintained over a short experimental session when the agent of approval was disliked than when he was liked.

A somewhat similar study was conducted with second- and fifth-graders by S. Tiktin and Hartup. In this instance, approval was dispensed either by generally popular children or by generally unpop-

ular children. The performance of children who were given approval by unpopular peers improved during the session more than did the performance of children praised by popular peers.

Why do unpopular or disliked children have a more enhancing effect on the performance of their peers than do liked or popular children? One hypothesis is that social situations containing some unfamiliar or unexpected element produce the highest work output. This hypothesis is consistent with the foregoing findings and also fits other data. It accords with results from recent experiments that tested problem solving in infants. Some of these experiments are reported in Chapter 6. These infants would work on solving simple problems as long as there was some element of novelty involved. When the baby was successively presented with the identical problem he had already solved, he refused to work on it.

Reinforcement from either markedly younger or older children was found to be more effective than reinforcement received from peers of the subject's own age. Another experiment showed that children who receive unexpectedly large or small amounts in a sharing task change their patterns of sharing more radically over time than do subjects who receive shared rewards at more-or-less expected levels.

IN THE SCHOOLROOM

Other studies of peer reinforcement have shown the effects of directly manipulating the interactions between children in the schoolroom. These studies represent forerunners of therapeutic pro-

Figure 14.3. Some frames from Hicks' film. He showed the film to preschool children and then gave them the same materials to play with. The children who had seen the film reenacted much of the aggression they had seen and in much the same way.

grams in which teachers and therapists could actively use the peer group as an adjunct in remedying problem situations.

In a study conducted by R. G. Wahler, the experimenter observed a group of nursery-school children and then selected five whose behavior was tied in some way to reinforcement emanating from their peers. Some of these children seemed to show a high rate of response associated with peer reinforcement. For this group the experimenter took aside a small number of the child's friends and asked them to help him by decreasing the regularity with which they paid attention to the child when he was behaving in a certain way. The other children in the group of five showed a particularly low rate of responding associated with attention and approval from peers, so for this group, the intervention consisted of asking the child's peers to increase the regularity of reinforcement. Within a few days, observation of the first group of children showed a drop in the frequency of the selected behavior, while records for the second group showed an increase. After the experimenter told the children's friends to treat them as they had before the experiment began, observation showed that the children's behavior returned to its original frequency.

A broad variety of studies clearly demonstrates that young children are responsive to reinforcement emanating from their peers; reinforcement control by peers is characteristic of children by at least the age of three. None of the findings indicates that the peer group uses its power at this early age to systematically subvert or contravene the objectives of parents and teachers. If anything, the contrary prevails. The Wahler study is particularly interesting because it suggests that teachers and parents may be able actively to enlist the aid of a young child's peers in modifying his behavior toward socially approved ends.

PEER MODELING

Peers also influence the behavior of young children through modeling, or imitation.

ANTISOCIAL MODELING

In a recent experiment, D. J. Hicks showed a group of preschool children a film in which a child behaved aggressively toward a large rubber doll. The child in the film struck the doll with a mallet, sat on it, and screamed at it. When the children who had seen the film were given the same kind of doll and mallet, they proceeded to enact many of the same aggressive behaviors. Although very little of the aggressive modeling was noticeable when the children were again tested with the play materials six months later, these results do show that at least the short-term impact of peer models on aggressiveness of young children is a decided one. And modeling not only can enhance the general level of the child's aggression but can influence the specific ways in which he displays aggression.

PROSOCIAL MODELING

Peer models can also influence prosocial behavior. Hartup and B. Coates designed a situation in which four- and five-year-old children were asked

to watch one of their classmates complete a series of ten maze-drawing problems. Between problems the model received a supply of tiny plastic trinkets, which he divided between himself and a mythical child "from another class at school." The model was actually the experimenter's confederate and had been coached to give away most of the trinkets to the "other child." The model came through as being highly altruistic. After the model had left the room the other children were asked to complete the same maze-drawing task. They also received trinkets and were given an opportunity to divide them with "the other child" in whatever way they wished. A control group of children, who had not seen the model, were given the same task, trinkets, and instructions. The children who had watched the altruistic model gave away many more of their trinkets than did the control-group children. Thus, there is straightforward evidence that a socially approved activity like sharing is under the influence of peer models by the time a child reaches four or five years of age.

Other investigators, working with children in the early grades of elementary school, have shown that peer models exert a potent influence on (1) problem-solving behavior in simple discrimination tasks; (2) patterns of self-reward in situations permitting the child to determine for himself how much he thinks he deserves for performing well; and (3) the tendency to resist temptation in situations where cheating could easily occur. Thus, in a variety of important behavioral areas, all related to the child's acquisition of accepted

social values, peer models clearly exert observable influences at very early ages.

CHOICE OF MODELS

Some peer models are more effective than others. B. S. Clark found that a peer who is perceived as successful is more effective as a model than a child whose success is indeterminate. Her subjects in a discrimination task were more likely to copy the solutions of a model they saw rewarded than one that was not rewarded.

In the Hartup and Coates study, two factors seemed to affect the tendency to copy the model's actions: the nature of the subject's previous interaction with the model himself and the nature of his interactions with the nursery-school peer group as a whole. It was found, for example, that children who usually received high levels of positive feedback in the nursery school (in the form of attention and approval from other children) more often imitated a child who had actually supplied some of this reward than one with whom no positive interaction had ever taken place. On the other hand, those children who ordinarily had little positive peer interaction in the nursery school seemed to imitate more readily a nonrewarding child than a rewarding one. These findings are depicted in Figure 14.4.

There are many other factors that affect the child's susceptibility to peer modeling. Psychologists know, for example, that the perceived competence of the model is related to amount of peer imitation. Also, children more readily imitate peer models who resemble themselves than mod-

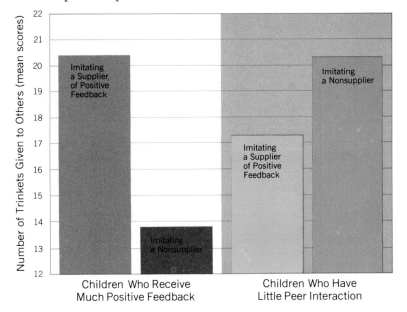

Figure 14.4. Whether children imitate a model or not depends on the interrelated factors of (1) the child's usual level of interaction with his peers, and (2) his relation with the particular model. In this study children watched models giving away many trinkets, then they were given the opportunity to distribute trinkets. The more they distributed, the greater the effect the model had had. (After Hartup and Coates, 1967.)

els who do not. With young children, however, much remains to be understood concerning the manner in which the child's social experience bears on his responsiveness to peers as models.

Peer Influences on Conformity

Young children are not particularly sensitive to normative influences from peer groups. Young children's groups do not generate the elaborate network of standards, rules, and shared interests that obtains in older children's groups. Preschoolers respond to rules laid down by others, but the rules have to be forcefully exerted from an external source. Jean Piaget referred to the preschool period as one of social egocentrism; lack of responsiveness to normative influence from peers is consistent with such a concept. During this period, the child responds to the influences of other children by direct reinforcement or modeling, but the sharing norm is not extensive.

Rudimentary self-generated norms are not totally absent in young children's groups, however. Primitive norms, in the form of spontaneous, loosely shared values, are clearly evident in some groups. H. Faigin, for example, found that two-year-olds reared in Israeli kibbutzim had already formed a clear "we-they" distinction; members of one nursery group defended one another in quarrels with outgroup children, and different groups seemed to share different patterns of interests. Similarly, it is not uncommon to note within American preschool classes that some enclaves share certain interests and some share others. There are groups who play "cowboys" and groups

who play "house." Shared interests and other simple traditions, such as ceremonies of greeting and conventions for seating during snack time, can be readily observed in young children's groups.

Research shows that direct conformity to the opinions and judgments of other children is not very common among four- and five-year-old children. In conformity tasks, such as taking turns in making comparisons between lines that differ slightly in length, false judgments from the experimenter's confederates have little effect on children between the ages of four and seven. There is an increase in conformity to false peer judgments during middle childhood and then a decline during adolescence. A study by P. R. Costanzo and M. E. Shaw, the results of which are summarized in Figure 14.5, shows these age changes in peer-induced conformity. As can be seen, middle childhood is the period of maximum sensitivity to normative influence from peers. It can reasonably be argued, as Piaget did, that the lack of conformity among preschool children is a further reflection of an egocentric social orientation.

In sum, preschool children's groups display loose, relatively uncomplicated norms in the form of shared standards and conventions, but direct person-to-person conformity is not very common until the elementary-school years.

The Child's Status in the Group

Although the groups formed by preschoolers are relatively loosely knit, their enclaves possess many of the formal properties of older children's groups. It has already been shown that at least

primitive norms are operative; another way in which preschool groups and groups of older children resemble each other is that they are all *structured*. Both observation and direct questioning of the children support the conclusion that all groups, regardless of age, possess a hierarchy and a structure. That is, some children seem to be popular, to have great capacity to influence and direct the behavior of other children, and to wield great amounts of what can only be called social power. Others seem less popular and less successful in influencing the activities of the group.

SOCIOMETRY

A number of techniques have been developed for studying these group structures. The general name for all of them is *sociometry*. With pre-schoolers, the most reliable and direct method of this kind is the picture sociometric. It involves showing the child photographs of each of his classmates and asking him to name the child in each picture and to pick out those children he likes best or likes least. The responses of four- and five-year-old children who are asked to name best-liked children are moderately stable over intervals of several weeks. Some investigators have even reported high stability over several months.

Rejection choices, on the other hand, are not very stable across time. Young children are unlikely to name the same child as disliked on two separate occasions. This fluctuation may be because rejection is associated with such socially disapproved behavior as aggressiveness, which itself fluctuates because it is reinforced erratically in most peer groups. Being liked is associated with such positive characteristics as friendliness and reinforcement of others, traits that are not likely to be subject to erratic pressures for change. Thus, there is a plausible reason why positive sociometric evaluations during the preschool years are more stable than negative ones. A sociogram showing positive choices in a group of young children is shown in Figure 14.7.

POPULAR CHILDREN

The correlates of sociometric status have been studied extensively in both preschool and elementary-school children. The traits that characterize the popular young child do not differ much from the traits that characterize his older counterpart. Popular children of any age are more friendly, outgoing, and sociable in their interactions with both peers and adults. They also appear to be well socialized, in the sense that they seem successfully on the road to the acquisition of core-culture values. They are, for example, more compliant with classroom routines and more altruistic, and they positively reinforce other children more frequently than do less popular children. This behavior does not mean that the popular young child is an overly sensitive, compulsive do-gooder; on the contrary, he seems to be comfortably in possession of socially acceptable values, and there is a kind of give-and-take in his interactions with other children. In other words, the popular child is a kind of mediator in his group; he is not constricted and prone to conformity.

Popular children are likely to display certain

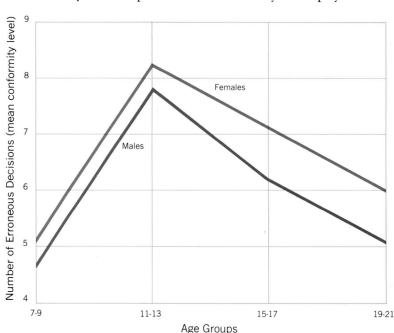

Figure 14.5. Children in the various age groups shown were asked to decide which of two lines was longest directly after the experimenter's confederate had made an erroneous judgment. There were sixteen pairs of lines. The mean conformity level in making these decisions is shown as a function of age. (After Costanzo and Shaw, 1966.)

Sociogram of a fifth grade—January

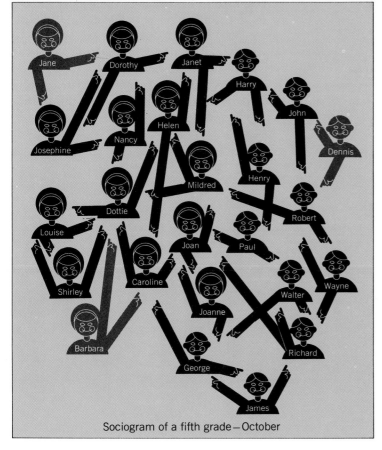

Sociogram of a fifth grade—October

Figure 14.6. Popularity and unpopularity are two quite different aspects of social choice; they are not opposite sides of the same coin.

Figure 14.7. The social structure of one classroom at two different times. Data were obtained by asking each pupil in the classroom to make first, second, and third choices among his classmates for a particular social activity.

kinds of dependency on their peers. This dependency is likely to be of a mature form, such as seeking help or approval for accomplishing something, rather than of an immature kind, such as clinging and affection seeking.

Although popular children are outgoing and friendly, unpopular children are not necessarily the opposite—that is, withdrawn and unfriendly. In fact, research shows that there is little relation between being rejected by the peer group and the child's degree of sociability.

UNPOPULAR CHILDREN

Children whose aggression is reality oriented and direct—for example, those who retaliate in a no-nonsense fashion when threatened—appear to be more popular than children whose aggression is attenuated and indirect. However, such aggressive acts as disrupting the activities of other children, disapproval of them, and unprovoked physical attack are major factors in being disliked. Aggression of this kind does not mean that a child will never be chosen as a best friend, but it does mean that he is likely to be frequently chosen as "someone that I don't like very well." This sounds paradoxical but it is not. Being liked and being disliked are two quite different aspects of social choice; they are not opposite sides of coin.

OTHER PERSONALITY FACTORS

Personality adjustment, intelligence, and social class begin to play a role in determining the child's sociometric status during the early elementary-school years. Many studies have shown that

popular children are brighter than unpopular children. Research with gifted children indicates that they generally occupy higher-status positions in their peer groups than do less gifted children; it has also been shown that mentally retarded children are seldom highly popular in mixed groups. Even in groups that do not include such exceptional cases, there appears to be a relation between IQ and popularity. Merrill Roff and S. B. Sells, for example, compared the IQs of popular and unpopular children in children's groups that had first been broken down according to socioeconomic class. In each of four social-class groups it was found that popular children were significantly brighter than the unpopular children—in some instances the mean IQ difference was as much as twenty points. (See Figure 14.8.)

Research with grade-school children also implicates social class as a factor in popularity. Regardless of the IQ of the children involved, there is a positive correlation between the social-class background of the child's family and his popularity. Children whose fathers hold prestigious jobs are more popular than children of fathers who have less desirable occupations.

Additional factors that differentiate the popular and unpopular grade-school youngster include academic performance, skill in such activities as sports and certain crafts, strength, and physical appearance. Strength and physical appearance, however, are of greatest significance to the child's popularity during adolescence.

Self-concept and self-esteem are related to popularity, although research shows that this relation

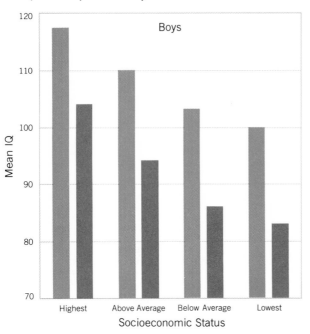

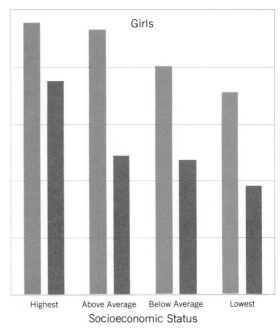

is not a simple, straightforward one. H. W. Reese found that children whose self-concepts were moderately positive—neither extremely high nor extremely low—were more popular with their peers than were children with very high or very low self-esteem. Children in the latter two groups are probably less popular for different reasons, although developmental psychologists are not sure about this. In all probability, the child who thinks poorly of himself does, in fact, have some undesirable characteristics that would account for his lack of popularity: he may be less bright, less successful in the classroom, more anxious, and so forth. It is more difficult to explain why a child who has a very high opinion of himself should be relatively unpopular. Possibly he may be rejected because he puts off his peers through overconfident attitudes. There is also the possibility, however, that among children with very high self-esteem are some who actually dislike their self-images and defensively disguise their feelings on research questionnaires and to their peers.

In thinking about all of the factors that are related to peer-group status in early childhood, one must recognize that the data presented here show only that there is a correlation between these traits and the manner in which the child is evaluated by his peers. These correlations have several possible interpretations. One might conclude that young children who are not gregarious and who are socially anxious are evaluated negatively by their peers for these very reasons. It could also be surmised, however, that the negative evaluations by peers produce increased with-

drawal, hostility toward peers, and insecurity. It is just as reasonable to think that peer disapproval reduces friendliness as to think that a lack of friendliness causes low peer evaluation.

The same is true of success experiences. Success at tasks valued by the peer group may enhance popularity. But, clearly, popular children have more frequent opportunities to be involved in success experiences (both in school and in the neighborhood) than do less popular children. Of course, it is also possible that a third factor—for example, physical attractiveness—may cause *both* success, by influencing others, and popularity.

The question being raised here is not of the chicken-and-egg variety. Rather, the problem consists of properly understanding the relationships existing between personal characteristics and popularity that have been found in research. In all probability, these relationships are reciprocal. Research does not show this reciprocity explicitly, but the logic of this argument is compelling: it is only reasonable to conclude that friendliness and attractiveness breed social success while, at the same time, social success enhances friendliness and attractiveness. Failure to recognize the reciprocity underlying findings concerning popularity could lead to very bumbling efforts by parents or teachers in their work with children.

SOCIALIZATION IN HOME AND SCHOOL

Research concerning the family experiences of children who are particularly successful in peer relations has been conducted mainly with children of elementary-school age. This research pre-

Figure 14.8. The relation between popularity and IQ. Generally, the higher the socioeconomic class and the higher the IQ, the better the chance for the child to be chosen as popular by his classmates. (After Roff and Sells, 1965.)

sents quite a consistent picture, although psychologists are presently able to say more about the development of boys' peer relations than they can about those involving girls. In an extensive study of the family antecedents of peer relations in boys, C. L. Winder and L. Rau found that (1) both the mothers and fathers of likable boys placed few demands for aggression upon their sons and infrequently used aggressive punishment with their children; (2) the mothers of likable boys seldom used deprivation of privileges as discipline, and were themselves confident and well adjusted; and (3) the fathers of likable boys, in addition to encouraging nonaggressive behaviors, indicated considerable satisfaction with their sons. This study shows that the distinctive aspects of the high-status boy's family experience include being discouraged in aggressiveness, being subjected infrequently to frustration and punishment, and receiving considerable supportive reinforcement. Parental warmth has also been shown to be important in the development of girls' peer relations, but this relation is presently most clearly established in the case of boys.

EFFECTS OF FATHER CONTACT

Boys who grow up with little father contact (because of either permanent or prolonged absence of the father from the home) have more difficulty in peer relations than do boys who live in homes in which the father is present. Indeed, recent research suggests that contact with the father during the first four years of life is particularly critical to the boy's peer relations during later childhood.

E. M. Hetherington found that when fathers leave the home permanently before the boy reaches his fourth birthday, the effects on his peer relations are significantly more pervasive than when the absence occurs later. Early father absence is associated with more passivity, less masculine play interests, and more solitary recreational interests than occur with boys from intact families or where the father's absence begins later. In fact, it appears that absence occurring after the boy is six years of age produces no detectable impact on his peer relations—at least as compared with behavior of boys whose fathers remain at home throughout all of childhood.

EFFECTS OF NURSERY SCHOOL

Much has been written concerning the effects of nursery-school experience on peer relations in early childhood. There is little question that peer adjustment improves from the beginning of such an experience to the end of it. Children are more effective in relating to each other after a year of organized social contacts than they are at the beginning. Developmentalists are not entirely certain, however, what impact early schooling has on the child's social development. Some studies, comparing school and nonschool groups, seem to show this impact, but the research comparisons have been faulty for one reason or another. For example, it has been difficult for researchers to obtain comparison groups whose parents *want* their children to go to nursery school but who, for reasons beyond their control, were unable to manage it. Also, developmental psychologists are not

certain that early gains in self-esteem, social skills, and peer status persist once a nursery-school child is placed in a kindergarten or first-grade class.

It seems reasonable that a nursery-school program fostering social play, effective techniques for social interaction, and positive feelings toward one's self should add to the child's total social adjustment. There is certainly no evidence to show that such experiences interfere in any way with later development. But for now, the evidence does not show that nursery schooling definitely improves later peer relations. Most parents whose children attend good nursery schools are enthusiastic in their support of early schooling and, in part, this enthusiasm derives from a belief that such schooling helps social development.

Preschool Social Life

No one who observes preschool children for any length of time can fail to appreciate the fact that they enjoy a rich and varied social life. There is a clear organization to be found in young children's groups, and there is considerable stability in their group life. There is much regularity in the factors that govern friendships and that govern the responsiveness of each child to peer influences.

Many of the differences in group behavior between the years of early and later childhood consist of differences in degree rather than in kind. Young children's groups possess norms, they possess structures, and there is a relatively clear basis for their organization. It is true that there is a looseness and an egocentric quality to young children's social interactions, but these characteristics are lost by the end of grammar school. Preschool children talk about their friends and perceive themselves as members of a peer culture, just as older children do. The intensity of this orientation may not be as great as it will be in later childhood and adolescence, but developmental psychology shows clearly that relations with peers begin as soon as real live peers are available and that the peer group can be a strong force in children's socialization from infancy onward.

Figure 14.9. Although developmentalists are not certain what impact nursery school has on a child's subsequent social development, most parents whose children attend good nursery schools are enthusiastic in their support.

Freud called the years of childhood the latent period, in which psychosexual energy lay dormant, in wait for the opportunity of phallic, heterosexual expression in adolescence and, later, in adulthood. Perhaps the childhood years are quiet sexually (although modern America seems to deviate from Freud's nineteenth-century Vienna in even this respect), but the child is certainly not dormant intellectually, socially, or emotionally. His entire cognitive structure evolves and stabilizes; the child develops new and more realistic ways to categorize his world, to operate in it competently, and to perceive its parts and the logical and causal relations that occur among them. Friendships and patterns of social behavior that will last even into old age are laid down in these years. School becomes a rewarding, useful experience, a tedious drudgery, or a meaningless task, to be merely endured or avoided at all costs. A sense of right and wrong evolves; and emotions either come increasingly under control or beat the child into illness. These are the years in which the child builds the intellectual, social, moral, and emotional superstructure that must all too soon support his meeting the challenge of adulthood.

Unit V
Growing Up: Later Childhood

It may seem peculiar to admit that little is known about some kinds of thinking because the one thing that all of us have studied all of our lives is our own thinking. But in a scientific sense, thought has been relatively little studied because the thoughts of one individual are not ordinarily available for inspection by another. Science is based on accessible information; inaccessible thought poses a very difficult scientific problem. Great credit is thus due to the few psychologists who, with courage and hard work, have begun to unravel the complicated web of thinking into processes that can be studied.

As stated in Chapter 11, the materials of thought are called *cognitive units*: the images, symbols, concepts, and rules. The *cognitive processes* are the operations or routines that the mind performs on these units. The processes include the encoding of information, the storing and retrieving of information from memory, the generation of hypotheses, their evaluation according to criteria, and deductive and inductive reasoning. Out of the interaction of these processes with these units there somehow emerges intelligent thought.

There are two philosophical attitudes toward thinking. One view assumes there is a psychological executive continually monitoring the cognitive processes, much as an architect supervises the construction of a house. The wood, nails, lights, pipe, and paint are the units; the hammering, wiring, plumbing, and painting are the routines. An alternative view assumes that the monitoring function is contained within the units and processes themselves. The actions in a chemical beaker provide a good analogy. The interaction of the chemical units hydrochloric acid and sodium hydroxide, facilitated by the process of ionization, produces the two products salt and water. There is no necessity for a force watching over this process to guarantee that the units combine in the proper way because the reaction is inherent in the nature of these chemicals. In general, American psychologists have been friendly to the second view, which regards thinking as a more-or-less mechanical interaction of basic psychological structures. The Europeans, especially Jean Piaget, assume, using the first view, that higher-order mental structures organize thought and keep it adaptive, coordinated, and efficient. This view has a strong intuitive appeal. The mind of a ten-year-old is stocked with hundreds of thousands of pieces of information; yet its awesome efficiency can quickly select the correct segment of knowledge and precise routine when asked questions like "How are a bird and a fly alike?" or "How many inches in four yards?"

The material in this chapter does not require commitment to either position. After discussing cognitive units and processes, intelligence as seen both by Piaget and by American psychometrists will be considered.

THE UNITS IN THOUGHT

The units of thinking consist primarily of images, symbols, concepts, and rules. Mental units are not actual things with substance, size, shape, or a definite location. A mental unit is, like tempera-

15
Intellectual Functioning in Childhood

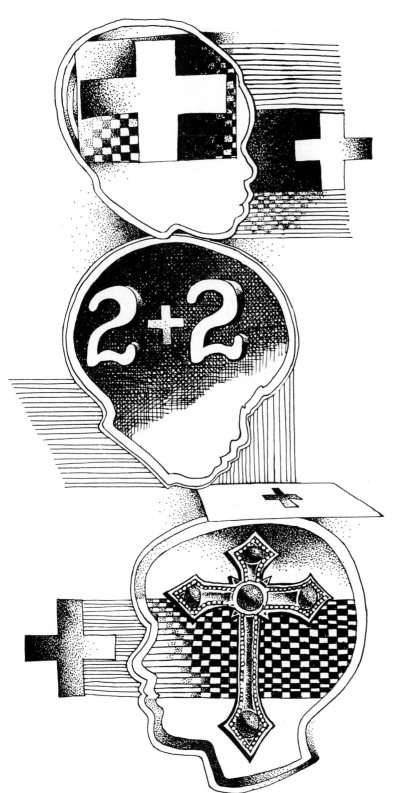

ture or gravity, an abstract potential entity that provides the child with the ability to make sense of experience, to aid remembering of past events, and to generate solutions to problems.

Images, the first mental unit to develop, and symbols, names for things and qualities, have been discussed in Chapter 11.

CONCEPTS

All concepts are symbols, but they are much more than that: they represent a set of common attributes among a group of symbols or images. The concept extracts a common meaning from a diverse array of experiences, whereas a symbol is only the name assigned to a particular class of events. Consider a drawing of a cross (+). The eight-month-old represents this event as an image. The three-year-old names it a cross or a plus sign and represents it as a *symbol*. An adolescent may regard it as a Christian cross and think of it in relation to religion and the church. In this case, the cross stands as a *concept*.

A concept represents a characteristic that belongs to different events; it is the mind's way of extracting some common traits from a variety of experiences. Take "religion" as a concept; there is no single thing called religion but rather many events that have, as one of their characteristics, a reference to God and church. Religion is the conceptual name given to that dimension.

RULES

A rule can function in one of two ways. Some rules state a relation between the dimensions of

Figure 15.1. The difference between images, symbols, and concepts can be illustrated by showing what two crossed lines (+) may mean to youngsters at various ages. *(top)* The 8-month-old represents this event as an image; the size and shape of the form and the relations of the parts to each other are what are impressed upon him. *(middle)* The 3-year-old, who names it a cross or a plus sign, represents it as a symbol. *(bottom)* An adolescent may think of the crossed lines as a Christian cross, related to religion and the church. For the adolescent, the cross then stands as a concept.

two or more concepts. Consider the simple rule "Candy is sweet," which states a relation between the two concepts candy and sweet: candy has many qualities, one of which is sweetness. Sweetness is a quality of many objects, one of which is candy. Therefore, candy implies sweetness, and vice versa.

A rule can also state a routine function that is imposed on concepts to produce a new concept. Multiplication, for example, is a rule imposed on two numbers to yield a new concept.

There is another division of rules into *informal* and *formal*. Informal rules refer to imperfect relations between two or more dimensions. "Candy is sweet" is an informal rule because occasionally one finds a candy that is sour. Most of a child's beliefs are informal rules. "Snakes are dangerous," "Water is wet," and "Men are tall" are all informal rules that describe the dimension shared by the concepts snake and danger, water and wet, man and tall.

Formal rules state a relation between dimensions that is always true and specifiable. The rules of mathematics and physics are the best examples. The formal rule $6 \times 11 = 66$ states a fixed relation between the concepts 6 and 11 when the routine of multiplication is imposed on them. Similarly, the formal rule that the weight of a piece of clay does not change despite alterations in its external shape states a fixed relation between the quantity of an object before and after a change in its appearance.

The images, symbols, concepts, and rules are the building blocks of cognitive activity. Al-

Figure 15.2. A collage representing formal rules—a relation between dimensions that is always true and specifiable (e.g., 6 x 11 = 66) —and informal rules—(e.g., men are tall).

though they are separated here in order to try to define each individually, they do not exist alone but rather in the intricate and usually changing webs of directed or undirected thought that psychologists refer to as the cognitive processes.

The Cognitive Processes

Cognitive processes include two very general types—undirected and directed. *Undirected thinking* refers to free associations, dreams, or reveries and includes the free-flowing thoughts that occur continually as the child walks home or stares out the window. There has not been much study of this exciting and important type of thought because it is difficult to probe the private, undirected meanderings of a child's mind.

Directed thinking refers to the processes that occur when the child tries to solve a problem—one posed for him by someone else or one he has set for himself. The child assumes that there is a solution to a problem, and he knows when he has arrived at an answer. The problem-solving processes typically involve the following sequence: encoding, memory, generation of ideas, evaluation, deduction, and, under special circumstances, reporting the answer to some other person or writing it down. The way in which children employ these processes changes dramatically from age three to age twelve, when they begin to think like adults. The richness of the child's supply of symbols, concepts, and rules increases, and this change is accompanied by a decreasing tendency to rely on images in problem solving. The child

Figure 15.3. Daydreaming is a kind of nondirected thinking; concentrating on some problem, such as the building of a model, involves directed thinking.

becomes increasingly concerned with the degree of agreement between his concepts and rules and those of other children, he becomes more apprehensive about making mistakes, and his memory improves dramatically.

ENCODING

Encoding, which eventuates in an understanding of the question posed in a problem, is the first process in all problem solving. Encoding involves selective attention to one event in a matrix of events and interpretation of the information provided by that event. The young child has difficulty focusing attention on more than one event at a time. If he tries to listen to or watch many things at once, he becomes confused. An adult can attend to several scenes or sounds with better efficiency because he can construct from his knowledge what might be happening on both channels. He is also more familiar with word sequences and has an easier time making a sensible construction from partial or partially understood sentences.

Children are always spontaneously interpreting information in the environment, but the nature of these interpretations changes with age. The infant and very young child usually translate experience into images; the older child is more likely to use symbols and concepts. As indicated in Chapter 11, each event is defined by its salient elements. The eyes are salient for a face, the legs are salient for an animal; a break in the continuity of a line is salient for a letter of the alphabet. The child regards a break in a line as a more important attribute of a letter of the alphabet than a change in the perspective of the figure. The symbols C and O are different letters, but C and Ͻ are the same letter. E. J. Gibson of Cornell University showed children unusual line designs, like those illustrated in Figure 15.4; the children were first shown one of the designs and were asked to pick out a design from the rest that was exactly like the standard. The children did not notice changes in the perspective of the design, for they would often treat ⊥ as similar to ⊥ , but they would rarely treat ⊥ as similar to ⊥ . The break between the vertical and the horizontal was an important feature of the stimulus. A second important feature was whether the lines were curved or straight, for the child did not regard ⊥ as similar to ⊥ or ⊥ .

The child's selectivity of attention is affected by his expectations of what he might experience. If a child knows what is likely to happen, he can prepare himself better for that event and improve the accuracy of his perception. In one experiment school-age children listened to a man's voice and a woman's voice saying different two-word phrases simultaneously (for example, "dog eat" and "man run"). The voices came from two loudspeakers placed eighteen inches apart. When the child was to report the words spoken by the man's voice, a man's picture was lighted; when he was to report the sentence spoken by the woman's voice, her picture was lighted. On some trials the picture of the face was lighted *before* the voices spoke; on other trials the picture of the face was lighted *after* the voices spoke. The results, reported in

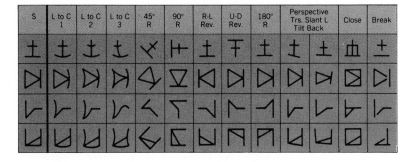

Figure 15.4. Salient features in line designs. Children are asked to pick out a graphic form from each line that matches the sample in the left-hand column. (After Gibson, 1962.)

Figure 15.5, show that the ability to report the words spoken by the indicated voice increased with age, but accuracy at all ages was much better when the children were told which voice to report before rather than after the voices spoke.

MEMORY FUNCTIONS

Memory has at least two functions: the storage of experience for a period and the retrieval of that information at a later time. For many years psychologists thought that all perceived events were registered in memory with equal strength. Thus, if a person could not remember something, the fault lay with his inability to recall it rather than with its initial poor registration. It now appears that one must distinguish between two memory processes—short-term memory and long-term memory. Short-term memory refers to an input that is available for a maximum of thirty seconds but typically for a much shorter period of time. Without a special effort to transfer information from short-term to long-term memory, it may be lost forever. Psychologists usually measure how much a child can remember either by asking him to *recall* what he saw or heard or by asking him to *recognize* it. When he recalls an event, he must retrieve all the necessary information; he is given no hints. When he is asked to recognize an event, he is presented with familiar and unfamiliar information and must select only that which seems familiar. An essay question requires recall; a multiple-choice question involves recognition. Children and adults perform much better when they have to recognize a familiar event than when they

have to recall it. But the difference is more dramatic in young children than in older ones. If a five-year-old is shown twelve pictures and is asked either to recall or to recognize them, he will recall four but will recognize all twelve. His recall is much poorer than his recognition.

There are several reasons why the child's recall is weaker than that of the adolescent or adult. First, young children have a less adequate set of cognitive units with which to label incoming information. Images, symbols, and concepts are the raw material of thinking. The naming of an event holds it in memory longer because that act requires increased attention to the event. It also facilitates rehearsal, the second aspect differentiating the young child from the adult: the child has not learned—or does not wish to use—the trick of rehearsal. He does not spontaneously repeat events to himself in order to aid their storage, nor does he self-consciously try to retain material; it may not occur to him that this trick has any value. He may not have learned that remembering things can be valuable.

Differences in the functioning of memory exist between adults, too, and within an individual, depending on the circumstances under which he is attending or trying to recall. Memory, which is continually reorganizing segments of knowledge into a more meaningful system, is the most elusive, yet one of the most central processes in thought. Its capacity for holding information is enormous, but it is fragile and vulnerable to slight interference. It is powerful, yet easily disturbed by anxiety, distraction, and fatigue. Anxiety influ-

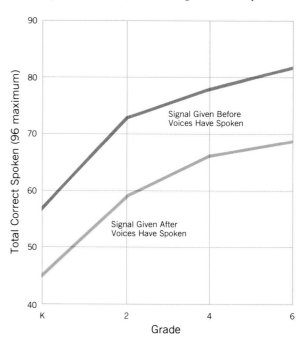

Figure 15.5. The role of expectation in attention. The amount of a message the child could repeat is plotted here as a function of whether the child had first received a signal telling him to attend to the message.

ences memory by interfering with focused attention, and quality of memory is affected by motivation. Recalling a name or date is effortful, and the person who is motivated to work longer or harder is likely both to store more information and to retrieve more.

GENERATION OF IDEAS AND HYPOTHESES

The comprehension of a problem and remembering of it are typically the first two processes in a problem-solving sequence. The third process moves toward the generation of possible solutions by generating alternative ways to solve the problem. This process is closely related to the notion of creativity. In order to generate ideas successfully, the child must possess the necessary units, be free from the fear of making a mistake, and possess the mystical ingredient called insight.

On the theory that creativity involves not only many ideas but unique ideas as well, a test was devised to assess creativity. It is illustrated in Figure 15.6. Fifth-grade children were shown these line drawings and asked to think up all the things they might represent. The child was classified as creative (1) if he came up with many possibilities for each drawing and (2) if some of his answers were unique among the answers given by the rest of the children.

The child is forced to think up ideas whenever he encounters a situation that he does not understand or a problem for which he has no immediate answer. The child sees his mother weeping or watches a bird unable to fly. Each sight creates a state of uncertainty because the child does not have a ready rule or concept that will explain these events. In order to find an answer, he dips into his bin of knowledge and searches for any information that will make sense of the event.

How does the child conclude that he has successfully explained an odd event or solved a problem? A seven-year-old sees his mother weeping for the first time in his life. The event is odd and stirs him to account for it. He automatically thinks of the conditions that make him cry: physical pain, fear, or loneliness. He checks the plausibility of each of these possibilities. The fear interpretation is rejected because it contradicts another rule he believes more firmly, namely, that adults are never afraid. He rejects the loneliness hypothesis for the same reason. But adults are capable of physical pain, and he decides that this interpretation is correct. He is satisfied. This example contains the three essential steps in an explanation.

1. The child searches his set of concepts and rules for possible causes of an event he does not immediately understand.
2. He checks each cause for consistency with his existing rules about the object or event. If the explanation he chooses contradicts an old rule in which he has strong faith, he is likely to reject the new interpretation.
3. If he finds an explanation that both matches his experience and does not contradict older rules, he is likely to accept it.

Two factors are critical—a set of available cognitive units appropriate to the event and the absence of a strong rule that would contradict the new hypothesis. Some children fail to generate good solutions because they cannot generate new ideas. If the child does have the capacity to gener-

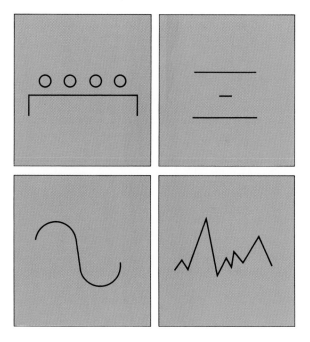

Figure 15.6. Stimuli used in testing children's creativity.

ate creative explanations, the two major obstacles to their production are (1) a set of firmly held ideas inconsistent with the best solution and (2) fear of criticism for suggesting an unusual idea or fear of being wrong. The most frequent reaction to this fear is to stop thinking about the problem. Every teacher recognizes this syndrome; each class has a few children who seem intelligent but who are overly inhibited. The teacher thinks they know more than they are saying, but the children censor many good ideas because they would rather avoid a mistake than risk the joy of success.

Young children often fail to be creative because they lack a repertoire of rich hypotheses. An important developmental change that takes place between seven and eleven years of age is the increasing ability to generate possible explanations of *hypothetical* events that violate the child's experience. Young children find it difficult to think about the following problem: "A three-headed fish flew four miles on one day and three miles on the next day. How many miles did he fly altogether?" The six-year-old may refuse even to work at this problem and rationalize his refractory attitude by reminding the interrogator that there are no three-headed fish, and fish can't fly anyway. The older child accepts the hypothetical state of affairs in the problem and begins to work at it. Adolescents usually fail to be creative because they fear criticism from their peers; adults fail because they hold a set of older beliefs inconsistent with the creative solution. Thus, the forces that inhibit creativity are not always the same at different stages in development.

Figure 15.7. Presented with an unfamiliar event, like the sight of his mother crying, a child will generate hypotheses to explain it based on his own experience. He knows that children sometimes cry because they are afraid or lonely, but he rejects these explanations in his mother's case because they contradict his long-held rules that adults are never afraid or lonely. People—adults and children—can cry if they are physically hurt, so this is the acceptable explanation.

□ *Conceptual Preferences* A child is brought into a typical schoolroom and asked to point to all the objects that "go together in some way"—all the objects that share a conceptual dimension. The child points to the chalk, erasers, and blackboard and, when asked why he selected these things, replies, "Because the eraser gets rid of the chalk on the blackboard." The content of his answer refers to school materials. The form of his answer emphasizes the *relation the objects bear to each other*. Another child points to the same three objects but says, "They are used to teach children." The common dimension is the function of the objects rather than the relation among them. This example illustrates two of the three major kinds of formal categories for concepts: superordinate, relational, and analytical.

A *superordinate* concept represents a shared attribute among the objects. The child who groups pears, apples, and bananas together under the conceptual label *fruit* is using a superordinate concept.

A *relational* concept is based on an interaction between or among members of the group. Grouping a man, woman, and child because they live together or associating a match with a pipe because the match lights the pipe are examples of relational concepts.

An *analytical* concept is based on a public, observable attribute that is part of each object in a group. Groups comprising all animals with four legs or all dresses with a single vertical stripe are illustrations of analytical concepts. As a child matures, he is more likely to use superordinate and less likely to use relational concepts in classifying familiar materials. Change in the use of analytical concepts depends on what materials are being used at different stages of development: if the child is working with objects or pictures of objects, the use of analytical concepts increases with age; if he is thinking about words that name objects, the use of analytical concepts decreases with age.

The set of pictures in Figure 15.8 was shown to a group of children from six to eleven years of age to test their preference for analytical, relational, or superordinate concepts. They were asked to group the two objects that belong together. *The number of analytical concepts employed increased with age.* The older children more often said that the watch and ruler go together because they both have numbers (analytical), whereas the younger ones said the man and watch go together because the man wears the watch (relational).

□ *Relative and Absolute Concepts* One obstacle in the adaptive use of concepts and rules by young children is the tendency to regard a concept as absolute rather than relative. When the four-year-old first learns the concept "dark," he regards it as descriptive of an absolute class of colors, namely, black and other dark hues. Thus, the phrase "dark yellow" makes no sense to him. The child learns that 1, 2, and 3 are small numbers and that 98, 99, and 100 are large numbers, so he may balk at regarding 99 as *smaller* than 100. It is difficult to teach the first-grader to see both the *absolute* and the *relative* aspects of a number because to him this implies that the same concept can have two different meanings.

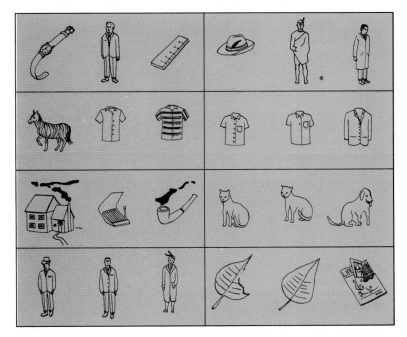

Figure 15.8. Sample items from a test to determine children's preferences for superordinate, relational, and analytical concepts. The children are asked to name the two objects in each group that belong together. (After Kagan *et al.*, 1964.)

EVALUATION

Evaluation influences the entire spectrum of mental work, including the quality of encoding, memory, and hypothesis generation. *Impulsive* children accept and report the first idea they produce and act upon it with only the barest consideration for its accuracy. Other children, whom psychologists call *reflective*, devote a long period of time to considering their ideas, and they censor many hypotheses. This dimension of difference can be seen as early as two years of age and seems to be a relatively stable component of personality over time. Reflective children are more afraid of making a mistake than impulsive children and check the quality of their thought more carefully. Thus, they are more accurate but less spontaneous.

Sample items from a test used to assess reflectivity and impulsivity are shown in Figure 15.9. The child is shown the top item as stimulus, then asked to pick the one from the other six items that is most like it. He is scored both on how long he takes to choose and on how many errors he makes. Impulsive children answer quickly and make more mistakes. From age five to age twelve there is a dramatic decrease in the number of errors American children make on this test and a corresponding increase in amount of time taken. It appears, then, that although the disposition toward impulsivity or reflectiveness is relatively stable, it can be modified through training. It has been shown that impulsive children exposed to an experienced, reflective teacher will change their tempo and become more reflective. Also, the decrease in impulsivity among American children as

they grow older reflects the generalized training that praises caution and frowns on mistakes.

DEDUCTION

The complementary processes of thinking of possible solutions and implementing the best solution usually occur together in time. Because deduction is the application of a rule—formal or informal—to solve a problem, the most important factor controlling the quality of deduction is the child's storehouse of rules, which, of course, increases with age. Some of the rules are formal: $8^2 = 64$; others are informal: thundershowers occur in summer. One of the important theoretical questions in the study of cognition centers on whether there are basic changes in the use of rules across the first dozen years. A simplistic point of view assumes that the child merely learns more rules each day, storing them for future use, and that there is no rule too difficult for a child of any age to acquire.

The alternative, but undoubtedly more truthful, assumption is that some rules are too complex for young children to understand and apply. This point of view assumes that there are stages in the development of thought. Jean Piaget is the best-known advocate of this position.

PIAGET'S THEORY OF INTELLECTUAL DEVELOPMENT

Piaget is the most influential theorist of intellectual development of this century. His writings have been prolific, and his views about intelligence are extremely provocative. Piaget's use of

Figure 15.9. Sample item from a test used to assess reflectivity and impulsivity. The child is asked to choose the one item among the six that is most like the sample at the top.

the term *intelligence* has a very specific meaning: it is "the coordination of operation." Piaget's *operation* is only partly similar to what has been termed here a *rule*. An operation, for Piaget, is the mental action one performs in adapting to the environment. One of the major characteristics of an operation is that it is *reversible*: it has a logically meaningful opposite. For example, addition has the reverse operation of subtraction; one can add two apples and three apples or perform the reverse operation of subtracting two or three apples from five apples. One can use a prism to split white light into its component parts or perform the reverse operation and combine the various colors into white light again. The gradual acquisition of these operations is, according to Piaget, the essence of intellectual growth. It follows that many of the statements classified as rules are not operations according to Piaget's definition, although a number of what are termed *formal* rules —for example, those dealing with arithmetical relations—do qualify as operations. However, the rule learned by a six-year-old that hitting his sister brings punishment does not have a reverse operation, so Piaget would not call it an operation.

PIAGET'S STAGES

As stated in Chapter 11, Piaget believes that the child passes through definable stages on his way to achieving the end state called *adult Western thought*. *Mental growth*, for Piaget, is the resolution of the tension between assimilation and accommodation. *Intellectual growth* is measured by the growing use of accommodation, the ability to

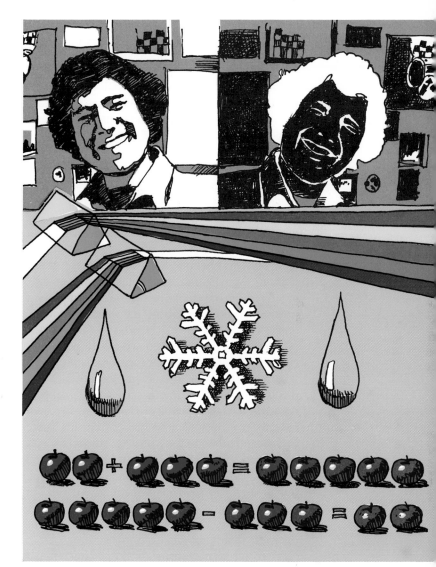

Figure 15.10. Reversibility, according to Piaget, is a most important characteristic of a cognitive operation; an operation must have a logically meaningful opposite, and the child's acquisition of both aspects of these operations defines his intellectual growth. The operation of addition, illustrated as one example here, has the reverse operation of subtraction.

alter old strategies or make new ones to solve unfamiliar problems. Flexibility of thought is the key to Piaget's view of intelligence.

He postulates four major stages of intellectual growth: sensorimotor stage (birth to eighteen months of life), preoperational stage (eighteen months to age seven), concrete operational stage (seven to twelve years), and, finally, the stage of formal operations (twelve years onward).

The *sensorimotor* stage exists prior to the child's acquisition of symbolic language. The intelligence of the infant is displayed in his actions. The child in the *preoperational stage* (eighteen months to seven years) possesses language (first symbols and then concepts), which begins to dominate his mental life. Although the three-year-old uses symbols, his thought is not usually organized into concepts and rules. This important process is completed during the stage of concrete operations.

Several important differences distinguish the child in the preoperational stage from the seven-year-old in the *stage of concrete operations.* The preoperational child does not have a *mental representation of a series of actions.* The five-year-old can learn to walk four blocks from his home to a neighborhood store, but he cannot sit at a table with a pencil and paper and trace the route he took. He does not have a mental representation of the entire sequence of actions. He walks to the store, making certain turns at certain places along the way, but he has no overall picture of the route that he traveled.

A second characteristic of the preoperational

Figure 15.11. A conservation experiment. The child is shown two rows of seven checkers, evenly spaced, and asked which row has more. Most children reply that they are the same. When one row is deformed and the checkers put in a small space, as shown, children under six or seven will say that the original row contains more.

stage is the absence of the operation of *conservation*, the rule that liquids and solids can be transformed in shape without changing their volume or mass. This operation appears only during the stage of concrete operations. The most famous of Piaget's clinical experiments demonstrates that the typical five-year-old does not believe a quantity of water remains constant (is conserved) despite changes in the form of the container that encloses it. A five-year-old child is shown two identical glasses filled to the same height with colored water. The adult asks the child if the two glasses have the same amount of water or unequal amounts. The child quickly acknowledges that both have the same amount of water. The examiner then pours the water from one container into a taller, narrower glass so that the water level is higher in the new container. When asked again whether the two glasses contain the same amount, the five-year-old says the taller container contains more water. (See Figure 15.11.) The seven-year-old insists that both have the same amount of water. However, the critical evidence that the seven-year-old has acquired the operation of conservation rests with the child's explanation: The seven-year-old says, "They are the same because you can put the water back in the other glass, and then the height will be the same." *The child is aware of the reverse operation that will restore the original situation.*

Some investigators see the problem of conservation as basically involving selective attention. In the water glass example, they argue that the child's real difficulty is in seeing that the new tumbler is different from the original one in *width* as well as in *height*. Thus, if he attends to the fact that the column of water is taller and does not notice that it is also narrower, the child will be led to the conclusion that there is more water. Using an approach derived from this line of reasoning, Rochel Gelman trained children to notice both critical dimensions involved in this type of transformation. With attention training there is evidence that children as young as five may be led to make conservation judgments.

A different mode of approach has been taken by Jerome Bruner and his colleagues, who have argued that the critical feature of the conservation concept is the recognition that it is the *same* water in both containers. The recognition of the *identity* of the water being transformed is thought to be basic to recognizing that its amount does not change.

But whatever the ultimate explanation of conservation (and probably of identity classes in general), it is clear that there are some very significant intellectual developments linked with this transition between modes of thinking.

A third intellectual hallmark of the preoperational child is that he cannot reason simultaneously about part of the whole and the whole itself. He lacks the operation of class inclusion. If a five-year-old child is shown eight yellow candies and four brown candies and is asked, "Are there more yellow candies or more candies?" he is likely to say, "More yellow candies." Piaget says that this reply indicates that the child cannot reason about a part and the whole simultaneously.

Figure 15.12. The preoperational child cannot simultaneously reason about the whole and a part of the whole. In a situation where the child is shown a dish of candies and asked whether there are more yellow candies or more candies, he will answer that there are more yellow ones.

Figure 15.13. The relevance of the operation of reversibility to biological and social phenomena is not clear—children discover that some aspects of life are not reversible.

The fourth characteristic that differentiates preoperational children from those advanced to the stage of concrete operations involves *serialization*—the tendency to arrange objects in order according to some quantified dimension, like weight or size. When asked to arrange eight sticks of differing length, for example, the five-year-old typically does not arrange them in a row according to their length, as does an older child. Serialization is critical for understanding the relation of numbers to one another and therefore necessary to the learning of arithmetic.

At about age twelve, a child's thinking moves into the stage of formal operations. A preoccupation with *thought* is the hallmark of this stage, which has several important attributes that differentiate it from the preceding stage of concrete operations. First, the child is capable of considering all the possible ways a particular problem might be solved and the possible forms a particular solution might assume. If he is thinking about the shortest way to get to the seashore, he can (and will) review all the possible routes, and he knows when he has exhausted all of them. Second, the thinking in this stage is self-consciously deductive. Third, the operations are organized into higher-order operations—ways of using abstract rules to solve a whole class of problems. We will return to this stage in Chapter 20 because it is the end point of intellectual development.

EVALUATION OF PIAGET'S THEORY

There is little doubt that Piaget's statements about the developmental changes in conservation of mass, class inclusion, or serialization are generally true for Western children. But the concepts with which Piaget has worked—mass, quantity, weight, volume, space, number, and time—and the operations he defines—reversibility, class inclusion, and serial ordering—are most relevant to mathematics and physics. Their relevance to biological and social phenomena, which seldom show reversibility or obey class inclusion rules, is less clear. The relation between a whole and its parts in mathematics is not necessarily applicable to living things or to the behavior of people. The concept of a crowd is more than the sum of the number of people in the crowd. The child discovers that life itself, unlike the quantity of water, is not conserved: there is no reversible operation that restores life when a child kills a butterfly.

Piaget's observations about certain sequences in cognitive development seem essentially correct, but it is still not clear how general these principles are and whether his emphasis on operations as the essence of a theory of thought is broadly applicable to all aspects of thinking.

THE CONCEPT OF INTELLIGENCE AND THE IQ TEST

Recently the field of child development has undergone a kind of renaissance and has begun to emphasize and explore thoroughly the learning processes of infants and young children. Not long ago the emphasis tended to be upon physical growth, physiological maturation, and the progressive achievement of developmental milestones. The concern was not so much with the understanding of mechanisms underlying physical growth as it was with the descriptive documentation of the relationships between age and such other attributes of the organism as height and weight.

MEASUREMENT OF INTELLIGENCE

Early in this line of study, child psychologists concerned themselves with the plotting of mental age with increases in chronological age. Put simply, the correct or normal mental age for a child of three years of age would be that which is typical or usual for most other children of that age. In order to determine whether a given child deviated from the typical and if so, by how much, it was necessary to devise behavioral norms, utilizing standard testing procedures, from birth on. Thus, a good deal of descriptive research was conducted, designed simply to catalogue what the usual six-month-old infant can and does do, what the one-year-old is capable of, and how three- and four-year-old children differ with respect to motor, cognitive, and social behaviors.

In assessing intelligence, the convention of creating a ratio of mental age divided by the child's chronological age was adopted, with mental age defined in terms of the age norms for typical performance on particular tests. When this ratio is multiplied by 100, the yield is the child's IQ—a quotient that represents his performance relative to numerous other children who have previously been tested under the same conditions. If a child of exactly three years of age achieves a mental age of three on such a test, his intelligence quotient

—IQ—will be 100, and if a three-year-old performs as well as most four-year-olds, his IQ will be 133. Thus the IQ provides no more than a descriptive statistic relating a child's present performance to that of other children of his chronological age. See Chapter 1 for a description of the methodology used by Alfred Binet in constructing his IQ test.

CHANGING VIEWPOINTS ABOUT IQ

For many years psychologists considered that an IQ score measured practically everything of importance in cognitive development. Creative abilities, productive thinking, and problem-solving were all assumed to be measured by performance on an IQ test. They also considered IQ to be constant; if a child's IQ score fluctuated from test to test or from time to time, blame was laid either on the test's technical makeup or on poor motivation or emotional upset during one or the other of the times the child was taking the test. A corollary belief was that it was not possible to train mental abilities.

On the basis of new evidence and experience, these ideas about IQ are now being modified, and the concept of what an IQ really measures is being redefined. One important basis for disgruntlement with the entrenched notions about IQ is their role in defining thinking processes: in the final analysis the processes are defined operationally by the measuring instrument used. In much psychological research—for example, studies attempting to correlate intelligence level with creative ability—intelligence *becomes* the IQ

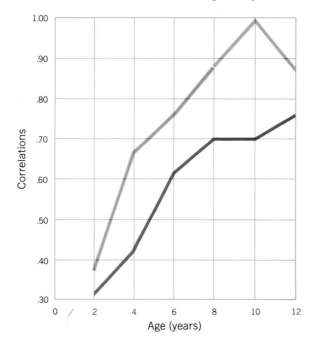

Figure 15.15. A study being conducted by J. Gaiter is providing stimulation – through activities such as those shown – to culturally deprived infants in order to enhance their cognitive and intellectual functioning.

Figure 15.14. Correlations between intelligence-test scores at various ages and IQ scores at age ten (Stanford-Binet) and at age eighteen (Wechsler). (Data from Honzik, Macfarlane, and Allen, 1948.)

score and creativity *becomes* the production of unusual titles to a certain story. Thus, when these studies seem to find that in bright students there is only a small correlation between intelligence and creativity, this puzzling result may well be nothing more than an artifact of the test construction.

IQ FLUCTUATION

Unfortunately, the early association of the psychological measurement of IQ with a program of various physical measurements caused many people to suppose that scales of intelligence produced scores that are essentially as accurate and immutable as physical measurements. A considerable mystique has prevailed since the early days of intelligence testing, and the assumption has often been made that intelligence is very highly determined by heredity and is only minimally affected by experiential circumstances. Today psychologists know that environmental circumstances can produce considerable variability in intelligence. They have also grown more suspicious—on the basis of long-term repetitive measurements of intelligence—of the alleged stability of intelligence in early life. On the basis of currently available data, it is clear that within the first year of a child's life one can do better in predicting the child's eventual intelligence level by examining the parents than by testing the infant.

Tests administered before the age of two are said to measure a child's DQ (developmental quotient) rather than his IQ. DQ tests measure behaviors such as activity level, motor coordina-

tion, manipulation, and walking ability; they are valuable in early identification of brain-damaged children, but there is *no* correlation between the DQ measures and later IQ scores.

The fluctuations in intelligence as determined by IQ scores are evident in the fact that approximately 20 percent of the American child population changes by at least 15 IQ points between the ages of six and ten, and some children, although not many, change as many as 50 points. External influences at the time of examination, including the manner of the examiner and the attitude of the child, can greatly affect the child's performance. By the same token, some changes in IQ scores from one testing to another are attributable to intervening circumstances. Two children of comparable DQs at eight months of age can be predicted to separate by about 20 IQ points by the time each is eight years of age if one child is reared in a slum home while the other is reared in circumstances that bestow unusual stimulation and provide desirable learning circumstances. This is not to say that there are no exceptions; indeed, there are so many instances of persons who grow up in the slums and/or have inferior educational facilities who achieve scholarly and other successes—and there are so many instances of middle- and upper-class children who have not succeeded in these ways—as to make one wary of predicting at all. But these facts, too, simply drive home the point that the standard intelligence test does not measure a static attribute of people and that there are numerous interacting determinants of any developmental outcome.

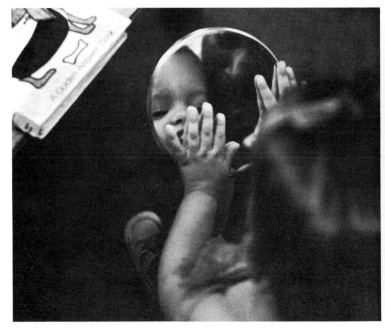

WHAT IQ DOES AND DOES NOT MEASURE

Most psychologists agree that intelligence is based on the ability to benefit from experience and the ease with which a child can learn a new idea or a set of new behaviors. It is generally assumed that everyone has a ceiling, a point above which he will not be able to profit from experience in a particular activity, and that this ceiling is governed by hereditary factors.

But a psychologist who evaluates the child's IQ by giving him an intelligence test does not ask many questions that require the child *to learn anything*. The majority of the questions on an intelligence test measure a skill or a segment of knowledge that he already possesses rather than his ability to learn a new concept or rule. Thus, the IQ test does not measure the basic attribute that most people acknowledge to be the central meaning of intelligence.

The New York City school system has recently discarded IQ tests for diagnostic purposes and has instituted a new set of tests, specifically designed by Educational Testing Service to measure *learning* ability. The child is first tested to determine what he knows; he is then given a task involving learning and is retested to determine how well and how fast he has learned. Studies that have attempted to correlate results of this test with achievement show conflicting results. However, use of the test indicates that some psychologists and educators, aware of the limitations of IQ tests, are attempting to find better and more accurate measures.

The intelligence test *is* a good measure of what a child knows how to do and what he has taken from his culture. It is also a reasonably good predictor of the child's grades in school. If the child has a strong motivation to improve the quality of his intellectual skills and has high standards for intellectual mastery, he is likely to have a higher IQ score than a child who is not highly motivated or has low standards. Because middle-class children are more consistently encouraged than are lower-class children to learn to read, spell, add, and write, a child's IQ, social class, and school grades all should be positively related to each other. This is the case. Moreover, the personality attributes of children who do well in school (persistence, lack of aggression, and responsible behavior) are similar to the characteristics of children from middle-class homes.

The IQ, as presently used, should be regarded, therefore, as an efficient and accurate way of summarizing the degree to which a child has learned the concepts and rules of middle-class Western society. The IQ score is useful because it can predict fairly well how easily a child of eight will master the elements of calculus or history when he enters college. However, the specific questions that are asked on an intelligence test have been chosen deliberately to make this prediction possible. The child is asked to define the word *shilling* rather than the word *peso*. He is asked to state the similarity between a *fly* and a *tree* rather than the similarity between *fuzz* and *Uncle Tom*. He is asked to copy a design rather than to defend

himself against the neighborhood bully. Current IQ tests, in short, have deliberately been designed to have meaning only for children raised in a particular environment.

The IQ tests used currently are not to be discarded merely because they are biased toward measuring skills that upper- and middle-class white Americans value and teach. But the parent and teacher should appreciate the arbitrary content of the test. If one's primary objective is to predict the child's success in school subjects, then the IQ test is the best instrument psychologists have devised so far. After the child is three or four years old, the test does a creditable job of predicting who will obtain good grades in elementary school, high school, and college. (For skills such as music or art there are special tests that are more appropriate.) Unfortunately, many persons believe that the IQ test measures a general factor of intelligence. If the original inventors of the test had called the test an index of academic, rather than intellectual, potential, there might be less controversy over the meaning of the IQ score.

Psychologists need more exact knowledge about the separate cognitive functions and how they are combined in thought, and everyone must come to realize that the actual, overt behavior of a child in a test situation depends as much on his motives, fears, and expectations as it does on the richness and quality of his mental structures. The relations between the answers that he writes on a test and the thought that produced those answers are still largely a mystery.

When did you become who you are today? Chances are that you consider yourself—your *youness*, the core elements of your *personality*—as having existed more or less intact throughout your life. We adults—most of us, certainly—see ourselves as travelers on a long journey that takes us through many strange lands and yields many different experiences. And yet, at the end of the journey, we see our identities as unchanged—we are still the same individuals who began the trip long ago. This viewpoint of the *continuity* of personality suggests that most of the structure of personality is laid down early and that our early experiences place rather stringent limits on what we can become.

Personality theorists, then, have spent most of their efforts studying the influence of the very early years on personality development, believing that by the time a child reaches the ripe old age of five or six, he has already become what he will be the rest of his life. One of Freud's greatest theoretical contributions was his insistence on the critical importance of the very early years in shaping later personality development. Yet the very strength of this insight led him to neglect the influence of the later period of childhood, those seemingly quiet years between six and twelve.

Freud was trained as a medical doctor, so his viewpoint toward personality development had strong biological overtones. In his later theorizing he intimated that ultimately all of man's psychological experience would be explicable in neurophysiological terms. Appreciating his bias, one can understand that Freud would expect the periods of greatest psychological development to be highly correlated with the periods of greatest physical growth. The child typically experiences two periods of maximal physical change—one period extending from birth to age three or four, the other beginning at the onset of puberty and lasting through adolescence. Freud thought that the great part of personality development (that concerned with sexual identity) occurred during these two segments of life, with the early period being the more critical. According to Freud, infant sexuality reached a peak of development roughly between two and four years of age and then gradually subsided. The rest of the prepuberty years he categorized as the *latent period*, a time of little or no sexual development.

Psychologists know now, however, from thousands of painstakingly gathered observations and studies made on children during this so-called latent period, that psychological growth is not suddenly turned off when toilet training is completed, to begin again suddenly when the pubertal juices begin to flow. They know that personality is the outcome of the interaction between what a person inherits and the environment in which he lives. The child continues to develop both sexually and socially during this period of time. Indeed, from the point of view of the child's socialization, later childhood is probably the most important growth period of all. But the growth is quiet, silent, and in many cases withdrawn from adult eyes.

16
Personality Development

PROFILE OF THE CHILD

At six, the child goes off to school and gains a freedom of movement that he perhaps never had before. At six, the child escapes for long periods of time from parental observation and begins to create his own private world, independent of adults. These are the peer years, that time of development when the child seeks out his own kind. He begins building the social structures and starts learning the social roles that are his map through the long journey into adulthood. For the first time in his life, the child may find that individuals outside his immediate family are of as much importance to him as are his parents and siblings. The parents, perhaps delighted to gain a measure of added freedom themselves, often yield the child up to his colleagues gladly; but, whether the parents like it or not, in middle-class America and Western Europe, the child almost always escapes from the parental eye at this age. Later, during adolescence, when physical, sexual, and social growth begin their final tumultuous spurts, the parents will take sharper notice of the changes occurring. During the placid days of late childhood, however, the changes occur so slowly, and often so far removed from the parents' observation, that the child does indeed appear to most adults to be in a latent stage of development.

During his early years, the child learns the rudiments of language, how to express his wants and needs, how to respond to changes in the environment. The child is open during this period; his needs are few and, for the most part, are regularly satisfied by his parents or other members of the family. But during the later years of childhood, the child learns how to manipulate his social environment by using language. He learns when to tell a lie to gain an advantage, as well as when to tell the truth. He learns to conceal things from his parents; he learns how to hide. These, then, are the *secret years,* and it takes an astute observer to penetrate the veil of secrecy and chart the enormous range of subtle changes that occurs in the child from age six to age twelve.

The society in which a child grows up can exert enormous influence on what he becomes. The description of personality development during the later years of childhood presented in this chapter is valid only for that broad segment of society called *middle-class America* (although it is a reasonably accurate description of children who grow up in middle-class Western Europe as well). Children from the upper or the lower classes, children in minority groups, such as black Americans, children who grow up in ghettos, and children from entirely different cultures follow somewhat different developmental paths than those explored here, and these differences will be pointed out whenever possible. The fact remains that most college students are white, middle-class Americans—as are their professors—and most of the observations made of children during the years six to twelve are made by middle-class American psychologists on middle-class American children. But because the majority of Americans are members of this normative community, the descriptions that follow are valid for the *average* American child.

THE ACQUISITION OF ROLES

When the six-year-old first skips off to school (or, more likely, is taken to meet his first-grade teacher by a doting mother), the process of role identification slips into high gear. The later years of childhood are those in which each person learns what is expected of him, to a great extent, in adult society. To a small degree children learn to meet these expectations in the classroom itself, from books and pictures and teachers who tell them what is good and what is bad, what they must do and what they cannot do. For the most part, however, such learning occurs on the playgrounds before and after school and during recess. Children in these years learn more from their peers than they do from adults.

One of the major means of learning social roles, surprisingly enough, comes from the games children play. An adult, watching children at play, may think they are merely wasting time, merely enjoying themselves, and the adult may envy the child his carefree time of life. Actually, the child is usually hard at work, gathering information about peer expectations, testing his strengths and learning his weaknesses, challenging his mind and his body in myriad ways. Child's play is usually very serious business indeed.

The young of most mammals seem to be genetically programmed to play during these critical years. Harry Harlow has made long-term studies of the socialization of monkeys; many of his findings seem pertinent to our study of that most advanced of primates, man. As described in Chapter 7, Harlow and his associates raised some infant monkeys with surrogate mothers; he also experimented with some monkeys by never exposing them to other young animals their own age. These young monkeys never learned to play the monkey games they should have; they never had the opportunity to acquire the social roles they would need in later life. As a result, such isolated monkeys found it almost impossible to fit within a group when, as "teen-agers," they were introduced to others of their kind. They tended to remain isolated for the rest of their lives and, for a variety of reasons, these lives were shorter than those of animals raised under more normal circumstances. In particular, monkeys raised with surrogate mothers found tremendous difficulty in forming mating pairs; the males did not know how to approach young females (or even that it was females that they should approach), and the females did not know how to entice and yield to the males.

Harlow also raised clutches of young monkeys in isolation from their mothers and all other adults. These animals were, if anything, overly socialized toward their peers, for the group in which they were raised took on the functions of both parents and playmates. Members of the group tended to cling to each other in "choo-choo train" fashion; they ran in packs and, at least until the onset of puberty, tended to reject newcomers when Harlow introduced them into the group. Peer-raised monkeys show precocious sexual development, too, the onset of both puberty and mating occurring significantly sooner in these animals than in monkeys raised with both adults

and peers. Interestingly, there are a few reports showing that children who spent their formative years in concentration camps, where they had little or no contact with any adults other than the prison guards, showed the same precocious development and the same difficulty in later years in establishing adequate roles with older people.

GAMES CHILDREN PLAY

Records of the types of games children play go back thousands of years, and many of the games popular today trace their histories back to the dawn of recorded time. While Socrates was lecturing to his older brothers, young Greek children were playing hide-and-go-seek among the trees in the groves of Academe. When Julius Caesar was young, he probably played tug-of-war outside the Roman Forum, and blind man's buff was known in England before Caesar's legions were.

In *Children's Games in Street and Playground*, Iona and Peter Opie not only trace the history of children's games but describe their social significance as well. The Opies, who talked to and observed more than 10,000 children, find two main objectives in all unorganized play. The first objective is social: "A game produces a structure within which a child is able to have relations with his own tribe." Children spend a great deal of time making rules for the games they play, and it is usually very important to them that the rules, no matter how silly they may appear to adults, be followed without deviation. A leader may break a rule—mainly by proposing an alternative—but a child with lower status in the group finds himself under tremendous pressure to conform. If he fails to do so, he is often expelled from the group and not allowed back in until he promises to keep the faith. This slavish attention to detail probably serves the child well in many ways. He learns that social commerce must be regulated if interactions are to be sustained for any length of time (at a younger age, children merely drift away from their peers if they don't like the rules). He learns that once a more-or-less formal structure has been enacted, he can relax and enjoy himself within its confines without having to worry about being rejected. And, as the Opies point out, rules provide a means by which a new arrival to the group may rapidly find his place.

The other function of most games, according to the Opies, is to allow the child to experience adult life in easy bits and nonthreatening pieces. Adults get most of their enjoyment of games from winning, not merely from experiencing. Children are quite different. Their games do not require umpires, and they seldom bother to keep score. Unless adults prompt them otherwise, children attach little significance to who wins or loses; they do not worry about prizes and are not concerned if a game is not finished. "Indeed," as the Opies write, "children like games in which there is a sizable element of luck, so that individual abilities cannot be directly compared. They like games which restart almost automatically, so that everybody is given a new chance." In a sense, games serve as microsimulations of the world around them. A child can experience competition of various kinds and compare his abilities to what

Figure 16.1. Rhesus monkeys raised together in isolation from parents and other adults form the characteristic "choo-choo train" position.

others can do without really being hurt by the comparison. As the Opies put it, "He can experience virtually all the incidents and emotions of life in play. He can throw stones or kiss, for instance, without risk."

The parent who attempts to organize children's games stands a very good chance of ruining their usefulness, for the adult typically does not see the game in the child's own terms. The father who pushes his son into a Little League baseball competition and then pressures the child to win often tells himself that he is teaching his son the importance of succeeding. In fact, he may be teaching the child the terrors of trying to compete, for parents will scold a child for losing, but his peers typically will not. It is the Opies' belief that nothing extinguishes self-organized play more effectively than an adult's action to promote it. They believe that it is not only natural but beneficial that a gulf should exist between the generations in their choice of recreation.

Games not only serve to instruct a child in how to relate socially to his peers (and, perhaps, in how better to avoid his parents) but also allow him to test his physical abilities both against his own standards and in comparison with those around him. Children need at least a minimal amount of exercise in order to promote the development of motor coordination, and many games that require muscular skill provide this exercise. Boys learn how strong they are—and how to keep this strength within limits—by fighting with each other. If Harlow's observations on monkeys have meaningful correspondence in human develop-

ment, the expression of such aggressive tendencies has important consequences for mature sexuality. The human male child who never learns to express himself physically in childhood fights may be too inhibited ever to establish a meaningful and rewarding heterosexual relationship. By learning to keep his aggressiveness within carefully controlled limits—to hit softly as well as to punch vigorously—the young male learns the importance of a physical gentleness that his wife may later appreciate.

Many games seem designed to let the child explore the capabilities of his own body for his own satisfaction. Follow-the-leader, skating, riding bicycles, tag, and even hopscotch typically are as much self-competitive as they are peer-competitive. The late-years child who sets out on his own expedition to a neighborhood nowhere-in-particular may climb a fence, walk along a narrow board over a ditch with hands outstretched to keep his balance, swing on a rope, jump a gulley, crawl through a drainpipe, and jump off a fairly high ledge—all merely to see if he can make his body do what he wants it to do. Some testing of his physical limits will come from peer-group taunts and dares, but he issues his own challenges as well. He learns persistence from answering either kind of challenge, but consistent self-testing may well lead to a kind of internal discipline later.

Although girls enjoy physical games as much as boys, their play tends to be neither as vigorous nor as aggressive. On the other hand, girls spend a great deal more time involved in social challenges than do boys. Girls talk at a younger age than do

Figure 16.2. Children's games show an amazing historical continuity.

boys, and during the later years of childhood they maintain verbal superiority over their masculine age mates. This verbal fluency is largely a product of the child's cultural environment, however; lower-class girls are usually less verbal than are middle-class boys. In a study conducted at the University of Michigan, Elton McNeil asked middle- and lower-class children to express emotions such as hate and anger in two ways: verbally and with bodily gestures. The lower-class children excelled at bodily expression, swinging their arms and legs freely, propelling themselves readily into an emotional state; these children were, however, comparatively tongue-tied when it came to expressing themselves verbally. As you might expect, the middle-class children were just the opposite. They were comparatively inhibited as far as gross movements of their limbs were concerned, relying on facial expressions to convey their emotions physically; but the agility of their tongue muscles more than compensated for the tight rein they kept over the rest of their musculature.

Modes of expression, ways of controlling one's environment, are surely learned during childhood. Throughout the rest of his life, the middle-class child will attempt to gain his rewards and pleasure through verbal expression, through talking and subtle gestures. The lower-class child is a more physical being and becomes a more physically oriented adult.

Given two youths with comparable physical development, motor coordination, and intellectual sharpness, the lower-class youth might well prove superior on the playing field simply because he

had learned the joys of bodily expression during his childhood while the middle-class youth had been taught to inhibit such pleasures. School performance during adolescence—and job choice (and success) later in life—may also be critically influenced during this stage of childhood. The world is predominantly middle class; schoolteachers (and employers) are predominantly middle class. The monetary and academic payoffs, then, come chiefly to those individuals whose childish games and whose interactions with peers and parents were such as to free their tongues and repress their arms and legs.

SEX ROLES

Sex roles and gender identification are also learned, at least in part, through the games children play during the years six to twelve. Watch three ten-year-old girls playing house. The oldest (or the most dominant) will assign the roles at her pleasure, switching them around from time to time to add interest to the game. "Let's plike I'm the daddy," she may say, slurring the words "play like" and forming a new verb in the process. In almost every culture where children have any free time at all, they "plike" adult roles. Grownups may take this imitation as the sincerest form of flattery, and perhaps the children mean this form of microsimulation as such, but it serves much the same useful socialization process as do the more formal games that the Opies describe. In playing house, the child picks up some of the essentials of the adult roles involved and, perhaps of greater importance, learns how to shift readily

from one role to another. If the little girl who is playing the mother wishes to go to the office and work and leave daddy at home to care for the baby, she is soon put straight by the other children playing the game. Mothers just don't leave daddies at home to do dishes or wash diapers.

When such a little girl reaches maturity and marries, it would be shocking to her if her husband suggested such a role reversal, for what individuals learn as being "proper" during their years of childhood takes on the aura of complete naturalness when they are adults. Indeed, the emotional components of role identification are conditioned so strongly during this period of people's lives that many would reject as being abnormal any man or woman who tried to indulge in significant role reversal. People learn the rules of social intercourse during this period of life, and knowing the rules gives them great freedom, for they need not think through each little action or reaction to their changing environments as adults; they merely stay within the rules, and they are home free.

Most children grow up in a circumscribed segment of society and so learn but a limited set of roles (and attitudes toward roles). Algebra and physics are learned primarily in schools, from books and teachers, and one can always go back to childhood events and determine almost precisely where one's knowledge of and attitudes toward such intellectual pursuits came from. Role learning does not come from studying books, however; the teaching is almost entirely informal, and the emotional conditioning associated with

sex and gender roles is so pervasive in the child's environment that it is practically invisible to later, rational inspection. Because individuals cannot consciously recover the learning experiences themselves, they often tend to think that their attitudes are genetic constants rather than structures built from thousands of microsimulations "pliked" together to form a superego.

Today everyone laughs at the argument against jet airplanes that goes, "If God had wanted man to fly, He'd have given him wings." But this generation's parents or grandparents did not find the joke too funny in the early days of aviation. The ten-year-old seldom questions *why* daddy goes to the office to work and mommy stays home to mind the children. That's merely the natural way things are done. As an adult, he is therefore unlikely to question what he sees as the Divine scheme of things. If he encounters a homosexual or a transvestite, a man with artistic talents or a woman with outstanding business or scientific abilities, the middle-class adult will typically reject such instances of role violation as evidence of unnatural tendencies that probably resulted from some kind of terrible mutation in the violator's genes. Natural behavior is, in reality, that behavior "pliked" during the later years of childhood, with the generous approval of peers and parents.

IMITATION

Parents do not usually set out deliberately to indoctrinate their children with the sorts of attitudes toward the world that the parents would like the children to have; yet, for all practical purposes, indoctrination is precisely what does take place in most families. Most adults cannot recall having their fathers and mothers tell them which political party they ought to belong to, but social scientists know from hundreds of studies that almost everyone ends up voting the way his parents do. How does this type of indoctrination take place? Part of attitude learning takes place through imitation. There is considerable evidence that the tendency to imitate one's elders is innately determined. According to a recent report from Phyllis Chesler, even a young kitten is more likely to adopt an unusual response (in this case, pressing a lever in order to get food) if, during its young kittenhood, it sees its mother or another adult cat perform the response.

A child tends to emulate or imitate those adults who occupy large chunks of his life space. Parents are important for several reasons: First, and perhaps foremost, because they loom so large in a child's world, because they are the adults with whom the child has greatest contact. But it is also true that parents are important because they have the power to reward and punish a child's responses. Although much attitude learning occurs at an overt level ("Big boys don't cry"; "Little girls don't say things like that"), much of it is covert and hidden. Parents tend to reward their children when they echo the parents' own attitudes and tend to be disinterested, bored, or even hostile when the child expresses some opinion that the parents do not share. The parents are not likely to see this type of response on their part as being a definite program by which they are incul-

cating their own values, but the result is the same as if it were planned.

DEVELOPMENT OF PREJUDICE

Parents may not consciously plan to teach prejudice to their children, but—as with other values—children are likely to acquire the prejudices of the people they identify with—especially their parents. However, children do not simply repeat, parrotlike, statements of bias they hear their parents say. Prejudice in children has been shown to be associated with a number of personality and background factors. Several studies, one of them by R. Tabachnick, have shown that self-esteem is related to prejudice: children who are satisfied with themselves tend to be less prejudiced than children whose self-esteem is low. Other personality factors that E. Frenkel-Brunswik found to be associated with prejudice in boys and girls (ages eleven to sixteen) are: rigid conformity to approved social values, including sex-role typing: both boys and girls disapproved strongly of passivity or "feminine behavior" in boys and of tomboyish girls; the boys feared to find traces of such weakness in themselves. The conformity displayed was active, in that these children *condemned* all behaviors and attitudes that were different from their own. Also, the children's low self-esteem was evidenced in feelings of helplessness in a world they considered to be chaotic and full of destruction.

Studies of the personality of prejudiced adults have shown that they tend to be highly conforming, inflexible, and authoritarian, so it is no sur-

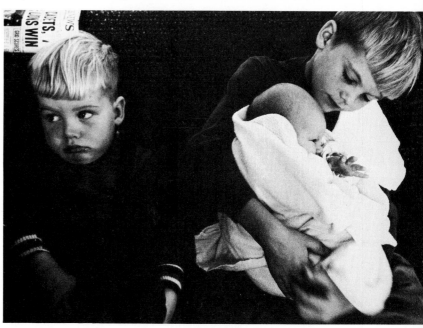

Figure 16.3. A newly arrived sibling may engender jealousy, but growing up in a family with brothers and sisters has been shown to be a factor in maintaining a happy home after marriage.

prise to learn that the parents of prejudiced children deal with them in an authoritarian way; they exercise strict control of the child's social relationships. Also, these parents seem to show little sufferance of children's "annoyance-value"; they can't be bothered to answer questions or reconsider decisions on the basis of feedback from the child. The family's treatment of the child need not be highly punitive; in fact, it has been shown that identification with prejudiced parents and internalization of their values is more likely to take place when a moderate amount of punishment is used than when there is little or a great deal. Even kindergartners display hostile attitudes toward people different than themselves, but it is during the early school years—when identification is operating strongly—that active prejudices become solidified.

SIBLING RIVALRY AND ONLY CHILD-HOOD

Children may learn a great deal about what will be expected of them in later life from their siblings, provided that the child's brothers and sisters are an important part of the family constellation during the child's formative years. The child's first real social frustrations typically come as a result of squabbles in which he has to give up something in order to maintain peace in the family. Studies have shown that children with older brothers and sisters are usually less aggressive, creative, and successful as adults than are only children or oldest children—perhaps because they had most of their aggressiveness and creativity beaten out of them by their elder siblings and

because success in American society typically results from a mixture of aggressiveness and talent. However, there are compensations: the boy who learns that his older brother deserves a large allowance simply because he is older or the girl who learns that her older sister may stay up later simply because she is more mature is also learning that there are almost always inequities in communal living. Thus, although older or only children may be more successful in a business or professional sense, they appear to be less fortunate in maintaining happy homes when married.

The only child, particularly one of well-educated parents, often seeks the companionship of imaginary playmates and spends more time daydreaming than does a child with many siblings. To begin with, the only child typically has more room, more privacy, and a greater share of such fantasy-inducing family resources as a radio, record player, tape recorder, television set, and even the family collection of books and illustrated magazines. The child may often use these resources as a buffer against too great a social exposure to the adult world. After parents have had several children, they probably give up trying to turn their offspring into instant adults by the time the children are old enough to walk and talk. Parents with several children know that no amount of pleading, scolding, or bribing will keep children from occasionally being childish. Parents with only one child to worry about typically learn this lesson too late to do them—or the child—much good. But whether through his own choice or as an answer to parental pressures, the only

Figure 16.4. An only child may have more comfort, privacy, and material things than a child growing up in a large family.

child may often be forced to develop a richer fantasy life—and may learn to draw more upon his own inner resources—than a child with a surfeit of siblings.

MISBEHAVIOR AND DELINQUENCY

Freud believed that one could learn a great deal about the normal development of a child by studying cases of obvious abnormality because the unusual may serve to set the usual in relief. Most people, for instance, seldom think of their stomachs as continuously functioning organs until they eat something that doesn't agree with them. In similar fashion, child psychologists often gain considerable insight into what is important in a normal family by seeing what has gone wrong in a family with severe problems.

Juvenile delinquents may be defined as children (usually below age seventeen) who have come to the attention of law enforcement agencies because they have committed some adjudicable crime. Delinquents come from all strata of society, although a disproportionate majority of those who are sent to some reformatory or training school are, in fact, from lower-class homes. It is probably the case that middle- and upper-class children commit as many crimes as do lower-class children, but the crimes are often qualitatively quite different, and the laws of the land have a decided middle-class bias. Crimes of violence and crimes involving property loss are more likely to be committed by lower-class children, who act out and aggress more readily than do middle-class children. Middle- and upper-class children are

more likely to have expensive legal assistance, too, and because the judges who sentence children to detention homes (or otherwise incarcerate them) are typically themselves middle class, they are more likely to take lower-class children from their homes ("for their own good") than they are to separate middle-class children from their parents. (Upper-class children are seldom bothered by such problems because their considerable wealth and the social standing of their family in the community offer them considerable protection.)

Although juvenile delinquency is typically seen as being a problem of adolescence, the fact is that the police regularly apprehend children under the age of thirteen on a large number of offenses, ranging from running away to murder. It is commonplace in large cities these days for gangs of children, ranging in age from seven to twelve (typically from ghettos), to roam the streets, terrorizing merchants and shop owners. Twenty or more such children in a gang may "hit" a ten-cent store, for instance, all racing into the store at the same time, grabbing whatever merchandise they are most attracted to, and then racing out onto the street within a minute or two after entering. Their sheer numbers make it impossible for the store detective—or for the local police—to deal with the problem.

It is a truism that for every juvenile delinquent, there is a delinquent home environment. Children are not born delinquent; they are made that way by their families, usually by their parents. It is also true that most parents of delinquents are unable to accept the fact that they are responsible for their child's acting as he does. Recent investigations in this area suggest that most children with severe behavior problems come from one of two types of family environment.

DELINQUENTS' FAMILIES

The first type of family setting that appears to breed delinquency is that in which the child is given no freedom whatsoever, in which every minute of the child's life is completely structured by the parents. Any signs of independence the child shows are instantly discouraged by the parents; they keep the child from having any friends outside the family circle by continually telling the child how bad or unsuitable his chosen friends are, by refusing to let the child see the friends or invite them to visit his home. If peers are allowed in the child's home, the parents are likely to supervise all such visits, to intervene in conversations and games, and to do their (perhaps unconscious) best to make such visits so unpleasant that the friends are not likely to come back. These parents lay down a thousand different ironclad rules that the child must obey. This type of repressive home situation breeds strong rebellion in many children, who break the law perhaps as much to get even with their parents as in a genuine attempt to gain some small measure of freedom. Such children, having once been caught and sentenced, may even prefer living in a detention home or in a hospital setting to staying at home.

The second type of family environment that predominates among delinquent children appears to be almost the exact opposite of the one just described and is more common among lower-class families. In this type of home, anything goes. The child's biological parents may or may not still be living together; if the father is gone, the mother may be living with one of a succession of husbands or boyfriends. In such homes, the parents have long since lost any means of disciplining the children or of controlling their behavior, so even seven-year-olds may come and go as they please at all hours of the day or night. Meals are haphazard events at best, and a large family may go for weeks or even months without once engaging in any activity (including meals) in which the entire family participates. Typically, the parents are so tied up in their own problems that they have little time to devote to the children, who must then find whatever psychological or social satisfaction they can from sources outside the family.

In many cases, particularly in those homes in which the original parents are no longer living together, the remaining parent may actively dislike or even hate the child and encourage various forms of delinquency in the hope that the child

will be taken away from the home by force of law. School truancy, curfew violation, aggression (usually in boys) resulting from too much alcohol or the use of drugs such as LSD or pep pills, and various kinds of theft are typically associated with the neglectful environment. Children from such homes may in some cases engage in illegal behavior in a vain attempt to force external agencies to bring some greatly needed structure into their lives. All children, particularly during the later years of childhood and early adolescence, test the limits of their social and physical environments. When they can find no limits at all, they are often in as much psychological trouble as if the limits they found were chokingly restrictive.

As different as these two family situations seem at first glance, they are similar in several important ways. Perhaps the most important similarity between overly permissive and overly restrictive parents is the tendency they both have to deny love and affection and support to the children and to attempt to control them almost entirely with punishment. When either type of parent is interviewed and asked to state what he thinks is fine or good or exemplary about his child (say, a ten-year-old girl picked up for shoplifting), the parent might hem and haw for some time before he finds one thing about the child that he believes is "good." These parents have no difficulty at all in telling what they think is wrong with the child, however. In many such interviews, even when the parents are encouraged to list the child's finer points, they are likely to combine the positives with a stinging negative: "Well, she's

Figure 16.5. One type of family setting that appears to breed delinquency is the repressive home, in which thousands of ironclad rules weigh the child down. These are most often middle-class homes.

really pretty good in school, but then, of course, she usually skips school anyway and she gets in so much trouble there . . ." For these parents, love is far too precious a commodity to be wasted on the likes of their offspring. Oddly enough, however, when these parents are asked whether they love the child, they assure the interviewer that they do.

HELP FOR DELINQUENTS

Attempts to help youthful offenders that do not include massive intervention into and reshaping of the family environment are usually doomed to failure. One promising new technique for helping such children involves training the parents in the proper use of what are called *techniques of behavior modification*. Children, particularly those between the ages of six and twelve, are most responsive to love and affection. Because, as we have said, the parents of most juvenile delinquents use punishment (which breeds rebellion) instead of positive methods of influencing the child's behavior (such as openly expressed interest or affection), the parents must be taught how to reward the child for doing good things.

Typically, the first task the therapist faces is that of getting the parents to realize how negative their behavior toward the child actually is. When asked, most such parents will insist that they do indeed show the child considerable love. Often it is necessary for the therapist to arrange for a record to be made of family interactions—usually a video or audio tape recording—and then play the record back to the parents, asking them as

they listen or watch to record each instance in which they rewarded the child for good behavior or said something good about him and each time they punished the child or said something bad about him. In such circumstances, these parents often sit through a ninety-minute recording of, say, dinner-table interactions without finding one instance where they were kind to or positive toward the child, yet they count fifty or a hundred instances of negative behavior.

Once the parents recognize the negative tone of their actions and are willing to attempt to change —offering the child love and affection as a reward for doing right (*positive reinforcement*) rather than making use solely of punishment for misbehavior—they can often be trained in better ways of influencing their offspring. A few illustrations of the proper use of the principles of behavior modification not only may serve to make the principles more understandable but may also illustrate the tremendous influence most parents actually have on their child's socialization.

Figure 16.6. The other type of home from which delinquents spring is totally unstructured; often there is no such thing as a family meal. These are usually lower-class homes.

CASES OF BEHAVIOR MODIFICATION

Gary was a nine-year-old, rather large for his age, who had gotten his parents in trouble because of aggressive attacks on other (usually smaller) children in the neighborhood. Although he had been toilet trained at a fairly early age, he still wet the bed almost every night; ridicule and punishment for such incontinence failed to break the habit. When his parents attempted any form of discipline, Gary would often fly into a rage and physically attack them. Video recordings of parent-child interactions showed that Gary's father and mother seldom offered him praise for anything he did well. His school grades, particularly in mathematical and scientific subjects, were well above average, but his report cards merely brought him criticism for those subjects in which he was not particularly successful.

In this case, the therapist began with one of the simpler problems, that of Gary's enuresis. A thorough medical examination showed that Gary did not suffer from any kind of physical disability that might explain the bedwetting. He was then told he could earn bonus money for each night that he did not wet the bed. The first few nights, the parents were told to wake him up every two or three hours, inspect his bed, and if it were dry, to ask him to go to the toilet and reward him with a dime for having gotten that far through the night without being enuretic.

More important, the parents were told to hug him and fuss over him each time they gave him the dime and to make it clear to Gary that their approval was even more important than the monetary reward. They were also told to mention to him several times a day how well he was doing whenever he had been able to get through a night without wetting his bed. This intervention was so successful that Gary was able to go the entire first week of treatment without once being enuretic. The parents were told to wake him but once a night during the second week, again to give him considerable praise for his accomplishment, and to reward him with fifteen cents. Gary again went the entire week without wetting the bed.

At this point, Gary was asked if he thought he could get through a full night without being awakened; he agreed to try. He was then given a quarter (and much praise and affection) for each successful night, and again he was able to go the full week without once wetting the bed. The next week he was given a quarter only if he could go two nights in a row without a mistake, and, in subsequent weeks, the time span between monetary rewards was increased considerably. The parents were careful to continue to give him praise every day, however, so that eventually the money no longer was necessary.

If behavior modification accomplished no more than teaching Gary how to be continent, it might be considered little more than a clever if rather limited technique. However, the parents reported considerable change in Gary's other behaviors. The aggressive outbursts diminished almost to zero, his schoolwork improved even in those subjects he did not particularly like, and he appeared

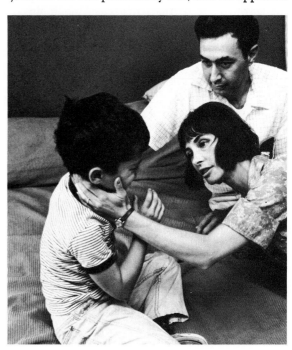

to be much more responsive to his parents' requests. In short, most of the other problems the parents had reported simply cleared up spontaneously. It would be easy to imagine that bedwetting was the basic reason for Gary's difficulties, but that probably was not the case. Rather, once the parents had learned how influential praise and affection could be in handling Gary, they began to make much greater use of positive reinforcement and less use of punishment. The parents reported that once the bedwetting was under control, Gary's general deportment changed so much that they were much happier to have him around the house than they had been before. The therapist noted, however, that the change in Gary was the result of a change in the way the parents were treating him. Once the parents had discovered the power of supportive love and affection, and Gary responded by ceasing many of his annoying behaviors, the parents found that they could openly give him the warmth that they had been unable to express to him before. It is little wonder, then, that Gary's other difficulties cleared up "spontaneously."

Gary came from a rather repressive, overly structured middle-class home. Lydia, however, was an eleven-year-old from a lower-class family. Her father had disappeared several years before. Her mother worked as a waitress in a local bar and was an alcoholic. Because her mother was gone nights and tended to sleep most of the day, Lydia had tremendous freedom. She went to school when she felt like it; but because she seldom felt like it, and because her mother never got up to see her off to school, she was truant more often than she was in class. When she was in school, she was in constant trouble. She smoked openly in the girls' restrooms, she wrote obscene words on the walls, she sassed her teachers, and she got into fights with other children. She came under the jurisdiction of the local juvenile court on a variety of offenses, including school truancy, running away from home, curfew violations, shoplifting, and insulting policemen. She was known to be sexually promiscuous and to smoke marijuana. Her language could make a sailor blush.

The therapist assigned to Lydia's case soon discovered that the mother did in fact wish that Lydia would run away and never come back. Most of Lydia's contacts with her mother were decidedly negative and usually consisted of the mother's telling Lydia to get lost and not be a bother. The mother was brought under a court order forcing her to cooperate in Lydia's treatment or risk a fine or a jail sentence herself. Once the chips were down, the mother proved to be fairly cooperative. Lydia and her mother both made lists of what kinds of things they wanted the other to do. Lydia was to get her allowance only if she went to school daily; her mother was to get up each morning in time to cook Lydia's breakfast and to see her off to school. Lydia then agreed not to bother her mother during the rest of the day and to keep her room in order.

The mother was given considerable practice in how to praise Lydia for good behavior, to say

"please" and "thank you" to the girl instead of merely shouting commands at her all the time. Lydia was given practice sessions in how to interact with other children and with adults in which she earned money and praise for not using obscene language. Lydia earned points for each day she attended school, for each day her teachers sent home a positive report of "no fighting," and for getting good grades; these points could be turned in whenever she had enough of them in exchange for new clothes, cosmetics, and records. The school authorities agreed to let her off the school grounds at lunchtime so that she could have a cigarette where the authorities couldn't see that she was smoking (another program was set up to help her cut down on the number of cigarettes she smoked each day). Both teachers and parent were instructed to give her frequent praise for good behavior and to ignore her bad behavior as much as possible. The year before therapy was started, Lydia had been absent from school without excuse more than 60 percent of the time and was failing almost every subject. After therapy began, she was truant but three days out of a hundred and her grades were mostly As and Bs.

In both cases prior to the beginning of therapy, the parents expressed a belief that their child was in some way abnormal and that his abnormality probably had some kind of physiological basis. The misbehavior that Lydia and Gary showed was, according to their parents, in no way due to any failing or lack of understanding on the parents' part, for hadn't they done everything possible to help the child? And yet the child had not responded. It is difficult in most such situations for parents to comprehend that they are primarily responsible for most things the child does and that they must change their own way of behaving toward them (and toward the rest of the world). Few parents ever suspect how mutable a child is, particularly during the critical years of later childhood; it is much easier to blame the child's genes, or bad companions, or poor schoolteachers —or even television—than to accept the blame themselves. To be a schoolteacher, one needs years of special training and a certificate showing that one knows one's business. To be a parent, the only license one needs is that obtainable from the local marriage bureau for five dollars—and not always that.

INFLUENCES ON PERSONALITY GROWTH

Parents are the single most important determiner of the normal child's attitudes toward the world around him. Next in importance come the siblings in the family and the child's age-group companions during his formative years, then close relatives, schoolteachers, and religious leaders, and finally heros and heroines the child reads about, hears about, or watches on television. For any given child, one may be able to find exceptions to this rank ordering, but in general it is a fairly accurate rating of influence. When parents are asked to draw up such a list, they often put such minor sources as television at the top of the list. In past generations, parents blamed their

Figure 16.7. Television actually has very little influence on children's personality development.

offspring's misbehavior on radio, comic books, pulp magazines, and, at the turn of the century, dime novels. These days, the "tube" bears the brunt of the projected blame.

TELEVISION

Research studies conducted both in the United States and abroad show that the mass media have little, if any, strong effect on most children. In several experiments conducted in Great Britain in the late 1950s, three psychologists at the University of London studied the differences between thousands of children who watched television and thousands who did not. Their findings suggest that British children view television much as do American children, although apparently for a little less time each day. Brighter children watch TV less than do duller children, and, in general, children prefer adults' programs to those specifically designed for children. The major effect that the psychologists report is that children who watch television go to bed, on the average, about twenty minutes later than children who do not. Beyond that one effect, their results are significant in what they do not find rather than in what they find.

Television appears to make the duller children a little more knowledgeable about the world and may slightly reduce the level of information of the more intelligent children. Television may give the brighter child a faster start on learning in his preschool years, but this effect seems to disappear during the later years of childhood. The British psychologists found no evidence of harmful physi-cal effects; no indication that television introduces a harmful amount of aggression, fear, or violence into a normal child; no data showing that it contributes significantly to a child's becoming delinquent; no evidence that television can turn an undisturbed child into a disturbed one. It may exacerbate a psychological problem already present or even give criminal suggestions to a child already well down the path toward criminality; this finding is of some importance because, in fact, addicts to television are, in a large proportion of cases, children who are already maladjusted and disturbed. One suspects, however, that if these children were not getting their "bad" ideas from television, they would be reading comics, watching movies, or reading pulp magazines—or even listening to their parents.

More recent studies in the United States by Wilbur Schramm (for many years director of the Institute for Communication Research at Stanford University) and by many other investigators suggest that the influence of television on American children is little different from its influence on their British counterparts. On the average, children spend a good deal less time watching television than they do watching their parents. What children make of television, and how it affects them, is determined to a large extent by what their parents teach them to make of it.

MARIJUANA

If television was the parental scapegoat of the 1960s, upon which all juvenile misbehavior was

Figure 16.8. Marijuana seems to be providing the cultural crisis of the seventies; its use has been shown to exist at the elementary-school level.

blamed, it seems likely that marijuana will provide the cultural crisis of the 1970s. A recent random sample of 1,104 men and women in a large American city showed that almost half of those adults between the ages of eighteen and twenty-four had used marijuana one or more times, whereas only some 5 percent of those adults thirty-five years of age and older reported ever trying the drug. (As was true of the data on television viewing, a high proportion of maladjusted or deviant adults admitted to smoking marijuana, but the *majority* of marijuana users appeared to be reasonably conventional, according to the indicators used in this study.) Although there are no reliable data on the smoking of marijuana by children in the age group six to twelve, a recent survey of high-school students in the state of Michigan indicated that better than 50 percent of them had tried marijuana at least once and that about 25 percent smoked it regularly. A better example of a "generation gap" could hardly be found. The long-term effects of the use of marijuana are as yet unknown (as are the long-term effects of viewing violence on television) and can only be guessed at; the social effects of the generation gap are probably more predictable. Parents with problem children will tend to blame the erratic and antisocial behavior of their sons and daughters on pot rather than realizing that marijuana probably does little more than heighten the problems instilled by the parents. Parents whose children turn out well will tend to give themselves all the credit (and perhaps rightly

so) for the child's having resisted this obvious social evil.

SEXUAL BEHAVIOR AND SEX EDUCATION

Although Freud claimed that sexual development is latent during the later years of childhood, it should be made clear that it is during this critical maturational period that a child's *attitudes* toward sex are firmly established. Until very recently, when sex education began appearing in more enlightened school districts, children were, for the most part, forced to learn the facts of procreation from their peers, from older siblings or friends, from sex manuals thrust into their hands by blushing parents who immediately excused themselves from the scene, from looking up dirty words in dictionaries, from careful search for forbidden treasures in the dusty recesses of public libraries, from pornography purloined from a parent's private collection, and from graffiti scrawled on restroom walls.

Although most middle-class American parents seem reluctant to discuss the facts of reproduction with their children, the parents' views on the subject are readily communicable. The very fact that this subject is seldom discussed openly and factually in most family settings leads a child to a double understanding—sex is both evil and desirable. The child whose hands are slapped for "playing with himself" needs little further evidence of his mother's or father's views on the matter. Sex is something to be practiced in secret, as his parents practice it in secret. It is something to be giggled

about with one's peers (with whom one performs certain physiological investigations when adults aren't around), but it is not a topic for dinner-table conversation, no matter how pressing one's questions about it may seem.

With the advent of sex-education classes in the schools, much of the delicious (if neurotic) wickedness of the topic seems to be disappearing. In many schools, the first instruction in human reproduction is given in the first grade, to be repeated at regular intervals throughout the rest of the child's precollege education. The instructional materials, for the most part, emphasize the biological aspects of conception and birth; more delicate questions, involving both moral and social aspects of sexuality, are typically left to the teacher to handle. It is the latter aspect of sex education that disturbs some parents, who insist that the teacher may instill too liberal or too immoral a viewpoint toward sexuality in their children. Such parents, like those who blame television for their child's delinquency, tend to overlook the fact that the influence of the teacher is very small in comparison to the influence the parents themselves exert on their children's morality. Although critics of sex education in the schools have been successful in having programs removed from some schools, it seems that these critics constitute a minority. In several recent surveys made in school districts in Northern and Eastern states, more than 70 percent of the parents polled voted in favor of continuing—and strengthening—programs already in existence.

Figure 16.9. Many children learn about sex through such sources as graffiti, although increasing numbers are now getting their sex education in the schools.

But what of sexual behavior itself in children aged six to twelve? According to the Freudian hypothesis, it should be nearly nonexistent. There are no adequate studies of the subject, but retrospective data such as those that Kinsey's investigators gathered suggest that the behavior is more hidden and secret than latent. Many children begin true masturbatory activities long before puberty; others engage in conspiratorial games carefully crafted to allow them to make as thorough investigation of matters sexual as their own bodies (and those of their partners) will permit.

One of the most pressing problems facing parents of young children is this: How much might one traumatic sexual encounter at an early age affect a child's later personality development? If a nine-year-old girl is teased into some kind of sexual play by an older male relative, what effect will it have on the girl's chances of establishing a happy home life of her own when she is grown? If a ten-year-old boy is seduced during a homosexual encounter with a camp counselor, is the boy then twisted inexorably toward homosexuality himself? There are no ready-made answers to such questions, and, as is the case in most matters dealing with human sexuality, there are very few data to apply. As a general principle, however, it seems wise to heed the old adage that one swallow does not make a summer. A child whose prior development has been at least normally healthy can probably withstand a traumatic sexual experience without showing any visible scars from it in later life. All the good work put in by parents

Figure 16.10. Today's adults remember having to do some kind of part-time job as children. Today's children take for granted many aspects of "the good life" that would have been undreamed-of luxuries to children a few decades ago.

during a young child's life is not likely to be swept aside by one chance encounter with a sex deviate. If, on the other hand, the parents have botched the child's upbringing rather badly, such a traumatic event may well serve to trigger off severe behavioral problems when the child is grown. It seems that almost all children encounter rather explicit (and often highly illicit) sexual situations between the ages of six and twelve and that most children survive rather nicely. The human sexual urges may occasionally be rather strong, but they are also almost innately directed along rather normal development pathways.

Today's Child—and Tomorrow's

Novelists and other writers (including psychologists) who make their livings evoking the nostalgia of yesteryear typically become rhapsodic about the period of later childhood. It is difficult for most people to remember much of what happened to them before they were in school, and the adolescent period is often tumultuous and unhappy; the years from six to twelve, however, they may remember with pleasure as being a peaceful period when they had much time and few responsibilities. How enticing such a carefree time often seems to the harried adult looking back through the mists of memory! But today's children lead quite different lives than did their mothers and fathers when they were young. Until the last decade or so, preadolescent children had little freedom and little money of their own, and it wasn't more than two decades ago that even

eight- to ten-year-olds were expected to have some kind of part-time job (delivering papers, cutting grass, helping clean house) to supplement their meager allowances. Household chores were commonplace, as were large homework assignments even for very young children, so that time was often at a premium. Having little time or money, children were restricted pretty much to remaining in the vicinity of their own homes. Lacking television's instant entrée into the adult world, they knew considerably less about the world than do today's children. Until recently, only the fortunate few ever got taken to expensive restaurants or vacation spots by their parents (at least in part because the parents themselves had neither the time nor the money to indulge in such pleasures).

Today's child is often given many of the material benefits of life that his parents had to struggle for (assuring themselves, as they did so, that their children would not have to work and slave so hard for such things). Because people all tend to undervalue those things that come to them too cheaply, today's child may well come to accept the good life as being little more than what the world owes him; he may turn more to social and intellectual pursuits for his pleasures than did his parents in their time. The gifts of time and good health and a highly challenging environment await tomorrow's children as they never did await the children of today and yesterday. What use the coming generation will make of these precious commodities, only tomorrow will tell.

In Europe, a woman was near death from a very bad disease, a special kind of cancer. There was one drug that the doctors thought might save her. It was a form of radium for which a druggist was charging ten times what the drug cost him to make. He paid $200 for the radium and charged $2,000 for a small dose of the drug. The sick woman's husband, Heinz, went to everyone he knew to borrow the money, but he could only get together about $1,000, which is half of what it cost. He told the druggist that his wife was dying and asked him to sell it cheaper or let him pay later. But the druggist said, "No, I discovered the drug and I'm going to make money from it." So Heinz got desperate and broke into the man's store to steal the drug for his wife.

Should the husband have done that? Why?

These questions have been answered by people of many ages and walks of life in many different cultures around the world. From their answers, there has emerged a surprisingly consistent view of what it means to be moral in judgment and action. This chapter discusses that view in detail not only because of the psychological relevance of morality but also because morality breaks down into precise developmental stages. You may begin to judge your own type of morality and stage of moral development if, before reading further, you pause to sketch out in some detail your moral view of the husband's actions and your reasons for feeling the way you do.

APPROACHES TO MORALITY

For many generations, morality was the central category for defining social relationships and development, and the social sciences were termed "the moral sciences." In the last few decades, morality has slipped in and out of focus as a central interest in child development. The important work of H. Hartshorne and M. A. May in the late 1920s on children's moral conduct and that of Jean Piaget in the 1930s on moral judgment were followed by two decades of relative inactivity in the area. In the 1930s and 1940s discussions of children's social adjustment absorbed thought about moral character, and discussions of socialization processes absorbed specific concerns about moral development. More recently, however, thoughtful educators and psychologists have become acutely aware of the inadequacies of dealing with moral issues in terms of mental health or group adjustment. The mental-health labels are not really scientific; they are ways of making value judgments about children in terms of social norms. And neither the mental-health nor the social-adjustment terms really allow a definition of the norms and values that are the most basic ideals for children. The barbarities of the socially conforming members of the Nazi system and the other-directed hollow men growing up in modern, affluent society have made us acutely aware of the fact that adjustment to the group is no substitute for moral maturity, a fact reflected in the consciousness of young adults today.

It is apparent, then, that the problems of moral development cannot be successfully considered in terms of personality development and adjustment. But what, then, can moral development mean for psychologists? The following discussion is based primarily upon the theory and research of thinkers in the tradition of cognitive develop-

17

Development of Moral Character

ment: J. M. Baldwin, John Dewey, G. H. Mead, Jean Piaget, and Lawrence Kohlberg.

Most contemporary psychologists and sociologists who write about moral values in child development and education start with the assumption that there are no universal, nonarbitrary moral principles and that each individual acquires his own values from what his particular culture deems to be right or wrong. Although there are major theoretical differences among sociological, psychoanalytical, and learning theorists, they all define moral development as the direct internalization of external cultural norms. Psychoanalytic theory sees morality as tied to development of the superego, and behavioristic learning theories assume that conditions of punishment and reward lead to learning the society's standards. Both approaches have focused upon guilt as the basic motive for morality: the child behaves morally in order to avoid guilt.

Many psychologists make another common assumption closely linked to the assumption of ethical relativity: that morality and moral learning are fundamentally emotional and irrational processes. Most textbooks assume that learning to accept rules and authority is a concrete nonrational process based on repetition, emotion, identification, and sanctions. The child is assumed to be controlled by primitive and selfish drives, which he is reluctant to give up, and the steady experience of authority and discipline is necessary to make him sublimate or unlearn these drives.

The cognitive-developmental approach to moral growth adopted in this chapter questions the assumption of the relativity of values. It claims that *ethical principles* are distinguishable from arbitrary conventional rules and beliefs. Moreover, these principles are the end point of an *invariant developmental sequence*, which is in many ways like the sequence in cognitive growth, as described by Piaget (see Chapters 6, 11, 15, and 20). That moral development is an absolute rather than a relativistic process is substantiated by its invariant unrolling in different social classes and in different cultures.

Against Relativism

Before presenting the evidence, it is important to demonstrate the logical confusions inherent in the relativistic position. The doctrine of ethical relativity assumes that different cultures or groups hold different fundamental moral values and that these values cannot themselves be judged as more or less adequate or more or less moral. When extended to individual differences within cultures, it holds that individuals, too, have different values resulting from differences in basic needs and that these values also are determined by extramoral considerations and so cannot be judged as more or less adequate morally. Explanations for differences in values must be sought outside any general conception of morality. The kinds of confusions that often arise, then, are between matters of fact—what *is*—and matters of value—what *ought to be*—because the relativistic position cannot define what ought to be.

To illustrate, a group of graduate students was asked to consider the moral dilemma at the start of this chapter. Part of a typical reply was as follows: "I think he should steal it because if there is any such thing as a universal human value, it is the value of life, and that would justify stealing it." When this student was asked, "Is there any such thing as a universal human value?" she answered, "No, all values are relative to your culture."

The student starts out by claiming that one ought to act in terms of the universal value of human life, implying that human life is a universal value in the sense that it is logical and desirable for all men to respect human life and that one can demonstrate to other men that it is logical and desirable to do so. If she were clear in her thinking she would see that the *fact* that all men do not always act in terms of this value does not contradict the claim that all men *ought* always to act in accordance with it. If the relativist could clearly separate the question "Are there universal moral values?" from the question "Ought there to be universal human values?" he could easily arrive at an affirmative answer to both questions.

EXISTENCE OF ETHICAL PRINCIPLES

For twelve years, Lawrence Kohlberg has been studying the development of moral judgment and character. His main study has followed the same group of seventy-five boys from early adolescence through young manhood. This study has been supplemented by a series of studies of development in other cultures and by a set of experimental studies, some designed to change a child's stage of moral thought, some to find the relation

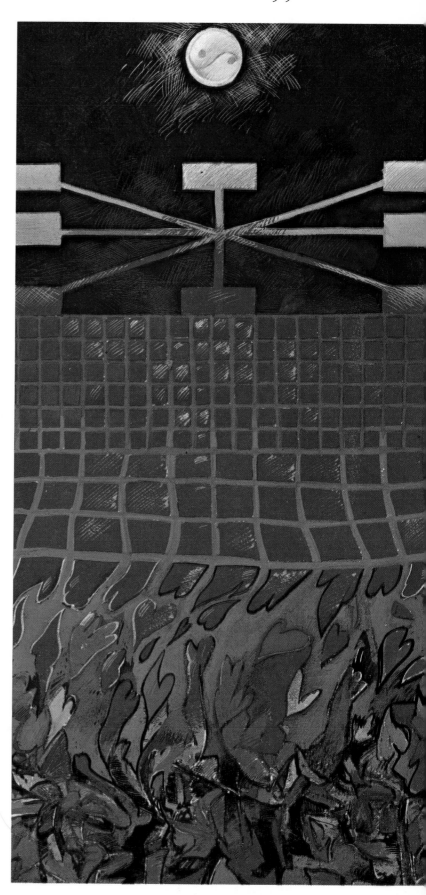

Figure 17.1. An abstract pictorial scheme representing the six stages of moral development as they apply to social reality. At Stage 1 *(bottom)* social power is diffuse. At Stage 2, individuals and their needs emerge and can be seen as separate units, but the units are unstable and exchange-oriented. At Stage 3, the social units are loose and flexible, and their relationships are benign. The unified grid pattern of Stage 4 suggests the orientation toward maintenance of order. In Stage 5 the unified grid breaks up into individual units, which are the starting point of a social-contract orientation. Stage 6 is based on universal principles of justice.

of an individual's moral thought to moral action.

The first assumption behind Kohlberg's approach has been that all humans, even young children, are moral philosophers. The child has a morality of his own. Adults are so busy trying to instill in children their own morality that they seldom listen to children's moralizing. If the child repeats a few of the adult's clichés and behaves himself, most parents think he has learned, or internalized, parental standards. This assumption, which underlies much anthropological and psychological study, can only be made if adults fail to talk to children. As soon as they do, they find that the children have many standards that do not come in any obvious way from parents, peers, or teachers. For example, Kohlberg describes his son's first real internal moral action; it occurred at age four. At that time his son joined the pacifist and vegetarian movement and refused to eat meat because, as the child said, "It's bad to kill animals." In spite of lengthy, Hawkish argumentation by his parents about the difference between justified and unjustified killing, the boy remained a vegetarian for six months. Like most Doves, however, his principles recognized occasions of just or legitimate killing. Kohlberg recounts how one night when he was reading aloud a book of Eskimo life involving a seal-killing expedition, his son got angry and said, "You know, there is one kind of meat I would eat, Eskimo meat. It's bad to kill animals so it's all right to eat *them*."

It is evident that the boy's attitude toward killing is not an internalization of the cultural rule "Thou shalt not kill" but is based on his immediate and natural empathy for other living beings. So, too, his punitiveness is not the result of the introjection of parental punishment but is based on the natural and primitive principle by which one bad act deserves another.

THE STAGES OF MORAL DEVELOPMENT

On the basis of theoretical and philosophical considerations and from *listening* to children of all ages and backgrounds explain their judgments about hypothetical moral dilemmas, Kohlberg constructed the six stages of moral development defined below. The six stages fall into the three levels shown: the premoral, conventional, and principled.

I. PRECONVENTIONAL LEVEL

At this level the child is responsive to cultural rules and labels of good and bad, right or wrong, but interprets these labels in terms of either the physical or the hedonistic consequences of action (punishment, reward, exchange of favors) or in terms of the physical power of those who enunciate the rules and labels. The level is divided into the following two stages:

STAGE 1: *The punishment and obedience orientation.* The physical consequences of action determine its goodness or badness regardless of the human meaning or value of these consequences. Avoidance of punishment and unquestioning deference to power are valued in their own right, not in terms of respect for an underlying moral order supported by punishment and authority (the latter being Stage 4).

STAGE 2: *The instrumental relativist orientation.* Right action consists of that which instrumentally satisfies one's own needs and occasionally the needs of others. Human relations are viewed in terms like those of the marketplace. Elements of fairness, of reciprocity, and of equal sharing are present, but they are always interpreted in a physical, pragmatic way. Reciprocity is a matter of "you scratch my back and I'll scratch yours," not of loyalty, gratitude, or justice.

II. CONVENTIONAL LEVEL

At this level, maintaining the expectations of the individual's family, group, or nation is perceived as valuable in its own right, regardless of immediate and obvious consequences. The attitude is one not only of *conformity* to personal expectations and social order but of loyalty to it, of actively *maintaining*, supporting, and justifying the order and of identifying with the persons or group involved in it. At this level, there are the following two stages:

STAGE 3: *The interpersonal concordance or "good boy–nice girl" orientation.* Good behavior is that which pleases or helps others and is approved by them. There is much conformity to stereotypical images of what is majority or "natural" behavior. Behavior is frequently judged by intention—"he means well" becomes important for the first time. One earns approval by being "nice."

STAGE 4: *The "law and order" orientation.* There is orientation toward authority, fixed rules, and the maintenance of the social order. Right behavior consists of doing one's duty, showing respect for authority, and maintaining the given social order for its own sake.

III. POSTCONVENTIONAL, AUTONOMOUS, OR PRINCIPLED LEVEL

At this level, there is a clear effort to define moral values and principles that have validity and application apart from the authority of the groups or persons holding these principles and apart from the individual's own identification with these groups. This level again has two stages:

STAGE 5: *The social-contract, legalistic orientation* —generally with utilitarian overtones. Right action tends to be defined in terms of general individual rights and in terms of standards that have been critically examined and agreed upon by the whole society. There is a clear awareness of the relativism of personal values and opinions and a corresponding emphasis upon procedural rules for reaching consensus. Aside from what is constitutionally and democratically agreed upon, the right is a matter of personal "values" and "opinion." The result is an emphasis upon the "legal point of view," but with an emphasis upon the possibility of changing law in terms of rational considerations of social utility (rather than freezing it in terms of Stage 4 "law and order"). Outside the legal realm, free agreement and contract are the binding elements of obligation. This is the "official" morality of the American government and Constitution.

STAGE 6: *The universal ethical-principle orientation.* Right is defined by the decision of conscience in accord with self-chosen *ethical principles* appealing to logical comprehensiveness, universality, and consistency. These principles are abstract and ethical (the Golden Rule, the categorical imperative); they are not concrete moral rules like the Ten Commandments. At heart, these are universal principles of *justice*, of the *reciprocity* and *equality* of the human *rights*, and of respect for the dignity of human beings as *individual persons*.

The full definition of stages is more detailed than is shown here and is based on separate treatments of thirty basic moral concepts that can be found in any culture. Some examples of the concepts are "motives for moral action" and "basis of respect for moral authority."

One of these concepts, the "value of human life," is defined below at each of the six stages generalized earlier. The quotations are from actual answers that typify children's judgments at

Figure 17.2. Stage 1 moral thought is based largely on doing good to avoid punishment.

that stage. The stages, however, define total ways of thinking, not attitudes toward a situation.

STAGE 1: No differentiation between moral value of life and its physical or social-status value.
Tommy, age ten (Why should the druggist give the drug to the dying woman when her husband couldn't pay for it?): "If someone important is in a plane and is allergic to heights and the stewardess won't give him medicine because she's only got enough for one and she's got a sick one, a friend, in back, they'd probably put the stewardess in a lady's jail because she didn't help the important one."
(Is it better to save the life of one important person or a lot of unimportant people?): "All the people that aren't important because one man just has one house, maybe a lot of furniture, but a whole bunch of people have an awful lot of furniture and some of these poor people might have a lot of money and it doesn't look it."

STAGE 2: The value of a human life is seen as instrumental to the satisfaction of the needs of its possessor or of other persons. Decision to save life is relative to, or to be made by, its possessor (differentiation of physical and interest value of life, differentiation of its value to self and to others).
Jim, age thirteen (Should the doctor mercy kill a fatally ill woman requesting death because of her pain?): "If she requests it, it's really up to her. She is in such terrible pain, just the same as people are always putting animals out of their pain."

STAGE 3: The value of a human life is based on the empathy and affection of family members and others toward its possessor. (The value of human life, as based on social sharing, community, and love, is differentiated from the instrumental and hedonistic value of life applicable also to animals.)
Tommy, age sixteen (same question): "It might be best for her, but her husband—it's a human life—not like an animal, it just doesn't have the same relationship that a human being does to a family.

You can become attached to a dog, but nothing like a human you know."
STAGE 4: Life is conceived as sacred in terms of its place in a categorical moral or religious order of rights and duties. (The value of human life, as a categorical member of a moral order, is differentiated from its value to specific other people in the family, etc. Value of life is still partly dependent upon serving the group, the state, or God, however.)
Jim, age sixteen (same question): "I don't know. In one way, it's murder, it's not a right or privilege of man to decide who shall live and who should die. God put life into everybody on earth and you're taking away something from that person that came directly from God, and you're destroying something that is very sacred, it's in a way part of God and it's almost destroying a part of God when you kill a person. There's something of God in everyone."

STAGE 5: Life is valued both in terms of its relation to community welfare and in terms of being a universal human right. (Obligation to respect the basic right to life is differentiated from generalized respect for the sociomoral order. The general value of the independent human life is a primary autonomous value not dependent upon other values.)
Jim, age twenty (same question): "Given the ethics of the doctor who has taken on responsibility to save human life—from that point of view he probably shouldn't, but there is another side, there are more and more people in the medical profession who are thinking it is a hardship on everyone, the person, the family, when you know they are going to die. When a person is kept alive by an artificial lung or kidney it's more like being a vegetable than being a human who is alive. If it's her own choice I think there are certain rights and privileges that go along with being a human being. I am a human being and have certain desires for life and I think everybody else does, too. You have a world of which you are the center, and everybody else does, too, and in that sense we're all equal."

Figure 17.3. Stage 2 moral thought is like that of the marketplace. Although elements of reciprocity are present, they exist in a pragmatic way: "You scratch my back, and I'll scratch yours."

STAGE 6: Belief in the sacredness of human life as representing a universal human value of respect for the individual. (The moral value of a human being, as an object of moral principle, is differentiated from a formal recognition of his rights.)

Jim, age twenty-four (Should the husband steal the drug to save his wife? How about for someone he just knows?): "Yes. A human life takes precedence over any other moral or legal value, whoever it is. A human life has inherent value whether or not it is valued by a particular individual."

(Why is that?): "The inherent worth of the individual human being is the central value in a set of values where the principles of justice and love are normative for all human relationships."

HOW VALUES CHANGE

The stages represent an invariant developmental sequence. Movement, when it takes place, is to the next higher stage. Children, however, are not likely to make all of their moral judgments at the same stage. Typically, as he develops, 50 percent of a child's judgments are at one stage, which can be designated as his current stage of moral development. The remainder of his judgments are divided between the preceding stage—the one he has almost moved out of—and the stage he will (may) move into next.

The age trends for the six stages are indicated in Figure 17.6. It is evident that the number of moral statements at Stage 1 and at Stage 2 level decrease with age; those at the Stage 3 and Stage 4 level increase until about age thirteen and then stabilize; and the number of statements at the highest two stages continue to increase from age thirteen to age sixteen, although at age sixteen

they still constitute a limited proportion of moral judgment. Because these age trends show that higher-level moral concepts and attitudes are acquired only in late childhood and adolescence, it is clear that they require an extensive foundation of cognitive growth and social experience. These aspects of moral development will be discussed in detail later in the chapter.

THEORETICAL BASIS

The *formal* criteria for development, which are applied to aspects of growth as diverse as motor development and maturity of personality, are increased *differentiation* and *integration*. These criteria also define movement from one stage of moral development to the next—within a philosophical framework that defines, on the basis of its assumptions, a universal morality.

The ethical philosophy that Kohlberg sets at the base of his theory is that of the formalist school; it has a long tradition, from the classics of Immanuel Kant to the recent papers of R. M. Hare. It stresses the distinctively *universal* nature of adequate moral judgments. That is, it defines *the right* for anyone in any situation. In contrast, conventional morality defines good behavior for a Democrat but not for a Republican, for an American but not for a Vietnamese, for a father but not for a son.

The way in which both the developmental and philosophical criteria are embodied in the stages of moral development is best indicated by the preceding examples of them for the moral worth of human life. The stages move toward *prescrip-*

Figure 17.4. Stage 3 moral behavior is that which is approved by others.

tivity because the moral imperative to value life becomes increasingly independent of the factual properties of the life in question. First, the person's furniture becomes irrelevant to his value, next whether he has a loving family, and so on. At the same time the stages show an increasing differentiation of moral considerations from other considerations. Simultaneously, movement through the stages is toward an increased universality of moral valuing of human life: at Stage 1, only important persons' lives are valued; at Stage 3 only family members'; at Stage 6 any life is to be morally valued equally. In this way the psychological explanation of why the child moves from stage to stage converges with a philosophical explanation of why one stage is "better" than another.

Along with the cross-cultural studies, to be discussed in the following section, a series of recent studies supports the theoretical basis for construction of the stages. The studies show that children and adolescents comprehend all stages up to their own but not more than one above their own. The material below, dealing with the aspect "motives for engaging in moral action," was used in a study conducted by J. Rest in 1968. Adolescents were asked to restate each of the pro and con statements in their own words and to rank the statements in order of how good they were. (The problem dealt with was the drug-stealing one, presented at the start of the chapter.)

STAGE 1: Action is motivated by avoidance of punishment, and "conscience" is irrational fear of punishment.

Pro: "If you let your wife die, you will get in trouble. You'll be blamed for not spending the money to save her and there'll be an investigation of you and the druggist for your wife's death."

Con: "You shouldn't steal the drug because you'll be caught and sent to jail if you do. If you do get away, your conscience would bother you thinking how the police would catch up with you at any minute."

STAGE 2: Action motivated by desire for reward or benefit. Possible guilt reactions are ignored and punishment viewed in a pragmatic manner. (Differentiates own fear, pleasure, or pain from punishment-consequences.)

Pro: "If you do happen to get caught you could give the drug back and you wouldn't get much of a sentence. It wouldn't bother you much to serve a little jail term, if you have your wife when you get out."

Con: "He may not get much of a jail term if he steals the drug, but his wife will probably die before he gets out so it won't do him much good. If his wife dies, he shouldn't blame himself, it wasn't his fault she has cancer."

STAGE 3: Action motivated by anticipation of disapproval of others, actual or imagined-hypothetical (e.g., guilt). (Differentiation of disapproval from punishment, fear, and pain.)

Pro: "No one will think you're bad if you steal the drug but your family will think you're an inhuman husband if you don't. If you let your wife die, you'll never be able to look anybody in the face again."

Con: "It isn't just the druggist who will think you're a criminal, everyone else will too. After you steal it, you'll feel bad thinking how you've brought dishonor on your family and yourself; you won't be able to face anyone again."

STAGE 4: Action motivated by anticipation of dishonor, i.e., institutionalized blame for failure of duty, and by guilt over concrete harm done to others.

Figure 17.5. Stage 4 is the "law and order" orientation— respect for authority.

(Differentiates formal dishonor from informal disapproval. Differentiates guilt for bad consequences from disapproval.)

Pro: "If you have any sense of honor, you won't let your wife die because you're afraid to do the only thing that will save her. You'll always feel guilty that you caused her death if you don't do your duty to her."

Con: "You're desperate and you may not know you're doing wrong when you steal the drug. But you'll know you did wrong after you're punished and sent to jail. You'll always feel guilty for your dishonesty and lawbreaking."

STAGE 5: Concern about maintaining respect of equals and of the community (assuming their respect is based on reason rather than emotions). Concern about own self-respect, i.e., to avoid judging self as irrational, inconsistent, nonpurposive. (Discriminates between institutionalized blame and community disrespect or self-disrespect.)

Pro: "You'd lose other people's respect, not gain it, if you don't steal. If you let your wife die, it would be out of fear, not out of reasoning it out. So you'd just lose self-respect and probably the respect of others too."

Con: "You would lose your standing and respect in the community and violate the law. You'd lose respect for yourself if you're carried away by emotion and forget the long-range point of view."

STAGE 6: Concern about self-condemnation for violating one's own principles. (Differentiates between community respect and self-respect. Differentiates between self-respect for achieving rationality and self-respect for maintaining moral principles.)

Pro: "If you don't steal the drug and let your wife die, you'd always condemn yourself for it afterward. You wouldn't be blamed and you would have lived up to the outside rule of the law but you wouldn't have lived up to your own standards of conscience."

Con: "If you stole the drug, you wouldn't be blamed by other people but you'd condemn yourself because you wouldn't have lived up to your own conscience and standards of honesty."

When the adolescents ranked the statements, they typically approved statements two or more stages above their own, but restated them in terms of lower-stage thinking. Stages below the subject's own were disapproved or ranked low. The reason that the young people prefer the next stage above their own to their own stage and to all the lower stages is because it is more differentiated and integrated than the lower stage but still comprehensible in terms of their development and experience.

The foregoing discussion explains why movement in moral thought is usually irreversibly forward; the explanation does not require the assumption that moral progression is wired into the nervous system or is directly caused by physical-natural forces. It also helps to explain why the step-by-step sequence of stages is invariant. This inner logical order is suggested by the interpretive statements in parentheses in the last sequence ("motives for engaging in moral action"). In these sequences each new basic differentiation logically depends upon differentiation before it; the order of differentiations could not logically be other than it is.

CULTURAL UNIVERSALITY OF STAGES

The stages of moral development appear to be culturally universal. Kohlberg studied non-Western as well as Western cultures, and his studies

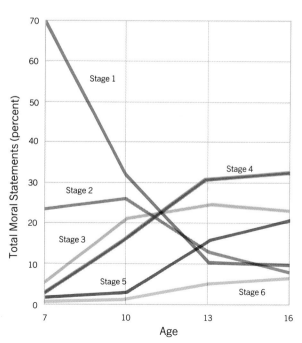

Figure 17.6. Age trends for use of the six stages of moral development. (After Kohlberg, 1963.)

suggest that the same basic ways of moral valuing are found in every culture—and that they develop in the same order.

The following dilemma, much like the drug-stealing one quoted earlier, was used in an Atayal (Malaysian aboriginal) and a Taiwanese village:

A man and his wife had just migrated from the high mountains. They started to farm but there was no rain, and no crops grew. No one had enough food. The wife got sick from having little food and could only sleep. Finally she was close to dying from having no food. The husband could not get any work and the wife could not move to another town. There was only one grocery store in the village, and the storekeeper charged a very high price for the food because there was no other store and people had no place else to go to buy food. The husband asked the storekeeper for some food for his wife and said he would pay for it later. The storekeeper said, "No, I won't give you any food unless you pay first." The husband went to all the people in the village to ask for food but no one had food to spare. So he got desperate and broke into the store to steal food for his wife.

Should the husband have done that? Why?

Children at Stage 2 in the Taiwanese village would reply to the above story as follows: "He should steal the food for his wife because if she dies he'll have to pay for her funeral and that costs a lot." In the Atayal village, funerals were not so expensive, and the Stage 2 boys would say, "He should steal the food because he needs his wife to cook for him." Both sets of these children made instrumental-exchange calculations. In each case, there was a distinctive difference in form between the child's thought and that of a mature adult, a difference that was definable independent of the particular culture.

An American boy, presented with a similar problem about the value of a human life, makes the same kind of instrumental valuing. The crux of the dilemma presented to the boy was: "Should the doctor mercy-kill a fatally ill woman requesting death because of her pain?" The boy answered, "Maybe it would be good to put her out of her pain, she'd be better off that way. But the husband wouldn't want it, it's not like an animal. If a pet dies you can get along without it —it isn't something you really need. Well, you can get a new wife, but it's not really the same."

It is this emphasis on the distinctive form (as opposed to the content) of the child's moral thought that allows one to call all men moral philosophers.

Figures 17.7 and 17.8 indicate the cultural universality of the sequence of stages. Figure 17.7 presents the age trends for middle-class urban boys in the United States, Taiwan, and Mexico. At age ten in each country, the greater number of moral statements are scored at the lower stages. In the United States, by age sixteen the order is reversed, so that the greater proportion uses higher stages (with the exception of Stage 6, which is rarely used). The results in Mexico and Taiwan are the same, except that development is a little slower. The most conspicuous feature is that Stage 5 thinking is much more salient in the United States than in Mexico or Taiwan at age sixteen. Nevertheless, it is present in the other countries, so it is not purely an American con-

Figure 17.7. Stages of moral development for middle-class urban boys of various ages in the United States, Taiwan, and Mexico.

struct. Figure 17.8 indicates results from two isolated villages, one in Yucatán, one in Turkey. The similarity of pattern in the two villages is striking. While conventional moral thought (Stages 3 and 4) increases steadily from age ten to sixteen, at sixteen it still has not achieved a clear ascendancy over premoral thought (Stages 1 and 2). Stages 5 and 6 are totally absent in this group. Trends for lower-class urban groups are intermediate in rate of development between those for the middle-class and those for the village boys.

IMPLICATIONS OF CULTURAL UNIVERSALITY

The first and most obvious implication of these findings is that many social-scientific notions of the cultural relativity of morals are false. Conclusions about cultural relativity have been based upon striking cultural differences in customs; they have not taken account of the meaning of such customs with regard to differences in principles or form of moral judgment. A comparison of American college students' quaint springtime rite of sitting-in in the 1960s with their quaint rites of panty-raiding in the 1950s would not tell us anything about moral changes unless we investigated the students' thoughts about the values involved in what they were doing. The results of Kohlberg's studies suggest that the same basic ways of moral valuing are found in every culture and develop in the same order.

A second implication of these findings is that basic moral principles are not dependent on a particular religion, or on any religion at all. No important differences in development of moral thinking were found among Catholics, Protestants, Jews, Buddhists, Moslems, and atheists. Children's moral values in the religious area seem to go through the same stages as their general moral values: a Stage 2 child is likely to say, "Be good to God and he'll be good to you." Both cultural values and religion are important factors in selectively elaborating certain themes in the moral life, but they are not unique causes of the development of basic moral values.

The data collected do not indicate that all values are universal but rather that *basic moral* values are universal. As an example, a Taiwanese boy recommends stealing the food "because if she dies, he'll have to pay for her funeral and that costs a lot." No American boy ever says that. But American boys will recommend stealing the drug because otherwise "there'll be no one to cook your food." In other words, big funerals are a value in Taiwan and not in the United States, but both the value of life and a stage of instrumental-pragmatic thinking about this value are culturally universal.

THE COGNITIVE-DEVELOPMENTAL APPROACH

Two basic assumptions of the cognitive-developmental theory will be stressed here. First, moral development has a cognitive core. Second, moral education or socialization does not transmit fixed moral values but rather stimulates the child's restructuring of his experience.

COGNITION AND EMOTION

To stress the cognitive core is not to dismiss the role of emotion in moral judgment. Discussions

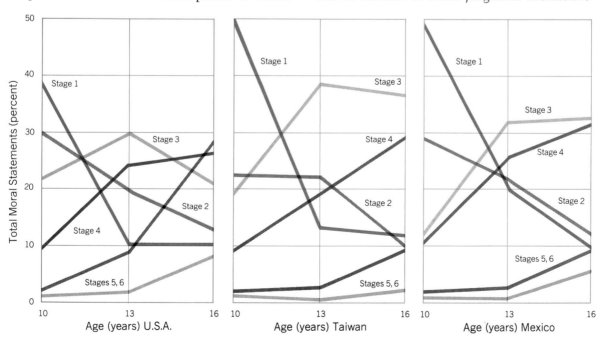

of cognition and emotion usually founder under the assumption that knowing and feeling are different mental states. The cognitive-developmental view holds that cognition and emotion are different aspects of, or perspectives on, the same mental events; that all mental events have both cognitive and emotional aspects; and that the development of mental dispositions reflects structural changes that are recognizable in both cognitive and emotional perspectives. Although moral judgments often involve strong emotional components, the presence of strong emotion in no way *reduces* the cognitive component of moral judgment. It is true, however, that the cognitive component may function differently under pressure of strong emotion than in emotionally neutral areas. An astronomer's calculation that a comet will hit the earth will be accompanied by strong emotion, but his calculation in these circumstances is no less cognitive than his calculation of a comet's path in outer space.

The role of emotion in moral judgment, however, is different than its role in a scientific judgment like the astronomer's. Moral judgments are usually made about sentiments and institutions and persons, and to a large extent they express, and are justified by, the judger's sentiments. The development of sentiment as it enters into moral judgment is, however, a development of structures with a heavy cognitive component. The developmental sequence dealing with "motives for engaging in moral action" (quoted earlier) illustrates this concept by showing how the sentiments of fear, shame, and guilt enter into moral

judgment. The emergence of self-condemnation as a distinctive sentiment in moral judgment is the final step in a series of cognitive differentiations. Studies that have produced data like the successive differentiations shown in that sequence demonstrate that the quality of the emotional component of moral judgment is determined by moral cognitive-structural development rather than the other way around. For example, two adolescents who are thinking of stealing something may have the same feeling of anxiety in the pit of their stomachs. One adolescent (Stage 2) may interpret the feeling as "being chicken" or "being afraid of the police" and so may ignore it. The other (Stage 4) interprets the feeling as "the warning of my conscience" and makes his decision on that basis.

MORALITY AND INTELLIGENCE

Empirical studies have shown that maturity of moral judgment is correlated with cognitive maturity but is clearly distinguishable from it. Among children of a given age, the correlations between IQ and moral maturity have ranged from .35 to .50 in various samples, but older children are generally more mature in moral judgment because they are more cognitively mature. IQ tests are actually poor tests of those reasoning processes relevant to moral judgment. In fact, age correlates better with maturity of moral judgment than does IQ. A certain level of cognitive maturity is necessary for a given level of moral judgment, but it does not, itself, assure moral judgment. In other words, all morally advanced children are bright, but not all bright children are morally advanced.

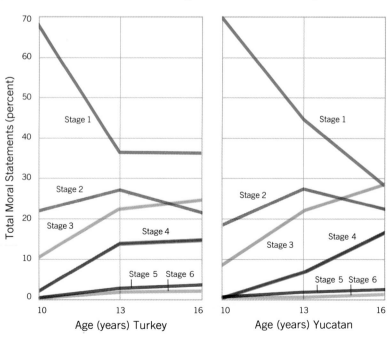

Figure 17.8. Stages of moral development found in boys in isolated villages in Yucatán and Turkey.

Moral judgment requires other aspects of personality and particular interactions between a personality and its intimate environment.

Social Interaction and Moral Growth

The second basic assumption of the cognitive-developmental theory—that moral stages represent the interaction between the child's structuring tendencies and the structural features of the environment—is also supported by study findings. They show that variations in the child's cognitive and social environment affect the rate of growth and maximum level of moral development but do not define the stages as such. Although one study has shown that if a child's parents are at the principled level, the child will reach the conventional (and principled) stage of moral judgment more rapidly than if his parents are at the conventional level, other studies have shown that passive exposure to the next stage of thinking is neither a necessary nor a sufficient condition for upward moral movement. Even where contact with the environment is demonstrably intense, as in the typical family, simple exposure cannot directly account for a child's movement through stages. If it did, conventional-stage parents would be as successful as principled-stage parents in bringing a child up to the conventional level. One reason why exposure is not a sufficient condition for upward movement is that a child at a given stage does not necessarily comprehend messages at the next stage. Studies show that the only children who comprehend messages one stage above their own already show substantial (20 percent) spon-taneous usage of that stage of thought and that it is these children who account for all of the learning about or assimilation of models one stage up. Presumably, then, movement to the next stage involves *internal cognitive reorganization* rather than the mere learning of additional content from the outside.

CONFLICT AS A CONDITION FOR CHANGE

Following one of Piaget's main theses about cognitive development, E. Turiel postulates that cognitive conflict or imbalance is the central condition for reorganization or upward movement in moral development. This position is supported by preliminary results from a series of experiments in which children heard varying combinations of contradictory arguments, but all flowing from the same stage—as illustrated by the statements relating to the drug-stealing episode in the sequence on "motives for engaging in moral action."

To test the hypothesis that moral-stage change depends upon conflict, M. Blatt and Kohlberg developed a four-month program of moral discussions for classes of children aged eleven to fifteen. The children discussed and argued hypothetical dilemmas. The teacher supported and clarified arguments that were at an average (Stage 3) level but challenged those below that level. When it seemed that most of the children understood these arguments and could extend them to new situations, the teacher began to challenge the Stage 3 level and to support and clarify Stage 4 arguments.

The children were given a test before and after

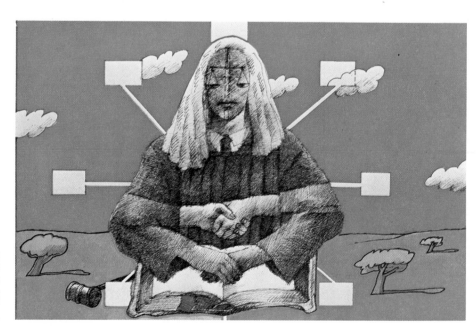

Figure 17.9. Stage 5 moral thought is the social-contract, legalistic orientation. Aside from what is democratically agreed on by the society, the right is a matter of personal values.

the program, and, of course, stories different than those involved in the classroom discussions were used for the tests. The tests showed that 50 percent of the children moved up one stage, 10 percent moved up two stages, and the remainder stayed the same. In contrast, only 10 percent of a control group moved up one stage during this period, and the remainder stayed the same. One year later the relative advance was maintained.

The contrast between results of passive exposure to higher moral thought and results from intentional induction of conflict illustrates the most important aspect of the role of interaction in moral growth.

ROLE TAKING

Another morally important interaction between the child and his environment involves the child's opportunities for role taking. Piaget's theory has stressed the peer group as the significant source of moral roles; some theories stress participation in the larger secondary institutions; others emphasize participation in the family itself. Research suggests that all these roles are important and that they all operate in a similar direction to stimulate moral development. Studies in three different cultures have found that middle-class children were more advanced in moral judgment than matched lower-class children. Middle-class and working-class children seemed to move through the same sequences, but the middle-class children seemed to move faster and farther. C. Holstein found that the amount of parental encouragement of the child's participation in family

discussion of moral-conflict situations was a powerful correlate of moral advance in the child. These types of discussions are more likely to take place in the middle-class families.

Why should the existence of environmental opportunities for social participation and role taking be basic for moral advance? The answer to this question also helps answer the question of why there are universal features of moral judgment in all societies. The answer is that there are universal structures of the social environment basic to moral development, just as there are universal structures of the physical environment basic to cognitive development (see Chapters 11 and 15). The same basic institutions exist in all societies: family, economy, social stratification, law, and government. In spite of cultural diversity in content, these institutions have universal functional meanings.

All institutions and societies are alike in the sheer fact of being societies—systems of defined complementary roles. Essentially, each of the moral stages defines (or is defined by) a new cognitive-structural mode of behaving—of taking a role—in conflict situations. To understand the development of role taking, one must consider not only the principle of empathy or welfare—the effects of action upon the others involved—but also the principle of justice—reciprocity and equality in human relations.

At every stage children perceive basic values like the value of human life and are able to empathize and take the roles of other persons, other living things. Even the young child experi-

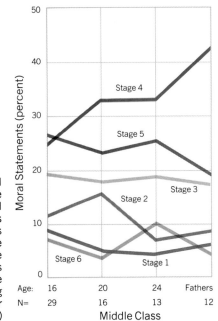
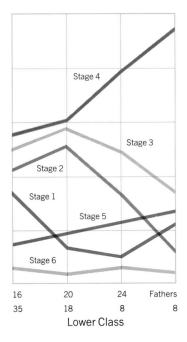

Figure 17.10. The influence of social class on moral development can be seen in these data, which show moral judgment profiles for middle-class males *(left)* and lower-class males *(right)* at different ages. Note the greater percentage of the three lower stages in the lower-class sample compared to the percentage of use of Stage 4 and Stage 5 thinking in the middle-class sample. (After Kohlberg and Kramer, 1969.)

ences the value of his parents' lives or of a pet dog's life as the result of primary empathy with other living things; he also has some experience of justice because reciprocity, too, is part of the primary experience of role taking in social interaction. The psychological unity of empathy and justice in moral role taking is apparent even at the very start of the moral experience.

In the anecdote related earlier, Kohlberg's four-year-old son empathically experienced the seals' predicament—he took the role of a seal. This role taking implied a Stage 1 sense of justice or reciprocity in the demand for an-eye-for-an-eye retribution for its Eskimo hunter. Such Stage 1 concepts of justice become differentiated, integrated, and universalized with development until they perhaps eventually become a Stage 6 sense.

It is the move from role taking to the resolution of conflicting roles that leads to the *principle* of justice. A moral conflict is a conflict between competing claims of men, and the precondition for a moral conflict is man's capacity for role taking. Where conflicts arise, the principles men use to resolve them are principles of justice. Usually, expectations or claims are integrated by customary rules and roles, and the principles for making rules and distributing roles (rights and duties) in any institution, from the family to the government, are principles of justice, or fairness. The most basic principle of justice is equality: treat every man's claim equally.

The concepts of role taking and justice, then, provide concrete meaning to the assumption that moral principles are neither external rules that have been internalized nor natural ego tendencies of a biological organism. Rather, they are the emergents of social interaction.

RELATIVISM REVISITED

The relativistic approach to moral development has received great apparent support from some studies.

The most definitive experimental study of children's moral character ever carried out was by Hartshorne and May in 1928. One focus of their study was honesty (resistance to cheating and stealing in experimental situations).

What Hartshorne and May found was:

1. *You cannot divide the world into honest and dishonest people. Almost everyone cheats some of the time.* Cheating is distributed in bell-curve fashion around a level of moderate cheating.
2. *If a person cheats in one situation, it does not mean he will or will not in another. There is very little correlation between situational cheating tests.* In other words, it is not a character trait that makes a child cheat in a given situation. If it were, one could predict he would cheat in a second situation if he did in the first place.
3. *People's verbal moral values about honesty have nothing to do with how they act.* People who cheat express as much or more moral disapproval of cheating as those who do not cheat.
4. *The decision to cheat or not is largely determined by expediency.* The tendency to cheat depended upon the degree of risk of detection and the effort required to cheat. Children who cheated in more risky situations also tended to cheat in less risky situations. Thus, noncheaters appeared to be primarily more cautious, not more honest, than cheaters.
5. *Even when honest behavior is not dictated by concern about punishment or detection, it is*

largely determined by immediate situational factors of group approval and example (as opposed to being determined by internal moral values). Some classrooms showed a high tendency to cheat, while other, seemingly identically composed, classrooms in the same school showed little tendency to cheat.

6. *Where honesty is determined by cultural value forces, these values are "relative," that is, specific to the child's social class and group.* Rather than being a universal ideal, honest behavior was more characteristic of the middle class and seemed less relevant to the lower-class child.

The Hartshorne and May findings, then, suggest that honest behavior is determined by situational factors of punishment, reward, group pressures, and group values rather than by an internal disposition of conscience or character.

These experimental findings clearly give strong support to the relativists' contention that moral character is a value concept and that moral behavior must be understood in the same way as any other behavior—as the result of the child's needs, group pressures, and situational demands.

The history of moral research since Hartshorne and May has been largely one of superficially bowing to their results and then denying in one way or another their radical implications in calling into doubt commonsense concepts of moral character.

It is interesting that many psychologists have started with a relativistic definition of morality without realizing that such a definition is subject to severe criticism. For example, Leonard Berkowitz offers the following definition: "Moral values are evaluations of actions generally believed by members of a given society to be either right or wrong." Under this definition Adolf Eichmann was a person of "good moral character" or with "strongly internalized moral values" according to the Nazi majority in his society. After the fall of the Third Reich, when opinion changed, Berkowitz's definition would make Eichmann a person with "weakly internalized moral values" or of poor character. Obviously, then, an explicitly relativistic conception of morality suffers from the corollary that an individual's morality changes when the expectations of the social order vary.

ABSOLUTE MORALITY

There is, however, a way toward a meaningful definition of moral *character* that can survive these criticisms. The point is that the basic moral terms used by people in making their own moral choices are the basic categories of moral judgment, which were set out in the preceding discussion about construction of moral stages. If a person is facing a decision like that of the husband with a dying wife, these terms include the value of life, consideration of the law, affectional and family role obligations, and the like. These terms are used by everyone in every culture; the major difference in how individuals use these terms depends on their stage or level of moral maturity—not on the changing whims of the social and political establishment. What often passes for conventional morality is actually only one of several relatively primitive stages in the sequence of moral development. The truly well-developed morality has advanced far beyond that stage to a basis in fundamental human principles, which are among the truest marks of maturity.

Figure 17.11. Stage 6 moral thought is based on self-chosen ethical principles that are universal and consistent: justice and equality of human rights, and dignity of human beings as individual persons.

There is a quiet war going on in the field of mental health that is directly affecting the theory and treatment of childhood maladjustment. An explosion of discontent has been directed primarily at the medical specialty of psychiatry, with clinical psychology also being caught in the fray. Critics say that traditional treatment has been not only inaccessible to most but also ineffective. According to the critics, behavior disorders are the result of a failure to learn, either because of a neurological handicap or because of improper teaching. Among such critics are neurologists, special educators, and a new breed of psychologists from the academic laboratories, all of whom have joined forces to repudiate the medical-disease model of the psychiatrist. Thus, the mental-health field is in the midst of a revolution. Although many professionals join in rebelling against the past, they choose very different and often diametrically opposite new approaches.

All this commotion makes it difficult to give an objective account of maladjustment in childhood. This presentation attempts to bridge the gap between the old and the new and to give the main theses of most major approaches to treatment fairly, although not comprehensively. The first section deals with normal problems encountered in growing up. The next section discusses the identification of special problems and some of the difficulties encountered in fitting behavior disorders into neat and precise categories. The next four sections might be thought of as outlining the four corners of a square because they represent the four major approaches to the understanding and treatment of maladjustment in childhood:

the biological-neurological view, the learning-theory approach, the psychodynamic (or traditional) view, and the sociological approach, which is still in its infancy. The final section is a plan for recognizing the many determinants of behavior and integrating the most powerful and important into a rational whole.

How Many Are Maladjusted?

There are two ways of arriving at an estimate of the amount of maladjustment in childhood: (1) by surveying behavior problems in large samples of children and (2) by collating data from mental-health workers about children referred to them. Unfortunately, the discrepancy between the estimates from these two sources is very large.

A variety of surveys have reached agreement on a figure of 8 to 12 percent as the proportion of maladjusted children in American schools. In public-health parlance, this percentage is a *prevalence* figure (both old and new cases counted together) rather than an *incidence* figure (occurrence of new cases), which means that some of these children overcome their problems spontaneously and so they would not reappear in a survey of the same population at a later time.

However, even with a generous allowance for spontaneous recovery, there remains a wide gap between the estimated number of maladjusted children and the number receiving help, which is consistently reported to be *less than 1 percent of the child population*. This small number reflects to some extent the lack of services and the critical shortage of trained manpower, particularly in poverty areas, where the need is often the greatest. It

18
Maladjustment in Childhood and Its Correction

is well established that parents in lower-income groups do not seek the help of mental-health personnel, partly because of inaccessibility but also because of the parents' preoccupation with more basic needs and their general feeling of futility about getting effective help at a price they can afford.

Even in the middle- and upper-income groups, there is resistance to seeking help. The difference between the child who appears at the clinic and the one who does not may lie less in the child than in how his parents and teachers react to his difficulties.

Frequently, it is the child's difficulty in school that finally stimulates action. In contemporary America, education appears to be the key to success, and nothing seems as serious as a learning problem; academic difficulty is now the reason for referral of at least three-fourths of the children between seven and fourteen who come to the attention of specialists in schools and clinics.

In view of what is known about the crucial importance of the first six years of life for both personality and intellectual development, it is paradoxical that referrals are few and far between in the preschool years. The problems that are recognized in the early years tend to be relatively serious developmental problems, such as mental retardation or infantile autism, while those that are more subtle, as well as more curable, go unnoticed. Because young children change so rapidly in their behavior, it is easy to hope that the problems will be outgrown. With the increase in early-education programs, particularly in poverty areas, it is probable that referrals in the young age group will increase because more who need help will be recognized.

NORMALITY

It is customary to start with definitions, but volumes have been written attempting to define the concept of normality—with very little success. Using any criteria, there is no such thing as a person who is totally normal in all respects and at all times, nor is anyone totally abnormal. Neither is there such an entity as an "emotionally disturbed child." Emotional disturbance is not a disease, like diabetes, that is either present or absent in a given individual. In current usage, "emotional disturbance" is an umbrella term that covers all degrees of behavioral problems in four major categories: antisocial aggressiveness, overwhelming fears, failures in learning, and infantile habits.

There is no sharp line of demarcation between normal and abnormal behavior. For example, little, if any, pathological behavior does not have a normal counterpart at a younger age. So, before diagnosing maladjustment, it is imperative that one know children—how they look, talk, and think, their abilities and limitations at different ages, their typical reactions, and the environmental stresses that they face. In short, one must examine normal problems and peculiarities.

CONFLICTS AND ANXIETIES

The first eighteen years of life can be conveniently divided into three equal periods of six years

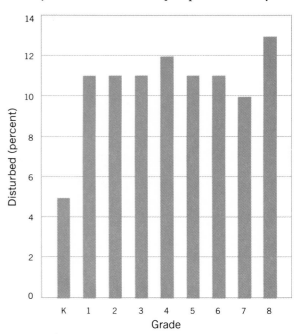

Figure 18.1. Percentage of emotionally disturbed children, by grade level, in one large elementary school system. (After Clancy and Smitter, 1953.)

each for this discussion: infancy as a foundation for childhood, childhood itself, and adolescence as what childhood foresees.

☐ *Infancy*   In addition to his physical needs, the infant needs people not only to love him but also to become objects for his love. He needs an environment that can give him stimulation and opportunity to explore as well as protection. For most infants these requirements are fulfilled, and so they develop a general feeling of well-being and basic trust in the outside world to serve as an underpinning for all later development.

It is worth taking a careful look at the two-year-old because so many difficulties of childhood have their source in this age period or represent a regression to this time of life. The normal two-year-old is characteristically stubborn and negativistic and, at the same time, fearful and dependent. With his emerging sense of himself, he is full of what he wants to do and resists directions, or even suggestions, coming from others. At this age he has no understanding of the laws of physical nature and assumes that anything is possible if one only tries hard enough. His infant experiences give him a lot of evidence for this opinion: yesterday he could not reach or turn the door handle; today he can. Then why won't a foot-long truck go into a two-inch garage? When his own stubborn efforts fail, the two-year-old looks to the mother as all-powerful and is enraged when she cannot stop the rain, produce ice cream from out of the air, or bring back a cartoon on television. He perceives external reality as the product of people, so people—namely the mother—are the hap-less sources of all the frustrations he encounters.

The limitations in concepts of size, time, and distance also render the young child susceptible to fears that have no basis in external reality. For example, it is common for a toddler to develop a morbid fascination with plumbing drains, vacuum cleaners, and other objects that make things disappear because the toddler has not learned that he is too big to disappear in a like fashion. The preschool child thinks only in concrete terms and interprets statements literally, with no judgment to temper what he sees and hears according to probabilities or logical impossibilities. When he hears mother complain that "ants eat everything up," he thinks that *he* could be consumed as well as the sugar. The young child also vastly overrates the power of his own words and thoughts. Because his first words usually resulted in something happening in reality, it takes a long time for him to understand that this magic occurred through the medium of communication with another person. To him, words and thoughts, which he rarely distinguishes, have all kinds of powers to affect reality, whether there is anyone around to hear them or not. This interpretation accounts, in part, for the child's fear of his own aggression, that is, fear over the idea that his bad wishes can be fulfilled.

One specific anxiety that is very common to the two-year-old but that may carry over into later childhood is "separation anxiety," elicited by the parents' leaving him or by his having to "leave" the parents by going to sleep. The two-year-old will put up a valiant fight, but he is bound to lose.

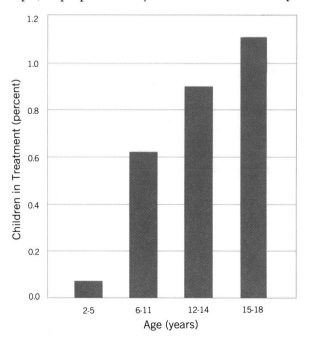

Figure 18.2. Percentage of emotionally disturbed children undergoing treatment. Note that until they start school—and manifest some learning problem—very few children receive help.

This inevitable frustration arouses his anger, which in turn increases his anxiety because of the fear of his own bad wishes and also because he assumes that the outside world is equally angry with him (which sometimes is true). Repeated experiences with disappearances and safe returns finally reassure him, but the normal separation anxiety will be unnecessarily prolonged if the parents mishandle it by (1) indulging the child so that he does not have the necessary reassuring reality experiences, (2) punishing the child for his upset, or (3) deceiving the child to avoid open distress at the time of separation.

Conflict between parent and child is inevitable. If the child's efforts toward compliance with parental demands are acknowledged and generously rewarded, his noncompliance need not become a battle of wills. On the side of the grownups is the child's passionate wish to be like them.

□ *Childhood* The child becomes increasingly more socialized as he approaches the age of six. He is more realistic in his concepts of causality, can distinguish fact and fantasy, can put himself in someone else's place, and accepts the standards of behavior set by his parents. Much of the change is achieved by direct teaching, but more is accomplished through identification. Normally, the child identifies with the same-sexed parent, and although such identification is advantageous in the long run, in the short run it creates conflicts for many children.

With the advent of school and a more meaningful social life with his peers, the six-year-old begins to break away from close ties with his parents. Life starts to be real and earnest and somewhat secret. He has his own business and becomes relatively uncommunicative about what goes on in his physically separate world. In one way the child feels great relief over his new-found independence; however, there are new strains on him for academic performance and appropriate behavior in a social group. With his emerging internalized conscience, he has to face self-criticism, which, hopefully, is liberally mixed with self-admiration. He has to go about the serious business of making friends and establishing his role as boy or girl outside the benign atmosphere of the loving family.

□ *Adolescence* The process of emancipation from family and home is accelerated by the onset of puberty, which poses a whole new set of problems. The child has to find an identity for himself, which means reexamination of everything that the parents hold dear. There are all kinds of choices to be made about college, interests, ideologies, and more. For a while the adolescent tries on personalities like one tries on clothes. At the same time, he has to come to terms with his sexual impulses and the inevitable anxieties surrounding masturbation.

Keeping these and other adolescent problems in mind, it is little wonder that the normal adolescent is so frequently moody, irritable, disagreeable, depressed, and alienated. At the same time as he is expressing these negative characteristics, the same adolescent may be highly creative, energetic, and capable of spurts of self-sacrifice and altruistic behavior. Like the two-year-old, the adolescent

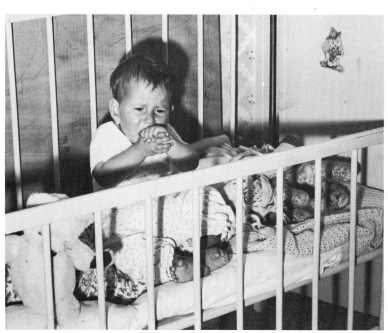

Figure 18.3. Anxiety and fears in an infant may be normal emotional reactions, related to specific situations. When fears become overwhelming, they indicate emotional disturbance.

fights, argues, and resists what others have to offer, but realistically he cannot manage his own affairs. However, unlike the two-year-old, the adolescent has some awareness of his own inconsistencies and feels none the better for it.

NORMAL PROBLEMS

Anxiety and conflict are inevitable in the growing-up process, no matter how normal the child or his parents. However, it should be made clear that behavior that is normal may still be undesirable. Although most children outgrow age-related problems, they do so because of environmental support and not simply because of the passage of time. Psychological attention should not be restricted solely to those children who are severely disturbed. Children's mental or emotional problems, however common, need to be taken as seriously as their transient physical illnesses.

ABNORMALITY

It is necessary to provide some guidelines to identify children who are in need of specialized help. One difference between normal and problem behavior is its persistence. When a behavior lasts beyond the expected age, is frequently displayed and easily aroused, and resists ordinary educational efforts to change, it should be investigated. Other criteria for abnormality of a behavior are how much it interferes with the relationships between the child and other people (peers as well as adults); to what degree it may handicap the child in the future (particularly in the case of learning

Figure 18.4. The normal child is bound to suffer a few emotional problems, such as short periods of unhappiness or depression.

disabilities); and how much suffering or loss of self-esteem it causes the child to feel. Some problems have predictable secondary effects. For example, school phobia is obviously serious because it prevents the child from receiving an education.

It is very tempting to look only at the external side of a child's problem. For example, parents often assume that a child's opinion of himself is based solely on the spoken statements of others. They may think that a child who wets his bed often will not be upset about his behavior if they are tolerant and keep the problem a secret. But children are quite capable of judging themselves, and a child may feel embarrassed and inferior because of a habit that he cannot control, even if it is a well-kept secret. The obvious pride that a chronic bedwetter shows after an occasional dry night also reveals his hidden shame about the many other nights of wetting. The inner effects of such chronic anxieties may deprive the child of normal pleasures and satisfactions, even though he is not in active conflict with the outside world and may be passing all the external tests of accomplishment.

The professional diagnostician decides whether or not a child needs treatment in terms of the child's progression, as opposed to fixation or regression. The child is a growing and developing entity, and as a consequence, his behavior is constantly changing. If he is at a standstill in some important respect, he is soon out of step with his peers. In severe cases, he goes backward—regresses. If he is progressing, moving toward maturity, the outlook is good.

THE PROBLEM OF LABELS

Given the vast array of problems that children present, there should be some kind of classification scheme so that workers in the field can share their experiences and evaluate the results of various approaches to treatment. The current classification schemes are notoriously messy and satisfy no one. Some workers contend that they must be entirely objective and classify only the surface behavior. An example of this approach would be the diagnosis "runaway reaction," which is listed as such in the official nomenclature proposed by the American Psychiatric Association. Other workers push for classification on the basis of underlying cause, as, for example, with a diagnosis of "minimal cerebral dysfunction," which can be manifested in a hundred different ways. Some workers say that diagnosticians should look for the ultimate, original cause, while others are satisfied with identifying the immediately preceding cause. To illustrate, a child might have a learning problem because of a visual-perceptual handicap that is amenable to specific remediation. Some workers would be content with this level of explanation, but others would feel it necessary to determine if the visual problem was organic or functional in origin.

Countless anecdotes can be told of different labels being given to the same child as his parents make their way from clinic to clinic, yet such stories do not indicate that one expert was right and the others wrong. First, a child can have more than one problem. For example, he may be mentally retarded *and* have emotional problems.

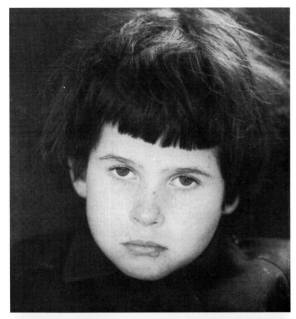

A second reason for variation in diagnostic labels has to do with the theoretical orientation of the diagnostician, which will be discussed in detail later in this chapter. A third reason for variation is that diagnostic terms are not uniformly defined. Even at the descriptive level, workers tend to use their own criteria for labeling, so the labels are more or less rigorous depending on their experience and predilections.

With all the controversy surrounding diagnostic definitions, one has to ask, "What's in a name?" Does a label change a child? Unfortunately, some diagnostic labels have such negative connotations that perhaps they *do* change one's perception of and attitude toward the child, so that one does act differently toward him. The child responds accordingly, in the fashion of a self-fulfilling prophecy. An example of such negative labeling is mental retardation, which is certainly the least desirable diagnosis of a child's problems. Some common feelings about this label are expressed in Jean Little's fictional account in *Take Wing:* Laurel must take her young son James to a clinic for diagnosis of his difficulties:

If the people at the clinic agreed that James was retarded, would he still be James?
Laurel had a recurring, unreasoning fear that the very words would somehow change him.
His mouth would hang ajar. His brown eyes would become fixed and dull. He would not laugh any longer. He would not ask for teeny tiny woman stories.

Another important consequence of diagnosis is in the kind of professional services the child will

Figure 18.5. One severe emotional disturbance is labeled "autism." Autistic children, like the ones pictured here, do not seem able to communicate with others. Until recently, there was little therapists could do to help them.

receive. If he is called "emotionally disturbed," he will be served primarily by the psychiatrist, the psychologist, and the social worker and perhaps be placed in a class for the emotionally disturbed. If he is "brain injured," he will be served by the neurologist, the psychologist, and the perceptual-motor consultant and be put in a class for the neurologically impaired. If he is "mentally re-tarded," he will be placed in a class for educable mentally retarded children. Many times a diagno-sis is made on a strictly pragmatic basis, that is, the label will make the child eligible for a particu-lar service. Applying a label to get help may be a satisfactory short-range solution, but professionals must take care that naming does not become a substitute for understanding.

BIOLOGICAL CAUSES OF MALADJUSTMENT

As mentioned before, child-guidance workers disa-gree strongly and often eloquently in their views about the importance of organic over functional factors in understanding childhood problems. This disagreement is particularly evident in the diagnosis of learning problems. Some workers ad-here to a disease model, asserting that children with minimal cerebral dysfunction are born with a different kind of brain, which processes incom-ing stimuli in such a way that the child's auditory and visual perception of the outside world is basi-cally altered. Such neurological terms as *dyslexia* (difficulty in reading) and *aphasia* (difficulty in understanding and using speech) suggest a dis-continuity with normal developmental processes. The causes for the neurological impairment may

be genetic variations, biochemical irregularities, brain insults from the birth process, or other ill-nesses or injuries sustained during the years that are critical for the development and maturation of the central nervous system.

There is also the possibility that early sensory deprivation causes irreversible alterations in cen-tral-nervous-system functioning. Evidence for this hypothesis is provided by the experimental effects of sensory deprivation on animal brains and also in the resemblances that have been noted be-tween brain-damaged children and institution-alized children. It is important to note that this diagnosis is usually made on the basis of external manifestations in behavior, with the possible early causes established in retrospect. There are no laboratory tests that can get inside the living brain, so such diagnoses are very difficult to prove or disprove. Because of this difficulty, many work-ers concerned with children's learning disabilities have tried to discard the medical model of or-ganic brain disease and replace it with diagnostic statements that describe the disability in terms of what specific problems can be remedied.

GENETIC DIFFERENCES

The idea that genetic variations are important in producing maladjustment is not a new one. The founders of both learning theory and psychoanal-ysis postulated constitutional or inborn differ-ences as important determinants of behavior—normal or abnormal. Studies have shown signifi-cantly higher correlation between incidence of schizophrenia in families than in nonrelated per-

sons and a higher correlation in family members who share the most genes (parents and children) relative to those who share only some genes (siblings). (See Table 3.2.)

Children are born with different temperaments, and these differences make children differently susceptible to their environments. Inborn differences mean that events readily assimilated by one child are traumatic for another. Unfortunately, too many people look at the causes of maladjustment in childhood in terms of two possibilities: organic defect or parental fault. Of course, there are parents who in fact do an undeniably poor job of rearing their children (even though some of these children still thrive to an astonishing degree). However, child development is a complicated process, and there are many failures in which the parents play only a secondary role.

Fortuitous outside events such as physical illnesses, family crises, disaster experienced vicariously by the child, and experiences initiated by people outside the family also are important in shaping behavior. Add to all these factors the distorted perceptions and misunderstandings created by the primitive thinking and unspoken fantasies of the young child and the inevitability of inner conflict between selfish desires and social allowances, and one can begin to appreciate that no one factor suffices to explain maladjustment.

SPECIAL EDUCATION

The treatment of children with neurological learning disabilities is in the hands of special-education teachers. Although drugs may be pre-scribed to alleviate anxiety or hyperactivity so that the child is more ready to learn, there is no medical cure or essential treatment. Professionals from fields such as optometry and occupational, physical, and speech therapy have developed remedial techniques, some of which have been absorbed by the teaching profession. Special programs are designed to counteract distractibility and hyperactivity by having small classes (eight to twelve children), with individual study booths, a plain environment, and work material that focuses attention on the individually selected learning task. The curriculum contains a great deal of preacademic or readiness instruction, which is presented in a highly structured way even though it may look like play. There is a great emphasis on order and routine, with clear-cut goal setting and mastery of one level before going to the next.

Motor activities include visual tracking of moving objects, reciprocal body movements (hopping, skipping), body balance (walking a balance board), spatial learning (up and down movements, running an obstacle course, crawling through tunnels), and learning left and right discrimination of various body parts. For eye-motor coordination, teachers use stencils and templates, pegboards and parquetry materials, puzzles, lotto-type games, and hidden-figure pictures. To reinforce the visual perception, children are presented with forms and letters cut out of felt or sandpaper so that they can feel as well as see them. Concepts such as size, number, left-to-right directionality, and position in space (up and down, in front or behind, in or out) are presented simulta-

Figure 18.6. Special education classes help children who have various disabilities or problems to cope with the world around them. The training attempts to improve both physical and cognitive capabilities.

neously in words, pictures, concrete objects, and body movement. Children with language disorders who have relatively better visual than auditory perception are taught in the reverse of the usual sequence, that is, starting with the visual symbol, then to the auditory association, and then to the meaning of the word.

Prescriptive teaching is the rule, that is, identifying the key deficits and the child's current level of functioning and presenting in an orderly manner learning tasks that guarantee success at each step of the way. It is presumed that once the child reaches the point of academic readiness, he can then proceed in the normal fashion and at the normal speed. There is no doubt that with the present acceleration of teaching at the primary grades, many children are presented with tasks for which they are not ready and so experience failure at a very young age. Such school failure alone can create emotional problems, but when such children are given extra time and help to catch up, the emotional problems disappear. There are other children, however, who continue to find academic work a struggle and are very frustrated by the usual school situation.

Maladjustment as Learned Behavior

Far from the advocates of the disease model stand the learning theorists, who look at problem behavior as something that the child has learned— or not learned. They do not look for causes, and the diagnosis is simply the problem behavior itself. This approach has its historical antecedents in the behaviorism made famous by J. B. Watson.

CONDITIONING

In 1920 Watson demonstrated that fears in children could be established by *classical conditioning*. His conditioning of eleven-month-old Albert to fear furred animals was described in Chapter 2. The second kind of conditioning, *operant* or *instrumental* conditioning, involves changing response patterns. The central thesis of this view is that man does not voluntarily choose behavior because of what he expects but involuntarily repeats behavior that was successful for him in the past, that is, behavior that was reinforced.

The principles of classical and operant conditioning are deceptively simple. How these principles operate in nonlaboratory situations poses many questions: What are the common denominators that account for the spreading effect (generalization) from one feared object to another in classical conditioning? Also, what kind of connection establishes the conditioned response? In Albert's case, the connection was a temporal one, but an older child might well have realized that there was no real connection between the noise and the animal, so he might have been conditioned to respond with fear to strange places rather than to furred objects. With increasing age, the child injects more of his own interpretations into the stimulus-response formula.

Another set of questions arises around the notion of reinforcement. Everyone agrees that a child is attracted to those things that give pleasure and avoids those that give pain, but leaving aside the physiological drives of hunger and thirst, what constitutes pleasure or pain? The external consequences of problem behavior in children—punishment, failure, shaming, loneliness—do not seem to qualify as bringing the pleasure that is presumed to keep the behavior going, unless one argues that any kind of attention may operate as a reward. On the other hand, looking at the well-adjusted child who attends to his studies, resists temptations, tells the truth, and is considerate of other people's feelings, one marvels that he will do so much for so little concrete reward. A situation that is satisfying to one child may not be to another, so the nature of reinforcements is a highly individualized matter, itself modified by learning.

Recently some very important contributions to the theory of reinforcement have been made by Albert Bandura and his co-workers in their studies of identification and social learning. They observed that a child may change his behavior because of vicarious reinforcement, that is, reinforcement he has observed rather than experienced. So a child's behavior is learned not only through the associations he has established between stimuli and the effects of his previous behavior but also through his perception of what other people do and what happens to them.

BEHAVIOR THERAPY

The term *behavior therapy* was coined by Hans Eysenck to describe a system of psychotherapy that systematically applies learning-theory principles to the problem of changing maladaptive behavior. One form or another of behavior therapy has been tried on almost every symptom of maladjustment seen in child or adult—with generally high rates of success. The changes after treatment are reported to be not only the elimination of undesirable behavior but also the establishment of new ways of behaving.

One of the first clinical applications of learning-theory principles was in the treatment of enuresis, or bedwetting. All kinds of appliances are on the market, but they all involve the same principle—waking the child with a buzzer, alarm clock, or slight shock at the first sign of urine. The child usually sleeps on an apparatus consisting of wire mesh foil pads separated by a piece of cloth. Moisture completes an electrical circuit, which sets off the waking device. In terms of conditioning, bladder tension is the conditioned stimulus, the buzzer is the unconditioned stimulus, and waking is the response to be associated with bladder tension. About 70 percent success has been reported, and it should be noted that when this method is going to work, success comes within a matter of weeks. The 30 percent failures are probably due to insufficient bladder tension preceding urination. Another example of how behavior therapy can be used in eliminating enuresis was discussed in Chapter 16.

□ *Counterconditioning* Phobias have been treated by *systematic desensitization, reciprocal inhibition,* or *counterconditioning,* which are all variations of the classical-conditioning theme. For example, W. P. Garvey and J. R. Hegrenes reported the use of treatment in eliminating a school phobia. The therapist and ten-year-old Jimmy, who was afraid of school, began treatment by coming to school early in the morning when no one else was present. Jimmy was told to report any uncomfortable feelings; when he said he was feeling afraid, the therapist immediately indicated that it was time to return to the car and generously praised Jimmy for what he had accomplished. Over a period of twenty days, Jimmy returned to school completely. The authors explained the success on the basis of counterconditioning: "Since Jimmy and the therapist had a good relationship, the presence of the therapist may be considered as a relatively strong stimulus evoking a positive affective response"; this positive response inhibited the anxiety response associated with school. Underlying the various mechanisms that the child behavior therapists employ, there is evidence that they must have considerable sensitivity in order to judge the child's anxiety and to win his affection and confidence. If the therapist rushes headlong, the child sees him as something else to fear rather than as an ally in a common cause.

□ *Modeling* Another approach to the treatment of phobias has been the use of models. Bandura explored this method with nursery-school children who were afraid of dogs. The treatment was eight brief sessions in which the fearful children watched an unafraid child interact more and more closely with a dog—approaching it, playing with it, petting it, and so on. The result: most of the children essentially lost their fear of dogs.

□ *Operant Conditioning* A major thrust in child behavior therapy has been in the manipula-

tion of the external consequences of behavior. Therapeutic application of operant-conditioning principles involves three elements: choosing a reward that is really effective for the child; delivering the reward on an immediate and regular basis contingent on certain behavior; and ensuring that reward is possible by detailing successive approximations toward the desired final outcome. Negative reinforcement or aversive conditioning has been used in the treatment of psychotic or aggressive behavior but only in combination with a generous reward system. Most behavior therapists are uneasy about punishment and prefer instead to withhold the positive reward in order to extinguish undesired behavior.

Operant-conditioning techniques were first tried in residential settings with seriously disturbed and severely retarded children. Behavior-modification strategy was then quickly picked up by teachers of special classes for emotionally disturbed children, and recently it has been used in home settings—after the parents have received special instruction. Behavior modification is not an office-type therapy that is administered once or twice a week; it depends on a major overhaul of the environment so that rewards are provided on a consistent basis. The particular rewards that are used depend on what will work for an individual child, and they range from the immediate delivery of candy to a system of check marks or credits that can be accumulated for the purchase of toys or special privileges. (See Chapter 16 for case studies of behavior modification.) In some instances, the reward that works is a matter of personal attention.

The reward system, particularly when it is something concrete, strikes some people as akin to bribery, but operant conditioners quite correctly argue that very few people work for nothing and that changing abnormal patterns of behavior is very hard work for disturbed children. The ultimate goal of therapy is that the child will switch from extrinsic reinforcers to intrinsic ones, which are, hopefully, self-perpetuating. It is presumed that once a child experiences mastery and success, he will continue to work to achieve them because they provide inner satisfaction.

One of the important features of behavior modification is the principle of successive approximations, ministeps toward the final outcome. The therapist starts with very small changes of behavior that go in the right direction but would ordinarily be overlooked because they are so far from the final goal. For instance, if one were to treat a chronic thumbsucker, one would look for those rare moments when the child was *not* sucking his thumb and, by rewarding these moments, hope to gradually extend their duration. It is a positive rather than a negative approach and ensures the child some degree of success from the beginning.

Behavior therapists vary in how much they use verbal instructions and explanations to reassure the child and to help him to understand what is going on, but they are all agreed that it is *not* necessary for the child to gain insight into the original cause of his problems. There is no prob-

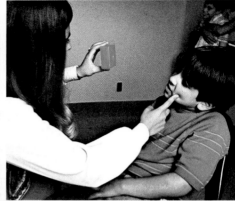

Figure 18.7. Operant conditioning therapy has recently begun to be used to treat autistic children. The children are rewarded when they communicate with the therapist. The rewards are both concrete and social approval, evidenced in affectionate handling of the children.

ing of the unconscious, and both cause and cure are seen as residing in the relation between behavior and its environmental consequences. The reported rate of success has been astonishingly high, and follow-up studies have been encouraging.

THE PSYCHODYNAMIC VIEW OF MALADJUSTMENT

The concept *psychodynamic* owes its origin to Sigmund Freud, who devoted the second half of his life to the study of the inner processes of the mind. His earlier training and career as a neurologist led him to devise a complicated structure of hypotheses intended to explain mental events in neurophysiological terms, but he soon gave up such theorizing as being too speculative. However, he retained the idea that there are energy forces (differentiated into the basic drives of sex and aggression) that clamor for expression and that give meaning to outside events. He pictured the mind as the arena for an active struggle among the push of primitive urges (the *id*), consideration of reality consequences (the *ego*), and self-regard (the *superego*, or conscience). Normal behavior represents a satisfactory blending of these three components, that is, gratifying basic needs in ways that are adaptive to reality and acceptable to the person. One of Freud's greatest contributions was his insistence that symptoms exist because at some point in the past they served a purpose. Freud said that the task of therapy was simply to discover, in respect to a senseless idea and a pointless action, the past situation in which the idea *was* justified and the action served a purpose.

Psychoanalysts distinguish between problems that are neurotic and those that are still tied to environmental events. By definition, a neurotic symptom is the expression of a wish that is so frightening or abhorrent to the person that it must be disguised; it is too strong to be totally knocked out by repression. For example, if a child is jealous and wishes the worst for a younger sibling, his subconscious feelings might show up in the form of exaggerated solicitude and anxiety that something terrible will happen to the sibling or to himself (as punishment). This anxiety might lead to a phobia in which the child has to stay home all the time in order to protect himself and the sibling. Because such a fear relates to a wish that goes on and on, reality does not reassure the child—in neurosis, the person behaves as if the past were present and the imagined were real.

ANXIETY

Because anxiety is the keystone of neurosis, it is important to take a close look at its causes. The most basic anxiety comes from a feeling of helplessness in the face of outside events or of overpowering inner urges, such as a towering rage or unexpected sexual excitement. To ward off this anxiety, the child tries to master his environment and to anticipate his inner feelings so that he is not caught off guard.

In the course of development, the child learns not only external and internal stimulus cues that signal danger ahead but ways to escape the dangers. Faced with an external danger, he can fight back, flee, or deny it—the last is not very effective. If the external situation arouses an internal stimulus associated with potential danger, *repression* is the first line of defense. Further defensive maneuvers may be called into action, such as *displacement* of the object (transferring the feeling to a different person or thing); *projection* (attributing the feeling to an outside source); or *reaction formation* (substituting the extreme opposite feeling in place of the original one). There are many other defense mechanisms that have been described, but they all have the common property of disguising the real problem. Everyone uses his particular set of defenses just to maintain his equilibrium, but in a neurosis, the defenses grow wild, occupying more and more room in the person's life space so that the individual becomes bound in on all sides—and some anxiety still leaks through nevertheless.

There is no easy way to distinguish between an internalized neurosis and bad habits or behavior stemming from an organic defect. To some extent a neurosis is diagnosed by the process of exclusion; that is, one first examines the environment closely to make sure that it is neither causing nor reinforcing the behavior, then one tries educational procedures of explanation, reassurance, and rewards for small steps in the right direction. When these reality procedures, which ordinarily have a positive result, work in reverse, this paradoxical effect is a good sign that there is some hidden cause that maintains the symptom. Other signs of neurosis are regression or substitution of symptoms, but these devices can only be detected

Figure 18.8. A form of anxiety commonly exists in boys who are in the phallic stage of psychosexual development and are in the throes of the Oedipus conflict. The boy longs to replace his father in his mother's affections and may fantasize his father's death. The thought that his wishes may actually cause his father to die can cause the child anxiety.

when a clinician watches a child closely over a period of time.

PSYCHODYNAMIC TREATMENT

The essence of psychodynamic treatment is to treat the underlying cause rather than the symptoms manifested. Many professionals do not choose psychoanalysis as the specific form of treatment but use psychoanalytic principles in residential treatment, group therapy, family therapy, or other types of psychotherapy. The principal means of dynamic therapy are (1) the child-therapist relationship, (2) working with the mother, (3) spontaneous play with conversation, (4) release and acceptance of feelings, and (5) interpretation.

It is essential that the child trust the therapist and that they share a common goal that the child understands. In the early stages the therapist tries to discover what bothers the child the most and what he would like to work on first. The actual problem that is bothering the child may not be the same problem that bothers the mother. For instance, the child may be failing at school but be *most* unhappy about his lack of friends. Thus, work with the parents is very important, not only so they will continue to support the treatment but also to help them better understand and communicate with the child.

In psychoanalytic therapy, the child's spontaneous play is used as a way of gaining understanding of his conflicts and feelings; the play is a natural substitute for the verbal associations of an adult. Some therapists feel that the release of feelings in play is itself therapeutic, but the evidence strongly indicates that these cathartic procedures—mere acting out—do not in themselves either reduce tension or change behavior. The dynamic therapist uses play observations to help the child identify and verbalize his feelings. Verbalization brings the behavior under some measure of control. The next step is to connect play feelings with real feelings in everyday life. After a while, recurring patterns begin to emerge. The therapist pursues these themes in order to understand their origin in the past.

An example of psychodynamic interpretation and treatment is the case of a charming little girl who developed a severe school phobia soon after starting first grade. On two occasions when she was dragged off to school, she vomited, fainted, and on returning home, remained happily content for the rest of the day. She could not say what she feared but only that school made her sick. Despite her school phobia, she was anxious to keep up with her classmates and particularly eager to learn to write like a grownup. This ambition provided an initial bond between therapist and child. One of the games suggested by the therapist was to play school. The little girl enthusiastically took the part of the teacher and portrayed her as vindictive, all-knowing, and all-powerful in contrast to the bad and stupid children. It became clear that the little girl was very jealous of the real teacher and had projected her own angry feelings. Further support for this hypothesis came when the child suddenly became afraid of the therapist and was quite convinced that the therapist (a

Figure 18.9. Play therapy is often employed in psychoanalytic treatment of children's emotional problems.

woman) was getting angry because she was not back at school. It was a short step to the idea that she was really jealous of *all* grownup ladies. With the insight that it was not really the teacher that was giving her the trouble, the child could return to school. In the second phase of the treatment, she was helped to acknowledge her jealousy of her mother and to make the all-important distinction between just thinking and really doing.

THE SOCIOLOGICAL APPROACH

The three major approaches so far presented—the biological, the learning theory, and the psychodynamic—have one thing in common: they consider the individual in terms of his unique history, problems, and home and school environment.

The sociological point of view greatly expands the scope of what should be regarded as significant environmental influences. According to this view, one should look far beyond the immediate life space of the individual child into the life spaces of the adults affecting his life, and so on, in ever-widening circles. Not only would diagnosis be deflected from the individual child, but the target and aim of treatment would have a much broader base; thus, individual treatment would be meaningless, not because of a controversy between the disease model and the learning model, but because the pathogenic agents are located in outlying social structures.

Spokesmen for this view attack current public-welfare programs for poor children and the public schools. The disproportionately high incidence of mental-health problems in poverty areas, the inac-

cessibility of treatment resources, and the pernicious effect of poverty on children have led to the establishment of community mental-health centers; expansion of day care, Head Start, and Upward Bound programs; as well as proposals for change in public assistance policies. As for the schools, the educators have been bombarded with recommendations and exhortations.

William Glasser proposes that the part played by the educational system itself in causing difficulties be investigated. He asks for a different relationship between child and teacher, with far more personal involvement and deliberate teaching of social responsibility to one another—not in terms of abstract principles but in terms of here-and-now events. He also attacks curricular offerings on the issue of relevance to the world outside (or failure to make the relevance explicit).

TREATMENT AND PREVENTION

Although it appears that there has been *no* increase in the severe, easily identified forms of maladjustment (beyond that expected from general population growth), there does appear to be an increase in the identification of mild or borderline maladjustment, reflecting both greater awareness of such problems and the fallout from the greater demands of our complex technological society. And there has been some progress in the treatment of children's problems. A great variety of treatment approaches have been tried and found useful. Unfortunately, the new methods have been used more to disavow than to revise or augment the old methods. For instance, one-to-one psychotherapy is currently presented to new students of the mental-health field as a thing of the past; the obvious fact that it cannot be made available to large numbers of children is cited as evidence. Nevertheless, for some it may well remain the treatment of choice, and it would be a pity to discard it because it is not good for everybody. In the mental-health field, there is an undeniable splitting into camps with little cross-fertilization of ideas. It is hard for any one person to acquire expertise in the therapy and practice of more than one major approach, with the result that each therapist wants to use his specialized techniques for any and all purposes. This universal application of a single approach leads to either an overevaluation of results or disillusionment because the treatment does not always work. More generalists in the mental-health field are needed who can move freely from camp to camp.

Unfortunately, very little is being done to prevent maladjustment; a major breakthrough in this area would require a unification of preventive efforts. The major means of prevention are (1) medical, (2) parent education, and (3) education of others who deal with children, including physicians, teachers, public-assistance workers, and juvenile authorities. In the area of medical prevention, there seems little chance of any breakthrough that will affect large numbers of children. The greatest hope lies in the prevention of mental retardation, with vaccination against German measles, improvement of prenatal care to prevent premature births, and making use of the new information about the inheritance of some metabolic disorders (such as phenylketonuria) and the chromosomal anomalies that cause such disorders as mongolism (Down's syndrome). However, it would be unwise to exaggerate the potential benefits of all these measures—perhaps the retarded population could be reduced by 10 percent.

With respect to behavior disorders, medical prevention offers little promise, which is one reason why there is so much objection to the medical-illness model. Even those who emphasize the biological components of inborn temperamental differences or variations of the minimal-cerebral-dysfunction theme say nothing about primary prevention. Like everyone else, they rely on changing the attitudes and behavior of parents and teachers to reduce the problems. The organicists seem to say: accept your child as born "different." The learning theorists seem to say: your child is what you make him. Similarly, teachers are warned of the dangers of the self-fulfilling prophecy but are simultaneously urged to make earlier and earlier identification of potential problems.

Parent education, the great hope of mental-health education for many years, has come under attack as disappointing in its results. No claims have been made that it is harmful—only that it may be useless. Recently there has been a move toward concentrating preventive efforts on particular times and places, utilizing such programs as Head Start. Work with parents of handicapped children has flourished, and much more sophisticated educational materials have been made available to parents with special interests and needs.

The new techniques of family therapy could be employed even more widely than they are for children with minor maladjustments. Although the problems might well disappear spontaneously, a good experience in brief family therapy would establish patterns of open communication for coping with future problems.

The education of teachers about the psychological needs of their students has been slighted in recent years with the tremendous push for academic excellence. Although they are taught to recognize signs of maladjustment, they are not given much insight into causes or into how the teacher, as a person, can help a child understand himself and feel more confident and worthwhile. Because school is a universal experience for all children (and one that inevitably has a certain amount of stress), more and more workers are looking to the schools as containing the hopes for prevention in the future.

In his important work on preventive psychiatry for adults, Gerald Caplan defined the concept of *crisis* as a time when an individual experiences a heightened desire for help and is more susceptible to influence by others. For children, too, there are times of extra stress when a little counseling can go a long way, especially on entry into a new school, in the process of choosing a college or a career, and so on. The development of child-care programs designed to help children with the *psychological* aspects of hospitalization and illness is an excellent example of strategic deployment of resources in prevention.

There are also unusual conditions that inevitably affect the children involved: parental divorce; death or mental or physical illness of a parent; presence of a handicapped brother or sister; parental unemployment or financial dependency, and the like. In such circumstances, there should be someone immediately available who can take the child's-eye view of the situation. Regrettably, such available people are extremely rare. Professional workers concerned specifically with the mental health of children are almost always tied up with the more difficult problems that have been officially referred to agencies, clinics, or special services in schools. The potential usefulness of workers as free-floating consultants has yet to be tapped.

In the last analysis, however, it is a lack of commitment that makes reform and extension of mental-health services difficult. It is clear that the techniques are available; it is not clear that there is either the way or the will to bring them into contact with the children who need them most. Fortunately, there is no trend toward increasing rates of mental illness among children. But the fact that the birth rate tends to be highest among those groups experiencing the highest rates of maladjustment means that the number of children in need of help is constantly growing disproportionally. Although it is true that many maladjustive disorders of childhood disappear eventually all by themselves—whether because of the innate tendency for personalities to become healthy or because what is abnormal behavior at one age will not be abnormal at another—this natural mechanism can be expected to account

for only a small proportion of mental-health needs. The solution to the problem becomes, in both the long and the short runs, a matter more of national commitment of resources than of psychological expertise and invention. Effective therapies are currently available; the resources to apply them are not.

Figure 18.10. Family therapy is a rather recent outgrowth of group-therapy techniques.

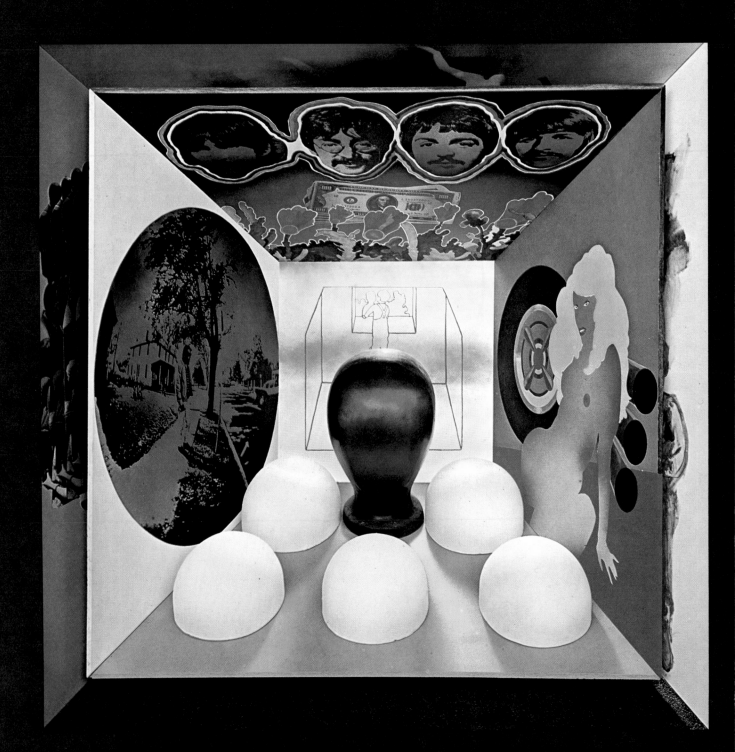

The personality that developed and established itself in late childhood faces its inevitable test in the biological necessity of finding sexual gratification and the corresponding psychological necessity of discovering love and security outside of the home. There is no choice. Biological maturation forces sexual opportunities; the disappearance of the childhood home requires the construction of another. Life's most personal joys as well as its sharpest pains arise from this inevitable confrontation between an innocent and imperfect personality and the rigor of biological and psychological development. At the same time, adolescence is a luxury dependent upon an economic and social establishment that requires from teen-agers no more than attendance at school and innocuous obedience to law. The rebels without a cause of the 1950s could hardly have existed without money enough to group around hot rods; the hippies of the 1960s required a setting permissive and philanthropic enough to allow them to exist; and the hordes of socially committed young soldiers against poverty and disease of the 1970s need a society that can afford concern for the underprivileged. The alternative is the early economic slavery of the Middle Ages in which both the problems and the possibilities of adolescence were dwarfed by the difficulty of simply staying alive. Given the freedom, adolescence is a time when an individual personality, formed in childhood, finds itself implemented physically and biologically and required, with or without its own consent, to achieve independence psychologically.

Unit VI
Adolescence and Youth

Adolescence begins biologically, and sex is its central theme. Long before emotional contradictions and social conflicts arise in the course of growth toward adulthood, hormonal changes begin to work their effects on the body. The main event is puberty, a phase of biological development in which germ cells come to be produced by the reproductive glands—the testicles in boys and the ovaries in girls. For a girl the first menstruation, an event of great psychological significance, provides a definite marker at puberty. For a boy the signs are less sharply defined—the appearance of pubic hair and general changes in the rate of growth of the body, particularly the sex organs, the penis and the testicles. Gradually, a girl takes on the graceful figure of a woman, and a boy develops the bodily structure of a man.

PHYSICAL CHANGES

Boys and girls produce both male hormones (androgens) and female hormones (estrogens). The proportions change, however, as the child nears adolescence, and at puberty there is a sharp increase in the production of androgens in boys and estrogens in girls. With the approach of puberty, the gonads become capable of producing hormones sufficient to cause accelerated growth of the genital organs and the appearance of secondary sex characteristics. In girls, the rhythm of the menstrual cycle is anticipated well before the first menstruation by a cyclic excretion of estrogens.

SEXUAL MATURATION IN GIRLS

In girls, physical changes associated with sexual maturation appear approximately in the following order, as described by F. K. Shuttleworth:

1. Enlargement of the breasts.
2. Appearance of straight, pigmented pubic hair.
3. Maximum rapid bodily growth.
4. Appearance of kinky pubic hair.
5. Menarche (the start of menstruation).
6. Growth of axillary (underarm) hair.

The normal age range within which menstruation first occurs is from ten to seventeen years, with an average of about thirteen years in the United States. It is rare for a girl (without a glandular anomaly) to reach the menarche before age nine or as late as eighteen. Three-fourths of girls are likely to have their first menstrual period during age twelve, thirteen, or fourteen.

The menarche does not give a complete indication of sexual maturity. After the first menstruation there may be irregularities in the menstrual cycle, and it appears that many girls begin to menstruate before their ovaries can produce eggs that are fertile and before their uteri are mature enough to support the bearing of children. C. S. Ford and Frank Beach cite evidence indicating that relatively few girls are capable of reproduction before the age of fifteen, and even then they are not as capable of becoming pregnant as they will be later.

19
Physical and Emotional Changes

ONSET OF PUBERTY IN BOYS

The following is an abridgment of a list by W. W. Greulich and his associates showing the order of appearance of some external changes in boys during the pubertal stage of growth.

1. The growth of the testes is accelerated, usually followed by that of the penis.
2. A conspicuous growth of long, downy hair on the pubes appears.
3. The down on the upper lip, especially at the corners, becomes slightly longer, coarser, and darker.
4. Long down appears on the sides of the face, in front of the ears.
5. The pubic region becomes covered with a moderate-to-dense growth of definitive pubic hair.
6. The voice deepens perceptibly.
7. Pubic hair spreads laterally to or onto the adjacent medial surface of the thighs, and terminal hairs are present along the linea alba.
8. The penis and testes attain almost their full adult dimensions.
9. The adult type of hairline begins to differentiate on the forehead.
10. Almost all or all of the terminal hair proper to the young adult is present on the forearms, arms, legs, and thighs.

According to most authorities, the average boy reaches sexual maturity about one and one-half to two years later than does the average girl. In a study by Hedley Dimock published in 1937, 65 percent of boys were rated as having attained puberty between ages fourteen and fifteen. In the most nearly comparable study of girls in the late 1930s, almost 50 percent of the girls had reached

puberty by the start of the thirteenth year and 85 percent by the end of the thirteenth.

PHYSIOLOGICAL DIFFERENCES BETWEEN THE SEXES

Girls not only reach sexual maturity earlier than boys but are biologically more mature than boys in other ways during the first fifteen years of life. As girls approach the teens, they are about two years ahead of boys in skeletal maturity, as measured by standard x-ray photographs of the hand and wrist (see Figure 5.7). They also display a number of secondary sex characteristics and reach mature stature earlier.

Young females are, on the average, made of sturdier stuff than young males. More males than females are conceived, but more males die before or during childbirth or during infancy. Girls survive physical hardships, such as malnutrition, better than boys.

Physical Versus Psychological Maturity

For more than a century there has been a trend toward earlier onset of puberty in areas where records have been kept. From 1850 to 1950 the age of menarche declined from about sixteen to thirteen years (see Figure 19.2). Available data concerning boys are not as complete as those for girls, but they also indicate that there has been a trend toward earlier maturation during the first half of the present century.

In keeping with earlier sexual maturation, present-day boys and girls are also taller and heavier age for age, before, during, and at the end of

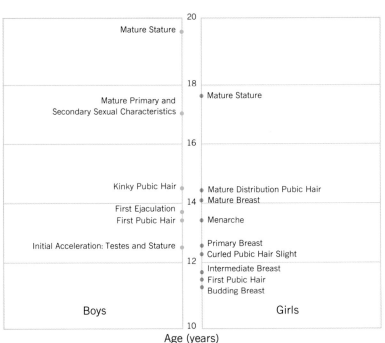

Figure 19.1. The typical sequence of sexual maturation in boys and girls, from age eleven to twenty. (After Shuttleworth, 1949.)

adolescence than they were some generations ago. These changes have been attributed to various influences, including a higher standard of living with improved nutrition. Another factor may be that the greater mobility of populations has brought genetic factors more freely into play; whereas most marriages used to take place between couples born and reared in the same locality, this situation is no longer so true.

A decrease of as much as three years in age of onset of puberty represents a radical change in the timetable of development. Childhood is shortened, and the demands of sexual and some aspects of social maturity are visited upon youth at an earlier age. This raises two questions: What changes, if any, have occurred in the meantime in the young person's social milieu as prescribed by adult society, and to what extent, if any, has accelerated physical maturation been accompanied by accelerated social and psychological development?

Earlier sexual maturity has not, by and large, been matched by a lowered age of induction into adult society. Laws pertaining to the "age of consent," voting, and the right to get a driver's license or to buy a glass of beer have remained much the same. Economically, the adolescent in today's urbanized society is, if anything, more dependent and has less opportunity for productive labor than at an earlier time.

Research on the question of psychological development at adolescence has come up with somewhat mixed answers. It has been shown that the

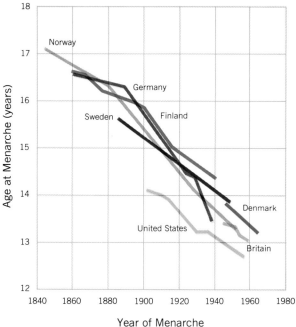

Figure 19.2. The decline in the age of menarche (onset of menstruation) in various European countries and the United States within the last 100 years. (After Tanner, 1968.)

sharp rise in the curve of physical growth is not accompanied by a corresponding sharp rise in intellectual growth. However, there have been some changes in social maturity over the years. Adolescents today, as compared with a few generations ago, are more precocious in their heterosexual interests: they date or demand the right to date at an earlier age, and they demand more privileges.

Some studies have compared compositions by adolescents about themselves and their aspirations written several decades ago with compositions written on the same themes by young people in the present decade. Such studies, while pointing out that adolescents today are willing to express an earlier development of heterosexual interests, do not show a consistent picture of increased maturity in self-evaluation, morals, or outlook on life.

Some dislocations between physical maturity and social-moral maturity in adolescence might be expected in any generation. Physical growth comes naturally. A young person does not learn to grow, but he must learn to adapt to changes wrought by growth. Such learning takes time, which means that there is an inevitable lag between physical developments and the process of adapting to them.

Prediction and Timing of Growth

One aspect of adolescent growth that is perplexing to most youngsters, and disturbing to many, is uncertainty about where things will end. A physical growth specialist, with proper equipment, can make predictions regarding the timing of sexual maturity and ultimate stature with some degree of certainty, using methods described in the following paragraphs. Unfortunately, such information is seldom available to the youngsters.

SKELETAL AGE

The maturity of the skeleton, as shown by degree of ossification of bone structure and expressed in terms of skeletal age, gives an indication of how mature a child is in the other aspects of his growth. For example, a girl who is chronologically ten years old may exhibit a skeletal age of twelve; this difference would signal an earlier than average onset of the menarche. When the extremities (epiphyses) of the long bones have become calcified, or closed, the potential for growth in height comes to an end. According to Nancy Bayley, a given skeletal age means that an individual has reached a given proportion of his eventual adult dimensions. Consequently, a young person's adult size can be predicted fairly accurately on the basis of his present skeletal age and size.

STATURE

The growth spurt in height in adolescents is often spectacular and, to the growing individual, may seem to be completely erratic. Yet it occurs within certain boundaries, some of which are more stable than others. According to measurements of boys by Donald M. Broverman and his colleagues, the beginning of the period of pubertal growth (ranging from age ten and a half to age fourteen and a half) is more variable than the

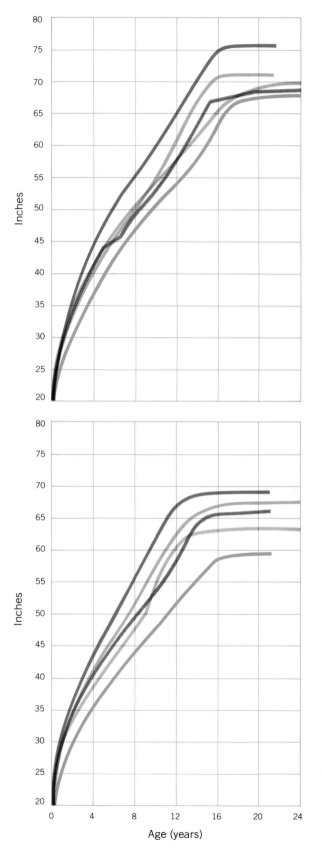

end (with a range of some three years, from age fourteen to seventeen). Thus, the boy who has the earliest start in pubertal growth has, potentially, a longer period of growth than the one with a late start.

A person's size at the beginning of adolescence predicts a great deal about how big he is likely to be at the end. Louis Stolz and H. R. Stolz found a correlation of more than .80 between height at the onset and at the end of the pubertal period. Because this coefficient is less than 1.00, it indicates that there are shifts in relative height, but it also indicates that a boy who is taller or shorter at the beginning of the pubertal growth cycle is more likely to be taller or shorter compared with others at the end.

PSYCHOLOGICAL REACTIONS TO PHYSICAL CHANGE

According to various reports, girls react to their first menstruation with feelings ranging from shock to joy. Shock is most likely to occur if the event comes as a surprise to a girl who is utterly unprepared for it. Many girls, by contrast, feel a glow of pride. Reaction to menstruation is influenced by a variety of factors other than the physical event itself. Her prior attitudes of accepting or rejecting her role as a girl, her own anxieties about sex, and the attitudes of her parents can all contribute to the happiness or horror of a girl's response to womanhood.

Practically every feature of the body becomes the focus, for some adolescents, of favorable or unfavorable opinion about his or her body, and

Figure 19.3. Curves of stature for five boys *(above)* and five girls *(left)* in the Berkeley Growth Study. Data are given for the tallest and shortest person of each sex as well as for three intermediary subjects. (After Bayley, 1956.)

negative feelings are expressed more often than positive ones. Girls worry more about their bodies than do boys, but for both sexes an adolescent's feelings about his or her unattractive physical characteristics rarely correspond with the way he or she is viewed by others.

BREAST DEVELOPMENT

The development of a girl's breasts, including their size and contour, plays an important role in her perception of herself as a female. Judging from the popular media, such as advertisements for brassieres, the dimensions of the Playmates of the Month, and the roving eyes of males, breasts are indeed of great importance, at least in the United States.

Breast development, from a bud stage to a more mature stage, has occurred in most girls before the menarche. With some exceptions, this development occurs before the appearance of pubic hair. A systematic study by E. L. Reynolds and J. V. Wines made repeated observations of breast development during a period of years. They found that development from bud to mature size occurs in about three years, usually between the ages of eleven and fourteen. Breasts classified as round or hemispherical in shape considerably outnumbered the flat and conical contours (see Figure 19.4).

MALE GENITALS

For many boys the size of their genital organs, notably the penis, has a profound meaning. Actual measurements show a great variation in penile size at all ages. Among boys thirteen years old in a study by William Schonfeld and G. W. Beebe, the average lengths of the shortest and longest penises (without erection and stretched) have been measured at 2.4 and 4.8 inches respectively. If standing height differed proportionately, these would be measurements for a boy about five feet tall at one extreme and one ten feet tall at the other. At age eighteen to nineteen, when most or all boys have completed their growth, the corresponding penis measurements were 4.25 and 6.1 inches.

If a boy has a small organ, or thinks he has, he is vulnerable to two widely held beliefs: first, that penis size gives a measure of manly physique, and second, that a man's ability to give sexual satisfaction to a woman depends upon the size of his genitals. In their long-term study of human sexual response, William H. Masters and Virginia Johnson found these beliefs to be myths. They found that the size of the penis was less consistently related to general physical development than was any other organ of the body. They found that the largest penis (5.51 inches in the flaccid state) in a sampling of 312 men was displayed by a man who was 5 feet 7 inches tall, while the smallest (2.36 inches) belonged to a man 5 feet 11 inches tall. They note also that increase in size of a small penis, when fully erect during coitus, is relatively larger than the increase in size of a large penis.

Masters and Johnson also found that in a man capable of a full erection, the physical ability to give sexual satisfaction is not dependent upon the size of the penis. The vagina, they report, is both

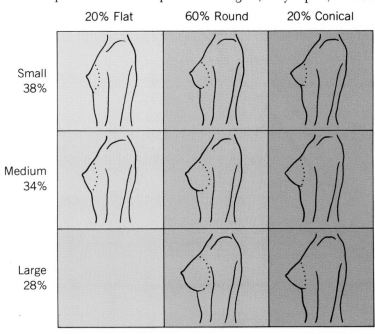

Figure 19.4. Classification of breast types. The percentage figures on the left indicate approximate distribution of the types among the population. (After Reynolds and Wines, 1948.)

distensible and contractible. Barring certain impediments (such as years of continence), the vagina of a normal woman who is sexually receptive
rapidly accommodates itself to the size of the
penis. It responds in a manner somewhat analogous to a handclasp that is accommodated to the
size of the other person's hand. According to
them, the size of the penis usually is a "minor
factor" in sexual stimulation of the female. Technique, not size, makes the difference.

OBESITY

About 10 percent of the child population has
been judged to be obese (as indicated by weight
relative to height), but in most groups the percentages are larger during adolescent years. For
example, Joseph Rauh and his associates report
the following percentages of children judged to be
obese at age fifteen: white male, 12.3; nonwhite
(practically all Negro) male, 7; white female,
15.3; nonwhite female, 21.3. X-ray measurements
of fat layers by E. L. Reynolds showed that girls
had a higher ratio of fat than boys into the late
teens, although there were variable gains and
losses during the middle teens. Reynolds notes
that fatness cannot be judged accurately simply
by measuring the external dimensions of the
body. The bodily contours are determined to varying degrees by fat, muscle, and bone and by the
shape of the skeleton. For example, a girl with a
wide bone structure may appear to have fat hips
when actually she has a thinner layer of fat than
do girls who look slimmer.

Many boys, for a time during adolescence, have

Figure 19.5. Studies have shown that
there is no direct relationship between
size of male genitals and physique.

fat deposits that seem inappropriate in a male. These deposits may occur in the thighs, the lower part of the trunk, the genital area, and the breasts. It is a great relief to a boy when these fat deposits prove to be temporary.

Obesity is the outcome of a multitude of factors, which vary from person to person. The simplest explanation is that a person is fat because he eats too much. But individuals vary greatly in their genetic predisposition to put on weight or to have large fat deposits in certain areas of the body and not in others. In psychological accounts, overeating has sometimes been explained as an unconscious reaction to emotional conflicts: it may be used, for example, as an escape from anxiety, as a means of compensating for lack of being loved, or as a protection (through physical unattractiveness) from sexual advances. Whatever the underlying motivation, overeating as an escape from emotional problems is likely to be self-defeating, at least in twentieth-century America.

EARLY AND LATE MATURING

As a group, early-maturing boys have a psychological advantage over late maturers, as shown in studies by Paul Mussen and Mary Jones. Such boys are likely to stand higher in the interrelated attitudes of acceptance by peers, self-acceptance, and positive feelings toward others.

Psychological reactions to early and late maturing result from an interaction between genetic factors, social attitudes, and attitudes toward self. William Schonfeld points out that many of the variations boys may regard as evidence of inadequate masculine physique are genetically determined physical variations within the normal range of development. When such is the case, a late-maturing boy need only bide his time. But in the meantime the values placed on athletic prowess and manly appearance (by boys and girls alike) may make him feel inferior to those who mature early. Feelings of inadequacy, and efforts to compensate for them, may persist even when the physical differences that made the boy feel inferior no longer exist.

Early or late maturing does not seem to have as much impact on girls as on boys. The early-maturing girl is somewhat conspicuous. She is far out of step developmentally with boys of her own age, and she may have to be on guard against the attentions of older boys who gaze at her appreciatively.

However, early maturing may be a source of satisfaction if a girl has favorite companions who also are early maturers. Early-maturing girls at seventeen may have a more favorable view of themselves and rate higher in popularity than they rated earlier in their teens.

PSYCHOLOGICAL ASPECTS OF SEXUAL DEVELOPMENT

Sexual development obviously has wide psychological and social ramifications beyond the overt aspects of sexual behavior. Human sexual behavior is governed not by hormones alone but, to an important degree, by the central nervous system, probably in an area known as the neocortex, which is the seat of learning, memory, imagination, and other forms of unstereotyped activity.

By virtue of the role of higher brain centers, human sexual behavior is very pliable and shows great variation. Interest in sex is not tied to the estrous cycle, as it is in most mammals. Human beings, notably the males, can be aroused by a wide variety of symbols, such as pictures, movies, and mere thoughts. A woman can continue to have orgasm after the menopause or after removal of the ovaries, and a castrated man may be able to have an orgasm even though he is unable to ejaculate.

Sexual intercourse as a means of enjoying physical and emotional intimacy—as distinct from being confined solely to procreation—is almost universally approved, as long as it occurs within a marriage. Among the persons who do not regard marriage as a necessary condition for intercourse, a large proportion (more girls than boys) still regard a loving relationship between the sexes as an essential condition. (Chapter 22 details the attitudes of average young people in contemporary American society about love and sex.)

All manner of motives and emotions may be associated with sexual activity: love, hate, jealousy, guilt, fear, anxiety, sorrow, joy. Sexual behavior may be spontaneous or it may serve such devious motives as revenge, rebellion, the need for mastery or security, or assuaging feelings of inferiority. When devious motives, which a person may not be aware of, are at work, what seems to be an exercise in sexual freedom may actually be compulsive behavior.

Figure 19.6. Although marriage is no longer considered a precondition for sexual relations by many girls, most still demand love and romance as requirements for sexual involvement.

SEXUAL ATTITUDES AND PRACTICES

Much has been said in recent years about the so-called sexual revolution. In assessing whether there really has been a revolution, it is much easier to take a census of overt sex practices than to find to what extent sexual activities are spontaneous or compulsive, free or fraught with fear and guilt. A more permissive attitude toward sex appears today in many forms, including relaxed censorship, relaxed dormitory rules in some colleges, and a greater expectation that girls should be responsible for contraception.

Practically all boys and probably a great majority of girls have had some sexual experience, at least some form of sex play, prior to adolescence. Glenn Ramsey found that by the age of twelve, about three-fourths of all boys have had experience with masturbation, and 98 percent report such experience by the age of fifteen. Moreover, by the age of thirteen, about 40 percent of boys have been involved in homosexual play. By late adolescence, according to Alfred Kinsey, about two-fifths of girls have had experience with masturbation, but the practice is not likely to be as continuous or as frequent as in boys.

PETTING AND INTERCOURSE

Practically all boys and girls have had some heterosexual contact with each other by the end of their teens, according to the Kinsey studies of the 1940s, and there is no reason to think that the percentages have changed greatly. Such experience varies, of course, ranging from holding hands to petting the genitals. By age twenty-one, in the population as a whole, approximately three-fourths of the boys and about one-third to one-half of the girls have experienced sexual intercourse, according to Kinsey and other studies.

A recent study by Eleanore Luckey and Martin Nass provides estimates on the percentages of young people who have had sexual encounters, or at least are willing to admit that they have. This survey included twenty-one colleges and universities in the United States and one major university in each of four foreign countries (Canada, England, Germany, and Norway). The average age of first intercourse reported by the American sampling was 17.9 years for males and 18.7 for females. See Table 19.1 for some results of the study.

Table 19.1. College Students Who Have Experienced Sexual Intercourse (1969)

Country	Boys (%)	Girls (%)
United States	58.2	43.3
Canada	56.8	35.3
England	74.8	62.8
Germany	54.5	59.4
Norway	66.7	53.6

PROMISCUITY

It would be a mistake to interpret the statistics regarding sexual activity as evidence of promiscuity. For example, a girl is represented in the 43.3 percentage cited in Table 19.1 whether she has had the experience many times or only once. The percentage leaves other things unsaid. A large proportion of these girls (46.6 percent) had coitus with only one partner, and as other studies have shown, this partner is commonly the one she intends to marry.

In Gallup polls conducted in the spring and summer of 1969, college students and individuals in the population at large were asked, "Do you think it is wrong for a man and a woman to have sex relations before marriage, or not?" The percentage of college students answering that it is not wrong was 68. In the population at large, 41 percent of persons aged twenty-one to twenty-nine gave the same answer. By contrast, of persons thirty to forty-nine years old, 21 percent said it was not wrong, and only 11 percent of those over fifty agreed that premarital intercourse was not wrong.

According to 58.6 percent of the college girls in the Luckey and Nass study, coitus should be considered appropriate at the eighteen- to twenty-year level only if the girl is married, and an additional 28.4 percent said that sex is appropriate outside of marriage only if the partners are officially or tentatively engaged.

Most significant, perhaps, in the Luckey and Nass survey is the finding that in spite of a so-called sexual revolution—and presumably a generation gap in sexual mores—about one-third of the boys and well over half the girls still described themselves as virgins.

Findings support the view that sexual mores have become more permissive during recent decades and that the double standard has begun to decline. There is less rigorous insistence that girls remain virgins until marriage—from the girls, their parents, and the prospective husbands.

Figure 19.7. In 1933 Romeo and Juliet, the symbols of young love, were played on the screen by adults in their thirties (Leslie Howard and Norma Shearer), who maintained a respectable distance. Today's changing sexual views may be symbolized by the casting and lovemaking of actual teen-agers in the 1968 film version and by the public display of affection among other young people in such places as college dorms.

HOMOSEXUALITY

There has been a drift toward a more thoughtful and sympathetic attitude toward homosexuality, although views on the subject are still controversial. One view is that homosexuality represents a form of mental illness. Homosexuality has also been described as a symptom of emotional maladjustment originating in childhood. One explanation is based on the Freudian theory of *reaction formation*—the unconscious substitution of a less threatening feeling for one that is unbearable. According to this view, a boy may, for example, feel abused by his father and other males and hate them; but he cannot safely express his hatred and so, through the work of an unconscious mechanism, he substitutes love for hate. If sexual impulses become linked with this love, he becomes a homosexual. Another theory is that the male homosexual feels deficient as a male and tries, unconsciously, to bolster his masculinity by sexually possessing another man.

Whatever the background might be, the male homosexual's existence in an inhospitable environment is risky and is often bleak, sad, furtive, and lonely, unrelieved by a stable relationship with any other person. The female homosexual also faces hazards, but she is likely to find it easier to establish a firm relationship, she can more readily accommodate either a heterosexual or a homosexual role, and she is not commonly regarded as dangerous.

According to Martin Hoffman, homosexuality, like heterosexuality, is interwoven with a complex

Figure 19.8 *(above)*. The traditional sex roles see the male as aggressive and athletic, the female as submissive and a helpmate to the male.

Figure 19.9 *(right)*. Many young females are rejecting the traditional role assigned to them and are beginning to assert themselves in ways usually associated with men.

Figure 19.10. The virtual elimination of male and female roles can be seen in such areas as the unisex trend in fashion.

array of factors—biological, social, and psychological—that vary from person to person. The homosexual person (or more correctly, a *given* homosexual person) may or may not be emotionally maladjusted. In any event, the conditions underlying homosexuality are so varied that an out-of-hand policy of moral condemnation, legal prosecution, or assigning a label of pathology is completely unwarranted.

Sex Roles and Sex Differences

There are many behavioral differences between the sexes besides those noted above. According to Kinsey, boys reach the peak of their sexual powers earlier than do girls, even though the menarche in girls comes earlier than the corresponding development in boys. Among other such behavioral differences are that boys desire orgasm more often than do girls; they resort more than girls to sexual fantasies; they are more responsive to symbols of sex; they reach a sexual climax in dreams more often; they require less constant physical stimulation to remain aroused; they more often have had sexual relations with more than one partner; they do not tend to insist, as girls do, that there should be a feeling of affection between the partners; and they prefer to go steady less often than do girls.

Differences between and among males and females are the result of both genetic and environmental factors. On the genetic side, G. Hardin reports that the production of the male hormone (androgen) may be eleven times higher in one person than in another. Frank Beach cites evidence suggesting that female brain functioning differs from male brain functioning, and it seems that at least part of the difference can be traced to the influence of hormones.

Differences in male and female sexual behavior are also influenced by what society deems to be appropriate sex roles. According to traditional standards in the United States (and those observed in many other areas), boys are aggressive, but girls are expected to be passive and to inhibit aggression. If a girl has hostile or aggressive impulses (as all normal girls have), she should, according to conventional standards, curb or hide them.

A girl may protest, but she should not hit. She should not compete aggressively or too openly with males. One result of such restrictions is that some girls do not do their best in contests with boys and do not, in high school, allow themselves to compete wholeheartedly for scholastic honors. By this standard, the girl should play a passive role in her heterosexual relationships. It is the boy who should take the initiative in petting, and he usually does. It is the girl who accedes, and if the approach threatens to go beyond the limits she allows, she is expected to serve as a calming conscience for two. In courtship, it is the man who is supposed to propose.

The feminine female is permitted to be dependent and conforming, but the masculine male is not supposed to have—or at least to show—such tendencies. The feminine type of girl should be capable of tenderness and compassion; she is permitted to cry, to be submissive, and to act

more helpless than a boy. The masculine male is supposed to be decisive, Spartan, able to suffer in silence, and guarded in showing his feelings (except, perhaps, anger).

Of course, there are wide variations in how boys and girls actually behave and in how they want to behave. But no one escapes from society's pressures to conform to its ideal masculine and feminine roles.

ANXIETY AND SEX

Personal concerns associated with sexual development are a source of much anxiety to some adolescents and are probably of some anxiety to all adolescents. Anxiety refers to feelings of uneasiness or distress that arise when a person is torn by inner conflict because of incompatible motives, when he is at odds with himself, or when he is threatened by an adverse evaluation of himself.

The conflicts underlying anxiety may involve motives of which the adolescent is aware, or they may arise out of motives that he does not recognize. Such is the case, according to Freudian psychology, when sexual impulses activate an unresolved Oedipus conflict. Here, sexuality is clouded by the effects of earlier feelings of rivalry, fear, and hostility. According to the view of Harry Stack Sullivan, sexual impulses may be enmeshed in long-standing attitudes toward the self. If, as a child, the adolescent was taught to regard sexual activity as bad and punishable, he feels threatened by his insistent sexual impulses—he is being threatened by his own badness, which, in the past, led to disapproval, insecurity, and anxiety.

Anxiety, according to this theory, may be augmented in a boy when he has sexual relationships with girls for whom he has no affection or respect.

Any impulse that is forbidden by an adolescent's conscience produces conflict, and the more rigorous the conscience, the more guilt and self-reproach there will be if the impulse wins out or threatens to do so. Such guilt is a form of anxiety. An interesting sidelight on scruples pertaining to sex is that some persons can forgive the transgressions of others but not their own.

Anxiety-producing conflict may also be precipitated by sex-role stereotypes such as those mentioned earlier. Regardless of inherent tendencies, differences between individuals of either sex, for example in disposition to be aggressive, are greater than differences between boys as a group and girls as a group.

A girl's predicament becomes especially acute in adolescence if she becomes aggressively rebellious in her struggle for independence but feels guilty about it. If she is openly aggressive, she risks disapproval by others, and disapproval by others is a source of conflict that often leads to disapproval of self. Even if she suppresses her aggressiveness or represses it by disavowing it and pretending to herself that it does not exist, it remains a threat. A boy who has a strong tendency to be dependent (presumably a feminine characteristic) also faces especially hard going in adolescence.

Boys or girls who do not fit into artificial notions of what a masculine boy or a feminine girl should be also face the danger of suffering in their

Figure 19.11. Individuals who are unsure of their sexual identities or of their attractiveness to the opposite sex often suffer anxiety, such as that felt by the traditional wallflower.

own eyes. Their difficulty involves added anxiety when they try to put on a false front, which, at best, is fragile and always in danger of exposure.

LOVE AND SEX

The romanticized notion of being in love retains —from Victorian and perhaps chivalric times—an idea of suspended sexuality; although sex is acknowledged to be, at bottom, the motivating force, the romantic version of love suggests that "real" love consists of loftier sentiments. Another, unromantic, view of love says that the lover has succeeded, through an unconscious process, in viewing the loved one as the embodiment of his idealized self—all the qualities he most deeply cherishes and would like to realize and possess within himself.

To a person who is or has been in love, accounts such as the above do not begin to tell the tale. An adolescent's first experience of being in love and having his love reciprocated comes as a revelation. When in full flower, love brings a rush of feeling—joy, ecstasy, exquisitely flavored fantasies, a desire to be near, to caress, to bring gifts, to comfort, to bestow happiness, to share, and to confide within the warm protection of mutual trust. For the boy and the girl in love, the well-being of the other is at least as important as his own—perhaps more important. When swept by a feeling of love, life loses its loneliness, fears seem less threatening, wounds from the past seem less hurtful, and the future looks more inviting.

But usually something a good deal less excitingly romantic may occur, and the condition may be short-lived. The typical girl is likely, according to her own account, to fall in love several times— from three to as many as six or more times—although, as she grows older, she may regard earlier episodes as infatuations. About one-fourth of the girls (median age about twenty) in a study by Albert Ellis said they had been in love with two men at the same time at least once.

As noted earlier, being in love is regarded by a large proportion of girls as a necessary condition for having sexual relations. This holds true both at the top and at the bottom of social and economic levels. David Knox and his co-workers found that in their expressed attitudes toward love, adolescent girls tend to be somewhat more realistic and conjugal than boys, while boys tend to be somewhat more romantic.

A professed state of being in love may mean many things. It may be a deep emotional commitment or a fragile infatuation. It may be genuine or largely a pretense. It may be a healthy form of self-fulfillment or a form of self-deception serving a variety of unrecognized needs, such as a need to put aside feelings of inferiority, to justify otherwise forbidden acts, to seduce or exploit, or to release tension. In like manner, blighted or unreciprocated love may leave a person jealous, vengeful, full of self-reproach, or only wounded and sad. The sadness, like adolescence itself, is temporary and disappears with growth. It lingers only in memory to enhance an appreciation in later years. The joys of reciprocated love survive, however; they are the single most important lesson of adolescence in forming adult maturity.

Put the personality of a child in the body of a man, furnish a need to be loved and a fierce desire to be independent, allow a need to be self-directing but leave out any idea of what direction to take, add an enormous amount of love but also the fear that it may not be accepted or returned, give physical and sexual powers without any knowledge or experience of how to use them —take these and place them in a society whose values and achievements are essentially incomprehensible and certainly unattainable and whose concerns are seemingly misplaced and insincere. Then you will have just begun to scratch the surface of adolescence.

Out of these contradictions comes growth for the lucky, healthy majority of adolescents. In living with conflicts and in occasionally resolving one or two of them or watching them disappear automatically with living, a child may grow gradually toward an ideal adult who is independent, free, humane and generous with others, self-directing, tolerant of complexity yet intolerant of injustice, at home with change yet committed to the highest principles.

No formula for human development can guarantee these attributes, but the experience of adolescence clearly fosters them. Successful adolescent development leads to an extension of rationality, to the integration of impulses into life, to the humanization of conscience, and to the stabilization of a sense of self both independent and related to others. Adolescence leads above all to a capacity for responsible commitment—to self, to others, to work, to family, to play.

This discussion of the tasks of adolescence will not describe the statistically typical teen-ager in American society, or for that matter in any society. Rather, it will characterize an ideal of adolescence at its best, as a process of profound inner and outer change that transforms the child into the emotionally sound, ethically responsible, and cognitively rational adult. Despite the infrequency with which this ideal is attained, it constitutes a standard against which the actual experience of adolescents in our society can be compared.

One primary concern of psychologists is the impediments to adolescence. The available facts indicate that far too few young Americans have available the familial, educational, and social resources necessary for the full unfolding of their personalities during adolescence. The impediments include cultural and social deprivation; overt and subtle discrimination; unimaginative, coercive, or simply inadequate educational resources; the absence of opportunities to innovate and experiment; irrational pressures toward conformity to peer group and adult authority; and the assumption by adults that all adolescent criticisms are perverse, trivial, irrational, and unworthy of being heard.

PSYCHOLOGICAL GROWTH VERSUS SOCIALIZATION
What happens in adolescence is important in its own right. A fortunate adolescence may help repair the damage of an unfortunate childhood, or a freezing of development in adolescence can constrict and warp the life of the adult. The view that adolescence is only a recapitulation and

20
The Tasks of Adolescence

working out of the themes of childhood does scant justice to these possibilities. To be sure, the preadolescent years are enormously important in defining where the adolescent begins, how much he has to work with, and what he must work on. Some boys and girls arrive at the teens so crippled by the experiences of childhood that only the most devoted remedial efforts can begin to overcome their handicaps; others reach adolescence with such abundant resources that only the grossest deprivations can arrest their development. But most are between these two extremes—resourceful yet troubled, eager to grow up yet rather afraid to, and in need of the confirming presence of an understanding but not overwhelming adult world. Human development is cumulative and layered. Adolescence is built upon the earlier stages of life but at the same time has its own tasks. Whether the adolescent accomplishes these tasks depends not only on his past but on his present—on what he is offered and on what he can make of it.

Psychological growth through adolescence must be distinguished from socialization during the years after puberty. There is ample evidence that many young Americans change in response to social expectations during their teens; there is less evidence that they grow psychologically. Socialization involves learning to understand the expectations of the social environment and to accommodate one's self to them. Psychological growth entails personality change, increasing inner differentiation and integration, real autonomy and flexibility, new capacities for self-determination—

growth toward a mature personality, as discussed in Chapter 24. Although not inherently incompatible, socialization and psychological growth are identical only in an ideal society. Real psychological development in adolescence often runs counter to unthinking accommodation to society as it exists. The experience of adolescent growth, then, does not inevitably lead to adjustment to the existing society. But it does lead to an adult who has overcome both his irrational rebelliousness and his irrational urge to conform, who can give his loyalty to a just society and work to reform an unjust one.

GROWTH IS ERRATIC

Psychological growth, especially in adolescence, is neither smooth nor automatic. It proceeds in fits and starts, has its upswings and downswings, and sometimes requires temporary reversals in preparation for the next advance. Nor is it guaranteed by time alone. The passage of time ensures physical growth and entry into adult social roles, but it does not ensure that the tasks of adolescence will be accomplished. Adolescence involves a major reorganization of personality, which requires abandoning old relationships, attitudes, and concepts of self. These changes cannot be accomplished without inner conflict and its symptoms: subjective turmoil and behavioral inconsistency. Indeed, total lack of conflict during adolescence is an ominous sign that the individual's psychological maturation may not be progressing.

Psychological growth requires appropriate environmental stimulation in adolescence, as at other

Figure 20.1. One of the tasks of adolescence is to work out one's psychological relationships with people, particularly with those who share one's daily life, such as parents, friends, and relatives.

stages of life, and the rates at which adolescents develop psychologically are even more idiosyncratic than the rates of their physical maturation. The age-graded social and educational institutions that deal with adolescents make little allowance for this variability, and many of the conflicts between the adolescent and his world stem from the fact that he is not ready—or has been ready too long—for what his world offers him and expects of him. The timetable of individual development, for example, rarely follows the uniform curriculum of the academic year that structures the lives of most adolescents. Nor does development during adolescence proceed at the same rate in all sectors. One teen-ager may be far ahead of his peers in his social development but behind intellectually. Another may exhibit great ethical precocity but have achieved little capacity to regulate his unruly impulses. Sexual maturity and responsibility may come years ahead of competence in work. In adolescence, developmental precocity and developmental lag are normal and routine.

INTRAPSYCHIC CHANGES

Adolescence can involve profound changes in the internal structure and organization of the personality. The change most frequently discussed by those concerned with intellectual development is the child's greatly extended capacity for rationality after puberty.

COGNITIVE CHANGES

As Jean Piaget and Bärbel Inhelder have suggested, the physiological onset of puberty coincides roughly with the emergence of new intellectual and cognitive abilities. At about the time of puberty, the individual first becomes capable of deductive and systematic thinking, of constructing hypotheses, ideologies, utopias, and models of reality with which he compares the world around him. At the same time, his historical sense expands, so that both the distant past and the far future acquire greater psychological immediacy for him. If encouraged and supported by his environment, the adolescent can develop his cognitive abilities in constructive and rational ways, developing an increased capacity for planning, for the mental rehearsal of alternate plans of action, and for guiding his behavior according to long-range purposes.

In Piaget's terminology the stage that begins at about age twelve is the *stage of formal operations* (Stage 4). The preceding stage, the stage of concrete operations, was discussed in detail in Chapter 15. There are several important attributes of thinking at the formal operational stage that differ from the thought processes of the earlier stage. First, the adolescent is capable of considering all the possible ways a particular problem might be solved and the possible forms a particular event might assume. If he is thinking about the shortest way to get to the seashore, he can (and will) review all the possible routes, and he knows when he has exhausted all the possibilities.

Consider the following question: "A man was found dead in the back seat of a car that had hit a telephone pole. What happened?" A seven-year-old thinks up a reason that satisfies him and states

Figure 20.2. Because all teen-agers advance intellectually at different rates, material that seems difficult for one student may seem simple and boring to another.

it: "The man hit a pole and was thrown into the back seat and was killed." An adolescent is more likely to generate all the possible causes of this event—the man could have been put into the car after it had crashed in order to make the scene appear an accident; he could have been put into the back seat by his companion after the crash; and so on. This ability to generate and to explore systematically all the possible hypotheses and then to check each for its probable validity is one of the hallmarks of the stage of formal operations.

Second, the adolescent's thought is self-consciously deductive; it resembles that of a scientist. He can think in terms of hypothetical propositions—even fanciful ones. Consider the following question: "They found a three-year-old skull of an animal with five feet and three heads that lived to be fifty. What is wrong with this statement?" The seven-year-old might say that it is silly because there are no animals with five feet and three heads; the adolescent will accept the fanciful hypothesis and attempt to reason out an answer.

Third, the adolescent organizes his operations into higher-order operations, ways of using abstract rules to solve a whole class of problems. Consider the different approaches to solving this problem: "What number is 30 less than 3 times itself?" The ten-year-old in the stage of concrete operations is likely to begin the problem by trial and error, trying first one number and then another, using the operations of addition and multiplication until he finally arrives at the correct answer. The adolescent has learned a higher-order

operation; he may set up the equation $x + 30 = 3x$ and quickly find the answer of 15. He has combined the separate operations of addition and multiplication into the more complex operations of the algebraic equation. If children and teen-agers are given a box full of objects and a bowl of water and asked to select the ones that float, the teen-ager will not test each object in the water but will apply a simplifying rule. He may first select all the wooden objects and may even apply some test (like knocking on them) to see if they are primarily made of wood. These more complex operations are called *combinative structures*. These structures seem to be necessary for understanding algebra and higher mathematics.

Thus, formal thought is a generalized orientation toward problem solving that involves isolating the elements of a problem and systematically exploring all the possible solutions, regardless of their hypothetical nature. Formal thought is rational and systematic. Moreover, the adolescent seems to reflect upon the rules he possesses and on his thoughts. It is not accidental that adolescence is the first stage in which the child begins to think carefully about himself, his role in life, his plans, and the validity and integrity of his beliefs. The adolescent's concern with the phoniness of his own ideals and those of adults, which is acute in our time, is not usually seen in children under ten years of age. The child in the stage of concrete operations deals largely with the present, with the here and now. The adolescent is concerned with the hypothetical, the future, and the

remote. An adolescent remarked, "I found myself thinking about my future, and then I began to think about why I was thinking about my future, and then I began to think about why I was thinking about why I was thinking about my future." This preoccupation with *thought* is one hallmark of the stage of formal operations.

As a result of these changes, the adolescent can achieve a new range and flexibility of mental processes. The lessons of the past, both personal and collective, can be applied with far more sureness to present and future events. Personal, interpersonal, and societal options, sometimes learned from others, sometimes learned from books, are rehearsed first in fantasy and then often tried out in behavior. New allegiances and loyalties become possible, not merely to concrete individuals and existing groups but to ideas, goals, and ideologies. It is in adolescence, then, that the intellect cuts loose from the concrete operations of daily life and becomes a powerful, generalized force in the governance of daily behavior. His capacity to use abstract ideas also permits him to use them defensively, in order to keep his own impulses and feelings at arm's length.

MORAL GROWTH

Closely related to the extension of rationality is the aspect of adolescence that is concerned with conscience. The morality of the child is first based upon simple egocentric or retributive assumptions, then on conventional concepts of "being good." But with adolescence, a major shift is

Figure 20.3. The adolescent in the stage of formal operations can quickly solve a mathematical word problem using algebra, while a ten-year-old still in the concrete operations stage must search for an answer through the tedious process of trial and error.

Figure 20.4. An artist's conception of the adolescent mind at work.

possible. If the experience of adolescence is facilitative, the previously unexamined moral edicts and precepts of parents come under critical scrutiny, as does the gap between parental precepts and practice. The egocentric or conventional morality of the child is gradually replaced by a more subtle ethical sense that for the first time may embody the abstract concepts of justice and of the sanctity of human life. These changes underlie some adolescents' capacity for uncompromising and even fanatical zealotry and their sometimes astonishing devotion to the highest ethical principles.

Especially at this period, adolescents become aware of the often radical discrepancies between what others tell them to do and what others actually do themselves—and no one is more likely to be the object of bitter criticism in this regard than parents. But however exclusively preoccupied he may seem to be with exposing the clay feet of his former idols, the adolescent is also in the process of reexamining his own internal values and codes of behavior. For a time, this process may require him to reject the moral lessons he assimilated as a child.

The stages of moral development as hypothesized and developed by Lawrence Kohlberg are reproduced here from Chapter 17 to promote a clearer understanding of the following discussion and illustrations.

I. Preconventional Level

At this level the child is responsive to cultural rules and labels of good and bad, right or wrong, but interprets these labels in terms of either the physical or the hedonistic consequences of action (punishment, reward, exchange of favors) or in terms of the physical power of those who enunciate the rules and labels. The level is divided into the following two stages:

STAGE 1: *The punishment and obedience orientation.* The physical consequences of action determine its goodness or badness regardless of the human meaning or value of these consequences. Avoidance of punishment and unquestioning deference to power are valued in their own right, not in terms of respect for an underlying moral order supported by punishment and authority (the latter being Stage 4).

STAGE 2: *The instrumental relativist orientation.* Right action consists of that which instrumentally satisfies one's own needs and occasionally the needs of others. Human relations are viewed in terms like those of the marketplace. Elements of fairness, of reciprocity and equal sharing are present, but they are always interpreted in a physical, pragmatic way. Reciprocity is a matter of "you scratch my back and I'll scratch yours," not of loyalty, gratitude, or justice.

II. Conventional Level

At this level, maintaining the expectations of the individual's family, group, or nation is perceived as valuable in its own right, regardless of immediate and obvious consequences. The attitude is one not only of *conformity* to personal expectations and social order but of loyalty to it, of actively *maintaining*, supporting, and justifying the order and of identifying with the persons or group involved in it. At this level, there are the following two stages:

STAGE 3: *The interpersonal concordance or "good boy–nice girl" orientation.* Good behavior is that which pleases or helps others and is approved by them. There is much conformity to stereotypical

Figure 20.5. Many adolescents begin to examine the discrepancy between what their parents teach and what they practice, how their parents actually live. Religious beliefs may be subjected to severe scrutiny in light of abstract concepts of justice.

MARTY GUNSAULUS 1970

images of what is majority or "natural" behavior. Behavior is frequently judged by intention—"he means well" becomes important for the first time. One earns approval by being "nice."

STAGE 4: *The "law and order" orientation.* There is orientation toward authority, fixed rules, and the maintenance of the social order. Right behavior consists of doing one's duty, showing respect for authority, and maintaining the given social order for its own sake.

III. POSTCONVENTIONAL, AUTONOMOUS, OR PRINCIPLED LEVEL

At this level, there is a clear effort to define moral values and principles that have validity and application apart from the authority of the groups or persons holding these principles and apart from the individual's own identification with these groups. This level again has two stages:

STAGE 5: *The social-contract, legalistic orientation* —generally with utilitarian overtones. Right action tends to be defined in terms of general individual rights and in terms of standards that have been critically examined and agreed upon by the whole society. There is a clear awareness of the relativism of personal values and opinions and a corresponding emphasis upon procedural rules for reaching consensus. Aside from what is constitutionally and democratically agreed upon, the right is a matter of personal "values" and "opinion." The result is an emphasis upon the "legal point of view," but with an emphasis upon the possibility of changing law in terms of rational considerations of social utility (rather than freezing it in terms of Stage 4 "law and order"). Outside the legal realm, free agreement and contract are the binding elements of obligation. This is the "official" morality of the American government and Constitution.

STAGE 6: *The universal ethical-principle orientation.* Right is defined by the decision of conscience in accord with self-chosen *ethical principles* appealing to logical comprehensiveness, universality, and consistency. These principles are abstract and ethical (the Golden Rule, the categorical imperative); they are not concrete moral rules like the Ten Commandments. At heart, these are universal principles of *justice,* of the *reciprocity* and *equality* of the human *rights,* and of respect for the dignity of human beings as *individual persons.*

You will recall that an individual's progression through the stages of moral development does not follow a consistent age-graded pattern, as usually occurs in the normal development of cognition. Adolescents, even the late adolescents attending a university, can range from Stage 2 through Stage 6 in moral development. Several studies have shown what differences in the stage of moral development imply for the actions of individuals in moral dilemmas. In an experiment conducted by Stanley Milgram, undergraduates were ordered by an experimenter to administer increasingly severe electric shocks to a stooge victim. The pretense was that the victim was a subject in a learning experiment. The principles of justice involved in Stage 5, the social-contract orientation, do not clearly prescribe a course of action here because the victim had voluntarily agreed to participate in the experiment and because the subject had contractually committed himself to perform the experiment. Only thinking characteristic of Stage 6 clearly defined the situation as one in which the experimenter did not have the moral right to ask them to inflict pain on another person. Accordingly, 75 percent of the students who had previously been judged to be at the Stage 6 level refused to shock the victim, while only 13 percent of those judged to be at lower levels refused to administer the shock.

A study of Berkeley students carries the same moral issue into political-civil disobedience. Norma Haan and Mahlon Smith administered moral-judgment interviews to more than 200 Berkeley students who were about to decide whether or not to sit-in in the administration building in the name of political freedom of communication. The situation was like that of the Milgram experiment. People at Stage 5, the social-contract interpretation of justice (the one held by the university administration), could take the position that a student who came to Berkeley came with foreknowledge of the rules and could go elsewhere if he did not like them. About 50 percent of the Stage 5 subjects sat-in. For Stage 6 students the issue was clear-cut, and 80 percent of them sat-in. For students at the conventional levels, Stages 3 and 4, the issue was also clear-cut, and only 10 percent of them sat-in.

These results will sound very heartwarming to readers who have been engaged in protest activities. However, there was at Berkeley another group almost as disposed to sit-in as the Stage 6 students: these were Stage 2 instrumental relativists, described at length in Chapter 17, of whom about 60 percent sat-in. Longitudinal studies conducted by Kohlberg and his associates have

Figure 20.6. Students may participate in sit-ins and protests for a number of reasons; such students can be either high or low on the scale of moral development.

shown that most Stage 2 college students are in a state of confusion. In high school most were at the conventional level (Stage 3 or 4); in college, however, they kick conventional morality and search for their own thing, for self-chosen values. But they cannot distinguish between an autonomous morality of justice and one of egoistic relativism, exchange, and revenge. However, the studies also indicate that all of the middle-class, Stage 2 college students developed out of Stage 2 again, to become principled adults. The ambiguity of the morality of protest activities is further indicated by a study of another, later sit-in at Harvard, one in which few Stage 6 students participated. In that case principles of justice did not dictate sitting-in in the relatively clear sense they did in the Berkeley situation. The point is that maturity of moral thought predicts maturity of moral action—not specific kinds of action like sitting-in.

Ideally, by late adolescence the ethic not only has progressed past the conventional stages of moral development but also is humanized, so that the adolescent recognizes and eventually accepts the fact that an ethical life is not simply a matter of obeying the rules but a matter of being one's best self. And at best, he learns to forgive himself and others for the fact that no one ever quite is.

EMOTIONAL GROWTH

Adolescents also inevitably acquire a new attitude toward the life of the impulses. The onset of puberty is marked by an influx of previously unexperienced sensations, desires, and fantasies accompanying the physical changes discussed in Chapter 19. These new energies and feelings are among the most important catalysts for adolescent development. They topple the balance established in late childhood and require a new equilibrium; they are among the challenges to which the adolescent experience is a response. But at the same time, they can be deeply upsetting to the early adolescent, the more so because his earlier childhood fantasies, now backed by his nearly adult sexual and aggressive drives, may seem threatening and even overwhelming to him.

In advanced societies, with their continuing taboos on the expression of childhood sexuality, the sexually maturing adolescent must learn to modulate, control, and yet be able to express his desires for sexual gratification, love, and intimacy. Equally important, adolescence brings new capacities and impulses for aggression. In both areas, the adolescent must learn to live with feelings and abilities that are both quantitatively and qualitatively new, and for which no childhood experience can ever have totally prepared him. These new impulses, feelings, and capacities must be integrated into a sense of self, a conception of personal responsibility, and an extension of rationality—all of which during adolescence are shaky, ambivalent, and incomplete.

It is around this issue of the control and the integration of impulse that the most dramatic and socially disruptive changes and alterations of behavior take place during adolescence. Compulsive masturbation, accompanied by fantasies,

often heavily laden with the remnants of child-hood preoccupations, may alternate with periods of asceticism. Rage and violence can be suddenly superseded by self-restraint and saintlike gentle-ness. But these apparently unpredictable changes, however bedeviling and anxiety provoking to adults, are not simply expressions of the perversity and irrationality of the adolescent; they are part of the normal dialectic of development, in which impulsive action and excessive self-control alter-nate in ever-narrowing cycles, eventuating in the slow development of a capacity to substitute flexi-ble internal controls for the external controls of childhood.

In considering the integration of impulse dur-ing adolescence, it is crucial not merely to empha-size the importance of self-control but also to point up the equal importance of release, free-dom, and acceptance—of learning to express sexu-ality and anger without guilt or anxiety. Uncon-trolled sexual and aggressive impulsivity among adolescents is a problem that demands immediate psychological attention. But equally weighty in the balance of human suffering are the less visible problems of sexual inhibition and overcontrol of anger, which can lead to lives of quiet constric-tion and incapacitation. The adolescent's learning to modulate and control sexuality and aggression moves him toward an adulthood in which the capacity for guilt-free sexual activity and unanx-ious expression of appropriate anger will be cru-cial for his well-being. If the adolescent experi-ence is good, the frequent terror of the early

Figure 20.7. Like Stevenson's Dr. Jekyll and Mr. Hyde, the adolescent often vacillates between self-control and emotional impulses that seem to overwhelm him.

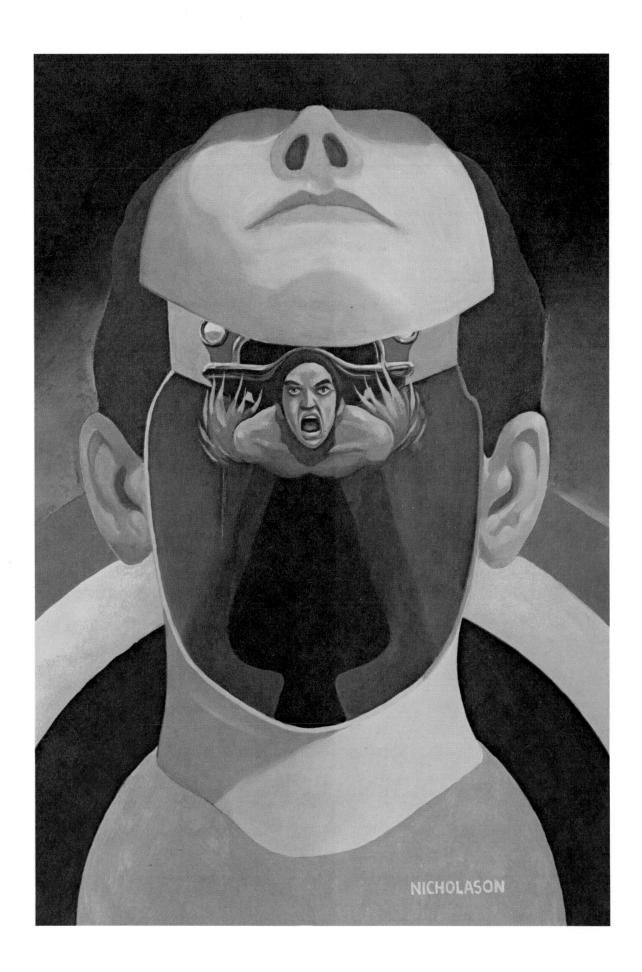

adolescent at his personally uncontrollable passions does not lead to massive self-restriction but evolves into a capacity to incorporate these passions and the energies that derive from them into personally and socially productive activities and relationships.

REDEFINING THE SELF

Adolescence involves major changes in the definition of the self. The childhood self is largely defined by parents and a few other key persons—family members, ministers, and teachers. It reflects in a relatively uncomplicated way the immediate world of persons crucial to the child and is based on relatively simple identification with these people or aspects of them. The adolescent self must be reexamined and reintegrated. On the one hand, it must be consistent with the adolescent's new capacity for rationality, the humanization of his conscience, and the integration of his impulses. On the other hand, it must be reconciled with the socially available possibilities for work, love, and play in modern society. This process, brilliantly described by Erik Erikson, touches all of the changes previously discussed. It entails the integration of emerging cognitive abilities and potentials for action; it involves the synthesis within the self of new values and purposes; it requires a capacity to live with aggression, instinct, and fantasy. Above all, it involves a movement away from the simple mirrorlike view of the self to a more integrated, more autonomous, and more individuated sense of identity, integrating the senses of uniqueness and independence with those of interdependence and solidarity with other people.

During adolescence itself, psychological pain, distress, worry, fear, confusion, shame, and guilt are probably more intense than during any other stage of life. Many adolescents show few outward signs of inner turmoil, and some may actually be able to weather adolescence with little conscious storm and stress. But for other adolescents, no matter how cocky or composed their surface, this stage of life involves times of intense psychological pain. Never before or after in life does the conscious gulf between actuality and aspiration, between the real-me and the social-me, and between feelings of loneliness and the need for love loom so wide or seem such a pit of deep despair.

ROLE CHANGES

The beginning of adolescence is marked not only by the obvious physiological changes and by the emergence of new cognitive capacities, but by a series of new interpersonal and social interactions. The emergence of primary and secondary sexual characteristics requires the adolescent to begin to develop new relationships with others that are appropriate to his new role as a potential adult and sexual being. Similarly, new cognitive capacities enable him to attain an expanded and qualitatively different view of the world, to construct new models of the future that will guide his personal and interpersonal behavior. At the same time, the attitudes of parents, teachers, and friends toward the adolescent change, and often change drastically. A new distance develops be-

Figure 20.8. The adolescent may show a calm exterior, which often hides a raging inner turmoil.

Figure 20.9. A rejection of conformity to family values and customs may be replaced merely by conformity to peer-group values and customs.

tween the postpubescent youth and his family, as if to recognize not only his developing sexuality but his forthcoming entry into the adult world. The impossibility of achieving within his family any complete or lasting satisfaction of his new impulses, values, and cognitive abilities serves to propel the adolescent away from his family toward friends, peers, and eventually adulthood.

RELATIONSHIPS WITH FAMILY

The chief interpersonal theme in early adolescence is the gradual move away from childhood dependency and immersion within the family toward ever-greater involvement with the extrafamilial world. For some young people this process of emancipation is fraught with visible tension, trauma, and conflict, but other adolescents are able to move away from their families with only internal turmoil, and much of that not conscious. Whether conscious or unconscious, acted upon or merely felt, intense ambivalence around issues of dependence and independence in early adolescence is routine. The actual behavior and attitudes of his parents in permitting him increasing freedom may bear little relation to the adolescent's feelings of being inwardly torn between his desire for independence and his usually less conscious wishes to remain a child, to be cared for, and to avoid the many deprivations and conflicts that adult life seems to entail. The provocativeness of adolescents toward parents who may offer little occasion for rebellion can often be understood in the context of the adolescent's own profound ambivalence. Indeed, it is through the acting out of this ambivalence in alternations between provocative self-assertion and childlike requests for succor that many adolescents gradually become able to emerge from their families.

But if the adolescent is capable of irrationality toward the adult world, adults prove no less capable of their own version of the same stance. In many societies the adolescent is one of the prime targets for adult projections. Within families, parents sometimes project their own unfulfilled dreams and forbidden wishes upon their children, subtly encouraging them to live in a way the parents cannot—and condemning them whether they do or do not. Many adult reactions to adolescents can only be understood as unwitting impositions onto the young of what the old have always really wanted to be. Promiscuity, irresponsibility, drug abuse, violence, and hedonism seem to be as much the wishes of adults for themselves as their ideas about the perversity of adolescents.

RELATIONSHIPS WITH PEERS

Among young Americans, relationships with peers play a major role in regulating impulses and emancipating the adolescent from childhood dependency. What Peter Blos has called "uniformism"—immersion into the peer group and acceptance of its norms as infallible and regulatory —may assist the adolescent to move away from his family while he still needs external sources of control. It often happens, however, that this dependency is clung to long after the need for it has passed, and conformity to peer-group norms merely replaces conformity to parental norms.

When this happens, adolescent development is foreclosed before real self-regulation and independence are achieved. The role of peer groups in social development is dealt with at length in Chapter 21.

THE END OF ADOLESCENCE

There is no exact criterion for the end of adolescence. In the following section, some of the qualities that distinguish the psychological adult from the child are discussed, and the emergence of these qualities constitutes a rough criterion for the end of adolescence. It is misleading to separate adolescence drastically from adulthood, for in most men and women, these two stages of life merge and blur: adolescence does not end, it fades away. And many creative adults retain adolescent qualities throughout their lives without being less adult—a passionate concern with ideals, openness to the turbulence of inner life, a speculative and theoretical bent. Furthermore, the fading away of adolescence does not mark the end of psychological growth but the beginning of a lifetime of further development, which will be discussed in Unit VII.

The steady prolongation of adolescence in our society also means that large numbers of young men and women become psychologically adult before they can become sociologically adult. They occupy an uncharted stage of life that has been interposed between the attainment of relative psychological maturity and their entry into the adult world of marriage and vocation. Their numbers are steadily increasing, and their special position

of disengagement from the structures of adult society makes of them a steady source of reforming zeal and critical commentary on the adult establishment. Their postponement of adulthood is less a response to their own unfinished developmental business than a requirement of prolonged higher education. These young men and women appear to be the harbingers of a new stage of life —youth—discussed at length in Chapter 23.

THE OUTCOMES

The gradual and imperceptible ending of adolescence is generally accompanied by the development of new psychological strengths that were not present to the same degree during adolescence itself. Central among the qualities that emerge from adolescence is the *capacity* for commitment, engagement, loyalty, and fidelity. Capacity is the concept that must be stressed: there are many in American society, as elsewhere, who possess a capacity to commit themselves to high purposes and intimate relationships but who have not found objects worthy of their commitment. Commitment does not necessarily entail conventionality or uncritical allegiance to what exists. On the contrary, in our disjointed modern world unexamined acquiescence in what exists often indicates a failure of adolescent development rather than its culmination. Commitment means a capacity for loyalty, devotion, and service to a set of imagined possibilities, some of which are within the realm of partial attainment; to a set of values and ideals relevant to the evaluation of action and intent; and to enduring relationships with people, groups,

Figure 20.10. One quality of character that should emerge from adolescence is a commitment to one's self: an understanding of one's basic worth and a conviction that this self is a worthy one. This commitment underlies all other commitments adolescents may make to others.

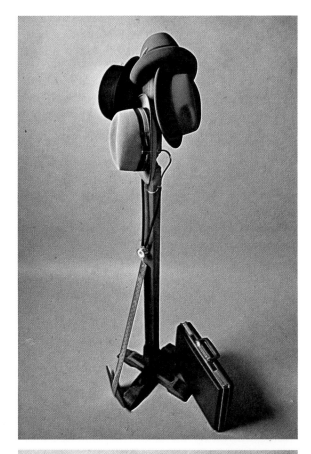

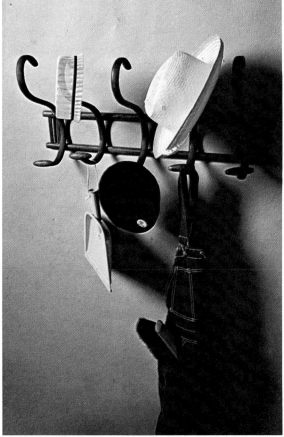

and institutions and to the purposes they serve.

In the modern world, especially for the more talented, privileged, and sensitive among today's youth, such commitments will often be fluid, open, and to a certain degree provisional; indeed, the dizzying pace of social change and the unpredictability of the future means that commitments to vocational skills, traditional values, and existing institutions are increasingly being replaced by commitments to general purposes, overriding values, historical possibilities, and styles of human relationship. Nevertheless, the ability and willingness to make such commitments without undue inner conflict and ambivalence, and to act effectively in their service, is one defining characteristic of the psychological adult (see Chapter 24).

☐ *Commitment to Self*   Underlying all other commitments is a commitment to self—not to the selfish pursuit of personal pleasure but to a basic sense of one's own values, founded on a realistic understanding of one's capacities, potential usefulness, and real and possible achievements. Not to be confused with vanity, narcissism, or false pride, this proper sense of self-regard is not so much a matter of ranking one's self relative to others (How good am I?) as of developing an awareness of one's own actual strengths (What am I good at? Whom am I good for?). It involves a willingness to be one's self, an effort to become more truly what one is, and a conviction that, in the end, *I am worth being.*

Such commitment to self is made possible by familial and societal experience and opportunities that enable the adolescent to test and define his

Figure 20.11. The field of career choices is wide open to the college graduate, while severely limited for the nonwhite, poor adolescent with little education.

real strengths and weaknesses and that provide realistic opportunities. It is undermined by forces that convince the individual of his inadequacy and worthlessness or that deprive him of realistic avenues for accomplishment and respect.

□ *Commitment to Work* Especially in an achievement-oriented society like modern America, a central aspect of commitment is commitment to a task. The meaning of the task will vary from man to man and woman to woman—the maintenance of a home and the rearing of healthy children, the reform of society, competent performance of a job, the achievement of a life's work, the writing of a poem, or the manufacture of goods. But however the task is defined, the postadolescent ideally turns from wondering what to do with life to the process of actually doing it; and in this turning, work is of crucial importance. What is crucial is the capacity to commit one's self to activity aimed at the achievement of competence in work, whether competence is defined in personal and idiosyncratic terms or in terms of the existing roles and rewards of society. As adolescence ends, the separation between grandiose fantasy and puny accomplishment that characterizes many adolescents' thinking is narrowed, and the adult is able to turn to the accomplishment of specific tasks.

□ *Commitment to Other People and to Play* Interpersonal commitment requires the capacity for mutuality, that is, for intimate reciprocal relationships in which the real needs and characteristics of each person are important to the other. For most, this capacity is actualized in marriage, where the complementarity of the sex roles is combined with a profound identification of each marriage partner with the other and with the creation of a new family. For others, this same capacity for mutuality is actualized primarily in friendship, in work, or in shared play.

This concept of commitment also entails a concern with the welfare of the wider community and above all care for the next generation. It is in adolescence that youth first feels itself part of a wider community; in adulthood, this feeling is translated into activities facilitative of the development of others. The relevant community is increasingly no longer the nation but the world. And in a time with cataclysmic possibilities for world destruction, commitment to the next generation will increasingly involve a commitment to avoiding worldwide holocaust. But for most, commitment to the community and to those who embody its future will be most concretely expressed in the capacity and willingness to bear and rear children thoughtfully and lovingly.

Finally, in a striving society that rewards and praises work, it is especially important to underline that one of the attainments of adolescence should be the capacity for invigorating play. The future will bring increased opportunities for leisure. The American legacy of Puritanism makes us tend to forget that one of the tasks of adolescence is the development of the capacity to live zestfully as well as purposefully, to be able to engage one's self fully with the world and with one's fantasies and passions, to be capable of free, buoyant, exuberant, and spontaneous pleasure. In

the absence of play, tomorrow's adults may be moral, virtuous, and responsible, but they will also be driven, compulsive, and grim.

THE RIGHT TO AN ADOLESCENCE

Although the characteristics discussed in the preceding section and in Chapter 24 distinguish the adult from the adolescent, no adult ever possesses all of these qualities in full: they are approximate criteria rather than a definition of what any one individual can be. They permit us to outline provisionally the hallmarks of successfully completed adolescence; however, we cannot provide fixed criteria for mental health during adolescence itself. The concept of mental health—slippery and elusive at best during other stages of life—is almost useless during adolescence. The adolescent routinely exhibits symptoms that reflect the routine trials of growing up but that would, in an adult, rightly be deemed ominous. Violent swings of mood and behavior, feelings of depersonalization and estrangement, hypermanic flights of ideas, and panicky feelings of inner breakdown can all merely be the signs of routine inner turmoil and need not foreshadow trouble.

The problem is complicated because some adolescent feelings and behavior are in fact ominous. Adolescence is the stage of life when a whole series of self-destructive and socially disruptive adaptations, from criminality to schizophrenia, first make their appearance. Separating these ominous developments from the normal difficulties of adolescents is an important task, though not an easy one. Even the most experienced psychologist finds such differentiation difficult. But the greater his experience, the more reluctant he will be to attach labels to adolescent behavior. Untold harm is done by adults who attach to some transient aspect of adolescent behavior a self-confirming label like delinquent, schizophrenic, homosexual, or psychopathic. The vulnerable adolescent, already confused as to who he is, may seize upon even such negative labels in a despairing effort to be *someone*. Many of the disturbances of adolescence that endure into adulthood are the products of such interaction between the adolescent's hunger for self-definition and the adult world's thoughtless willingness to label him on the basis of a single act or episode.

The goal of all interventions with adolescents, then, should be to strengthen and confirm *them* in *their* development. Some adolescents may need special help, but the purpose of this help should not be to cure them of their illness (much less their adolescence); rather, it should be to restore to them their capacity to proceed in their growth without special help. Too much help can be enfeebling, just as too much understanding without respect for the individual can be demeaning. Even today, much of what passes for counseling of adolescents displays basic ignorance of adolescent development by undercutting the adolescent's normal questioning, rebellion, and search. Such counseling socializes, but it does not foster psychological growth.

Many teen-agers find it easier simply to allow themselves to be socialized rather than to undertake the more painful task of growth toward adult

Figure 20.12. Attaching labels to temporary adolescent behavior may result in the adolescent's acquisition of other behaviors associated with that label.

autonomy. Many who arrive at adolescence are so scarred by their childhoods that they lack the courage and the resources for unaided growth in the years of adolescence. And in every adolescent there exist elements of childishness and underlying dependence. For all these reasons, the adolescent himself is often reluctant or at least ambivalent about the adolescent experience. As adults who work with adolescents know, the forces within the adolescent that oppose growth are often powerful; well-meaning help is often refused, understanding is often rejected. Yet it is precisely because of the adolescent's own ambivalence that he needs the stimulation, challenge, and support of adults if his development is to be confirmed.

Some of the responsibility for the foreclosure of adolescence lies in part within the family. During adolescence, parents sometimes attempt to retain total control or, worse, totally abdicate involvement—postures that effectively stymie the adolescent's growth. Some responsibility for the foreclosure of adolescence also lies within our educational system, which too rarely touches, much less strengthens or consolidates, the adolescent's capacity for rationality, ethicality, empathy, and humanitarian concern. It too often opts for safety and conformity in the short run at the expense of judgment and independence in the long run. It too often equates obedient conformity with real psychological maturity. Some responsibility for the failure of adolescence also lies within our social institutions, which tolerate or perpetuate injustices that deprive important minorities in American society of equal rights and opportunities and so alienate from society many of the adolescents whose ethical sense is most compelling. Often, all of these factors interact in a vicious circle, as with that large group of young Americans, most of whom are black, who are simultaneously deprived of family support, educational opportunity, and social dignity.

But even for those adolescents whose families can provide them with status and influence, the adolescent experience is often far less than it could be. The displacement of parental ambition onto children, the misguided mystique of popularity, the conformist pressures of many teen-age peer groups, the overvaluation of admission to prestige colleges, the heavy penalties that teenagers must pay for conflicts with authority and for academic mistakes—all of these factors conspire to prevent the unfolding of personal potential.

Adolescence is, of all the later stages of life, the one that can most readily permit profound and benign transformations of personality. A challenging, responsive, and confirming environment can enable an adolescent to undo vast damage done in earlier childhood, to heal the wounds of parental inconsistency, ignorance, or neglect, and to move beyond these handicaps to a responsible and satisfying maturity. Adolescence can provide a second chance—the opportunity to move away from the malignancies of family pathology, social disorganization, and cultural deprivation in order to pursue the goals of becoming independent, self-directing, tolerant and humane, and ethical.

However, several recent, extensive studies suggest that the number of adolescents who achieve a decisive articulation of the self is diminishing. Elizabeth Douvan and Joseph Adelson found that a serious testing of values and ideology occurs only in a minority of the adolescents. It appears that real independence is accomplished in lower-class and some upper-middle-class youngsters because these two extremes are so different from the core adolescent culture. But in studying the "silent majority" of adolescents, they found only token parent-child conflict and therefore token maturity and autonomy. They found that the peer group for many adolescents is only used to learn and display social skills—a kind of playpen designed to keep the children out of harm's way. Although for many, the peer group is an arena for confrontation of self, for many more it acts to hinder differentiation and growth. Douvan and Adelson conclude: "If this amiable but colorless form of adolescence is indeed a new thing in our country, then we would have to single out as one important reason the extraordinary attentuation of today's adolescence. . . . Nowadays the adolescent and his parents are both made captive by their mutual knowledge of the adolescent's dependency. They are locked in a room with no exit. . . . [The adolescent] keeps the peace by muting his natural rebelliousness through transforming it into structured and defined techniques for getting on people's nerves. The passions, the restlessness, the vivacity of adolescence are partly strangled, and partly drained off in the mixed childishness and false adulthood of the adolescent teen culture."

Most of us spend our social lives in interaction with people who are like us in important ways. We grow up in neighborhoods, which are clusters of persons with jobs of roughly similar status or prestige, with similar educational histories, and therefore with shared ways of perceiving, thinking, and behaving. We usually go to neighborhood schools through elementary and high school and so interact outside the family with people much like ourselves. Our parents and our friends' parents usually have about the same amount of money to spend on goods and services and often spend that money in the same way. In other words, we grow up in a certain *subculture*. And we learn—internalize—the values of these subcultures as children and adolescents. In American society distinctive subcultures—that is, patterns of values and beliefs—are associated with the various levels of social status. The experience of adolescence, then, will differ markedly from social class to social class.

Social-class subcultures differ from one another in many dimensions. One of the most useful ways of characterizing these differences is in terms of values and beliefs associated with *achievement*. B. Rosen has identified three value orientations central to the motivation of behavior in achievement situations: activistic versus passive; individualistic versus collectivistic; and future versus present. Activism (the belief that one can manipulate the physical and social environment to his own advantage), individualism (the belief that an individual need not subordinate his own needs to

the family group), and a future orientation (the belief that one should forgo short-term satisfactions and rewards in the interest of long-term gains) are more characteristic of higher social-status groups in our society than of groups lower in the socioeconomic spectrum.

Teen-agers from upper-middle-class families (professional and managerial occupations) and from lower-middle-class families (semiprofessional, semimanagerial, white-collar, and skilled-crafts occupations) are more likely to have learned as children that their lives were under their own control and that occupational achievement and the external symbols of success could be theirs by their own efforts. From infancy and childhood, the upper-middle-class adolescent's experiences have fit him for having a career. The notion of a career implies, perhaps implicitly, personal development or self-actualization. The lower-middle-class adolescent will have been exposed to experiences that make him look forward to a *job*, not a career. He will have learned to value the security, stability, and respectability of this kind of life style. Both these subcultures engender attitudes and behaviors in young people that correspond to those demanded by educational institutions. The idea of prolonged schooling makes sense in adolescence as a means either of developing one's potentialities or of getting a decent job in the future.

The delay of immediate gratification in the interest of future success demanded by education does not make as much sense to the adolescent

21
Social Development

from a working-class family (semiskilled or unskilled blue-collar workers) or from a lower-class family whose stability depends upon irregular maternal employment in marginal work roles or upon welfare funds. Although the fathers of working-class families are regularly employed, they rarely move up; neither responsibilities nor pay change much from year to year, so the father discards his belief (if he ever held it) in the middle-class American dream. It is understandable, therefore, that activism and a future orientation do not prevail in the socialization of children in this milieu. Work in school and later on is not likely to be valued in its own right but only as a means of providing goods and services that lead to satisfaction in the extended family. In the lower-class subculture a collectivistic orientation is more likely to prevail, so loyalty to the family may stand in the way of the adolescent's making decisions that would permit him, from the middle-class point of view, "to better himself." Moving away, going to school someplace else, taking advantage of opportunities that weaken bonds with members of the extended family, all more-or-less taken for granted by the middle-class adolescent, are rarely possible for the lower-class youth.

A passive, even fatalistic, set of beliefs is likely to characterize the adolescent from the lower-class background. "Luck" is a frequent explanation for accomplishments and setbacks: as L. Rainwater has said: "In the white and particularly in the Negro slum worlds little in the experience that individuals have as they grow up sus-

tains a belief in a rewarding world. The strategies that seem appropriate are not those of a good, family-based life or a career, but rather strategies for survival." In a survival-oriented economy, it is the gratifications of the present that are important. There are few opportunities for the child or the adolescent to learn that active, individual effort might pay off in the interest of some long-term goal—whether it be studying now for an A on a report card or earning money to save for a car. Report-card marks only matter to college registrars, and any money put away is likely to be found and used by the family for an unexpected expense—a doctor bill or a broken water heater.

The child enters adolescence with experience in three kinds of social groups—the family, the peer group, and larger organizations such as the school. He plays a *role* in each of these groups (which are, themselves, systems of interrelated roles). For each role in a social system, there is a set of role definers—persons with whom the individual interacts and who define the role for him by modeling appropriate behaviors and by providing consequences for his behavior (reinforcers). An individual is said to have *internalized* the culture of a given group when he comes to govern his own behavior on the basis of the group's standards. The teen-ager thus comes to judge himself—his appearance, his academic achievement, his social capacities—by the standards of those who define the roles in his social groups. Among these role definers are parents, peers, and teachers. But what happens when, for example, the teen-ager encounters a teacher who impresses him and the teacher

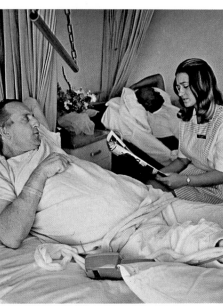

Figure 21.1. Middle-class teens actively pursue future goals by preparing for careers and adult tasks.

attempts to influence him toward continuing his education, while his family wants him to start earning money?

Many of the persistent questions of adolescent psychology deal with the changes in influence of various social-role definers during adolescence. Psychologists want to know what happens when noncomplementary or even contradictory and conflict-inducing pressures are brought to bear on the adolescent.

The Role of the Adolescent in the Family

Compulsory education laws and the demand for more highly trained specialists (of which they are a reflection) have increased dramatically the length of time the middle-class child is dependent economically upon his parents. This economic dependence has increased the time that middle-class parents remain powerful role definers. Through the provision or withdrawal of approval, attention, and praise, the typical middle-class parent begins to stress independent action and personal responsibility well before adolescence. Rules governing conduct are likely to be verbalized explicitly. When the child misbehaves, he is likely to be asked why he did so, and if he is to be punished, the parents are likely to first explain why. By these means, the parents teach the child—both explicitly and implicitly—that he can and should control his own behavior on the basis of an internalized set of (the parents') standards.

As the middle-class child grows into adolescence, he will participate increasingly in decisions that affect him. By late adolescence, decisions

about relations with peers, jobs, and having money are made either by the adolescent himself or by him in consultation with his parents. In adolescence, as before, the child is rewarded for indications that he is learning to cope with his own problems. Middle-class parents, then, train children for independence. They monitor the child's responses and reward appropriate independent behaviors. E. C. Devereux has shown that when such monitoring does not occur (when parents are overly permissive) or when opportunities for independent decision making and action are not provided because the parents make all decisions themselves, stormy parent-child relations and excessive peer conformity are likely to be the result. On the whole, however, adolescence in middle-class families is a more peaceful and less overtly conflict-filled period than it is often held to be. Manifestations of rebelliousness are by no means universal in adolescence.

Working-class parents begin independence training later than do middle-class parents and, throughout childhood and adolescence, do not permit much participation by their offspring in establishing rules for behavior. They also are less likely to provide an explicit rationale for rules that are enforced. Although there seems to be less direct supervision of even very young children in lower-class families, parents value obedience in the family context and are inclined to attain it through coercion. Physical punishment is used much more in the lower class than in other social strata. These practices are consonant with M. L. Kohn's finding that working-class parents value

Figure 21.2. The lower-class teen-ager, like his parents, often lives on a day-to-day basis, concerned only with staying alive at the present, having no particular plans for the future.

obedience to authority more than acting in accord with a set of internal standards. The result is that "independent" actions by lower-class adolescents usually take place away from the watchful eyes of the family. When issues of autonomy do arise at home, a sullen obedience is a predictable result.

It should by now be clear that the role of the adolescent in the family group varies considerably with social class because the behavior of the relevant group of role definers—in this case, parents—varies as well. It should be noted, too, that the earlier independence training and the focus on conformity to internal standards characteristic of middle-class socialization are reflected in middle-class activism, individualism, and a future orientation, which, in turn, influence the aspirations toward career or job: a career more often requires individual unsupervised responsibility for decision making and its consequences.

The two words most frequently mentioned in discussions of adolescence are undoubtedly *rebelliousness* and *conformity*. Some accounts of adolescent development assume that conformity to parents' wishes decreases in adolescence and that unreasoning conformity to peer wishes increases. Other discussions assume that conflict between peer and parental wishes is an inevitable accompaniment of adolescence. However, no available evidence directly and unequivocally demonstrates any absolute decrease (or increase) in conformity to parental demands with the onset of adolescence. In the matter of conforming to peers, evidence from a number of studies reviewed by W. W. Hartup suggests that conforming to peer ma-

Figure 21.3. Parents' supervision of children and adolescents in middle-class homes is generally aimed at training the children for independence. By providing praise or displaying disapproval, and by explaining why they are pleased or displeased, the parents generally succeed in having the children internalize the parents' standards of behavior. This pattern is not generally present in lower-class homes.

jorities increases in childhood, reaches its maximum in the years around puberty, and actually decreases in later adolescence. However, even though the absolute amount of conformity to peer groups may decline in adolescence, the peer group continues to constitute an important source of role definition.

It may be that the decrease in conformity is related to the onset of the cognitive stage of formal operations (see Chapters 15 and 20 for the discussion of Piaget's theory of cognitive development). Because at the stage of formal operations adolescents are able to consider the many possibilities inherent in any given situation, they may conform less because they can consider consequences other than those resulting from nonconformity to their peers.

A few studies have compared adolescent conformity to parents' and to peers' values; C. V. Brittain's results suggest, for example, that adolescents conform to peers in matters pertaining to the youth culture such as friendship choice, fads of language, and what to wear but conform to parental values in matters that pertain to achievement, including academic performance and job or career aspirations. Evidently, the role of peer-group member conflicts less with the role of family member than is commonly thought to be the case. Cliques and crowds of adolescents are for the most part formed within, rather than across, social-class lines, so occasions for conflict arising from differences in socialization are not numerous. Perhaps more important is the fact that the roles of peer and son or daughter are enacted in

relative isolation from one another, and whatever discrepancies exist between the adolescent's at-home behavior and his behavior away from home remain outside the parents' immediate scrutiny.

The Role of the Adolescent in the Peer Group

Those youngsters who are popular with their peers before adolescence are likely to be popular adolescents as well; indeed, popularity rankings from year to year throughout childhood and adolescence are almost as stable as IQ scores. Popularity is highly related to conformity to peer-group values; to be accepted by a peer group, an adolescent must accept its norms and fads. Both before and during adolescence the characteristics having most to do with peer acceptance are those that define appropriate sex-typed behavior in our society. Athletic participation and skill, standing up for one's rights when aggressed against, and sexual and, in some groups, drinking prowess are valued in the male. The popular girl is one who is physically attractive, who has a "good reputation," who is fun to be with, and who has social skills that might be labeled warmth, empathy, or nurturance. Because these characteristics bring with them the positive consequences of peer acceptance, they are in turn strengthened. Thus, the sex-role learning that occurred in peer groups prior to adolescence and in the home is strengthened by adolescent peer-group socialization. The stability of popularity rankings probably is attributable to this continuity in socialization.

The new element that adolescence brings to

peer relations and to sex-role development is sexual maturation and heterosexual behavior. The structure of peer groups changes in adolescence to accommodate these developments. D. C. Dunphy, who has studied urban adolescent peer groups, described the process well:

Initially this [peer] group is the unisexual clique, which represents the continuation of the preadolescent "gang" and at this stage is a group comparable in size to the family. In order to achieve and maintain membership in this group, the individual must show his readiness to conform to the group's authority. This is made easier through his identification with the clique leader who embodies many of the social skills and personality traits admired in the group. The clique establishes and reinforces the individual's drive to achieve heterosexuality, since it is, or becomes, a subsystem of the crowd; the crowd in its turn is only a subsystem of a hierarchy of crowds . . . About middle adolescence there is a major transformation of the clique system which has persisted in a relatively stable form. A new clique system evolves . . . Groups become heterosexual, members having established a significant relationship with a member of the opposite sex. The crowd persists long enough to ensure that the basic role characteristics underlying this relationship are thoroughly acquired. It then breaks up into cliques of loosely associated couples as members move toward marriage.

Dunphy found, as have other observers, that group members generally deny the existence of a group leader and of a status hierarchy within the group. Nevertheless, the formation of such hierarchies has been studied in some detail. The effective initiator and expediter of group activities is the leader. He generally becomes the leader by virtue of some combination of personal attributes

Figure 21.4. Cliques and gangs play an important part in the adolescent's social development.

and material resources germane to the group's activities. In male cliques, high status generally is accorded to the assertive, actively sociable, and intellectually able boy. However, in some groups it may be unique social or athletic skills or the possession of a car or money or access to a suitable place for the group's activities that take precedence in the determination of status. Changes in group goals are likely to lead to fluctuations in the status hierarchy. Thus, status rankings over the months and years are less stable than are popularity rankings.

It is during high school that cliques become subsystems of crowds and that crowds themselves may be ranked according to status. In the leading crowd are those who embody the virtues that bring young people to the forefront of their cliques or that made them popular with classmates as younger children. Middle-class students are likely to be overrepresented in leading crowds in proportion to their numbers in the student body as a whole. Because crowds are composed of cliques and cliques are largely neighborhood affairs, crowd members tend to have the same social-class backgrounds. Girls, who cannot use the power of athletic accomplishment to surmount social-class barriers, are less likely than boys to attain membership in cliques and crowds of

higher prestige within the high-school social system. Racial and ethnic backgrounds are also barriers to moving up in the hierarchy of crowds. Indeed, social systems in large high schools where there is a mixture of racial or ethnic groups often are almost totally segregated. Gifted athletes of minority background frequently may cross the line and be accepted into crowds composed of students in the majority, but there are few, if any, other accomplishments that permit achieving such changes.

Indeed, interscholastic athletic competition probably serves as a major integrative force in adolescent social systems. If there is any general principle for the resolution of intergroup conflict, it must be that of bringing opposing factions to act together in the pursuit of some goal that transcends factional concerns. Athletics is the only major activity that brings high schools—as total social systems—together in the pursuit of common goals.

PROBLEM BEHAVIOR

Although everyone says that not all adolescents should be blamed for the actions of the few whose bad behavior makes the headlines, the term "bad behavior" carries implicit assumptions that need clarification. Whether the given bad incident is an automobile accident, drug usage, drinking, pregnancy out of wedlock, dropping out of school, or delinquency in general, many people assume: (1) that the actual behavior involved is qualitatively different from the behavior engaged in by "good kids"; (2) that the behavior is the

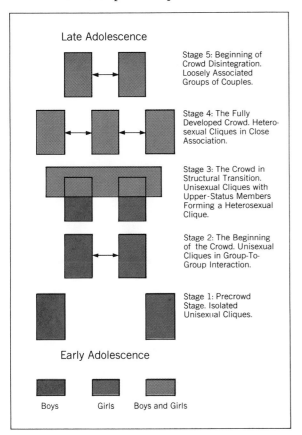

Late Adolescence

Stage 5: Beginning of Crowd Disintegration. Loosely Associated Groups of Couples.

Stage 4: The Fully Developed Crowd. Heterosexual Cliques in Close Association.

Stage 3: The Crowd in Structural Transition. Unisexual Cliques with Upper-Status Members Forming a Heterosexual Clique.

Stage 2: The Beginning of the Crowd. Unisexual Cliques in Group-To-Group Interaction.

Stage 1: Precrowd Stage. Isolated Unisexual Cliques.

Early Adolescence

Boys Girls Boys and Girls

Figure 21.5. Five stages of group development in adolescence. (After Dunphy, 1963.)

product of disordered, antisocial, and amoral individuals—bad kids—acting individually or in the grip of a crazed gang; and (3) that either the causes of the problem are unique and not comparable to those of other behavior *or* its causes are totally nonunique expressions of "generational conflict" or "rebellion against authority." These assumptions will be investigated in the following paragraphs.

INCIDENCE OF ADOLESCENT DELINQUENCY

It is commonly reported and commonly believed that juvenile delinquency has increased steadily over the past decade and that the great majority of delinquencies are committed by lower-class adolescents. These assertions are based upon statistics accrued by law-enforcement, judiciary, and probation agencies. Several lines of evidence converge to warrant the conclusion that these statistics are not an appropriate data base from which to draw conclusions about increments in delinquency rates or about the social class from which delinquents are drawn. A. V. Cicourel has warned that official statistics reflect many variables other than the commission of illegal acts. For example, because more crimes are expected in lower-class neighborhoods, more police are likely to be assigned there. Thus, more delinquencies will be identified *and* adjudicated in lower-status neighborhoods. When middle-class youths are apprehended, they are more likely to be referred to their parents without an official report, arrest, or court hearing because of political and other pressures that can be brought to bear by parents of high socioeconomic status. Even when a middle-class youth has committed four or five offenses, and some action is required, judicial disposition is likely to be less severe because officials feel that the families involved are likely to make good on promises to reform the adolescent personally or with the help of psychiatrists and other middle-class institutions.

Official delinquency statistics, then, reflect the conceptions and customs of a variety of agencies. How, then, can one check on the incidence and social-class breakdown of juvenile crime? A number of studies have asked adolescents in public-school settings, under anonymous conditions, to indicate their involvement in illegal acts. The results of these studies reveal no social-class differences in the frequency *or* severity of misdemeanors and felonies reported. M. and C. W. Sherif have corroborated these self-reports in their more direct observational studies of adolescent cliques at all social strata: "Frequently, doing things on their own as adults involved activities deemed improper for the age level, even immoral or illegal. This was true in middle and high rank neighborhoods as well as low rank, even though most of the groups and their members were not labeled as 'delinquent' by police." Because the amount of detected delinquency accounts for something like 3 to 5 percent of all self-reported offenses, even a small increase in the amount of attention that law-enforcement authorities pay to it could create what may seem to be a "delinquency wave" even though there had not been the slightest change in adolescent behavior.

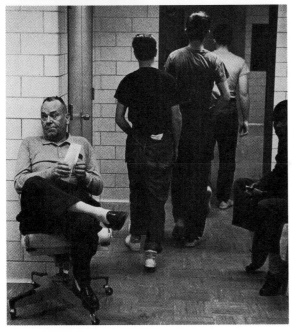

DETERMINANTS OF DELINQUENCY

Official statistics minimize the frequency of law-violating behavior among adolescents in general and exaggerate the proportion of law violations attributable to youths of lower social strata. Because most psychological and sociological studies of the causes of delinquency compare delinquents (officially defined—apprehended and recorded) with nondelinquents (youth without *records* of violation), they are not likely to be very revealing. Indeed, owing to the composition of "delinquent" and "nondelinquent" samples, it is not surprising that the findings of such studies read like descriptions of social and cultural differences between the lower and middle class.

One set of theories based on official statistics that attempts to find the causes of juvenile delinquency assumes that socialization into lower-class culture per se leads to law violation and entanglements with the middle-class authority structure. According to this view, lower-class focal concerns with toughness, outsmarting others, seeking excitement, autonomy, and fatalism generate delinquent behavior. Because status within the peer group requires conformity to the norms associated with these focal concerns, delinquent behavior is seen as normal within this context and so cannot easily be characterized as asocial, amoral, or the product of psychological disorder. Another set of hypotheses assumes that lower-class adolescents accept middle-class goals but are not given opportunities to pursue them. Lacking legitimate means, they turn to illegitimate ones to attain success goals. It is, of course, possible that in particular situations both points of view may have merit. However, contemporary research has pointed up the inadequacy of definitions and sample selection based upon "official delinquency," so it is now clear that the emphases in the theories cited have been misplaced.

Studies of adolescent drinking behavior provide a good illustration of many of the points made above. Drinking is illegal for adolescents of high-school age in most states. Summarizing the studies of the incidence of drinking among adolescents, Margaret Bacon and Mary Brush Jones report that the number of teen-agers who drink on at least some occasions varies from 86 percent in Nassau County, New York, to 44 percent in rural Kansas. However, the widespread illegal activity remains underground in most communities until an automobile accident or some other incident that is associated with drinking makes the headlines. In the public rumblings that follow, action is often recommended and taken on the basis of an implicit assumption that *all* teen-age drinking involves drunkenness and uncontrolled behavior. The particular adolescents who become publicly involved are likely to be stigmatized. Psychological disorder, rebelliousness, and the lack of "wholesome things to do" will be aired as causal possibilities.

Actually, every study of the problem has found that the drinking patterns of teen-agers reflect directly those of their parents and of the community in which they live. About two-thirds of all adults in the United States drink on occasion, and drinking is more prevalent among persons of higher social status than of lower ones. Bacon and Jones found that:

The tendency for teen-agers on the whole to drink moderately if they drink at all, to begin drinking at home with their parents, to follow generally the rules their parents set, makes rebellion an unlikely explanation. It has been found, for instance, that urban teen-agers drink more than rural ones, just as urban adults drink more than adults in rural areas; that boys drink more than girls, just as men drink more than women; that teen-agers from certain income groups or certain religious backgrounds drink less than others, just as adults from these same groups do. In all these ways, teen-age drinking patterns imitate adult drinking patterns. And imitation cannot really be considered rebellion, even if it may seem badly timed.

Adolescents are most likely to have had their first drink in their own homes at their parents' invitation, and most subsequent drinking is likely to take place at home or in the homes of friends. They have learned from their parents and other adults to perceive drinking as an explicitly social affair. Norms of acceptable drinking behavior in the peer group are, for the most part, continuous with adult norms for adult drinking behavior and so keep drinking behavior in line. Thus, when drinking behavior among adolescents does take place in the secrecy of the peer group, social control is by no means absent.

Adolescent drinking provides an illustration of ways in which behavior that poses problems for adults often is tied to the values and customs of the larger society. Where adolescents are con-

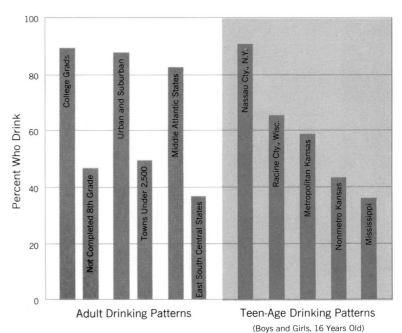

Figure 21.6. Teen-age drinking patterns clearly reflect those of adults. Drinking here does not imply excess; the category includes those who drink occasionally or socially. (After Cahalan *et al.*, 1967, and Bacon and Jones, 1968.)

cerned, adults tend to ignore these connections; they are too ready to consider any problem behavior as an *adolescent* problem and to label the adolescents involved as "problems." The adolescent has had more than a decade of exposure to adults whose behavior, legal and illegal, serves as a model for adolescent experimentation and adolescents' control of one another's behavior. Problem behavior, legal or illegal, cannot be modified without reference to the behavior patterns of adults or the patterns that constitute the peer social system in adolescence.

IDENTITY CONFUSION

When, by late adolescence, an individual has not attained that sense of inner unity and fittedness with a role in his society that Erik Erikson calls identity, he is prone to the developmental disturbance Erikson calls *identity confusion*. This disturbance is especially likely to occur if there is in the individual's history a long-standing sense of hopelessness and doubt of his ethnic and sexual identity. Erikson describes the internal signs of this state as a painfully heightened sense of isolation; a disintegration of the sense of inner continuity and sameness; a sense of overall ashamedness; an inability to derive a sense of accomplishment from any kind of activity. When they are extreme, these characteristics are called symptoms, and the constellation of them bespeaks disturbance. In more moderate forms, they are characteristic of the normal identity crisis. In either case, some of the characteristics of identity confusion stand out in descriptions of the runa-

way, the dropout, the uncommitted, the hippie, and otherwise alienated groups of young people.

ALIENATION AND ACTIVISM

The superficial stereotypes of rebellious youth drawn by magazines and television make it easy for adult observers to avoid seeing important differences between adolescents whose behavior appears to challenge established proprieties. These adults tend to group hippies and yippies and motorcycle gangs into one category. For anyone who discards stereotypes, it is clear that, for example, the characteristics of activists depart significantly from those of other groups whose actions present problems to many adults. Kenneth Keniston has shown that student activists are not drawn from disadvantaged, status-anxious, underprivileged, or uneducated groups; on the contrary, they are selectively recruited from among those young Americans who have had the most socially fortunate upbringings. Activists tend to come from upper-middle-class families that are politically and religiously liberal. The available evidence indicates that many activists are simply taking action to promote values their parents hold; this is the opposite of rebellion. Adolescent activists, then, are committed to social change within the system. As Keniston says, "These students object to our society not because they oppose its basic principles, but because it fails to implement these principles fully at home and abroad."

Teachers from working-class and lower-middle-class backgrounds face special difficulties in coping with activists; these teachers are predisposed to conceive of protest as lack of submission to authority rather than in terms of the principles or causes espoused by the activist. They ignore the possible legitimacy of the demand or cause—and are able to ignore it because they have labeled the activist as a troublemaker and so can just lump him with other troublemakers—delinquents, communists, hippies. The result of such a repressive stereotyping process is that adolescents who were committed to the ideals of a given system turn away from society to search for meaning in private experiences that they believe will be free of society's corrupting influence.

ALIENATION AND DROPPING OUT

Some alienated youth at upper social strata, unlike the protesters, tend to reject their parents' political and social values; seeing their elders as having sold out to a corrupt system. They reject available roles in the system and seek self-definition through intense subjective experiences. Some withdraw psychologically from family and high school or college. Others drop out in a physical sense as well and explore the possibilities of distinctive modes of living, for example, in a hippie commune. Both psychological and physical dropouts seek personal experiences outside the system, some turning to hallucinogenic drugs and/or other forms of mystical experiences. (In contrast, drug use among adolescents of lower-status backgrounds involves heroin as opposed to the hallucinogenics. Drug use in the lower class has been characterized by N. E. Zinberg as *oblivion-seeking* as opposed to the *experience-seeking* of the ado-

Figure 21.7. Activism and use of drugs, especially to drop out, are two reflections of the adolescent's feeling of alienation from his society.

lescent of higher social status. At both status levels drug taking is a group activity.)

The external manifestations of the hippie and similar subcultures are widely known to and widely imitated by adults and younger adolescents in American society. Many young adolescents adopt aspects of the appearance, dress, and other practices of the subculture, including drug usage, even though they do not cognitively comprehend—let alone share in—the hippies' value stance. The externals of hippiedom provide an available alternative identity, however, and it would be surprising if some young adolescents did not try it on, even when the fit with their own past histories, temperament, and probable futures is not a very good one.

ALIENATION OF THE BLACK ADOLESCENT

Alienation among lower-class, and especially among black, adolescents is different than the upper-middle-class alienation. The black adolescent's attempts at self-definition have for centuries been shaped in the context of prejudice and poverty; he has been continually prohibited from access to the opportunities that make it possible for the white adolescent to find a niche in society that matches his attributes and aspirations. Lower-class Negro identity is largely based upon alien status. While bombarded with images of the aspirations toward and concrete and symbolic outcomes of occupational success in America, the black person traditionally has been told that he is not worthy of them. Erikson has said that an individual belonging to an oppressed and ex-

ploited minority that is aware of the dominant cultural ideals but prevented from emulating them is apt to fuse the negative images held up to him by the dominant majority with the negative identity cultivated in his own group. The traditional Negro identity, then, may be said to be a negative one, that is, one based upon lack of fit with the ready-made roles of middle-class America and one characterized in many Negroes by self-hate, debasement, and a fatalistic stance toward the world.

But not all Negroes are blacks—the use of this new label signals the shaping and increasing availability of a new alternative, rooted in black history in America and in Africa. Whether the five- and six-year-olds who are now being taught that "black is beautiful" will emerge from adolescence with more positive self-definitions probably depends as much upon the nature of the educational and vocational opportunities really open to them at that time as it does upon that childhood teaching. Indeed, among the newly alienated black adolescents are those who, with considerable racial pride, have tried an active stance toward "the system" and found it unresponsive: "I can't lose by rioting. Done lost. Been lost. Gonna be lost some more. I'm sayin' to the Man 'You includin' me in this game or not?' And I know his answer, so I'm getting ready to get basic."

THE SCHOOL DROPOUT

In 1920, 80 percent of the school population failed to graduate from high school. This proportion has declined steadily and, should the same rate of retention prevail, it has been estimated that the figure will drop to 20 percent by the end of the century. Nevertheless, for a society that values universal education and is faced with increasing specialization and automation, such a proportion is extremely high. One in six upper-middle-class adolescents fails to finish high school; among lower-middle- and working-class groups, the proportion is one in four; only one of two lower-class adolescents completes high school. And although 80 percent of dropouts are white, the proportion of dropouts among black youth is twice that of whites. Adequate descriptive statistics are difficult to come by, but H. L. Voss, A. Wendling, and D. S. Elliott estimate that between 50 and 75 percent of dropouts possess sufficient general intelligence and reading ability to complete high school. Socially, such a high dropout rate represents an unaccountable waste of human resources; psychologically, it may be presumed that dropping out is caused by, and in turn contributes to, the alienation of (largely urban, lower-class, black) youth from the larger society.

Because most dropouts, like "official delinquents," are from the lower socioeconomic strata, it is not surprising that most studies comparing their characteristics with those of nondropouts are indistinguishable from descriptions of lower-class culture. When dropouts were matched with nondropouts on social status (and also on minority group status, school background, sex, and age), L. S. Cervantes uncovered more profound and informative differences. Families of dropouts, as opposed to families of graduates, could be characterized by their relative isolation from other families, by less family interaction, and by poor intrafamilial communication. Dropouts were more likely than graduates to express overt alienation from others and from social institutions and "to exhale feelings of inadequacy, worthlessness, frustration, and failure."

IS EDUCATION THE ANSWER?

Cervantes' study shows clearly that certain family environments predispose young persons to respond finally to educational systems by dropping out. Because the most important of the predisposing effects occur well before adolescence, it is important not to identify the dropout problem as

Figure 21.8. The black adolescent's alienation is particularly profound; a feeling of inadequacy, worthlessness, and failure often overwhelms the individual in his search for identity.

an adolescent one. Identifying the problem and solving it, however, are two separate tasks. Part of the solution lies in compensatory educational programs, which begin in elementary school and even before. The increasing number of programs such as Head Start for lower-class urban youth does not, however, make the need for change at the secondary level any less critical. Diversification of educational opportunities inside and outside of school buildings already is an important possibility. But diversification is an objective that may be sought in the service of many different goals. Certainly the goal of getting ahead in the world is a worthy one. But another important goal, which education today has not taken account of, is the promotion of personal development and growth. And it is in the service of this goal that diversity in educational systems is sought by an increasingly large number of upper-middle-class families—both parents and their sons and daughters.

This goal adds to the burden of educational reformers if one takes Erikson's view of adolescent growth seriously, for it implies that there must be an increased willingness to recognize di-

verse ways, styles, manners, and modes of taking advantage of opportunities when they are offered. High schools based upon the model of obeisance to authority in the name of authority are not up to this task. E. Z. Friedenberg believes that the majority of American high schools foster acquiescence and not growth. He says of adolescents:

They are trying to realize and clarify their identity; the school, acting as a mobility ladder, assumes instead the function of inducing them to change or alter it. They want to discover who they are; the school wants to help them "make something out of themselves." They want to know where they are; the school wants to help them get somewhere. They want to learn how to live with themselves; the school wants to teach them how to get along with others. They want to learn how to tell what is right for them; the school wants to teach them to give the responses that will earn them rewards in the classroom and in social situations.

If high schools fail to promote adolescent growth, a growing number of teen-agers are able to look to the college or university to help them fuse their identities. The following chapter presents case studies of adolescent development that occurred during the four years leading out of adolescence.

TUITION AND ROOM

CHANGE UNDER $30⁰⁰
WINDOWS 13 TO 17
CHECKS·GRANTS·ETC.

CHANGE OVER $30⁰⁰
WINDOWS 18 TO 23
CHECKS·GRANTS·ETC.

Having lived through part or all of adolescence yourself, you may have found some of your own experience mirrored in the general principles of the preceding chapters. As a further aid to understanding your own development as well as the psychological stage of adolescence, the experience of adolescence will now be examined through the eyes and the words of several adolescents, each of whom has something in common with all of us. The accent is on healthy experience, although some of the following experiences seemed abnormal and frightening to the individual at the time they occurred. The emphasis is on growth, whether forced by the environment in the natural course of events or provided by the ingenuity of the individual confronted with a seemingly insoluble conflict.

The time of transition to college is a potentially profitable point at which to observe the basic processes of personality development. An adolescent's personality is often still organized in terms of the cognitive immaturities and imaginative constructions that originally developed in childhood. His public self, which appears to be well socialized, is often dependent upon the presence of specific environmental conditions. When the environment changes abruptly—as when the adolescent leaves home to enter college—the immature, undeveloped self may reassert itself. The events that follow during the four years a youngster spends in the different and special social systems of college are a decisive time for personal growth or failure. This chapter takes advantage of the special observational situation provided by thrusting adolescents abruptly into college in order to identify some of the core experiences of adolescence that foster or force adjustment.

CHALLENGE AND RESPONSE

One of the most important mechanisms leading to development (as contrasted with maturation) involves the general concept of challenge and response. When presented with a new situation, a child or adolescent will, if he is to develop, devise a new scheme or operation to deal with the new problem. Piaget's concept of accommodation (Chapter 11) deals with this development in the area of cognitive growth, but the need to alter old strategies or to construct new ones to solve new problems can be seen as more general. Nevitt Sanford has said that people do not change unless they encounter a situation in which the devices they already possess cannot be used to adapt to the situation. When this encounter occurs, they must either innovate or fail to develop.

This chapter will point up some of the processes by which normal development takes place by examining adolescents who were subjects in a four-year research study of college students. These intensive, individual studies were carried out by Peter Madison, and most were published in 1969 by Addison-Wesley in Madison's *Personality Development in College*. The challenges of this new environment and the students' responses to them illustrate their development. Two boys' experiences are dealt with in this section.

Sidney was a precocious intellectual whose parents were very concerned that he be a success in

22
Cases of Adolescent Development

life and who valued intellectual achievement highly. At age four Sidney had prided himself on using words (like "diagonally") that the housekeeper could not understand. During his four years of college he carried off every possible honor and was one of the outstanding graduates of a major university.

Bob, too, had been a great success in high school. But he was from a small town that was geographically isolated, and he was so untraveled that he had never seen a Negro at the time he was graduated from high school. He enrolled in the engineering curriculum at a prestigious cosmopolitan university, where he found himself for the first time socially and culturally outclassed. The challenges he faced almost overwhelmed him for some time, and eventually he faced a developmental crisis.

EXPECTATION AND FACT

Direct confrontations between a person's expectation and facts that contradict this expectation are a major impetus to change and development. The psychology of learning has identified the conditions under which this change will take place: the stimulus situation must arouse an expectation of certain consequences; the expectation is based upon what has happened before under similar stimulus conditions; when this expectation is contradicted by failure, the behavior—or expectation—is weakened and finally extinguished.

Psychotherapy uses a parallel term, corrective emotional experience, to describe a like pattern. For example, a patient who, as a child, had learned to fear his father's criticism may have his fears aroused by his therapist, who shares several contextual characteristics in common with the father. If, in the face of the patient's expectation, the therapist clearly and decisively refuses to engage in any criticisms that may be fear arousing, the same sort of weakening of an emotional response takes place.

Direct confrontations between expectation and experienced fact occur often in everyday life and serve as mechanisms by which one's ideas and feelings are changed. Let us examine relevant excerpts from Sidney's and Bob's careers in order to see how this mechanism operates.

Sidney had planned to major in physical science, intending a career in medicine. But he wrote in his diary (which he contributed to the research project):

October 1: In math class on Saturday I was confronted with a theory I did not understand, and felt inadequate. I am very distressed at not comprehending.

October 17: I am enjoying German and European literature more than my science and math courses ... Although I would enjoy liberal arts more, I will probably spend my life with science because I can earn more money that way.

October 25: I had a frustrating

physics lab. Another student kept telling me about the errors I was making.

November 20: I find that it is a struggle to bring myself to do math and physics: they are so boring, so meaningless.

January 24: No more math for me — too repulsive. I felt dreadful before the physics exam: unprepared and without knowledge, and nauseous.

As a sophomore, Sidney reflected upon the academic experiences of his first year:

I took mostly science and math courses in my first term and although I finished in the upper 5 percent of my class, I found that I was not a scientist and certainly not a mathematician. I was best at the liberal arts. The course I enjoyed most was an introduction to the European literatures, and my enjoyment was corroborated when I got an A+. My critical abilities were increased by the course, as was my appreciation of literature. I found, nonetheless, that it was the ideas

and not the style which fascinated me. Philosophy, as I suspected in looking over my real interest and abilities, was my subject. I was overjoyed to realize that I could major in that field which I was most interested in.

Bob, who was an outstanding track man in high school, shows how direct confrontation can change an athletic interest:

I was tops in high school, and I did well in the state, but the competition here — well, there are about ten on the team — it's been a little, you might say, shaking to me.

In his third year of college Bob dropped track:

It was more a matter of frustration than anything else because I worked very, very hard at track all during the last summer and got down to a point where I was running better than I ever had in my life. I could run a 4:20 mile without any problems; I could probably have made the

*squad in just about any other
college, and here I was running
ninth on the track squad, so it
just got kind of frustrating—
seeing me finish from a
hundred yards back all the time.*

For Bob, the evidence that he wasn't that good a runner was decisive. A change of self-image followed automatically and uncontrollably. For Sidney, being in a math class was a situation associated with great success in elementary and high school. He was known to friends and teachers as being superior in mathematics, and he enjoyed the feeling of superiority. Being in a college-level math class automatically aroused expectations of similar success, but the failure even to understand some of the work was decisively contradictory. A succession of such experiences automatically led to a changed expectation: being in a math class aroused feelings of repulsion, and in physics classes Sidney came to feel "nauseous."

DEVELOPMENTAL SYNTHESES

Close study of many students suggests that the original choice of college majors serves primarily personal developmental functions—so much so that careers and majors chosen in adolescence should be viewed as serving personality rather than vocational functions. This developmental function in adolescence is most observable in what we call the *developmental synthesis*. The synthesis seems to take place during the period between the first choice of a college major and the final one. The synthesis involves a temporary choice that seems to allow the developmental changes in personality necessary to making the final choice. For example, Sidney did not go directly from medicine-physics to his final choice of sociology; he spent an intervening period of several years in philosophy. Another subject, Trixie, an adventurous girl who had decided as a child that she would be the first woman to land on the moon, chose astronomy as her starting major. As a senior, Trixie decided that her real career interest was in English, and she later enrolled in graduate school in that subject. But she spent an intervening two years in psychology.

As a freshman, Sidney was too materialistic to entertain seriously a career as a college teacher of sociology, which he finally became. His intervening major, philosophy, was not just a neutral place to pause. To Sidney, philosophy was a tool by which he changed himself through a study of the ethics of materialism. His diary entries show that dissatisfaction with the materialistic basis of his interest in medicine began shortly after he entered college:

*October 17: I see how much money
motivated my desire to be a doctor.
Although I would enjoy liberal arts
more, I will spend my life with
science, probably because of money.
October 25: I have been question-*

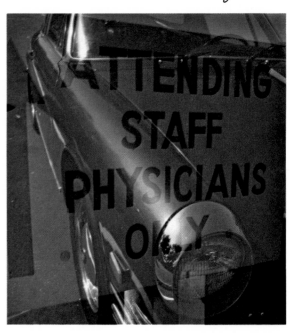

ing my motives for going into medicine: money and freedom of position seem to be the central reasons.

His first course in philosophy showed him how to analyze his materialistic values:

November 10 (freshman year): a study of philosophy to decide what is important to me is my most urgent need. I should major in recognition of truth ... My future career is not determined entirely by materialism. I constantly try to convince myself (sometimes successfully) that medicine is altruistic, fascinating, intellectually stimulating ... and free.

Trixie's intervening stay in psychology before proceeding to her final choice of English shows a similar pattern. Astronomy, her original choice, is a highly masculine profession; there are few women astronomers. She had originally identified English, her final choice, as "unadventurous," "feminine," and hopelessly "ordinary." She could not move from one to the other without making some changes in her own personality. Psychology proved to be a major that could simultaneously fill *both* her masculine and feminine needs; it also

functioned as one of the influences supporting the strong feminization that the college environment was helping to bring about in her personality. Here is her own account:

My most obvious change during college has been in major fields of interest. I registered first as an astronomy major. After taking Introductory Psychology the first semester of my sophomore year, I decided to become a Psychology major. Not until this fall (senior year) did I realize that I should have been an English major. I have been a step or two behind myself all the way: my decisions have been made completely on irrational bases. My interest in astronomy was part of my romantic adventure concept. It also tied in with my third-grade interest in prehistoric times and the evolution of Earth, and with my reaction against religion and my father — in the seventh grade I began to use science in support of my atheism, and idealized the scientist as an independent seeker of the (godless) truth. This concept persisted as an irrational ideal right up through my junior year here. After a C in math I stubbornly persisted in calculus and got a D ... My science binge has persisted in the courses I have taken in the psychology department, too, Physiological Psychology being an example. I have had little nudgings every once in a while as to the correctness of my choice, but only this year have I thought out my long-term interests and admitted my mistakes. Now I have idealized writing...

By the end of her senior year, Trixie's personality had developed in a more feminine direction, in part through her involvement in the study of personality, and she finally developed a response to English:

Literature is the one field, incidentally, in which I have felt satisfied and interested this year.

Early vocational choices and corresponding fields of study are primarily developmental phenomena. Boys with high status needs may declare for law or medicine; others who need to share in the image of hard, active masculinity may start in fields like mathematics, engineering, forestry, or physics. Engaging in the activities required by these majors may be instrumental in so reducing the spurious needs they support as to allow a new motivational basis for a different career.

DEVELOPMENTAL FRIENDSHIPS

A deep friendship with a person who differs significantly from one's self can be highly influential, as the experiences of both Sidney and Bob suggest.

Sidney's description of his friend Jay shows one of the prerequisites of such influence; there must be a very strong emotional attachment to the friend:

I first met Jay in the eighth grade. At this time he was the creative genius of the class, producing poetry and short stories far beyond his chronological age and apparent mental skills. I read some of his early things. They are truly amazing...

I believe I influenced Jay, but not to the extent that he influenced me. Conversations which we held, delving into philosophical, moral, and ethical questions of the meaning of life, could not help but direct his way of thinking. We both value psychology, philosophy, and literature very highly. He had many friends; I had few and still fewer intimate ones. There's a charm about him, an unusual charm which makes you like him, no matter what... I have great respect for the potential greatness of Jay. Matter-of-fact, I think our friendship was largely based on a belief in each other's possibility for greatness. Jay represented to me from the very first time I met him, and I'd heard of him even before I met him, the very opposite of what I was. Rich, attractive, sure of himself, successful in everything, people all around him, the epitome of social success...

As the foregoing implies, Jay provided Sidney with an adolescent ideal of what he would like to become: to be socially and romantically successful, to be athletic, intelligent, creative, to be personally charming, sure of himself. When they were graduated from high school together, the influence continued; Sidney applied to the same college as did Jay. Jay also provided a pathway into the curriculum and social life that profoundly influenced Sidney's college career. Jay's influence led Sidney into the courses in philosophy and literature that humanized Sidney and helped to change his materialistic values. Jay led him into a special honors program that provided one of the bases for Sidney's extraordinary academic success. Most importantly, Jay's joining an independent social group rather than a fraternity helped Sidney to do likewise and discover that he could be politically and socially successful in an independent group.

THE PEER GROUP

Sidney's personality and his religious beliefs led to his rejection by the peer group. His diary tells how dependent the adolescent is upon acceptance and support by peers and of the anguish of rejection:

September 14: I constantly feel envy, envy toward those who have accomplished what I have not. I gave my entire person to the interviews for the Freshman Council and failed. I again prostituted what I believe in order to get what I want...

December 8: Three weeks ago we marched to fraternity row, drunk, shouting "Abolish antisemitism!" I have had many talks with the rabbi here, and he claims Judaism is search and not dogma. Is this bullshit? Will I be socially driven out of atheism as I was socially (probably) driven into it? Will I be brave and join the nonfraternity group, or will I succumb to my social failings and to life and join a fraternity?

January 31: I saw Edward after the fraternity rushing was over—a broken and unhappy child. I despise a system which shocks me into the realization of jingle existence. I hope I do not join a fraternity. I have almost tallied myself out of it.

March 15: I have felt moist with tears shed or repressed over acceptance by others. By my continual presence, I feel my welcome is being worn out, as a comrade, an idol, an intellectual, or a human.

April 2: I find that I did not make the Service Club (although I surrounded myself with boisterousness, which should have impressed them), and I was saddened.

A later acceptance by a peer group brought not only support but strong developmental effects:

I made up my mind not to join a fraternity in my freshman year. The original reasons were concerned with Jay (my closest friend from high-school days), with religion, and with social acceptance. Jay and I felt that the frats were rather anti-intellectual.

Perhaps I should explain just what the nonfraternity group is, and what it means to me here. This college has long been dominated by fraternities. They have run the social life, they've been a haven for the college's institutionalizing of anti-intellectualism, of nonserious, rowdy academic life. They've been the other half of the intellectual-barbarian dichotomy which pervades most of the life of every student here. They have the run-of-the-mill evils of fraternity systems: religious and racial discrimination, social stratification, and highly selective joining processes.

Several years ago the university founded a nonfraternity group, an organization which would allow anyone to join, thus

eliminating the standard fraternity evils; but more than that, it founded an organization which would institutionalize the academic part of life here, not just provide the sort of three-meal-a-day haven which the fraternities provide. This nonfraternity group has been tremendously successful in its aims. Of 150 members, about 70 are very serious students, leaders of the class in academic and non-athletic extracurricular activities. As far as I'm concerned, these people make up the cream of the crop here. We also have 50 faculty members who eat many of their meals with us. It's through this organization that I've had the pleasure of meeting and becoming friends with many of the faculty members and administrators. Without the independent group, I would have been tremendously unhappy here because I would have had to participate in the rock-and-roll, in the heavy drinking, and in the attitude that studies come second and social life comes first. The group has enabled me to grow in many ways, to express myself as a person, and has fostered, rather than hindered, my development as an intellectual. I am sure there are many other people here who didn't join the independents and have gone the other way because of their fraternity environment.

After two years of participation in the nonfraternity group, Sidney was elected vice-chairman and was president of its chess club, with strong consequent effects upon his self-image:

Another thing, by then (junior year) I had gained stature such that almost everyone knew who I was; people respected me. I could sit down to dinner with anyone, and they'd look up to me as sort of a wise person — ask my advice about things.

DEVELOPMENTAL ANXIETY AND CRISES

As discussed at length in Chapter 20, too often the personal crises and intense anxieties that young people experience are labeled as abnormal phenomena. Studies of development have shown that for most adolescents anxiety and personal crises are not at all pathological but rather are characteristic of rapid normal growth—and may even be indispensable to it.

In terms of both personality-test-score changes and research-staff judgments during the four-year study, Bob's development was among the most remarkable in the sample of students studied. After a freshman year constrained by the shock of college, Bob began to develop at a pace that climaxed in a personality crisis that was quite acute throughout his senior year. Following are some samples of his distress as recorded in his diary:

I guess what I like least about myself are my vacillating ideas. I never seem to get a clear viewpoint of what I am doing, or what I want to do, or what I have done.... When I was running for president last spring, there was never any point in the campaign that I was absolutely sure that this was what I wanted. And it just seems that this is the way everything happens. I can't really seem to make heads or tails out of what I am doing. It is a feeling of being lost... no sense of direction. For a few minutes you feel like you have got to start doing something, but when you get on something, a few minutes later you want to turn around. What good are you doing when you don't know where you are going?

I'd say when I first came to college I had a single purpose in mind, and now I have lost all purpose entirely. That's an oversimplification, of course, but what I've learned and what I've seen and done over the past four years have all just led to a state where I don't really know what I want. I can sit down every other week and mark down a new goal, and still not be any more sure of which way I want to go.

Sidney's freshman-year anxieties would be difficult to understand in any frame of reference that automatically views anxiety as a pathological phenomenon:

September 11: My past seems to have died. I stand alone before my life-to-come, full of doubts and fears of inadequacy.

September 14: Last night at a college mixer I found myself lost and inadequate, terribly insecure. My status as a man was deeply shaken.

October 11: I long for home with a powerful longing. I am obsessed and burdened with fantasies, thoughts, dreads. I feel a longing to return home and recapture a dead childhood. Help me!

October 31: I feel depressed and lonely. I called home last night to console myself. My mother is distant; love, which I need badly, escapes me. I feel great tension and nervousness in the wake of exams. I must now call my date. Terror again seizes me. I alternate between depression and morbidity. I must find meaning and stability in a world which I fear is meaningless and unstable. I need help. I fear the need of help — help!

December 16: I am going home for Christmas with horror. I feel horror at the social rejection and loneliness which is certain to engulf me at home. I am leaving college in fear. My past is suffocating me. Have I committed some crime which demands that I get air, air, air?

Sidney turned out to be one of the most effective students in the group and eventually experienced highly positive personality changes. The crises evidenced in his diary were not symptomatic of pathology. To grow means to change from what one has been, and rapid change is naturally unsettling. The movement from one point in developmental life to another very often requires a disintegration of certain parts of the personality before a reintegration is possible. An adolescent who is not to some degree anxious and who does not experience crises is an adolescent who is developmentally on the shelf.

The Socialization of Sex

Sex is unique in its power to illuminate the interaction between biology and development and to lay bare the meaning of identity in the human personality. Research such as that conducted by Frank Beach has shown that motives like sex, which begin as pure biology in each person's life history, undergo a fundamental transformation. The mature personality is governed primarily by the socially learned components of sex—the love and closeness components, which come to play a major role in directing the biological urges.

As Sigmund Freud intimated, sex has a kind of archaeological function to the personality theorist: traces of childhood learning are more evident in its adult forms than in other aspects of the person. In American society, at least, sex is a special window through which to observe directly the interaction between the child and the adult he becomes. In observing sexual development, psychologists are studying the motive that most clearly reveals how man's biology can be socialized and the central processes by which identity as an adult human comes about—or fails to.

THE UNSOCIALIZED ADOLESCENT SEX MOTIVE

Confidentially written replies to anonymous questionnaires about their childhood sex experiences and their early adolescent sex interests reveal that few youngsters arrive at puberty with anything resembling what most adults describe as normal sex motives. Until recently, the adult world has practiced a mass deception—on their children and themselves—in which a stereotype of normal sexual behavior is agreed upon; each deceiver privately knows that he, himself, does not fit into the stereotype, but the mass nature of the deception lets him suppose that most others do. The excerpts below are not from a collection of abnormal cases but from a random assortment of college sophomores in a very ordinary class in a typical state university.

The purpose in presenting the personal case data that follow is to illustrate some of the most common and typical but nevertheless unsocialized end products of sex learning as understood by cognitively immature children. It is a survey of how things are with the adolescent just at the point when he is getting seriously into the dating and peer-group experiences that will—if he is lucky—socialize and humanize his sex motives. The section following this one will examine the socialization of sex.

In the following uncensored excerpts, each paragraph under a particular heading represents the account of a different person.

IGNORANCE ABOUT SEX

□ *Girls*

As a child some of the kids would talk about "fucking." At first I would just connect it with something wrong. Later on it was associated with sexual acts. My mother told me vaguely about these things at the end of the sixth grade.

It must have been about age eight or nine that I had a long talk with a girl who was two-three years older than I. She told me quite a bit about sex. It really frightened me. Mostly she explained about menstruation and she mentioned rape and I had no idea what it was and she didn't explain it. I learned very little from my parents but mostly from talking with other girls.

I used to think a woman just got pregnant. God just put it there because he wanted her to have a baby—kind of like the Virgin Mary, I guess.

□ Boys

At age 13, I was with two male friends who were talking about girls and sex. One mentioned that the male's penis was inserted into the female's vagina, and that constituted intercourse. I was amazed, surprised, shocked, and embarrassed, but I was careful to not let on that I had not already known this. I knew differences between boys and girls existed before this, but this was the first time everything became clear.

When I was 12 I heard a neighbor girl say "fuck" when she made a bad play in a ball game. I asked her what this meant ... I was extremely curious. I told her I had to know and she wouldn't tell. Finally, I ran in the house and got a dictionary, but, of course, didn't find it. Seeing that I really wanted to know, she finally told me. She told me something about a boy inserting his penis in the girl's vagina and "moving around" as she called it. I shuddered to think that my parents did this. I was shocked to say the least.

CHILDHOOD SEXUAL EXPERIENCE

☐ Girls

I think I was about five years old... One of the boy's fathers (our next door neighbor) would get me alone and make me watch him masturbate. This scared me, and I'd try to run away. I did not like it at all. I always thought he was really abnormal.

When I was about 12, a man presented me in an office staircase with the exposure of his penis. He was an older man of about 40. He also played with it. I was extremely scared. I did not tell anyone for a long time.

On two different occasions a boy in our neighborhood tried to rape me. I was in first and second grade and didn't know what was going on. He took me some place and took all my clothes off and pulled his pants down. I thought he looked rather strange. He started to come close to me and I got scared so I ran away.

☐ Boys

Our attractive baby sitter (I was 10) frequently caressed my body when she put me to sleep. She spent a great deal of time hugging and stroking my front. Today I have a very pleasurable feeling if someone pets my front (stomach, chest, genitals).

I can't really recall any sexual experiences in childhood. I don't believe I had any until college.

One day I rubbed the genitals of a girl who lived next door. We were in my back yard behind a tree. I put my hand in her pants and ran my

*finger around her. I had
similar experiences on occasion
with my sister.*

The responses quoted above and many other data from the sex questionnaires filled out by nineteen-year-olds indicate the unsocialized nature of the sex motive in most adolescents. Among other points, they show:

1. Sex may first be encountered in terms of something frightening. There's a surprising amount of ignorance of female masturbation.
2. First explanations of the act of intercourse may cause shock.
3. Parental and adult intercourse is hard for children to imagine and may be very upsetting.
4. Misconceptions that would be unthinkable in other aspects of personality abound in the adolescents' views and feelings about sex.
5. Frightening childhood sexual experience is more common than adults suppose because children often do not reveal seductive overtures by adults.
6. Sibling sex play does take place.
7. Picture sex and storybook sex can be so strongly experienced as to be more arousing than the prospects of intercourse.
8. Sadistic sexual fantasies modeled after presentations in the mass media are common to both sexes.
9. What adolescents find arousing is likely to be part of the passing ideology of types of boys and girls who are considered "in."
10. Much less sexual excitement is aroused by primary sex stimuli (nudity, genitals) than by the forms in which sex is presented in the mass media.
11. Girls are as concerned about orgasm adequacy as boys are about potency.

HOW SEX MAY BECOME SOCIALIZED

The principle underlying the socialization of sex is simple and basic: in a deep, positive relationship between a boy and a girl, the negative or asocial feelings about sex can be transformed into a sex-closeness-love motive. Left to their own devices, many adolescents heal themselves of the crazy sexual misadventures that beset the child in our culture.

Florence's story, in her own words, will be used as an example. As a child, Florence was told that sex was dirty and immoral. Worse, her first adolescent sexual experiences were frightening. She had a too rough and quick introduction to sex. That she overcame the consequences of these fears is testimony to the special power of deep personal relations between boy and girl for the personality development of the adolescent.

☐ *Original Sexual Learning*

*Questions which I did have about
sex were answered by my mother
in a twisted, euphemistic fashion.
When I did become aware of the
truth from other people, my trust
and faith in my mother was lost.
Now, as then, I simply am unable
to talk with her frankly about sex.
Communication between us on the
subject of sex has been and will be
nil. Thus, when I went into high
school, I thought about sex with*

feelings of guilt and shame...
During my freshman year in high
school I got to know boys four and
five years older than me... I
became fascinated by and interested in these older boys. Of course,
their ideas were quite different
from mine. It was during this
time that I first became aware
of sex as personally involving me.
Once I engaged in necking and
petting with John, the biggest,
strongest guy in the group. This
was the first time anything like
this had happened to me, and I
was very naive and absolutely
too young mentally for this. I
developed a great guilt complex
and fear that I can see as very
evident even now. After this
happened my next monthly
period did not occur. I knew
better, but guilt plus naivete
and imagination made me think
that God had performed a
miracle to punish me, and I was
now pregnant. For about six
weeks I lived in fear, guilt,

anxiety, and uncertainty. I feel
that the episode with John
added a great feeling of fear to
my already existing shame-guilt
complex about sex. The fear was
in part due to my ignorance,
for which I blame my mother.

☐ Sexual Readjustment

I spent the summer following
my freshman year in college in
Bermuda, and it proved to be the
most educational few months I
have ever experienced... I met
Ray... I went home thinking about
him and soon we met... He was so
interesting and did so much. He
told me about his skiing in Colorado,
surfing here, photography, mountain
climbing, and also about _him_. His
fight for independence from his
parents was really causing him
trouble. They... wanted Ray to act
a certain way, do certain things,
and just fall into a pattern. He
had quite an unpleasant home as
a result. Immediately, I was full

of feeling for him... I sensed that he needed somebody, and I wanted very much to be the object of his dependence...

We went everywhere together, and a mutual understanding grew. I loved all of the adventures we had — surfing, shopping, sleeping on the beach, skin diving, or climbing to a mountain pool to swim. Soon it turned out to be quite convenient if I would sign out for weekends and merely stay with him. We worked and lived together. As before, affection and sex entered into the situation. He did not push me, and I began to lose that ugly fear. Our relationship was really turning into something wonderful. Then he began to expect more and more. I wanted to be able to give and love him. Yet this idea of morals that had plagued me and always been there arose. We had many arguments about it but I just couldn't. It was a beautiful

feeling to wake up having his chest to rest my head on. We would always fall asleep to soft music, and talked many nights until three or four in the morning. Once we came very close to intercourse, but I suddenly felt great fear and began sobbing and crying. Ray... would sit down and try to explain and make me understand how he felt and how he thought. He was not void of morals or standards; in fact, his were much more correct and logical than mine. Ray was the first person to make me understand that morals are a personal, circumstantial type of thing rather than blind, hard-and-fast rules. It changed me a great deal... I ended up staying an extra month in Bermuda.

A year later in the midst of a deep relationship with a new boy, Steve, Florence reflected upon the meaning of her summer with Ray and commented upon her current sex interests:

I've found someone like Ray in many ways. My first interests in Steve were quite unrelated to sex. Now, I find myself instigating and pushing for more sexual satisfactions. Steve, like Ray, has a slow, sure, and very fine approach. My only regret with Steve is that I did not discover him earlier.

My sex interest now is very high as compared to one year ago. I think that my relationship with Ray helped and benefited me in this. My likes and dislikes in gentle approach is derived directly from Ray.

Florence has sensitively described the development of the sex-closeness-love motive and shown its special power for transforming sex fears into positive sex interest by embedding sex in a larger emotional context of closeness and love. Such embedding in a sweeping organization is a fundamental developmental mechanism.

The case of Jim shows that the kind of closeness Florence experienced can be more basic than sex—even for a boy accustomed to quite a different kind of relation to girls from early adolescence.

Jim had his first intercourse at fifteen with a prostitute, and he continued relations with prostitutes throughout high school and his first year of college. Then he met Linda:

In the beginning of my sophomore year I met a freshman girl who came to mean everything to me. I used to see her each day when she'd come over to eat; finally, I asked her out—a turning point in my life. She was pretty, had long blond hair, and dressed differently. She didn't wear the status type of clothes most college coeds do, but her clothes were not out of place. She was different from any other girl I had ever met ...

Linda taught me to appreciate art, drama, and certain forms of music, and introduced me to many new ideas taken from her studies—studies that I would never have come in contact with myself. In turn, I taught her to appreciate hikes and picnics and getting close to nature. I even took her fishing with me a couple of times; she loved it. She painted and I fished; usually she had better luck than I did.

We saw each other constantly, but grew into love slowly. Our love-making reached peaks that I had never before experienced, nor have I since. You will not believe this, but we never had intercourse in the fourteen months we went together. We didn't think twice about going to bed nude and staying there for hours, but she didn't want intercourse. I think she was afraid of becoming pregnant. She used to say that if she became pregnant before graduating, she would destroy her parents, as they had sacrificed so much to put her through, so I didn't push her. We'd just lie there for hours talking, caressing, and being with each other... The funny thing is that while we never had intercourse, it didn't matter; I always felt satisfied anyway, as long as I was with her.

Thereafter, sex as a mere physical outlet had a different meaning for Jim:

Intercourse with a prostitute lacks the most important element of a sexual relationship: the development of a rapport, a communication between the sex partners. The partners share not only their bodies, but their feelings and thoughts. _They share._

IDENTITY: THE SELF-SOCIETY RELATIONSHIP

Erik Erikson's concept of identity has emerged as the central idea for understanding not only youth, to which the concept is most often applied, but the relation between self and society at any age. The relation is simply more visible when disrupted, as it is in the young and in adults caught up in such social upheavals as war. The underlying processes to which Erikson's concept refers are not particularly perceptible when they are working smoothly, as they typically are for the child as long as he exists within the social context of his family and the extended context of the high school and the community with which the family is linked. And later, when the individual has found his place in the adult world, the processes underlying the self-society relationship once more become silent—almost unnoticed because they work without explicit attention on anyone's part. Occasional failures of smooth functioning cause such surprise and mystification that we call them mental illness and invent all sorts of hypotheses, often genetic and medical ones, to explain away these puzzling and disturbing individuals. It was Erikson's insight that any major dislocation of the person from his social matrix could bring about the same kind of symptoms. It was no accident that he came to the identity concept while treating crises arising from combat.

The personal dislocations from society, which are frequent for adults caught up in war, have their parallel in youth, when the individual no longer has the full support of his original social structure nor yet of the one he is moving into.

The concept of identity has two facets: it refers to a person's feelings about himself on the one hand and, on the other, to how his self-estimate relates to estimates of him by significant others in his social context. The estimates involve dimensions that the current society considers fundamental to a personality. The dimensions are further organized into functional subgroupings, which are usually termed *roles*. Being "a male" or "a female" is one such fundamental role. Roles provide the significant connections between self and society: through participation in the established roles of society the individual is not only linked meaningfully to the social order but, in turn, is defined by it.

MASCULINE IDENTITY

The transition from boyhood to masculine, sexual adulthood is a classic problem of late adolescence. The case of Hugh shows some of its hazards as well as the talent of one youth for seeking out conditions that allowed him to develop normally. □ *Original Sexual Learning* Following a childhood in which Hugh's mother taught him that sex was dirty and immoral, he met Margot:

Margot is a hometown girl whom I dated my last year in high school. She is much younger than me but is very grown up in her attitudes. Margot is a beautiful and popular girl whom I am very proud to date, and I am very close to her. She is the first girl I ever dated; I didn't even go to dances in high school unless asked by a girl for those functions in which girls were supposed to invite boys.

This (freshman) year I have dated little because my relation to Margot, which has continued during vacations home, seems too happy to give up. In the dorm this year I first met attitudes of free love toward girls that differ very much from my own. This spring I began to develop the physical side of my relation to Margot, but felt conflicts over this.

This (sophomore) year I had my first sexual experience — with Margot. She seduced me rather than the other way around. During the past year we have spent a great deal of time in very heavy petting. I vividly recall the whole scene. We had spent the afternoon walking near the campus and had come back to my room, gotten involved in heavy petting, and ended up nude in bed. I was terribly unsure about proceeding further, and we both decided it would be better not to in the dorm. We had planned a weekend away, and she finally said, "Why can't we go a day early and stay in a hotel and get this over with?" And we did.

I was impotent in that first occasion and caught a certain amount of berating from Margot for this, or at least questioning. She asked, "What's the matter?" I succeeded in having intercourse with her, but it was not wholly satisfactory for either of us. It was her first experience too. From this time on we carried on a lukewarm affair through the rest of the year. When she visited here, she came to my dorm room, and when I visited her home we attempted relations in the car. These were never satisfactory, usually because of impotence on my part. Margot often berated me during that time, saying, on one occasion, that she felt as though she were in bed with only half a man.

This (senior) fall I met Rosalind, a girl who was several years older than me, at an extended weekend party... Rosalind was domineering... It was purely a physical attraction for both of us. This developed into eight or ten subsequent nights spent at Rosalind's apartment. It was never satisfactory from my standpoint, and probably not from hers since I had repeated difficulty with premature ejaculation. Because of my failure to fulfill an adult masculine role, the whole thing began to have a good deal of anxiety overtones for me, and her attitude and behavior became even more domineering. I really began to worry greatly about ever being able to function in a sexual relationship.

My ghastly experience with Rosalind was repeated later this year with Ada, also a sexually experienced girl. Her deprecatory treatment of me reminded me terribly strongly of Margot. I was worried about my impotence, whether I could really ever perform sexually, and became more and more disturbed by the situation with this girl. One day it got to the point where I felt numb and unable to get my studies done at all, and this scared the hell out of me. I had real visions of cracking up.

☐ **Sexual Readjustment**

In the spring of this (senior) year I met Diana through a mutual friend ... Diana's most striking characteristic was her passiveness.

She was agreeable to whatever I wanted to do. I had the feeling that she was less critical of me than these others had been. I was surprised on our first kiss that she immediately went to a French kiss, and I wondered if she would be sexually receptive too. About the fourth date we ended up in my room, and I asked her to stay. She was coy but ended up staying. We petted and went to sleep, but neither of us made an attempt to carry it to intercourse. The following weekend we ended up in her apartment, having intercourse that was mutually very satisfying. I was really overjoyed.

After graduation I began to work. I felt a conviction that I could succeed with a girl. A married friend introduced me to Julia, who immediately struck me as being a physically attractive girl and as a very warm person. I was very much attracted to her. She impressed me as a very open, honest person, a woman not given to coy

machinations, to playing a helpless role, to making snide, undercutting remarks or to aggressive
manipulation, and yet in no sense
hesitant about saying what she
thought. We found we shared
interests in art and in how we felt
about our college experience and
the future.

I felt at once relaxed with
Julia. She didn't expect me to be
anything in particular; therefore,
I really didn't have to be. It's
hard to say why she gave me this
feeling, and yet it was very
clearly true. I found that I
could be very spontaneous and
open with her, even on our first
date. We read plays together with
my married friend. In the way
she glowed when she talked about
her interest in art she was much
like Margot.

I never had the feeling that I
would win her by some kind of
manipulation. I felt a great
sharing of common interests,
common approaches to things.

I didn't feel I was going to have
to perform or to prove myself
socially, sexually, or in any
other way — but that I could be
myself with her.

After a couple of months our
relationship became physically
involved ... After I asked her to
marry me, we began to have intercourse. She used an oral contra-
ceptive, and our relationship was
very satisfactory for both of us
and has continued so since our
marriage.

Hugh's case illustrates one natural course in
development of identity. Like Florence in the
preceding section, Hugh seemed to have an instinct for finding his own readjustment. The
young are their own best therapists. The conditions of the readjustment proved to be the same:
when the anxiety-provoking habit is embedded in
a different context—a deeper personal relation in
which there is closeness, sharing, and, above all,
acceptance—this overriding positive context
changes the fear and permits the development of
the new, mature sex role.

FEMININE IDENTITY

Traditionally, the late adolescent challenge of
sex-role identity has not been as sharp for girls

because sexual potency has not been a clear-cut social expectation or defining criterion for femaleness—nor has sexual adequacy been a central part of the girl's self-image. Dating and generally being popular have usually been sufficient.

Changing sexual mores, however, have introduced a new criterion for femininity for the gradually increasing number of girls who now engage in sexual intercourse as a part of normal dating relations: some discover that they do not achieve orgasm and are as concerned as the male has been about potency. Ramona's experience shows that under certain conditions the same mechanisms found in Hugh's case also operate with a girl.

Part of Ramona's childhood sexual learning was a fearful image of "women . . . victimized through treatment by males lurking everywhere," given her by her mother. Also, she was seduced into a homosexual relation by an older girl. As a consequence, Ramona arrived at puberty in much the same state of uncertainty as was Hugh after his experiences with Margot, Rosalind, and Ada. Her further development took a similar form:

Sophomore year. My greatest fear was my possible homosexuality. *Sophomore summer*. I was nearly seduced by a boy with whom I shared intellectual interests. Being with him gave me palpitations, and the place he accidentally touched me on the thigh burned deeply for hours. We experienced ecstatic kisses, and weeks of this had no tingling. We went to the park one sunny day and he almost made me. Afterwards we gratefully kissed goodbye, and I flew homeward feeling like a million dollars. For the first time I felt truly female, so female I knew then I never need fear my role again. It was so natural and smooth; so easy to desire when one is desired. *Senior year*. A big wheel asked me over to his house and I let him seduce me . . . . I loved the flattery and ate up the attention for which I was so hungry . . . I adored his dominance. *May 12*. This semester has been the first time I could be content just with a boy showing tenderness toward me without his having to commit himself . . . I can feel wanted in a relationship that is temporary.

To change in matters of sex is no different than with other motives: The old fear must be aroused in a new context that leads to a decisive contradiction. In adolescence, the boy-girl relation proves to be an embedding context in which fundamental personality developments take place. Its power as a mechanism for change in adolescents seems infinitely greater than any form of psychotherapy.

IDENTITY AND VOCATIONAL COMPETENCE

For the male in our society, competence in a vocational role is as fundamental a dimension of identity as is his masculinity in the sex role. Again, the male is held to a more sharply defined criterion. The condition of the late-adolescent boy is much more complex and drastic than we realize. Consider his situation: Like all adolescents, he is in transition from the personality supports of family and high school and peer groups to the still distant adult world. He is like a climber crossing a bridge of thin ice over a crevasse between two solid rocks. Typically, he is still hung up on unrealistic, childhood-determined vocational goals. Further, the college curriculum tells him very little about whether he will either like a projected field of work or do well in it. The college faculty, too, are poor role models for all but the few future professors in the student body. Yet by the end of his sophomore year, the registrar's office insists that he commit himself to a department and an implied career, a commitment that he has neither the experience nor the facts at hand to make; he can only guess.

Sidney's case, already familiar to the reader, illustrates many of the foregoing points. We have seen how he began as a science major intending a career in medicine because he childishly imagined that he needed the safety and material security implied by that role. When he changed to philosophy, he found that he lacked the competence to perform at the high level he expected of himself:

March 2 (sophomore year): I have been in a state of intellectual depression since the end of fall term. It came from a philosophy paper, the first major paper that I have written in philosophy. When I turned it in I thought it was a top-notch paper, but it was returned with "a bit dubious" written on it. That broke the bubble. It has taken me a long time to come out of that. I now have a lot of trouble regaining interest in what I am doing, of the sort I had last year and fall term of this year....

I don't know how I will decide about the future. Apparently the basis that I have to decide upon is as superficial as what grade I got on a paper. If this is the case, I'm not ready to decide.

Sidney's simultaneous failure to make it with the dominant peer group deepened his identity crisis. During his first two years of college Sidney was an unhappy, often depressed young man. One would scarcely have anticipated that he would graduate as an enormously competent and highly self-confident scholar.

Upon graduating, he wrote:

> I look forward to the rest of my life with great relish. I have the feeling every day that my life is before me and I can do with it what I will — possibilities of success are almost unlimited. I feel that I have tucked neatly away now one corner of my life, the sexual, social ... an that, by my love, my engagement, and my marriage that chapter of my life has been completed ...

Indeed there *had* been a personality change: Sidney now had an identity. The turning point was the discovery in his junior year that he could achieve his highest level of competence in sociol-ogy. Also, he found models for identification in the faculty role:

> Something was happening in the meantime, something quite a bit more general. I saw that these people around me, these intellectuals who were not medical doctors, who were not engaged in materially successful enter-prises, were nevertheless happy, healthy, respectable, and highly admirable in the way they were putting their intellects to work. Such a life, then, for the first time, really seemed possible to me.

The combination of identification with suitable models in a socially valued role, a role in which a person both feels himself to be competent and is acknowledged by others to be competent, has the powerful effect one sees in Sidney's case. Despair and depression, a feeling of nonbeing, turn into supreme self-confidence, optimism, and personal well-being. When these are tempered and honed by the realities of adult experience, one facet of maturity will emerge.

Our own day has seen the emergence of a new and unique stage of psychological development—youth. Interposed between the end of adolescence and the beginning of adulthood, youth is a stage peopled by the mature but not traditionally committed. These young adults have survived the rigors of adolescence but have not yet accepted the mold of marriage, home, children, and job that characterizes normal adult society.

In order to clearly set out the reasons for the emergence of a new stage of life at this time and to define the characteristics of these young people, it will be best to recapitulate the three types of change that routinely occur during the course of human life. The first, *maturation*, refers to the biological, physiological, and anatomical changes in the human body and brain—changes that underlie, make possible, and in many instances require changes in psychological functioning and social role. The second, *socialization*, describes the processes, in all societies, by which individuals pass through age-graded social roles whose requirements they must learn. For example, in every society some distinction is made between what is expected of the prepubescent child and the postpuberty young man or woman. Behavior and attitude both change in response to these age-graded patterns of social expectation. And finally, there is the process of *psychological development* or growth. Although psychological development is premised upon maturation and is often stimulated by socialization, it is not identical with either. One can mature physically and learn the social ropes without automatically growing in a psychological sense. By psychological development is meant a process of increasing psychic complexity, differentiation, and individuation. The development is seen psychologically in qualitative and largely irreversible shifts in levels of functioning, and behaviorally in increased flexibility and adaptability to the environment, along with increased autonomy and capacity for self-direction.

In discussing an emergent stage of life, we will concentrate on psychological development because maturation occurs almost without regard to social and historical setting, and, similarly, in all societies, the great majority of individuals are socialized—that is, they pass through the age-graded social roles that their societies provide for them. Psychological development, however, does not always keep up with the passage through each socially defined stage of life. Clinical practice and research have shown that many individuals become fixated at one stage of life and fail to make the next step forward in human growth. One of the causes of this failure is an environment that is harshly depriving or that fails to provide the stimulation necessary for growth. Such environments can not only retard psychological development; at times, they may arrest it entirely.

But there are also environments that are particularly rich and facilitating. In fact, the recent conditions of some societies have made it possible for larger and larger numbers of individuals not only to develop normally but also to undergo a longer and more complex period of psychological

23
Youth: A Separate Stage of Life

development. As a consequence, the entirely new stage of youth is emerging.

HISTORICAL BACKGROUND

Philippe Ariès, in his recent provocative study *Centuries of Childhood*, reexamined the concept of the life cycle from the Middle Ages to the present. He concluded that in the Middle Ages even the concept of childhood as it is defined today was virtually unknown. There was a clearly admitted infancy, lasting until approximately the age of seven. But thereafter, people whom we would consider children were simply assimilated into the adult world. The art and social documents of the Middle Ages show children and adults mingling together in one unified community, wearing the same clothes, performing the same functions, undifferentiated with regard to status or psychological development. The vast majority of children—and adults—were, of course, totally unschooled. But even those who obtained some minimal schooling so as to become priests or clerks were taught in ungraded schools where children, adolescents, and adults all intermingled.

EMERGENCE OF CHILDHOOD

It was only in the seventeenth and eighteenth centuries that a concept of childhood as a separate stage of life slowly began to appear. There was a new and sentimental view of childhood along with new theories of education concerned with promoting the child's moral and intellectual development, with protecting him from the evils

Figure 23.1. The child as a miniature adult.

and corruptions of adult society, and with preserving his real or imagined childhood virtues. At the same time, schools became increasingly graded by age, and both the average length of schooling and the number of children who received formal schooling increased.

From historical evidence it seems clear that childhood became a separate stage of life only when large numbers of people entered the bourgeoisie, the amount of available leisure increased, and the rate of infant mortality decreased. As the bourgeoisie prospered, there was less need for their children to work in order to ensure the family's economic survival. The lowered childhood mortality rate allowed parents to devote themselves less cautiously to each child. And the new mercantile capitalism required that a larger portion of the citizenry be literate and fluent with numbers: thus, more children had to go to schools.

Ariès' analysis of the emergence of a concept of childhood has far-reaching implications for understanding the relationship between historical change and psychological development. For although Ariès speaks explicitly of concepts of childhood, the experience of childhood changed as well, although perhaps less dramatically. In the Middle Ages, most children died before the age of six, and those who survived were apprenticed out or put to work. They were often treated with what we would now consider shockingly little tenderness, protectiveness, attention, or care. Parents seem to have invested far less emotional energy in their children than they do at present: children were rarely spoken of as precious possessions to be cherished and protected.

But as a stage of childhood began to emerge, a larger proportion of those between the age of six and fourteen were deliberately segregated into schools; they were increasingly sheltered from the demands of adult work. Children found new freedom to play and to experiment and had systematic opportunities to develop new interpersonal and technical skills. In advanced Western societies, the process of segregation of childhood is now virtually complete, but it has only been in this century that it has finally been extended from the aristocracy and bourgeoisie to the working and lower classes. The full institutionalization of childhood is marked by universal primary education. In the span of four centuries, we have moved from an era in which childhood was not recognized to an era in which we take it completely for granted and protect it with an array of legal, social, and educational institutions.

EMERGENCE OF ADOLESCENCE

The concept of adolescence is of even more recent origin. Only after childhood had been demarcated from adulthood was adolescence interposed between them. Adolescence as we think of it today emerged only in the nineteenth and twentieth centuries, and the extension of adolescence as a stage of psychological growth is far from complete even today. Puberty, in the sense of biological maturation has, of course, occurred in all societies, but in early Western societies, it seemed to go largely unnoticed. When children

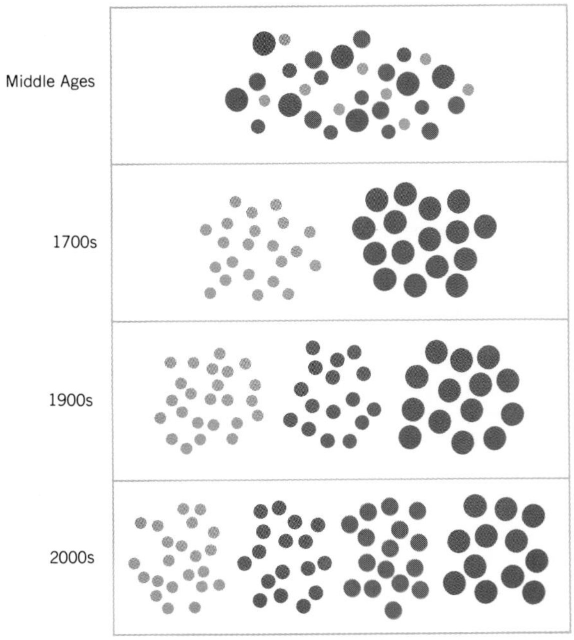

Figure 23.2. Changes in the pattern of populations as new life stages emerge.

are considered neither innocent nor importantly different from adults, the fact of puberty constitutes neither a fall from innocence nor a change in status, and it therefore has little special meaning.

When a postpuberty stage of life was first noted in the eighteenth and nineteenth centuries, concepts of adolescence centered on two images: the *cherubino*—the androgynous youth—or the *recruit*—the young soldier in training. Only in our century (specifically, after World War I) did the modern concept of adolescence appear. And even today, images of adolescence are fluid and changing. Media that portray adolescents still alternate among earlier images of the adolescent as awkward, acned, and anguished and newer images that view the adolescent either as deviant, wild, and uncontrolled or else as an idealistic and accurate critic of society, the repository of the future's hope.

The recent emergence of the *concept* of adolescence does not mean that no one ever had an adolescence before the concept emerged. Clearly, the potential for this experience is part of our endowment as human beings, and many men and women have passed through what would now be recognized as an adolescent experience. But three things have changed in the last century. First, adolescence as a stage of life has been socially recognized and acknowledged. Second, society has begun to sanction and support adolescence, increasingly buttressing it with educational, familial, institutional, and economic resources. Third, these new resources, coupled with other changes in society, have opened up to an ever-larger proportion of young people the possibility of continuing psychological growth during the years from thirteen to eighteen. Protection from adult responsibilities has been granted, educational institutions have been created to fill this duty-free time, and a positive image of a postchildhood, preadult stage of life—adolescence—is now almost universally held. Table 23.1 shows how these and other aspects of adolescence have emerged in the last century.

As with the recognition of childhood, the emergence of adolescence is closely related to social, economic, and historical changes. Increasing industrialization has allowed those past the age of puberty to be freed from the requirements of

Table 23.1. Changes in Adolescent Status

From	To
A short pubertal period between childhood and adulthood.	An increasingly longer period (four to seven or eight years) of preparation for the assumption of adult responsibility.
The experiencing of rigid rites and ceremonials as tests of readiness for adult status.	Relatively little emphasis upon such procedures, except for religious observances (confirmation) during early adolescence and some social recognition ("coming-out" parties) for girls at the end of adolescence.
Early marriages and the raising of large families for the benefit of the societal group.	No restriction upon age of marriage or size of family.
Mating controlled by parental authority.	Individual freedom of mate selection.
Specialized training of upper-class boys for war or political leadership.	Many-sided education as preparation to engage in one or another occupational or citizenship activity.
Little, if any, education for girls beyond some training in homemaking.	Increasing trend toward equalization of educational opportunity for the two sexes.
Great emphasis upon superiority in physical strength and endurance.	Concern about the mental as well as the physical health of young people, and decreasing emphasis upon mere physical strength and endurance.
Educational advantages available to a relatively small number of young people.	Educational advantages available to all.
Schooling, for the most part, the responsibility of parents, religious institutions, or national organizations, usually on a fee basis, especially for adolescents and young adults.	Nontuition, citizen-supported education available for all from the preschool level through adolescence and, in some communities, through the college or university level.
No recognition of individual differences among children except in physical structure and constitution.	A recognition and acceptance of the fact that young people are different as well as alike, physically, mentally, and emotionally.
Almost complete disregard and nonunderstanding of young people's developing interests, aptitudes, and needs.	Increasing interest in, and study of, the developmental pattern of the needs, wants, interests, and aptitudes of maturing children and adolescents.
Emphasis upon the submission of young people to the authority and will of parents and other elders.	Encouragement of individual freedom of behavior from early childhood through adolescence within the framework of the general welfare of a democratic society.

Source: L. Crow and A. Crow, *Adolescent Development and Adjustment.* 2nd ed. (New York: McGraw-Hill, 1965), p. 28. Copyright © 1965 by McGraw-Hill, Inc. Used with permission of McGraw-Hill Book Company.

Figure 23.3. How the movies have depicted the "typical teen-ager" over the years: *(from top to bottom)* Mickey Rooney as Andy Hardy; the Dead End Kids; Annette Funicello; James Dean; Sandra Dee as "Gidget."

farm and factory labor. Indeed, the rising standards of economic productivity today make the adolescent, especially the uneducated adolescent, almost impossible to employ. The new attitudes toward adolescence are expressed in laws that make full-time employment before the age of sixteen or eighteen illegal. Growing affluence provides individual families and society as a whole with the wealth needed to support these economically unproductive adolescents in school. And all of these changes have happened, on a mass scale, almost within living memory; even the child labor laws were passed in America only in the twentieth century.

PERSPECTIVE ON CONTEMPORARY SOCIETY

Industrialization has also increased societal demands upon adult personality, and a phase of adolescent psychological development appears to help the individual meet these demands. To start with the obvious example, highly developed technical skills are necessary if the individual is to find a respected job within an industrial economy. Furthermore, the young must often be trained in skills with which their parents are unfamiliar. All of this requires an increasingly protracted period of relatively formal education, extending long past the age of puberty.

Equally important, industrial society demands special *psychological* characteristics of its citizens. The individual in a complex, changing, highly organized, industrial or industrializing society must have a highly developed sense of independence, adaptability, and self-direction. He must be able to leave his parents and relatives to set up a home of his own, which is often as distant psychologically from his first home as it is geographically. And in a rapidly changing society, the individual must learn to deal virtually by himself with continual novelty and change. He must be able to postpone immediate gratification, operate at a high level of symbolic thought and action, and be gratified by relatively intangible rewards. What psychologists know of successful adolescent development tells them that, by and large, the experiences of this life stage help to promote precisely the qualities of independence, adaptability, and self-direction required in modern society.

The increasing extension of adolescence as a concept does not mean that adolescent development is in any way complete. Those who have attempted to study representative groups of American teen-agers have usually concluded that most show marked signs of foreclosure, blocking, stagnation, or resistance to the process of internal development and change that we consider desirable in adolescence. Elizabeth Douvan and Joseph Adelson, working from intensive interviews with a large sample of American teen-agers, conclude that growth toward real emotional autonomy, detachment from the family, and the development of a personal ethical and moral code of behavior and thought occur only in a "bold, sometimes stubborn, often unhappy minority."

Emergence of the Stage

Although the life cycle is defined as an ordered sequence of psychological development, this defi-

nition does not imply that life is an escalator up which all men move regardless of social setting and historical circumstance; rather, it is a ladder from which many individuals fall and many more get off without reaching the top. Obviously, some exceptional individuals will grow psychologically almost regardless of their environment, but, for continuing psychological development, most people need social confirmation, support, protection, and challenge. These requirements constitute the stimulus to psychological growth. When such facilitations are missing, psychological development is retarded or at times stopped altogether. Certain societies, or certain subcultures within a society, may systematically retard development during childhood and adolescence, with the result that members of these societies may be, on the whole, less developed psychologically than members of other contemporary cultures and groups. Other societies or subcultures, under new historical conditions, may be able to extend the ladder of psychological development or speed up the climb.

At this time in history, in the more advanced nations, the contours of still another stage of life, one that intervenes between adolescence and adulthood, is now becoming visible—the stage of youth. This chapter will attempt to give to the ancient but vague term "youth" a more specific psychological meaning.

HISTORICAL FRAMEWORK

Social and historical factors, as well as psychological ones, are critically important in understanding the prolongation of youth. Two factors are of

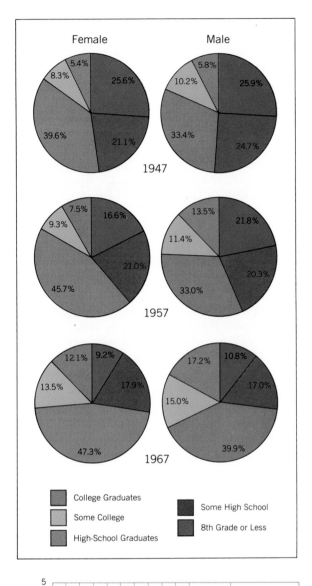

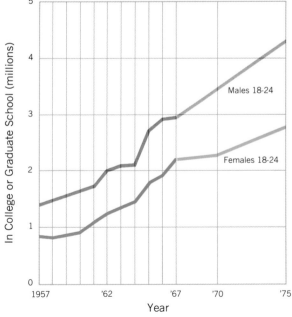

obvious importance. The first is the rapid and progressive increase in the amount of education in the advanced nations. Historically, it is completely without precedent for 80 percent of the citizens of a society to continue their education through high school, for approximately half of them to enter institutions of higher education, for half of these freshmen to graduate eventually from some institution, and for approximately half of all college graduates to go on for graduate and professional education. These figures mean that somewhere between one out of eight and one out of sixteen young people are destined for education *beyond* the college level: two generations ago only this proportion even had a hope of *entering* college. This extraordinary prolongation of education in American and other technologically advanced societies provides a major facilitation for the entry of young men and women into a postadolescent but preadult stage of life.

Second, because this is an era when social change is more rapid, more unrelenting, and more thoroughgoing than in any other recent historical era, the individual's relationship to his personal, social, and cultural tradition is cast into doubt. The technologies and methods of the past are becoming obsolete at an ever-increasing rate, but more important, the ideologies, values, and systems of symbolic interpretation that were taken for granted by one's parents and grandparents often seem largely irrelevant and useless. The most articulate of today's youth thus express a vivid, even anguished, feeling that their cultural inheritance may not be adequate either to the

contemporary world or to the future world in which they hope to live out their lives. Politically, this feeling is expressed in slogans about the "exhaustion of the old ideologies" and the "need to rebuild" a future. Psychologically, a similar feeling is reflected in the perception of the parental generation as old-fashioned, out of date, behind the times, and inadequate as models for life today. A rapid change in values in any era leads the young toward a search for new values, new institutions, and new models of life that will seem more relevant than the values of their parents.

PSYCHOLOGICAL FRAMEWORK

Although writers like Sigmund and Anna Freud, Harry Stack Sullivan, Peter Blos, Erik Erikson, and Helene Deutsch have provided enormously important insights into the nature of adolescent development, most of what they say applies with greater accuracy to the young teen-ager than to the older one; with the increasingly earlier onset of puberty has come an increasingly earlier sophistication. The concepts of adolescence have been stretched too much, and so we need to examine the development of what has sometimes been called late-late adolescence in its own right. One advantage of separating the youth from the adolescent is that it frees us from assuming a fundamental developmental similarity between the twenty-one-year-old apprentice or graduate student and the fourteen-year-old eighth-grader.

Kenneth Keniston recently studied in some depth an elite group of young radical activists, most of whom were in their middle twenties. In a

Figure 23.6. Youth across the nation are expressing their dissatisfaction with the way of life established by their parents and grandparents.

sociological sense, none of these young men and women was an adult: that is to say, none was involved in the institutions of marriage and career that are normally used to differentiate the adult from the adolescent. But psychologically, many of these young men and women seemed already to have accomplished what are considered the traditional tasks of adolescence—emancipation from original family; relative tranquility concerning sexuality; the formation of a stable and relatively integrated self-identity; a capacity for commitment, intimacy, and play; a considerable synthesis in the moral and ethical areas; and a history of having passed through and beyond earlier adolescent rebellion. Despite these developmental accomplishments, however, the particular young men and women Keniston studied continued to place enormous emphasis on psychological change, on remaining open, fluid, and in motion, on not foreclosing their development in any way, and on not becoming prematurely integrated into the established society. In this respect, they were not adult. These young men and women seem to be in an uncharted stage of life that intervenes between the end of adolescence proper and the beginning of adulthood.

It is obvious that not everyone between the ages of twenty and thirty can be said to be in this stage of life. On the contrary, these youths constitute but a small minority of their age group. However, their number is increasing among college and graduate students, among Peace Corps and Vista volunteers, among college and graduate student dropouts, among young radicals, and in

Figure 23.7. Youth, the stage of life emerging between adolescence and adulthood, is peopled by different personality types, including hippies, Peace Corps volunteers, professional students, and militants—whose common theme is uneasiness with the prevailing values of their society.

the hippie world. Although they have mastered most of the tasks we consider central to the completion of adolescence, these young men and women are reluctant, unprepared, or unready to enter adulthood. They are characteristically preoccupied with their relationship to what they term the system or the establishment, asking themselves and others how, when, where, or indeed whether they can ever enter it. They are still but a minority of their age group, yet they exercise an influence all out of proportion to their numbers.

The concepts of developmental theory have yet to include an understanding of this stage of life. Existing theories of adolescence are useful in characterizing the *earlier* lives of such young men and women. Peter Blos' concept of protracted adolescence clearly applies to some in this age group; Blos says some adolescents are unwilling to accept adulthood because of fear and overweening narcissism. However, most of today's youths seem to base their delay of adult commitment on an accurate and rational analysis of the faults, inconsistencies, and problems of their society. Erik Erikson's concept of a psychosocial moratorium, a pause in the developmental sequence, is highly relevant to many of these young men and women, but with the major qualification that most of them show few signs of the acute identity diffusion that Erikson has said probably inspired such a moratorium. Anna Freud's discussions of adolescence are relevant to understanding these young men and women in their mid-teens but have less applicability to the older age group dis-

cussed here. The concepts of postadolescence developed by Helene Deutsch and Harry Stack Sullivan generally assume that the postadolescent is in the process of making precisely the marital and vocational commitments that these youths are profoundly unwilling to make.

PSYCHOLOGICAL CHARACTERISTICS

There appear to be several psychological characteristics that define youth as a stage of life. First, the central conscious focus of concern that unifies these youths is the *ambivalent testing of the connection of self and society*. What most distinguishes the youth from the adult is that the nature of the youth's bonds with society remains unsettled. The adult is committed to an enduring style of relationship with established institutions. The style itself may be deviant, revolutionary, criminal, conformist, or accommodating, but it is nevertheless set. The youth is still exploring his fundamental position toward society. Thus, youth's psychohistorical position is that of *disengagement from society*. Whatever his formal relationship to society, whether student, dropout, revolutionary, or service volunteer, his inner position is one of noncommitment to existing institutions. This disengagement is not necessarily followed by rejection. The attitude these youths hold is most often a questioning one, a feeling of a personal unreadiness rather than a radical rejection of society.

Another characteristic of this stage of life is the adoption of *youth-specific identities* that are not expected to outlast their youthful usefulness.

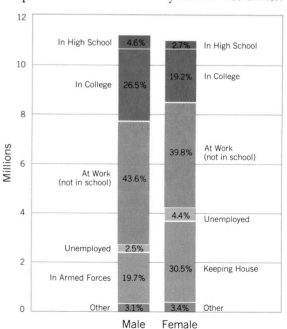

Figure 23.8. Where the eighteen- to twenty-four-year-olds are.

These identities differ from the more enduring identities of the adult in that the young men and women who hold them recognize that they are temporary, self-limiting, and transient. Young radicals, for example, do not expect to remain *young* radicals all of their lives but are prepared neither to become professional (old) radicals nor to enter into some nonradical relationship to the establishment. Although the identities of youth are limited temporally, they differ from the shallower, more fluctuating enthusiasms of adolescence in that they last many years, inspire deep loyalty, and generally provide a vantage point outside of the system from which youth can explore both society and self, testing the two against each other and attempting to find some lasting pattern of relationship. As soon as a more definitive engagement with society occurs—whether this engagement takes the form of a more enduring commitment to revolution and social change, a more enduring acceptance of the existing society, or an intermediate position—youth is over.

PSYCHOLOGICAL TASKS

Because the most prominent issue in youth is the ambivalent relationship between self and society, the psychological work of youth consists of two tasks: first, a renegotiation of the relationship between the individual and his past and the existing society; second, a *reformulation* of that part of the personality that represents and reflects social reality and cultural inheritance.

Let us consider first the renegotiation of the relationship between the individual and society.

There are enormous individual differences in how this renegotiation is accomplished. One youthful solution involves a determined attempt to change the society or some part of it so as to bring society in line with the individual's principles and needs. This, of course, is the solution of radicals, activists, and reformist youth, whether of the right or the left. Another, contrasting, solution is a systematic attempt to change one's self so as to fit with less anxiety or discomfort into the existing system. A third approach during youth is the effort to locate or carve out some special niche within the society where the qualities of the self can be preserved, enhanced, or acted upon.

The polar extremes during youth, then, are defined by societal activism and personal self-reform—by the revolutionary and the patient, as character types. The pure revolutionary seems to accept his own core values as given and seeks to transform the world in their image. The pure patient, the self-reformer, nominally accepts the demands of society and attempts to transform himself so as to meet them. But clinical experience has shown that these apparently opposite positions are often secretly related. For one thing, both self and society are infinitely complex, changing, and ambiguous. There is no such thing as perfect congruence or total conflict between them. Equally important, the ambivalence inherent in human development means that no one can ever hold either himself or society as totally responsible. As is known, the psychoanalytic patient of this age, although nominally committed to a rigorous program of self-transformation, often harbors an obdurate attribution of blame to society. And even the most radical revolutionary must suppress his own deep and subconscious doubts about whether his critique of society is much more than an expression of some personal inadequacy. Indeed, without this profound ambivalence about both self and society, youth does not occur. The young man or woman who is sure that he is right and society is wrong is, by his certainty, committed to the adult role of revolutionary or exile. Ambivalence, then, is an essential characteristic of youth; alternations between programs of self-change and social transformation are the rule.

The second basic psychological task of youth involves the analysis, synthesis, consolidation, and reformulation of the social and cultural aspects of the personality. At one level, this reformulation might be thought of as involving a further elaboration of ethical and moral orientations and principles (the superego), but for purposes of our analysis, it will be best to examine in detail the portions of the personality that reflect society and the cultural inheritance. In addition to the powerful dictates of parental teaching, everyone possesses an image, or an internalized representation of society, consisting of his accrued and elaborated experience with social institutions and their representatives, with their potentialities and defects. Everyone carries within him some notion of the social order, of how it works, of how it affects him, and of what he can expect from it. In most men and women, this image is largely implicit and rarely articulated; in all people, it is related to

other internalized images in fundamentally important ways.

Part of the intrapsychic work of youth, then, involves a reexamination, a redefinition, and a rearticulation of the internalized culture. Consciously, the focus during youth is often on questions of social ethics, personal integrity, problems of compromise and accommodation, the relationship between value and practice, the effect upon the self of involvement in social institutions, and the relative priority of struggles at self-reform and promotion of social change. A youth is likely to be concerned with the price of success; the real meaning of achievement; the possibilities of reward for effort; ethics and work; and the price in integrity of social effectiveness. The youth is also likely to be engaged in earnest efforts to root out personal characteristics that seem, in retrospect, to have developed from no firmer foundation than an effort to gain popularity or social approval. And the most intellectual youth often develop an idealized image of the social order toward which they strive in their personal and political actions. Finally, the more sophisticated youth self-consciously examine the entire cultural inheritance, the traditional political, social, and moral symbols that they have inherited from parents and society. In short, the adolescent reexamines his superego, but the youth reexamines his cultural inheritance as a whole.

PSYCHODYNAMICS

From a psychodynamic point of view, there appear to be two contrasting pathways into the

Figure 23.9. The revolutionary versus the patient.

stage of youth. One is the pathway from psychological strength, a pathway that leads some young men and women whose development has been unusually successful to be dissatisfied with their society and what it offers them. These young people seek to continue their own process of inner development and to postpone for a period of years or even decades their entry into the constraints of established society. On the other hand, there are clearly many who enter youth for neurotic reasons; these youths are unable to accept or come to terms with either the society that exists or the self they possess for unconscious reasons, whose origins lie in unexplored and uninterpreted childhood experiences. Keniston's studies have led him to conclude that most youths fall somewhere between the two poles; they show a mixture of both neurotic reluctance and principled unwillingness to accept the adulthood their society attempts to force upon them.

SOCIAL TASKS

Because youth involves efforts to transform, differentiate, elaborate, and modify the internalized representation of society, the behavior of youth typically entails an active exploration of the social order by a deliberate self-exposure to new groups, new places, and new social strata. Youth is a time of geographic and social-class mobility, during which the individual may identify far more profoundly with those of other classes, regions, and historical eras than with those of his own. This exploration sometimes requires deliberate self-immersion in poverty, in the underlife, even in de-

Figure 23.10. Social exploration may take the form of going on the road, joining a commune, trying the methods of Eastern philosophy, or choosing to live in poverty.

pravity. It frequently involves exaggerated geographic mobility, continual and even compulsive movement on the road.

The active testing of both self and society during this stage of life is characterized at times by a euphoric omnipotentiality—a sense that all things are possible, a feeling of utter freedom, a vista of limitless horizons and opportunities, and a conviction (not without some basis in reality) that the self is malleable, plastic, and open and can be shaped and bent in virtually any direction. This euphoria alternates with feelings of complete estrangement, absurdity, uprootedness, and disconnectedness that result from the inner ambivalence of youth. As yet undefined by specific social roles and institutional obligations, youth is a stage of life in which feelings of exile, meaninglessness, unrelatedness, homelessness, uselessness, and aimlessness are common and intense.

The central psychological achievement of youth is the acknowledgment of both self and society without denying either. Just as men and women sometimes achieve with each other a mutuality in which the separate uniqueness of each is a precondition for loving the other, so in youth, acknowledging the independent reality and valid claims for both self and society is a precondition for achieving a social engagement in which self and society exist as distinct yet interlocked entities.

There is as yet no adequate vocabulary to define the tasks and goals of youth—and its dangers. But the essence of youthful failure is a kind of alienation, either from self or from society. On the one hand, youth is constantly tempted by a total repudiation of the existence and importance of social reality, a quest for moral purity, and an insistence on total integrity. This intense and total rejection of society can be seen in some drug-culture, hippie, and alienated youth today. The rejection is also manifested in the revolutionary position that seeks the destruction of existing society, no matter what the human price. This solution preserves personal idealism and self-integrity at the expense of social engagement and effectiveness.

At the other extreme, youth can fail by totally acquiescing to social demands, by denying the claims of the self and abandoning personal integrity. Karen Horney and her followers have written eloquently of this state as "alienation from the real self"; Erich Fromm's concept of the marketing personality also describes it well. Here, social involvement is purchased at the price of denial of selfhood and integrity.

MOVING FROM YOUTH TO ADULTHOOD

Youth must end as the individual moves into a more enduring pattern of relationship with society. As youth ends, the amateur becomes the professional, and the individual accepts a social role that is likely thereafter to define his relationship to society. This social role may be a deviant one—revolutionary, criminal, mental patient, artist, innovator, or crank. But when youth ends, the individual's relationship to society is relatively settled.

The ending of youth may provoke a new period

of turmoil and crisis. To define a position vis-à-vis society commonly entails the fear of selling out, becoming frozen to a social role, bogging down in marriage and career, abandoning future growth— and for many the chilling fear becomes the icy reality.

YOUTH IN A SOCIAL CONTEXT

Youths whose privileged social position, affluence, superior intelligence, ethical commitments, or psychological disturbances make them most sensitive to historical currents of the time are especially unlikely to be automatically socialized and absorbed into the existing social system. In face of the rapid social change, all young people must reexamine and redefine their personal relationships to the past, including the cultural past, before they are ready to move ahead in the task of creating their own future. The reexamination of the cultural tradition by the more perceptive of the young has important and desirable consequences for the society at large. It means that the obsolete is continually being winnowed out from the enduring, that the problems and future direc-

tions of the society are continually being scrutinized, and that the society at large is assured a critical commentary upon its own functioning. American society urgently needs this commentary, even if it does not always like it.

Put more generally, the opening of a stage of youth to larger numbers of young men and women may turn out to be a part of the essential dynamic of social change and reform in modern societies. Within the past decade, youths have played a major role in social change in this country. They have exposed—in a way no previous group in American history has done—the disgraceful legacy of slavery and segregation in American society; they have been the key catalysts for the agonized reappraisal of American foreign policy, especially with regard to the war in Vietnam; and they have precipitated a wave of university reforms, involving a long-overdue recognition of the students' dignity, judgment, and maturity. It is almost certain that in the future, youth will continue to play a comparable role, a role that is valuable and may even be necessary for our society.

The Command Generation in their late thirties, forties, and early fifties—what are they like? The grown-up people who fancy themselves to be in charge of the various destinies of the world have in common that they have survived adolescence and youth but have not yet slipped into old age and senescence. Some are mature; some only strive toward maturity. All, however, are continually changing as they meet and either master or fall victim to the challenges of adulthood. Theirs is both the power and the anxiety of responsibility; the threat and the opportunity of independent challenge; the freedom from the legal and moral constraints of adolescence; and the necessity of preparing to grow old. Youth looks upon the life of the adult with amazed or amused disdain, but it is the adult who cannot disdain the problems of life, not the least of which may be youth.

Unit VII
Adulthood

What does it mean to be mature? No matter how old you are, assume for the moment that you are on the threshold of maturity. Before reading in this chapter what psychological theorists have said about maturity, spend a moment making a rough list of what maturity means to you. Try to write down what seem to you to be your own outstanding characteristics, good or bad, and then note beside them how they will have changed by the time you are psychologically mature.

Chances are that you have forecast maturity as a time when the problems of the present have disappeared, the worries are fewer, and the powers, greater. Most people see maturity as the ability and the opportunity to deal effectively with other people, with their environment, and with themselves. These assumptions are correct, but there is a great deal more to maturity.

All complete theories of personality have included a statement of what it means to be mature, what it means to function psychologically in an ideal fashion. By classifying these theories into types, or models, and removing the semantic stumbling blocks, it is possible to compare them in order to isolate their commonalities: major and basic agreements among them. These areas of agreement can then be considered the universals of mature functioning. But the comparison will also reveal basic differences between the theories, illustrating that one man's maturity may be another's archaic conformism or needless surrender to age. Metaphorically, an orange and a lemon are both citrus fruits, contain vitamin C, grow on trees, thrive in the same kind of soil under the same climatic conditions, and both are edible. All these are commonalities between oranges and lemons. They are important. Yet, to the eater, all these factors may fade in the face of the fact that an orange is sweet, but a lemon, bitter.

ALLPORT'S MATURE PERSON

The late Gordon Allport of Harvard stated the essence of maturity more insightfully than any other theorist. His ideas, in one form or another, have obtained nearly universal acceptance among students of the healthy adult personality. Gordon Allport made maturity a psychological issue. His struggles with the problem are all the more interesting because he made them public twice in his long career. The first statement of his notions of maturity came in the 1930s, while he was still a young man, and consisted of an easily remembered list of attributes of maturity. The later statement, from a chronologically older but psychologically wiser psychologist, came in the 1960s. The later statement is so much more varied, accepting, insightful, and human that the student can find no better definition of maturity than by reflecting on Allport's later views and their departure from an ordered list of attributes.

Allport's final statement found the mature person to be simultaneously both of himself and of others—in the realest sense of an involvement in mankind. Far from a retiring, older aesthete, the mature personality described by Allport is in and of the world—not only a participant in his own and others' strivings, activities, and ambitions but

24
The Mature Personality

fundamentally an *active* participant. His own personal, psychological house put into active and effective order, the mature personality relates warmly to other human beings, their goals, aspirations, and human hopes. The fully extended self, at maturity, accepts itself and others both objectively and compassionately. Allport recounts the anecdote in which Socrates arose in the middle of a performance of *The Clouds* in order to give his fellow spectators a better opportunity to compare his real features with those of the mask of the character lampooning him on the stage. His objective appraisal and acceptance of himself and his concern for the wishes and foibles of others characterized his maturity. In our day, Eugene McCarthy and, in some ways, Robert Kennedy seemed to share this characteristic.

Beyond public relating, Allport's mature personality has a realism based on experience with both success and failure. In the deepest sense, the mature personality must face his limits, come to grips with them, see them in the perspective of his abilities and successes, evaluate them, and learn to live with them; he must use them, appreciate them, and acquiesce to their limitations while reveling in their capabilities. A deep religiosity characterizes the mature personality, in the sense of recognition and acceptance of real for real, of sham for sham, of the possible and the impossible, of the desirable and the undesirable, of the attainable and the unattainable—all in and of themselves for their own inherent worth as human capacities and frailties shared by the self with mankind as a whole. In this sense, the mature personality embraces a unifying philosophy of life, which, in its essence, involves the capacity for death. Thus Erik Erikson's concept of ego integrity at the end of life readying man for his death harks back, as we shall see, to Allport's thinking on maturity.

THEORIES OF MATURITY

All theories of personality are no more than theories. No psychological construct can claim to define maturity outside of context, a context that includes cultural, ethical, and behavioral considerations and is oriented to an era of history and feeling. Many of the theories of maturity are summarized in Table 24.1. Before discussing their content, we shall categorize their substance and intent.

Salvatore Maddi has identified three basic ways of theorizing about the mature personality. These three models primarily emphasize *conflict, fulfillment,* or *consistency.* The *conflict model* assumes that an individual is continuously and inevitably in the grip of a clash between two great, opposing forces. Life, according to this model, is necessarily a compromise—at best involving a dynamic balance of the two forces, at worst involving the foredoomed attempt to deny the existence of one of them. In the *dynamic balance* of the two opposing forces rests the secret of the mature personality.

There are two versions of the conflict model. They differ in identifying the opposing forces. In the *psychosocial* version, the source of one force is within the individual, while the other comes from

Figure 24.1. Conflict can occur between the individual and his family or it can involve the individual in society.

Table 24.1. Theories of Maturity

Models	Forces	Goals	Theorists
Conflict			
Psychosocial	Two—one in person, the other in society	To achieve a dynamic balance of the forces	Sigmund Freud Erik Erikson
Intrapsychic	Two—both within person	To achieve a dynamic balance of the forces	Otto Rank Rollo May Andreas Ángyal David Bakan
Fulfillment			
Actualization	One—within person	To realize one's inherent potential	Carl Rogers Abraham Maslow
Perfection	One—within person	To live up to culturally defined (internalized) ideals of excellence and meaningfulness	Alfred Adler Gordon Allport Erich Fromm
Consistency	None	To balance one's expectations with the feedback from one's environment	George A. Kelly David C. McClelland Donald W. Fiske Salvatore Maddi

groups or societies outside him. In the *intrapsychic* version, both forces exist within the person. Both theories based on the conflict model consider the content and goal of the two postulated forces to be given by nature and to be unchangeable.

The *fulfillment* model assumes only one psychological force, resident within the individual, and interprets mature living as the progressively greater expression of this force. Although conflict is possible in the fulfillment model, it is neither necessary nor continuous. Indeed, when it occurs, it represents an unfortunate failure in mature living. In this model, the mature personality is one that expresses fully the one individual force, without being bogged down in conflict.

As with the conflict model, there are two differ-

ent versions of the fulfillment model. In the *actualization* version, the force is in the form of an inherited blueprint determining the person's special capabilities; living maturely comprises the processes of realizing these capabilities. The *perfection* version, on the other hand, turns from determinants to internalized but culturally universal ideals of what is fine, excellent, and meaningful in life. The governing force of the personality comprises the individual's strivings toward the postulated ideals of perfection.

Theories of personality based on the *consistency model* make surprisingly little or no statement of what constitutes maturity. They emphasize the formative influence of feedback from the external world. If environmental feedback is consistent with what the individual expects—what

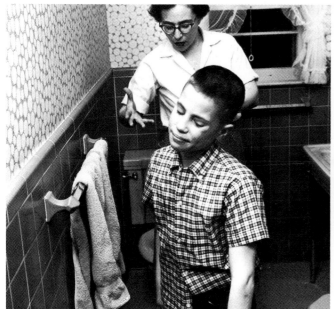

has been customary—he is quiescent. But if there is uncomfortable inconsistency between the feedback and the individual's expectancy, there is pressure to decrease the inconsistency. Life is therefore an extended attempt to maintain consistency. It is possible to derive statements about maturity from such theories because whatever constitutes the best way of maintaining consistency between expectations and outcomes is presumably satisfactory and hence mature. But consistency models will not be further discussed here because they fail to make specific statements about what actions and attitudes serve to maintain the postulated balance in individual cases.

CONFLICT STATEMENTS OF MATURITY

For conflict theories, maturity involves the ability to minimize inevitable but painful, debilitating, and frustrating conflict, that is, to strike the most effective compromise between the conflicting forces.

PSYCHOSOCIAL CONFLICT THEORIES

In the psychosocial version of conflict theory, one force in the individual opposes another in society. The specific nature of the compromise between the two forces determines the individual's degree of maturity. It is assumed that, by nature, the individual invariably desires things and behaves in ways that are contrary to society's rules and requirements. But the social force is considered the stronger because it is based on the power of countless institutions and eras of culture. Thus, the individual must adjust to the roles, responsi-

Figure 24.2. According to Freud, the mature person learns to resolve conflict through work and love.

bilities, and mores of the society in which he lives. The better the adjustment, the more mature the personality.

□ *Sigmund Freud* The strongest expression of the psychosocial conflict position is to be found in the writings of Sigmund Freud. When asked what the good life entails, Freud answered simply, *"Lieben und arbeiten"*—"To love and to work." By love Freud meant primarily the heterosexual love that leads to procreation and family life. Other forms of love, as in friendship and nurturant devotion of parenthood, are also implied. This definition accords with the ordinary experience of mature love. Freud's mature working entails productive and constructive furtherance of the ends of civilization and culture. To work and to love in Freud's sense involve healthy adjustment, fitting in, and carrying one's share of personal and social responsibility.

Freud traces the growth of personality from birth, when the infant's personality involves only an *id*—Freud's summary term for life, sexual, and aggressive instincts that clamor for satisfaction irrespective of the rights, needs, or wishes of anyone else. Soon the child develops to the point where he has a functioning *ego*, an organized and effective basis for operating in the outside world. Then he is potentially a lethal weapon: a seething cauldron of selfish desires (id) that can be put into effective action (ego). At this point he becomes such a burden to his parents and other members of society that his freedom of expression must be curtailed—in short, he must be socialized. Through punishment for unrestricted ex-

pression of the id and more positive instruction in what is acceptable, he develops a *superego*, or conscience, which is the internalized version of society's taboos and sanctions.

The child, then, must find his way out of this dilemma: He faces the possibility of guilt and punishment from the superego for nothing more than free expression of his true nature; he cannot change his true nature—his instincts are set by the terms of his biological inheritance. But society and its internalized representative, the superego, are so powerful that the threat first of punishment and later of guilt is too strong to be faced. He must compromise, and the form of that compromise must be either to inhibit his instincts from expression or to somehow change them into a more socially acceptable form. Such inhibition is accomplished by *defenses*, the most powerful of which is called *sublimation*. Attempting to compromise by wholesale inhibition of instincts constitutes psychopathology, not maturity. What is considered mature is to transform or *sublimate* instinctual desires and expressions into socially acceptable, constructive thoughts and actions.

Two comparisons will help to clarify this developmental trend. Whereas the small boy, according to Freud, wants to possess his mother sexually and kill his father to remove him as a rival, the mature man wishes to possess sexually only someone outside his family and to protect his interests from other males in general, not his father in particular. Again, whereas the small child wants food and water even if that means depriving others of them, the mature adult tries to satisfy

his life instincts while also caring that enough is produced and available for others.

From a developmental viewpoint, it is important to recognize that for Freud the original selfish and antisocial nature of the instincts does not change. The instincts come up against a defense system erected by the ego in cooperation with the superego. The instincts are either defended against and kept from experience or sublimated so that they are more acceptable. The defense process works so well that most persons lose all conscious awareness of their underlying primitive drives. Maturity, for Freud, requires defenses—a somewhat pessimistic conclusion following from the original assumption that psychosocial conflict is inevitable and continuous.

The psychopathological attempt to ease conflict by denying any expression to instincts also requires defenses. The difference between psychopathology and maturity is in the nature of the defenses. Those of psychopathology are restrictive and crippling; they permit insufficient instinctual gratification and generate neurotic discomfort. The defenses of maturity block expression of instincts just enough to keep anxiety guilt at a low level and to avoid the negative judgment of society.

□ *Erik Erikson* Erik Erikson has elaborated upon Freud's view to yield a more differentiated picture of maturity. It must be emphasized that Freud considered development to be more or less over by the time puberty is reached. Freud divided the prepuberty years into four major stages —the *oral, anal, phallic,* and *latency* periods of

psychosexual development (see Chapter 7)— whereas the entire time of adulthood is lumped together as the *genital* period. While generally subscribing to Freud's views for the prepuberty years, Erikson also divides adolescence and adulthood into four developmental ages, which overlap considerably. He called these the ages of (1) *ego identity versus role diffusion,* (2) *intimacy versus isolation,* (3) *generativity versus stagnation,* and (4) *ego integrity versus despair.* The first term in each comparison obviously indicates what is ideal, or mature. Erikson's elaboration of Freud's view of mature loving and working then includes: (1) a clear and continuing sense of who one is and what one's goals are (ego identity); (2) ability and interest in relating closely in both the physical and the psychological sense (intimacy); (3) ability and desire to be productive and to nurture and devote one's self to others, as to children (generativity) and to productive work; and (4) an overarching acceptance of and satisfaction in one's life (ego integrity). The truly mature adult is one who has so thoroughly experienced having-been that he is able to face and accept not-to-be, the end of life.

INTRAPSYCHIC CONFLICT THEORIES

Intrapsychic conflict theories stress harmony much more than adjustment in discussing the mature personality. Both forces in conflict are posited as universally inherent in each human psyche, in contrast to Freud's assumption that one intrapsychic agency, the superego, arises from outside, societal influence.

Figure 24.3. The id and the superego.

□ *Otto Rank* The clearest example of an intrapsychic conflict theory was formulated by Otto Rank. He assumed that there exists in each person a *fear of life* and a *fear of death*. The fear of life manifests itself in a wish not to be separated from people and things and an unwillingness to face change; the fear of death is manifested by the drive to be an independent, masterful individual. If the fear of life becomes the stronger of the two, the fear of death will be denied, and the person will be what Rank calls an *average man*. The average man is a conformist socially and fails generally to impress himself upon his activities in terms that would express his individual worth. If it is the fear of death that becomes strongest, the fear of life will be denied, and the person will become *neurotic*. The neurotic is isolated and rejecting of others rather than truly individual; in his distaste for conformity, he finds no way to relate to people and things outside himself. The average man and the neurotic are both psychopathological personalities, according to Rank. In fact, the former is considered sicker than the latter.

Rank calls the truly mature person the *artist*, though this term is used broadly to denote one who has a creative approach to life—not necessarily one who paints, sculpts, or writes. The artist puts his talent into his work and his genius into his life. The artist minimizes both the fear of life and the fear of death by becoming an individual, differentiated being who can relate to and be accepted and respected by other people. The artist neither rejects nor conforms to outside frames of reference but tries to interact with them in his own individual way. He can both change those frames of reference and be changed by them. The emphasis in this view of maturity is on harmony between the two intrapsychic forces, which, if achieved, leads to harmony with the external world.

□ *Angyal, Bakan, and May* Three other personality theories correspond very closely to Rank's position. Andreas Angyal focuses upon the tendency toward *autonomy* and the tendency toward *surrender*, both of which have to be served to reach maturity. David Bakan refers to the *agentic* and *communal* tendencies in man. Although the words used by these theorists are somewhat different, their views of what constitutes maturity are really much alike. Indeed, many modern existentialists, among them Rollo May, hold the same views. May refers to life as a series of choice points, in which one can move ahead, change, and strike out toward the unknown or can choose to remain with the known. Although choosing the unknown leads to *existential anxiety*, relying on what is familiar leads to *ontological guilt*. May's existential anxiety is related to Rank's fear of death; ontological guilt, to the fear of life.

FULFILLMENT STATEMENTS OF MATURITY

Although fulfillment theorists recognize that conflict can occur, they view it as arising from some failure of society toward the individual. Conflict may, in fact, jeopardize the attainment of maturity by bogging the person down in defensive operations aimed at coping with the external

Figure 24.4. An artist's conception of Rank's fear of life and fear of death.

threat and by keeping him from the task of fulfilling himself, which is the only valid process leading to true maturity.

ACTUALIZATION-FULFILLMENT THEORIES

Actualization-fulfillment theories conclude that *it is the mark of maturity to follow one's preordained blueprint wherever it may lead, in freedom and without compromise.* What is best for the person to be and to do is what he is best suited for by virtue of the conditions of his individuality.

□ *Carl Rogers* The purest expression of this view is found in the personality theory of Carl Rogers. His statement on maturity is contained in the concept of the *fully functioning person.* The characteristics of such a person are (1) *openness to experience*, the state where every stimulus from the organism or the external environment is freely relayed through the individual without any distortion by defenses; (2) *existential living*, the ability to live fully and vitally in each moment, as if it were one's last; (3) *organismic trusting*, a willingness to do one's own thing spontaneously without requiring a full and rational understanding of one's actions before performing them; (4) *experiential freedom*, the subjective sense that one is free to choose among alternative courses of action in defining one's life; and (5) *creativity*, the capability for producing new and effective thoughts, actions, or things. In this view of maturity, there is nothing of compromise, conflict, defense, adjustment. Nor is there emphasis on a carefully constructed and policed harmony of disparate tendencies. Instead, the person is viewed as constructing his own life, with a strength and sureness contributed by the burgeoning development of his inherent potentialities.

The fully functioning person is not antisocial or isolated; he can appreciate and enjoy people but does not neurotically need them. This view of maturity is a more self-reliant one than is possible within the restrictions of the conflict model. All that a person needs from society in order to develop into a mature person is *unconditional positive regard*: acceptance, respect, appreciation, and tolerance. All else that is needed will come about through the natural tendency of potentialities to press for expression. Because these potentialities were originally subject to natural selection, there is nothing in them, according to Rogers, that is inherently dangerous to self or others. This position is opposite to that of Freud.

But it frequently happens that society fails the person by giving him only *conditional positive regard*; he is taught that some of the things he does are acceptable while others are not. Because all things he does are expressive of inherent potentialities, he is left in a state of conflict, which he can reduce only by denying a real part of himself, defensively withholding from consciousness any realization of the unacceptable parts of himself. Whereas in psychosocial conflict theories, some form of defensiveness is considered necessary to attain maturity, in actualization-fulfillment theories, conflict defines maladjustment or psychopathology.

□ *Abraham Maslow* The other notable theorist in this area is Abraham Maslow, who agrees very closely with Rogers. He calls the mature person *self-actualized* and numbers among his characteristics: *realistic orientation; acceptance* of self, others, and the natural world; *spontaneity; task orientation*—as opposed to self-preoccupation; *sense of privacy; independence;* vivid *appreciativeness; spirituality* that is not necessarily religious in a formal sense; sense of *identity with mankind;* feelings of *intimacy* with a few loved ones; *democratic values;* recognition of the *differences between means and ends; humor* that is philosophical rather than hostile; *creativeness;* and *nonconformism.* Although this list of characteristics is long and heterogeneous enough to escape easy integration into an organized picture of personality, the mature personalities envisaged by both Maslow and Rogers are similar.

Self-actualized individuals are rare. Any single individual may number only one or two among his friends and acquaintances throughout a whole lifetime. Because they make full use of their freely developed potentialities, self-actualized individuals are likely to be well placed and influential in the world. For these two reasons, Maslow turned to the spheres of public service and to historical biography in his studies of and search for self-actualized individuals. Among the persons in history considered self-actualized by Maslow are individuals as diverse as Abraham Lincoln, Eleanor Roosevelt, and Walt Whitman.

PERFECTION-FULFILLMENT THEORIES

The humanistic quality of actualization-fulfillment theories stands in contrast to the idealistic framework of perfection-fulfillment theories, in which the governing force is defined as the attempt to achieve ideals of what is true, good, and beautiful.

□ *Alfred Adler* A notable example of the perfection-fulfillment position can be found in the theory of Alfred Adler, who postulated a basic human tendency to strive for perfection. Adler was especially preoccupied with the sort of striving for perfection that requires overcoming some real or imagined inferiority—as when the eloquent Demosthenes overcame stuttering by practicing speaking with stones in his mouth. Adler assumed that the push toward perfection concerns not only the individual but also the society in which he participates. By working toward the perfection of his society, the person is also working toward his own perfection.

The person who achieves maturity will combine an *active,* initiating approach to life with a *constructive* style of interaction with people. Somewhat less mature is the *passive-constructive* person, who is charming rather than ambitious. But to be either *active-destructive*—rebellious— or *passive-destructive*—despairing—is immature. The resulting life style of the mature person resembles that of Rank's artist, although no compromise aimed at easing conflict is implied.

Whether a person will reach full maturity or not depended for Adler on the *family atmosphere* in which he grows up. If the atmosphere is one of cooperation, mutual trust, and respect, the child will be encouraged to overcome inferiorities in a manner that is constructive for him and for

Figure 24.5. Actualization-fulfillment theory sees man carried along on a preordained route; perfection-fulfillment theory sees man as a being that strives or climbs toward his goals. A good analogy is the elevator versus the stairway.

others. If competition and distrust are the rule, he will be destructive in trying to overcome inferiorities. The family ambience described echoes Rogers' emphasis on unconditional positive regard.

□ **Gordon Allport**   Another important perfection-fulfillment theorist is Gordon Allport, who was discussed earlier. Generally, Allport believed that the road to maturity requires a turning, in early childhood, from primary reliance on *opportunistic* functioning, which is biologically defined and has to do with physical survival, to primary reliance on *propriate* functioning, which stresses trying to become what one deeply believes one should be. This shift in functioning is facilitated by forms of unconditional positive regard, and an individual may fail to make the shift if he has been maimed by an exceptionally depriving environment.

□ **Erich Fromm**   The final perfection-fulfillment theorist to be considered is Erich Fromm. Like Allport, Fromm distinguishes between man's *animal nature* (opportunistic functioning) and *human nature* (propriate functioning). Anyone who continues into adulthood giving free rein to his animal nature is psychopathological. Maturity, the expression of one's human nature, requires some of the same things emphasized by Maslow and Allport: to find bases whereby one can feel *rooted*; to *belong* to some people or frame of reference; to give and receive *love*; and to develop some basis for *self-esteem*. Fromm agrees with the others that in order to ensure this sound development, the youngster must experience love, acceptance, and respect from the significant adults in his life.

If he is thus graced, the person develops a *productive orientation*, Fromm's term for maturity. Immature orientations may be *receptive, exploitative, hoarding,* or *marketing.* The receptive, exploitative, and hoarding orientations are similar to Freud's oral-incorporative, oral-aggressive, and anal character types, respectively. This similarity is not surprising, for Fromm was deeply influenced by Freud early in his career. The marketing orientation, however, expresses Fromm's originality as a theorist and his emphasis upon perfection and the failure to achieve it. The marketing person treats himself and others as if they were commodities to be bought and sold to the highest bidder. He becomes what it is expedient to be, behaving opportunistically rather than functioning in a principled manner. In extreme degrees, all of the orientations but the productive one are considered psychopathological.

It is difficult to describe succinctly the productive orientation because it amounts to a conglomerate of mild forms of the other orientations. It borrows such characteristics as *acceptance, responsiveness,* and *devotion* from the receptive orientation; *activeness, initiative,* and *pride* from the exploitative orientation; *practicality, frugality,* and *carefulness* from the hoarding orientation; and *purposefulness, flexibility,* and *efficiency* from the marketing orientation. The productive orientation is a sound basis for creative, responsible, committed functioning—in short, for maturity.

Figure 24.6. According to Adler and Rogers, family atmosphere is most important for the child's psychological development and his ultimate achievement of emotional maturity.

The Common Denominator

The above exploration of the salient points in each type of theory permits the student to relate these theories to each other and to see both the common grounds that exist and the unalterable oppositions.

There are some human characteristics that all these theorists consider (with varying degrees of emphasis) to be mature. The ability to be intimate—to give and accept love, affection, sexual response—is considered necessary. The ability to be sociable—to have friends, to be devoted to and nurturant of those close to one—is considered positive, as long as there is no implication of conformity in the sociability. It is also agreed that some clear, vivid sense of who one is—what one's aims and powers are, what is best for one—is characteristic of maturity. Almost a direct result of all these characteristics is an interest in and an ability to do productive work. These agreements reflect a view of maturity that has been accumulated over centuries.

That some of these conclusions have a commonsense ring does not, of course, demean the personality theories or theorists. Theorists—those seeking to explain the physical world as well as those trying to understand the intricate human personality—ask themselves questions based on sometimes commonplace observations. Isaac Newton noted that things always fall down. We all know that; but he set out to explain why. A psychologist might observe the vast amounts of literature and music devoted to love, the time that boys and girls spend circling and sensing each other, the despair of those unloved, and he may ask why love is so important to man and what happens to produce people who cannot love.

There are basic differences among the theories. One sharp theoretical difference is echoed concretely in society today: some theories emphasize rationality and planfulness as vital to maturity (psychosocial conflict, intrapsychic conflict, and perfection-fulfillment theories), whereas others (actualization-fulfillment theory) see the mature person as trusting his intuition and reacting spontaneously. This conflict between trust in stability, dependability, predictability and belief in flexibility and spontaneity might be an apt definition of the generation gap.

Another striking difference among the theories has a deep philosophical implication: they offer diametrically opposed views of the nature of man. Psychosocial conflict theories see the mature personality as a veneer that only masks man's immutable, selfish animal nature. Fulfillment theories hold man's nature to be basically good, needing only support to blossom and noninterference to express itself.

Although these differences reveal real and deep divisions among theorists of personality, they do not alter the substantial agreement among the theorists as to what constitutes maturity. Each theory takes a somewhat different view of maturity, but that is perhaps proper, given the complexity of adult human life.

Figure 24.7. The generation gap may well be defined by the gap between spontaneity and predictability.

Bertrand Russell enjoyed a longer period of adulthood than most of us will have, but also a life filled with change and experience—intellectual, emotional, political, spiritual, philosophical. His autobiography chronicles his private and public concerns, and the following excerpts illustrate that adults are not the stable end product of a sequence of development; rather, adulthood is a part of the sequence.

Russell went to prison for six months in 1918 because of his pacifist activities; he was forty-six years old: "I became filled with despairing tenderness toward the young men who were to be slaughtered, and with rage against all the statesmen of Europe. . . . In the midst of this, I was myself tortured by patriotism. Love of England is very nearly the strongest emotion I possess, and in appearing to set it aside at such a moment, I was making a very difficult renunciation. Nevertheless, I never had a moment's doubt as to what I must do. . . . I knew it was my business to protest, however futile protest might be."

In the early 1930s Russell wrote a book titled *Which Way to Peace?* in which he maintained the pacifist position that had sent him to jail in World War I. But in 1940 he decided he ". . . had to support what was necessary for victory in the Second War, however difficult victory might be to achieve, and however painful its consequences. . . . Although my reason was wholly convinced, my emotions followed with reluctance. My whole nature had been involved in my opposition to the First War, whereas it was a divided self that favoured the Second. I have

never since 1940 recovered the same degree of unity between opinion and emotion as I had possessed from 1914 to 1918."

Although Bertrand Russell was an extraordinary man, all adults have potential for change, and although the course their development takes may not influence the conduct of public affairs, the changes within them—the growth of the individual—may be what defines the course of civilizations.

Russell wrote in the 1920s: "When the War was over, I saw that all I had done had been totally useless except to myself. I had not saved a single life or shortened the war by one minute. . . . for myself, I had acquired a new philosophy and a new youth. I had got rid of the don and the Puritan. I had learned an understanding of instinctive processes which I had not possessed before, and I had acquired a certain poise from standing so long alone."

Defining Adult Growth

The study of psychological development has too long ignored adult growth. The two prevailing commonsense theories about normal development in adults neatly contradict one another. The theory proposed depends on the age, social status, and life style of the theorist. Some say that adulthood is a terminal state of existence: after raising the kids, becoming definitively involved in a job, settling into a long-term marriage, and adopting a comfortable temperamental style, the adult maintains an incredible constancy until aging and se-

25
Personality and Intellectual Change

nility work their effects. The other theory says that this constancy is a foolish and defensive stance in the face of life's variety; that it is necessary to bend to life in order not to break; that is better to shift gears frequently rather than drone along; and that changing times call for flexible people. Common sense, then, may not help much in defining adult growth, but it certainly provides extreme alternatives.

Because the obvious and dramatic growth of children, even in most ordinary circumstances, occurs within a comparatively few years, child development is easily observed and therefore relatively easy to study. But adult change, growth, and development are intricate and are muted by the long years over which they occur. Investigating adult development immediately raises a number of philosophical problems, and the varieties of adult development lead to very practical problems of research design.

Central to any attempt to define change in adulthood is the problem of defining adulthood —or maturity—itself. In the preceding chapter many theories of maturity were discussed. Although some of their hypotheses and conclusions contradicted each other, there was enough coincidence to permit an outline of the characteristics that define a mature adult—at least in Western society in the last half of the twentieth century.

Ideally, a developmental theory should aspire to rise above particular times and places in history, particular contents of individual lives or societies, and particular outputs valued by some but

not by others. Some aspects of the study of child development, discussed in earlier units of this book, have succeeded reasonably well in this aim. Both Piaget's stages of cognitive development and Kohlberg's levels of moral development have demonstrated that their invariant sequences of stages can be found in many different cultures. Similar theories defining the stages of adult development do not have the same universality, as discussed later in this chapter.

There is one theorist of development, however, whose work, perhaps more comprehensively and definitively than any others so far, has identified the properties of the evolutionary development of an individual life in an objective, noncultural context. Although Heinz Werner's work is not easy to understand because it is highly abstract, his theoretical framework provides the best point from which to view and assess many of the findings about the years of adult development. Werner's work is summarized in the following paragraphs so that the empirical studies discussed later in the chapter may be related to his theory.

Werner's Theory

Werner deals with *processes* of human life rather than with *qualities*. One of these processes, which continues throughout life, is a development from *syncretic* (global) functioning to differentiated functioning and finally to functioning that is both *differentiated* and *articulated*. This sequence may be enacted in miniature each time a person is confronted with an unfamiliar situation, but it is also meant to describe an ongoing direction in human development over a lifetime. For example, earlier it was shown that infants' motor development proceeds from reflexes involving the entire body to a one-year-old's ability to pick up a marble with his thumb and forefinger. The change is ongoing—from a global muscular response to a differentiated and purposeful articulated use of the muscles.

A metaphor for the sequence in adult life might be the following: A fourteen-year-old who is about to learn algebra buys a textbook for his course. He looks at the book, knowing that it represents a field of mathematics, a well-defined and coherent area of human thought, yet the printing, the black marks on the paper, are all but unintelligible to him. He starts his course and begins to differentiate the signs and operations and can begin to solve equations; at this point he is operating in a differentiated way but one that is not yet articulated. If he finishes the course and takes another in geometry, he will learn that these algebraic expressions can define a geometrical shape. His early global understanding that there exists a discipline called "algebra" is now differentiated—he knows what algebra can and cannot do —yet also articulated—he can, if he chooses, design his own mathematically expressed shapes.

Another important process is the movement toward *dominance* over one's environment. A person develops from being a *reactor* to being an *operator*; his developing capability allows him to be progressively better at selecting structures and

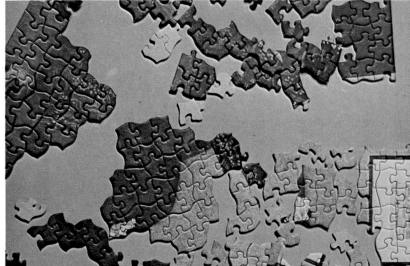

Figure 25.1. The progression from global functioning to functioning that is both differentiated and articulated can be analogized in the assembling of a jigsaw puzzle: the person at first knows only that the jumble of parts represents a coherent whole; he then works to differentiate those pieces into understandable parts, and finally he associates all the parts into a whole that he now understands.

organizing means to achieve intended ends. But simultaneously there is a movement from *egocentricity* to increased *perspective* of others' points of view and of the relationship between one's own viewpoint and that of others. Two other ongoing processes are a development from *lability* to *stability* in terms of his own structure and from *rigidity* to *flexibility* in terms of his response to the environment. All together, Werner's properties of the life process constitute a comprehensive coverage of various broad aspects of individual functioning.

The optimal adult, then, in Werner's context imposes more organization on his environment than his environment imposes on him; he views events and feelings from the perspective of others as well as from his own; and his functioning is both discrete and articulated while still being both flexible and stable.

All of these characteristics are *formal* properties of individual development and as such are logically independent of time, content, specific behavioral output, or a particular set of values. They do not require that a particular content or life style be endorsed as the valued one toward which normal development should proceed. The "good" man need not be chosen before research can proceed. Life is viewed broadly as an ongoing, evolutionary process, developing along specific lines but with a wide variety of contents and styles.

RESEARCH STUDIES IN ADULT DEVELOPMENT

Before the results of empirical investigations of adulthood can be considered, their limitations must be considered. Some difficulties will be remedied in time as more longitudinal studies are able to report their results, but because lives cannot be conducted in laboratories, some problems will never be solved.

First, the character of adult life can only be known by comparing the adult with both the adolescent and the aged person. But no studies have done both simultaneously. Obviously, different characteristics will emerge from a comparison of youths and adults than from a comparison of adults and the aged. Consequently, psychologists' understanding is still segmented and does not reflect a clear comprehension of the total life span.

LONGITUDINAL METHOD

Many psychologists say that the most penetrating and the most certain information about the meaning of development is provided by longitudinal study of changes in the same person from childhood to old age. This type of longitudinal study, however, has limitations—particularly when content, rather than process, is being measured. The results of such measurement over a thirty-year period may very well reflect a generalized cultural shift that actually characterizes all age groups living at that time in history rather than an individual, age-related development. If there were longitudinal data for eighty-year-olds, we could conclude that they naturally had developed a liking for musical comedy and an uneasiness about heights, when in fact these changes would have been due to the invention of television and the airplane.

CROSS-SECTIONAL METHOD

Much of the research reported to date employs the cross-sectional method, that is, comparison of different age groups at the same point in time. Behavioral or attitudinal differences between people of various ages are then assumed to be developmental changes.

Neither the longitudinal nor the cross-sectional method provides certain and pure information about adult development because each is affected by historical and cultural shifts in values and outlooks. For example, shifts in the behavior of subjects in a longitudinal study who are between twenty and fifty years of age may be the result of either age changes or general cultural changes between 1940 and 1970. The cross-sectional method may reflect the effects of a person's having been young in the 1920s compared with those of growing up in the 1950s. For these reasons, it is difficult to say what differences between twenty- and fifty-year-olds are really individual developmental changes.

If identical differences between age groups were found by both methods, we could say with some degree of certainty that the results were age related. We would see that persons at two different ages of vulnerability were affected in the same way at two different times in history (see Figure 25.2). For this reason many psychologists say that the ideal design for investigating age-related changes would involve both the longitudinal and the cross-sectional methods. Figure 25.3 shows graphically how a change in cultural values can be corroborated by using both study methods.

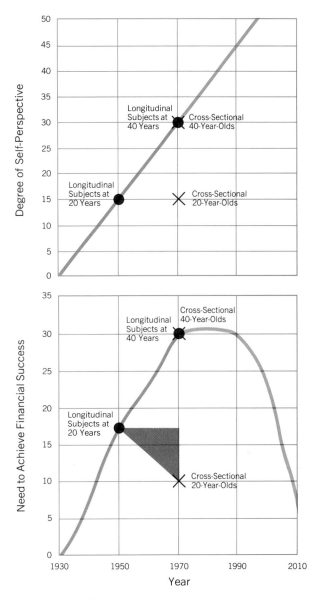

Figure 25.2. Drawn from hypothetical data, this graph illustrates a developmental change in degree of self-perspective that is corroborated by both a longitudinal and a cross-sectional study. The conclusion that can be drawn from these results—that the degree of self-perspective increases between age twenty and age forty— is independent of any cultural shift. It is assumed that the study was done in 1970. All the longitudinal subjects and the cross-sectional forty-year-old subjects would have been born in 1930; the cross-sectional twenty-year-old subjects would have been born in 1950.

Figure 25.3. Drawn from hypothetical data, this graph illustrates a developmental change, seen both in the longitudinal and the cross-sectional study, that reflects a cultural shift. The need to achieve financial success is much less important to twenty-year-olds born in 1950 than it was to the longitudinal twenty-year-olds, born in 1930; yet the forty-year-old cross-sectional subjects and the forty-year-old longitudinal subjects, who were born in the same year (1930), show the same need to achieve financial success. It is assumed that the study was done in 1970.

The real limitations to measuring adult development have been noted; it must also be noted that adult subjects almost never arrange themselves into neat, captive groups and so are not easily secured as subjects. Children in a classroom come neatly age ordered and have very little to say about whether or not they wish to participate in a psychological study, but it is hard to find a willing group of thirty-five-year-olds all in one room. Even in the face of all these difficulties, some studies have been completed, and the existing empirical findings will now be reviewed. Most studies have not been conducted with the guidance of a comprehensive theory, but Werner's dimensions of the life process will help in understanding many of them.

STUDIES OF ADOLESCENCE TO ADULTHOOD

Much of the longitudinal research concerned with the transitional period between adolescence and adulthood has focused on *consistency* in behavior or attitudes rather than on changes. The question that researchers most often ask is: If the adolescent's relative position on some dimension (compared to other adolescents) is known, can his adult position (compared to other adults) be predicted? The answers from various studies are generally in reasonable agreement with each other. However, almost all the evidence is too weak to permit prediction of any individual adolescent's adult status. Achievement behavior (particularly in men), interest in intellectual mastery, and general level of both social and physical re-

sponsiveness are all moderately consistent between adolescence and adulthood. Developments in these areas are not usually dramatic.

The period of transition from adolescence to adulthood is usually the time when personal heterosexual problems get solved. Jerome Kagan and Howard Moss interpreted most of their results in this light. They found consistency during this transition for sex-typed behaviors, such as aggressiveness in boys and passivity in girls, and inconsistency when the earlier behavior was incompatible with the individual's sex, such as dependency in boys. In this sense, development proceeds in a direction toward society's ideal types. But notice that a cultural change in the definition of sex-appropriate behavior, such as is taking place in the present generation of youth, would reduce the probability of repeating this finding with other longitudinal groups at a later time in history.

Mervin Freedman conducted a longitudinal study in which Vassar girls were tested as undergraduates and later as alumnae. He found that as adults they had become more capable, cooperative, efficient, resourceful, conscientious, patient, helpful, sympathetic, calm, deliberate, spontaneous, and, of course, talkative. These changes again recall familiar trends in middle-class, white womanhood.

Jeanne Block and Norma Haan used a longitudinal method that permits the assessment of the saliency of different aspects of the personality within its total organization. They investigated the general personalities of adults as compared to

their personalities when they were adolescents and found greater equanimity and effectiveness in the adults. Their overall results support the conclusion that personality functioning is reorganized between adolescence and adulthood—and in ways that are consistent with Werner's characterizations of the ongoing life process. The functional organizations of adulthood reflected the following characteristics relative to those of adolescence: (1) Adults showed greater possibilities of regulating environmental impact by self-impositions. The adults were more productive and satisfied with themselves; they gave advice more, aspired to more, fantasied less, and were less inclined to withdraw when they were frustrated. (2) The adults also exhibited greater perspective about themselves and about the positions of others. They were more giving, introspective, sympathetic, philosophically concerned, and evaluative of their own and others' motivations. They were also found to be less sensuous, rebellious, competitive, and pushing of limits, and the women were less self-indulgent. In Werner's terms, the adults' responses were both more discrete and more articulated—they were more concerned with being objective; they were personally less rigid; and at the same time they were more dependable and therefore more stable.

Three main life events, with varying cultural meanings and contents, usually occur during the early adult years—occupational commitment, marriage, and parenthood. Most societies mark entry into adulthood by these three occurrences;

Figure 25.4. Longitudinal studies that have focused on the transition from adolescence to adulthood have found consistency in sex-typed behaviors—aggression in boys and passivity in girls—but if such studies are carried out with this college generation's children, the findings will most likely be very different.

however, there is a wide range from one culture to another as to when these events occur. Unfortunately, the impact of these events in *furthering* adult development has not been adequately studied, even though maturing effects are commonly ascribed to all three.

CAREER CHOICE

Career choice in American society is most frequently a process of successive commitment and rejection until a person finally achieves an acceptable match between a possible reality and his personal interests and capabilities. Most investigators have found that the process of vocational choice is more a matter of rejecting alternatives —as the young person becomes increasingly differentiated, discrete, and stable in his thinking— than a discovery of new choices. Undoubtedly, the young adult's finer discriminations, compared

to the adolescent's often unrealistic globality, is accompanied by more intense commitments to fewer interests.

In a longitudinal study, E. K. Strong found that the interest patterns of four different groups of Stanford students were quite stable eighteen years later. Most of Strong's subjects were satisfied with their vocations in their late thirties. The eighteen-year interval brought an increase for the entire sample in two scales that are concerned with controlling and managing others: public administrator and personnel manager. These findings are consistent with trends for the same period found in more general studies of personality change and reflect again the movement toward greater imposition of self on the environment. In their late thirties, Strong's subjects thought that "freedom to direct their own work" was the most important factor in their work satisfaction.

MARRIAGE

A vast psychological literature concerned with marriage and parenthood exists in this country, but almost none of it is focused on the specific contributions that these events may make to adult development; rather, the failures in marriage and parenthood have been the subject of most studies. Even when more benign situations have been examined, the target of study has usually been the development of the child, as the offspring of various kinds of marriages and conditions of parenthood, rather than the development of the adults involved. Marriage and parenthood, unlike career commitment, have definite beginnings in most societies, but neither has the characteristics of a drastic structural reorganization of the personality. One reason is that complex rehearsal for both roles takes place years in advance of their occurrence: dating, playing house, and so on. Because pregnancy is a biological as well as a deeply personal and social event, it seems likely to have the most universal effects upon female development; fatherhood, which seems to have interested almost no one, is more a social experience.

Some time ago, marriage research uncovered a process of disenchantment after marriage, which has been attributed to the effects of the relationship itself. Couples report less marital satisfaction, intimacy, and reciprocal settlement of disputes after some years of marriage than they do earlier. However, the personal adjustment of each member of the marriage team is unaffected. This inconsistency between self-adjustment and adjustment in the relationship raises a question about the truth—or, more likely, the actual meaning—of the initial reports of enchantment. Some psychologists have suggested that American society has romanticized young love to such an extent that relative disillusionment later is inevitable. Werner's views suggest that real marital experience would result in increased perspective and differentiation so that later ratings of marital satisfaction would inevitably be more objective.

Because the question to be answered concerns the developmental effects of being married, data about differences between the premarital and postmarital states are needed. Catherine Chilman and D. L. Meyer report that both male and female married undergraduates have higher personality test scores for needs of achievement, humanism, and scientism and lower scores for narcissism, sex, and succorance than single undergraduates. Married students report happier personal lives than do single students. These findings agree with several other studies and suggest that the marital experience with its mandatory accommodations promotes greater perspectivism.

PARENTHOOD

Empirical results illuminating the developmental effects of parenthood and pregnancy are scanty. Most research is concerned with the pathological effects of pregnant women's anxiety, the severity of their psychosomatic symptoms, and their postpartum depressions. Unwed mothers have frequently been the subjects of such studies, but only recently have the fathers been considered.

Figure 25.5. Researchers say that some disillusionment after marriage is inevitable.

Martin Heinstein reports that women who had recently given birth were more willing to discuss the negative aspects of their pregnancy (much like the postnuptial subjects). They also reported they felt less dependent on their own mothers and expected more of their own performance with their babies and children. K. L. Kogan, Erling Boe, and Edward Gocka found that postpartum unwed mothers moved toward greater self-reliance and warmth and less self-indulgence. These observations are consistent with the interpretation of the experience of pregnancy and motherhood as serving to promote control of one's own experiences, self-perspective, and greater differentiation of self.

STUDIES IN INTELLECTUAL CHANGE

By the time the adolescent becomes the adult, intellectual growth is no longer occurring at a rapid rate. In fact, early investigations suggested that full intellectual capacity was reached by the early twenties, followed by a plateau and then by a slow decline. The supposition of intellectual peaking in early adulthood seemed strengthened by H. C. Lehman's finding that scientists and scholars made their maximum contributions when they were very young. Recent research has asked more specific questions, so it is now apparent that the early reports were in error in important ways. Early studies reported the results of cross-sectional studies, but more recent ones are longitudinal. The first longitudinal reports that showed gains by older adults were studies of superior individuals, and so for a time continued gains

Figure 25.6. Parenthood brings new responsibilities into the adult life.

were thought to characterize only the gifted. Later investigations by Nancy Bayley and others have included persons of more average accomplishment, and even in these circumstances gains in adult intellectual functioning have been observed.

At present it appears safe to report that gains in verbal IQ continue until at least the late thirties and perhaps even as late as fifty years of age. Performance IQ begins to decline for females in the late twenties but not for males. The eventual and probably inevitable declines during the fifties all involve speed and perhaps immediate memory.

Wayne Dennis has recently studied the productivity of a large number of gifted but not necessarily outstanding artists, scientists, and scholars in sixteen different areas of work, all of whom lived to be seventy-nine years of age or older. His results do not agree with previous findings, in part because the earlier studies did not adequately control for the subjects' age at death. Dennis found that—with the exception of persons in the arts—the decade of the twenties was roughly the period of least productivity. The forties was the decade of highest output for nearly all areas of work. The productivity of scholars showed little decrement even after the age of sixty, but that of scientists decreased, and the output of persons in art, music, and original literature dropped appreciably. There are great individual differences, however, and many renowned exceptions.

It is commonly observed that the disequilibrium of moving into an actual vocation, even after years of apprenticeship as a student for that profession, produces discernible reorganization in the intellectual and personality realms. Discontinuity is shown by the fact that IQ predicts school grades rather well, but neither IQ nor school grades are very accurate predictors of adult achievement.

Various forms of personality functioning may relate to gains and losses in IQ. For example, adult ego defenses that can distort or negate input have been related to a decrease in IQ within a group of subjects who were rank ordered at early adolescence and again at middle adulthood; improvement in IQ was correlated with the individual's ability to cope with his world and himself.

It may be that an IQ test with little cultural content and mainly formal items would be an acceptable tool for assessing the cognitive growth of children. But an adult's deployment of intelligence, for all the reasons advanced earlier in this chapter, is undoubtedly an integrated, articulated, discrete, selective, many-splendored display, requiring more than formal tests for its evaluation. It is thus difficult to take the reported decline in some concrete skills in middle adulthood very seriously. Out in the real world and away from the artificial requirements of timed school tests, the adult engages in a functional reorganization of his intellectual hierarchy: elegance, depth, comprehensiveness, and lively appropriateness in terms of his intentions are more valued than speed and concreteness.

A prime example of functional reorganization can be found in age changes in scores for the

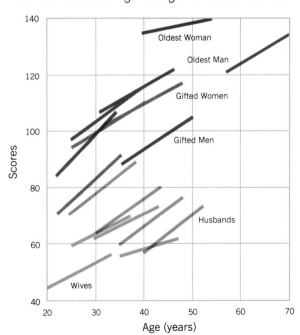

Figure 25.7. Mean scores on the Concept Mastery Test, administered to 1,103 gifted men and women and their spouses about twelve years apart. The test is not concerned with measures of speed; it calls for knowledge of symbols and abstractions and the ability to use these in relation to each other. The data give strong evidence that intelligence of the type measured continues to increase at least through fifty years of age. (Adapted from Bayley and Oden, 1955.)

Figure 25.8. Productivity throughout adulthood is symbolized in such famous figures as Leonard Bernstein, Henry Moore, and André Malraux.

Digit-Symbol Substitution Test, part of the widely used Wechsler intelligence tests. The task requires that a person perform as many number-symbol pairings—by marking the symbols below the printed numbers—as he can within a timed period. A chart showing which symbol should go with each number is available in plain sight. Clearly the task is clerical, but a person can speed himself up, if he sees fit, by memorizing the digit-symbol pairings. However, he can do a reasonable job by checking the code key each time if he is not greatly concerned about doing well on this particular test or if he regards it as a trivial measure of his ability. The skill measured by this test is, by the consensus of no less than ten studies, the one most likely to deteriorate with age. However, the deterioration may simply be a function of decreased speed.

Bayley's attention to the less cognitive aspects of intellectual change led her to correlate various scales of the California Psychological Inventory with the Wechsler subtest scores. One personality scale, Good Impression, probably reflects a formal, organized ego attitude toward self-presentation, although it is regarded by the author of the test as more of a test-taking attitude. In any case it reflects concerns about others' evaluations—the examiner's or those of the world at large. Bayley's data for thirty-six-year-olds show that males with the highest scores on the Good Impression scale do poorly and females with the lowest scores, well on the Digit Symbol test. (The same pattern obtains for the Digit Span Test, which requires the subject to repeat a series of numbers immediately after the examiner says them.) This pattern could reflect the low status of substituting symbols for the adult male and the disorganizing effects of the adult female's concern with making a good impression when she is having her intelligence tested.

Most intelligence tests were originally conceived with the child in mind. For adults, the items were made more difficult simply by allowing less time or by adding more esoteric information. Moreover, most tests are constructed so that abilities rather than integrated functions are assessed. Psychology's present improved understanding of the qualitative differences between the child's and the adult's cognitive and personal functioning suggests that different methods of observation should be used for adults. Even more basically, qualitatively different conceptualizations may be necessary. Intelligence and self and personality are not likely to be as separable in adulthood as they are in childhood. Haan found a number of close relationships between intelligence and independently observed coping functions in adulthood, but Moriarty found only very attenuated associations with preschool children.

LATER ADULTHOOD

Because a later chapter covers aging, the present discussion will deal only with findings about the middle and later adult years, from forty to sixty. The extensive studies conducted at the University of Chicago, which have been most comprehensively reported by Bernice Neugarten, have provided us with the most detailed and extensive descriptions of this time in life. Neugarten has

said that the mass media's use of the label "the Command Generation" to identify this time in life is apt. The middle-aged adult, as Neugarten and others describe him, seems to epitomize Werner's counterbalanced life processes of greater imposition of self on the environment and increased perspective in regard to one's own point of view. Neugarten reports that the middle years are a period of maximum capacity and ability to handle a highly complex environment.

These adults are characterized by an increasing personal and social distance from the young but regard themselves as bridging the gulf between young and old and between the past and the future. They interpret each age group to the other with greater tolerance and objectivity than either can muster for itself. Middle-aged people reconstruct their view of their own place in life along a scale running all the way from time-since-birth to time-left-to-live and begin to consider the relative importance of the tasks left to be done. Middle age is the time people take stock: men redefine their career goals and reevaluate the state and use of their bodies (Neugarten calls this body monitoring); women reconstruct their view of themselves as mothers and begin the rehearsal for widowhood, the inevitable response to the difference in life expectancies between men and women. All of these add up to increased perspective about one's self in a family, in a society, and in one's limited time in history.

Men in American society become more receptive to affiliative and nurturant feelings, and women become more responsive and less con-

strained about expressing aggressive and egocentric tendencies. It seems that the increased perspective of a middle-aged person about himself and his increased ability to organize his environment permit him to ignore some social sanctions about sex.

Neugarten has also investigated the psychological effects of menopause in women—the most discernible middle-age counterpart of biological changes and development in children. She discovered that menopause involves few or no basic personality functions.

The Chicago studies have also focused on the age-status system—a frame of reference, implicitly held by people in the society, for defining the proper time to perform certain life events, such as marriage, childbearing, and retirement. The investigation has shown that this system becomes more important with age; older people feel more strongly that certain behaviors should be relegated exclusively to certain age groups. It is not clear whether this reflects increasing rigidity or increasing awareness among the middle aged.

Problems in Defining Adult Change

Social psychology has been concerned with the way an adult can be influenced; industrial psychology has studied the way he works; and personality psychology has attempted to describe his motivations, his feelings, and, more recently, his cognitive style. Psychoanalysis was founded on the model of the *troubled* adult, and its view of development still largely consists of reconstruction of the child and adolescent that the adult must have been. However wide-ranging and rich in contribution these disciplines have been, they have not yet led to a comprehensive or widely accepted conceptualization of adult development, and it seems unlikely that they ever will. The developing adult will probably not be understood until investigation focuses directly upon the subtle internal dialogue of change and self-consistency across the span of some forty years.

STAGE THEORIES

Some theories, such as Erik Erikson's (discussed in Chapter 1 and at length in Chapter 23) and Jane Loevinger's, employ the concept of stages that has proven so useful in research on children. They presume timings or schedules of change. If the various stages occur in a fixed sequence or are universally associated with various events of adult life, then an objective statement of adult development has been secured. Erikson's eight stages of man link the adult stages of intimacy with heterosexual love and marriage, generativity with parenthood, and integrity with aging; the psychosocial content of each is considered optimal for its particular period of life. There is, of course, no reason to think that these events have the same essential meaning in all cultures or that the nature of social existence is such that all persons must necessarily confront these tasks, or confront them in any fixed order.

Loevinger's six stages—impulse ridden, opportunistic, conformist, conscientious, autonomous, and integrated—are expected to occur in a fixed sequence, and presumably the last four would most often characterize persons during the adult years. Loevinger has not indicated the conditions of progression from one stage to another, but development in both Erikson's and Loevinger's stages seems to be linked with particular social experiences and contexts. Neither set of stages is defined in the formal terms of structure, organization, and process that characterize Piaget's cognitive stages (see Chapters 11, 15, 20) and Kohlberg's moral stages (see Chapter 17). The formal aspects of the Kohlberg stages have permitted demonstration of their cross-cultural existence and their invariant, developmental sequence. It is doubtful that the social-content aspects of the other two positions could permit of such broad application.

Whether adult development can ever be typified by conceptualizations of formal stages remains open to question. Kohlberg has set out several criteria of stage conceptualization: (1) It involves change in the form, pattern, and organization of response and not just in its frequency or intensity. (2) It involves newness, that is, a qualitative difference in response. (3) It is irreversible; the individual, except in very unusual stressful or damaging circumstances, does not respond in accordance with his earlier modes. (4) The stages appear in a sequence that does not vary from individual to individual. (5) Each successive stage integrates critical formal aspects of previous

stages into a more articulated organization. Because stage theory is only concerned with conceptualizing the changes in the structure, form, and organization of responses, it rises above particular contents, times, and places. The developmental criteria are progressive, evolutionary changes with age that can be empirically defined and observed wherever they exist. No evidence presently available suggests that there are structural changes in adult life equivalent to those of childhood—at least as structural progression is now understood. This kind of change seems to occur only when the growing child's cognitive grasp of his world and himself proves to be dramatically inept and objectively unsupportable in his own view. Normally, this is not encountered by an adult. If it is, however, the resulting reorganization may be peculiar or even psychotic.

SOCIOLOGICAL AND LEARNING THEORIES

Sociologist Howard S. Becker sees the crux of adult development in the interplay of two processes: (1) situational adjustment, which explains change—situations are always shifting—and (2) personal commitment, which explains stability. Becker's view puts change and stability in dynamic interchange. The adult develops, perhaps reluctantly, in order to adjust to a change in the social scene. Commonalities in adult change are found in common social tasks. In this way, Beck-

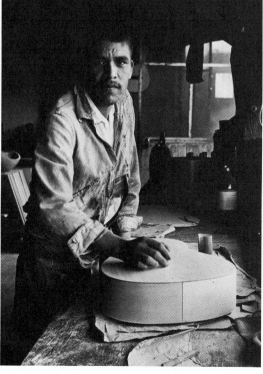

er's postulation is not markedly different from the exploration of personality change generally offered by stimulus-response psychology. I. E. Farber, for example, has recently stated the position that no theory of change, and therefore of development, is needed beyond a general theory of learning. Adult change occurs when the environment presents positive or negative contingencies —rewards or punishments for the occurrence of changes. The adult as a reactor automatically changes by learning whatever is best for him and his own peculiar self-interest.

DIALECTICAL THEORIES

A position that is less radically environmental sees adult development as a *selective* interaction of the adult with his environment: when the adult is confronted with new, contradictory, or possibly unsettling information, he will respond in a way that preserves his personal continuity. In responding, he may himself change to some degree but he may also alter his environment. This kind of dynamic interchange (as opposed to a mechanized view of growth as expansion) underlies the psychoanalytic view of the ego and Erikson's eight stages of man.

THE IMPORTANCE OF ADULT CHANGE

Most of the human life cycle is spent as an adult, and the quality of life during that time—its via-

bility along with its promethean qualities—is critical to its holder and to mankind. For better or for worse the questions and the answers of science have increasingly greater impact and wider meaning to citizens and policy makers. In its investigation of the adult, however, social science has not always lived up to its own dedications of representing life. An atrophied, technological model of the adult, representing more than anything else an American commitment to mechanical efficiency, often guides research. The movement inherent in life itself, whether it is developing or destructively turning on itself, has not been captured. Moreover, science has not always lived up to its own requirements of objectivity in conceptualization when it has considered the ideal state of the fully developed adult. Metaphysical questions, impossible for science to resolve, are persistently raised in describing the ideal man in his various and competing guises. Science will probably eventually come to the investigation of the open-ended evolutionary qualities of adult life, lived out in the midst of myriad social contexts— none of which is now, or may ever be, optimally supportive of life processes. Students of adult development will need to direct their attention to the commonalities of all men in order to explain eventually why some social arrangements, and not others, allow the adult years to be ones of glorious evolution rather than dull, defensive fixedness.

A tightly wound green coil covered with coarse, hairlike material—who would suppose from its appearance that it contains the potential for developing into a broad, finely divided leaf, a fern frond with all of the characteristics of its species, a capacity and a necessity for reproduction, a continuing tendency to grow upward toward the sun, and the ability to feed and develop itself through photosynthesis?

These potentialities will naturally develop by themselves if nothing occurs to inhibit them. But if there is too little water, too much sun, the encroachment of other plants, the hungry mouth of a sheep, or inadequate food in the soil, the potential for growth may be destroyed, stunted, or warped and the fern frond prevented from realizing itself as the great, broad, deeply fringed, light-seeking leaf that it has the potentiality and the tendency to become.

To many psychologists, human beings are analogous to this fern. They have a potential for full development, called the *actualizing tendency*. Under appropriate circumstances, they will grow and develop until their full potential is realized. Every living person is involved in an active process of growing, but there are also inhibiting forces that can distort or terminate growth and delay or prevent the actualization of a person's potential.

PSYCHOLOGICAL MALADJUSTMENT

Many elements can impede or distort the tendency of a human being to actualize himself. From the point of view of this chapter, these warpings constitute psychological maladjustment. It is important to distinguish *psychological* maladjustment (and adjustment) from other meanings of maladjustment. There is ample evidence, for example, that a psychologically healthy person is not necessarily well adjusted to a social or political dictatorship. Similarly, a psychologically well-adjusted person would not be well adjusted to life in an urban ghetto, and the student who is well adjusted to an outdated and rigid educational institution is not necessarily psychologically healthy.

We are not simply talking about adjustment to any and every situation. Neither are we focusing simply on problems of social concern—drug addiction, alcoholism, robbery, promiscuity, homosexuality, car theft, and the like. These are *social* maladjustments—failures to adjust to society, which are not necessarily serious *psychological* maladjustments. However, psychological maladjustment is involved in varying degrees in each of the individuals exhibiting these social problems. The youth who smokes pot because it seems to be the way to belong to his group represents a very different problem from the youth who takes drugs because he must escape from himself. The person who engages in homosexual behavior in prison may have a very different problem from the person who has no sexual interest in the opposite sex while feeling a compelling interest in his or her own. Although individuals who display serious social problems usually show at least some degree of psychological maladjustment, the two concepts are definitely not synonymous.

Psychological maladjustment—or adjustment—refers to certain inner states that can be care-

26
Continuing Growth Versus Maladjustment

fully and accurately defined. A person is psychologically maladjusted when his organism denies to awareness or consciousness—or has a distorted awareness of—significant experiences in his life. Consequently, these experiences are not adequately symbolized in his consciousness or accurately organized into the concept he has of himself. Thus, there occurs a real discrepancy between what he has experienced and the recognition and acceptance of this experience- in his awareness. As a consequence, his behavior is based on a very inadequate awareness of the data available to him. Behavior based on such inadequate data is certain to be less than satisfying to either his primary or his higher needs.

Consider, for example, a person who reports that he never gets angry. Things that make other people angry, he says, simply do not upset him. Instead, he behaves in a rational and calm fashion in situations where he is insulted, treated unjustly, or made the subject of an attack. However, on these same occasions he suffers a violent headache. To anyone observing his behavior when he is attacked, it seems evident from the flush on his face and the look in his eyes that he is both hurt and angry. Because the experiences are completely denied in his awareness, his system must find some other form of expression, and the headaches are the result.

Another example of psychological maladjustment is a man who is obviously highly dependent upon his wife but who, in his own perception and consciousness, believes he is nothing of the sort: In his eyes he is independent of his wife and is a thoroughly self-directing individual. However, if his wife leaves home to visit friends, even for a day or two, he becomes ill. Consciously he regrets very much that these illnesses often demand his wife's return. The truth is, however, that his organism has experienced strong feelings of dependence and probably of resentment at his wife's absence, and he engages in behavior that is designed to bring his wife back to his side.

Another, more serious, maladjustment can be illustrated by the case of an adolescent boy brought up in a rigidly religious home where sex was never mentioned except in terms of evil thoughts—thoughts that no normal person would have. This boy therefore has no interest in sex and engages in no sexual behavior. Yet one night he creeps into the house next door, enters the room of the daughter of the house, and starts to bludgeon her and tear off her clothing before he is apprehended. Caught, he assures the police and the psychologist that he could not possibly have done this, that he must not have been himself. It certainly was not in any way his own self's behavior. Like any adolescent boy he must have been full of sexual desires and tensions related to sex. These were denied to his conscious mind, but his organism behaved in ways to satisfy those unconscious desires and tensions.

CAUSES OF MALADJUSTMENT

Why would an individual be unable to admit to consciousness some of the things that he is experiencing? The most plausible explanation may at first seem a strange one: He denies experiences to awareness in order to *satisfy some of his basic needs for growth and development.*

In order to actualize himself, the human being, especially the infant, needs an affectionate and caring love—not a pseudolove or a possessive love —from someone close to him, usually his parents. He also needs an acceptance of himself as he is, with his curiosities, impulses, fears, angers, affectionate feelings, and desire to be in close relationship. Perhaps most important of all, he needs to be in relationship with people who are *real*, who are not shutting important experiences out of their own awareness. But very frequently the only love and acceptance he can gain is highly conditional—he will be loved and accepted only if he behaves in certain ways, has only certain proper feelings and attitudes. To buy this love and acceptance he tries to conform to the standards set for him, even though they go directly contrary to his own experiencing. Here is the beginning of the individual's estrangement from himself, the root cause of psychological maladjustment.

The person may introject from his parents, from others, or from society in general values and standards that run contrary to his own experience but that bring him acceptance. It is when he acts in terms of these expectations, denying to awareness the experiences of his own organism, that he is on the road to psychological maladjustment. He learns to distrust his own experience as a guide and therefore is at the mercy of those who, knowingly or unknowingly, have caused him to accept their values and expectations as his own. It is because of this conformity that an individual comes to be guided by a concept of himself that is not truly his own and behaves in ways that are strange or unsatisfying because they are not based on all of his sensory data. His experiencing is no longer the basis of his behavior as it was in infancy. Then he cried when he was hungry, cooed when he was satiated, explored himself when he was curious, and in general knew what he found valuable; he knew equally well what he found unsatisfying and acted in terms of his experience.

GROWING OUT OF MALADJUSTMENT: A CASE STUDY

The basic aspects of psychological adjustment are most clearly seen as a person is becoming healthier. As he moves further and further away from a split between his experience and his partly false concept of himself, he can perceive more clearly just what it is that has prevented his growth and how it is that he has been able to leave it behind.

There is no better way to understand growth than to study actual cases of it. Read the following letter, written by a young woman in the act of growing.

Dear ———: I don't know how to explain who I am or why I am writing to you except to say that I have just read your book and it left a great impression on me. I just happened to find it one day and started reading. It's kind of a coincidence because right now I need something to help me find *me*. I do not feel that I can do much for others until I find me.

I think that I began to lose me when I was in high school. I always wanted to go into work that would be of help to people but my family resisted, and I thought they must be right. Things went along

smoothly for everyone else for four or five years until about two years ago. I met a guy that I thought was ideal. Then nearly a year ago I took a good look at us, and realized that I was everything that *he* wanted me to be and nothing that *I* was. I have always been emotional and I have had many feelings. I could never sort them out and identify them. My fiance would tell me that I was just mad or just happy and I would say okay and leave it at that. Then when I took this good look at us I realized that I was angry because I wasn't following my true emotions.

I backed out of the relationship gracefully and tried to find out where all the pieces were that I had lost. After a few months of searching had gone by I found that there were many more than I knew what to do with and I couldn't seem to separate them. I began seeing a psychologist and am presently seeing him. He has helped me to find parts of me that I was not aware of. Some parts are bad by our society's standards but I have found them to be very good for me. I have felt more threatened and confused since going to him but I have also felt more relief and more sure of myself.

I remember one night in particular. I had been in for my regular appointment with the psychologist that day and I had come home feeling angry. I was angry because I wanted to talk about something but I couldn't identify what it was. By 8 o'clock that night I was so upset I was frightened. I called him and he told me to come to his office as soon as I could. I got there and cried for at least an hour and then the words came. I still don't know all of what I was saying. All I know is that *so much hurt* and *anger* came out of me that I *never really knew existed*. I went home and it seemed that an *alien* had taken over and I was hallucinating like some of the patients I have seen in a state hospital. I continued to feel this way until one night I was sitting and thinking and I realized that this alien was the *me* that I had been trying to find.

I have noticed since that night that people no longer seem so strange to me. Now it is beginning to seem that life is just starting for me. I am alone right now but I am not frightened and I don't have to be doing something. I like meeting me and making friends with my thoughts and feelings. Because of this I have learned to enjoy other people. One older man in particular—who is very ill—makes me feel very much alive. He accepts everyone. He told me the other day that I have changed very much. According to him, I have begun to open up and love. I think that I have always loved people and I told him so. He said, "Were they aware of it?" I don't suppose I have expressed my love any more than I did my anger and hurt.

Among other things, I am finding out that I never had too much self-respect. And now that I am learning to really like me I am finally finding peace within myself. Thanks for your part in this.

Let us paraphrase a number of crucial statements that summarize the feelings and attitudes expressed in the letter and try to gain a more general understanding of growth by discussing them.

I was losing me. Her own experiences and their meanings were being denied, and she was developing a self that was different from her real experienced self, which was becoming increasingly unknown to her.

My experience told me the work I wanted to go into, but my family showed me that that was not its meaning. This phrase shows how a false concept of self is built up. Because she accepted her parents' meanings as her own experience, she came to distrust her own organismic experience.

She could hardly have introjected her parents' values on this subject had she not had a long previous experience of introjecting their values. As she distrusted more and more of her own experience, her sense of self-worth steadily declined until she had very little use for her own experience or herself.

Things went along smoothly for everyone else. What a revealing statement: Of course things were fine for those whom she was trying to please. This pseudoself was just what they wanted. It was only within herself, at some deep and unknown level, that there was a vague uneasiness.

I was everything he wanted me to be. Here again she was denying to awareness all her own experiencing—to the point where she no longer really had a self and was trying to be a self wanted by someone else.

Finally my organism rebelled and I tried to find me again but I couldn't, without help. Why did she finally rebel and take a good look at her relationship with her fiance? One can only attribute this rebellion to the actualizing tendency that had been surpressed for so long but that finally asserted itself. However, because she had distrusted her own experience for such a long period and because the self by which she was living was so sharply different from the experiences of her organism, she could not reconstruct her true self without help. The need for help often exists when there is such a great discrepancy.

Now I am discovering my experiences—some bad according to society, parents, and boyfriend, but all good as far as I am concerned. The locus of evaluation that formerly had resided in her parents, in her boyfriend, and others, she is now reclaiming as her own. She is the one who decides the value of her experience. She is the center of the valuing process, and the evidence is provided by her own senses. Society may call a given experience bad, but when she trusts her own valuing of it, she finds that it is worthwhile and significant to her.

An important turning point came when a flood of the experiences that I had been denying to awareness came close to the surface. I was frightened and upset. When denied experience comes close to awareness, anxiety always results because these previously unadmitted experiences will have meanings that will change the structure of the self by which she has been living. Any drastic change in the self-concept is always a threatening and frightening experience. She was dimly aware of this threat even though she did not yet know what would emerge.

When the denied experiences broke through the dam, they turned out to be hurts and angers that I had been completely unaware of. It is impossible for most people to realize how completely an experience can be shut out of awareness until it does break through into awareness. Every individual is able to shut out and deny those experiences that would endanger his concept of himself.

I thought I was insane because some foreign person had taken over in me. When the self-concept is so sharply changed that parts of it are completely shattered, it is a very frightening experience, and her description of the feeling that an alien had taken over is a very accurate one.

Only gradually did I realize that this alien was the real me. What she was discovering was that the submissive, malleable self by which she had been living, the self that had been guided by the statements, attitudes, and expectations of others, was no longer hers. This new self that had seemed so alien was a self that had experienced hurt and anger and feelings that society regards as bad, as well as wild hallucinatory thoughts—and love. As she goes further into self-discovery, it is likely that she will find out that some of her anger is directed against her parents. The hurts will have come from various sources; some of the feelings and experiences that society regards as bad but that she finds good and satisfying are experiences and feelings that probably have to do with sexuality. In any event, her self is becoming much more firmly rooted in her own gut-level experiences. Another person put something of this in the phrase "I am beginning to let my experience *tell me* what it means instead of *my* trying to *impose* a meaning on it." The more the individual's concept of himself is rooted in the spontaneously felt meanings of his experiencing, the more he is an integrated person.

I like meeting me and making friends with my thoughts and feelings. Here is the dawning of the self-respect and self-acceptance of which she has been deprived for so long. She is even feeling affection for herself. One of the curious but common side effects of this change is that now she will be able to give herself more freely to others,

to enjoy others more, to be more genuinely interested in them.

I have begun to open up and love. She will find that as she is more expressive of her love she can also be more expressive of her anger and hurt, her likes and dislikes, and her "wild" thoughts and feelings (which will turn out to be creative impulses). She is in the process of changing from psychological maladjustment to a much healthier relationship to others and to reality.

I am finally finding peace within myself. There is a peaceful harmony in being a whole person, but she will be mistaken if she thinks this reaction is permanent. Instead, if she is really open to her experience, she will find other hidden aspects of herself that she has denied to awareness, and each such discovery will give her uneasy and anxious moments or days until they are assimilated into a revised and changing picture of herself. She will discover that growing toward a congruence between her experiencing organism and her concept of herself is an exciting, sometimes disturbing, but never-ending adventure.

CONTINUED GROWTH

We have just participated in an actual case of growing out of trouble. In addition to troubled people who are trying to move toward normality, there are thousands of normally functioning individuals who are looking for opportunities to move in the direction of even greater normal personal growth. Everyone has problems, but it is not because of their problems that many forward-looking, well-functioning people in education, the arts, industry, psychological work, homemaking, and many other occupations are seeking ways in which they can develop themselves more fully.

Fifty years ago psychologists, psychiatrists, and others interested in development were little known and even less regarded. Gradually such professional people were used more extensively by deviant individuals who were forced to turn to them and by some desperate individuals who turned to them voluntarily. As this work continued, the possibility of personality and behavioral change gradually became real to a significant part of our population. Then increasing numbers of people in personal trouble began to seek psychotherapy, psychoanalysis, group therapy, and other forms of help—and not only because of mental illness, but also and even primarily because of mental stagnation.

We have now proceeded to the point where the normally functioning person, often a leader in his profession or occupation, is coming increasingly to realize that he has more potential for growth than he has utilized, and he wants to develop himself further. Consequently, there has been a burgeoning development of encounter groups, sensitivity training, T-groups, and growth centers, where people go for periods ranging from a week-end to two weeks or more in order to further develop their own potential. Individuals are embarking on searches for richer personal development, greater authenticity, more capacity for living fruitfully in interpersonal relationships, and greater development of creative potential. Thousands of such individuals are engaged in organized activities that they hope and believe will be of help in continuing their own growth as persons. In most cases, their hopes are fulfilled.

THE GROWTH PROCESS

Drawing upon the experiences of those who are involved in the search for continuing psychological growth, perhaps a tentative definition of the concept of continuing development for the individual can be reached.

In the first place, continued growth requires an openness to experience. The person tends to become more aware of his feelings, attitudes, and thoughts. He becomes less defensive and tends to shut out of awareness fewer of the reactions that he is experiencing. He thus has more internal data at his command and those data are more accurate. Because he is not defensive, the growing person also perceives external reality with more accuracy. There are fewer external facts that threaten him; therefore, he can approach a real situation with less bias, less need to shut out those facts that might change his belief system or self-concept. Abraham Maslow points out that such individuals are more efficient in their perception of reality. Such perceptions include not only the obvious and easily observable but the mysterious and unknown as well. Individuals moving in the direction of psychological growth are less threatened by the unknown or the mysterious. They are able to say it—and see it—like it is.

This greater openness to realities within and without is a flowing, ever-changing process. It is never a static goal that can be fully achieved.

Because the data available in the psychologically growing person, both from internal and from external sources, are much greater than those available to the psychologically stagnant person, he tends to live in an existential rather than a stereotyped fashion. For the person involved in continuing personal growth, each moment is new. The complex configuration of inner feelings, attitudes, and reactions and the complex perception of the realities that exist in this situation at this moment have never before existed in just this fashion. Consequently, the growing person begins to realize, "What I will be in the next moment and what I will do grows out of that moment. It cannot be predicted in advance either by me or by others."

One of the basic characteristics of the psychologically growing person is that he sees life as a continuing process. That people can be almost continually in process is a new cultural concept—one that is very difficult for individuals to absorb and that is frequently frightening to them.

For generations and centuries the individual has learned the facts of his environmental reality, the values that are true, and the behaviors that are right and wrong, and he has tended to live his life in these more or less static terms. This kind of living is no longer adequate for the incredibly rapid change of our technological society. Yet we have had very little experience with the nature of living in a process fashion, and those who are attempting to do so are psychological pioneers. It is probable that creative spirits throughout all generations have lived in this fashion, but now

circumstances seem to demand it of the ordinary individual. The psychologically growing person must become a participant in, and an observer of, the ongoing process of his own organismic experiencing—rather than a self who controls experience, twisting and distorting it to fit a preconceived structure.

The final characteristic of the psychologically growing person is that he finds his own organism an increasingly trustworthy means of arriving at the most satisfying behavior in each existential situation. By doing what simply feels right in the immediate moment, he discovers in general that his feelings are a competent and trustworthy guide for his behavior. Because he is open to his experience, he has access in a given situation to all of the data that he needs for determining his behavior: his perceptions of the social demands, institutional demands, and personal expectations; his recognition of his own complex and possibly conflicting needs and desires; his memories of similar situations; and his perception of the uniqueness of this situation. He thus becomes increasingly able to permit his total organism to consider each stimulus, need, and demand, to weigh its relative intensity and importance, and to discover the course of action that must and will come closest to satisfying all his needs—now.

Because he is more at home in his own experience and more comfortable with the self that emerges from it, the psychologically growing person has ample energy to deal with problems outside of himself, and he tends to focus primarily on those problems rather than being vigilantly and eternally self-conscious. He is able to work toward satisfying his curiosities, achieving answers to problems that concern him, and taking action in areas where he can have impact. Because he is more integrated within himself, he is able to focus outwardly more effectively.

As our society becomes more affluent, as man's physical needs become easily satisfied, men are freed to pursue the goals that stand higher in the hierarchy of their needs. They are turning to a variety of resources in order to achieve within themselves the flow of enhancing psychological growth.

The growing person is more able to live in and with his feelings and reactions. He uses all of his organic equipment to sense, as accurately as possible, the existential situation within and without. He is more able to trust his total organism to use these data effectively in guiding his behavior. He is more able to experience all of his feelings and is less afraid of any of his feelings; he is his own sifter of evidence but more open to evidence from all sources; he is actively engaged in the process of being and becoming himself but is discovering that this individual process is the best way of being realistically social; he lives more completely in the moment but is finding that this is the soundest living for all time. He is more nearly a fully functioning organism, and because of the awareness of himself that flows in and through his experiences, he comes closer to being a fully functioning person. In short, he grows.

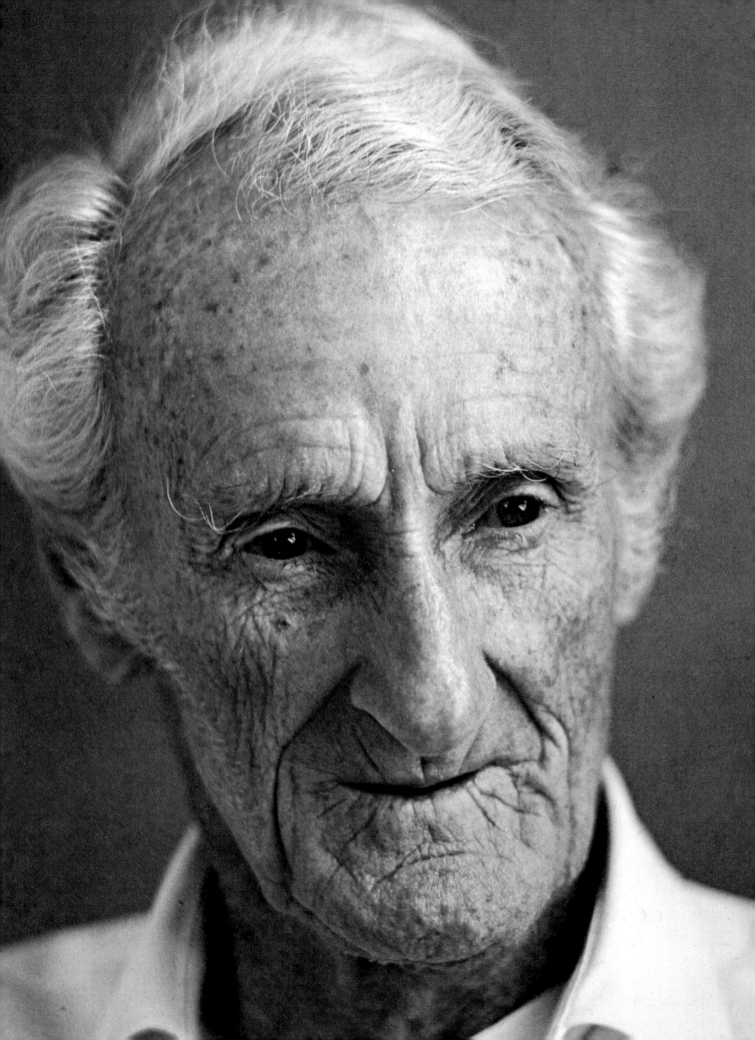

There is more to aging than just growing old. Old age may come slowly or rapidly—gradually or suddenly. Some people seem to slide gracefully and even beautifully into old age, while others seem almost overnight to be transformed by some malevolent experience, real or imagined, into suddenly very old, helpless creatures. Regardless of how it comes, old age is inevitable; it is everyone's personal fate if he is lucky—or unlucky —to live long enough.

An old man of seventy-five is very different from a man of fifty-five, as this chapter will make clear in detail, but he is still a human being. The older man has more memories and a longer history, but he still lives in the present. The older man has less physical ability to influence his world, but he still has the human capacity and desire to control. The older man may have lost those he loved to death or distance, but he still needs to love and be loved. The old man may have no friends left, but he still has the capacity for friendship.

Aging involves at least three kinds of changes —biological, social, and psychological. The developmental processes underlying these changes may be no different in kind than those underlying growth during the mature years. But the outcome of these processes is dramatic: they produce old and, eventually, dead people.

Biological aging refers to changes in an organism's vulnerability: the chances of survival diminish with the passage of time. Someone who is old biologically has, on the basis of physiological, chemical, and anatomical measurements, only a short time left to live. Biological aging is an approach to biological—final—death.

A person's *psychological age* is measured by his capacity to adapt to demands of the environment and of other persons. Psychological age is, of course, influenced to some extent by biological age, but it is mainly determined by other factors, such as a person's motivation or disposition to employ his capacities.

Social age refers to an individual's social habits relative to society's expectations. Age grading of behavior is a complex social process that is only partly determined by biological and psychological age. Because the individual has been socialized and so has incorporated certain group expectations, he may show behavior expected for his age even though his potential capacities may be for totally different behaviors. For example, in some societies a woman dons black clothes and retires from active society at the death of her husband— without regard to her own biological or social capacities—simply because she has incorporated —and must follow—the norms of her culture. A society sets up varying standards for forms of speech, polite behavior, deference, and authority as being appropriate to different age groups. Against these norms, a person is judged as acting too young or too old for his age.

BIOLOGICAL DETERMINANTS

Each animal species lives, on the average, only a certain length of time, but there are large individual differences around the average. The lifetimes of men, for example, range from a few minutes to

**27
Aging**

well over one hundred years. To some extent, an individual's life span is determined genetically. For instance, if one had long-lived grandparents, it appears that one has a small advantage in living longer than the average. Individual genetic factors also appear in the fact that the life spans of identical twins are more similar than those of fraternal twins or siblings.

ENVIRONMENTAL INFLUENCE

The environment in which a person lives—the food, temperature, demands for activity, quality of the air, and the like—also affect his chances of living a long life. At the present time, variations in man's environment are probably more important in determining length of life than are individual differences in heredity. Life expectancy at birth for a male in the United States is sixty-eight years; in India it is close to forty. However, if the environment were to become more homogeneous and favorable, man's unique individual heredity would become more important.

An emergent biological factor is seen in the increasing difference in life expectancy between the sexes. Although the average life expectancy has lengthened in America during this century, women have gained more than men, so that a female at birth now has an average life expectancy four to five years longer than a male (about seventy-two for the female and sixty-eight for the male). The reason for the female gain is by no means clear, but it does illustrate an emergent characteristic. One may expect more emergent characteristics as man's environment changes, and

although some may be favorable, others may not. For example, the tendency for modern man to live a sedentary life may be unfavorable. If man can more accurately assess his biological endowment as well as his individual requirements, he may be able to contrive environments that increase his life span.

TISSUE AND CELL CHANGES

Wrinkled skin and other changes in appearance with age are apparently the result of changes in the connective-tissue fibers that lie between cells of the body. The great artist and anatomist Leonardo da Vinci saw these changes clearly and was able to reduce the drawing of individuals of different ages to rules, based on specific anatomical changes. Changes in appearance are in part determined genetically but can be modified by the environment: Continued exposure to sun, for example, can cause faster thickening of connective tissue, producing a permanently leathery skin.

Many cells of the body continue to divide with age, providing a mechanism for replacing cells that die. But some of the most important ones do not: brain cells and heart muscle cells do not divide and cannot be replaced. The cells of the brain are as old as the body and are undoubtedly critical in determining aging. Some of the basic biological changes that occur with age are shown in Figure 27.3.

SOCIAL DETERMINANTS

There is no doubt that patterns of aging vary with social class. Poor people are generally exposed to

Age	Expectation of Life in Years			
	White		Nonwhite	
	Male	Female	Male	Female
0	67.6	74.7	61.1	67.4
1	68.3	75.1	62.9	68.9
5	64.5	71.3	59.3	65.3
15	54.8	61.5	49.7	55.5
25	45.6	51.8	40.7	46.1
35	36.3	42.2	32.3	37.1
45	27.3	32.9	24.5	28.8
55	19.4	24.2	17.9	21.4
60	16.0	20.1	15.1	18.2
65	12.9	16.3	12.6	15.5

Figure 27.1. The projected years of life remaining for those at different ages. Note the discrepancies between men and women and between whites and nonwhites. (Data from Metropolitan Life Insurance Co.)

Figure 27.2. Physical signs of aging, as observed by Leonardo da Vinci.

Figure 27.3. The percentage of change with age for various physiological functions, based on 100 percent at age 30. (After Shock, 1962. From "The Psychology of Aging," by Nathan W. Shock. Copyright© 1962 by Scientific American, Inc. All rights reserved.)

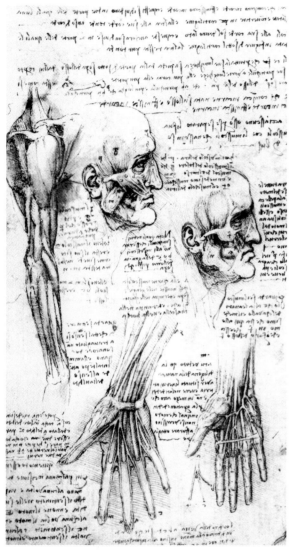

more injurious environmental conditions than are the middle- or upper-class rich, and the consequences are poorer health and earlier aging. Poor people also become more vulnerable psychologically as they grow old. Their range of choices as to where and how they can live is increasingly constricted with advancing age. Because, in a real sense, it is choice that makes us human, the aged poor, robbed of choice, decay even more rapidly. Aging may thus be accelerated among the poor because adverse events are more likely to occur and because poor old people have fewer options with which to handle events.

Because of the diverse ethnic and racial origins of the American population, there is great heterogeneity in what people expect their social roles to be when they are old. A Chinese in Taiwan knows what respect is due him and what powers he wields as an elder. A Chinese in San Francisco cannot be assured that his role will be so clearly defined or its dictates obeyed by his Americanized progeny. Similarly, a sixty-year-old woman from Eastern Europe will hold a different expectation of her role than a woman from North Africa.

Despite the ethnic diversity, however, there do appear to be behavior patterns in American society that are deemed appropriate for different ages. The characteristic tasks that children encounter—called *developmental tasks*—reflect such patterns. Most children go to school, are taught to read, and learn to play certain games at about the same age. Experts have recently begun to view as developmental tasks the whole sequence of common tasks or problems encoun-

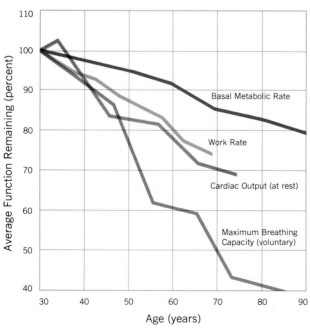

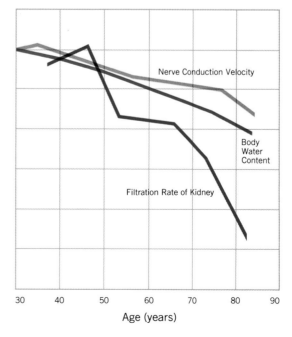

Figure 27.4. Aging is often accelerated among the poor.

tered throughout the entire life span. It seems that all of life—childhood and adulthood—is structured by a commonality of response to the sequence of experiences.

THE STRUCTURE OF EXPERIENCE

Most people manage to work their way through the progression of tasks that commonly structures experience. However, some individuals cannot master a given task at its characteristic time and may suffer anxiety or even breakdown by being out of step. For example, children who cannot read by the second grade, people who do not marry by age thirty, and childless forty-year-old couples are all out of step with the normally accepted progression of white, American, middle-class life.

THE TASKS OF MIDDLE AGE AND AFTER

Once a person completes the task of marriage and child-rearing, he becomes aware of the end of one epoch and of the beginning of another. He is faced with the necessity of adapting to a new phase of life. In middle age, about age forty-five or fifty, many married women must face the reestablishment of their identity. The children are grown and have left the household; the woman's primary role is no longer mothering; the size of the household has shrunk; and the constraining daily activities associated with school-age children are no longer necessary. How can a woman understand the purpose of such a changed life? At this age she may also be passing through the biological menopause, and her own attractiveness and desir-

Figure 27.5. Women's attitudes and general views toward menopause. (After Neugarten, 1968.)

ability as a female may come into question in fact or at least in her mind. "Who am I?" and "What will I do next?" are common questions for the middle-aged woman. Quite often she goes back to work in order to reestablish herself.

Bernice Neugarten, in an extensive study, has found that menopause itself presents no special psychological problems to the average woman adjusted to living in her community. Some of the attitudes that the women she studied expressed are shown in Figure 27.5. Crises of menopause are apparently limited to a small group of women who have special hormonal or personality disturbances. For women who have a strong identity and a variety of current social roles, the cessation of the possibility of reproduction can be a largely unemotional event.

For the man, retirement is the key happening that often initiates a period of uncertainty and the need to reestablish his personal worth. During his work life, a man characteristically invests more and more of his energy into his job, gradually withdrawing from other activities—even from those near and dear to him, his family. Because of his highly specialized work role, a man is vulnerable to psychological disorganization when he is faced with retirement. Retirement may mean a loss of income, but more damaging psychologically are losses of a man's friends, his status, and whatever feelings of worth he owes to his job. Most men adapt well to retirement after a year or two. Many would not consider going back to work after the ambiguous adjustment phase is over. Other friends and activities take up his time;

he finds rewards in other activities; and he often finds that he can be admired as a person, not only as a worker.

The task for women at the empty-nest stage and for men in retirement consists of redefining their selves and re-creating new activities—usually a new style of life. Of course, such broad generalizations neglect many of the subtle stimuli an aging person must deal with. The mirror reflects a face no longer young, hair gone or gray, a fat and wrinkled physique—these changes all necessitate psychological adaptations if the person feels much the same as he did when he was youthful. A particularly intense problem faces a woman who has let her self-esteem depend wholly on her physical attractiveness.

One of the concerns of aging is the increasing need to limit activities as energy declines and the need for rest increases. Understanding his growing limitations is especially difficult for a person used to crowding much into a day. Older people begin to place more emphasis upon conservation of achievements made earlier in life—and on conservation of physical being. The ill health and death of a person's peers, which serve as reminders of his own vulnerability, seem to heighten the tendency to conserve. From this retreat often follow the complexities of the desire to be able to withdraw from life honorably and with dignity.

FRIENDS AND INTIMACY

Although older people do begin to disengage from many social roles, activity seems to be positively related to life satisfaction. That is, individu-

The Worst Thing about Middle Age	Percent
Losing Your Husband	52
Getting Older	18
Cancer	16
Children Leaving Home	9
Menopause	4
Change in Sexual Feelings and Behavior	1

What I Dislike Most about Being Middle-Aged	
Getting Older	35
Lack of Energy	21
Poor Health or Illness	15
Feeling Useless	2
None of These	27

The Best Thing about the Menopause	
Not Having to Worry about Getting Pregnant	30
Not Having to Bother with Menstruation	44
Better Relationship with Husband	11
Greater Enjoyment of Sex Life	3
None of These	12

The Worst Thing about the Menopause	Percent
Not Knowing What to Expect	26
The Discomfort and Pain	19
Sign of Getting Older	17
Loss of Enjoyment in Sexual Relations	4
Not Being Able to Have More Children	4
None of These	30

How Menopause Affects a Woman's Appearance	
Negative Changes	50
No Effect	43
Positive Changes	1
No Response	6

How Menopause Affects a Woman's Physical and Emotional Health	
Negative Changes	32
No Effect	58
Positive Change or Improvement	10

How Menopause Affects a Woman's Sexual Relations	
Sexual Relations Become More Important	18
No Effect	65
Sexual Relations Become Less Important	17

als who are active in a number of social roles tend to report greater life satisfaction than disengaged or unengaged persons. One important social relationship for an aging person is to have an intimate friend in whom to confide personal problems and accomplishments; individuals who have someone who will listen sympathetically or at least at great length can apparently better handle the myriad personal and health crises of aging. Loneliness—personal and social and intellectual—is the most wicked scourge of the aged.

FAMILY LIFE

Interpersonal relationships of a married couple—or with other family members—are continually changing throughout the life span. Data about married life after sixty-five do not support the idea that relationships, even at this point in life, remain stable. Many marriages improve after retirement, but others decline in quality. One important element in the late life of marriage is the man's increasing dependency on his wife and his reaction to his loss of "power" as he leaves the work force. If he can adapt well to his role loss and to his greater dependency on his wife for psychological support, his satisfaction with the marriage may go up. Similarly, if his wife has a supportive attitude about his increasing dependence, her satisfaction with the marriage may increase relative to the days when he was spending many hours away from home to earn a living. On the other hand, if a man resents his dependency on his wife and her seeming dominance, and she uses his dependence as a weapon against him, their life together after retirement may degenerate into bickering and nagging. Their long marriage may terminate, to the utter surprise of friends and children, in a late-life divorce.

SEXUAL ADJUSTMENTS

Sexual adjustments in a marriage may also change in late life. Although survey data indicate a decline in sexual activity with age, many married couples enjoy regular sexual intercourse throughout their married life, well into their nineties. Other couples, for whom sexual adjustment was always marked with conflict, may cease to have sexual relations after middle age, and they may not have intercourse for thirty years. Individual differences are great, so it is possible to find examples of almost any type of sexual adjustment in late life. Although the hormonal and other somatic changes that occur with age are almost universal, the influence of religious differences, marital adjustment, and personality on sexual behavior in late life is very important.

One of the important factors in older adults' sexual behavior is simply the availability of sex partners. Because there are many more widows than widowers, there is an excess of potentially sexually active women. But because of the lower mobility of aged persons, and the lack of men, many widows must adjust by sublimating their sexual desire.

REMARRIAGE

Remarriage in old age can create surprisingly intense problems. Grown children of a widowed

Figure 27.6. Friends and family — or lack of them — play an important part in the aged person's life.

mother or father are frequently reluctant to see the parent marry again—for a variety of reasons. Remarriage of an older parent with a "stranger" may seem to derogate the previous long-lasting marriage and family life of which they were a product. Inheritance of property or disposal of sentimental objects may well be a factor. So strong are their children's feelings about remarriage that some aged couples find themselves eloping to avoid the negative attitudes and family tensions.

PERSONALITY DIFFERENCES

The characteristic problems that face adults in the later phases of the life span evoke different responses depending upon the personalities of the individuals. Generally, the style with which the person met previous life issues will characterize how he solves problems in his old age.

A variety of individual personality types appear to adapt well to aging. It is not only the mature personality, who seeks information and develops constructive approaches in his life, who adapts well. Surprisingly, persons who have had a passive style, who have leaned heavily on others, age well. Another personality type that seems to adapt successfully is the highly armored type of individual; because such persons have always protected themselves by ignoring reality, they defend themselves against the anxiety-evoking problems of aging by simply denying that they exist.

Individuals who adapt most poorly to late-life problems are those who are passively hostile and those who intrinsically hate themselves. Self-

haters blame themselves for every turn of events and often are so preoccupied with self-blame that they make no plans of action. Passively hostile persons view themselves as being victimized by other persons and events. They have always been angry do-nothings, and their satisfactions are not likely to increase in later life.

The major problems of late life—whether they be lack of money or serious illness and impending death—can produce high anxiety. The manner in which a person has handled ambiguous problems that produce anxiety during his adult life is likely to typify his responses in old age. The aged are real people who behave much as they always have —a loving, giving person still is affectionate, an old paranoid is still a paranoid, and an old roué still lusts after new women. For psychologically mature persons, though, growing older seems to bring a reduction of rash emotional responses and greater mastery of self. The resulting candidness of the very aged is generally surprising to young persons; a mature, aged person can seem very cool to the young. The aged are often quite prepared to discuss topics that would seem to be daring or sensitive areas to young persons; they may be very open in discussing their old age, lack of money, sexual desires, active hostilities, or benign prejudices, and even their impending death.

CHANGES IN GOALS

As was stated earlier, the normally developing individual will, by definition, successfully adapt to many problems and crises over his life span. One by-product of normal coping with many develop-

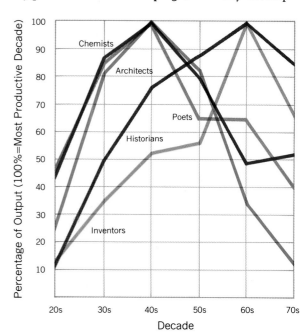

Figure 27.7. Productivity for certain professions, expressed as a percentage of the output of the most productive decade. The 738 subjects for whom data were collected all lived to age seventy-nine or beyond; most were born after 1600. The data came from important source books in each area. The subjects are not uniform with regard to degree of eminence, and the units of productivity vary widely, e.g., a sonnet versus a history of Rome. (After Dennis, 1966.)

mental tasks seems inevitably to be the evolution of goals and life strategies. Results of research indicate that older men often report themselves to be more satisfied with their earlier lives than are younger men. Thus, growing older can permit many individuals to accept their pasts and perhaps to renounce without excessive regret the unobtained goals. Young people's goals are more remote, and they are more driven and motivated. One could say that the task of the younger person is to become, whereas the task of the older person is to be. After having developed acceptance—say, following retirement—the older person has less need to be defensive in his relations with other persons and so has less need for the masking artifices of conversation; he can be more candid than a young adult.

Another effect of evolving goals in late life is that an older person, who is less driven to achieve his own goals, will display a concern for providing younger persons with the opportunity for achievement. Normally developing persons in middle age, for example, will help others younger than themselves to develop autonomously. On the other hand, there are many crochety old-timers around who figure that because they came up the hard way, youth had better suffer, too.

It is not often that an individual can continue a high level of productivity into the seventies and eighties. One study found an exception in writers, who apparently still find opportunities for career achievements in late life. Figure 27.7 shows the productivity of men in various fields at different ages. More typically, however, scientists and pro-

Figure 27.8. Achievement in old age is symbolized by such well-known figures as Pablo Casals, Aaron Copeland, and Marc Chagall.

fessional persons must gain satisfaction less from their own contemporary achievements than from the achievements of their direct heirs or of younger persons whom they sponsor and support. They can, of course, remember and hope; a great many major awards—such as the Nobel prizes— are often based on work done twenty or thirty years earlier.

New turns of interest may appear in late life to replace the achievement-directed activities of earlier years. Youth's desire for play may be recaptured and embellished in older adults. The need for play and the associated interpersonal contact exists at all ages. Even in terminally ill, bedridden patients the desire for play exists and can be cultivated. Play activities in such instances may provide the medium for important effective exchanges around life's important issues.

MOTOR SKILLS

One of the most pronounced characteristics of the very aged is their slowness of movement. This slowness is frequently disconcerting in situations where the older adult cannot pace his own activities but must respond to the demands of the environment, such as in automobile traffic, in pedestrian crosswalks or escalators, and in coping with automatic machines. Automobile driving may become a serious problem, because everything a very aged person may do is generally slower than the demands of traffic signals and other drivers. It is not always just a problem of slower reactions or poorer attention. The problem may be sensory: the very aged driver, for example,

Figure 27.9. Recent studies have shown that most aged persons enjoy living with others of their own age-group. Many residential centers are now being built to accommodate these people.

is very susceptible to glare. Most older people avoid driving at night for the simple reason that they cannot see well.

Older persons—like us all—try to adapt so that their physical limitations do not preclude their participation in life's activities. In many circumstances, visual, hearing, and motor deficits are not great handicaps if the person has time enough to adapt. Slowness of response remains an issue, however, as do sensory impairment and inability. These problems are inevitably confounded by the aged's inability to shift attention rapidly. Talking with the old is frustrating, unless the topic never changes.

HOUSING AND LIVING ARRANGEMENTS

One of the newer findings coming out of studies of the aged is that living with persons of about the same age appears to result in higher satisfaction with life than does living among persons of a wide range of ages. All things being equal, individuals enjoy contact with others of the same age and situation. Thus, if income permits, older people prefer to live adjacent to others of the same age where they can make intimate new friends with whom they can exchange accounts of similar life experiences and share current problems. They still want to be in the vicinity of an adult child, however. There seems to be validity to the principle that most aged persons should live near their children but not with them because no matter how congenial intimate daily contact with one's children might be, prolonged contact can evoke tensions and problems. Independent living, with its greater variety of options, is apparently more comfortable for the aged, as it certainly is for their children and grandchildren.

The middle-aged adult is developmentally in the middle. He faces the tasks of his children as well as those of his aged parents. When aged parents change their residence, the grown children must help them to adapt to the new communal living. Often, the younger adult tries to dissuade his parents from living with other retired persons; from his view it seems an "old folks' home." The parents and children must both sift their attitudes and resolve their goals and expectations in order to develop the most suitable living arrangements. Surprisingly, some individuals very late in life will report that they have never been happier than when living in a community of other aged adults. Perhaps the significant thing is the opportunity for congenial daily contact with empathetic persons in similar circumstances.

MALADJUSTMENT

Not all individuals adapt well to the crises and problems of late life. Some persons who have never before been mentally ill may develop problems of surprising intensity in late life. These problems need not necessarily be caused by physical deterioration; there are purely emotional disorders that occur for the first time in late life—and from which individuals can recover. Hospitalization is rare, however; only about 1 to 2 percent of the population over sixty-five ever become mental-hospital patients. Generally speaking, the widowed, single, and divorced occupy more beds in institutions than do married persons. It seems clear, then, that it is not only the behavior of an older adult that dictates whether or not he will be institutionalized; much depends on the supportive nature of his environment—whether there is anyone outside the institution who can and wants to care for him.

Depression appears to occur with greater frequency in older adults than in younger ones, often as a reaction to real or supposed losses. It is a particularly serious problem in men, who tend to become severely depressed because of changes in their physical well-being. Attempts at suicide are much higher in aged men than in any other population group, and such attempts often follow a health-related depression. Not only do many more old men than young adults attempt suicide, the proportion of successes is much higher among the old—when they decide, they really mean it. Suicide rates are much lower for women than for men, and the factors responsible may be cultural as well as biological. Women may be more willing, by training and experience, to accept the dependent relationships necessitated by poor health.

There are no accurate figures about the extent of mental illness in the aged population because there are no adequate measuring instruments. Some persons who see aged relatives undergoing severe intellectual deterioration, with a tendency to forget and to wander, may form a stereotype of the aged on this basis. And this stereotype may influence their expectations about their own old age. In fact, relatively few persons ever suffer such

Figure 27.10. Institutionalization of old persons sometimes takes place not because of physical or mental disability—but simply because there is no one outside the institution to take care of—or care for— the old person.

progressive and serious deterioration of intellectual functioning.

The Terminal Stage and Death

In theory, the final developmental task of life is to face death. Old people know they will die, of course, just as do the young; but no one expects to die tomorrow or next week or next year. In fact, the longer an aged person lives, the more he expects to live still longer.

The terminal decline in an individual may last for a few days or for a few years. A person's characteristics during this phase may be largely influenced by the dominant biological character of the terminal illness. An abrupt change in mental functioning is coming to be regarded as characteristic of impending death.

The last days of life for a person who has been told that death is imminent can be a dynamic, evocative stage. Often individuals have a wave of recall of early life events; for some, disturbing dreams occur. The realists, as well as those who use fantasy to face life, have the task of dying to face. It is quite possible that some who have lived their life by denial will attempt to end it by denial; they will dispute the diagnosis. It will help the terminally ill person to be surrounded by persons who are aware of the dynamics of this stage of life. How he faces the facts of his life will depend in part upon the intactness of his competence, that is, the extent to which the terminal illness leaves his mind unclouded.

The terminal stage of life presents four problems. First, the person must somehow manage his reactions to the symptoms of his terminal illness, must adapt to the changes in his body and the pain and limitations on his mobility. Second, the awareness of the terminal illness requires that he adapt to an impending separation from his loved ones and friends. Third, because he is leaving his life behind, he must adjust his perception of the contents of his life as he lived it to the way that he would liked to have lived it. And fourth, he must adapt to a transition to an unknown state. Even though religious teachings may influence his reaction to the thought of impending death, the transition itself remains a mystery to human beings.

Individuals, of course, vary in how they approach the end of life. Some welcome it, some simply accept it, some deny it, some disdain it, and some are filled with fear. The inner experience of reviewing one's life is not idle reminiscence; it is important to adapting to the end of life. When dying people talk to others about the past, they are attempting to weave their experiences into a new and finally acceptable perspective on their lives. The recognition of one's approaching death may open the dam to a stream of unresolved conflicts from past life. These conflicts may bring emotions of such intensity that psychiatric care becomes necessary as an adjunct to the physical care.

One of the aspects of the terminal stage, mentioned before, is the abruptness of change that may occur in mental functioning. Individuals who have shown stable mental capacities into their nineties may, within a few months of death,

show sudden losses in mental capacities as the illness encroaches upon the biological functions of the nervous system. The old person may eventually lose awareness of his state and of other individuals.

Generally, then, a person dies in this order: socially, psychologically, and biologically. The circumstances of his terminal illness may require protracted hospitalization and so separate the individual from his previous social roles. Thus, social death may occur early in protracted illnesses. Psychological death occurs later, when an individual is no longer aware of other persons and no longer has any affective relationships. Biological death occurs last, but it also is distributed over time because cells of the body are differently susceptible to oxygen want and toxicity.

AFTER DEATH

The grief of surviving aged relatives or friends is both a psychological and a physiological problem. The psychosocial accompaniments of grief may be physiologically stressful and so provoke serious medical complications. Mortality rates show that more widows and widowers die during their first year of bereavement than married persons of the same age; the stress associated with the grief thus appears to be a powerful physiological phenomenon. The distress may be reduced when the bereaved person has other intimate friends.

Coping with bereavement is a special problem for very old persons. They are faced with the necessity of adapting to the death of friends, brothers and sisters, and even their children. Our mobile society, with its emphasis on youth, has not prepared individuals for the final developmental task of facing their own death. Recently, however, the reluctance to discuss death has been breaking down, and it is becoming possible to examine objectively the cultural and psychological aspects of dying. Religion and a firm and continuing society of thoughtful friends remain the best comfort, however.

Personal psychological preparation for death is still a mystery and will likely always be one. Objectively speaking, the test of any preparation for one of life's developmental tasks is whether or not it works; and it is impossible to determine whether or not the dead have been successful. Any account or theory of preparing for death must be judged by very personal standards. The poet Dylan Thomas wrote to his dying father:

Do not go gentle into that good night
Old age should burn and rage at close of day

A religious individual will prefer one theory, the existentialist another, and the materialist yet a third. Theories, then, are only exercises in personal artistry. The only sure preparation for the end of life is a life well lived.

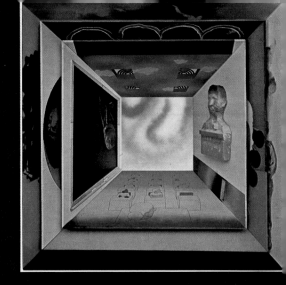

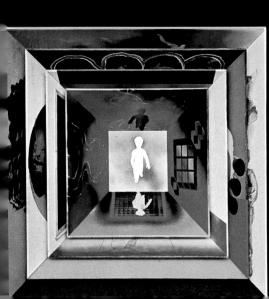

All individual lives are different. Each life, from birth through death, is a unique process, lived out by one person and lived in his own particular manner. From the moment of conception, individuals differ in a host of ways—their physical size, the color of their skins, their potential for intelligent behavior, their temperament, and even their predispositions to various diseases. As soon as an individual comes into the world, however, his inherited characteristics become subject to the influence of his environment—his family and his culture. These external forces will determine many of the characteristics of the individual's life—his chances of going to college, for example—and even of his final place in earth—in most parts of the world there are separate cemeteries for Protestants, Catholics, Jews.

In order to make sense and order out of millions of individual human lives, social and behavioral sciences categorize people. Broad classes of characteristics are drawn, and individuals sharing those characteristics are placed in the class regardless of their individuality in other respects. Predictions are made about the class of individuals, with the hope that they will apply to some extent to each of its individual members. Some categories are relatively easy to make, and some predictions about people in the category are almost obvious. Social class, for example, is a way of categorizing individuals according to a variety of characteristics, notably their family's income, type of employment, residential location, and educational level. Once a person is categorized this way, a great deal more is predictably known about him

and his future than went into making the categorization. A lower-class boy, compared to an upper-class boy, can be predicted to have a variety of different opportunities and experiences, which shape the contents of his life into an entirely different mold. The amount of education he will attain, his companions in grammar school, his interests and aspirations, even his eventual political preferences can be predicted from his class membership with amazingly little error and with distressingly few exceptions.

Some examples of classifying individuals for the purpose of predicting are not so obvious, but they succeed nevertheless. The order in which children are born determines, to some extent, their future. First-born children are many times more likely than later-born children to enter occupations requiring great independence of judgment.

Right from conception, then, there are physical and potential differences, and from birth there are social, cultural, and institutional constraints on the life that will be lived. These factors do not obscure individuality; rather, they group very different individual personalities together on the basis of just a few shared characteristics. The fact remains, however, that the content of an individual life is highly and multiply determined from the very start. Unique as it is, a life is nevertheless the product of determining forces.

Developmental psychology teaches that the processes of growth and development are the same for all individuals. Regardless of one's unique personality, regardless of one's social class, regardless of the color of one's skin, regardless of

Epilogue:
The Life Cycle in Perspective

one's cultural background, one's development consists of the same *stages*, encountered at about the same age and resolved in the same manner, as does the development of every other living person. An individual's development and that of the one person in the world who is most different from him run in parallel channels. Developmental stages are the processes in growth that all humans share in common.

In order to explore this aspect of developmental psychology, take four crucial episodes—infancy, childhood, adolescence, and maturity—from the lives of two hypothetical but representative individuals, one from a wealthy white family and one from a poor black family in the same large city. We could as well compare a poor white boy with a rich black boy; the results would be the same. The content of their lives will be poles apart, as different as two lives can be, but the stages of their development, their resolutions, and their implications will nevertheless be the same.

The poor infant is likely to encounter many inadequacies in his infancy, ranging from poor diet to overcrowded living conditions. The rich boy, on the other hand, is most likely to be provided with everything that infancy requires in the way of physical objects and care. But both these infants will be loved, stimulated, and encouraged. And both their bodies and their behavioral capacities will develop according to the same maturational schedule. At this stage of life, barring actual damage, the two quite separate lives unfold along the typical and immutable developmental timetable of infancy. If the two infants were suddenly brought together, they would approach each other as if there were no differences between them.

It is in childhood that the socioeconomic accidents of history and birth begin to create monstrous differences between the contents and experiences of these two lives. The physical environments of the two children may be as different as can be imagined, the one filled with all that the parents can think of to give the child, the other severely deprived. The problems that the children face in their daily lives will range from a battle to find enough to eat in the one case to a desperate attempt to relieve well-fed, pampered boredom in the other. And their human environment may include several persons from outside the family—in the role of servants in the one case and as a multitude of half-brothers and half-sisters but perhaps no father in the other.

To be sure, extreme deprivation may thwart the one child's efforts to take full advantage of his capacity, yet the developmental stages through which the two children pass are identical. The specific contents and experiences, of course, must differ radically because the surroundings that determine them are so different. But each child, for example, learns a language during this period. The language of one child will be different in many words, phrases, and expressions from that of the other child, but both languages require the mastery of just as difficult a syntax and at least initially just as large a vocabulary. Both acquire a language that is appropriate to at least as many situations, crises, and traumas. There are further developmental homogeneities as well. Both children learn in this period to master their physical environments insofar as possible. It is true that quite different environments are mastered, but the important point developmentally is that mastery and competence develop in each case out of interaction with the available environment—successes with it and failures. It matters little developmentally whether the mastery is over the rats of a garbage heap in the alley behind a tenement or over the clean and inoculated family dog; whether over dilapidated stairs and broken windows or over expensive electronic gadgets. Mastery and competence develop.

Also, both children develop their personalities through identification with the significant adults and peers who populate their worlds. One identification may be with the mother and the leader of the local street gang, whereas the other is with the father and the Little League coach; doubtless, the results of these identifications for later personality will be very different. But in each case, identification does take place, and aspects of the personality are laid down that will follow the child as long as he lives and that will continue to influence the contents of further development. Radically different environments and life situations make for radically different contents and life styles, but the processes of development remain intact and the same for all people.

The opportunities as well as the frustrations of adolescence will also be different for these two people, but the developmental lessons that emerge from them will be substantially the same.

Again, it is a matter of the immutable march of underlying stages, despite variance in their specific outward manifestations. Both children face and solve their sexuality on the way to becoming effective adults, although the access to sexual relationships and the specific approvals or shames connected with them may vary greatly. At this stage of development both children face the necessity of independence from the family, at least in their private lives and thoughts, and both achieve some degree of independence, although its physical form will be different. Both learn to succumb to or master frustration, be it over a better job after school or a faster yacht at the club. Both face the decisions, determined by outside factors in both cases, connected with school; for the rich youth, college, desired or not, is nearly a certainty, while for the poor one, continuing in school at all is an often unachievable and at best mixed blessing. And each approaches obligation, if only in the form of the armed forces draft, although in the one case it is tantamount to slavery and in the other a lesson in the astute exercise of special privilege. The core developments are thus the same, although the contents and even the degree to which development takes place will vary. Regardless of their degree, the advancements or regressions of adolescence are developmentally homogeneous.

Although the specific contents of maturity—what it means to be an effective, mature adult in a cultural and social setting—will differ for these two people, and although it is likely that their individual degrees of maturity in their own set-

tings will also differ, the developmental question of maturity applies equally well to each of them. Kohlberg's scale of moral judgment will be found to describe the morality of each of the boys as adults, although the things they value and the degree to which they advance through the stages may not be at all the same.

With maturity comes the greatest and least understood of the developmental challenges— freedom. Previous stages are in a real sense forced on the individual as long as he remains healthy and intact physically and mentally. The accidents of conception—which particular set of hereditary determinants successfully penetrates the ovum— are immutable. The developments of infancy and childhood are largely forced by physical growth and the constancies of human cultures, which structure the physical and social environments. The transition to adolescence is marked by sexual maturing; one cannot choose, like Peter Pan, to remain a child. These transitions and episodes arise without effort or seeking by the individual; they come from the commonalities of human growth and human experience. But that is not so with the mature years. Adults can all too easily hide away from development.

Perhaps the young adults who people the emerging stage of youth can best illustrate the possibilities of freedom. By virtue of the generosity and affluence of the time in which they live, these youths are free to explore themselves and their world without the confinements of daily work, without moment-to-moment demands from outside themselves, and without instantly pressing problems of survival or the need for progress. Many of these people, society's luxury, have chosen not to hide. They have temporarily chosen not to assume the responsibilities of career and family that poorer and less fortunate individuals are forced into and that less brave individuals choose as a way of hiding from themselves and from the problems of their society. These youths are looking into themselves and into their society, and some are actively seeking ways to better both.

Post-youth adults, too, have the option of freedom. If they are lucky enough to be free from the necessity of daily physical toil for survival and to belong to a group against which few prejudices are exercised by society, they have a choice between facing the world and thereby continuing to develop or hiding away from it in a secure but challengeless job, rounds of television, and perhaps pills or liquor. It is as easy to hide in modern American society as it is to convince one's self that meaningless tasks constitute a day's work. These people constitute the Hiding Majority.

Developmental psychology as yet knows little about these options for freedom or bondage, just as it knows little about the effects of enforced societal bondage on the poor or minority adult. Continued growth in maturity presents an as yet unsolved challenge to developmental psychologists. It is likely that, as knowledge of infancy and childhood expands, so also will the ability to probe the problems and potentialities of normal, free adults.

Everyone is his own psychologist. Ask anyone if he understands people, and he will surely reply, "Yes." He has to believe that he does, because he has to interact with people most of his waking time. But the intuitive generalizations that people build up are only partly true, or at best true under particular circumstances. Thus, although such maxims as "Absence makes the heart grow fonder" are often accurate, frequently "Out of sight, out of mind" is a truer statement. The task of the psychologist is to determine what general laws do apply to behavior and under what circumstances each is true or not true.

Some psychological statements hold for everyone or for people within a given culture. If a gun is fired behind a person, he will assume a certain tensed-up posture. If you are introduced to another adult and hold out your right hand, he will take it. There are some situations in which the behavior of almost everyone is restricted or controlled by the specific stimulus or the total situation, but most behavior is not so obviously determined. Many factors can affect behavior, and several may contribute to one act. For example, a dog may react to a stranger by wagging its tail and barking while slowly backing away. It has been argued that the multiple determination of behavior makes its scientific study more difficult than the study of other phenomena. It may simply be that different kinds of factors can determine a reaction and that psychologists today can isolate and identify these factors only under very limited conditions and often only in the laboratory, not in everyday life.

PSYCHOLOGICAL OBSERVATIONS

We might think that the psychologist should have no trouble observing the phenomena he wants to study. They are all around him all the time. Psychologists do use their everyday experience with other people as well as their own inner experiences as part of the grist for their mill. But observations of such phenomena are unsystematic and frequently biased. These experiences are most useful as a source of hunches to be confirmed by more carefully controlled observations.

KINDS OF OBSERVATIONS

Professional psychologists may observe behavior *under natural conditions*. Some study personal products—autobiographies, compositions, and letters. Some make such systematic observations of behavior under natural conditions as how many drivers stop completely at a "Stop" sign or how many go through without stopping, and at what speeds. The growing field of ethology was initiated by the observations of American, German, and British scientists on the behavior of animals, birds, and insects in nature. Nursery-school children are observed on the playground.

A common source of data is *ratings*, which may be made by peers or by superiors (teachers, job

Appendix:
Methods and Measurement

supervisors). Observations are often made by experts by means of interviews in connection with selection for school admission or for a job.

Other kinds of observations require the subject himself to furnish the data. The psychologist does not necessarily accept the subject's statement as the ultimate truth, but he does take it for what it is, that is, for what the subject says about himself. One such well-known method is the *survey*, as in public opinion polling. In surveys, a carefully selected sample of people is asked questions, and the responses are considered to be estimates for the population from which the sample was drawn. This method, however, is not always as simple as it initially seems: the data gathered from such polling during presidential elections must be interpreted carefully if the surveyor wants to maximize his accuracy of predicting the election. For example, he gives more weight to responses given by the kind of people who are likely to go to the polls on election day.

Other methods of observation include *inventories* and *tests*. Much can be learned by asking subjects about their past life, about their interests, and about how they see themselves. By having a subject solve various problems or perform certain tasks, it is possible to estimate his intelligence and skills. Notice that in these tests the psychologist uses the person's actual performance in the testing situation, whereas in self-report inventories, the psychologist uses what the person says now about his prior behavior.

Finally, the psychologist can observe the physiological functioning of people. He can record pupil size, heartbeat, breathing pattern, blood volume in the finger, skin conductance, and electrical activity in the brain.

The Observation, the Index, and the Variable

It is apparent that psychologists do not lack methods of observation. The more critical problem is making something out of their observations. The researcher is never interested in his observations just for their own sake: he wants to do something with them. He is interested in estimating something. To make a reliable estimate, he has to make a series of observations. If he is estimating an ability in a person, he asks the subject to answer many questions and takes the person's total score as an index of the person's ability. He has learned from past experience that this score is more dependable than the score from any one item (question) in his test. Similarly, the

experimenter studying learning in rats will observe a number of rats and take their average performance as his index.

THE OBSERVER'S PERSPECTIVE

One of the major problems of psychology is that its phenomena depend more upon the observer than do the phenomena of other sciences. You have undoubtedly heard about the objectivity of the scientist; you have heard about science's requirement that observers agree on what they see and that scientists must be able to repeat their own experiments and those of other scientists before the findings become accepted as part of scientific knowledge. But there are often discrepancies between phenomena as perceived by different people. You may see a friend as less likable than he sees himself as being, or as less so than his wife sees him. Thus, the objectivity of psychologists' observations is of a different sort than that in the physical sciences.

Psychologists seek consensus on phenomena as seen by some designated person or persons. You may see a mother grab her child who is running out into the street. You may think she is trying to protect her child from being hurt. But a moment later you may hear her say as she spanks the child, "Don't you ever hit your little brother again!" and you realize that she was reaching for the child to punish him for something else. Someone else who had observed the incident from the beginning might report that the child had been running into the street simply to escape from his mother. In this event, the essential psychological phenomena are the experiences of the child and of the mother. If we could get into the child's mind, what would we find that he was trying to do? What would a mother tell a close friend that she was doing? The phenomena you observed as a disinterested third party might also be of interest in terms of how people interpret the behavior of others. But for each of these viewpoints—yours, the child's, and the mother's—the psychologist needs to obtain dependable observations on what the phenomena were from that particular perspective. Psychologists seek objectivity in the sense of agreement on what the phenomena are from some perspective.

There are, therefore, several perspectives from which the psychologist's data can be produced. The psychologist must treat the data from each perspective as a separate set of phenomena. In some instances, he may find that two different perspectives yield data that agree closely with each other, but until he has such empirical evidence, he must recognize the conceptual independence of each point of view. One of the major sources of disagreement between psychological observations made by different methods is simply a result of utilizing different perspectives, each perspective producing its own phenomena.

Finally, there are the stimuli themselves. In tests, the stimuli are the separate questions, problems, or items. A person's score on a vocabulary test will vary a little with the particular test used, that is, with the particular words included in it. A person's score on a questionnaire about proneness to anxiety will also vary with the particular instrument—and may vary a great deal, especially when the different questionnaires have been constructed by different psychologists with varying ideas about anxiety and its manifestations.

Psychology has many methods for collecting data and many concepts it wants to study. Like any science, it must find methods appropriate for each concept and must make sure that the methods really do produce data relevant to the concept. The discussion above has indicated that the target concepts at which measurement is aimed should be concepts associated with a stated perspective: how a person sees himself, how others see him, and so on. Within each perspective, the methods of measurement must use conditions and stimuli that are congruent with the concept as it has been spelled out. Thus, it is apparent that each global variable, like learning, intelligence, love, or emotionality, takes various forms when seen from different viewpoints, and within each viewpoint, the variable's manifestations may vary with the conditions and with the stimuli. The enormous task faced by psychology is to create a conceptual framework into which all these pieces can be fitted. As things stand today, it is no wonder that different methods for measuring what is thought to be the same variable typically disagree with each other to a major degree.

PROBLEMS IN OBSERVING

From what has been said above and from his own experience, the reader can readily accept the assertion that psychological observations by laymen are very likely to be biased when compared to those made by a more objective observer. We would not expect a mother's description of her child to agree with a teacher's or with a neighbor's. We would not expect an applicant for a job to describe his deficiencies with utter frankness. It is hardly necessary, then, to warn the reader about the possibilities for strong *observer effects* (effects associated with a particular perspective or particular conditions) in data based on reports by observers who are personally involved or have not been trained in systematic observation.

ERRORS IN OBSERVATION

One might think that a trained psychological observer would encounter little difficulty in making observations objectively because he has experience at doing so, but such observations are not easy. First, let us consider an experimental study in which the psychologist is not studying the subject himself but rather is trying to draw conclusions about people in general—for example, a study to determine the threshold for hearing a sound, that is, the lowest intensity that a human subject can detect auditorially. The experimenter begins with a sound he is sure the subject can hear and then gradually lowers its intensity, asking each time, "Can you still hear it?" The subject will tend to continue reporting affirmatively even when the intensity is reduced considerably. Next, the experimenter begins at a very low intensity, perhaps telling the subject that he will hear nothing for a while. In this series, the subject is likely to report

As she sees herself: ten years younger than her age. Competent yet desirable.

As her husband sees her: older than she actually is.

As the camera sees her: she is thirty-seven and chic but looks inhibited.

As she thinks others see her: sophisticated and sexy, a focus of masculine approval.

not hearing the sound even when its intensity has reached the level at which, in the series with descending intensity, he was still reporting that he heard it. This example shows the possible *error of habituation*.

Now suppose that the experimenter again begins with very low intensity but instructs the subject to attend very carefully and to be sure to report the sound just as soon as he hears it, even if it is very faint. This instruction is likely to produce *errors of expectation*. For example, after the subject has been making his reports for a few minutes, perhaps from one series with increasing intensities and then with a decreasing series, the experimenter can make it appear that the next series will be one with ascending intensities but actually not have any sound at all. Under these conditions, many subjects will, sooner or later, report hearing a sound. They may indicate uncertainty, but their report will be positive.

A person is very likely to hear or see something that he is set to hear or see, whether it is there or not. Experimental procedures have to be carefully planned to control such effects or to measure them so that appropriate corrections can be made in the data. Another form of this kind of bias is the *stimulus error*. When an observer knows something about the actual stimulus, his knowledge may influence and distort the report of his experience.

When a person's expectation comes from what someone else says or does, we often refer to it as *suggestion*. When a person with prestige, a person we respect, says something, we tend to believe him. If you go to your doctor for treatment and he gives you a pill and says, "This will make you feel better," you are likely to start feeling better even if the pill contains nothing but a little sugar. Doctors have known about this effect for some time, and researchers studying the effects of drugs have to design their experiments to control such influences. In the typical design, subjects in an experimental group are given the drug and those in the control group are given a placebo, a pill with no effect. The experimenter then determines whether the observed effects in the experimental group are greater than those in the control group.

EXPERIMENTER EFFECTS

The subject is not the only person in an experiment influenced by expectations. If a medical researcher knows which subjects are in the experimental group and which in the control, his observations of the subjects or his report of what they say may be influenced by this knowledge. For example, suppose that an experimenter believes he has found the cure for a disease that was formerly untreatable. He wants very much to obtain results demonstrating his cure, and he is likely to see effects whether they are there are not. To guard against this tendency, medical research is often performed using a double-blind design. Not only the subject but also the observer is functionally blinded: neither knows whether the subject got the experimental drug or the placebo. Only a third person, such as the pharmacist preparing the pills, holds the secret. Of course, in such experiments, the pills must be indistinguishable; the experimental drug and the placebo must be prepared so that they have the same size, color, and taste.

Psychologists know that an experimenter can unwittingly affect his empirical data in accordance with his expectations. In a standard demonstration, subjects are asked to judge each of a series of photographs of people as to whether the person has been experiencing success or failure. The subject is told that this is a test of empathy, of how well he is able to put himself into someone else's place. Then the person doing the exper-

Figure A.1. The same scene or person may be perceived differently by different observers.

iment instructs some assistants (who are really the subjects of most interest in this experiment) that they are repeating a well-known experiment. Some of these assistants are told that their subjects will give an average rating of moderate success; others are told that the average reported will be that of moderate failure. Each assistant administers the test to ten to twenty subjects. The results clearly demonstrate the effect (and the experiment has been done many times): experimenters expecting ratings in one direction obtain just that. It must be noted that the obtained averages do not reach the averages that the assistants have been led to expect, but the effects are unequivocal. Also note that the conditions are such as to facilitate the appearance of such an effect. The subjects are given a task that they cannot do—they cannot judge success or failure from the typical picture found in a news magazine—and it is under such circumstances that outside influences are likely to have the most effect on judgments.

These discoveries are very sobering. Experimenter biases in observations often occur in the physical and biological sciences as well as in the behavioral sciences. Seeing early data in an experiment may produce expectancies affecting data collected later. Even experimenters studying simple animal behavior may get results biased toward their expectations. If the experimenters believe their rats to be particularly bright, their rats will learn faster than those of experimenters with the opposite expectation. The effects may be small, as in the experiments with human subjects, but they are obtained consistently and they are sufficiently large to affect the interpretations of experiments.

Remedies for such biasing influence are available. The researcher can use assistants who do not know what he hopes to find out and who do not have any clear expectations or any reason for obtaining results of a given kind. Even better are automated procedures. By recording the instructions on tape, for example, the possibilities for subtle communication can be reduced and the experimenter can make sure that his experimental and control subjects are treated the same way except for the critical variable he is studying.

Errors of Measurement

Measurements always contain errors. That is, measurements always are influenced by factors that the experimenter would like to eliminate. There are three major types of error in measurement. One is *observer bias*, which we have consid-

ered above. In that category, we can also include many experimenter effects that influence the behavior of the subject. A sophisticated experimenter who is aware of such dangers and has a good knowledge of the experimental literature can devise experimental procedures for minimizing the possible influence of such errors.

Another kind of measurement error, *design error,* occurs when the experimenter measures something that does not exactly coincide with what he wants to measure. A psychologist studying dreams might ask people in the middle of the day to report a dream they had the night before. A better procedure would be to ask the person to record his dreams as soon as he wakes in the morning. Experimenters have shown that an even better procedure is to wake the person immediately after he has dreamed. The researchers have compared reports made in the morning with reports by subjects who were awakened during the night just after they had dreamed and have found that much of the detail has been lost between these two recall points. But note that even the report immediately after the dream is of an experience occurring many minutes earlier. Psychologists have yet to obtain records of dreams while the subject is dreaming them.

The third kind of measurement error, shared by psychologists and all other scientists, is simple *imprecision*. In physics, the speed of light has been measured by many experimenters over the course of several decades. With increasing technical skill and sophistication, the precision of the measurement has increased steadily. Most psychological measurement, however, has nowhere near such precision.

Precision is the degree of agreement among repeated observations; it is the same as the concept of reliability. Lack of precision is due to uncontrolled factors that affect the observations. Sometimes the experimenter may know what these factors are; sometimes he may not. After the experimenter has done the best he can in eliminating unwanted factors or in controlling their influence, he assesses the reliability of his observations. If the reliability is still unsatisfactory, he seeks to improve his measuring techniques.

The kind of imprecision considered above is random error of measurement, that is, disagreements between measurements repeated under conditions that are identical as far as we can tell. Another kind of imprecision is systematic, as in measuring weight with a spring balance that always yields too low a value or in measuring length with a yardstick that has expanded from heat and moisture. This kind of error can generally be controlled by checking the calibration against a standard instrument not subject to the same kinds of distortion. But note that systematic bias can only be detected when the experimenter uses an independent set of measuring operations that he trusts more than the one being used.

MEASURING

Observing is seeing and recording what is seen. Measuring is going from observations to indices; it is assigning numbers to things in accordance with certain rules. The rule for measuring a book may be that if one end of a ruler is lined up with the bottom edge, the height is taken as that inch mark on the ruler that comes closest to the top of the book. The rule for measuring speed of learning may be to assign the number of the trial on which the organism first completes the task successfully. These rules are arbitrary, in that alternative rules are usually available. The experimenter chooses the rule that seems most rational to him, the one that seems best to index the attribute he is studying. In more technical words, measuring is mapping observations into a number system, an abstract model. The resulting values can then be manipulated according to the rules permissible for the system: sometimes we can add, subtract, and multiply them; however, sometimes we run great risks by even adding them, as we shall see below. Psychology uses several number systems, or scales. The first, the *nominal*, involves simply assigning numbers for identification purposes, as in assigning license plates to automobiles. Scientifically, such numbers have no utility—it is senseless to subtract or divide them—and we could use letters or any other marks as well.

An excellent example of a nominal scale is the set of numbers assigned to the members of a football team. If the quarterback wears the number 15, is he but a third as big, or strong, or powerful as the defensive back who wears number 45? Can we subtract a center (number 54) from a tackle (number 74) and get a halfback (number 20)? No, these numbers are merely symbols used to help differentiate one player from another. These numbers cannot be manipulated in any really meaningful way.

The next type of scale is the *ordinal*, in which numbers are assigned to people or events in terms of how they rank along a given dimension. For example, even if we did not have a yardstick handy, we could line up the members of a foot-ball team in order of their height. We would not be able to say that the fullback was three inches shorter than the flanker back, but we could say that one was taller than the other.

When we have an absolute unit of measurement, then and only then can we make absolute comparisons. For example, if we compared the salaries paid to professional football players, we could say that a man who received $20,000 for the season was paid exactly twice what a man paid $10,000 received. Money is an example of a *ratio scale*, the most powerful type of scale a scientist can use. Distance measured in inches or centimeters and weight measured in pounds or grams are examples of other ratio scales. A ratio scale comprises equal units (the difference between $100 and $101 is exactly the same as the difference between $996 and $997, namely, $1); and, as we all know, it has an absolute zero point, too. Neither an ordinal scale nor a nominal scale has equal units or an absolute zero point.

When we make our measurements with a ratio scale (as scientists almost always prefer to do), we can manipulate the numbers we get in any way we wish—add them, subtract them, or compare them in any way we find meaningful. When we deal with scales other than the ratio, we have to make certain assumptions about the numbers that sometimes are hard to justify. Intelligence and personality tests are often scored like college quizzes—that is, the subject is given one point for each correct answer. But are psychologists justified in such procedures? Do the items in an intelligence test represent equal units of ability, even though some are easy and some are difficult? Does the difference between IQs of 100 and 110 represent just the same difference in ability as the difference between IQs of 90 and 100? No one really knows. All we can say is that some assumptions usually seem to work and that, at worst, they do not lead psychologists too far astray.

RESEARCH DESIGNS

We have considered the kinds of observations made by psychologists and the possible sources of error in them. We have seen that observations are converted into numbers. But what kinds of plans underlie the making of observations and the recording of numbers? There are two major types: the *correlational* and the *experimental*.

CORRELATIONAL DESIGN

A correlation tells us the degree of relatedness between two things. For example, let us take two

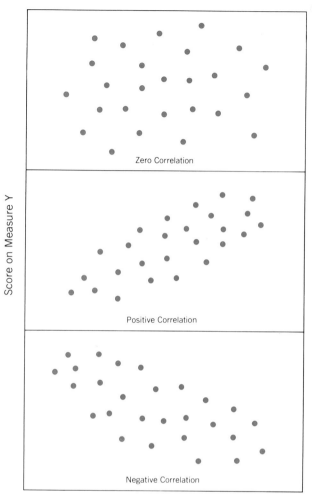

Zero Correlation

Positive Correlation

Negative Correlation

Score on Measure Y

Score on Measure X

Figure A.2. A scatterplot, or correlation plot, is a graphic device that displays the relation between two sets of scores. The scores on one measure are entered according to the index on one axis; the other set of scores is entered according to the index on the other axis. To the extent that the position of a point along one axis is a good predictor of position along the other axis, the points tend to cluster in a line (high positive correlation or high negative correlation).

college students, Mark and Mary. Suppose you happened to notice that, during a certain period of a week or so, almost every time you saw Mark anywhere, you also saw Mary. You saw them together at several parties, at a football game, in the student union, at several meals, and even in a class or two. The appearance of Mark at any given place is obviously correlated with the appearance of Mary; that is, the two events tend to occur together most of the time. If someone told you that he went to a party and saw Mary there, you might be willing to give rather good odds that Mark was there too. Thus, knowing that a correlation exists, you could *predict* the occurrence of one event (seeing Mark) from the occurrence of the other (seeing Mary). In loose terms, a *positive correlation* between two things merely means that they go together, much as we might presume that Mark and Mary were "going together." A correlation tells us nothing about *why* the two events tend to be associated, however.

There are *negative correlations* as well as positive ones. If Mark and Mary had been engaged but had had a violent argument and broken up with great hostility toward each other, you could predict fairly well that if you went to a party and saw Mary, Mark would not be there. Negative correlations allow you to predict the *nonoccurrence* of events with just as much accuracy as positive correlations allow you to predict their occurrence. We seldom invite our enemies to dinner.

The single most important thing to remember about correlations is that they tell us nothing at all about causality, although most people intuitively believe that they do. Take Mark and Mary, for example. We automatically assume that if we see them together all the time, they must be going steady, that is, they must be mutually attracted. If Mark's mother looked at the situation, she might imply a different causality—namely, that Mary was throwing herself at Mark and thus causing them to be seen together all the time. Mary's mother, of course, might believe just the opposite, that the causality was all Mark's doing. In point of fact, all these assumptions could be false. It might be that both Mark and Mary were cheerleaders and therefore were thrown together a great deal by factors outside their control although neither one particularly liked the other.

It is a psychological truism that "positive traits correlate positively." In his famous study of gifted children, Terman found that high IQs were positively correlated with such other factors as better than average health, larger than average size, good looks, superior adjustment, and success. It is easy for most of us to see that good looks do not cause high intelligence, or vice versa; rather, the same genetic factors that lead to one probably also cause the other. It is not so simple for us to see that the high positive correlation between smoking cigarettes, for example, and getting lung cancer does not in and of itself *prove* that smoking causes the illness—it merely gives us a hypothesis that must then be tested experimentally. With only the correlation to deal with, it is scientifically just as tenable to hypothesize that perhaps incipient lung cancer causes a person to become a heavy smoker (because the nicotine tends to deaden the pain from already-irritated lung tissue). The noted British scientist Hans Eysenck has cogently argued that the correlation between smoking and lung cancer is probably due primarily to genetic factors that predispose a person likely to get the disease also to take up smoking. He points out, too, that the correlation between lung cancer and air pollution is much higher than that between cancer and smoking tobacco, a fact most people tend to forget. Obviously, smoking is an unhealthy habit that for sound physiological reasons should be discouraged. Moreover, experimental evidence may eventually show that smoking is indeed a significant contributing cause of lung cancer. But the point of the present discussion is that the causal relationship between smoking and various diseases in humans cannot be *proved* by mere correlations.

Mathematically speaking, correlation coefficients run from +1.0 to −1.0, the extreme coefficients indicating either a perfect positive or a perfect negative relationship. A correlation of zero implies that there is no relationship at all between the two variables being measured. A positive correlation of .85 denotes a much stronger relationship between the events than, say, a coefficient of .35; that is, if the correlation between seeing Mark and also seeing Mary is .85, you can predict their behavior much more accurately than if the correlation is .35. To discover why the correlation exists, you must make use of the experimental method.

EXPERIMENTAL DESIGN

Suppose a psychologist noticed that students who drank a cup of coffee just before taking a long examination seemed to be more alert toward the end of the test than did students who had had nothing to drink. At this point, he merely has noticed a correlation between ingestion of coffee and alertness. If he then performed an experiment in which one group of students (the experimental group) was given coffee while another was given a placebo drink that looked and tasted like coffee (the control group), and subsequently the experimental group was indeed more alert, he would be on the track of a causal connection. He might then assume that it was the caffeine in the coffee that caused the effect and repeat the experiment, giving regular coffee to an experimental group and caffeine-free coffee to the control group. If again the experimental students were more alert, he would be relatively sure that the caffeine did cause the alertness, but he still would not know why.

Next, he might inject caffeine solutions into rats to see if their nervous systems reacted differently than when they were injected with a control solution such as a weak salt solution. If he found that caffeine does indeed act as a neurological excitant, he could safely conclude that coffee causes alertness because the caffeine in it excites the brain in a certain fashion. In all these studies, he would make use of control groups to prove that his results were due to the experimental variable he was manipulating (the coffee or the caffeine) rather than being due to such extraneous variables as the students' knowing they were participating in an experiment or the rats' becoming excited merely because they had been stuck by a needle. No single part of planning an experiment is more important than the wise selection of control groups. The more extraneous variables an experimenter controls for, the greater faith he can have that his experimental variable is doing what he thinks it is doing.

STATISTICAL ANALYSES

Once the experimenter has gathered his observations on his experimental and his one or more control groups, how does he proceed toward a finding and an interpretation? He uses two kinds of statistics, *descriptive* and *inferential*.

DESCRIPTIVE STATISTICS

The psychologist uses descriptive statistics to reduce a mass of data to more manageable terms and to make these data more readily understandable. Suppose we gave a history quiz made up of 100 questions to a class containing thirty-nine students. After grading the quiz, we find that the highest score was 65, the lowest, 40; the *range* of the scores is therefore 25 (65 − 40 = 25). We can now plot a *frequency distribution* of the scores by laying them out as shown in Figure A.3. We can see that one student made a score of 40, that no one made scores of 41, 42, 43, or 44, that three students made a score of 55, and that only one student scored 65. Now, look at the shape of this frequency distribution. It is clear that most students scored about 55, with relatively few scoring at either extreme. In most tests of this type, the scores do tend to pile up in the middle of the distribution. For example, roughly two-thirds of the scores on IQ tests fall between 85 and 115, although the range of the test can be as much as 200 points.

Now suppose we want to compare this class' performance on the quiz with that of another class that took the same test. How could we most meaningfully make such a comparison? One simple way is to find out what the average performance by each group was, then compare the averages. By definition, the average performance is always in the middle or center of the distribution, so when we seek an average of some kind, we are really looking for what psychologists call a *measure of central tendency*. One such measure of central tendency is the arithmetic *mean*; to find it, you merely add up all the scores and then divide by the number of people who took the test. In the case of the history class, the mean of the distribution is 54. In order to justify calculating a mean on mathematical terms, you must use a measurement scale that has equal intervals.

Sometimes the scores on a given scale are so oddly distributed that a mean would give a distorted idea of where the center of the distribution actually was. For example, if you went into a large urban ghetto and randomly asked eleven people

their annual income, you might accidentally select ten very poor people plus one slum landlord who was in the ghetto to collect rent. The poor people might do well to earn $1,000 a year each; the landlord might easily make $1 million. If we add their incomes together, we would get $1,010,000; if we took the arithmetic mean of this figure, we would find that their average annual income was about $92,000. Mathematically, this is a true statement; socially, it is a gross distortion of the facts. In such cases, psychologists make use of a different statistic, the *median*, which is that score in the exact middle of the distribution. In the case of the history class, the median score was 55; in the case of the ghetto dwellers, it was $1,000. When the data you are gathering come from an ordinal scale, you cannot use the mean; you must make use of the median.

A third measure of central tendency occasionally used by psychologists is the *mode*, which is that score made most frequently in any distribution. In the case of the history class, the modal score was 57. Notice that in the distribution of quiz scores, the mean, median, and mode were all different, although closely related to each other. In a perfectly symmetrical distribution, such as the one shown in Figure A.4, the mean, median, and mode might be 50. However, compare this distribution with that in Figure A.5, whose mean, median, and mode are also 50. The range of the two distributions is also the same. Yet what a difference between the two in terms of how the scores are dispersed about the center. In Figure A.4, the bulk of the scores are packed tightly about the middle; in Figure A.5, the scores are spread out evenly from one end to the other. It

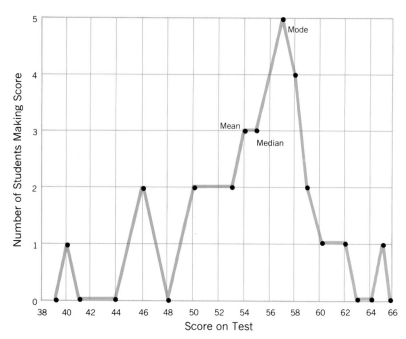

Figure A.3. Frequency distribution of scores.

would be misleading to compare these two distributions merely by talking about their similar means or medians; rather, we need some additional descriptive statistic that tells us how the scores vary about the center point. One such statistic is the *variance* of the distribution. To find the variance, we first calculate the mean, then subtract each score from the mean, square this difference for each score, add all the squares together, then divide by the number of scores we had in the first place. Figure A.6 shows how this is done with a very small distribution of scores. A more useful statistic for most psychological purposes is the *standard deviation*, which is merely the square root of the variance.

Both the variance and the standard deviation tell us something important about the shape of the distribution. If they are relatively large, the scores are widely spread out (as in Figure A.5). If

they are relatively small (as in Figure A.4), the scores are closely packed about the center of the distribution. To calculate either the variance or the standard deviation, we must use a measurement scale with equal intervals.

Measures of central tendency and of variation are used to describe a set of observations (such as test scores) for a single variable (the history quiz itself) or to compare two sets of observations (the scores of one history class compared to those of another) on the same variable. If we wish to determine the relationship between two variables (the heights of a team of football players and their test scores on a quiz), we would calculate the mathematical correlation between the two sets of numbers. This number, which, as we said above, varies from +1.0 to −1.0, is called the *correlation coefficient*.

INFERENTIAL STATISTICS

Descriptive statistics are important, but inferential statistics are even more so, for they provide the researcher with ground rules or conventions for determining what conclusion can be drawn from his data. Consider a man tossing a coin high in the air 100 times. If it lands heads up 53 times, is the coin biased? What if it lands heads up 79 times? Statisticians have worked out methods for determining the probability of obtaining any given result with any given number of tosses of an unbiased coin. More exactly, if the probability of

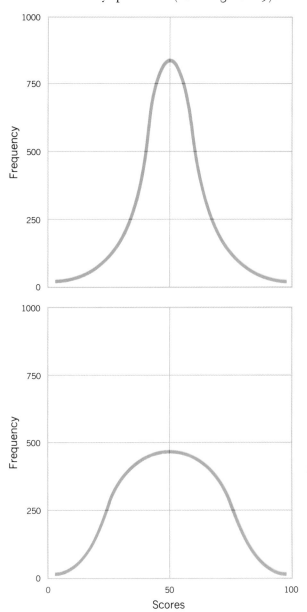

Figure A.4. A distribution of scores with low variance.

Figure A.5. A distribution of scores with larger variance.

Scores	Mean = 6	
3	6 − 3 = 3	$3^2 = 9$
4	6 − 4 = 2	$2^2 = 4$
5	6 − 5 = 1	$1^2 = 1$
5	6 − 5 = 1	$1^2 = 1$
6	6 − 6 = 0	$0^2 = 0$
6	6 − 6 = 0	$0^2 = 0$
7	7 − 6 = 1	$1^2 = 1$
7	7 − 6 = 1	$1^2 = 1$
8	8 − 6 = 2	$2^2 = 4$
9	9 − 6 = 3	$3^2 = 9$

Sum of Squares = 30
÷
Number of Scores = 10
= 3 (Variance)
$\sqrt{3}$ (Standard Deviation)

Figure A.6. The computation of variance.

heads is .50, there are tables to indicate how often, in (say) 100 tosses, one can expect to obtain 28 heads, 53, 79, or any other number of heads from 0 to 100. Probability is a complex technical topic and our intuitions about it are not always correct. For example, if a coin is really not biased, and if it lands on heads 5 times in a row, the chance of its landing heads the next time is still .50; the fact that there has been a run of heads does not affect the best bet on the next trial, provided the toss is honest.

The history of modern probability theory begins in the late 1700s, when a group of French gamblers hired the noted mathematician Pierre Simon, later Marquis de Laplace, to help them determine what odds they should give on such games of chance as a roulette wheel. The odds on most such devices (as well as on such card games as poker and bridge) have long since been worked out, which is one reason the casinos in Las Vegas continue to make money year after year. Take a roulette wheel, for instance. There are the 36 red and black squares, plus a zero and a double zero that are usually colored green. If you place a dollar bet on the number 3, you would expect to win (on the average) one time in 38. Yet when you win, the casino pays you but $35 (they also give you back the dollar that you bet). In short, for each 38 turns of the wheel you would pay the casino $38, but you would expect to get back only $36. The odds in favor of the casino are 38 to 36. No matter how much one individual may win on one occasion, if he keeps on playing the game for a sufficiently long time, he will end up losing—provided, of course, that the wheel is honest. In Las Vegas, the gambling houses usually go to considerable lengths to make sure that their games are honest—it is the safest way they have of making sure that they make a profit.

When we say that a roulette wheel is honest, what we are saying is that there are no biasing factors present that make it more likely that the roulette ball will fall into one numbered pocket more than any other. If one of the pockets was substantially larger than all the rest, the wheel would be biased in favor of this number. But suppose the biasing factor were more difficult to detect; for instance, suppose the roulette ball were made of metal and one of the pockets had a tiny magnet hidden beneath it. How could you, as an external observer, detect the presence of this biasing factor?

The detection of such biasing or controlling factors is what the business of inferential statistics

is all about. Let us go back to the coin-flipping example. The odds of getting a head on any given toss are 50/50; that is, a head will turn up one-half of the time. To find the odds of getting two heads in a row, we multiply the odds for getting one event (a head) by the odds of getting the second (another head); $\frac{1}{2} \times \frac{1}{2} = \frac{1}{4}$. If you got two heads in a row, would you begin to think the coin was biased? No, because such an event occurs about one-fourth of the time. The odds of getting three heads in a row are $\frac{1}{2} \times \frac{1}{2} \times \frac{1}{2}$, or $\frac{1}{8}$, still respectable odds that would not make us suspicious about the coin. If we got four heads in a row, the odds would be $\frac{1}{16}$ that such an event occurred by chance alone, and now we might start muttering to ourselves about our luck (if we were betting on tails).

At what point would our suspicions become so aroused that we would insist on inspecting and perhaps analyzing the coin? Such a decision obviously would be arbitrary and would vary from one individual to another. Psychologists, like most other scientists, have adopted an arbitrary convention: If the odds against a given event's occurring are 1 in 20—that is, if we would expect the event to occur by chance alone only 5 percent of the time—then we are willing to admit that there is a significant likelihood that the results cannot be explained merely in terms of chance variation. If the odds against the event's occurring are 100 to 1—that is, if we would expect the event to occur by chance alone only 1 percent of the time—then we are strongly convinced that something other than chance probably accounts for the results.

Suppose that we ran an experiment in which an experimental group of rats was injected with caffeine and the control animals were injected with a weak salt solution, and we found that the experimental animals learned a maze, on the average, in 30 trials (that is, the mean number of trials to learn the maze was 30), while the control animals, on the average, took 38 trials. What can we infer from these means? Does the difference between the two means really make a difference? Or could we have obtained these differences by chance alone?

To test our hypothesis that the caffeine injection enabled the experimental animals to learn faster, we would usually make use of an inferential statistic called the t test. The t test allows us to use the means and standard deviation to calculate the odds that such a difference between two means was due to chance alone. If the odds were

1 in 20, we would know that we would obtain such a difference by chance alone only 5 percent of the time, so we could accept our hypothesis that caffeine increases speed of learning a maze at what psychologists call the 5 *percent level of confidence* (sometimes also called the *.05 level of significance*). If the odds were 100 to 1, we could accept the hypothesis at what we call the 1 *percent level of confidence* (sometimes also called the *.01 level of significance*). In both cases what we are saying is that we are reasonably confident that our results have some real psychological significance.

If our results (using the *t* test or perhaps some other, more complicated inferential statistic) do not reach the .05 level of significance, then by convention we assume that our hypothesis was not accurate because the odds are too great that the results could be due to chance variation.

As you might guess from the lengthy and rather complicated description we have given of this topic, the proper use of descriptive and inferential statistics is at the heart of many scientific methods, and anyone wishing to do professional work in any of the social, behavioral, biological, or physical sciences must have at least a rudimentary understanding of such matters.

FINDINGS, FACTS, AND THEORIES

No one experiment ever proves anything. A soundly designed and executed experiment can, at best, change our subjective probability that a statement is correct. When we have studied an experiment and found it convincing because its methodology conforms to acceptable scientific standards, we have more confidence that some relationship holds or that it does not hold. Scientific methods are sophisticated common sense. They are the use of rational thinking derived from basic, generally accepted assumptions.

There have probably never been, in psychology, truly crucial experiments that provide a clear basis for choosing between propositions derived from two opposed theories. Such experiments are very rare in any science. The final test in science is replication. A scientific finding becomes established when it has been obtained in several experiments (and the more, the better)—experiments conducted by different experimenters in different places but with the same basic methods. Psychology has few such firmly established findings or facts. Psychologists, and especially students just beginning in research, do not like to repeat the studies done by others; they naturally prefer to do something original, such as repeating an experiment but with a modification of a basic condition. Hopefully, this situation will change so that psychology can become a more mature science.

Science builds on models. Psychologists use statistical models and measurement models in collecting and processing their data and statistical models in evaluating their findings. Psychologists use conceptual models to guide their research, to determine what data to collect and what to look for in the data after collection. These conceptual models become theories, structures that permit interpretation of natural phenomena. We understand what we observe by referring observations to theories. Working the other way, we make predictions derived from these theoretical models. As long as our observations agree with our predictions, we tend to accept the theory. But when these predictions are not consistent with observations, we must change our theory or seek another one that fits more observations. The true goal of science is not the prediction and control of events but the understanding of them. Prediction is merely the way we test our understanding of the world around us, and control of that world is the practical reward of our efforts.

UNIT I THE MEANING OF DEVELOPMENT

● CHAPTER 1 THE CONCEPT OF DEVELOPMENT

ARIÈS, P. *Centuries of Childhood: A Social History of Family Life*. R. Baldic (tr.). New York: Knopf, 1962.

FREUD, S. *Civilization and Its Discontents*. New York: Norton, 1930.

————. *Collected Papers*. London: Hogarth Press, 1925, Vols. I–V.

JENSEN, A. R., AND W. D. ROHWER. "Syntactical Mediation of Serial and Paired-associate Learning as a Function of Age," *Child Development*, 36 (1965), 601–608.

KOHLBERG, L., AND E. TURIEL. *Research in Moral Development: The Cognitive-Developmental Approach*. New York: Holt, Rinehart and Winston, 1971.

MILLER, N. E., AND J. DOLLARD. *Social Learning and Imitation*. New Haven, Conn.: Yale University Press, 1941.

PIAGET, J. *The Origins of Intelligence in Children*. M. Cook (tr.). New York: International Universities Press, 1956.

SPELT, D. "The Conditioning of the Human Fetus In Utero," *Journal of Experimental Psychology*, 38 (1948), 338–346.

● CHAPTER 2 MECHANISMS OF DEVELOPMENT

ANASTASI, A. "Heredity, Environment, and the Question, 'How?' " *Psychological Review*, 65 (1958), 197–208.

BAER, D. M. "Laboratory Control of Thumbsucking by Withdrawal and Re-presentation of Reinforcement," *Journal of Experimental Analysis of Behavior*, 5 (1962), 525–528.

COLEMAN, J. *The Adolescent Society*. New York: Free Press, 1963.

ERIKSON, E. H. *Childhood and Society*. 2nd ed. New York: Norton, 1963.

FOSS, B. (ed.). *Determinants of Infant Behavior*. New York: Wiley, 1961.

MC CANDLESS, B. R. *Children: Behavior and Development*. 2nd ed. New York: Holt, Rinehart and Winston, 1967.

NEWMAN, H. F., F. N. FREEMAN, AND K. J. HOLZINGER. *Twins: A Study of Heredity and Environment*. Chicago: University of Chicago Press, 1937.

STEVENSON, H. W., E. H. HESS, AND H. L. RHEINGOLD (eds.). *Early Behavior: Comparative and Developmental Approaches*. New York: Wiley, 1967.

WHITE, R. W. "Motivation Reconsidered: The Concept of Competence," *Psychological Review*, 66 (1959), 297–333.

UNIT II THE BEGINNING OF THE LIFE CYCLE

● CHAPTER 3 PRENATAL DEVELOPMENT

COGHILL, G. E. *Anatomy and the Problem of Behavior*. Cambridge, Mass.: Cambridge University Press, 1929.

Bibliography

CRICK, F. H. C. "The Genetic Code," *Scientific American*, 207 (1962), 66–74.

DOBZHANSKY, T. *Genetics and the Origin of Species.* 3rd ed. New York: Columbia University Press, 1951.

EYSENCK, H. J., AND D. B. PRELL. "The Inheritance of Neuroticism: An Experimental Study," *Journal of Mental Science*, 97 (1951), 441–465.

FULLER, J. L., AND W. R. THOMPSON. *Behavior Genetics.* New York: Wiley, 1960.

GOTTESMAN, I. I. "Heritability of Personality: A Demonstration," *Psychological Monographs*, Vol. 77, No. 9 (1963).

HIRSCH, J. (ed.). *Behavior-Genetic Analysis.* New York: McGraw-Hill, 1967.

HOOKER, D. *The Prenatal Origin of Behavior.* Lawrence: University of Kansas Press, 1952.

KALLMAN, F. J. *The Genetics of Schizophrenia.* New York: Augustin, 1938.

NEWMAN, H. H., F. N. FREEMAN, AND K. J. HOLZINGER. *Twins: A Study of Heredity and Environment.* Chicago: University of Chicago Press, 1937.

PATTEN, B. M. *Human Embryology.* 2nd ed. New York: McGraw-Hill, 1953.

RUGH, R., AND L. SHETTLES. *From Conception to Birth: The Drama of Life's Beginnings.* New York: Harper & Row, 1971.

SHETTLES, L. *Ovum Humanum.* New York: Hafner, 1960.

SKODAK, M., AND H. M. SKEELS. "A Final Follow-up of One Hundred Adopted Children," *Journal of Genetic Psychology*, 75 (1949), 85–125.

WATSON, J. D. *Double Helix: Being a Personal Account of the Discovery of the Structure of DNA.* New York: Atheneum, 1968.

● CHAPTER 4 THE WORLD OF THE NEWBORN CHILD

BRACKBILL, Y., AND S. G. THOMPSON. *Behavior in Infancy and Early Childhood.* New York: Free Press, 1967.

FANTZ, R. L. "The Origin of Form Perception," *Scientific American*, 204 (May 1961), 66.

GESELL, A., AND H. THOMPSON. *The Psychology of Early Growth.* New York: Macmillan, 1938.

LIPSITT, L., AND C. C. SPIKER. *Advances in Child Development and Behavior in the First Year of Life.* New York: Academic Press, 1964.

PRECHTL, H. "Behavioral Studies in the Newborn Infant," *Advances in the Study of Behavior*, 1 (1965), 91.

STEVENSON, H. W., E. H. HESS, AND H. L. RHEINGOLD (eds.). *Early Behavior: Comparative and Developmental Approaches.* New York: Wiley, 1967.

WATSON, J. B., AND R. R. WATSON. *Psychological Care of Infant and Child.* New York: Norton, 1928.

UNIT III THE DAWN OF AWARENESS: THE FIRST TWO YEARS

● CHAPTER 5 PHYSICAL DEVELOPMENT

BAYLEY, N. *Bayley Scales of Infant Development.* New York: The Psychological Corporation, 1969.

———. "Individual Patterns of Development," *Child Development*, 27 (1956), 45–74.

CONEL, J. L. *The Postnatal Development of the Human Cerebral Cortex.* Cambridge, Mass.: Harvard University Press, 1939–1963, Vols. I–VII.

DENNIS, W. "Causes of Retardation Among Institutional Children: Iran," *Journal of Genetic Psychology*, 96 (1960), 47–59.

ERIKSON, E. H. *Childhood and Society.* 2nd ed. New York: Norton, 1963.

GREULICH, W. W., AND S. I. PYLE. *A Radiographic Atlas of Skeletal Development of the Hand and Wrist.* 2nd ed. Stanford, Calif.: Stanford University Press, 1959.

LENNEBERG, E. H. *Biological Foundations of Language.* New York: Wiley, 1967.

OLSON, W. C., AND B. O. HUGHES. "Concepts of Growth: Their Significance for Teachers," in A. Coladarci (ed.), *Educational Psychology: A Book of Readings.* New York: Holt, Rinehart and Winston, 1955.

● CHAPTER 6 PERCEPTUAL AND INTELLECTUAL WORLD

AMBROSE, A. "The Development of the Smiling Response in Early Infancy," in B. M. Foss (ed.), *Determinants of Infant Behavior.* New York: Wiley, 1961, Vol. I, pp. 179–196.

ARONSON, E. "Coordination of Auditory and Visual Spatial Information in Early Infant Perception." Unpublished Manuscript, Center for Cognitive Studies, Harvard University, 1969.

BOWER, T. G. R. "The Development of the Object Concept," in J. Mehler (ed.), *Handbook of Cog-*

nitive Psychology. Englewood Cliffs, N.J.: Prentice-Hall, 1970.

————. "The Development of Object-permanence," *Perception and Psychophysics*, 2 (1967), 411–418.

————. "The Visual World of Infants," *Scientific American*, 215 (1966), 80–92.

BOWLBY, J. *Attachment*. London: Hogarth Press, 1969.

ENGEN, T., L. P. LIPSITT, AND H. KAYE. "Olfactory Responses and Adaptation in the Human Neonate," *Journal of Comparative Physiology and Psychology*, 56 (1963), 73–77.

FREEDMAN, D. G. "The Infant's Fear of Strangers and the Flight Response," *Journal of Child Psychiatry*, 2 (1961), pp. 242–248.

GIBSON, E. J., AND R. D. WALK. "The Visual Cliff," *Scientific American*, Vol. 202 (1960), 64–71.

KLIMPFINGER, S. "Ueber den Einfluss von Internationaler Einstellung und Uebung auf die Gestaltkonstang," *Archiv fuer die gesamte Psychologie*, 88 (1933), 551–598.

LIPSITT, L. P. "The Concepts of Development and Learning in Child Behavior," in D. B. Lindsley and A. A. Lumsdaine (eds.), *Brain Function: Brain Function and Learning*. Berkeley and Los Angeles: University of California Press, 1967, Vol. IV.

————. "Learning in the Human Infant," in H. W. Stevenson, E. H. Hess, and H. L. Rheingold (eds.), *Early Behavior: Comparative and Developmental Approaches*. New York: Wiley, 1967, pp. 225–247.

MENEGHINI, K. A., AND H. W. LEIBOWITZ. "The Effect of Stimulus Distance and Age on Shape Constancy," *Journal of Experimental Psychology*, Vol. 74 (1967), 241–248.

MUNDY-CASTLE, A. C., AND ANGLIN, J. "The Development of Looking in Infancy." Unpublished paper presented at SRCD, Santa Monica, California, April, 1969.

PAPOUŠEK, H. "Conditioning During Early Post-natal Development," in Y. Brackbill and S. G. Thompson (eds.), *Behavior in Infancy and Early Childhood*. New York: Free Press, 1967.

PIAGET, J. *Construction of Reality in the Child*. New York: Basic Books, 1954.

WERTHEIMER, M. "Psychomotor Coordination of Auditory and Visual Space at Birth," *Science*, Vol. 134 (1961), p. 1692.

WHITE, B., AND R. HELD. "Plasticity of Sensori-motor Development in the Human Infant," in J. F. Rosenblith and W. Allinsmith (eds.), *The Causes of Behavior*. 2nd ed. Boston: Allyn and Bacon, 1966, pp. 60–71.

● CHAPTER 7   SOCIAL DEVELOPMENT

AUSUBEL, D. F. *Theory and Problems of Child Development*. New York: Grune & Stratton, 1958.

BOWLBY, J. *Child Care and the Growth of Love*. 2nd ed. Baltimore: Penguin, 1965.

ERIKSON, E. H. *Identity, Youth and Crisis*. New York: Norton, 1968.

FREUD, S. *A General Introduction to Psychoanalysis*. Garden City, N. Y.: Doubleday, 1938.

FRIES, M. C. "Psychosomatic Relationships Between Mother and Infant," *Psychosomatic Medicine*, 6 (1944), 159–162.

GOLDFARB, W. "Psychological Privation in Infancy and Subsequent Adjustment," *Journal of Orthopsychiatry*, 15 (1945), 247–255.

HARLOW, H. F. "The Nature of Love," *American Psychologist*, 13 (1958), 673–685.

HARRIS, I. D. *Normal Children and Mothers*. Glencoe, Ill.: Free Press, 1956.

PIAGET, J. *The Origins of Intelligence in Children*. M. Cook (tr.). New York: International Universities Press, 1956.

RHEINGOLD, H. "The Modification of Social Responsiveness in Institutional Babies," *Monographs of the Society for Research in Child Development*, Vol. 21, No. 2 (1956).

SCHAEFER, E. S., AND N. BAYLEY. "Maternal Behavior and Personality Development—Data from the Berkeley Growth Study," *Child Development*, 13 (1960), 155–173.

SEARS, R. R., E. E. MACCOBY, AND H. LEVIN. *Patterns of Child Rearing*. New York: Harper & Row, 1957.

SKEELS, H. M., AND M. H. DYE. "A Study of the Effects of Differential Stimulation in Mentally Retarded Children," *Proceedings of the American Association of Mental Deficiencies*, 44 (1939), 114–136.

SPITZ, R. A. *The First Year of Life*. New York: International Universities Press, 1965.

————, AND K. M. WOLF. "Anaclitic Depression," in *Psychoanalytic Study of the Child*. New York: International Universities Press, 1946, Vol. II.

SULLIVAN, H. S. *The Interpersonal Theory of Psychiatry*. New York: Norton, 1953.

THOMAS, A., S. CHESS, R. G. BIRCH, M. E. HERTZIG, AND S. KORN. *Behavioral Individuality in Early Childhood*. New York: New York University Press, 1963.

● CHAPTER 8   EMOTIONAL DEVELOPMENT

BOWLBY, J. "Separation Anxiety," *International Journal of Psychoanalysis*, 41 (1960), 89–113.

BRACKBILL, Y., AND S. G. THOMPSON (eds.). *Behavior in Infancy and Early Childhood*. New York: Free Press, 1967.

BRIDGES, K. M. B. "Emotional Development in Early Infancy," *Child Development*, 3 (1932), 324–341.

BÜHLER, C. *The First Year of Life*. New York: John Day, 1930.

ENGEL, G. L. "Anxiety and Depression-Withdrawal —The Primary Effects of Unpleasure," *International Journal of Psychoanalysis*, 43 (1962), 89–97.

GOODENOUGH, F. L. *Anger in Young Children*. Institute of Child Welfare Monograph Series, No. 9. Minneapolis: University of Minnesota Press, 1931.

HEBB, D. O. "On the Nature of Fear," *Psychological Review*, 53 (1946), 259–276.

JERSILD, A. T., AND F. B. HOLMES. *Children's Fears*. Child Development Monograph, No. 20. New York: Columbia University Bureau of Publications, 1935.

MANDLER, G. "Emotion," in R. Brown *et al.*, *New Directions in Psychology*. New York: Holt, Rinehart and Winston, 1962.

MORGAN, G., AND H. N. RICCIUTI. "Infants' Responses to Strangers During the First Year," in B. M. Foss (ed.), *Determinants of Infant Behavior*. London: Methuen, 1969, Vol. IV.

RHEINGOLD, H. L. "The Effects of a Strange Environment on the Behavior of Infants," in B. M. Foss (ed.), *Determinants of Infant Behavior*. London: Methuen, 1969, Vol. IV.

SCHACHTER, S., AND J. SINGER. "Cognitive, Social, and Physiological Determinants of Emotional State," *Psychological Review*, 69 (1962), 379–399.

SCHMALE, A. H. "A Genetic View of Affects," *Psychoanalytic Study of the Child*, 19 (1964), 287–310.

SHERMAN, M. "The Differentiation of Emotional Responses in Infants, I and II," *Journal of Comparative Psychology*, 7 (1927), 265–284, 335–351.

SPITZ, R. A. "Anxiety in Infancy," *International Journal of Psychoanalysis*, 31 (1950), 138–143.

TOMKINS, S. S. *Affect, Imagery, and Consciousness: The Positive Affects*. New York: Springer, 1962, Vol. I.

WATSON, J. B., AND J. J. B. MORGAN. "Emotional Reactions and Psychological Experimentation," *American Journal of Psychology*, 28 (1917), 163–174.

● CHAPTER 9   ORIGINS OF LANGUAGE

BELLUGI, U., AND R. BROWN (eds.). *The Acquisition of Language*. Chicago: University of Chicago Press, 1970.

BROWN, R. *Words and Things*. Glencoe, Ill.: Free Press, 1958.

ERVIN-TRIPP, S. "Language Development," in M. Hoffman and L. Hoffman (eds.), *Advances in Child Development Research*. New York: Russell Sage Foundation, 1966, II, 55–105.

FLAVELL, J. H. *The Development of Role-taking and Communication Skills in Children*. New York: Wiley, 1968.

JAKOBSON, R. *Child Language, Aphasia and Phonological Universals*. The Hague: Mouton, 1968.

LENNEBERG, E. H. *The Biological Foundations of Language*. New York: Wiley, 1967.

———— (ed.). *New Directions in the Study of Language*. Cambridge, Mass.: MIT Press, 1964.

LEOPOLD, W. F. *Speech Development of a Bilingual Child: A Linguist's Record*. Evanston, Ill.: Northwestern University Press, 1939–1949.

LEWIS, M. M. *Infant Speech*. New York: Humanities Press, 1951.

VYGOTSKY, L. S. *Thought and Language*. Cambridge, Mass.: MIT Press, 1962.

WEIR, R. H. *Language in the Crib*. The Hague: Mouton, 1962.

WERNER, H., AND B. KAPLAN. *Symbol Formation*. New York: Wiley, 1963, Part II.

UNIT IV THE FORMATIVE YEARS: BEFORE
    STARTING SCHOOL

● CHAPTER 10 PHYSICAL GROWTH

BAYLEY, N. "Mental and Motor Development from
Two to Twelve Years," *Review of Educational
Research*, 9 (1939), 18–37, 114–125.

————, AND A. ESPENSCHADE. "Motor Development
from Birth to Maturity," *Review of Educational
Research*, 14 (1944), 381–389.

BRONSTEIN, I. P., *et al.* "Obesity in Childhood,"
American Journal of the Disturbed Child, 63
(1942), 238–251.

BRUCH, H. *The Importance of Overweight*. New
York: Norton, 1957.

CONEL, J. L. *The Postnatal Development of the
Human Cerebral Cortex*. Cambridge, Mass.: Harvard University Press, 1939–1963, Vols. I–VII.

ERIKSON, E. H. *Childhood and Society*. 2nd ed. New
York: Norton, 1963.

ESPENSCHADE, A. "Motor Development," *Review of
Educational Research*, 17 (1947), 354–361.

GUTTERIDGE, M. "A Study of Motor Development of
Young Children," *Archives of Psychology*, Vol.
244 (1939).

● CHAPTER 11 DEVELOPMENT OF PERCEPTION
                AND COGNITION

BOWER, T. G. R. "Phenomenal Identity and Form
Perception in an Infant," *Perception and Psychophysics*, 2 (1967), 74–76.

BRAINE, M. D. S., AND B. L. SHANKS. "The Development of Conservation of Size," *Journal of Verbal
Learning and Verbal Behavior*, 4 (1965),
227–242.

BRUNER, J., R. OLVER, AND P. GREENFIELD. *Studies in
Cognitive Growth*. New York: Wiley, 1966.

FOSS, B. M. (ed.). *Determinants of Infant Behavior*.
New York: Wiley, 1963, Vol. II, pp. 113–134.

GIBSON, E. J., AND R. D. WALK. "The Visual Cliff,"
Scientific American, 202 (1960), 64–71.

GIBSON, E. J., J. J. GIBSON, A. D. PICK, AND H. A.
OSCAR. "A Developmental Study of the Discrimination of Letterlike Forms," *Journal of Comparative and Physiological Psychology*, 55 (1962),
897–906.

GIBSON, J. J. *The Senses Considered as Perceptual
Systems*. Boston: Houghton Mifflin, 1966.

HOCHBERG, J., AND V. BROOKS. "Pictorial Recognition
as an Unlearned Ability: A Study of One Child's
Performance," *American Journal of Psychology*,
75 (1962), 624–628.

HUDSON, W. "Pictorial Depth Perception in Sub-cultural Groups in Africa," *Journal of Social Psychology*, 52 (1960), 183–208.

INHELDER, B., AND J. PIAGET. *The Early Growth of
Logic in the Child*. New York: Harper & Row,
1964.

PIAGET, J. *The Construction of Reality in the Child*.
New York: Basic Books, 1954.

VYGOTSKY, L. S. *Thought and Language*. Cambridge,
Mass.: MIT Press, 1962.

WERNER, H. *Comparative Psychology of Mental Development*. New York: International Universities
Press, 1957.

● CHAPTER 12 DEVELOPMENT OF LANGUAGE

BELLUGI, U. "Linguistic Mechanisms Underlying
Child Speech," in *Proceedings of the Conference
on Language and Language Behavior*. New York:
Appleton-Century-Crofts, 1968.

BERKO, J. "The Child's Learning of English Mor-
phology," *Word*, 14 (1958), 150–177.

BROWN, R. *Social Psychology*. New York: Free Press,
1965.

————, AND U. BELLUGI. "Three Processes in the
Child's Acquisition of Syntax," in E. H. Lenneberg (ed.), *New Directions in the Study of Language*. Cambridge, Mass.: MIT Press, 1964.

CAZDEN, C. "The Acquisition of Noun and Verb Inflections," *Child Development*, 39 (1968), 433–
448.

FRASER, C., U. BELLUGI, AND R. BROWN. "Control of
Grammar in Imitation, Comprehension, and Production," in R. C. Oldfield and J. C. Marshall
(eds.), *Language*. Baltimore: Penguin, 1968.

● CHAPTER 13 DEVELOPMENT OF PERSONALITY

BANDURA, A., D. ROSS, AND S. A. ROSS. "Imitation of
Film-mediated Aggressive Models," *Journal of Abnormal and Social Psychology*, 66 (1963), 3–11.

BELLER, E. K. "Dependence and Independence in
Young Children," *Journal of Genetic Psychology*,
87 (1955), 25–35.

BOEHM, L. "The Development of Independence: A Comparative Study," *Child Development*, 28 (1957), 85–92.

BROWN, D. G. "Sex-role Development in a Changing Culture," *Psychological Bulletin*, 55 (1958), 232–242.

ERIKSON, E. H. *Childhood and Society*. 2nd ed. New York: Norton, 1963.

FESTINGER, L. A *Theory of Cognitive Dissonance*. Evanston, Ill.: Row-Peterson, 1957.

HARTLEY, R. E. "Sex-Role Pressures and the Socialization of the Male Child," *Psychological Reports*, 5 (1959), 457–468.

HILL, W. F. "Learning Theory and the Acquisition of Values," *Psychological Review*, 67 (1960), 317–331.

JOHNSON, M. M. "Sex Role Learning in the Nuclear Family," *Child Development*, 34 (1963), 319–333.

KAGAN, J., AND H. A. MOSS. "The Stability of Passive and Dependent Behavior from Childhood Through Adulthood," *Child Development*, 31 (1960), 577–591.

KAHN, M. L. "Social Class and Parent-Child Relationships: An Interpretation," *American Journal of Sociology*, 68 (1963), 471–480.

LORENZ, K. *On Aggression*. New York: Harcourt, Brace & World, 1966.

MC NEIL, E. B. *The Concept of Human Development*. Belmont, Calif.: Wadsworth, 1966.

MUSSEN, P. H. "Early Socialization: Learning and Identification," in G. Mandler *et al.*, *New Directions in Psychology*. New York: Holt, Rinehart and Winston, 1967, III, 53–110.

SEARS, R. R., E. MACCOBY, AND H. LEVIN. *Patterns of Child Rearing*. New York: Harper & Row, 1957.

WATSON, G. *Social Psychology*. New York: Lippincott, 1966.

● CHAPTER 14 SOCIAL DEVELOPMENT WITH PEERS

CLARK, B. S. "The Acquisition and Extinction of Peer Imitation in Children," *Psychonomic Science*, 2 (1965), 147–148.

COSTANZO, P. R., AND M. E. SHAW. "Conformity as a Function of Age Level," *Child Development*, 37 (1966), 967–975.

FAIGIN, H. "Social Behavior of Young Children in the Kibbutz," *Journal of Abnormal and Social Psychology*, 56 (1958), 117–129.

FREUD, A., AND S. DANN. "An Experiment in Group Upbringing," in R. Eisler *et al.* (eds.), *The Psychoanalytic Study of the Child*. New York: International Universities Press, 1951, Vol. VI, pp. 127–163.

HARLOW, H. F., AND M. K. HARLOW. "The Affectional Systems," in A. M. Schrier, H. F. Harlow, and F. Stollnitz (eds.), *Behavior of Nonhuman Primates*. New York: Academic Press, 1965, Vol. II, pp. 287–334.

HARTUP, W. W. "Friendship Status and the Effectiveness of Peers as Reinforcing Agents," *Journal of Experimental Child Psychology*, 1 (1964), 154–162.

————, AND B. COATES. "Imitation of a Peer as a Function of Reinforcement from the Peer Group and Rewardingness of the Model," *Child Development*, 38 (1967), 1003–1016.

HETHERINGTON, E. M. "Effects of Paternal Absence on Sex-typed Behaviors in Negro and White Preadolescent Males," *Journal of Personality and Social Psychology*, 4 (1966), 87–91.

HICKS, D. J. "Imitation and Retention of Film-mediated Aggressive Peer and Adult Models," *Journal of Personality and Social Psychology*, 2 (1965), 97–100.

HOROWITZ, F. D. "Incentive Value of Social Stimuli for Preschool Children," *Child Development*, 33 (1962), 111–116.

PARTEN, M. B. "Social Participation Among Preschool Children," *Journal of Abnormal and Social Psychology*, 27 (1932–1933), 243–269.

PATTERSON, G. R., R. A. LITTMAN, AND W. BRICKER. "Assertive Behavior in Children: A Step Toward a Theory of Aggression," *Monographs of the Society for Research in Child Development*, Vol. 32 (1967), Whole No. 113.

PIAGET, J. *The Moral Judgment of the Child*. London: Kegan Paul, 1932.

REESE, H. W. "Relationship Between Self-acceptance and Sociometric Choice," *Journal of Abnormal and Social Psychology*, 62 (1961), 472–474.

ROFF, M., AND S. B. SELLS. "Relations Between Intelligence and Sociometric Status in Groups Differing in Sex and Socio-economic Background," *Psychological Reports*, 16 (1965), 511–516.

TIKTIN, S., AND W. W. HARTUP. "Sociometric Status and the Reinforcing Effectiveness of Children's Peers," *Journal of Experimental Child Psychology*, 2 (1965), 306–315.

WAHLER, R. G. "Child-Child Interactions in Free Field Settings: Some Experimental Analyses," *Journal of Experimental Child Psychology*, 5 (1967), 278–293.

WINDER, C. L., AND L. RAU. "Parental Attitudes Associated with Social Deviance in Preadolescent Boys," *Journal of Abnormal and Social Psychology*, 64 (1962), 418–424.

UNIT V GROWING UP: LATER CHILDHOOD

● CHAPTER 15 INTELLECTUAL FUNCTIONING IN CHILDHOOD

BALDWIN, A. L. *Theories of Child Development*. New York: Wiley, 1967.

GELMAN, R. "Conservation Acquisition: A Problem of Learning to Attend to Relevant Attributes," *Journal of Experimental Child Psychology*, 4 (1965), 227–242.

GIBSON, E. J. "Development of Perception: Discrimination of Depth Compared with the Discrimination of Graphic Symbols," in J. C. Wright and J. Kagan (eds.), "Basic Cognitive Processes in Children," *Monograph of the Society for Research in Child Development*, Vol. 28. Minneapolis: University of Minnesota, 1963.

PIAGET, J. *Logic and Psychology*. New York: Basic Books, 1957.

———. *The Origins of Intelligence in Children*. New York: International Universities Press, 1952.

———. *Play, Dreams and Imitation in Childhood*. C. Gattegno and F. M. Hodgson (trs.). New York: Norton, 1951.

WRIGHT, J. C., AND J. KAGAN (eds.). "Basic Cognitive Process in Children," *Monographs of the Society for Research in Child Development*, Vol. 28, No. 2 (1963).

● CHAPTER 16 PERSONALITY DEVELOPMENT

CHESLER, P. "Maternal Influence in Learning by Observation in Kittens," *Science*, 166 (1969), 901–903.

FREUD, S. *The Basic Writings of Sigmund Freud*. A. A. Brill (ed.). New York: Modern Library, 1938.

HARLOW, H. F. "The Nature of Love," *American Psychologist*, 13 (1958), 673–685.

HARRIS, D. B., H. G. GOUGH, AND W. E. MARTIN. "Children's Ethnic Attitudes. II. Relationship to Parental Beliefs Concerning Child Training," *Child Development*, 21 (1950), 169–181.

HIMMETWEIT, H. T., A. N. OPPENHEIM, AND P. VANCE. *Television and the Child: An Empirical Study of the Effect of Television on the Young*. New York: Oxford University Press, 1958.

KINSEY, A. C., W. B. POMEROY, AND C. E. MARTIN. *Sexual Behavior in the Human Female*. Philadelphia: Saunders, 1953.

———. *Sexual Behavior in the Human Male*. Philadelphia: Saunders, 1948.

MANHEIMER, D. I., D. G. MELLINGER, AND M. B. BALTER. "Marijuana Use Among Urban Adults," *Science*, 166 (December 19, 1969), 1544–1545.

MC NEIL, E. B. "Psychology and Aggression," *Journal of Conflict Resolution*, 3 (1959), 195–293.

OPIE, I., AND P. OPIE. *Children's Games in Street and Playground*. New York: Oxford University Press, 1969.

RADKE-YARROW, M., H. G. TRAGER, AND J. MILLER. "The Role of Parents in the Development of Children's Ethnic Attitudes," *Child Development*, 23 (1952), 13–53.

SCHRAMM, W., J. LYLE, AND E. B. PARKER. *Television in the Lives of Our Children*. Stanford, Calif.: Stanford University Press, 1961.

● CHAPTER 17 DEVELOPMENT OF MORAL CHARACTER

BERKOWITZ, L. *The Development of Motives and Values in the Child*. New York: Basic Books, 1964.

BLATT, M. "The Effects of Classroom Discussion Upon Children's Moral Judgment," in L. Kohlberg and E. Turiel (eds.), *Moral Research: The Cognitive-Developmental Approach*. New York: Holt, Rinehart and Winston, 1971.

DURKHEIM, E. *Moral Education*. New York: Free Press, 1961.

HARE, R. M. *The Language of Morals*. New York: Oxford University Press, 1952.

HOLSTEIN, C. "The Relation of Children's Moral Judgment to That of Their Parents and to Communication Patterns in the Family." Unpublished dissertation, University of California, Berkeley, 1969.

HARTSHORNE, H., AND M. MAY. *Studies in the Organization of Character*. New York: Macmillan, 1930.

KANT, I. *Fundamental Principles of the Metaphysics of Morals*. T. K. Abbott (tr.). New York: Liberal Arts Press, 1949.

KOHLBERG, L. "The Development of Moral Character and Ideology," in M. Hoffman (ed.), *Review of Child Psychology*. New York: Russell Sage Foundation, 1964.

———. "Stage and Sequence: The Cognitive-Developmental Approach to Socialization," in D. Goslin (ed.), *Handbook of Socialization Theory and Research*. Chicago: Rand McNally, 1969.

———, AND E. TURIEL. *Research in Moral Development: The Cognitive-Developmental Approach*. New York: Holt, Rinehart and Winston, 1971.

PIAGET, J. *The Moral Judgment of the Child*. London: Kegan Paul, 1932.

REST, J. "Developmental Hierarchy in Preference and Comprehension of Moral Judgment." Unpublished dissertation, University of Chicago, 1968.

TURIEL, E. "Developmental Processes in the Child's Moral Thinking," in P. Mussen, J. Langer, and M. Covington (eds.), *New Directions in Developmental Psychology*. New York: Holt, Rinehart and Winston, 1969.

• CHAPTER 18 MALADJUSTMENT IN CHILDHOOD AND ITS CORRECTION

BANDURA, A. "Behavioral Psychotherapy," *Scientific American*, 216 (March 1967), 78–86.

CAPLAN, G. *Principles of Preventive Psychiatry*. New York: Basic Books, 1964.

EYSENCK, H. J. "Learning Theory and Behavior Therapy," *Journal of Mental Science*, 105 (1959), 61–75.

FREUD, A. "Assessment of Childhood Disturbances," in R. Eisler *et al.* (eds.), *The Psychoanalytic Study of the Child*. New York: International Universities Press, 1962, Vol. XVII.

FREUD, S. *The Disposition to Obsessional Neurosis*. Standard ed. London: Hogarth Press (1913, 1958), Vol. XII.

———. *General Theory of the Neurosis*. Standard ed. London: Hogarth Press (1917, 1963), Vol. XVI.

GARVEY, W. P., AND J. R. HEGRENES. "Desensitization Techniques in the Treatment of School Phobia," *American Journal of Orthopsychiatry*, 36 (1962), 147–152.

GLASSER, W. *Schools Without Failure*. New York: Harper & Row, 1969.

HEWETT, F. M. *The Emotionally Disturbed Child in the Classroom*. Boston: Allyn and Bacon, 1968.

PIAGET, J. *Play, Dreams and Imitation in Childhood*. C. Gattegno and F. M. Hodgson (trs.). New York: Norton, 1951.

ROSENTHAL, R., AND L. JACOBSON. *Pygmalion in the Classroom*. New York: Holt, Rinehart and Winston, 1968.

UNIT VI ADOLESCENCE AND YOUTH

• CHAPTER 19 PHYSICAL AND EMOTIONAL CHANGES

BAYLEY, N. "Skeletal Maturing in Adolescence as a Basis for Determining Percentage of Completed Growth," *Child Development*, 14 (1943), 5–46.

BEACH, F. "It's All in Your Mind," *Psychology Today*, 3 (1969), 33–35, 60.

BROVERMAN, D. M., I. K. BROVERMAN, W. VOGEL, R. D. PALMER, AND E. L. KLAIBER. "Physique and Growth in Adolescence," *Child Development*, 35 (1964), 857–870.

COLEMAN, J. S. *The Adolescent Society*. New York: Free Press, 1961.

DEUTSCH, H. *The Psychology of Women*. New York: Grune & Stratton, 1944–1945, Vols. I–II.

DIMOCK, H. S. *Rediscovering the Adolescent*. New York: Association Press, 1937.

ELLIS, A. "A Study of Human Love Relationships," *Journal of Genetic Psychology*, 75 (1949), 61–71.

FORD, C. S., AND F. A. BEACH. *Patterns of Sexual Behavior*. New York: Harper & Row, 1951.

GREULICH, W. W., *et al.* "Somatic and Endocrine Studies of Puberal and Adolescent Boys," *Monographs of the Society for Research in Child Development*, Vol. 7, No. 3 (1942).

HARDIN, G. "Biology and Individual Differences," in *Child Psychology*. Chicago: University of Chicago Press, 1962, Vol. LXI.

HOFFMAN, M. *The Gay World: Male Homosexuality and the Social Creation of Evil*. New York: Basic Books, 1968.

KINSEY, A. C., W. B. POMEROY, AND C. E. MARTIN. *Sexual Behavior in the Human Female*. Philadelphia: Saunders, 1953.

———. *Sexual Behavior in the Human Male*. Philadelphia: Saunders, 1948.

KNOX, D. H., AND M. J. SPORAKOWSKI. "Attitudes of College Students Toward Love," *Journal of Marriage and the Family*, 30 (1968), 638–642.

LUCKEY, E. B., AND G. D. NASS. "A Comparison of Sexual Attitudes and Behavior in an International

Sample," *Journal of Marriage and the Family*, 31 (1969), 364–378.

MASTERS, W. H., AND V. E. JOHNSON. *Human Sexual Response*. Boston: Little, Brown, 1966.

MUSSEN, P. H., AND M. C. JONES. "Self-conceptions, Motivations and Interpersonal Attitudes of Late- and Early-maturing Boys," *Child Development*, 28 (1957), 243–256.

———. "Self-conceptions, Motivations and Interpersonal Attitudes of Early- and Late-maturing Girls," *Child Development*, 29 (1958), 495–501.

RAMSEY, G. "The Sexual Development of Boys," *American Journal of Psychology*, 56 (1943), 217–233.

RAUH, J. L., D. A. SCHUMSKY, AND M. T. WITT. "Heights, Weights and Obesity in Urban School Children," *Child Development*, 38 (1967), 515–530.

REYNOLDS, E. L. "The Distribution of Subcutaneous Fat in Childhood and Adolescence," *Monographs of the Society for Research in Child Development*, Vol. 15, No. 2 (1951).

———, AND J. V. WINES. "Individual Differences in Physical Changes Associated with Adolescent Girls," *American Journal of Diseases of Children*, 75 (1948), 329–350.

SCHONFELD, W. A., AND G. W. BEEBE. "Normal Growth and Variations in the Male Genitalia from Birth to Maturity," *Journal of Urology*, 48 (1942), 759–777.

SHUTTLEWORTH, F. K. "The Adolescent Period," *Monographs of the Society for Research in Child Development*, Vol. 3, No. 3 (1938).

———. "Sexual Maturation and Physical Growth of Girls Age Six to Nineteen," *Monographs of the Society for Research in Child Development*, Vol. 2, No. 5 (1937).

STOLZ, H. R., AND L. M. STOLZ. *Somatic Development of Adolescent Boys*. New York: Macmillan, 1951.

SULLIVAN, H. S. *The Interpersonal Theory of Psychiatry*. New York: Norton, 1953.

● CHAPTER 20 THE TASKS OF ADOLESCENCE

BLOS, P. *On Adolescence*. New York: Free Press, 1962.

DOUVAN, E., AND J. ADELSON. *The Adolescent Experience*. New York: Wiley, 1966.

ERIKSON, E. H. "Growth and Crises of the Healthy Personality," *Psychological Issues*, Vol. 1, No. 1 (1959).

FRIEDENBERG, E. Z. *The Vanishing Adolescent*. New York: Dell, 1962.

INHELDER, B., AND J. PIAGET. *The Growth of Logical Thinking*. New York: Basic Books, 1958.

KOHLBERG, L. "The Child as Moral Philosopher," *Psychology Today*, 2 (September 1968), 24–30.

LIDZ, T. *The Person*. New York: Basic Books, 1970.

MILGRAM, S. "Some Conditions of Obedience and Disobedience to Authority," *Human Relations*, 18 (1965), 57–76.

PIAGET, J. *The Moral Judgment of the Child*. London: Kegan Paul, 1932.

RIESMAN, D. *The Lonely Crowd*. New Haven, Conn.: Yale University Press, 1950.

SANFORD, N. *Where Colleges Fail*. San Francisco: Jossey-Bass, 1967.

WHITE, R. W. *Lives in Progress*. New York: Dryden, 1952.

● CHAPTER 21 SOCIAL DEVELOPMENT

BACON, M., AND M. B. JONES. *Teen-Age Drinking*. New York: Crowell, 1968.

BRITTAIN, C. V. "An Exploration of the Bases of Peer-Compliance in Adolescence," *Adolescence*, 2 (1968), 445–458.

CERVANTES, L. S. *The Dropout: Causes and Cures*. Ann Arbor: University of Michigan Press, 1965.

CICOUREL, A. V. *Social Organization of Juvenile Justice*. New York: Wiley, 1968.

DEVEREUX, E. C. "Role of Peer Group Experience in Moral Development," in J. P. Hill (ed.), *Minnesota Symposia on Child Psychology*. Minneapolis: University of Minnesota Press, 1970, Vol. IV.

DUNPHY, D. C. "Social Structure of the Urban Adolescent Peer Group," *Sociometry*, 26 (1963), 230–246.

ERIKSON, E. H. *Identity, Youth and Crisis*. New York: Norton, 1968.

FRIEDENBERG, E. Z. *Coming of Age in America: Growth and Acquiescence*. New York: Knopf, 1963.

HARTUP, W. W. "Peer Interaction and Social Organization," in P. H. Mussen (ed.), *Carmichael's Manual of Child Psychology*. New York: Wiley, 1970.

KENISTON, K. "Sources of Student Dissent," *Journal of Social Issues*, 22 (1967), 108–137.

KOHN, M. L. "Social Class and Parental Values," *American Journal of Sociology*, 64 (1959), 337–351.

ROSEN, B. C. "Race, Ethnicity, and the Achievement Syndrome," *American Sociological Review*, 24 (1959), 47–60.

SHERIF, M., AND C. W. SHERIF. *Reference Groups*. New York: Harper & Row, 1964.

VOSS, H. L., A. WENDLING, AND D. S. ELLIOTT. "Some Types of High School Dropouts," *Journal of Educational Research*, 59 (1966), 363–368.

ZINBERG, N. E. "Facts and Fancies About Drug Addiction," *The Public Interest*, 6 (1967), 75–90.

● CHAPTER 22 CASES OF ADOLESCENT DEVELOPMENT

FORD, C. S., AND F. A. BEACH. *Patterns of Sexual Behavior*. New York: Harper & Row, 1952.

HARLOW, H. F. "Sexual Behavior in the Rhesus Monkey," in F. A. Beach (ed.), *Sex and Behavior*. New York: Wiley, 1965, pp. 234–265.

LEWIN, K. *Dynamic Theory of Personality*. New York: McGraw-Hill, 1935.

MADISON, P. *Personality Development in College*. Reading, Mass.: Addison-Wesley, 1969.

●. CHAPTER 23 YOUTH: A SEPARATE STAGE OF LIFE

ARIÈS, P. *Centuries of Childhood: A Social History of Family Life*. R. Baldic (tr.). New York: Knopf, 1962.

BLOS, P. *On Adolescence*. New York: Free Press, 1962.

DEUTSCH, H. *The Psychology of Women*. New York: Grune & Stratton, 1944, Vol. I.

DOUVAN, E., AND J. ADELSON. *The Adolescent Experience*. New York: Wiley, 1966.

ERIKSON, E. H. *Identity, Youth and Crisis*. New York: Norton, 1968.

———. "Youth: Fidelity and Diversity," in E. H. Erikson (ed.), *The Challenge of Youth*. New York: Anchor, 1963.

KENISTON, K. *Young Radicals: Notes on Committed Youth*. New York: Harcourt, Brace & World, 1968.

SULLIVAN, H. S. *The Interpersonal Theory of Psychiatry*. New York: Norton, 1953.

UNIT VII ADULTHOOD

● CHAPTER 24 THE MATURE PERSONALITY

ADLER, A. *The Practice and Theory of Individual Psychology*. New York: Harcourt, Brace & World, 1927.

———. *What Life Should Mean to You*. Boston: Little, Brown, 1931.

ALLPORT, G. W. *Becoming*. New Haven, Conn.: Yale University Press, 1955.

———. *Pattern and Growth in Personality*. New York: Holt, Rinehart and Winston, 1961.

ANGYAL, A. "A Theoretical Model for Personality Studies," *Journal of Personality*, 20 (1951), 131–142.

BAKAN, D. *The Duality of Human Existence*. Chicago: Rand McNally, 1966.

ERIKSON, E. H. *Childhood and Society*. 2nd ed. New York: Norton, 1963.

FREUD, S. *Civilization and Its Discontents*. New York: Norton, 1930.

———. *Collected Papers*. London: Hogarth Press, 1925, Vols. I–V.

———. *New Introductory Lectures to Psychoanalysis*. W. J. H. Sprott (tr.). New York: Norton, 1933.

FROMM, E. *The Art of Loving*. New York: Harper & Row, 1956.

———. *Man for Himself*. New York: Holt, Rinehart and Winston, 1947.

———. *The Sane Society*. New York: Holt, Rinehart and Winston, 1955.

MADDI, S. R. *Personality Theories: A Comparative Analysis*. Homewood, Ill.: Dorsey Press, 1968.

MASLOW, A. H. "Deficiency Motivation and Growth Motivation," in M. R. Jones (ed.), *Nebraska Symposium on Motivation*. Lincoln: University of Nebraska Press, 1955.

———. "Some Basic Propositions of a Growth and Self-actualization Psychology," in *Perceiving, Behaving, Becoming: A New Focus for Education*. Washington, D.C.: Yearbook of the Association for Supervision and Curriculum Development, 1962.

MAY, R. "Contributions of Existential Psychotherapy," in R. May, E. Angel, and H. F. Ellenberger (eds.), *Existence: A New Dimension in Psychiatry and Psychology*. New York: Basic Books, 1958.

MURRAY, H. A. *Explorations in Personality: A Clinical and Experimental Study of Fifty Men of College Age*. New York: Oxford University Press, 1938.

RANK, O. *Will Therapy and Truth and Reality*. New York: Knopf, 1945.

ROGERS, C. R. *On Becoming a Person*. Boston: Houghton Mifflin, 1961.

————. "A Theory of Therapy, Personality, and Interpersonal Relationships, as Developed in the Client-centered Framework," in S. Koch (ed.), *Psychology: A Study of a Science*. New York: McGraw-Hill, 1959, Vol. III.

● CHAPTER 25   PERSONALITY AND INTELLECTUAL CHANGE

BAYLEY, N. "Cognition and Aging," in K. W. Shaie (ed.), *Current Topics in the Psychology of Aging: Perception, Learning, Cognition and Personality*. Morgantown: West Virginia University Library, 1968, pp. 97–119.

————, AND M. ODEN. "The Maintenance of Intellectual Ability in Gifted Adults," *Journal of Gerontology*, 10 (1955), 91–107.

BECKER, H. "Personal Change in Adult Life," *Sociometry*, 27 (1964), 40–53.

BLOCK, J., AND N. HAAN. *Ways of Personality Development*. New York: Appleton-Century-Crofts, 1970.

CHILMAN, C. S., AND D. L. MEYER. "Single and Married Undergraduates' Measured Personality Needs and Self-rated Happiness," *Journal of Marriage and the Family*, 28 (1966), 67–76.

DENNIS, W. "Creative Productivity Between the Ages of Twenty and Eighty Years," in B. Neugarten (ed.), *Middle Age and Aging*. Chicago: University of Chicago Press, 1968.

ERIKSON, E. H. *Childhood and Society*. 2nd ed. New York: Norton, 1963.

FARBER, J. E. "A Framework for the Study of Personality as a Behavioral Science," in P. Worchel and D. Byrne (eds.), *Personality Change*. New York: Wiley, 1964, pp. 3–37.

FREEDMAN, M. "Studies of College Alumni," in N. Sanford (ed.), *The American College*. New York: Wiley 1962, pp. 847–893.

HAAN, N. "Proposed Model of Ego Functioning: Coping and Defense Mechanisms in Relationship to I.Q. Change," *Psychological Monographs*, Vol. 77 (1963), Whole No. 571.

————. "The Relationship of Ego Functioning and Intelligence to Social Status and Social Mobility," *Journal of Abnormal and Social Psychology*, 69 (1964), 594–605.

————, AND A. FITZGIBBONS. "Interests," in N. Haan (ed.), *A Handbook for the Assessment and Measurement of Educational Outcomes*. Berkeley, Calif.: Far West Laboratory for Educational Research and Development, 1967.

HEINSTEIN, M. "Expressed Attitudes and Feelings of Pregnant Women and their Relations to Physical Complications of Pregnancy," *Merrill-Palmer Quarterly*, 13 (1967), 217–236.

KAGAN, J., AND H. A. MOSS. *Birth to Maturity*. New York: Wiley, 1962.

KOHLBERG, L. "A Cognitive-Developmental Approach to Socialization," in D. Goslin (ed.), *Handbook of Socialization*. Chicago: Rand McNally, 1968, pp. 347–480.

————, AND R. KRAMER. "Continuities and Discontinuities in Childhood and Adult Moral Development," *Human Development*, 12 (1969), 93–120.

LEHMAN, H. C. *Age and Achievement*. Princeton, N.J.: Princeton University Press, 1953.

LOEVINGER, J. "The Meaning and Measurement of Ego Development," *American Psychologist*, 21 (1966), 195–206.

NEUGARTEN, B. (ed.). *Middle Age and Aging*. Chicago: University of Chicago Press, 1968.

STRONG, E. K. *Vocational Interests 18 Years After College*. Minneapolis: University of Minnesota Press, 1955.

WECHSLER, D. *The Measurement and Appraisal of Adult Intelligence*. 4th ed. Baltimore: Williams & Wilkins, 1958.

WERNER, H. *Comparative Psychology of Mental Development*. New York: International Universities Press, 1948.

● CHAPTER 26   CONTINUING GROWTH VERSUS MALADJUSTMENT

MASLOW, A. H. *Motivation and Personality*. New York: Harper & Row, 1954.

MAY, R. *Love and Will*. New York: Norton, 1969.

ROGERS, C. R. *Freedom to Learn*. Columbus, Ohio: Merrill, 1969.

————. *On Becoming a Person*. Boston: Houghton Mifflin, 1961.

————, *et al. Person to Person*. Lafayette, Calif.: Real People Press, 1967.

SEVERIN, F. T. (ed.). *Humanistic Viewpoints in Psychology*. New York: McGraw-Hill, 1965.

● CHAPTER 27 AGING

BIRREN, J. E. *The Psychology of Aging*. New York: Prentice-Hall, 1964.

CURTIS, H. J. *Biological Mechanisms of Aging*. Springfield, Ill.: Charles C Thomas, 1966.

NEUGARTEN, B. L. (ed.). *Middle Age and Aging*. Chicago: University of Chicago Press, 1968.

————, V. WOOD, R. J. KRAINES, AND B. LOOMIS. "Women's Attitudes Toward the Menopause," *Vita Humana*, 6 (1963), 140–151.

SHOCK, N. W. (ed.). *Aging . . . Some Social and Biological Aspects*. Washington, D.C.: American Association for the Advancement of Science, 1960.

SUNDOWN, D. *Passing On: The Social Organization of Dying*. Englewood Cliffs, N.J.: Prentice-Hall, 1967.

APPENDIX METHODS AND MEASUREMENT

COURTS, F. A. *Psychological Statistics: An Introduction*. Homewood, Ill.: Dorsey, 1966.

HAYS, W. L. *Statistics for Psychologists*. New York: Holt, Rinehart and Winston, 1963.

ROSENTHAL, R. *Experimenter Effects in Behavioral Research*. New York: Appleton-Century-Crofts, 1966.

Contributing Consultants

Aronfreed

Bayley

Bellugi

Bissell

Birren

JUSTIN ARONFREED, a professor of psychology at the University of Pennsylvania, received his B.A. in 1951 from the University of Pennsylvania and his Ph.D. in 1956 from the University of Michigan. He is an associate editor of *Child Development* and is the author of *Conduct and Conscience: The Socialization of Internalized Control over Behavior* (Academic Press, 1968). Dr. Aronfreed's current interests include "the experimental and theoretical investigations of the development of children's capacity for representational thought: the variety of forms of cognitive representation and their mental transformations."

NANCY BAYLEY, recently retired as research psychologist at the University of California Institute of Human Development, is well known for her work in the physical developmental processes in children and adults. Dr. Bayley received her B.S. and M.S. degrees from the University of Washington and her Ph.D. from the State University of Iowa in 1926. She is past president of both the Society for Research in Child Development and the Western Psychological Association. In 1966 she received the Distinguished Scientific Contribution Award from the American Psychological Association, of which she is a fellow. Dr. Bayley's professional interests have included mental and physical development of intelligence and motor abilities, physical growth and maturation of the skeleton, factors affecting personality and emotional adjustments, and interrelationships among all these variables.

URSULA BELLUGI joined the staff of the Salk Institute of Biological Studies in 1968 as a research assistant and is now a member of the institute, specializing in studies of the foundation of language and language acquisition. She is also an assistant professor in residence in the Department of Psychology at the University of California at San Diego. Dr. Bellugi received her B.A. in 1952 from Antioch College and her Ed.D. in the language acquisition area of the Human Development Program at Harvard in 1967. She has taught courses relating to psycholinguistics at Harvard, the University of California at Berkeley, and Rockefeller University. The young, German-born professor is married to Professor Edward S. Klima, professor of linguistics at UCSD, and they have two sons.

JAMES E. BIRREN is director of the Gerontology Center and a professor of psychology at the University of Southern California. He is a graduate of Chicago Teachers College and earned both his M.A. (1942) and his Ph.D. (1947) at Northwestern University. His awards, publications, and professional activities are too varied and numerous to list in this brief biography, but he is past president of both the Gerontological Society and the Western Gerontological Society and is editor-in-chief of the *Journal of Gerontology*. In 1968 he received the American Psychological Association's Distinguished Scientific Contribution Award.

JOAN S. BISSELL received her B.A. in social relations from Radcliffe College in 1967 and her Ed.M. and Ed.D. degrees from the Laboratory of Human Development at the Harvard Graduate School of Education in 1968 and 1970, respectively. Her doctoral dissertation, "A Survey of Pre-School Compensatory Education," dealt with program and child characteristics related to effectiveness in preschool programs for disadvantaged children. In the future she plans to continue doing research in developmental and educational psychology.

T. G. R. BOWER, presently setting up a laboratory at Edinburgh University in Scotland, is most known for his studies of perceptual development in infants. Dr. Bower earned his M.A. at Edinburgh in 1963 and his Ph.D. at Cornell in 1965. His particular interest has been in the development of object permanence, the concept of the object, and the ability of the infant to distinguish such distance cues as binocular disparity, constancy, and motion parallax. Before taking his present post at Edinburgh, Dr. Bower had his own perceptual development laboratory at Harvard.

J. ANTHONY DEUTSCH, professor of psychology at the University of California at San Diego, is an active researcher in the area of physiological psychology. His work has dealt mainly with the mechanisms of thirst, intracranial self-stimulation, and the physical basis of memory and learning. Czech born, he did his undergraduate and doctoral studies at Oxford University, where he spent eight years on the faculty before going to the Center for Advanced Study in the Behavioral Sciences at Stanford University in 1959. After spending some time on the faculty at Stanford, he moved to New York University in 1964, and in 1966 he returned to California to take up his present post at UCSD. Dr. Deutsch's first book, *The Structural Basis of Behavior*, was published in 1960. More recently, he coauthored a textbook, *Physiological Psychology* (Dorsey Press, 1966), with his wife, Diana.

SUSAN M. ERVIN-TRIPP, professor of rhetoric and research psychologist at the Institute for Human Learning, University of California at Berkeley, earned her B.A. in art history at Vassar, followed directly by an M.A. in psychology and a Ph.D. in social psychology at the University of Michigan; her dissertation was on the effects of language on message content in French bilinguals. While teaching child language and working on the development of children's scientific concepts as an instructor at the Harvard School of Education, Dr. Ervin-Tripp became interested in the possibilities of using the new theories of linguistics for analysis of child speech. At Berkeley she has continued working with bilingualism and has extended her research to the large developmental study of grammar.

JOSEPH GLICK, head of the developmental program at the City University of New York, received his B.A. from Brandeis and his Ph.D. from Clark University. Before assuming his present position in the fall of 1970, Dr. Glick taught at Yale University and the University of Minnesota. His main interests lie in the field of cognitive development, especially in cross-cultural differences in cognition.

NORMA HAAN is an associate research psychologist at the Institute of Human Development and a lecturer in the School of Social Welfare at the University of California at Berkeley. She received her B.A. in education at Western Washington College in 1943, her M.S. in psychology at the University of Utah in 1948, and did her graduate work in clinical psychology at the University of California and in school psychology at San Francisco State College. She is the author of numerous publications, with topics ranging from coping and defense mechanisms to moral reasoning and activism in adolescents.

Bower.

Deutsch

Ervin-Tripp

Glick

Haan

Haith

Hartup

Hill

Jersild

Kagan

MARSHALL M. HAITH, a lecturer in developmental psychology at Harvard University, holds a Ph.D. in experimental child psychology from the University of California at Los Angeles. Dr. Haith has published numerous papers and articles in professional journals and is a member of the Society for Research in Child Development, the Committee for Correspondents in Infancy, and the Centre for Advanced Study in the Developmental Sciences. Before his present position he taught at the University of Connecticut at Waterbury. His special fields of investigation include visual perception in infants and visual-information processing and memory in children and adults.

WILLARD W. HARTUP is associate director of the Institute for Child Development and a professor of child psychology at the University of Minnesota. He received his B.S. and his M.A. degrees in psychology from Ohio University. In 1955 he earned his Ed.D. in human development from Harvard. Dr. Hartup has participated in a number of editorial activities, including his present role as consulting editor to both the *Journal of Experimental Child Psychology* and the *Journal of Genetic Psychology and Genetic Psychology Monographs*. Dr. Hartup also belongs to several scientific and professional societies and is active in government and community councils related to child psychology.

JOHN P. HILL, an associate professor of psychology at the Institute of Child Development at the University of Minnesota, earned his B.A. at Stanford in 1958 and his Ph.D. at Harvard in 1964. Before coming to Minnesota in 1963, Dr. Hill interned at the Massachusetts Division of Child Guardianship and was a psychiatry and mental health fellow at the Massachusetts General Hospital and Human Relations Service, Wellesley and Boston. His main fields of study are socialization, infancy, and community mental health.

ARTHUR T. JERSILD, professor emeritus since 1967 at Columbia University, is well known for his popular textbook, *Child Psychology* (Prentice-Hall, 1968), which is now in its sixth edition and has been translated into many languages. Dr. Jersild is a 1924 graduate of the University of Nebraska, which awarded him an honorary LL.D. in 1962. He earned his Ph.D. from Columbia University in 1927 and taught there from 1930 until his retirement in 1967. He has been editor of *Child Development Monographs* and the Prentice-Hall Psychology Series, and he is currently associate editor of the *Journal of Genetic Psychology* and *Genetic Psychology Monographs*. Among Dr. Jersild's numerous publications are several book-length monographs, dozens of journal articles, and four books.

JEROME KAGAN, a professor of human development at Harvard since 1964, is noted for his research in cognitive and personality development. He did his undergraduate work at Rutgers and earned his B.S. in biology and psychology in 1950. He received his doctorate from Yale in 1954. Dr. Kagan received the Hofheimer Prize for Research from the American Psychiatric Association in 1963 as a result of research done at the Fels Institute, published in his book *Birth to Maturity* (Wiley, 1962), coauthored by H. A. Moss. Among his numerous publications are basic textbooks in psychology and in child development.

KENNETH KENISTON, professor of psychiatry and psychology and director of the Behavioral Sciences Study Center of the Yale Medical School, is well known for his studies of personality development in adolescence and early adulthood. He is a Harvard graduate and earned his D.Phil. at Oxford University as a Rhodes Scholar in 1956. Dr. Keniston's most recent book, *Young Radicals: Notes on Committed Youth* (Harcourt, Brace and World, 1968), is a study of the psychological and social forces in the lives of a group of young antiwar activists. In addition, he has studied college dropouts, student drug users, and students who interrupt their college careers to work in such services as VISTA and the Peace Corps. Dr. Keniston is a member of the Task Force on Adolescence and Youth of the Joint Commission on Mental Health for Children and is a consultant to a number of projects on student drug use, campus unrest, and sexual behavior.

WILLIAM KESSEN, a professor of psychology and research associate in pediatrics at Yale University, received his Ph.D. from Yale in 1952. He is particularly interested in the behavior of the newborn infant and the child in the first year of life. In 1964 he received a grant from the Carnegie Corporation of New York to conduct research on the preference for complexity in infants and young children. This research is based on the theory that children seek an optimal amount of complexity in their lives and that children will learn in order to present themselves with more complex problems. Dr. Kessen is the author of *The Language of Psychology* with George Mandler (1959) and of *The Child* (1965).

JANE W. KESSLER is a professor of psychology and director of the Mental Development Center at Case Western Reserve University. She was graduated from the University of Michigan in 1940 and was awarded her M.S. degree from Columbia University and her Ph.D. from Case Western Reserve University. Dr. Kessler served ten years as chief psychologist at the University Hospitals in Cleveland. She is currently

president of the Ohio Psychological Association and belongs to a number of other professional organizations. She is the author of *Psychopathology of Childhood* (Prentice-Hall, 1966) and numerous articles and book chapters dealing with problems of child development, normal and abnormal. She is married to a psychiatrist, and they have one son, who is studying music at Harvard.

LAWRENCE KOHLBERG, a professor of education and social psychology at Harvard University, received his Ph.D. from the University of Chicago. He has taught at both Chicago and Yale and has also served as a fellow of the Institute for Advanced Study in the Behavioral Sciences, Palo Alto, and as director of the Child Psychology Training Program. In 1969 Dr. Kohlberg received the National Institute of Mental Health Research Scientist Award, and he has published numerous papers and articles in the fields of education, sex-role attitudes, and cognitive development. He is perhaps most well known for his research in moral development and for his delineation of developmental stages in this area.

LEWIS P. LIPSITT, professor of psychology at Brown University, received his Ph.D. from the University of Iowa Institute of Child Behavior and Development. Dr. Lipsitt is a founder and coeditor of *Advances in Child Development and Behavior* and has served on the boards of editors of the *Journal of Experimental Child Psychology*, *Child Development*, and the *Monographs of the Society for Research in Child Development*. He is also on the scientific advisory panel of the Center for Advanced Study in the Developmental Sciences in Minster Lovell, England. Dr. Lipsitt is the author of numerous papers that have been published in professional journals. His two major fields of interest are discrimination and verbal process learning in older children and infant behavior and development.

Keniston

Kessen

Kessler

Kohlberg

Lipsitt

Maddi

Madison

McNeil

Munsinger

Ricciuti

SALVATORE R. MADDI, a professor of psychology at the University of Chicago, received his B.A. and M.A. degrees in psychology from Brooklyn College. He did his doctoral work in clinical psychology at Harvard, receiving his Ph.D. in 1960. He is currently involved in a longitudinal study of personality change in men and women training to become priests and nuns; the study, in its fourth year, is focusing on the effects of the total institutional approach to personality change and on the possibility for deep and lasting personality change after childhood. Dr. Maddi is a frequent contributor to professional journals and is a consulting editor to the *Journal of Abnormal Psychology*. He is also the author of *Personality Theories: A Comparative Analysis* (Dorsey, 1968) and (with D. W. Fiske) *Functions of Varied Experience* (Dorsey, 1961).

PETER MADISON is a professor of psychology at the University of Arizona and also works as a part-time psychotherapist at the Southern Arizona Mental Health Center. Dr. Madison is a graduate of the University of Oregon and did his graduate work in social relations (M.A., 1947) and clinical psychology (Ph.D., 1953) at Harvard. Dr. Madison's main interest is personality development, especially the relationship between childhood personality and the student's response to college life. He has pioneered a new type of undergraduate laboratory course in which the procedures used both teach theoretical content and directly affect the student's own personality. His recent book, *Personality Development in College* (Addison-Wesley, 1969), traces the personality development of college students who participated in a long-range study.

ELTON B. MCNEIL, professor of psychology at the University of Michigan, also received his Ph.D. in clinical psychology from Michigan after graduating from Harvard. His interests span the fields of delinquency, violence, mental health, education of the gifted, human conflict, sex, neurosis, and psychosis. He is a frequent contributor to scholarly journals and is the author of numerous books, including *Human Socialization* (Brooks/Cole, 1969), and *The Psychoses* (Prentice-Hall, 1970).

HARRY MUNSINGER, an associate professor of psychology at the University of California at San Diego, has concentrated his research in the area of visual perception and has published numerous journal articles on that topic. He is a graduate of the University of California at Berkeley and received his Ph.D. in 1962 from the University of Oregon. Before coming to UCSD Dr. Munsinger held posts at the University of Illinois, Yale University, and the Veterans Administration Hospital at Palo Alto. He serves on the editorial board of the *Journal of Experimental Child Psychology* and is a psychology editor for Holt, Rinehart and Winston.

HENRY N. RICCIUTI is a professor of human development and family studies at Cornell University, where he has taught for the past eleven years. He is also director of the Cornell Research Program in Early Childhood Education, a component center of the National Laboratory in Early Childhood Education, sponsored by the U.S. Office of Education. His research and teaching interests center on the influence of experience and of related biological factors on early development in human infants, with particular reference to social-emotional and cognitive processes. Prior to coming to Cornell, Dr. Ricciuti was a research associate at the Child Research Council, University of Colorado Medical School, and at the Educational Testing Service in Princeton. He received his Ph.D. in psychology in 1949 from Fordham University.

CARL R. ROGERS, resident fellow at the Center for Studies of the Person, La Jolla, California, is internationally known as the originator of client-centered psychotherapy, which he developed while head of the Counseling Center at the University of Chicago. For twenty years his research and writing have been in the fields of psychotherapy, personality theory, and education, and increasingly in the last five years he has been involved in both the theory and the practice of encounter groups (sensitivity training). He is the only psychologist in the United States to receive from the American Psychological Association both its Scientific Contribution Award and its Award for Professional Contribution. Dr. Rogers, the author of many books and articles, has been professor at Ohio State University, the University of Chicago, and the University of Wisconsin. His most recent books are *On Becoming a Person* and *Freedom to Learn: A View of What Education Might Become*.

PAULINE S. SEARS, a professor of psychology at the Stanford University School of Education, holds a Ph.D. from Yale University. She has held teaching positions at Harvard, Yale, and the State University of Iowa. Her particular interests are in parent-child relations, achievement motivation, and child projection techniques.

HAROLD W. STEVENSON has been professor of child psychology and director of the Institute of Child Development at the University of Minnesota since 1959. He is a 1947 graduate of the University of Colorado and earned both his M.S. and his Ph.D. degrees in psychology from Stanford. Before assuming his present position, Dr. Stevenson taught at Pomona College and at the University of Texas. He is currently president of the Society for Research in Child Development and a member of the Behavioral Sciences Committee, National Research Council of the National Academy of Science, and is involved in a variety of other professional organizations and activities.

LELAND H. STOTT, a member of the Merrill-Palmer Institute faculty since 1944, has concentrated his research on longitudinal studies in personality development. Dr. Stott was born in Utah in 1897. He did missionary work in Pago Pago and taught school in a one-room log schoolhouse in Idaho before pursuing his education at Brigham Young University, where he received his B.A. in psychology in 1927. He earned his M.A. at the University of Utah in 1929 and his Ph.D. at the University of Illinois in 1933. He taught for nine years at the University of Nebraska before joining Merrill-Palmer.

SHELDON H. WHITE, a professor of education and cognitive psychology at Harvard University, received his M.A. from Boston University and his Ph.D. from the State University of Iowa. Before assuming his present position, he was a research fellow at the Center for Cognitive Studies at the University of Chicago, a consultant to the Educational Testing Service at Princeton University, and a research assistant at the Institute of Child Behavior at the State University of Iowa. His special interests include learning and attentional processes in children. Dr. White has served as consulting editor for the *Journal of Experimental Child Psychology* and is presently on the editorial boards of the *Journal of Child Psychology and Psychiatry* and *Developmental Psychology*.

Rogers

Sears

Stevenson

Stott

White

Glossary

a

aberration. Any departure from that which is normal.

accommodation. The tendency to change one's schemes or operations or to make new ones in order to include new objects or experiences. See also *assimilation*.

active-constructive personality. According to Alfred Adler, the fully mature individual. See also *active-destructive personality*; *passive-constructive personality*; *passive-destructive personality*.

active-destructive personality. Alfred Adler's term for the immature and rebellious individual. See also *active-constructive personality*; *passive-constructive personality*; *passive-destructive personality*.

active sentences. Sentences using active verb forms, such as *John hit the ball*. See also *passive sentences*.

actualization-fulfillment theory. The version of the fulfillment theory of personality holding that the personality force is in the form of an inherited blueprint determining the person's special abilities. See also *personality, fulfillment theory of*.

actualizing tendency. The potential for the fullest development that, under appropriate circumstances, will occur.

adjustment. The achievement of harmony between an individual and his environment.

adolescence. The stage of the human life cycle lasting from the onset of puberty until psychological and biological maturity are attained.

adulthood. The stage of the human life cycle that begins when the individual achieves biological and psychological maturity and ends with the gradual onset of old age.

affect. An overall term comprising feeling, mood, emotion, and temperament.

afterbirth. The placenta, its attached membranes, and the rest of the umbilical cord, delivered in the final stages of labor.

age. See *biological age*; *chronological age*; *mental age*; *psychological age*; *social age*.

aggression. Feeling and behavior of anger or hostility.

albinism. Congenital absence of skin pigmentation.

alleles. Pairs of genes on corresponding chromosomes that affect the same traits. When the two alleles are identical, a person is said to be *homozygous* for that trait. When the alleles carry differing instructions he is said to be *heterozygous*.

alienation. A feeling of estrangement from and hostility toward society based in part on a discrepancy between expectations and promises and in part on the actual experience of the role one is playing.

ambivalence. Simultaneously holding conflicting reactions toward a person or object.

amnion. The translucent sac in which the developing prenatal organism lies.

amniotic fluid. The fluid in the amnion in which the developing prenatal organism is suspended; it protects the organism from external pressure.

anal stage. In psychoanalytic theory, the second stage of psychosexual development, during which the child's interest centers on anal activities. See also *genital stage*; *oral stage*; *phallic stage*.

analytical concept. A concept based on a public, observable attribute that is part of each object in a group. See also *relational concept*; *superordinate concept*.

androgens. The male sex hormones. See also *estrogens*.

androgynous. Having characteristics of both sexes.

anencephaly. The lack of a brain at birth.

anger. Generally, an emotional response involving aggressive behavior or impulse directed toward some person or object, usually caused by the thwarting or frustration of a desired goal.

animism. The belief that inanimate objects are alive.

anoxia. A severe oxygen deficiency that seriously interferes with normal metabolism.

anterior pituitary gland. The front part of the pituitary gland, an endocrine gland situated at the base of the brain. The anterior pituitary produces hormones that regulate growth and others that regulate the functions of the other endocrine glands.

anxiety. A feeling of uneasiness or distress that arises when a person is torn by inner conflict because of incompatible motives, when he is at odds with himself, when he is threatened by an adverse evaluation of himself, or when he feels apprehension over a possible danger to himself. See also *fear*.

aphasia. The loss or impairment of the ability to use speech resulting from lesions in the brain.

arithmetic mean. The sum of all scores divided by the number of scores. See also *median*; *mode*.

articulation. The manner of uttering the separate vowel and consonant sounds that make up speech.

artist. Otto Rank's term for the mature individual who minimizes both the fear of life and the fear of death by becoming an individual, differentiated being who can relate to and be accepted by other people. See also *average man; neurotic.*

asceticism. Rigorous abstention from self-indulgence.

assimilation. The incorporation of a new object into an existing scheme. See also *accommodation.*

atavism. A carryover from an older phylogenetic ancestor; a genetic throwback.

attention. The focusing of perception on a certain stimulus or stimuli while ignoring others.

audiogenic seizures. Rhythmic seizures, such as epileptic fits.

autism. A schizophrenic syndrome characterized by absorption in fantasy to the exclusion of interest in reality.

auxiliary verbs. Verbs that accompany the main verb in a sentence and that usually express person, number, mood, or tense.

average man. Otto Rank's term for a psychopathological individual in whom the fear of life overcomes the fear of death. He is typically conformist and fails generally to impress himself upon his activities in terms that would express his individual worth. See also *artist; neurotic.*

axillary hair. Underarm hair.

b

babbling. Speech patterns found in infants, comprising repetitive sequences of alternating consonants and vowels.

basic trust. According to Erik Erikson, the feeling that one's physical and psychological needs are being satisfied and that the world is a fine and pleasant place. Such a feeling is necessary for a child to develop a mature personality.

behavior. Any activity of an organism.

behaviorism. The school of psychology holding that the proper object of study in psychology is behavior alone, without reference to consciousness. Behavior theorists are particularly interested in learning mechanisms. See also *cognitive theory; psychoanalytic theory.*

binocular disparity. The incongruent views the two eyes receive because of their different positions in space.

binocular fusion. The integration of the two different views of the eyes.

biological age. Age measured in terms of an organism's physical vulnerability. See also *psychological age; social age.*

blastocyst. The cluster of cells that begins to differentiate itself into distinct parts during the germinal period of prenatal development.

blastula. The cluster of cells that make up the prenatal organism the first few days after conception.

body stalk. During the germinal period of prenatal development, the structure that differentiates to become the embryonic disk and the umbilical cord.

brain waves. The rhythmic, spontaneous electrical discharges of the living brain.

breech delivery. A birth in which the baby's buttocks appear first, then his legs, and finally his head.

c

Caesarean section. A surgical operation through the walls of the abdomen and uterus for the purpose of delivering a child.

central nervous system (CNS). The brain and spinal cord.

cephalocaudal development. The progressive growth of the body parts in a head-to-foot direction. See also *proximodistal development.*

cerebral hemispheres. The two symmetrical halves of the cerebrum that constitute the bulk of the human brain.

cervix. The canal connecting the vagina and the uterus.

childhood. The stage of the human life cycle lasting from the end of infancy until the onset of puberty.

chorion. The protective and nutrient cover of the amnion, which contains the developing organism in the womb.

chorionic villi. Capillaries that link the developing umbilical veins and arteries of an embryo with the uterine wall; they eventually become part of the placenta, along with the surrounding maternal tissues.

chromosomes. The chainlike structures within the nucleus of the cell that carry genes, the transmitters of hereditary traits.

chronological age. Age in years.

class. See *social class.*

class inclusion, operation of. The ability to reason simultaneously about part of the whole and the whole itself.

classical conditioning. An experimental method in which a conditioned stimulus is paired with an unconditioned stimulus in order to condition a particular response.

cleft palate. A congenital fissure in the median line of the roof of the mouth.

clinical method. The psychological method of study that involves using such techniques as interviews, questionnaires, and various types of tests. See also *experimental method; observational method.*

cognition. Knowing the world through the use of one's perceptual and conceptual abilities.

cognitive development. The development of a logical method of looking at the world, utilizing one's perceptual and conceptual powers.

cognitive processes. The operations or routines that the mind performs utilizing cognitive units. The processes include the encoding of information, the storage and retrieval of information in memory, the generation of hypotheses, their evaluation according to criteria, and inductive and deductive reasoning. See also *deduction; directed thinking; encoding; hypotheses; induction; memory; undirected thinking.*

cognitive theory. The basis of the school of psychology that concentrates primarily on the development of human thought processes. See also *behaviorism; psychoanalytic theory.*

cognitive units. The materials of thought: images, symbols, concepts, and rules. The units enable one to make sense of experience and to generate solutions to problems. See also *concept; image; rule; symbol.*

coitus. Sexual intercourse.

combinative structures. Mental rules for carrying out complex thought operations.

commitment. A capacity for loyalty, devotion, and service to a set of imagined possibilities, some of which are attainable; to a set of values and ideals relevant to the evaluation of action and intent; and to enduring relationships with people, groups, and institutions and to the purposes they serve.

concept. A type of symbol that represents a set of common attributes among a group of other symbols or images. See also *analytical concept; relational concept; superordinate concept.*

conceptual chaining. Conceptually grouping successive pairs of items, each pair on a different basis, resulting in indirect linking of two or more items sharing no common characteristics.

conceptualization. The process of concept formation in which various items are grouped into units on the basis of commensurable characteristics.

concordance rate. In genetics, the proportion of cases in which both members of a pair of relatives show the same expression of a trait.

concrete operational stage. The stage of cognitive development that occurs from about seven to twelve years of age and during which the child develops the operations of conservation, class inclusion, and serialization. See also *class inclusion, operation of; conservation; formal operational stage; preoperational stage; sensorimotor stage; serialization.*

conditional positive regard. The attitude of society toward the individual in which society finds some of the individual's actions acceptable and other of his actions unacceptable. See also *unconditional positive regard.*

conditioning. See *classical conditioning; operant conditioning.*

conflict theory of personality. See *personality, conflict theory of.*

conformity. Responses governed by prevailing attitudes and opinions.

congenital. Present at birth.

congenital activity types. The term Margaret Fries applied to the basic temperaments found in infants. She identified three types: the active, the moderately active, and the quiet.

connective tissue. Fibers that lie between cells of the body.

consciousness. Cognizance of the immediate environment plus the ability to utilize encoding, memory, and logic at will.

conservation. A child's ability to ignore irrelevant transformations, as in shape in relation to volume.

consistency theory of personality. See *personality, consistency theory of.*

constancy. The fact that an object perceived from different points of view still looks like the same object.

contraception. The prevention of pregnancy by artificial means.

control group. A group used for comparison with an experimental group, with the exception that the independent variable is not applied to the control group.

conventional stage. A stage of moral development in which the individual strives to maintain the expectations of his family, group, or nation, regardless of the consequences. See also *postconventional stage; preconventional stage.*

coordination. Such aspects of motor performance as accuracy of movement, poise, smoothness, rhythm, and ease.

correlation. The relationship between two variables as measured by the correlation coefficient. See also *negative correlation; positive correlation.*

correlation coefficient. A statistical index for measuring correspondence in changes occurring in two variables. Perfect correspondence is $+1.00$; no correspondence is 0.00; perfect correspondence in opposite directions is -1.00.

correlational design. A type of psychological investigation in which the interrelationships among response measures are sought. See also *experimental design.*

cortical development. The development of the areas of the brain that control sensory and motor functions.

creativity. The seeking and discovery of new relationships and new solutions to problems.

critical periods. Specific times in development during which a child is best able to learn a specific lesson; also, in fetal development, crucial points at which various specific physical features and organs develop, so that environmental influences during those periods can adversely affect their development.

cross-sectional study. A study technique that examines a number of subjects who are all at the same point in development. See also *longitudinal study.*

cyclicity. The continual, rhythmic repetition of a cycle.

d

declarative sentences. Sentences that make a statement, as opposed to those that ask a question or that make a request.

deduction. The process of arriving at a conclusion that follows necessarily from the premises. See also *induction.*

defense mechanism. A reaction to frustration or conflict in which the individual deceives himself about his real motives and goals to avoid anxiety or loss of self-esteem.

deoxyribonucleic acid (DNA). The complex molecules of which genes are composed; thought to be responsible for genetic inheritance.

dependence. The desire or need for supporting relationships with other persons. See also *independence.*

dependent variable. A variable that changes in response to the independent variable; in psychology, the dependent variable is behavior.

depression. The emotional response of extreme sadness.

depth perception. The perception of the distance of objects from the observer.

descriptive statistics. A simplified method of summarizing measurements. Descriptive statistics include the number of subjects; measurement of the average, including the mean, median, and mode; and measurements of variability, including range and standard deviation. See also *inferential statistics.*

design error. An error occurring when an experimenter measures something that does not coincide exactly with what he wants to measure, as when a psychologist studying dreams uses written reports as data.

development. A process involving all the orderly changes that occur during progress toward maturity.

developmental psychology. The branch of psychology concerned with the description and explanation of changes in an individual's behavior that are a result of maturation and experience.

developmental synthesis. A period in adolescence during which the subject temporarily chooses a course of action that seems to allow the development of changes in personality necessary for making a final choice of a course of action.

diaphyses. Ossification centers in the shafts of bones. See also *epiphyses.*

differentiated functioning. Functioning on a specific level rather than on an overall one, such as the infant's being able to pick up an object with just two fingers when he previously had to close in on it with his whole body. See also *syncretic functioning.*

differentiation. The process by which forms of behavior become more complex and specialized.

Digit Span Test. A portion of the Wechsler intelligence test. It involves repeating a series of numbers after the examiner says them.

Digit-Symbol Substitution Test. A portion of the Wechsler intelligence test. It involves pairing numbers and symbols in certain ways and is chiefly a clerical test.

directed thinking. Thinking aimed at solving a problem. See also *undirected thinking.*

discrimination. The process of distinguishing between two events, ideas, or objects.

disequilibrium. According to Piaget, the result of the conflict between cognitive level and environmental output; disequilibrium is induced whenever the organism encounters a situation that produces two or more mutually opposed, partially adopted responses that cannot be applied simultaneously. See also *equilibration.*

distribution. An array of the instances of a variable arranged by classes according to their value.

dizygotic (DZ) *twins.* Twins that develop from two separate eggs; fraternal twins. See also *monozygotic* (MZ) *twins.*

DNA. See *deoxyribonucleic acid.*

dominant gene. A gene whose hereditary characteristics always prevail. See also *recessive gene.*

double-blind design. An experimental design, used primarily in drug research, in which neither the investigator nor the patient knows which group is drugged and which drug is being administered.

Down's syndrome. A congenital physical condition associated with mental retardation; characterized by thick, fissured tongue, flat face, and slanted eyes.

dysfunction. Disturbance and impairment of the functional capacity of an organ or system.

e

ectoderm. The upper layer of the embryonic disk; it is the source of cells for the skin, the sense organs, and the nervous system. See also *endoderm; mesoderm.*

EEG. Electroencephalogram or electroencephalograph.

egg cell. See *ovum.*

ego. According to Freud, that part of the personality that corresponds most closely to the perceived self. It functions by reconciling the conflicting forces of the id and superego. See also *id; superego.*

ego identity. According to Erik Erikson, a clear and continuing sense of who one is and what one's goals are.

ego integrity. According to Erik Erikson, an overarching acceptance of and satisfaction with one's life.

egocentrism. Having excessive concern with the self rather than society.

electroencephalogram (EEG). A graphic record of the electric activity of the brain obtained by placing electrodes on the skull.

emboîtement theory. The idea that the prefabricated baby is contained somehow in the mother's ovaries (the view held by the *ovists*) or in the father's sperm (the view held by the *homunculists*).

embryo. The growing prenatal organism during the six weeks following the germinal period. See also *fetus.*

embryology. The study of the development of the individual from conception to birth.

embryonic disk. During the germinal period, the part of the prenatal organism that will eventually become the embryo.

emotion. Visceral changes (chiefly in the autonomic nervous system and the endocrine system) that result from the subjects' value response to a given stimulus. Emotions are the physiological forms in which men experience their estimates of the harmful or beneficial effects of stimuli.

encoding. The first step in problem solving. It involves selective attention to one event and interpretation of the information provided by that event. See also *cognitive processes.*

encounter group. An intensive group that emphasizes development and improvement in interpersonal communication.

endocrine gland. A ductless gland that secretes hormones into the bloodstream or lymph system.

endoderm. The lower layer of the embryonic disk; it is the point of origin for the muscular, circulatory, and skeletal systems. See also *ectoderm; mesoderm.*

epinephrine. A hormone secreted by the adrenal medulla that stimulates the sympathetic nervous system.

epiphyses. Ossification centers located at the ends of bones. See also *diaphyses.*

epistemology. The branch of philosophy that is concerned with discovering the nature of knowledge and knowing.

equilibration. According to Piaget, the coordination of cognitive level with environmental output so as to reduce disequilibrium. See also *disequilibrium.*

erogenous zones. A term Freud used to refer to certain areas of the body thought to be more pleasurable than others. Freud included in this category the mouth and lips, the anal region, and the genital organs.

error of expectation. An error in psychophysical testing in which the subject reports receiving a stimulus before he actually does because he has been warned that it is coming.

error of habituation. An error in psychophysical testing in which the subject continues to report receiving stimulation after it is no longer present.

estrogens. The female sex hormones. See also *androgens.*

estrous cycle. The periodic waxing and waning of sexual desire and receptivity (with accompanying physiological changes) in the female animal.

ethical principles. Moral propositions that are the end point of an invariant ethical developmental sequence. They are of an absolute nature as opposed to arbitrary rules and beliefs, per the cognitive-developmental approach to morality.

ethical relativity. The doctrine stating that different cultures or groups hold different fundamental moral values and that these values cannot themselves be judged as more or less adequate or more or less moral.

ethics. Moral values and ideals. See also *morality.*

executive independence. David Ausubel's term for the infant's ability to satisfy some of his behavioral needs for himself.

existential anxiety. According to Rollo May, the anxiety that arises from choosing the unknown. See also *ontological guilt.*

existential living. According to Carl Rogers, the ability to live fully and vitally in each moment, as if it were one's last.

existentialism. The philosophy that man forms his own nature in the course of his life, with man's situation in the universe seen as purposeless or irrational.

experiential freedom. According to Carl Rogers, the subjective sense that one is free to choose among alternative courses of action in defining one's life.

experimental design. A type of psychological investigation in which information is sought through the use of controlled experiments. See also *correlational design.*

experimental method. The psychological method of study that involves the investigation of the effects of particular variables on behavior.

extraversion. Orientation outward from the self; a preference for the company of others. See also *introversion.*

eye-hand coordination. The ability to coordinate vision with motor activities so that one can accurately reach for and grasp objects.

f

Fallopian tube. Either of the tubes that carries the ova from the ovaries to the uterus.

family atmosphere. The relationship between parents and children in a family and the way in which the children are reared.

fear. A strong emotional response involving agitation and feelings of unpleasantness, coupled with a desire to flee. According to John B. Watson, it, along with love and rage, is one of the inherent or primary emotions. See also *anxiety.*

fear of death. According to Otto Rank, the fear that manifests itself in isolation and rejection of others and in a distaste for conformity. An excess of this element results in a *neurotic* personality.

fear of life. According to Otto Rank, the fear that manifests itself in a wish not to be separated from people and things and an unwillingness to face change. An excess of this element results in an *average man.*

fertilization. The union of an egg cell with a sperm.

fetus. The prenatal human organism from approximately eight weeks after conception to birth. See also *embryo.*

fixation. Stereotyped repetitive responding. In Freudian theory, if a child encounters excessive frustration in any of the psychosexual stages, he may become fixated at that stage.

formal operational stage. According to Jean Piaget, the fourth stage of thought, which begins at about age twelve. It is the period during which logical thinking begins and is the final step toward abstract thinking and conceptualization. See also *concrete operational stage; preoperational stage; sensorimotor stage.*

formal rules. Statements of relations between units or classes that are always true and specifiable, such as the rules of mathematics. See also *informal rules.*

formal thought. A generalized approach toward problem solving that involves isolating the elements of a problem and systematically exploring all the possible solutions, regardless of their hypothetical nature.

fraternal twins. See *dizygotic (DZ) twins.*

frequency distribution. A distribution showing the frequency with which each particular score occurs in a population of scores.

frustration. A subjective experience or response to the blocked gratification of an individual's needs.

fulfillment theory of personality. See *personality, fulfillment theory of.*

fully functioning person. Carl Rogers' term for an individual characterized by openness to experience, existential living, organismic trusting, experiential freedom, and creativity.

g

galvanic skin response (GSR). A change in the electrical resistance of the skin.

gamete. A sex cell; an egg or a sperm.

gene pool. The totality of alleles carried by members of a breeding population; the population genotype.

generativity. According to Erik Erikson, ability and desire to be productive and to nurture and devote one's self to others.

genes. The basic units of heredity, carried on the chromosomes.

genetics. The branch of biology concerned with the transmission of hereditary characteristics.

genital organs. The male and female sex organs.

genital stage. In psychoanalytic theory, the final stage of psychosexual development, during which heterosexual interests are dominant. This stage begins in adolescence and lasts throughout adulthood. See also *anal stage; oral stage; phallic stage.*

genotype. The characteristics of an organism that are inherited and that can be transmitted to offspring. Also, the traits or characteristics common to a biological group. See also *phenotype.*

germinal period. The first stage of prenatal development. It is roughly the first two weeks after conception, during which the developing individual is primarily engaged in cell division. See also *embryo; fetus.*

gestation period. The amount of time the prenatal organism spends in the uterus; the period from conception to birth.

gifted children. Children with high IQs, generally above 130.

global functioning. See *syncretic functioning.*

gonadotropic hormones. Secretions of the anterior pituitary that stimulate activity in the gonads.

gonads. The sex glands; the ovaries in females and the testes in males.

grammar. The study of the underlying rules and systems of a language.

group therapy. Psychotherapeutic treatment of several patients simultaneously.

growth. The process of becoming larger, becoming increasingly complex in body structure and functioning, and approaching mature size, organic structure, and body build. See also *psychological growth.*

guidance. Advising, counseling, testing, and corrective teaching of persons to help them to adjust to society and to achieve personal satisfaction.

h

habituation. The process of becoming accustomed to a particular set of circumstances or to a particular stimulus.

handedness. The tendency to use either the right or the left hand predominantly.

hedonic. Seeking pleasure and avoiding pain.

heredity. The totality of characteristics biologically transmitted from parents and ancestors to offspring at conception.

heritability. The percentage of trait variance in a population that is attributable to genotypic differences among individuals.

heterosexuality. Sexual intercourse with or attraction toward members of the opposite sex.

heterozygote. See *alleles.*

hierarchic integration. Heinz Werner's term for the way in which an individual interrelates a variety of separate skills or ideas into a coherent whole.

higher-order operations. Ways of using abstract rules to solve a whole class of problems.

homeostasis. The condition of physiological equilibrium within an individual.

homologues. The two chromosomes of a pair.

homosexuality. Sexual intercourse with or attraction toward members of the same sex.

homozygote. See *alleles.*

homunculists. In the seventeenth and eighteenth centuries, biologists who held that man starts in the head of the sperm, which uses the womb as an incubator in which to grow. See also *ovists.*

hormone. A substance produced and secreted by any of the endocrine glands.

hypotheses. Tentative assumptions that explain, or aid in explaining, given data.

i

id. According to Freud, that part of the personality consisting of primitive instincts toward sexuality and aggression. The id seeks immediate gratification regardless of the consequences but is held in check by the superego. See also *ego; superego.*

identical twins. See *monozygotic (MZ) twins.*

identification. The process by which a person takes over the features of another person whom he admires and incorporates them into his own personality.

identity. A sense of one's self. See also *object identity.*

image. A mental representation, based on a set of primary elements, of a specific object or event. See also *concept; symbol.*

imprinting. Behavior attached to stimuli very early in life and generally not reversible. It occurs at critical stages in development.

impulsivity. Uncontrolled action; acting without first thinking.

inbreeding. The interbreeding of closely related individuals, especially to preserve and fix desirable characteristics and to eliminate undesirable characteristics from a stock.

independence. Self-reliance. See also *dependence.*

independent assortment. See *law of independent assortment.*

independent variable. The variable that is controlled by the experimenter in order to determine its effect on the dependent variable.

induction. The process of reasoning from particulars to generals or from parts to wholes. See also *deduction.*

infancy. The stage of human development lasting from birth until the organism is able to exist independently of its mother, capable of feeding itself, of walking, and of talking.

inferential statistics. Statistics used to make generalizations from measurements. See also *descriptive statistics.*

informal rules. Statements of imperfect relations between two or more units or classes. See also *formal rules.*

instinct. Unlearned, biologically based behavior.

intelligence. The ability to conceptualize effectively and to grasp relationships. Also, according to Jean Piaget, the coordination of operations.

intelligence quotient (IQ). An index to the rate of mental growth of a child obtained by dividing chronological age into the mental-age score achieved on a test and then multiplying by 100.

intensive-group experience. A general term that encompasses groups in which individuals are taught to observe their interactions with others and the nature of the group process. See also *encounter group*; *sensitivity group*; *T-group*.

intermodal transfer. Perception of one sense made by means of another.

internalization. The incorporation of beliefs, attitudes, and ideas into the personality.

intimacy. According to Erik Erikson, ability and interest in relating closely in both the physical and the psychological senses.

intonation. Pitch patterns in speech.

intrapsychic conflict theory. The version of the conflict theory of personality holding that the two opposing forces of life both exist within the individual. See also *personality, conflict theory of*; *psychosocial conflict theory*.

introversion. Orientation inward toward the self; a preference for one's own thoughts and activities rather than association with others. See also *extraversion*.

invariant developmental sequence. Any developmental process in which movement is always to the next higher stage.

inventory. A test for assessing the presence or absence of certain traits, behaviors, interests, attitudes, or values.

IQ. See *intelligence quotient*.

isogenic population. A population in which all members are genetically identical.

jealousy. The emotional response felt by a person who thinks he is being actually or potentially displaced by someone else in his relationship with a special person.

justice. Reciprocity and equality in human relations.

kibbutz. An Israeli collective farm.

kleptomania. A persistent neurotic impulse to steal.

Klinefelter's syndrome. A congenital physical condition in men that occurs when the individual has two X chromosomes and one Y. The symptoms include sterility, small testes, and mental retardation.

knee-jerk reflex. See *patellar reflex*.

l

lability. In psychology, the tendency to shift erratically from one emotional state to another. See also *stability*.

labor. The process by which a baby is expelled from his mother's body.

laboratory experiments. The method of psychological study in which the essential features are careful description and control of the stimulus materials presented to an organism and a restricted and repeatedly measurable response.

language. An abstract system of word meanings and syntactic structures that facilitate communication.

lanugo hair. A fine, woolly fuzz that appears briefly in the later months of fetal development.

latency period. In psychoanalytic theory, a stage in psychosexual development that appears between the phallic and genital stages and during which sexual drives become temporarily dormant.

law of effect. The principle stating that responses followed by a satisfying state of affairs will tend to be repeated under similar circumstances in the future and that behaviors that produce neutral or disagreeable effects will tend to diminish in frequency.

law of independent assortment. Gregor Mendel's second law of inheritance, which describes the simultaneous inheritance of two or more traits that are determined by single genes.

law of segregation. Gregor Mendel's first law of inheritance, which maintains that each phenotypic trait is governed by a separate pair of elements that divide and recombine when producing offspring.

learning. A relatively permanent modification of behavior resulting from experience.

level of confidence. In the *t* test, expression of the assurance with which a null hypothesis can be rejected, often expressed as a percentage. If the desired result could occur by chance one in twenty times, the level of confidence is 5 percent.

level of significance. In the *t* test, expression of the confidence with which a null hypothesis can be rejected, usually expressed as a decimal fraction. If the desired result could occur by chance one in twenty times, the level of significance is .05.

libido. According to Freud, a basic psychological energy inherent in every individual; this energy supplies the sexual drive, whose goal is to obtain pleasure.

life expectancy. The number of years, based on a statistical average, that a person is expected to live in a given culture.

localization. In audition, the localization of sounds in space by means of the physical and temporal differences between the sounds arriving at the two ears.

long-term memory (LTM). The permanent information-storage system of the human mind, as opposed to short-term memory.

longitudinal study. A study technique in which the same individual is examined over a long period or over a complete developmental stage. See also cross-sectional study.

love. In the general sense, an intense emotional response involving a feeling of affection toward a person or persons. According to John B. Watson, it, along with fear and rage, is one of the inherent or primary emotions.

LTM. See long-term memory.

maladjustment, psychological. The denial to awareness or consciousness, or a distorted awareness of, significant experiences in life.

maladjustment, social. The failure to adjust to society.

malnutrition. Substandard nutrition due to faulty or unbalanced intake of nutritives.

manic-depressive psychosis. A psychotic reaction characterized by extreme variation in mood, from a highly elated state to depression and back.

marketing orientation. Erich Fromm's term for the immature personality that is characterized by treating himself and others as if they were commodities to be bought and sold to the highest bidder.

masturbation. Achievement of sexual gratification by manual stimulation.

maturation. The process by which an individual approaches his mature size, organic structure, and body build.

mean. See arithmetic mean.

measure of central tendency. In testing, the measure of the average performance—usually the median, the mode, or the arithmetic mean.

measurement. The assignment of units or numbers to events, objects, or traits.

median. The middle score when all the scores are arranged from highest to lowest. See also arithmetic mean; mode.

meiosis. The process of cell division in which the daughter cells receive half the normal number of chromosomes, thus becoming gametes.

memory. The mental activity of reliving past events. It can be considered as having two functions: The storage of experience for a period of time and the revival of that information at a later time.

memory trace. Believed by some to be a physical change in the nervous system that accompanies learning. It is thought to fade with time and lack of use.

menarche. The first menstruation in an adolescent girl.

Mendelian population. A community of interbreeding organisms that is reproductively isolated from other organisms of the same species.

menopause. The period in a woman's life when menstruation ceases.

menstrual age. The age of a prenatal organism calculated from the first day of its mother's last menstrual period.

menstruation. The cyclic discharge of blood and discarded uterine material that occurs in sexually mature females.

mental age. A summary evaluation of an individual's mental attainment based upon testing. One who scores as well as the average twelve-year-old is said to have a mental age of twelve, regardless of his actual age.

mental retardation. A condition of mental deficiency, usually defined as being below 70 in IQ.

mental units. See cognitive units.

mesoderm. The middle layer of the embryonic disk; it develops into the alimentary canal and various digestive glands. See also ectoderm; endoderm.

middle age. Roughly, the period of life between the ages of forty and sixty.

mode. A measure of central tendency. The most frequent score in a frequency distribution. See also arithmetic mean; median.

model. An object or area similar in structure to the object or area being investigated. Information about the model will yield information about the object of study.

modeling. Imitation of a model; in children, modeling is usually patterned after parents, peers, or admired adults.

mongolism. See Down's syndrome.

monozygotic (MZ) twins. Twins that develop from the same fertilized ovum; identical twins. See also dizygotic (DZ) twins.

mood quality. The amount of pleasant, joyful, friendly behavior in an infant as contrasted with unpleasant, crying, unfriendly behavior.

morality. A sense of what is right and wrong.

moral judgments. Judgments as to the rightness or wrongness of actions.

mores. Social norms of behavior invested with great moral importance. They involve matters of health, sex, religion, property, and other activities that are deemed important.

Moro response. The newborn infant's involuntary response to having his head fall backward—he stretches his arms outward and brings them together over his chest in a grasp gesture.

morpheme. In speech, the smallest sound unit having a lexical or grammatical meaning.

mortality rate. Statistical rate of death.

mosaicism. The occurrence of different chromosome counts in different cells of the same organism.

motion parallax. The different relative motions that objects at different distances appear to have as a person moves his head.

motivation. A general term referring to factors within an organism that arouse and maintain behaviors directed toward satisfying some need or drive or toward accomplishing a goal.

motor skill. Any skill, such as walking or riding a bicycle, that requires muscular coordination.

myelin sheath. A white fatty covering on many neural fibers that serves to channel impulses along fibers and to reduce the random spread of impulses across neurons.

myelinization. The process by which neural fibers acquire a sheath of myelin.

n

nasals. Vocal sounds characterized by resonance in nasal passages. See also *stops.*

negative correlation. A relationship between two variables in which high values in the first correspond to low values in the second and vice versa. See also *positive correlation.*

negative reinforcement. In operant conditioning, the termination of an aversive stimulus as the result of a response. See also *positive reinforcement.*

neocortex. An area of the brain thought to be the seat of learning, memory, imagination, and other forms of unstereotyped activity.

neonate. A newborn infant.

neurosis. A mental disorder that prevents the victim from dealing effectively with reality. It is characterized by anxiety and partial impairment of functioning.

neurotic. Otto Rank's term for a psychopathological individual in whom the fear of death overrides the fear of life. He is generally isolated and rejecting of others rather than truly individual. See also *artist; average man.*

nominal scale. A scale in which numbers are simply assigned to persons or objects, as in numbering members of athletic teams. See also *ordinal scale; ratio scale.*

nondisjunction. The failure of a pair of chromosome homologues to separate and be distributed to different gametes during meiosis.

normative observation. The study of individuals by comparing them to standards or norms for the age group to which they belong.

normative studies. Those developmental studies designed to determine what behaviors may normally be expected at various stages in the life cycle.

norms. Prescriptions for correct behavior.

number. The singularity or plurality of grammatical components in a sentence.

nutrition. The process by which an organism takes in and utilizes food substances.

o

obese. Overweight.

object identity. The principle that an object is identical only with itself.

observational method. The psychological method of study that involves controlled observation of behavior and the transformation of such observations into measurable units or ratings. See also *clinical method; experimental method.*

observer effects. Effects associated with a particular perspective or set of conditions.

Oedipal conflict. According to Freud, a conflict that appears during the phallic stage. It consists of sexual attraction to the parent of the opposite sex and hostility toward the parent of the same sex.

olfaction. The sense of smell.

ontological guilt. According to Rollo May, the guilt that arises from relying on what is familiar.

openness to experience. According to Carl Rogers, the state in which every stimulus from the organism or the external environment is freely relayed through the individual without distortion by defenses.

operant conditioning. A type of conditioning in which an organism's responses change as a result of the application of reinforcement or reward. It is based on the principle that organisms tend to engage in behavior that succeeds in producing desirable outcomes.

operation. According to Jean Piaget, the mental action one performs in adapting to the environment.

opportunistic functioning. According to Gordon Allport, functioning on a biological level and being primarily concerned with survival. See also *propriate functioning.*

opposition. See *thumb opposition.*

oral stage. In psychoanalytic theory, the first stage of psychosexual development. In this stage gratification centers around the mouth and oral activities. See also *anal stage; genital stage; phallic stage.*

ordinal scale. A scale in which objects or qualities are ranked with ordinal numbers: first, second, third, and so forth. See also *nominal scale; ratio scale.*

organismic age. The age of an individual as determined by the combining and averaging of his height age, weight age, mental age, and other such factors.

organismic trusting. According to Carl Rogers, a willingness to react spontaneously without requiring a full and rational understanding of one's actions before performing them.

orgasm. A period of intense physical and emotional sensation usually resulting from stimulation of the sexual organs and generally followed in the male by the ejaculation of semen.

ossification. The replacement of cartilage by true bone.

ossification centers. The diaphyses and epiphyses, where ossification begins.

ovaries. The female reproductive organs, in which egg cells are manufactured.

ovists. In the seventeenth and eighteenth centuries, biologists who adhered to the theory that a prefabricated baby is contained somehow in the mother's ovaries and that the sperm merely serve to incite the expansion of the already-made baby. See also *homunculists.*

ovum. The female sex cell.

p

parallax. The apparent movements of two objects in the field of vision, one closer than the other, that occur when the head is moved from side to side.

parasocial speech. In a young child, talking to one's self. This behavior, thought to be social in origin, occurs most frequently when others are listening or when the child encounters difficulties.

passive-constructive personality. According to Alfred Adler, the unambitious but somewhat mature individual. See also *active-constructive personality; active-destructive personality; passive-destructive personality.*

passive-destructive personality. According to Alfred Adler, the immature and despairing individual. See also *active-constructive personality; active-destructive personality; passive-constructive personality.*

passive sentences. Sentences containing passive verb forms, such as *The ball was hit by John.* See also *active sentences.*

patellar reflex. The involuntary response that occurs when the patellar tendon is tapped. Commonly known as the knee-jerk reflex.

patient, the. A character type that nominally accepts the demands of society and attempts to transform himself in order to meet them. See also *revolutionary, the.*

patterns of behavior. Organized ways of behaving in certain situations.

Pavlovian conditioning. See *classical conditioning.*

pediatrician. A medical doctor who specializes in the development, care, and diseases of children.

peer. Another of one's own age or status.

peer group. The group of persons that constitutes one's associates, usually of the same age and social status.

penis. The male copulatory organ.

perception. The awareness of one's environment obtained through interpreting sense data.

perfection-fulfillment theory. The version of the fulfillment theory of personality that maintains that the personality force takes the form of internalized but culturally universal ideals of what is good and meaningful in life. See also *personality, fulfillment theory of.*

permanence. The principle that objects continue to exist even when they can no longer be seen.

personality. An individual's characteristic pattern of behavior and thought, including an accordant self-concept and a set of traits consistent over time.

personality, conflict theory of. The theory holding that an individual is continually and inevitably in the grip of a clash between two great opposing forces and that the secret of mature personality lies in the dynamic balance of the two opposing forces. See also *intrapsychic conflict theory; psychosocial conflict theory.*

personality, consistency theory of. The theory maintaining that maturity, and life itself, is an extended attempt to maintain consistency between environmental feedback and the individual's expectancy.

personality, fulfillment theory of. The theory maintaining that maturity lies in the full expression of one psychological force, lying within the individual. See also *actualization-fulfillment theory; perfection-fulfillment theory.*

phallic stage. In psychoanalytic theory, the third stage of psychosexual development, during which gratification centers on the sex organs. The Oedipal conflict also manifests itself during this stage. See also *anal stage; genital stage; oral stage.*

phenotype. The observable characteristics of an organism. See also *genotype.*

phenylketonuria. An error of metabolism caused by a recessive gene that gives rise to a deficiency in a certain enzyme. It can cause mental retardation if it is not caught in time.

phenylthiocarbamide (PTC). A chemical that, because of hereditary differences, can be tasted by some individuals and not by others.

phocomelia. Deformation of the limbs such as that caused by maternal use of the drug thalidomide.

phonetics. The study and classification of speech sounds.

placebo. An inert preparation often used as a control in experiments.

placenta. The organ that forms in the uterine lining and through which the developing prenatal organism receives nourishment and discharges waste.

polygenic system. The complex of genes involved in determining a polygenic trait.

polygenic trait. A hereditary trait that is controlled by more than one gene pair.

positive correlation. A relationship between two variables in which high values in the first correspond to high values in the second and low values in the first correspond to low values in the second. See also *negative correlation.*

positive reinforcement. In operant conditioning, the presentation of a rewarding consequence contingent on the desired response. See also *negative reinforcement.*

postconventional stage. A stage of moral development in which the individual defines moral values and principles in relation to their validity and application rather than in relation to the dictates of society or of any particular group. It is characterized by self-chosen ethical principles that are comprehensive, universal, and consistent. See also *conventional stage; preconventional stage.*

postpartum. Immediately after birth; the first week of life.

precision. The degree of agreement among repeated observations; reliability.

precocity. Unusually early development of a function.

preconventional stage. A stage of moral development in which the child responds to cultural rules and labels of good and bad only in terms of the physical or hedonistic consequences of obeying or disobeying the rules. See also *conventional stage; postconventional stage.*

prenatal. Before birth; the stage of human development lasting from conception to birth.

preoperational stage. According to Jean Piaget, the stage in a child's development occurring from eighteen months to seven years of age, during which he begins to encounter reality on the representational level. See also *concrete operational stage; formal operational stage; sensorimotor stage.*

primary process thinking. Freud's term for thought that is directed toward the satisfaction of basic needs; such thought is highly intuitive and emotional.

problem solving. Thinking directed toward the goal of solving a problem.

productive orientation. Erich Fromm's term for psychological maturity.

propriate functioning. According to Gordon Allport, the striving to become what one deeply believes one should be. Propriate functioning characterizes the mature individual. See also *opportunistic functioning.*

protracted adolescence. The concept that Peter Blos applies to adolescents who are unwilling to accept adulthood because of fear.

proximodistal development. The progressive growth of the body parts in a center-to-periphery direction. See also *cephalocaudal development.*

psychoanalysis. A method of psychotherapy developed by Freud. It emphasizes the techniques of free association and transference and seeks to give the patient insight into his unconscious conflicts and motives.

psychoanalytic theory. The basis of the school of psychology that emphasizes the development of emotions and their influence on behavior. See also *behaviorism; cognitive theory.*

psychological age. Age measured in terms of a person's capacity to adapt fruitfully to demands of the environment and of other persons. See also *biological age; social age.*

psychological growth. Personality change; the increasing of inner differentiation and integration, the acquisition of autonomy and flexibility, and the development of new capacities for self-determination.

psychological inertia. A force that increases the likelihood of a person to stay in his own social milieu and that makes any drastic change unlikely.

psychopath. A person suffering from a mental disorder.

psychosexual development. In Freudian theory, the sequence of stages through which the child passes, each characterized by the different erogenous zones from which the primary pleasure of the stage is derived. See also *anal stage; genital stage; oral stage; phallic stage.*

psychosis. Severe mental disorder.

psychosocial conflict theory. The version of the conflict theory of personality maintaining that one of the two opposing forces of life resides within the individual while the other comes from groups or societies outside of him. See also *personality, conflict theory of; intrapsychic conflict theory.*

psychosocial moratorium. According to Erik Erikson, a pause in the developmental sequence caused by acute identity diffusion.

psychotherapy. The treatment of mental and emotional disorders by the application of psychological methods.

PTC. See *phenylthiocarbamide.*

puberty. The period of life during which an individual's reproductive organs become functional and secondary sexual characteristics appear.

pubic hair. The hair that appears in the genital areas during adolescence.

q

quickening. The first fetal movements that a mother can readily perceive.

r

race. An aggregate of persons who share a set of genetically transmitted and physically identifiable characteristics.

rage. An emotional response involving intense anger and feelings of hostility. According to John B. Watson, it, along with fear and love, is one of the inherent or primary emotions.

random error of measurement. Disagreements between measurements repeated under conditions that are apparently identical.

range. A measurement of variability in a frequency distribution. It is obtained by subtracting the lowest score from the highest.

rapid eye movement (REM). During sleep, eye movement that usually occurs during dreaming.

rating. An estimation of an individual made by another.

ratio scale. A measurement scale composed of equal units and having an absolute zero point. The measurements of length and weight in feet and pounds are examples of ratio scales. See also *nominal scale; ordinal scale.*

reaction formation. A defense mechanism involving the replacement in consciousness of an anxiety-inducing impulse or feeling by its opposite.

reaction time. The interval of time that elapses between the instant a stimulus is presented and the individual's reaction to it.

recall. The form of remembering in which previously learned material is reproduced with a minimum of cues. See also *recognition.*

recessive gene. A gene whose hereditary characteristics will not prevail when paired with a dominant gene. See also *dominant gene.*

recognition. The form of remembering in which the previously learned material is merely recognized as such without actually being recalled. See also *recall.*

Refsum's disease. A congenital disease that causes the enzyme phytanic acid to accumulate in the body; accumulation of the enzyme leads to degenerative changes in the nervous system.

regression. Currently immature behavior appropriate only to an earlier stage of development.

rehearsal. Repeating or reviewing information to be learned. Rehearsal prolongs the retention of material in short-term memory and aids in transferring it to long-term memory.

reinforcement. In operant conditioning, the experimental procedure of immediately following a response with a reinforcer. See also *negative reinforcement; positive reinforcement.*

reinforcers. Consequences of behavior that result in the repetition of the behavior that produces them.

relational concept. A concept based on an interaction between or among members of a group. See also *analytical concept; superordinate concept.*

REM. See *rapid eye movement.*

representational level. The level of cognitive development at which the child begins to use symbols as well as images.

repression. In psychoanalytic theory, the defense mechanism of forcefully rejecting unpleasant memories or impulses from conscious awareness.

response. A segment of an organism's behavior, either operant or elicited by a stimulus.

retina. The light-sensitive portion of the eye containing the rods and cones, the receptors for vision.

reversibility. Having a logically meaningful opposite, such as addition and subtraction.

revolutionary, the. A character type that seeks to transform the world in the image of his own core values. See also *patient, the.*

Rh antigens. Substances in the blood that stimulate production of antibodies.

Rh factor. An agglutinizing factor present in the blood of most humans; when introduced into blood lacking the factor, antibodies form. Such a situation occurs when an organism with Rh positive blood inherited from its father resides within a mother whose blood is Rh negative. A first-born child is rarely affected, but subsequent children may require transfusions.

role. See *sex role; social role.*

rooting reflex. The newborn infant's involuntary movement of his mouth toward any source of stimulation in the mouth area.

rote learning. Memorization of meaningless verbal material.

rubella. German measles. Rubella in a pregnant woman can cause damage to the developing child if she contracts it during the first two months of pregnancy.

rule. A statement of a relation between the dimensions of two or more concepts; also, a statement of a routine function that is imposed on concepts to yield a new concept. See also *formal rules; informal rules.*

rhythmicity. See *cyclicity.*

S

scheme of action. A general response used to solve a variety of problems.

schizophrenia. A form of psychosis in which the patient becomes withdrawn and apathetic. Hallucinations and delusions are common.

sebaceous. Fatty, oily; sebaceous glands secrete oily matter for lubricating hair and skin.

secondary sex characteristics. Physical characteristics that appear in humans around the age of puberty and that are sex differentiated but not necessary for sexual reproduction. Such characteristics include breast development and the appearance of pubic hair in girls and the appearance of facial and pubic hair, enlargement of the penis, and deepening of the voice in boys.

segregation. See *law of segregation.*

self-actualization. According to Abraham Maslow, the need to develop one's true nature and fulfill one's potentialities.

self-esteem. The amount and quality of the regard that a person has toward himself.

semen. The fluid produced by the male testes that contains the spermatozoa.

sensitivity group. A training group that may resemble either a T-group or an encounter group.

sensorimotor reflexes. The basic reflex repertoire with which the infant is born—the Moro response, rooting reflex, patellar reflex, and so on.

sensorimotor stage. According to Jean Piaget, the stage in a child's cognitive development during which he is essentially involved in perfecting his contact with the objects that surround him. It generally occurs from birth to two years of age. See also *concrete operational stage; formal operational stage; preoperational stage.*

separation anxiety. In an infant, the strong negative reactions and efforts to regain proximity that often follow separation from the mother. Also known as separation protest.

serialization. The tendency to arrange objects in order according to a quantified dimension, such as weight or size.

serotonin. A substance thought to mediate transmission of impulses from one nerve to another.

sex roles. Patterns of behavior deemed appropriate to each sex by society.

shame. An emotion characterized by feelings of guilt, embarrassment, and avoidance.

short-term memory (STM). Memory with limited capacity and short duration. See also *long-term memory (LTM).*

sibling. A brother or sister.

significant. That to which a signifier refers.

signifiers. Things (words or objects) that refer to other things.

skeletal age. A measure of the maturity of the skeleton, determined by the degree of ossification of bone structures.

skelic index. The index that measures the ratio of lower limb length to sitting height.

social age. Age measured in terms of an individual's social habits relative to society's expectations. See also *biological age; psychological age.*

social class. A social strata or category differentiated from other such strata on the basis of such economic considerations as wealth, occupation, and property ownership.

social deprivation. The lack of economic, educational, and cultural opportunities.

social role. A set of expectations or evaluative standards associated with an individual or a position.

socialization. The process by which individuals pass through age-graded social roles whose requirements they must learn.

societies. Systems of defined complementary roles.

sociogram. A graphic portrayal of relationships within a group.

sociometry. The study of group structures and relationships.

speech. Verbal communication.

spermatozoon. The male sex cell.

spirants. Vocal sounds that are not stops, fricatives, nasals, flaps, trills, or semivowels. Examples are *sh* and *th.*

stability. In psychology, the tendency to stay in an even emotional state. See also *lability.*

stage of concrete operations. See *concrete operational stage.*

stage of formal operations. See *formal operational stage.*

stages. Periods in which the function and relative emphasis of a given type of behavior differ from those of other periods of time.

standard deviation. The square root of the variance in a frequency distribution.

standard score. A derived score based on the number of standard deviations between the original score and the average score.

startle response. A reaction to stimuli in infants outwardly characterized by eye widening, jaw dropping, cooing, squealing, or crying and inwardly characterized by changes in heart rate, respiration, and galvanic skin potential.

stature. Natural height in an upright position.

stereogram. A set of two plane pictures, each of which is slightly different from the other; adults looking at a stereogram are not aware of these differences but instead perceive objects as being at different distances.

stimulus. Any form of environmental energy capable of affecting the organism.

stimulus error. In experimentation, a problem that occurs when an observer knows something about the actual stimulus so that his knowledge may influence and distort his report of his observations.

STM. See *short-term memory.*

stops. In speech, consonants in which the breath passage is completely closed at some point, as in *d* or *b*. See also *nasals.*

strain. A reproductively isolated population within a given species.

sublimation. The substitution of a socially acceptable activity for an unacceptable one.

suctorial. Functioning as a sucker for imbibing or adhering.

suggestion. The exertion of influence through constant reiteration that one do something or believe something.

superego. According to Freud, that part of the personality that restrains the activity of the ego and the id. See also *ego; id.*

superordinate concept. A concept representing a shared attribute among a group of objects. See also *analytical concept; relational concept.*

surprise paradigm. The idea that if one presents an organism with an event that violates its expectations or beliefs, then it will be surprised. See also *startle response.*

surrogate mother. Someone or something that takes the place of a mother in an organism's life.

survey method. Collection of information by questioning a large selection of people.

symbol. An arbitrary name or tag for an object, idea, or event, or a class of objects, ideas, or events. See also *concept; image.*

syncretic functioning. Functioning on a general and overall level rather than on a specific one, such as reacting to a stimulus with one's whole body rather than with only the area stimulated. See also *differentiated functioning.*

syntax. The underlying rules of sentence formation in a language.

systematic imprecision. Consistent error in measurement due to some imperfection in the measuring device.

T

T-group. An intensive group that emphasizes human-relations skills.

t test. A statistical test used to calculate whether a difference in scores is significant or due to chance. See also *level of confidence; level of significance.*

tag question. A question that requests confirmation of the statement it follows, such as *It's my turn, isn't it?*

temperament. The behavioral style of an individual; in infants, a level of activity and responsiveness.

tense. A distinction of form in a verb to express past, present, or future.

terminal illness. A disease that results in death.

test. A set of questions and/or tasks used to measure individual differences.

testes. The male reproductive organs, in which spermatozoa are manufactured; testicles.

thalidomide. A drug once used by women during pregnancy to assuage morning sickness; it caused deformation of the limbs in the children.

theory. A set of logically interrelated statements used to explain observed events.

thinking. The active process of conceptualization, involving integrating percepts, grasping relationships, and asking further questions. See also *directed thinking; undirected thinking.*

threshold of responsiveness. The level of stimulation necessary to evoke a discernible response.

thumb opposition. The ability to oppose the thumb to the fingers and to bring the fingertips in contact with the ball of the thumb.

thyroxin. A hormone produced by the thyroid gland; it regulates metabolism.

torporous. Sluggish; lethargic; apathetic.

toxicity. Having the quality of a poison.

trace. See *memory trace.*

tracking. The act of following an object with one's eyes.

trauma. An experience that causes serious physical or psychological shock to an organism.

Turner's syndrome. A congenital physical condition resulting from the individual's having only one X chromosome and no Y chromosomes. The afflicted individual looks like an immature female and is characterized by a lack of reproductive organs, abnormal shortness, and mental retardation.

U

umbilical cord. The cord that connects the prenatal organism with the placenta.

unconditional positive regard. The acceptance, respect, appreciation, and tolerance that society offers an individual. See also *conditional positive regard.*

unconditioned response. The response given naturally to an unconditioned stimulus.

unconditioned stimulus. A stimulus that, without training, elicits a response.

undirected thinking. Free association, dreaming, daydreaming, reverie, and so forth. See also *directed thinking.*

uniformism. Peter Blos' term for immersion of the individual into the peer group and his acceptance of its norms as infallible and regulatory.

unpleasure. R. A. Spitz's term for the negative reactions of the infant in the first six weeks or so of life.

uterus. The female organ in which the prenatal organism develops and is nourished prior to birth.

V

vagina. The female genital region and copulatory organ.

value. Any object, experience, or response that one seeks to obtain and/or keep.

variable. See *dependent variable; independent variable.*

variance. The square of the standard deviation. To find the variance, the mean is calculated, then each score is subtracted from the mean, the difference for each score is squared, all the squares are added together, and, finally, this figure is divided by the original number of scores.

vocalization. The utterance of sounds, as in speaking, babbling, crying, and so on.

W

Wechsler Adult Intelligence Scale. A widely used individual intelligence test.

womb. See *uterus.*

X

X *chromosome.* A chromosome that, when paired with another X chromosome, programs a gamete to develop as a female.

Y

Y *chromosome.* The chromosome that determines that an individual will be male.

yolk sac. A nonfunctional sac that forms during the germinal period of human prenatal development.

youth. A stage of the human life cycle experienced by persons who are psychologically and physically mature but who are not sociologically mature, in that they have not made any commitments to career or family. This stage intervenes between adolescence and adulthood.

Z

zygote. The one-celled product of the union of a sperm cell with an egg cell.

Index

101—Stephen McCarroll/John Oldenkamp Studio. 103—(*Top, center*) William Macdonald/John Oldenkamp Studio. (*Bottom*) Stephen McCarroll/John Oldenkamp Studio. 104—(*Top*) Marcia Keegan. (*Bottom*) Ken Heyman. 105—Armstrong/Fountain; reprinted from "Differences in Walking in the European Longitudinal Samples," *Human Biology*, 38 (1966), 369, by C. B. Hindley, A. M. Filliozat, G. Klackenberg, D. Nicolet-Meister, and E. A. Sand. By permission of the Wayne State University Press. Copyright © 1966 by Wayne State University. All rights reserved. **Chapter Six:** 106—William Macdonald/John Oldenkamp Studio. 108—(*Top two photographs*) George Zimbel/Monkmeyer Press. (*Bottom three photographs*) Jason Lauré. 109—Jason Lauré. 112—Tom Suzuki. 113—Armstrong/Fountain. 114—From T. G. R. Bower, "The Visual World of Infants," *Scientific American*, 215 (December 1966), 72. Copyright © 1966 by Scientific American, Inc. All rights reserved. 115—Stephen McCarroll. 116—Courtesy Eric Aronson. 117—Thomas G. Lewis; adapted from *Principles of Perceptual Learning and Development* by E. J. Gibson. Copyright © 1969, New York: Appleton-Century-Crofts, Educational Division, Meredith Corporation, p. 354. Data from R. Aherns, *Zeitschrift für experimentelle und angewandte Psychologie*, 1954, p. 445. 118—William Macdonald/John Oldenkamp Studio. 119, 120—Jason Lauré. 122—Photographs by Jane Cowles; diagram, Armstrong/Fountain. 124—Armstrong/Fountain; adapted from T. G. R. Bower, "The Development of Object-Permanence: Some Studies of Existence Constancy," *Perception and Psychophysics*, Vol. 2, No. 9 (1967), 413; 125—Stephen McCarroll. 126, 127—Courtesy Burton L. White. 128—Suzanne Szasz. **Chapter Seven:** 130—John Oldenkamp/Photophile. 133—Gerri Blake. 135—Carl Aldana. 136, 137—William Macdonald/John Oldenkamp Studio. 138—Armstrong/Fountain; adapted from Nancy Bayley, "Research in Child Development: A Longitudinal Perspective," *Merrill-Palmer Quarterly*, 22 (1965), 205; courtesy Merrill-Palmer Institute and Institute of Human Development of the University of California at Berkeley. 140—Courtesy Regional Primate Research Center, University of Wisconsin. 142—Armstrong/Fountain; adapted from H. L. Rheingold, "The Modification of Social Responsiveness in Institutional Babies," *Monograph of the Society for Research in Child Development*, 21 (1956), 23. Copyright © 1956 the Society for Research in Child Development, Inc. All rights reserved. 143—Louis Goldman/Rapho Guillumette Pictures. 144—William Macdonald/John Oldenkamp Studio. 145—(*Top*) William Macdonald/John Oldenkamp Studio. (*Bottom*) John Oldenkamp/William Macdonald. 146—William Macdonald/John Oldenkamp Studio.

Chapter Eight: 148—William Macdonald/John Oldenkamp Studio. 151—Stephen McCarroll/John Oldenkamp Studio. 153—(*Top, center*) William Macdonald/John Oldenkamp Studio. (*Bottom*) Armstrong/Fountain; adapted from G. Morgan and H. Ricciuti, "Infants' Responses to Strangers During the First Year," in B. M. Foss (ed.), *Determinants of Infant Behavior*, Vol. IV. New York: Wiley, 1969. 154, 155—Armstrong/Fountain; adapted from A. T. Jersild and F. B. Holmes, *Children's Fears*. Child Development Monograph No. 20. New York: Teachers College, Columbia University, 1935. 156—William Macdonald/John Oldenkamp Studio. 157—William Macdonald/John Oldenkamp Studio. 158—Robert J. Smith/Black Star. 159—(*Top left*) Harry Crosby. (*Top right, bottom*) William Macdonald/John Oldenkamp Studio. 160—Harry Crosby. **Chapter Nine:** 162—Constructions by Gerri Blake; photograph by William Macdonald/John Oldenkamp Studio. 164, 165—William Macdonald/John Oldenkamp Studio. 167—Gerri Blake. 168—Armstrong/Fountain; adapted from Mildred Templin, *Certain Language Skills in Children*, Institute of Child Welfare Monograph No. 26, University of Minnesota Press. Copyright © 1957, University of Minnesota. 170—Gerri Blake. 171—Thomas G. Lewis. 172—Armstrong/Fountain; test items from Kuhlman-Anderson Tests, 6th ed., reproduced with permission of the copyright holder, Personnel Press, Inc., Princeton, N.J. 173—Armstrong/Fountain; adapted from E. H. Lenneberg, *Biological Foundations of Language*. New York: Wiley, 1967, p. 134. 174—(*Top*) Dorothy Levens, professor of psychology and director of the Nursery School, Vassar College, Poughkeepsie, New York. (*Bottom left*) Peter Keen/courtesy *Aramco World* magazine. (*Bottom right*) Wayne McLoughlin. 175, 176—Thomas G. Lewis; adapted from *Language Development: Form and Function in Emerging Grammars* by Lois Bloom, by permission of The MIT Press, Cambridge, Massachusetts. Copyright © 1968 by the Massachusetts Institute of Technology. 179—(*Top*) William Macdonald/John Oldenkamp Studio. (*Bottom*) John Oldenkamp/William Macdonald.

Unit IV, **Chapter Ten:** 180—Karl Nicholason. 182—John Oldenkamp/William Macdonald. 184—(*Top*) Toge Fujihira/Monkmeyer Press. (*Bottom*) Stephen McCarroll/John Oldenkamp Studio. 185—Joan Sydlow/Monkmeyer Press. 186—Armstrong/Fountain; adapted from N. Bayley,

"Growth Curves of Height and Weight by Age for Boys and Girls, Scaled According to Physical Maturity," *Journal of Pediatrics*, Vol. 48 (1956). 188, 189—William Macdonald/John Oldenkamp Studio. 191—John Oldenkamp/William Macdonald. 192—William Macdonald/John Oldenkamp Studio. 193—John Oldenkamp/William Macdonald. **Chapter Eleven:** 194—Rey Hernandez. 196—John Oldenkamp. 198—From W. Hudson, "Pictorial Depth Perception in Sub-cultural Groups in Africa," *Journal of Social Psychology*, 52 (1960), 183–208. 199—From *Child Development and Personality*, 3rd ed., by Paul Henry Mussen, John Janeway Conger, and Jerome Kagan. New York: Harper & Row, 1969, p. 295. 201—William Macdonald/John Oldenkamp Studio. 202—John Oldenkamp. 203—Joyce Fitzgerald. 205—William Macdonald/John Oldenkamp Studio. 206—Dorothy Levens, professor of psychology and director of the Nursery School, Vassar College, Poughkeepsie, New York. 208—Carl Aldana. **Chapter Twelve:** 210—Harry Crosby. 213—Roger Mayne. 214, 215—Darrel Millsap/Millsap and Kinyon. 216, 217, 218, 219—William Macdonald/John Oldenkamp Studio. 221—Darrel Millsap/Millsap and Kinyon. 222, 223—William Macdonald/John Oldenkamp Studio. **Chapter Thirteen:** 224—John Oldenkamp/William Macdonald. 226—(*Top, center*) Myron Papiz. (*Bottom*) © 1967 United Features Syndicate, Inc. 227—Myron Papiz. 229—Joyce Fitzgerald. 230—Ken Heyman. 232, 234—William Macdonald/John Oldenkamp Studio. 235—Burk Uzzle/Magnum. 236—Steve McCarroll/John Oldenkamp Studio. 237—Ken Heyman. 238—(*Top*) Hiroji Kubota/Magnum. (*Bottom*) Charles Harbutt/Magnum. **Chapter Fourteen:** 240—John Oldenkamp/William Macdonald. 242—(*Top*) Suzanne Szasz. (*Bottom*) courtesy Regional Primate Research Center, University of Wisconsin. 243—Armstrong/Fountain; adapted from M. B. Parten, "Social Participation Among Preschool Children," *Journal of Abnormal and Social Psychology*, 24 (1932–1933), 243–269; copyright © 1932–33 by the American Psychological Association and reproduced by permission. 245—(*Top, center*) Myron Papiz. (*Bottom*) William Macdonald/John Oldenkamp Studio. 247—Courtesy of David J. Hicks, Department of Psychology, Chico State College. 248—Armstrong/Fountain; adapted from W. W. Hartup and B. Coates, "Imitation of a Peer as a Function of Reinforcement from

Excerpt from D. C. Dunphy, "The Social Structure of Urban Adolescent Peer Groups," *Sociometry*, 26 (1963), 236. (*Top*) Bob S. Smith/Rapho Guillumette. (*Center*) Rogers/Monkmeyer Press. (*Bottom*) Welden Anderson/Photophile. 391—Armstrong/Fountain; adapted from D. C. Dunphy, "The Social Structure of Urban Adolescent Peer Groups," *Sociometry*, 26 (1963), 236. 392—Jim Jowers/Nancy Palmer Agency. 393—(*Top*) Charles Harbutt/Magnum. (*Center*) Jim Jowers/Nancy Palmer Agency. (*Bottom*) Wayne Miller/Magnum. 394—Armstrong/Fountain; data on adult drinking patterns from D. Cahalan, J. H. Cisin, and H. M. Crossley, *Drinking Practices: A National Survey of Behavior and Attitudes Related to Alcoholic Beverages* (Social Research Project Report No. 3). Washington, D. C.: George Washington University, 1967. Data on teen-age drinking habits from M. Bacon and M. B. Jones, *Teen-age Drinking*. New York: Crowell, 1968. 396—(*Top*) Roland Scherman. (*Bottom*) Steven Waterman/Photophile. 398—Richard B. Klein/Nancy Palmer Agency. **Chapter Twenty-two:** 400—Michael Alexander. 402–427—Quotes from Peter Madison, *Personality Development in College*, 1969, Addison-Wesley, Reading, Mass. 402—Harry Crosby. 404, 408—Stephen McCarroll/John Oldenkamp Studio. 410—John Dawson. 412—Stephen McCarroll/John Oldenkamp Studio. 416—William Macdonald/Photophile. 417—Stephen McCarroll/John Oldenkamp Studio. 423—William Macdonald/John Oldenkamp Studio. 425—Stephen McCarroll/John Oldenkamp Studio. 426—George Zimbel/Monkmeyer Press. **Chapter Twenty-three:** 428—Michael Alexander. 430—(*Top*) Historical Pictures Service, Chicago. (*Center*) The Bettmann Archive. (*Bottom*) Culver Pictures. 431—Armstrong/Fountain. 433—(*From top to bottom*) The Bettmann Archive; The Bettmann Archive; Culver Pictures; The Bettmann Archive; Culver Pictures. 435—Armstrong/Fountain; data from the January 1969 issue of *Fortune* magazine by permission, © 1968 Time, Inc. 436—(*Top, center right*) Michael Alexander. (*Center left, bottom*) Roland Scherman. 437—(*Top, bottom*) Michael Alexander. (*Center right*) Peter Keen/courtesy of *Aramco World* magazine. (*Center left*) Peace Corps photo by James Pickerell. 438—Armstrong/Fountain; data from the January 1969 issue of *Fortune* magazine by permission, © 1968 Time, Inc. 441—Karl Nicholason. 442—Michael Alexander. 444—Philip Kirkland.

Unit VII, Chapter Twenty-four: 446—Karl Nicholason. 448—NASA. 451—(*Left*) Ken Heyman. (*Right*) Harry Crosby. 452—Harry Crosby. 454, 457—Philip Kirkland. 459—Stephen McCarroll/John Oldenkamp Studio. 460—(*Top left*) Rogers/Monkmeyer Press. (*Top right*) Bern Keating/Black Star. (*Center, bottom left*) Harry Crosby. (*Bottom right*) Bruce Roberts/Rapho Guillumette. 462—(*Left*)

John Oldenkamp. (*Right*) William Macdonald/John Oldenkamp Studio. **Chapter Twenty-five:** 464—Rodin Museum, Paris; SCALA, New York/Florence. 465—Quotes from *The Autobiography of Bertrand Russell* by Bertrand Russell. Boston: Little, Brown, pp. 6, 7, 38, 287, 289; copyright © 1951, 1952, 1953, 1956 by Bertrand Russell; copyright © by George Allen and Unwin Ltd. By permission of Atlantic-Little, Brown and Co. 467—William Macdonald/John Oldenkamp Studio. 469—Armstrong/Fountain; hypothetical data from Norma Haan. 471—William Macdonald/John Oldenkamp Studio. 472—John Oldenkamp. 473—(*Top*) Toge Fujihira/Monkmeyer Press. (*Bottom*) William Macdonald/John Oldenkamp Studio. 474—Harry Crosby. 475—Armstrong/Fountain; adapted from N. Bayley and Melita H. Oden, "The Maintenance of Intellectual Ability in Gifted Adults," *Journal of Gerontology*, 10 (January 1955), 91–107. 476—(*Top*) Schmick/Monkmeyer Press. (*Center*) Roth/Rapho Guillumette Pictures. (*Bottom*) Dourdin/Rapho Guillumette Pictures. 478—Karl Nicholason. 480, 481—Harry Crosby/Photophile; John Oldenkamp. **Chapter Twenty-six:** 482, 486, 488, 490, 493, 494—John Oldenkamp. **Chapter Twenty-seven:** 496—Harry Crosby. 498—Armstrong/Fountain; data courtesy of Metropolitan Life Insurance Company. 499—(*Top*) courtesy The Royal Library, Windsor Castle, England. Copyright reserved. (*Bottom*) Armstrong/Fountain; adapted from "The Psychology of Aging" by Nathan W. Shock, *Scientific American*, 206 (January 1962), 110. Copyright © 1962 by Scientific American, Inc. All rights reserved. 500—(*Top*) Bruce Roberts/Rapho Guillumette Pictures. (*Bottom*) Alan Mercer. 501—Adapted from B. Neugarten, "A New Look at Menopause," *Psychology Today*, December 1967, p. 44. 502, 503—Harry Crosby. 504—Armstrong/Fountain; adapted from W. Dennis, "Creative Productivity Between the Ages of 20 and 80 years," *Journal of Gerontology*, 21 (1966) 3. 505—(*Top*) Henle/Monkmeyer Press. (*Center*) Bernheim/Rapho Guillumette Pictures. (*Bottom*) Izis/Rapho Guillumette Pictures. 506—Harry Crosby. 508—(*Top*) Rita Freed/Nancy Palmer Agency. (*Bottom*) Ken Heyman. 510—Harry Crosby. 511—Lines from Dylan Thomas, *Collected Poems*, copyright 1952 by Dylan Thomas. Reprinted by permission of New Directions Publishing Corporation. **Epilogue:** 512—Karl Nicholason. 515, 516, 517—Gerri Blake. **Appendix:** 520—Stephen McCarroll/John Oldenkamp Studio. 524, 526, 527—Armstrong / Fountain. **Contributing Consultants:** 542-547—Karl Nicholason.

We wish to thank the following persons and institutions for their contribution.

Eric Aronson, Harvard University; Phoebe Cramer, University of California at Berkeley; Douglas Freundlich, Harvard University; Juarlyn Gaiter, Brown University; Louis Gluck, University of California at San Diego; John W. Hagan, University of Michigan; Paul Hamlyn, Ltd., London; Tryphena Humphrey, University of Alabama; Lewis Lipsitt, Brown University; Boyd McCandless, Emory University; James McConnell, University of Michigan; Anne Meyer, Harvard University; Keith Moore, Harvard University; Alex Mundy-Castle, Harvard University; Providence Lying-in Hospital, Rhode Island; George Reynolds, University of California at San Diego; St. Vincent's Home for Infants, Providence, Rhode Island; Einar Siqueland, Brown University; Nancy Stein, University of California at San Diego; William H. Terry, Time-Life Broadcast, Inc.; and Burton White, Harvard University.

CRM Books

Richard L. Roe • *Publisher, Social Sciences*
John H. Painter • *Publisher, Life and Physical Sciences*
Phillip M. Whitten • *Revision Manager*
Genevieve Clapp • *Ancillary Materials Manager*
Lynne Fulton, Diana Vennard • *Editorial Coordinators*

Jean Smith • *Editorial Director*
Arlyne Lazerson, Larry McCombs • *Senior Editors*
Cecie Starr • *Editor*
Jacquelyn Estrada, Johanna Price • *Associate Editors*
Lee Massey • *Promotion Editor*
Paul Bailiff, Kathleen Benson, Cynthia MacDonald,
  Martha Rosler, Roberta Savitz • *Editorial Assistants*
Beth Lanum, Cindy Lyle, Evelyn Shapiro • *Promotion Editorial Assistants*
Carolyne Hultgren • *Editorial Coordinator*
Nancy Hutchison • *Rights and Permissions Supervisor*

Rick M. Connelly • *College Marketing Manager*
Frederic W. Squires • *College Operations Manager*
Carol Walnum • *College Sales Supervisor*
Sharon Broad, Anne Bradley, Gail Dedman, Connie Rogers, Kathleen Quinn,
  La Delle Willett • *College Sales Coordinators*
Marti Rice • *Staff*

Barbara Blum • *Director of Production*
Robert E. Hollander • *Production Manager*
Patricia Bouchard, Catherine Hunink • *Production Associates*
Joyce Couch • *Promotion Production Supervisor*
Shelley Bennett, Phyllis Bowman, Sheridan Hughes,
  Vicki Wing • *Production Assistants*

Tom Suzuki • *Director of Design*
Leon Bolognese • *Art Director*
John Isely • *Promotion Art Director*
Donald Fujimoto • *Senior Designer*
Reynold Hernandez • *Designer*
Sally Collins, Catherine Flanders, Dale Phillips • *Associate Designers*
Pamela Morehouse, Paul Slick • *Assistant Designers*
Linda Higgins, Kurt Kolbe • *Staff*
Ken Melton • *Design Operations Supervisor*
Mary Whiteside, Janie Fredericks • *Operations Assistants*

Eugene W. Schwartz • *Operations Analyst*

Lynn D. Crosby • *Office Manager*
Rochelle Pinnell • *Assistant*

Officers of Communications Research Machines, Inc.
Nicolas H. Charney • *Chairman of the Board*
John J. Veronis • *President*
William J. Boff • *Vice-President*
James B. Horton • *Vice-President*
Walter C. Rohrer • *Vice-President*

Developmental Psychology Today **Book Team**

Richard L. Roe • *Publisher, Social Sciences*
Arlyne Lazerson • *Editor*
Jacquelyn Estrada • *Associate Editor*
Martha Rosler • *Editorial Assistant*
Diana Vennard • *Editorial Coordinator*

Donald Fujimoto • *Designer*
Pamela Morehouse • *Assistant Designer*
Dale Phillips • *Associate Designer*

Barbara Blum • *Director of Production*
Patricia Bouchard • *Production Associate*
Phyllis Bowman • *Production Assistant*

This book was set in Electra typeface by
Kingsport Press, Inc., Kingsport, Tennessee.

Transparencies were processed and assembled by
Robert Crandall Associates, New York, New York.

The text was printed in web offset lithography by Kingsport Press, Inc.

Text paper is Glatcotext Web, furnished by
Perkins & Squier Company, New York, New York.

The book was bound in Holliston cloth by Kingsport Press, Inc.